MARRIAGES AND DEATHS

from the *Baltimore Patriot,*

1820 - 1824

Michael A. Ports

CLEARFIELD

Published for Clearfield Company by
Genealogical Publishing Company
Baltimore Maryland
2015

ISBN 978-0-8063-5738-6

Introduction

More than forty years ago, when this novice genealogist first ventured into the library of the Maryland Historical Society seeking his roots, Robert Barnes noticed his apparent confusion and took the time to show him around, explain the layout, and introduce him to the various collections and finding aids. Robert then asked specific questions about which families he sought and offered numerous helpful suggestions on how to get started effectively and efficiently, further suggesting that he join the Maryland Genealogical Society and attend their upcoming genealogical workshop for beginners. The workshop transformed that novice into an avid and zealous researcher, who has continued assiduously over the decades, enjoying his membership in the society and his friendship and collaboration with Robert Barnes. A few weeks after the workshop, Robert invited the novice to join him for a research trip to the York County Historical Society, again taking the time to introduce those facilities and their holdings. In the intervening years, Robert assisted countless others searching for their Maryland roots, quickly gaining the reputation as the expert, if not the foremost expert, on Maryland genealogy. In addition, Robert is a prolific transcriber, compiler, and author, well known for his series on marriages and deaths from Baltimore newspapers, starting in 1796 through 1819. The present work is dedicated to Robert Barnes, thanking him for his friendship and numerous kindnesses to this genealogist and for his services to all genealogists over the years. Robert, thank you.

On Monday, December 28, 1812, from his offices at 29 South Calvert Street, Ebenezer French began publishing the *Baltimore Patriot*. The Republican newspaper supported the political philosophies of Thomas Jefferson and James Madison; one of its primary competitors was the *American & Commercial Daily* Advertiser. In August 1813, Mr. French changed the name of the newspaper to the *Baltimore Patriot & Evening Advertiser*. From 1817 to 1838, the newspaper ran under the title of *Baltimore Patriot & Mercantile Advertiser*. In April 1838, merging with the *Baltimore Gazette & Daily Advertiser*, the new publishers used the title *Baltimore Patriot & Commercial Gazette*, reverting back to the original name *Baltimore Patriot*, during a portion on 1858. Numerous libraries and archives have originals or microfilmed copies of various issues, including the Enoch Pratt Free Library, Library of Congress, Maryland Historical Society, and Maryland State Archives. In addition, several paid internet services have copies of the newspaper. The following transcription includes the complete marriage and death notices for the years 1820 through 1824. Typically, the marriage notices include the date of the marriage ceremony and the names of the bride, groom, and officiating minister, sometimes including, the place of the marriage, the father of the bride or groom, and the occupation of the groom. The death notices usually include the name of the deceased, date and place of death, and age of the deceased, sometimes including the cause of death, names of surviving husbands and parents, numbers of surviving children, occupation of the deceased, circumstances surrounding an unusual death, the date and location of the funeral, place of burial, religious affiliation, and other biographical information. Many death notices include eulogies, extolling the virtues of the deceased and lamenting their death, some with added poetry or quotes from scripture. Including the complete notices, rather than a short abstract or summary, provides more context surrounding the customs and mores prevailing in Baltimore at the time. The notices were copied, some by hand and others by photocopy, sometimes from microfilm and other times from originals, at numerous libraries and archives, over more than thirty years, before being transcribed here.

Many of the marriage and the death notices in the *Baltimore Patriot* concern people who married or died outside of Maryland, in virtually every U. S. state and territory and in numerous countries in Africa, Asia, Central and South America, as well as Europe. This transcription, however, includes all those notices having a Maryland connection. Notices having no Maryland connection usually concern European nobility or other notables, national politicians, federal government officials, American Revolutionary War veterans, and people who died under unusual or sensational circumstances or at very advanced ages.

The transcription corrects most of the punctuation errors in the notices, usually with the addition or deletion of commas, but does not correct the misspellings, no matter how obvious. However, the names of many of the officiating ministers are spelled in a variety of imaginative ways, especially the Reverends Helfenstein, Kurtz, and Mareschal. Whenever obvious, the surnames of the officiating ministers are corrected. The transcription consistently abbreviates the titles Reverend, Doctor, Professor, Junior, Senior, and Esquire, as Rev., Dr., Prof., Jr., and Esq., regardless of how they appear in the original. The transcription similarly abbreviates all military and naval ranks, such as Lt., Capt., Maj., Col., Gen., etc. The transcription presents the notices more or less in chronological order.

A few of the marriage and death notices appear in more than one issue of the newspaper, sometimes with identical notices and sometimes with substantially different information. For the duplicate noices, both dates of publication appear with the notice. Substantially different notices appear separately; however, minor differences between otherwise duplicate notices as well as other comments are noted between open braces, { }, following the first appearance.

On Tuesday, March 4, 1823, the editors printed the following notice.

> *Marriages. – The printers are frequently imposed upon by accounts of sham marriages, though every precaution is used, and I have thought it would be expedient to require a dollar for each publication, in order to prevent imposition. Nothing can be more mortifying, and frequently distressing, for a lady to see her name in the paper, coupled with a person, who not only may be odious to her, but actually of a character calculated to prohibit such alliance; and a man is liable to the same mortification. Then, on the other hand, a gentleman may see himself actually married in the paper to a lady who has repulsed him, or coupled with a fair dame who is his aversion. In any light you may be pleased to view it, the imposition is a base one. N. Y. Adv.*

The editors apparently copied the foregoing from an out-of-town newspaper; but, nonetheless felt the problem of false marriage notices was sufficient to mention it. One should think that problems with intentionally false death notices were much less likely. In addition to submitting intentionally false information to the newspaper, submitters may have erred in supplying the information, the printer may have erred in publishing the notices, and this transcriber could have erred in copying the notices. Remembering that published transcriptions of newspaper notices are at best tertiary or even quaternary sources, the careful researcher will take the time and effort to corroborate the information in the notice with information from multiple other sources.

The editors frequently published coroner's reports, providing details about deaths from drowning, murder, accident, suicide, and other causes. All of the coroner's reports that name the victim or provide clues to the victim's identity follow the submitted marriage and death notices. The table of coroner's reports includes a few deaths noted in news articles. The index includes the surnames of everyone mentioned in the notices, except the names of the officiating ministers and coroners.

Many thanks are offered to Joe Garonzik, of the Genealogical Publishing Company, for his professional advice and counsel. Special thanks are offered Marcia Tremonti for her patience and encouragement through this challenging and difficult endeavor.

Report of Interments

On January 9, 1821, the Health Office published in the *Baltimore Patriot* a Report of Interments, in the City of Baltimore, from the first of January 1820, to the first of January, 1821. A summary of that report follows.

Month	Males	Females	Total	Colored
January	55	66	121	45
February	45	51	96	34
March	77	60	137	42
April	48	50	98	25
May	37	36	73	24
June	52	40	92	26
July	112	101	213	60
August	90	84	174	37
September	106	90	195	55
October	85	72	157	52
November	81	73	154	52
December	66	48	114	36
Total	854	771	1,625	488

The above numbers reflect interments, and not necessarily deaths, that occurred in Baltimore City during the year. Nearby residents of Baltimore County may have been buried in a city cemetery. Similarly, relatives of Baltimore City residents who died elsewhere may have had the remains returned for burial in the city. And, of course, the remains of deceased crew members or passengers of the numerous ships arriving at Baltimore may have been buried in a city cemetery. Moreover, the remains of at least some persons who died at Baltimore City were removed for burial elsewhere. Regardless, the number of interments should be a reasonable proxy for the number of deaths during the year.

It is surprising that so few of those interments were noticed in the local newspaper. In 1820, notices of the deaths of only 83 men and 74 women appear in the *Baltimore Patriot*. Of course, the published notices are not always clear whether death occurred within the city limits or the remains of the deceased were buried in the city. Regardless, notices of slightly less than ten percent of the interments reported by the Baltimore Health Office appeared in the local newspaper.

The ages of those 1,625 persons interred during the year reported by the Health Office are summarized below.

Age of one year and under	390
Between the age of one and two years	116
From two to five	48
From five to ten	77
From ten to twenty	113
From twenty to thirty	177
From thirty to forty	210
From forty to fifty	133
From fifty to sixty	107
From sixty to seventy	62
From seventy to eighty	35
From eighty to ninety	47
From ninety to one hundred	9
Over one hundred	3
Stillborn	98
	1,625

It is striking that 604, or 37 percent, of the total interments were either stillborn or children under two years of age. The Health Office also reported the cause of death for each of the interments.

Asthsma	1	Gravel	3
Abscess	2	Haemorrhage	2
Abscess of the Brain	1	Hydrothorax	2
Abscess of the Liver	1	Hives	1
Appoplexy	18	Incarcerated Hernia	1
Anasarca	1	Jaundice	4
Affection of the stomach & head	1	Intemperance	29
Burn	6	Insanity	9

4

Catarrh	9	Inflammation of the Lungs	3
Cancer	7	Inflammation of the Bowels	5
Cramp Cholic	2	Inflammation of the Brain	6
Casualty	10	Indigestion	1
Child Bed	20	Infantile unknown	66
Cholera Morbus	175	Liver Complaint	11
Cholic	10	Lock Jaw	4
Cholic Cramp	3	Mortification	24
Cholic Bilious	2	Marasmus	6
Consumption	328	Murdered	4
Convulsions	90	Old Age	78
Croup	73	Palsey	17
Decay	22	Pleurisy	39
Dropsy	43	Pleurisy Bilious	3
Dropsy in the Breast	5	Quinsey	3
Dropsy in the Head	8	Rheumatism	2
Drowned	20	Scrofula, or King's Evil	4
Dysentery	56	Scalded	1
Dyarrhaea	2	Still Born	98
Drinking Cold Water	4	Sudden Death	12
Epilepsy	1	Sphacelus	2
Fever Bilious	9	Suicide	4
Fever Intermittent	5	Thrash	1
Fever Nervous	5	Teething	20
Fever Bilious Intermittent	45	Ulcer	1
Fever Scarlet	4	Whooping Cough	27
Fever Typhus	73	Worms	32
Flux	8	Unknown	2
			1,625

The three largest causes of death include consumption, cholera morbus, and stillborn, accounting for 37 percent of the total. Including burns, casualties, drowning, intemperance, murder, and suicide, 73, or 4.5 percent of the deaths were accidental, self-inflicted, or otherwise nonmedical. Remarkably, the Health Office did not know cause of only two of the deaths that year. The reader should recognize the names of many of he causes of death; however, because many of the medical terms now are obsolete, the definitions of some of the more obscure medical terms follows.

Abscess: a swelling in soft tissue filled with pus caused by an infection, such as a boil.

Apoplexy: paralysis caused by stroke. Sudden deprivation of all the internal and external sensation and of all motion unless of the heart and thorax.

Bilious fever: intestinal or malarial fevers.

Biliousness: nausea, abdominal pains, headache, and constipation. Also, jaundice associated with liver disease.

5

Bloody flux: blood in the stools, see dysentery.

Bronchial catarrh: acute bronchitis.

Catarrh: inflammation of mucous membranes of the head and throat, with a flow of mucous. Bronchial catarrh was bronchitis; suffocative catarrh was croup; urethral catarrh was gleet; vaginal catarrh was leukorrhea; and epidemic catarrh was the same as influenza.

Child bed fever: also known as puerperal fever is a form of septicaemia caused by lack of hygiene during the delivery of a baby. It was widespread in hospital deliveries in the middle of the 19th century where it was spread by doctors from patient to patient until the importance of good hygiene was finally accepted.

Cholera: an acute, infectious disease caused by *Vibrio comma*, characterized by profuse diarrhea, vomiting, and cramps. Cholera is spread by feces-contaminated water and food.

Cholera infantum: a common, non-contagious diarrhea of young children, occurring in summer or autumn. It was common among the poor and in hand-fed babies, i.e. babies who were fed on mixtures of bread or flour and water, possibly with admixture of cows' milk, which might be infected, or condensed milk, which was vitamin deficient. Such brews of "pap" in addition to being nutritionally inadequate were easily infected with bacteria. Death frequently occurred in three to five days. Synonyms include summer complaint, weaning brash, water gripes, choleric fever of children, and cholera morbus.

Colic: abdominal pain and cramp. Renal colic can occur from disease in the kidney and affects the ureter; gallstone colic arises from stones in the bile duct. Strictly a disorder of the colon but loosely any disorder of the stomach or bowels, attended with pain, also gripes and bellyache.

Consumption: a wasting away of the body; formerly applied especially to pulmonary tuberculosis, caused by the bacterium *Mycobacterium tuberculosis*. In physick, a wasting of muscular flesh. It is frequently attended by a hectic fever and is divided by physicians into several kinds, according to the variety of its causes. It also is called marasmus.

Convulsions: violent, involuntary muscular contractions of the extremities, trunk, and head, whereby the body and limbs are preternaturally distorted.

Croup: a spasmodic laryngitis seen mainly in children and associated with a cough and difficulties in breathing. Synonyms: include roup, hives, choak, stuffing, and rising of the lights.

Dropsy: observable swelling from fluid accumulation in body tissues, now called oedema.

Dysentery: inflammation of the intestine. There are two varieties: amoebic dysentery and bacillary dysentery. Synonyms include flux, bloody flux, contagious pyrexia (fever), and frequent griping stools.

Epilepsy: a disorder of the nervous system, either with mild and occasional loss of attention or with severe convulsions and loss of consciousness, commonly caused by oxygen starvation during a difficult birth.

6

Gravel: a disease characterized by small stones which are formed in the kidneys, passed along the ureters to the bladder, and expelled with the urine.

Hives: an allergic skin disorder, often attended by severe itching.

Hydrothorax: congestion of the lungs, see also dropsy.

Inflammation: the classic definition comes from the Roman physician Celsus who described four symptoms: swelling, heat, redness, and pain.

Jaundice: a yellow pigment deposited in the skin, whites of the eyes, and mucous membranes, caused by an increase of bile pigments in the blood A distemper from obstruction of the glands of the liver which prevents the gall from being duly separated from the blood.

Kings evil: scrofula, a tubercular infection of the throat lymph glands. The name originated in the time of Edward the Confessor, with the belief that the disease could be cured by the touch of the king of England. A scrofulous distemper, in which the glands are ulcerated, commonly believed to be cured by the touch of a king. In the late 19th and early 20th centuries the infected gland was lanced and drained, often leading to a noticeable scar on the neck as the wound might continue to seep for a time.

Lockjaw: tetanus, an infectious, often fatal disease caused by the bacterium *Clostridium tetani*, which enters the body through wounds.

Marasmus: progressive emaciation caused by malnutrition in young children.

Mortification: infection, often used for gangrene or necrosis, also, a state of corruption, or losing the vital qualities, gangrene.

Palsy: a privation of motion or feeling or both, proceeding from some cause below the cerebellum, joined with a coldness, flaccidity, and a wasting of the parts. If affecting all the parts below the head, except the thorax and heart it is called a paraplegia; if in one side only, a hemiplegia; and, if in some parts only on one side, a paralysis. This definition could include conditions arising from spinal injuries and stroke as well as conditions such as Bell's palsy and cerebral palsy.

Pleurisy: inflammation of the pleura, the lining of the chest cavity. Symptoms are chills, fever, dry cough, and pain in the affected side.

Quinsy: an acute inflammation of the soft palate around the tonsils, often leading to an abscess. Synonyms include: suppurative tonsillitis, cynanche tonsillaris, paristhmitis, and sore throat. Also, a tumid inflammation in the throat, sometimes producing suffocation.

Scrofula: tuberculosis of the lymphatic glands, especially those in the neck. A disease of children and young adults.

Sphacelus: gangrene, also a gangrenous or necrosed part or mass.

Teething: Teething infants sometimes suffered infections of the gums as the teeth erupted leading to pain and swelling. If the infection became systemic, it could lead to convulsions, diarrhea, and even death. Another explanation of teething as a cause of death is that infants were often weaned at the time of teething and may have encountered contaminated milk or food.

Thrush: a disease in which there are white spots and ulcers in the mouth, and on the tongue, caused by a parasitic fungus, *Candida albicans*.

Typhoid fever: an infectious disease producing intestinal inflammation and ulceration, usually encountered in the summer months. It is caused by the bacterium *Salmonella typhosa*. The name came from the disease's similarity to typhus.

Typhus: An acute, infectious disease caused by the parasite *Rickettsia prowazekii*, transmitted by lice and fleas and sometimes called bilious fever. It is marked by high fever, stupor alternating with delirium, intense headache and dark red rash. The epidemic or classic form is louse borne; the endemic or murine is flea borne.

Marriage and Death Notices	Date
On Thursday evening last, by the Rev. Mr. Fenwick, Enos McFaul, Esq. to Miss Mary, daughter of James Collins, Esq. all of this city.	01/01/1820
Departed this life on Friday evening, 24th Dec., in the 70th year of her age, Mrs. Rosanna Dorothy Cook, long a respectable inhabitant of this city.	01/01/1820
Departed this life on the 27th of Dec., Mrs. Johannah Forrester, in the 65th year of her age, after six weeks illness, which she bore with Christian fortitude.	01/03/1820
By the Rev. Dr. Glendy, on the evening of Thursday last, Dr. John Buckler, to Miss Eliza, eldest daughter of James Sloan, Esq., all of this city.	01/03/1820 01/04/1820
On Thursday evening last, by the Rev. Mr. Bartow, Mr. Joseph Roach, to Miss Henrietta Medcalf, all of this city.	01/04/1820
On Saturday last, by the Rev. Mr. Babade, Mr. John Charles King, to Miss Louisa Jane Nathalie, daughter of Mr. L. F. Leloup, all of this city.	01/04/1820
At Easton, on the 20th ult. by the Rev. Mr. Scull, Mr. William C. Skinner, to Miss Mary D. Watts, both of that place.	01/04/1820
At the residence of Robert Dennis, Esq., in Dorchester county, on the 22nd ult., Mr. Robert Dennis Waters, aged 22 years and 7 days, much lamented by his relations and friends.	01/04/1820
At Nashville, on the 14th December, by the Rev. Edmund Lanier, Mr. William George, late of Baltimore, to Miss Martha Ann, daughter of Mr. John Cox, of that town.	01/05/1820
Last evening, by the Rev. Mr. Bartow, Garrett Garrettson Worthington, Esq. of Baltimore county, to Miss Julia, daughter of Hezekiah Price, Esq. of this city.	01/05/1820
At Annapolis, on Saturday night last, suddenly, Mrs. Elizabeth Brewer, consort of John Brewer, Esq., Register of the Western Shore Land Office.	01/05/1820
Mr. Alexander Soper, to Miss Mary Ann Mahew, both of Prince George's county, Md.	01/06/1820
On Thursday evening last, by the Rev. Dr. Glendy, Mr. Chilian Ashmead, to Miss Hannah Hide, of this city.	01/08/1820

Marriage and Death Notices	Date
On Thursday evening last, by the Rev. Mr. Baer, Capt. James H. Martin, to Miss Louisa Caroline, daughter of the late Mr. Thomas Wood, all of this city.	01/08/1820
On Tuesday evening last, at Fox Hall, Prince George's co., Md., by the Rev. Mr. M'Cormick, Capt. George Talbott, of Fairfax co., to Mrs. Elizabeth Neale, of the former place.	01/08/1820
On Saturday morning last, at 6 o'clock, after a long and afflicting illness, Mrs. Isabella James, aged forty nine years. She was a woman of the most estimable qualities and respected character, in whose death her friends and neighbors have experienced a grievous loss; her husband and children an irreparable one. The needy and distressed never applied to her in vain - she was the comforter of the sick and afflicted - as a wife, a mother, and a mistress, she was kind and affectionate – and we trust she has gone to meet her reward in the bosom of her father and her Lord.	01/10/1820
On Thursday evening last, by the Rev. Mr. Bartow, Mr. Elias Avery, to Miss Mary Ray, all of this city.	01/11/1820
On Tuesday evening last, by the Rev. Mr. Burgess, Mr. John Hoffman, Merchant, to Miss Margaret Ann Peterson, daughter of the late Capt. John Peterson, all of this city.	01/12/1820
At his seat, in Annapolis, Md., on the 27th ult., Gen. Osborn Williams, a distinguished soldier of the Revolution.	01/12/1820
On Thursday, the 6th inst., at Holly, the residence of Mr. Lewis Foulk, Baltimore county, by the Rev. Bishop Black, of Halifax, John Brown, Esq. of Denton, Caroline county, to Miss Eliza Grey, daughter of the late Robt. Bonsall, of New York.	01/13/1820
Last evening, by the Rev. Mr. Snyder, Mr. Andrew Entz, to Miss Sarah Kauffman, all of this city.	01/14/1820
By the Rev. Dr. Glendy, on the evening of Thursday last, Mr. Ephraim A. R. Robinson, to Miss Ellen M. Hanna, all of this city.	01/15/1820
On the 12th instant, by the Rev. Mr. Childs, Mr. Mark Grafton, of this city, to Miss Keziah Hall, daughter of Mr. Edward Hall, of Baltimore county.	01/15/1820
On Tuesday, the 11th inst., by the Rev. William Ninde, Andrew F. Henderson, Esq. to Miss Susan, daughter of Wm. Ward, Esq., all of	01/15/1820

Marriage and Death Notices	Date
Cecil county.	
On Sunday morning last, in St. Peter's church, by the Rev. Mr. Henshaw, Mr. Andrew McLaughlin, to Miss Francis Ann Barnum, daughter of the late David Barnum, all of this city.	01/17/1820
On Thursday last, Capt. M. S. Bunbury, long a respectable inhabitant of this city – he has left a family to lament his loss. Capt. B. was respected by all who knew him, for his excellent disposition, and his friends and acquaintances have cause to lament his loss. "An honest man is the noblest work of God" and Capt. B. was that man.	01/17/1820
On Friday evening last, by the Rev. Mr. Bartow, Mr. Benjamin Child to Miss Esther Bailey, all of this city.	01/18/1820
At Annapolis, Mr. Thomas Wayman, to Miss Elizabeth Crutchley.	01/19/1820
On the 19th inst., of a pulmonary affection, which she bore with truly Christian fortitude and submission, Miss Ann Appleby, aged 28 years. It seems often to be the will of Providence, that those who were the most eminently qualified to adorn and benefit society, should be the first to be torn from it. Worth is frequently shrouded in a delicate tenement, which makes it more easily yield to the storms and chilling blasts that assail it. But the reflection is consoling that it will be transplanted to a more genial clime, when no adverse winds will ruffle its beautiful foliage, or parching siroc destroy its delightful fragrance. Miss A. embraced the religion of the Gospel in early life; it was the comfort of her days of health and the support of her dying hours. It carried her tranquilly, without a misgiving fear, "thro the dark valley of the shadow of death." It tempered her natural disposition; softened her manners, and through around her that halo, which should always encircle virtue. Alas! She has gone, and left us to weep her loss, but "Her spirit soars "Beyond the skies and leave the stars behind "Lo! Angels lead her to the happy shores "And floating paeans fill the buoyant wind." W.	01/21/1820
At his seat in St. Mary's county, Md., on the 4th inst., Philip Key, Esq., in the 70th year of his age.	01/21/1820
At Fredericktown, Md., on the 19th ult., Mr. Thomas Little, in the 29th year of his age.	01/21/1820
On Thursday evening last, by the Rev. Dr. Roberts, Mr. John Medairy,	01/22/1820

Marriage and Death Notices	Date
to Miss Rachel, daughter of Alexander Russell, Esq. all of this city.	
At Charleston, S. C., on Thursday the 13th, by the Rev. Dr. Gadsden, M. P. Mitchell, Esq., of this city, to Miss Ann Eliza, daughter of Joshua Brown, Esq., of the former place.	01/22/1820
Yesterday morning, about 7 o'clock, after a long and painful illness, Mrs. Ann Pason Millard, consort of Mr. Joseph Lee Millard, aged 58 years, for a long time a respectable inhabitant of Fell's Point; leaving a disconsolate husband and four children to lament their loss. But their loss is her great gain.	01/22/1820
At Prospect Hill, Prince George's county, Md., on Tuesday 18th instant, by the Rev. Mr. Gaes, George W. Duval, Esq. to Miss Elizabeth H., daughter of Nathaniel Soper, Esq.	01/25/1820
On Monday evening last, by the Rev. Dr. Elbert, Mr. Ezekiel Wilson, to Miss Jane Childs, both of this city.	01/26/1820
At Boston, Samuel Eliot, Esq., aged 81: one of the most eminent merchants, enlightened citizens, and benevolent men, of our metropolis, and the age we live in.	01/26/1820
Last evening, Campbell S. Askew, in the 42nd year of his age.	01/26/1820
On Tuesday evening, 25th inst., by the Rev. J. M. Duncan, Mr. John P. Coulter, to Deborah, eldest daughter of Mr. James Symington, all of this city.	01/27/1820
On Tuesday evening, the 25th inst. by the Rev. Mr. Grist, Mr. Miller Speakman, of the District of Columbia, to the truly amiable Miss Rebecca Young, of Baltimore county.	01/27/1820
On Wednesday, the 26th instant, Capt. James Gibson, of Mathews county, master of the sloop Pike, now in this port, at an advanced age. The deceased was a native of Virginia; through a long, useful, and chequered life, supported a spotless reputation, and was universally esteemed for his benevolence and urbanity of disposition. "His heart was formed in a superior mould – it was his own worst enemy."	01/27/1820
On Wednesday evening, 26th inst., by the Rev. Thomas Birch, Mr. Thomas A. Conway, to Miss Catherine Richard, all of this city.	01/28/1820
In Warwick, R. I., on the 10th inst., Mrs. Susanna Cornell, in the 51st year of her age, consort of Mr. Abner Cornell, of Westport, Mass., and	01/28/1820

Marriage and Death Notices	Date
daughter of Mr. William Brown, of the county of Kent, Maryland.	
In this city, last evening, Mr. David Hans, in the 25th year of his age, a young man whose virtues endeared him to his friends, and his loss will be severely felt by his widowed mother, of whom he was the sole stay and support. His friends and acquaintances are requested to attend his funeral at 3 o'clock this afternoon.	01/29/1820
On Thursday evening last, by the Rt. Rev. Bishop Kemp, Mr. Richard Gawthrop to Miss Charlotte Young, all of this city.	01/31/1820
Last evening, by the Rev. Dr. Samuel K. Jennings, David Meredith Reese, M. D. to Miss Frances Brown Harris, both of this city	01/31/1820
On Wednesday, the 19th instant, at his late dwelling in Octoraro Hundred, Cecil county, Brother Samuel Chew Hall, a worthy member of Harmony Lodge No. 56, much lamented by his brothers.	01/31/1820
Departed this life, on Friday evening last, in the fortieth year of her age, Mrs. Margaret Merryman, consort of Job Merryman, of this city. She beheld with a mind tranquil and serene, the approach of death; and with a mind full of faith, resigned her spirit into the hands of her Redeemer, to receive that reward promised to the righteous. "Rejoice ye in that day, and leap for joy, for behold, your reward is great in Heaven." Luke, vi, 26.	02/01/1820
On the 25th inst., Mr. John Sprigg, of Montgomery county, to Miss Mary Dorsey.	02/02/1820
At Havana, on the 24th ult., after a few days illness, Mr. Thomas P. Goodwin, of this city. Inexorable death has again caused to bleed afresh the wounds of his afflicted relatives; but a few months before, the brother-in-law of Mr. Goodwin, George P. Stevenson, having also fallen a victim to the same fatal climate. Those who were favored of the acquaintance of Mr. Goodwin will bear testimony with the writer of this imperfect tribute to his memory, to his amiable worth and benevolent disposition, and whilst it behooves us, the survivors, to bow in humble submission so the decrees of an over-ruling Providence, the affectionate heart, treasuring the remembrance of his virtues, will long feel with sensibility the melancholy blank he has left in society. "No farther seek his merits to disclose, "Or draw his frailties from their dread abode; "There they alike in trembling hope repose, "The bosom of his Father and his God."	02/02/1820

13

Marriage and Death Notices	Date
At Boston, Don Juan Stoughton, his Catholic Majesty's Consul in this town for above thirty years, aged 75. Universally respected during his life, his death is universally lamented.	02/02/1820
On the 27th Jan. by the Rev. Bishop Kemp, Mr. Joseph Harrop, to Mrs. Ann Keatinge, both of this city.	02/03/1820
On Wednesday afternoon, much lamented, Mr. Joseph Thornburgh, of this city, an aged member of the society of Friends. The funeral will take place tomorrow morning, the 4th inst., at 10 o'clock, from his late residence in Sharp street. The friends of the deceased are invited to attend.	02/03/1820
Last evening, by the Rev. Dr. Cole, Mr. John Coats, Jr., to Miss Jane E. Sterret, both of this city.	02/04/1820
On Thursday evening last, by the Rev. Mr. Force, Mr. Asa Needham, merchant, to Miss Ann Eliza Lynch, all of this city.	02/04/1820
On the 9th instant, at his residence in Ontario county, N. Y., Valentine Brother, Esq., a representative in the assembly, from that county, and formerly a resident of Fredericktown, Md.	02/04/1820
Suddenly, on the morning of the 25th ultimo, Mr. Hugh Montgomery Stewart, a native of Ayrshire, Scotland, aged 67; a gentleman of the strictest integrity and honor, and gifted with superior talents, which had been highly cultivated.	02/04/1820
On Sunday, 30th ult., at Washington, by the Rev. Mr. Munroe, Mr. Lewis J. Hunter, of Baltimore, to Miss Sophia Greene, of the former place.	02/05/1820
On Monday evening last, by the Rev. Mr. Bartow, Mr. Samuel Elms, to Mrs. Rebecca Rainey, all of this city.	02/05/1820
On Thursday evening last, by the Rev. Dr. Jennings, Mr. Lemuel W. Gosnell, of this city, to Miss Providence, daughter of Mr. Isaiah O'Dell, of Baltimore county.	02/05/1820
On Thursday evening last, by the Rev. Dr. Roberts, Mr. John House, to Miss Catherine Grover, all of this city.	02/05/1820
On Thursday evening last, by the Rt. Rev. Dr. Kemp, John Marshall, Jr., Esq., of Virginia, son of the Chief Justice of the United States, to Elizabeth Maria, daughter of Dr. Ashton Alexander, of this city.	02/05/1820

Marriage and Death Notices	Date
On Friday, the 4th inst., after a severe illness, Mrs. Catherine Foltz, widow of the late Wm. Foltz, in the 31st year of her age.	02/05/1820
Last evening, by the Rev. Dr. Kurtz, Mr. George August Tegtmeyer, to Miss Ann Catherine Raab, all of this city.	02/07/1820
On Thursday 27th ult., by the Rev. Mr. Sparks, Mr. Ebenezer M. Covington, to Miss Maria Carman, both of Queen Ann's county, Maryland.	02/07/1820
On Thursday, 27th ult., by the Rev. Mr. Martindale, Mr. Charles Langdon, to Miss Elizabeth Duhamell, both of Queen Ann's county, Maryland.	02/07/1820
Mr. Richard D. Armengast, to Miss Elizabeth Cox, both of Baltimore county.	02/07/1820
Mr. Henry Myer, of Washington county, Md., to Miss Catherine Bixler, daughter of Mr. Christian Bixler, of Baltimore county.	02/07/1820
On Thursday last, Mr. Henry Sprengle, to Miss Catherine Fuhrman, daughter of Mr. Jacob Fuhrman, both of Baltimore county.	02/07/1820
On the 25th ultimo, Mr. Stephen Biddle, to Miss Maria Cook, daughter of Mr. Aaron Cook, all of Dorchester county, Maryland.	02/07/1820
On Tuesday, the 1st inst., by the Rev. Mr. Balch, Mr. Henry Albers, of Baltimore, to Miss Rebecca Brooks, of Georgetown.	02/07/1820
On Saturday, the 5th inst., by the Rev. Mr. Wyatt, Mr. Josiah Harrop, to Miss Elizabeth Wilkins, both of this city.	02/08/1820
On Tuesday evening last, by the Rev. Mr. Angie, Mr. Walter B. Brooke, of Prince George's county, to Mary Victor, daughter of James Middleton, Esq., of Charles county.	02/08/1820
On Tuesday, 1st inst., by the Rev. Mr. Childs, Mr. Edward Gorsuch, to Miss Sarah B. Stansbury, all of Baltimore county.	02/09/1820
On Thursday last, in the 60th year of her age, Mrs. Wilhelmina Dorothea Ratien, wife of Mr. Richard Ratien, of this city.	02/12/1820
Yesterday, in the 45th year of his age, Mr. Thomas Turner. His friends and acquaintances are requested to attend his funeral this evening at 3 o'clock, from his late residence in Wilk street.	02/12/1820

Marriage and Death Notices	Date
On Thursday evening last, by the Rev. Mr. Waugh, Mr. Jacob Waters, to Miss Mary Ann Harrison, all of this city.	02/12/1820 02/14/1820
On Sunday evening last, by the Rev. Mr. Waugh, Capt. Joshua K. Harrison, to Miss Mary Ann, eldest daughter of Mr. Thomas Curtain, all of this city.	02/14/1820
On Sunday morning, the 13th inst., in the 60th year of her age, Mrs. Catherine Rawlings, after a long and tedious illness, which she bore with great patience and resignation.	02/15/1820
Last evening, by the Rev. Dr. Elbert, Mr. George Peale, to Miss Louisa Urie, both of this city.	02/16/1820
On Saturday morning last, in the 64th year of his age, Captain Joseph Leonard, born in England, but many years an inhabitant of Maryland.	02/16/1820
On Thursday evening last, by the Rev. Dr. Roberts, Mr. Jesse Armager to Miss Julianna Lash, all of this city.	02/17/1820
At Hagerstown, Md., Mrs. Catherine Schnebly, wife of Mr. Daniel Schnebly, in the 32nd year of her age.	02/18/1820
On Thursday evening last, by the Rev. Mr. Waugh, Mr. Frederick S. Littig, to Miss Hannah W., second daughter of Mr. William Pitt, all of this city.	02/19/1820
On the 17th day of February, 1820, Mrs. Ann Way, consort of Capt. John Way, of this city, at the early age of 24 years. Scarcely had one year passed, since with mirth and hilarity, were celebrated the connubial rites of her, whose funeral obsequies her friends have been called on to perform. Five days a mother, and just about to present the consecrated chalice to her lips, when an unexpected blow dashed it from her hand, and summoned her to the appointed place of rendezvous for all. So short the notice, as hardly to admit a parting kiss or farewell sigh – as scarcely to permit the short lived mother to utter a dying wish for her babe. Yet was the decree received without a murmur or complaint; and the gloom produced by the absence of husband, father and mother, was dissipated by the hopes of *"another and a better world."* Her life was such as made her many friends, and enabled her to cry, at the trying hour of death, *"Where is thy boasted Victory, Oh Grave!"* "Thus at the shut of ev'n, the weary bird "Leaves the wide air, and in some lonely brake, "Cowers down, and dozes 'till the dawn of day,	02/19/1820

Marriage and Death Notices	Date
"Then claps her well-fledg'd wings, and bears away!"	
At Hagerstown, Mrs. Harriet Hall, wife of Mr. John Hall, in the 28th year of her age.	02/19/1820
At his residence on Ringgold's Manor, Capt. John Ashbury.	02/19/1820
Last evening, by the Rev. Mr. Bare, Mr. Matthew R. Stone, to Mrs. Mary Askey, all of this city.	02/21/1820
At Easton, Md., Mr. George Stevens to Miss Ann Chapline.	02/22/1820
At St. Michaels, Md., Mr. James Wrightson to Miss Sarah Auld.	02/22/1820
On Friday, the 18th inst., after a short illness, Miss Mary Garts, daughter of the late Charles Garts, Esq., of this city.	02/22/1820
At his residence, on the evening of the 21st inst., after a long and painful illness, Capt. Samuel Lowry, in the 55th year of his age, long a respectable merchant of this city – he has left a widow and a large family, who will long deplore the loss of an affectionate husband and father.	02/22/1820
On The 19th inst., after a short illness, at her residence, near Baltimore, Ann Palmer, consort of Abraham Palmer, in the 37th year of her age, a member of the society of Friends. By the death of this truly amiable and pious lady, her husband has lost a very affectionate and virtuous bosom friend and companion, her children a tender and affectionate mother, and her acquaintances a kind, benevolent, and charitable neighbor; yet they have a consolation in the belief, that she is now reaping the rewards of a well spent life, in the arms of her precious Redeemer.	02/22/1820
On the 15th inst., Mrs. Priscilla Boteler, wife of Dr. Boteler, of Shepperdstown, Va., and daughter of Mr. Alex. Robinson, of this city. Mrs. Boteler has left to the care of her bereaved husband, four small children. She lived only twenty-three years; but the tenor of her short and useful life, gives to the grieving relatives and friends who witnessed her bodily sufferings, for some time past, the comforting assurance that her troubles now are over; and that her earthly trials were of short duration, because she was soon fitted for the awful change which has taken place. When vigorous life flowed through her veins, she did not forget her God; when she passed through the valley of the shadow of death, her God did not leave her or forsake her, but enabled her to maintain a successful conflict with the king of terrors, and to exhibit to those, who gathered instruction at her deathbed scene a bright example	02/22/1820

Marriage and Death Notices	Date
of resignation, piety and hope. *"Blessed are the dead who die in the Lord."*	
At New Orleans, on the 6th of January last, after a severe illness, Mrs. Sophia D. Harris, formerly of the Philadelphia and Baltimore Theatres.	02/22/1820
On Saturday morning last, at Philadelphia, Isabelle, consort of John Alexander Brown, late of Baltimore. She was a native of Ireland, aged 23 years, and has left a disconsolate husband with three small children and a numerous circle of relatives and friends, who alone knew how to appreciate her worth and the loss they have met with.	02/22/1820
Last evening, by the Rev. John Duncan, Evan T. Ellicott, merchant of this city, to Harvey M. Bond, youngest daughter of the late Oliver Bond.	02/24/1820
On Saturday evening last, 19th inst., Mr. Tudor James, in the 48th year of his age.	02/24/1820
On the 1st inst., at her usual residence in Churchill, Queen Ann's county, Mrs. Sarah Elizabeth Taylor, consort of Dr. Parran Taylor, in the 19th year of her age, of a lingering pulmonary affection, which she bore with an unusual fortitude and resignation to the last, when she gave up her sole with composure to the author of its existence, with a lively assurance of a welcome reception on the right hand of the hope of her salvation.	02/24/1820
On Tuesday evening last, by the Rev. Mr. Healey, Mr. Chaplin Conway to Mrs. Sarah Fanvell, all of this city.	02/25/1820
On Thursday evening last, by the Rev. Mr. Fenwick, Mr. Wm. Harding, to Miss Elizabeth Stewart, all of this city.	02/26/1820
On Thursday evening last, by the Rev. Mr. Toy, Mr. Hirem Wiley to Miss Elizabeth Koonts, all of this city.	02/26/1820
On the 15th inst., at Chestertown Ferry, by the Rev. Mr. Thomas, Mr. John S. Foreman, to Miss Susan Skinner, both of Queen Anne's county, Md.	02/26/1820
On the 17th inst., at Centerville, Md., by the Rev. Mr. Martindale, Mr. Thomas R. Perkins, to Miss Ann Kennard, both of that place.	02/26/1820
On Thursday evening, by the Rev. Dr. Roberts, Mr. Edward Green, to Miss Lydia Ann Sumwalt, both of this city.	02/26/1820

Marriage and Death Notices	Date
On Thursday evening last, by the Rev. Mr. Force, Mr. John W. Culisen, to Miss Margaret Mifflin, all of this city.	02/28/1820
On Thursday morning, by the Rev. Mr. Williams, Mr. John Wright, Esq., to Miss Jemima Frederica Barhan, all of Baltimore county.	02/28/1820
On Thursday evening last, by the Rev. Mr. Force, Capt. Thomas Hook, to Miss Sarah Dorsey, both of Baltimore county.	02/28/1820
On Thursday evening last, by the Rev. Albert Helfenstein, Mr. William Hurst to Miss Rebecca Turner, both of this city.	02/29/1820
On Tuesday evening, by the Rt. Rev. Bishop Kemp, Granville S. Townsend to Sarah, youngest daughter of the late David Brown, Esq., of this city.	03/01/1820
On Sunday evening last, by the Rev. Maybury Parks, Mr. Joseph Mather to Miss Elizabeth Parker, all of this city.	03/02/1820
On Tuesday last, by the Rev. A. Helfenstein, Capt. Isaac D. Johns to Miss Susannah S. Loudenslager, both of this city.	03/02/1820
On Sunday, the 15th ult., by the Rev. Mr. Warfield, Capt. Richard Kenney to Miss Mary Kenney, both of Talbot county, Md.	03/03/1820
On Tuesday, the 15th ult., by the Rev. Mr. Skull, Mr. Robinson Stitchnickey, to Miss Eliza Manship, both of Talbot County, Md.	03/03/1820
On the 15th ult., Mr. Richard J. Harrison, Esq., to Miss Sarah B. Hackett, both of Queen Anne's county, Md.	03/03/1820
At Annapolis, Md., on Thursday evening last, by the Rev. Mr. Guest, Dr. Walter W. Wyvill, of Anne Arundel county, to Miss Margaret Murdoch, all of that city.	03/03/1820
On Thursday evening, the 24th February, by the Rev. Mr. _____, Mr. Thomas Sands, to the amiable Miss Elizabeth Tunis, a niece of Seany Busic, all of Queen Ann's county, Maryland.	03/03/1820
On Sunday evening last, by the Rev. Mr. Henshaw, Mr. Daniel Mandeville, merchant of Philadelphia, to Miss Harriet, third daughter of Geo. Warner, Esq., of this city.	03/03/1820
Suddenly, on Wednesday evening last, Mr. Peter Wilhelm, in the 25th year of his age,	03/03/1820

Marriage and Death Notices	Date
On Wednesday evening last, by the Rev. Mr. Bartow, Mr. Moses Millum, to Mrs. Sarah Seeman, all of this city.	03/04/1820
On Thursday last, by the Rev. P. Davidson, Mr. John W. Walker, of Baltimore, to Miss Rachel Crabs, of Frederick county.	03/06/1820
At Friend's Meeting House, Alexandria, D. C., on the 2nd inst., John E. Carey, merchant of Baltimore, to Ann, daughter of Thomas Irwin, of the former place.	03/08/1820
On Sunday evening last, by the Rev. Mr. Bartow, Mr. Thomas Hassell to Mrs. Elizabeth Ware.	03/08/1820
On Tuesday last, by the Rev. Dr. Glendy, St. Clair Sutherland, Esq., to Mrs. Jane Donaldson, all of this city.	03/08/1820
On Sunday evening last, by the Rev. Dr. Roberts, Mr. Barney Miller, to Miss Jane Conway, all of this city.	03/08/1820
In this city, on the 2nd inst., in the 24th year of his age, Mr. Elijah Weaver.	03/08/1820
At Fredericktown, on Thursday evening, 24th ult., by the Rev. Mr. Higgins, Mr. Cutsail, aged 78, to Miss Fogle, aged 17, all of that county.	03/09/1820
By the Rev. Dr. Glendy, on the evening of Thursday last, Mr. Edward Keene, to Miss Elizabeth Barnett, both of Baltimore county.	03/10/1820
This morning, in the 70th year of his age, Mr. Adam Trumbo, long a respectable inhabitant of this city. His relatives and friends are respectfully invited to attend his funeral from his late residence in Biddle street, near the Reisterstown road, at 3 o'clock Tomorrow.	03/11/1820
On Thursday evening last, by the Rev. D. E. Reese, Mr. James P. Woods, to Miss Matilda A. Partridge, both of this city.	03/13/1820
On Friday, 10th inst., after a short, but severe illness, Dr. John Caldwell, in the 26th year of his age.	03/13/1820
On the 9th inst., at his residence on Long Green, Mr. James Gittings, Jr., in the 50th year of his age.	03/13/1820
In Caroline county, Md., William Wilson, a member of the society of Friends, aged 40 years.	03/13/1820

Marriage and Death Notices	Date
Last evening, by the Rev. Mr. Valiant, Mr. Nathaniel Batchlor, to Miss Harriet Ashly, all of this city.	03/14/1820
On Sunday evening last, by the Rev. Geo. Dashiell, Mr. Robert M'Causland, of Harford county, to Miss Ann Higinbotham, late of Ireland.	03/14/1820
On Sunday evening last, by the Rev. Dr. Roberts, Mr. Josias Pool, to Miss Barbara Feckley, all of this city.	03/14/1820
In this city, last evening, after a long and tedious illness, which he bore with Christian fortitude, Mr. Jonathan Alden, aged 45 years. His friends and acquaintances are respectfully invited to attend his funeral tomorrow afternoon at 3 o'clock precisely.	03/14/1820
On Tuesday evening, the 14th inst. by the Rev. Dr. Jennings, Mr. Peregrine Love to Miss Mary Rook, all of this city.	03/15/1820
At Annapolis, on Tuesday evening last, Mr. Thomas Gardiner to Miss Susan Brewer, all of that city.	03/17/1820
On Thursday last, by the Rev. Dr. Roberts, Mr. Edward G. Disney to Miss Elizabeth G. Hall, both of this city.	03/18/1820
On the 11th inst., by the Rev. Mr. Bartow, Mr. Henry Lainhart, to Mrs. Mary Cline, both of this city.	03/18/1820
Suddenly, on Friday last, at 11 o'clock, John M'Ginnis, long a respectable inhabitant of this city. His friends and acquaintances are invited to attend his funeral this evening at half 3 o'clock, at his late dwelling, Fish Market space.	03/18/1820
On Saturday, the 18th inst., in the 52nd year of her age, Mrs. Anne McClellan, consort of Robert McClellan, of this city, leaving a disconsolate husband and family, to mourn their irretrievable loss. She beheld with tranquil serenity the approach of death, and with a mind, full of faith, resigned her spirit into the hands of her Redeemer; we trust to receive that reward promised to the righteous. *"Rejoice ye in that day and leap for joy – for behold your reward is great in Heaven."*	03/20/1820
In Dorchester county, E. S., on Friday, 3rd instant, Capt. William Morgan, formerly of Baltimore, in the 30th year of his age, after a painful, lingering illness, which he bore with patient, Christian fortitude. He was a man beloved and esteemed by all who knew him.	03/20/1820

Marriage and Death Notices	Date
On Monday evening last, by the Rev. Mr. Bartow, Mr. Alexander Jackson, to Miss Harriet Craig, all of this city.	03/22/1820
In Talbot county, Md., Miss Eleanor S. Dent, in the 22nd year of her age, late of Baltimore.	03/22/1820
On Thursday evening last, by the Rev. Mr. Waugh, Mr. Robert Graves, to Miss Lydia Humes, all of Fell's Point.	03/24/1820
On Thursday evening last, by the Rev. Geo. Dashiell, Mr. Daniel Kauffman, to Miss Eleanora Clark, both of this city.	03/25/1820
On Thursday evening last, by the Rev. Mr. Healey, Mr. John Z. Thomas, to Miss Matilda Louisa Seeley, all of this city.	03/25/1820
On Monday, the 20th inst., at his residence in Calvert county, Henry Hunt, Esq., aged 75 years, long a respectable inhabitant of that place. His death will long be lamented by a large circle of friends and acquaintances, but especially by his children, who mourn indeed for the death of a dear and affectionate parent. The poor will have cause to mourn, as he was a friend of the needy and distressed.	03/25/1820
At Easton, Md., on Tuesday morning, 7th inst., about 7 o'clock, at the residence of Mr. Wm. Harrison of James, Miss Eleanor S. Dent, in the 22nd year of her age. Miss Dent came from Baltimore to this shore in June last, supposed then to be in the last stage of a decline.	03/25/1820
At Havana, of the fever, about the 22nd of February, Dr. Joshua W. Ridgely, a practitioner near Little River, N. C. It is stated that he was a native of Maryland, and that his parents probably reside in Ohio. [Some papers belonging to him have been received by the Department of State.]	03/25/1820
On Thursday evening last by the Rev. John Hagerty, Mr. Daniel Hartman, to Mrs. Charlotte Spinks, both of this city.	03/27/1820
On Thursday night, the 23rd inst., by the Rev. Mr. Toy, Mr. Edward Stone, to Miss Eliza Robinson, both of this city.	03/27/1820
At New Orleans, in February last, Mr. James Abercrombie, late of the Philadelphia and Baltimore Theatres.	03/27/1820
At Friend's Meeting, Mount Pleasant, Jefferson county, Ohio, Benjamin Thomas, late of Baltimore, to Joanna Terrel, of the former place.	03/28/1820

Marriage and Death Notices	Date
On Wednesday evening last, by the Rev. Dr. Glendy, Mr. William Munroe, to Miss Susanna Reese, both of this city.	03/28/1820
On Sunday evening last, by the Rev. Dr. Glendy, Mr. Wm. Moorhouse, to Miss Catherine Mincher, both of this city.	03/28/1820
On Thursday evening last, by the Rev. Mr. Williams, Mr. Richard Rawlings, to Miss Nancy Fernerden, both of Anne Arundel county.	03/28/1820
On the 22nd ult., off the Capes of Virginia, on his passage from the West indies to this port, Mr. Francis Woodward, in the 25th year of his age.	03/28/1820
On Thursday evening last, by the Rev. Mr. Healey, Mr. David Williams to Miss Phoebe Powell, all of this city.	03/30/1820
At Friends Meeting, Mount Pleasant, Jefferson County, Ohio, Benjamin Thomas, late of Baltimore, to Joanna Terrell, of the former place.	03/30/1820
On Tuesday evening last, by the Rev. Mr. Bartow, Mr. John H. Speck to Miss Angelica Bennett, all of this city.	03/30/1820
On Sunday evening last, by the Rev. Mr. Kurtz, Mr. Wm. Solomon, to Miss Eliza Myers, all of this city.	04/04/1820
On Sunday evening last, by the Rev. Mr. Bartow, Capt. William Shanks, to Miss Charlotte Howell, all of this city.	04/04/1820
On the 1st inst., Mrs. Jane W. Hall, in the 45th year of her age. Who through the chequered scenes of life was amiably virtuous, and in death victorious – leaving a disconsolate daughter to lament the demise of a fond parent.	04/04/1820
Mr. Benjamin White, Jr. to Miss Rebecca Darby, of Montgomery county, Md.	04/06/1820
On Monday evening last, by the Rev. James I. Higgins, Dr. John H. McElfresh to Miss Theresia Mantz, daughter of Mr. Francis Mantz, all of Fredericktown.	04/06/1820
On Thursday evening last, by the Rev. David M. Schaeffer, John H. Harding, Esq., to Miss Eleanor Mantz, daughter of Mr. Francis Mantz, all of Fredericktown.	04/06/1820
Last evening, after a lingering illness, which she bore with Christian meekness and fortitude, Mrs. Elizabeth Forbes, in the fifty eighth year of her age, sincerely regretted by a numerous circle of friends and	04/06/1820

Marriage and Death Notices	Date
relatives. It may be truly said of this departed lady, that in her character were centered those benevolent and pious qualities, which so plainly mark the Christian. Her suavity of manners, her even and friendly disposition, endeared her to all who knew her – while her firm and unshaken faith in her Redeemer, during a long series of bodily suffering, gave to her mind an ease and tranquility, experienced only by the pious.	
Last evening, 9 o'clock, Mr. John Morris Bennett, aged 34. His friends and acquaintances are invited to attend his funeral tomorrow morning at ten o'clock from the Hotel near Pratt street Bridge.	04/06/1820
On Wednesday evening last, by the Rev. Mr. Force, Mr. John Snyder, to Miss Eliza Spry, all of this city.	04/07/1820
At White-Haven, in Dorchester county, on Monday morning, the 27th ult., in the 35th year of her age, Mrs. Alice, the beloved consort of Capt. James Colston.	04/08/1820
At his residence in Talbot county, on Friday night, the 24th ult., after a short illness, Mr. Zebulon Dixon, at an advanced age.	04/08/1820
On the morning of the 29th of March, at Fowling Creek Mills, very suddenly, Mrs. Ann Dukes, consort of Levi Dukes, Esq., of Caroline county.	04/08/1820
By the Rev. Dr. Glendy, on Thursday last, Mr. Richard Dent, to Miss Maria Eckles, all of this city.	04/08/1820 04/10/1820
On Thursday evening last, by the Rev. Dr. Roberts, Mr. Richard Bradshaw to Miss Ann Beck, both of this city.	04/10/1820
On Tuesday, the 4th inst., at Nottingham, by the Rev. Ralph Williston, John Reed Magruder, Jr., Esq., of Upper Marlboro, to Miss Eliza Waring, grand daughter of the late Robert Bowie, formerly Governor of Maryland.	04/10/1820
On Monday, the 3rd inst., by the Rev. Mr. Henshaw, Dr. John Arnest, of Virginia, to Miss Juliet Nicholson, of this city.	04/10/1820
At Fredericktown, Mr. John T. Spurrier, aged 24.	04/10/1820
At Easton, Md., Mrs. Sarah H. Kerr, consort of John Leeds Kerr, Esq. Mrs. Brannock, wife of James Brannock.	04/10/1820
At Queenstown, Md., Miss Elizabeth Troup, daughter of Dr. John I.	04/10/1820

Marriage and Death Notices	Date
Troup.	
Yesterday morning, Mr. James Bryden, in the 59th year of his age. Mr. Bryden was a native of Scotland, but for more than 30 years has resided in the United States, the greater part of that time in this city.	04/12/1820
On the 11th inst., of a Consumption, Mr. George Gillespy, a native of Ireland, and for the last five years, an inhabitant of this city. The slow, but certain, approach of death which his disease indicated from its commencement, afforded ample time for pious reflection, and the participation of those sacraments, instituted by his blessed redeemer, for the remission of sin. He lived and died a member of the Roman Catholic Church. *Requiescat in pace.*	04/14/1820
On the 14th inst., Miss Margaret Reed, in the 45th year of her age, after a long and painful illness, which she bore with truly Christian patience and resignation.	04/14/1820
Of a consumption, on Tuesday, the 11th instant, Miss Mary Ann Monihan, in the 21st year of her age – her sufferings were many, which she bore with true Christian patience and resignation.	04/15/1820
On the 6th inst., Mr. William Heddrick, to Miss Mary Morris. Mr. Jacob Trayer, to Miss Ruth Algeyer. Mr. Henry Burkepile, to Miss N. Freeland. Mr. George Ebough, to Miss Sarah Jenoweth, all of Baltimore county.	04/17/1820
On Sunday last, George Shock, aged 52, and John Ely, aged 51. The have both been biscuit bakers from their youth, and each had a hand in baking at least 50,000 barrels of Flour in his time – they were buried within two feet of each other on Monday afternoon, between 4 and 5 o'clock, P. M., in the Methodist burying ground.	04/18/1820
On Friday evening last, after a severe illness, which she bore with Christian resignation, Mrs. Elizabeth Lawson Starr, in the 52nd year of her age.	04/18/1820
On Tuesday, the eleventh inst., in the fifty ninth year of his age, at the country residence of his brother, Capt. William Bryden, about two miles from the city, Mr. James Bryden, a native of Edinburgh, Scotland – formerly the proprietor of the Fountain Inn, Light street, and for many years keeper of the Tontine Coffee House, N. Y. In Mr. Bryden's voyage through life, we have a striking instance of the mutability of human affairs – the very little dependence that can be placed on riches,	04/18/1820

Marriage and Death Notices	Date
"which take wings and fly away."	
In Fredericktown, Mr. Ephraim H. Maynard, to Miss Elizabeth, daughter of Dennis Poole.	04/19/1820
At Easton, Md., Mr. Samuel Pickering, of Baltimore, to Miss Eliza Applegarth, of that Town.	04/19/1820
At his residence in Somerset county, Md., after a short illness, Benjamin F. A. C. Dashiell, Esq.	04/19/1820
Last evening, by the Rev. Dr. John Glendy, Mr. Samuel H. Shaw, to Miss Jane G. Jenne, all of this city.	04/21/1820
At Rochelle, 17th March, James Benson, of Maryland, a seaman on board the Brandt, who was suffocated in the cabin, while fumigating the ship to destroy the Rats.	04/21/1820
On Tuesday evening last, by the Rt. Rev. Ambrose Mareschal, Mr. John I. Gross to Miss Elizabeth Worthington.	04/22/1820
On Thursday evening, by the Rev. Dr. Roberts, Mr. Benjamin Rickets, to Miss Rebecca Waters, both of this city.	04/22/1820
In Harford county, Thursday evening last, by the Rev. Mr. Reed, Mr. Robert Thompson, of Baltimore, to Miss Susan Sutton, of the former place.	04/22/1820
On Thursday evening last, by the Rev. Dr. Roberts, Mr. James Hammersley, to Miss Sophia Jane Martindale, all of this city.	04/24/1820
On Thursday evening last, by the Rev. Mr. Waugh, Mr. Thomas P. Stran, of this city, to Miss Ann Follin, of Alexandria.	04/24/1820
On Thursday evening last, by the Rev. Mr. Geo. Dashiell, Mr. Alex. Manro, Merchant, to Miss Mary Ann Armstrong, daughter of James Armstrong, Jr., Esq., all of this city.	04/24/1820
Last evening, by the Rev. Dr. John Glendy, Mr. William Ogden Niles, eldest son of Hezekiah Niles, Esq., editor of the Register, to Miss Sophia, daughter of Samuel Vincent, Esq., all of this city.	04/24/1820 04/22/1820
On Thursday evening last, by the Rev. Mr. Shane, Mr. Hugh Garvin, of Franklin county, to Miss Ann Jones, of this city.	04/25/1820

Marriage and Death Notices	Date
On Sunday evening, 16th inst., by the Rev. Mr. Moranville, Mr. Alexander J. Hunter to Mrs. Ellen Feinour, all of Fell's Point.	04/25/1820
On Sunday evening last, by the Rev. Mr. Chambers, Mr. James Brown to Miss Jane Ensor, both of Baltimore county.	04/25/1820
On Saturday evening, 22nd instant, in the 53rd year of her age, Mrs. Ann Matchett, consort of Mr. George Matchett.	04/25/1820
On Tuesday evening, by the Rev. Dr. Glendy, Mr. James Broughton, of Cecil county, to Miss Catherine, daughter of the late Samuel Patterson Wallace, of the same place.	04/26/1820
Suddenly, on Monday morning, in the sixty first year of his age, John Caldwell, a native of Philadelphia, but for the last 20 years a resident in Baltimore. Eulogy is deemed unnecessary. His numerous friends will pay the best tribute to his memory by their grief for his loss, and the cherished recollection of his estimable qualities.	04/26/1820
On the 24th inst., by the Rev. Mr. Latta, Capt. E. P. Kennedy, U. S. Navy, to Miss Ann P. Harden, of Christiana, Delaware.	04/27/1820
A New Orleans, in March last, Mr. Alvan Munroe, Printer, aged 25, recently of Baltimore.	04/27/1820
Last evening, by the Rev. Dr. Kurtz, Mr. Henry Keiffel, to Miss Eliza Lingenfelter, all of this city.	04/28/1820
At Annapolis, Mr. Isaac Holland to Miss Mary Shepherd.	05/01/1820
At Fredericktown, Mr. Thomas Burrows to Miss Elizabeth Winters.	05/01/1820
In Harford county, on Sunday evening last, by the Rev. Mr. Richardson, Mr. William Everet, to Miss Mary Worrick.	05/02/1820
At St. Thomas, on the 22nd March, Mr. James Cooper, in the 31st year of his age, long a respectable inhabitant of this city – his death is much regretted by his relations, as well as a large circle of acquaintances, to whom he was endeared by his many amiable virtues.	05/02/1820
On Friday, the 7th inst., Mr. Hollingsworth Vandevere, Sr., of a long and lingering illness, aged 90 years. He was born in the state of Maryland, but was for the last 28 years, a respectable citizen of Pendleton District, S. C.	05/02/1820

Marriage and Death Notices	Date
On Sunday evening last, by the Rev. Mr. Richards, Mr. Ebenezer Graves, aged 68, to Mrs. Susannah Flint, aged 44, all of this city.	05/04/1820
Last night, after a lingering and painful illness, Mr. John Shultz, in the eighty ninth year of his age – his friends and acquaintances are respectfully invited to attend his funeral from his late dwelling, in German street, at 9 o'clock tomorrow morning.	05/04/1820
At Annapolis, Mr. Isaac Holland, to Mrs. Mary Sherbert. Mr. Henry Williams, of Magothy, to Miss Louisa Wheedon. Capt. K. White, of Baltimore, to Miss Elizabeth Ross.	05/05/1820
On the 28th ultimo, after a short illness, at Tuscarora Mills, near Martinsborough, Va., Mr. George Weller, Sr., in the 71st year of his age – for many years a respectable citizen of Baltimore. *"Mark the perfect and the upright, for the end of that man is peace."*	05/05/1820
At Haster's tavern, on the Princeton turnpike, about two miles from this city, on Friday evening, a young woman, whose name, from a certificate signed by a Mr. Ford, of Elizabethtown, in her favor, as an industrious, honest and sober person, in whose family she had lived for nearly two years, is Maria Johnson – she was found on the road sometime in the afternoon of said day in a senseless state, with a phial still containing a small quantity of laudanum. She was genteely dressed, of a good person, and appears from 18 to 23 years of age. Her ridicule contained two certificates of her character and two or three dollars in cash. This is inserted to apprise her friends of her melancholy fate.	05/05/1820
On Thursday evening last, by the Most Rev. Archbishop Mareschal, Dr. James D. Middleton, of Charles county, to Miss Catherine M. E., eldest daughter of Mr. Owen McManus, of this city.	05/06/1820
On Thursday evening last, by the Rev. Mr. Waugh, Mr. Andrew Montgomery, to Miss Priscilla A. Lawes, all of this city.	05/06/1820
At Alexandria, D. C. on Tuesday evening last, by the Rev. Mr. Allen, Mr. George Kerrl, merchant of Baltimore, to Miss Susannah, eldest daughter of Thomas Mundell, Esq., of Prince George's county, Maryland.	05/06/1820
On Thursday evening last, by the Rev. Mr. Burch, Mr. Abraham Lee to Miss Sarah Roberts, all of this city.	05/06/1820
Miss Elizabeth Worthington, the daughter of Col. Nicholas and Catherine Worthington, departed this life in the city of Annapolis, on	05/06/1820

Marriage and Death Notices	Date
the 29th ultimo, after a most painful and distressing illness, respected and lamented by all who knew her.	
Died lately at Cambridge, Ohio, Mr. Jacob Gomber, formerly of Fredericktown.	05/06/1820
On Thursday evening, the 27th ult., by the Rev. Dr. Jennings, Mr. Abraham Stansbury, of Baltimore county, to Miss Elizabeth Whitaker, of this city.	05/08/1820
On Sunday evening last, by the Rev. Mr. Kurtz, Mr. Charles Grover, to Mrs. Savannah Crook, all of this city.	05/08/1820
Yesterday, about 12 o'clock, after a lingering illness, Mr. Richard Summerville, in the 42nd year of his age – his friends and acquaintances are respectfully invited to attend his funeral, from his late residence, at the corner of Bridge and Green streets, O. T., at 4 o'clock this afternoon.	05/08/1820
On Thursday, the 20th ult., Mr. George Gilmier, of Cedar Grove, Frederick, Md., to Miss Elizabeth Wise, of York county.	05/09/1820
On Thursday, the 20th ult., Mr. George Weaver, to Miss Rachel Baumgardner, both of Baltimore county.	05/09/1820
On Thursday, the 20th ult., Dr. Dedrick G. Pfeiffer, of Manchester, to Miss Solome Foltz, daughter of Mr. John Foltz, of Baltimore county.	05/09/1820
On Tuesday, the 25th ult., Mr. Francis Mathias, to Miss Ann Cocky, both of Frederick county.	05/09/1820
At Pittsburgh, on the 27th ult., Mr. William Savory, a native of Baltimore, after a few days illness.	05/10/1820
Last evening, by the Rev. Dr. Kurtz, Mr. Jacob Mayer, of Lancaster, Pa., to Miss Louisa Dannenberg, of this city.	05/12/1820
On Thursday evening, by the Rev. Dr. Kurtz, Mr. Abraham Busch, to Miss Hannah Martinberry, both of this city.	05/12/1820
At Havana, after three days illness, Mr. John Wilmot, of Baltimore.	05/12/1820
At Annapolis, after a painful illness, Mr. Horatio G. Munroe, merchant.	05/12/1820
At Cumberland, Md., Mr. Samuel Magill, to Miss Emma Whitehead.	05/13/1820

Marriage and Death Notices	Date
In Washington county, Md., Mr. Abraham Brown, to Miss Ann Riner.	05/13/1820
On Thursday evening, by the Rev. Mr. Bartow, Mr. Nicholas Dorry, to Miss Mary De Putrow, all of this city.	05/13/1820
On Sunday evening last, by the Rev. Mr. Waugh, Mr. John Norwood, to Miss Margaret Samuels, both of this city.	05/16/1820
On Monday evening last, by the Rev. Mr. Bartow, Mr. Mason Garrison, to Miss Margaret Ritchie, all of this city.	05/17/1820
Last evening, by the Rt. Rev. Mareschal, Arch Bishop of Baltimore, Mr. John F. Hamtramck, of the U. S. army, son of the late Col. Hamtramck, to Miss Mary Antoinette, daughter of David Williamson, Esq., of this city.	05/17/1820
On the 14th instant, by the Rev. Mr. Gilliss, Zachariah Berry, Jr., Esq., to Miss Priscilla M. Gantt, daughter of Levi Gantt, Esq., all of Prince George's county, Md.	05/17/1820
At Annapolis, Dr. Stevens Gambrill, to Miss Elizabeth Gambrill, both of that city.	05/17/1820
On the 7th inst., near Ellicott's Mills, after a short, but severe illness, in her thirty-fourth year, Mrs. Sarah Hardesty, consort of Joseph Hardesty.	05/17/1820
On Thursday, the 11th inst., in the 76th year of her age, Mrs. Rachel Haslett, a native of Ireland.	05/17/1820
On Tuesday evening last, by the Rev. Mar. Waugh, Mr. Peter G. Johnston, to Miss Adeline Smith, all of this city.	05/18/1820
At Annapolis, Mr. Marmaduke W. Conner, to Miss Sarah Wessels. Mr. Nelson Nicholls, to Miss Rachel Ann Nicholls. Mr. Davis Ephraim Gaither, Esq., to Miss Sarah E. Goldsborough.	05/19/1820
On Thursday evening last, by the Rev. Mr. Burch, Mr. Andrew Dayhuff, to Miss Rebecca, eldest daughter of A. W. Watkins, all of this city.	05/19/1820
On Thursday evening, the 18th instant, by the Rev. Mr. Bartow, John I. Hoxton, Esq., of Prince George's county, to the amiable Miss Margaretta Gover, of this city.	05/19/1820
At Wilmington, N. C., suddenly, in consequence of taking a decoction of the roots of Jamestown weed and Jessamine, *administered by a negro*, on the 25th ult., in the 34th year of his age, Mr. Peter De Witt, of	05/19/1820

Marriage and Death Notices	Date
the city of New York, and for a few months past, a resident of this place.	
By the Rev. Dr. Glendy, on the evening of Thursday last, Mr. Robert Galloway, to Miss Eleanor Bowen, all of this city.	05/20/1820
At Washington city, Mr. John Woods, to Miss Margaret Hody, both of that city.	05/22/1820
On the 16th inst., at Benfield, Charles county, Maryland, Dr. James Thos. Johnson, to Miss Emily Newman, all of that county.	05/22/1820
At Williamsport, Md., Mr. Skipwith C. Wilson, to Miss Sarah Weisel. Mr. Adam Seidels to Miss Maria Mann.	05/22/1820
At New-Market, Frederick county, on the 13th inst., by the Rev. James L. Higgins, Mr. David Scott, of Baltimore, to Mrs. Ann C. Hall, of the former place.	05/22/1820
In Baltimore county, Mrs. Hannah Gorsuch, aged 61.	05/22/1820
A day or two ago, Mr. Adam Baer, a respectable citizen of Washington City; a dealer in Hardware and Ironmongery, and a native of Frederick county, in Maryland. He was on a small vessel on the Potomac, and was knocked overboard by the boom and drowned.	05/22/1820
On Wednesday evening last, by the Rev. Mr. Bartow, Mr. Israel Brady to Miss Harriet Ensor, all of this city.	05/24/1820
On Tuesday evening last, by the Rev. Mr. Bartow, Capt. Abraham Lavitt, of the ship Support, to Miss Mary Barber, of this place.	05/24/1820
On Sunday night, aged 35 years, Mr. Dennis Kennedy, long a respectable inhabitant of this city. He has left, to deplore their loss, a wife and four children.	05/24/1820
On the 24th ult., in the 56th year of his age, at the Sulphur Springs, Greenbrier county, Va., Mr. William Bedford, formerly of the firm Bedford & Morton, merchant, of this city.	05/25/1820
On Thursday evening, by the Rt. Rev. Bishop Kemp, Stevenson White, Esq., to Miss Priscilla H. Ridgely, daughter of Gen. Charles Ridgely, of Hampton.	05/27/1820
On Thursday evening last, by the Rev. Mr. Bartow, Mr. James Johnson	05/27/1820

Marriage and Death Notices	Date
to Miss Mary Ann Stevens, all of this city.	
At Perry Point, in Cecil county, Md., on the 25th inst., by the Rev. Wm. Stephenson, Mr. Joseph Couden to Miss Ann, second daughter of John Stump, Esq.	05/29/1820
Departed this life, yesterday morning, Mr. James McQuinn, late of Ireland, after a short, but painful illness, which he bore with Christian fortitude, in the 22nd year of his age.	05/29/1820
At Friends Meeting-house, Kings Creek, Eastern Shore, Wright Anderson, of Caroline county, to Margaret Atwell, of Talbot county.	05/30/1820
At Frederick town, William H. McCannon, Esq., to Miss Eleanor G. Cockey, daughter of John Cockey, Esq. Mr. Frederick Delaplane to Miss Frances Jane Huff. Ephraim Gaither, Esq., of Montgomery county, to Miss Sarah Goldsborough, of Annapolis.	05/31/1820
On Sunday evening last, by the Rev. Mr. Valiant, Mr. Beale Spurrier, Jr., to Miss Elizabeth Denton, all of this city.	05/31/1820
On Sunday evening last, by the Rev. D. E. Reese, Mr. John Halfpenny, to Miss Sarah Watson, all of this city.	05/31/1820
Yesterday morning, after a painful illness, in the 54th year of her age, Mrs. Mary M'Donald, consort of Mr. Alexander M'Donald. Her friends and acquaintances are respectfully invited to attend her funeral from her late residence, corner of Ann and Alisanna streets, F. Point, this afternoon, at half past 4 o'clock.	05/31/1820
On the 29th instant, aged 40 years, Andrew Hazlehurst, Esq., a native of Philadelphia, but for many years a respectable merchant in this city. He has left a numerous circle of friends, to cherish the recollection of his benevolent character and unostentatious virtues.	05/31/1820
At Havana, Mr. Charles Henry Martin, aged 23, son of Dr. Ennals Martin, of Easton, Maryland.	05/31/1820
On the evening of the 30th ult., by the Rev. Mr. Waugh, Mr. Samuel Lucas to Miss Mary, eldest daughter of Joseph Benson, Esq., all of this city.	06/02/1820
On Thursday evening last, by the Rev. Dr. Roberts, Mr. John Thompson, to Miss Sarah Ann Alderdice, both of this city.	06/02/1820

Marriage and Death Notices	Date
On the 30th May, at Elkton, Md., by the Rev. Mr. Bell, Mr. Lewis Thomas to Miss Jane Gutherie, of Delaware.	06/03/1820
On Thursday last by the Rev. Mr. Tidings, Mr. John Harford, to Miss Rebecca Merrick, both of Baltimore county.	06/05/1820
Departed this life, on the morning of the 2nd inst., aged 10 years, Adeline Sophia Keyser, only daughter of George Keyser – it was a bud of brightest promise, but the cold relentless hand of death has torn it from its parent stem, ere it had time to blossom; thus forever destroying the fond visionary hopes of those, to whom she was endeared by many virtues. The writer of this feeble tribute to her memory, lov'd her living, and laments her dead. I see her pure and spotless soul By angel pinions borne on high; Behold it reach its heavenly goal, And claim a mansion in the sky! Freed from the world and death's alarms. Take her, dear Savior, to thy breast; Shield her with thy Almighty arms, And grant her there eternal rest.	06/05/1820
On Monday morning last, by the Rev. Mr. Tidings, Mr. Levy Hagerty, of Baltimore, to Miss Rebecca Rockhold, of Belle Air, Harford county, Maryland.	06/06/1820
On Monday evening, the 15th of May, by the Rev. Mr. Waugh, Capt. George Gilpin, of Alexandria, to Mrs. Margaret Smull, of Baltimore.	06/06/1820
On the 1st June, at Wye House, by the Rev. Mr. Hubbard, Edward S. Winder, Esq. to Elizabeth, eldest daughter of the Hon. Edward Lloyd.	06/07/1820
At Cincinnati, Ohio, Mr. John Buffum, recently of Baltimore.	06/07/1820
On Tuesday evening last, by the Rev. Mr. Henshaw, Mr. Robert A. Taylor, to Miss Mary Ann, eldest daughter of Henry Schroeder, Esq., all of this city.	06/08/1820
Last evening, by the Rev. Mr. Burch, Henry S. Mallory, of the U.S. army, to Miss Ellen B. Hawkins, of this city.	06/09/1820
At Louisville, Ken., Mrs. Mary Hewes, aged 36, wife of Mr. Daniel Hewes, recently of Baltimore.	06/09/1820
At Hagerstown, on the 30th ult., in the 19th year of her age, Miss Louisa	06/09/1820

Marriage and Death Notices	Date
Johnson, daughter of Capt. John Johnson, of that place.	
On Thursday, 1st inst., by the Rev. Mr. Duncan, Mr. Stephen McCoy, to Miss Sarah Williamson, all of this city.	06/10/1820
On Thursday evening last, by the Rev. Mr. Waugh, Maj. William Newton, of Dorchester county, Md., to Miss Maria Gavitt.	06/12/1820
In Talbot county, Mr. John R. Ruth, of Caroline county, to Miss Ann G. Loveday, of Easton, Md.	06/12/1820
On Saturday morning, the 10th inst., after a long and painful illness, Mr. John G. Brown, son of Dr. Brown, of this city.	06/12/1820
At Port-au-Prince, on the 24th May, 1820, Mr. John A. Rutter, a seaman belonging to the schooner Dandy, of Baltimore, Capt. Allen Fish. His friends will hear of something to their advantage, by applying to Buck & Hedrick, No. 81 Smith's wharf.	06/12/1820
At Springfield, in Frederick county, on Wednesday, the 24th of May last, Col. William Luckett, in the 81st year of his age. Averse from the active turmoil of the world, the deceased passed the last years of his life in the bosom of his family, in the reciprocal interchange of affectionate offices. The strict propriety of his deportment won for him the regard of his neighbors; esteem for his virtues was co-extensive with the circle of his acquaintance. As he lived for the most part estranged from perturoations of time, so he died with his affections alienated from its concerns, and fixed upon things imperishable and eternal.	06/12/1820
On the 6th instant, on his passage from New Orleans in the ship Lucy Ann, Mr. Joseph Whiting, a native of New Hampshire, but for a few years past a resident of Marietta, Ohio. His friends, who, it was understood from him, reside in this city, will obtain further information by applying on board said ship at Ramsay's wharf.	06/13/1820
Last evening, by the Rev. Mr. Snyder, Mr. Christian Nagle, printer, to Miss Elizabeth Martha Machen, all of this city.	06/16/1820
Last evening, by the Rev. Mr. Waugh, Mr. Samuel Sherwood, printer, to Miss Joana Forrester, of this city.	06/16/1820
On Tuesday evening, the 13th inst., by the Rev. Slingby Linthicum, Mr. Abner Linthicum, son of Abner Linthicum, Esq., of Anne Arundel county, Md., to Miss Rachel Stewart, daughter of Charles Stewart, Esq., of the same county.	06/17/1820

Marriage and Death Notices	Date
On Tuesday evening last, by the Rev. D. E. Reese, Mr. Adam Shott to Miss Elizabeth Kliendenstin, both natives of Germany.	06/17/1820
On Thursday evening, by the Rev. Mr. Shane, Mr. Henry F. Hultz, of Bremen, Germany, to Miss Martha Ann Brown, of this city.	06/17/1820
On Saturday Morning, by the Rev. Mr. Stansbury, Mr. Samuel B. Owings, to Miss Mary Adeline Johnson, all of this city.	06/19/1820
In Salem, on Monday last, John Dodges, Esq., aged 36. Thus has passed to a higher sphere of action, one of our most active and enterprising merchants, and most useful citizens. No one was more industrious and indefatigable in his pursuits.	06/19/1820
On Sunday evening last, by Rev. Dr. Elbert, Mr. James Smith to Miss Jane, eldest daughter of Wm. Atkins, Esq., of Harford county, Md.	06/20/1820
On the 14th inst., at Greenwood, the seat of Philip Rogers, Esq., Mrs. Mary Hesselius, aged 83 years.	06/20/1820
On Thursday evening last, George Buckey, Esq., to Miss Mary Cook, both of Frederick county.	06/21/1820
On Tuesday morning, at 6 o'clock, after a short, but distressing illness, Mrs. Eleanor Smith, aged 31 years, consort of Capt. Stephen Smith.	06/21/1820
At Philadelphia, William C. Poultney, Merchant, late of Mohele.	06/22/1820
At St. Jago de Cuba, Capt. Robbins, late commander of the brig Wasp, at Philadelphia.	06/22/1820
On Tuesday last, by the Rev. Enoch Fenwick, Mr. James Murry to Miss Lucy C. Murry, only daughter of William A. Murry, all of this city.	06/23/1820
At Washington, Dr. David Ott.	06/23/1820
On the 18th, at his late residence, Springfield, Baltimore county, in the 46th year of his age, Mr. Henry Green, long a respectable member of the Methodist Episcopal Church.	06/24/1820
Yesterday morning, about 1 o'clock, at his seat near this city, James Stirling, in the 69th year of his age, long a respectable inhabitant of this place.	06/26/1820
After a short illness, in St. Mary's county, Md., on Wednesday, the 14th	06/26/1820

Marriage and Death Notices	Date
instant, Mrs. Elizabeth Manning, consort of Mr. Cornelius Manning.	
Suddenly, yesterday morning, Mrs. Margaret Banks, in the 46th year of her age, consort of Capt. George Banks, of this city. In the exit of this amiable woman, her acquaintances are bereft of a dear, tender and valuable friend.	06/27/1820
On Saturday night, about 11 o'clock, Mrs. Mary Lyons, consort of Mr. M. Lyons, of this city, aged 24 years and one month.	06/28/1820
Died, in Annapolis, on Sunday night last, aged 66, Gen. John Gassaway, a distinguished Revolutionary hero.	06/28/1820
On Thursday evening last, by the Rev. Jennings, Mr. William M'Neir, to Miss Ann Hall, both of this city.	07/01/1820
On Thursday evening last, by the Rev. Jennings, Mr. John Watchman to Miss Elizabeth Kempfer, all of Baltimore.	07/01/1820
On Wednesday last, Mrs. Mary Maria Bromwell, after a lingering and painful disease, with which she suffered for the last five months. In her case, it may be said in truth, that "tribulation" served "to work patience – patience, experience – and experience hope;" and that hope did "not make her ashamed;" was not followed by disappointment, seeing it was consummated in the "love of God shed abroad in her heart."	07/01/1820
Last evening, by the Rev. Dr. Roberts, Mr. George Riggs, merchant, to Mrs. Rebecca Norris, both of this city.	07/03/1820
On Thursday evening last, by the Rev. D. E. Reese, Mr. William Adams to Miss Eliza Jane Dennit.	07/05/1820
By the Rev. D. E. Reese, on Sunday evening last, Mr. Jacob Gracie, to Miss Ann Maria Mott, all of this city.	07/05/1820
On Friday last, Mrs. Catherine Maria Yeiser, aged 65 years, of a painful and lingering complaint, which she bore with the greatest patience and resignation, with the fullest assurance of her peace with God.	07/06/1820
On Thursday last, in the 56th year of her age, Mrs. Ann Martindale.	07/06/1820
On Tuesday evening, 4th of July, by the Rev. Dr. Kurtz, Mr. Thomas Miller to Miss Elizabeth Henning, all of this city.	07/07/1820
On Wednesday evening last, by the Rev. Dr. Elbert, Mr. James Lee to	07/07/1820

Marriage and Death Notices	Date
Mrs. Harriet Smith.	
Last evening, Michael Macky, long an industrious and respectable inhabitant of this city. He lost his wife on Sunday morning last, and without any previous indisposition, he gradually sunk into the grave, broken hearted. By their economy and industry, they had acquired a competency, and appeared to enjoy it – but an epileptic affection recently showing itself on the wife, led them to doubt their permanent happiness; and, on Sunday morning last, a violent convulsion effected their short separation, as they were moral and religious, in an exemplary degree, we must hope that they have met in Heaven.	07/07/1820
Departed this life, yesterday at noon, Mr. James Labes, of the house of Jabes & Jacobsen, in the 66th year of his age. Mr. L. was a native of Prussia, born in Dantzic, and for many years a respectable merchant of this city.	07/07/1820
In Baltimore county, on Monday last, after a short illness, Mr. George Miles, Jr., aged 35.	07/07/1820
At Hagerstown, Mr. Isaac Wells to Miss Elizabeth Herring.	07/08/1820
On Thursday evening last, by the Rev. Dr. Roberts, Mr. John D. Turner, of Philadelphia, to Miss Adeline Holmes, of this city.	07/08/1820
Yesterday morning, in this city, after a long illness, Mr. James C. Hughes, of Havre de Grace, Md.	07/08/1820
Departed this life, on Saturday, July 1st, at Green Hill, in Montgomery county, Md., Mrs. Eliza R. Washington, consort of George C. Washington, Esq., and daughter of the late Thos. Beall of Geo., Esq.	07/08/1820
Last evening, by the Rev. Mr. Valiant, Mr. Hemphill, of Baltimore county, to Mrs. Elizabeth Wells, of this city.	07/10/1820
On Monday evening last, by the Rev. Dr. Jennings, Mr. George Hart to Miss Catherine Kempfer, all of this city.	07/10/1820
On Sunday, the 9th inst., by the Rev. Dr. Jennings, Mr. Francis Wilson, to Miss Matilda Dungan, both of Baltimore county.	07/11/1820
On Sunday evening last, by the Rev. Dr. Roberts, Mr. William Fusselbaugh, to Miss Mary Donovan, all of this city.	07/11/1820
On Sunday evening, the 9th inst., after a long and painful illness, in the 24th year of her age, Mrs. Evelina Barney, wife of Mr. Stephen J.	07/12/1820

Marriage and Death Notices	Date
Thompson.	
On Sunday last, Mrs. Hobson, in the 40th year of her age, consort of Capt. George Hobson, of this city, after a long and painful illness, borne with most exemplary patience and resignation to the will of her Heavenly father.	07/12/1820
In Easton, Md., Isaiah Rowland Moore, son of Wm. M. Moore, of that place, in the fifth year of his age, of a most distressing illness, from accidentally drinking a small portion of a solution of Corrosive Sublimate, which was prepared for the purpose of destroying Bed Bugs! This most afflicting circumstance ought to be a caution to all, how they leave poisons in any form, in the way of children, as the draught, once taken, too often has resisted the antidotes, however judiciously and speedily administered.	07/12/1820
On Wednesday last, after a short, but distressing illness, James Ellicott, of this city, a valuable and much beloved member of the Society of Friends. Honesty, faith, and benevolence were the presiding tokens that illuminated through the shadows of this world, his passage to the tomb; but they are now unhappily destined to shed their light only upon his ashes. An only child is all the family he has left to weep over his corpse, but all who knew his amiable qualities will feel his loss, and we trust find consolation in the melancholy remembrance of his virtues. Death speaks with an awful and commanding energy.	07/13/1820
On the 6th inst., Mr. Adrian Oudesluys, aged 45 years, a native of Holland, and many years a respectable citizen of Baltimore.	07/13/1820
At Hagerstown, Daniel Scheely, Esq., to Miss Margaret Rench.	07/14/1820
On Sunday, the 9th inst., at his late residence, in Prince George's county, Md., Francis Magruder, Esq.	07/14/1820
Departed this life, on the 6th instant, Izak Proctor, one of the most respectable members of the Society of Friends: a man of stern integrity and good principles. In the removal of this good and amiable citizen, the city has sustained no small loss. Whether in the domestic, social, or religious circle, his presence was animating and useful. Born with the passions common to other men, his glory was in disciplining and governing himself. In his early life, he appeared, as latterly, to be thoughtfully inclined towards good; and, at 12 or 14 years of age, a great admirer and favorite of Anthony Benezet.	07/14/1820

Marriage and Death Notices	Date
In Washington county, Md., Rev. John Clapper, to Miss Susanna Longman, both of Pleasant Valley.	07/15/1820
On Tuesday evening last, by the Rev. Dr. Kurtz, Mr. John C. Rau, to Miss Elizabeth, daughter of Mr. Peter Sauerwein.	07/20/1820
In Savannah, Mr. Richard W. Edes, Printer, late of this city, to Miss Sarah T. Davies, of the former place.	07/21/1820
At Hagerstown, on Sunday last, by the Rev. Mr. Kurtz, Mr. Noah Carter, to Miss Susanna Huinrickhouse.	07/21/1820
At Waynesburg, on Tuesday evening, the 27th ult., by the Rev. Mr. Buchannan, Dr. James Brotherton to Miss Helen Mentoria Hammit, only daughter of the late David Hammit, of Washington county, Maryland.	07/21/1820
At New York, on Sunday last, Mr. Francis H. Woolsey, of the firm Panton & Woolsey.	07/21/1820
Washington, Pa., July 17th. On Sunday, the 10th inst., Mr. John Davidson, a student of Jefferson College, was killed by lightning in Canonsburg. While standing with three young men of his acquaintance, in the street opposite the house lately kept by Mr. Keyhoe, the lightning struck a tree under which they stood, passed down to about the height of Mr. Davidson's head, when the electric fluid left the tree, and struck him to the ground a lifeless corpse. His hat and part of his clothing were cut to pieces, but his silk handkerchief, which was contained in his hat, remained uninjured. Those in company with Mr. Davidson were knocked down with the shock, and remained insensible for a short time, when they recovered. The deceased had been a student at the college about two years. We understand his family relatives live near Greencastle in this state. His remains were interred the next day, in the most respectful manner, under the superintendence of his fellow students.	07/24/1820
On Sunday evening last, by the Rev. Mr. Bartow, Mr. Andrew Armstrong to Miss Harriet Bivens, all of this city.	07/27/1820
At Easton, Md., Mr. Thomas Meconckin to Miss Susan Jones.	07/27/1820
On Tuesday evening last, by the Rev. Mr. Waugh, Mr. John Casson to Miss Caroline Hodskiss, all of this city.	07/27/1820
On the 13th inst., in Anne Arundel county, Miss Elizabeth Allein, of a	07/27/1820

Marriage and Death Notices	Date
lingering illness, which she bore with Christian fortitude and resignation.	
At Savannah, Patrick Stanton, Esq., merchant, in the 33rd year of his age.	07/27/1820
On Sunday evening last, by the Rev. Mr. Birch, Mr. John Hodgkinson, to Miss Ann Skillman, both of this city.	07/28/1820
At Hagerstown, after a short, but painful illness, Miss Mary Ann Hoffman Lawrence, eldest daughter of Upton Lawrence, Esq., of that place, in the 14th year of her age.	07/28/1820
On Thursday evening last, by the Rev. Mr. Valiant, Mr. George Brister, of Richmond, Virginia, to Miss Susanna Lusby, of this city.	07/29/1820
On Thursday evening last, by the Rev. Mr. Bartow, Mr. John Taylor to Miss Sarah Ann Rutter, all of this city.	07/29/1820
On Thursday evening last, by the Rev. Mr. Valiant, Mr. Thomas Townsend, to Miss Margaret Corner, both of this city.	07/29/1820
At the Indian Queen Hotel, in this city, Mr. Wm. Nicol, from Northumberland county, Virginia, after a lingering illness of twelve months, which he bore with Christian fortitude to the last moment.	07/29/1820
On Thursday evening last, by the Rev. Mr. Burch, Mr. James Burland, to Miss Ann Stretch, both of this city.	07/31/1820
On the 25th ult., at the house of Ira Emmons, Esq., at Octorora, Cecil county, Maryland, Maj. Asa Emmons. Having descended the Susquehanna River with Lumber, and having sent the same on to the Baltimore market, he was seized with the bilious fever, which put a period to his existence, in the 45th year of his age.	08/01/1820
On Sunday morning, the 30th inst., Mrs. Louisa Snowden, consort of Richard Snowden, Esq., of Prince George's county, and daughter of the late Dr. Charles Alexander Warfield. No one ever more deservedly possessed the sincerest affect on of family and relations, and all who had the happiness of her friendship.	08/01/1820
At Louisville, Ky., on the 13th July, after a long illness, Mr. Benjamin Arcambal, formerly of this city.	08/01/1820
On Tuesday, the 17th inst., at his residence, in the 64th year of his age, Col. George Handy, Register of Wills for Somerset county, which office	08/02/1820

Marriage and Death Notices	Date
had had held with high reputation for a considerable number of years.	
On Tuesday evening, Aug. 1, at the Meadows, in Baltimore county, by the Rev. Mr. Keech, Maj. William Stansbury, Merchant of Baltimore, to Miss Rebecca J. Bosley, daughter of Elijah Bosley, Esq.	08/03/1820
On the 21st June last, in Tennessee state, James P. Caldwell, Esq., late of Baltimore, to Miss Martha, daughter of Dr. Samuel Dabney, Tennessee, late of Virginia.	08/03/1820
Near Washington City, of an indisposition of some duration, Rev. Notley Young.	08/03/1820
On the 28th ult., Dr. John Thomas, of the vicinity of Centreville, Queen Anne's County, Maryland.	08/04/1820
On Thursday evening last, by the Rev. Dr. Kurtz, Mr. Robert Green, of Patapsco Neck, to Miss Margaret Ann Moss, of Fell's Point.	08/05/1820
Departed this life, on Saturday morning last, the 29th of July, of a pulmonary consumption, Dr. John Norris Scott, in the 22nd year of his age.	08/05/1820
At Port Tobacco, on Friday last, the 29th instant, Mrs. Clarissa Carroll, the amiable and excellent wife of Dr. George N. Carroll. She has left an affectionate husband and several young children to deplore their irremediable loss.	08/05/1820
At Port-au-Prince, on the 17th ult., Mr. John M. Sewell, a native of Anne Arundel county, and for some years a respectable merchant of this city.	08/07/1820
On Thursday evening last, by the Rev. Mr. Tidings, Mr. James Belford, to Miss Mary Bennett, both of this city.	08/09/1820
On the 3rd instant, by the Rev. Mr. Burgess, Mr. Edward McFarland Mooney, to Miss Eliza Savage, all of this city.	08/09/1820
On the 5th instant, John B. Merryman, in the 25th year of his age, after a short, but severe illness, which he bore with all the fortitude and resignation that became the Christian.	08/09/1820
Departed this transitory life, on Tuesday, the first day of August, Mrs. Pamela Sefton, in the 57th year of her age, after a long and painful illness, which she bore with Christian fortitude and resignation. Her loss is sincerely regretted by a numerous circle of relatives and friends.	08/09/1820

Marriage and Death Notices	Date
On Monday morning, Aug. 7th, Mrs. Mary, consort of Mr. Wm. Fulton, aged 53.	08/10/1820
At Darien, Geo. John Johnston, Esq., in the 29th year of his age. Honesty, industry, integrity, frugality, and hospitality, were ever conspicuous traits in the character of the deceased. *"In death lamented, and in life beloved."*	08/10/1820
Died, on Tuesday, at Bell Air, at the residence of Jonathan Swift, the Rev. James Muir, Senior Pastor of the First Presbyterian Church in Alexandria.	08/10/1820
On Tuesday, the 8th inst., Mrs. Catherine Sleigh, in her 68th year, after a painful confinement of one year, which she endured with exemplary Christian piety. She expired without apparent pain – without a sigh – without a groan – "blessed are the dead who die in the Lord."	08/11/1820
On Thursday evening last, by the Rev. Mr. Waugh, Mr. Thomas Bailey, to Miss Ann Maria Catherine Reese, all of this city.	08/12/1820
On the afternoon of Saturday last, Mrs. Eleanor Murphy, consort of the late much lamented Capt. John Murphy, and long a respectable inhabitant of this city. She bore her afflictions with a firmness and stability of mind, which could only be exhibited by one possessing a well-grounded hope of immortality and eternal life, through the merits of a Redeemer. While six orphan children are thus left to mourn the bereavement of an affectionate and tender parent, a large circle of friends and acquaintance, who knew her worth as a mother, friend, and associate, unfeignedly regret her demise, and condole with those whose loss is irreparable.	08/14/1820
Yesterday afternoon, after a distressing indisposition upwards of six months, which she bore with Christian patience and fortitude, Mrs. Catherine Hillen, consort of John Hillen, Esq., of this city.	08/14/1820
Yesterday, Mr. Hugh McKaa, aged 34. His funeral will be this day, between 4 and 5 o'clock, from his late dwelling, in Frederick st., at which time his friends and relations are invited to attend.	08/14/1820
In Harford county, on Thursday, the 10th inst., in the 35th year of his age, Hugh Allen, of this city.	08/14/1820
Suddenly, on Sunday evening, Edward Allen.	08/15/1820
On Sunday night last, in the 67th year of her age, Mrs. Henrietta James,	08/15/1820

42

Marriage and Death Notices	Date
an old and respectable inhabitant of this city.	
On Tuesday, the 7th instant, at his residence in Easton, in the 64th year of his age, Col. George Handy, Register of Wills for Talbot county.	08/15/1820
In Biddeford, Capt. William Freeman, aged 56. He put a period to his existence by hanging.	08/15/1820
On Sunday evening last, by the Rev. Mr. Battee, Capt. Peter Dorsey, to Miss Maria Canada, all of Patapsco Neck.	08/16/1820
On Saturday evening last, at his residence in Brooklyn, L. I., Francis Guy, Esq., Landscape Painter, recently of Baltimore, in the 61st year of his age.	08/16/1820
On Thursday, the 17th inst., by the Rev. Dr. Wyatt, Mr. Benjamin Buck to Miss Jane Herbert, both of this city.	08/19/1820
Suddenly, on board of his schooner, on his way to Baltimore, a few days ago, Lewis Medley, Esq., of Leonardtown, Md.	08/19/1820
On Monday last, at Mount Pleasant, Mrs. Lucy Graham, wife of Lt. John H. Graham, of the U. S. Navy.	08/19/1820
Last evening, by the Rev. Dr. Roberts, Mr. Thomas Duer, Merchant, to Miss Mary Ann, daughter of John W. Wilson, all of this city.	08/21/1820
At Quincy, Mass., by the Rev. Whitney, Mr. Harrison Dawes, of Baltimore, to Miss Lucy Greenleaf, daughter of Mr. John Greenleaf.	08/22/1820
Yesterday, at noon, of an illness of some weeks, Mr. Edward McNulty, son of the late John McNulty, of this city, in the 23rd year of his age. His friends are invited to attend his funeral, this day at 4 o'clock, from his late residence, in N. Calvert st.	08/22/1820
On the 22nd inst., Richard Clayton, aged 63 years, long a respectable inhabitant of this city.	08/23/1820
Last evening, by the Rev. Mr. Bartow, Mr. James Graham White to Mrs. Sophia Boury, all of this city.	08/25/1820
On Wednesday evening by the Rev. Mr. Wyatt, Mr. Charles Mayger, to Miss Mary Thomas French, all of this city.	08/25/1820
On the 24th of June last, near Havre, in France, Henry Osgood, Esq., of	08/25/1820

Marriage and Death Notices	Date
the firm of H. & R. H. Osgood, of this city.	
On Thursday evening, by the Rev. Dr. Roberts, Mr. Joseph Janvier to Miss Debora Neal, both of this city.	08/26/1820
On the 22nd inst., by the Rev. Mr. M'Cormick, Mr. Elijah Knox, of Charles county, Md., to Miss Martha Milstead, of Washington city.	08/26/1820
At Mount Jefferson, the residence of her father, in the vicinity of Baltimore, on the 22nd instant, Miss Mary Ann Biays, daughter of Col. Biays, in the 17th year of her age.	08/26/1820
At the house of David Mills, in Dorchester county, Md., on Thursday, Aug. 17, Miss Soahia Beasten. Although she had been for some time in ill health, yet her death was sudden and unexpected.	08/26/1820
It became our painful duty yesterday, to announce the death of Henry Osgood, Esq., merchant, of this city; and, although we are not much in the habit of bestowing obituary commendation, yet, in respect to this gentleman, it is proper that something more should be said, than that he had lived and died. His solid and unassuming merit was highly estimated by a numerous acquaintance; his friends will not soon forget his amiable traits, by which he was endeared to them – and his sterling integrity enabled him to leave behind him, that good name, *the gain whereof is better than fine gold.* Equally estimable in all the relations of life, in the nearest and dearest, his loss will be especially afflicting; and an amiable family must look for their best consolation to the assurance, that their separation is but temporary, and that, in *"another and better world"* their reunion will be certain. His disorder was a pulmonary consumption, that surest, although not always hasty warrant from the King of Terrors. He sought, by a change in climate, a restoration of health; embarking first for Savannah, and thence for Havre, in France. In vain – the arrow of death had sped. From a foreign land, he took his departure, for that other and perpetual state of existence, of which his belief was settled. "On some fine breast, the parting sole relies; Some pious drops the closing eye requires; E'en from the tomb the voice of nature cries, E'en in our ashes live their wonted fires." "Alas! He, hapless, no such blessings knew; No weeping kindred sighed their last adieu; By strangers mourn'd, the parting spirit flies, And swift revisits its paternal skies."	08/26/1820

Marriage and Death Notices	Date
By the Rev. Wm. Maffit, at Salona, the Rev. Thomas B. Balch, of Maryland, to Miss Susan Carter, of Virginia.	08/29/1820
On board the schooner Good Return, on his passage from Aquadilla, P. R., to this port, Capt. Francis Lane, of Newburyport, Mass., aged 35 years.	08/29/1820
On the 27th inst., of a short, but severe illness, which she bore with Christian resignation, Mrs. Elizabeth Wortman, consort of David Wortman.	08/29/1820
On Friday afternoon, 18th instant, in the Parish Church, Princess Ann, E. S. Maryland, the Rev. Henry R. Judah, of Fairfield, Con., to Miss Mary Jane L. Reece, daughter of the late Rev. Joshua Reece, deceased.	08/30/1820
In St. George's Parish, Harford county, much regretted by her numerous friends and acquaintance, Mrs. Catherine Jack, in the 50th year of her age.	08/31/1820
On Thursday evening, by the Rev. Mr. Kurtz, Mr. David Ring to Miss Sophia Benteen, all of this city.	09/01/1820
On the 25th ult., at the house of Mr. Edward Austin, Somerset county, Md., after an illness of three weeks, the Rev. Oliver S. Wilson, a Preacher of the Baptist denomination, in the 22nd year of his age. Though young, he was eminent, both as a Minister and a Christian. On his deathbed, he expressed those consolations, which the doctrines of the Cross only are calculated to give – he set his seal to the truths he taught in the pulpit, by declaring that Christ is an everlasting friend, and that having Christ, we have all – he expressed a strong desire to depart and be with Jesus, and that the sickbed was a Bethel to his soul. Thus it pleased the Master of the Vineyard to take this young laborer from the field, and transplant him to joys immortal. This loss will be severely felt by the Church for which he preached; and he is universally lamented in the circle of his acquaintance. The harvest is truly great, but the laborers are few. Pray ye, the Lord of the harvest, *to send forth more laborers.*	09/01/1820
Last evening, by the Rev. George Dashiell, Mr. Joseph P. Van Lear to Miss Ann B. Booth, both of Washington county, Md.	09/05/1820
Last evening, in the 45th year of his age, Mr. George Crosdale, merchant of this city.	09/05/1820

Marriage and Death Notices	Date
On Friday morning last, Mrs. Sarah Lee Jennings, in the 20th year of her age, after a long and painful illness of twelve months.	09/05/1820
In Queen Ann's county, Mr. John Nabb, formerly of Talbot.	09/05/1820
In Talbot, Mr. Garey M'Neal.	09/05/1820
On Sunday evening last, by the Rev. Mr. Bartow, Mr. John Lucas, to Miss Elizabeth Riley, all of this city.	09/06/1820
On the 29th ult., at Georgetown Cross Roads, in Kent county, Maryland, of a lingering illness, Daniel Bodartha, Esq., Attorney of Law, about 30 years of age, a native of West Springfield, Mass. He was a member of Experience Lodge No. 64, and was interred pursuant to his request, by the brethren of the craft, in masonic order. His relatives and friends will be gratified to learn, with what exemplary patience he endured his tedious illness. Having long had warning of his complaint, he was sensible of its nature, and manifested the most entire resignation to the Divine will.	09/06/1820
On Tuesday evening, by the Rt. Rev. Bishop Kemp, Charleston M. Thurston, Esq., to Juliana, youngest daughter of Christopher Hughes, Sr., Esq.	09/07/1820
In Cecil county, on Tuesday evening, 29th ult., Mr. Adam Steever, merchant of Baltimore, to Miss Elizabeth Steele, of the former place.	09/07/1820
On Saturday evening, the 26th ult., at the residence of his son, in Prince George's county, Md., Mr. Charles Maddox, in the 83rd year of his age.	09/07/1820
On Sunday evening last, by the Rev. Dr. Roberts, Mr. James Thomas, to Miss Elizabeth Kirkpatrick, all of this city.	09/08/1820
On Thursday evening last, by the Rev. Mr. Birch, Mr. Stephen T. Mare, of Dorchester county, Md., to Miss Mary Coffin, of Nantucket, Massachusetts.	09/08/1820
On Sunday last, Mrs. Margaret Magrauran, wife of Mr. James C. Magraudan. May angels conduct her to heaven.	09/08/1820
On the 31st August, by the Rev. Mr. Birch, Mr. George Shock, to Miss Machia Biddison, both of this city.	09/09/1820
On Thursday evening last, by the Rev. Dr. Glendy, Mr. Alexander Somerville, merchant, of Nashville, to Miss Caroline Matilda, eldest	09/09/1820

Marriage and Death Notices	Date
daughter of Col. William Stewart of this city.	
This morning, suddenly, at his residence near Fort McHenry, Mr. Thaedeus Jackson, aged 34 years. His friends and acquaintances are requested to attend his Funeral, tomorrow, at 1 o'clock, P. M., from the residence of Capt. D. Schwarzauer, Federal Hill. It being his request, it is expected that his Masonic Brethren, members of Washington Lodge No. 3, will attend to his burial with the honors of Masonry, requesting all the lodges of Masons to join in the procession.	09/09/1820
On the 27th ult., in the prime of life and usefulness, Caleb Taylor, Druggist, of this city.	09/11/1820
On the 3rd inst., Samuel Williams, Esq., lumber merchant.	09/11/1820
On Tuesday morning, after a long and painful illness, Mrs. Eliza Truman, in the 26th year of her age.	09/11/1820
On Saturday last, at half past 3 o'clock in the morning, Mary Davis, wife of John Davis, aged 35 years.	09/11/1820
On Tuesday evening, Wm. Cox, of Delaware county, in the 24th year of his age.	09/11/1820
On the 5th inst., at his residence, in Prince George's County, Maryland, after a long and painful illness, which he bore with a truly Christian fortitude, Mr. Jasper M. Jackson, Sr., formerly and for many years a respectable merchant in Georgetown, in the District of Columbia.	09/11/1820
Last evening, by the Rev. Mr. Elbert, Mr. William B. Jones to Miss Mary Ann Elizabeth Jones, all of this city.	09/15/1820
On Tuesday, the 12th inst., after a short illness, Miss Margaret Chapman, daughter of Christopher Chapman, of this city. The death of this amiable girl affords another striking instance of all sublunary prospects. But a few days since she was in the bloom of health, the object of her parents fondest hopes, and the delight of her numerous acquaintances, who in mourning the irreparable loss they have sustained, have the consolation to believe that she has been translated to a more congenial and blissful state of existence.	09/15/1820
In the 27th year of his age, on board the ship Ceres, M'Lean, on his passage from New Orleans to Philadelphia, Mr. David B. Finley, merchant of St. Francisville, Louisiana, and late of Baltimore. In the death of this estimable young man, the wide circle of his relatives and	09/15/1820

Marriage and Death Notices	Date
friends, have sustained a loss which cannot be repaired – he was endeared to them and to all who knew him, by every amiable quality which could attract affection and secure esteem – liberal, high minded and generous to an extreme – regardless of self, and only studious to promote the happiness of his friends – his short, but useful life was one unceasing effort to do good to others; his charity was as unbounded as the wants of those who applied to him for relief – as a merchant, his conduct was regulated by the strictest standard of honesty and integrity – as a man, his life was an unvarying effort at a conformity with the principles of religion, which had been early implanted in his mind, and which, in a country (Louisiana) where these principles are rarely observed, shown more bright and beautiful from the contrast with which they were surrounded. After several years absence, he was returning to his native city, and within a few days of his revival – when in the midst of his anticipations of a speedy reunion with his family, after a long separation, it pleased his God to take him from this world of care, to a happier and better one, where his friends fondly trust he is now, in the full enjoyment of that happiness, which is the reward of a well spent life.	
On Wednesday, the 6th inst., of a short, but severe illness, which she bore with Christian resignation, Miss Ann Eliza Leothold.	09/15/1820
On the 13th instant, at his farm, in Prince George's county, Md., after a short, but severe illness, Mr. Robert Orme, aged about 75 years.	09/16/1820
On the 4th inst., by the Rev. Mr. Mann, Edmund H. Contee, Esq., of Charles county, Md., to Eleanor, daughter of James Clerkee, Esq., late of Bromont, Charles county, Md.	09/18/1820
At Easton, Md., on Thursday, the 7th inst., by the Rev. Lott Warfield, Mr. Richard Frampton, to Mrs. Mary Martindale.	09/20/1820
In this city, last night, David B. Solomon, aged 13, son of Mr. Benjamin Solomon. Seldom is it the lot of a youth, of so tender an age as this, to establish a character; and even rarely is it in the power of such as one to give any correct indication, of what would have been that character. In the case of this young man, it will be the testimonial of all who knew him, that he displayed traits most promising – that he evinced a good and affectionate heart, a correct judgment, and a disposition to make himself useful and agreeable as a son, a brother and society. He was remarkably attentive to those pursuits, which were calculated to make him acquainted with the details of useful business; and he ever evinced a heart, warmed with the best and most honorable feelings. The parting adjuration to his friends might be resolved into the emphatic language of	09/20/1820

Marriage and Death Notices	Date
Mason: "Tell them, tho' 'tis an awful thing to die, 'Twas even to thee; yet the dread path once trod, Heaven lifts its everlasting portals high, And bids the pure in heart behold their God."	
On the 11th inst., James Walker, of Charles, in the 43rd year of his age.	09/20/1820
Departed this life, on Sunday morning, the 16th inst., at her late residence on Elk Ridge, after ten days sickness with the bilious disease, Mrs. Mary Leatherwood, aged 70 years. She has left a number of relations and a large circle of acquaintances to lament her death. As she lived, so she died, tranquil in mind, and at peace with all mankind. In this lady, were remarkably exemplified characteristics of the Christian. Universally benevolent, tender towards all under her direction, hospitable to the stranger and distressed – her house always open to receive the weary pilgrim, and her substance ready to be dealt out to the needy. Her peculiar delight was to entertain the saints of the most high, and the Ministers of the Gospel. Her industry and economy of life, rarely excelled by her sex – for many years a professor of the religion of Christ, and a warm adherent of to the doctrines of the Gospel, and that she had not followed a cunningly devised fable, was the more evident in her last illness; although aged and somewhat infirm, she was entirely free from peevish and fretful passions; exhibited remarkable patience and pious resignation, had resolved herself into the will and providence of God, entertained no fear of death, but a joyful hope and pleasing prospects of blissful immortality; and thus enjoying the consolations of the grace of God. She closed her eyes and breathed her last without a struggle or groan. Let me die the death of the Righteous, and let my last end be like his.	09/20/1820
On Saturday morning, 9th September, at her seat, Shoal Creek, in Dorchester county, Maryland, Mrs. Elizabeth G. Ennalls, in the 89th year of her age.	09/20/1820
On the 7th instant, at his residence, in Anne Arundel county, Md., Mr. John Welsh, Sr., in the 77th year of his age, an old inhabitant of the state of Maryland, and a late member of the Baptist Church. His sore affliction, which lasted for 14 days, he bore with Christian fortitude, never murmured or complained, and was perfectly in his senses to the last.	09/20/1820
On Tuesday evening last, by the Rev. Dr. Roberts, Mr. Henry Green to Miss Eleanor Durkee, all of this city.	09/22/1820

Marriage and Death Notices	Date
At Augusta, Geo., on the 9th inst., Mr. James Caruthers, of Savannah, formerly of this city, in the forty fourth year of his age.	09/22/1820
On Thursday evening last, by the Rev. Dr. Wyatt, Geo. H. Newman, Esq., to Susan, eldest daughter of the late Andrew Buchanan, Esq., of this city.	09/23/1820
On Thursday evening, by the Rev. Dr. Roberts, Mr. Robinson J. Renshaw, Merchant of this city, to Miss Margaret Eliza Waltham, of Kent County, Eastern Shore, of Maryland.	09/23/1820
On Sunday evening last, by the Rev. Bishop Kemp, James Brant, Esq., to Miss Harriet Mitchell, second daughter of Mrs. Mitchell, all of this city.	09/25/1820
On the 22nd inst., at St. Mary's Church, Burlington, New Jersey, by the Rev. Dr. Wharton, Mr. John Loney, of Baltimore, to Miss Esther C. Stockton, daughter of the late Samuel W. Stockton, Esq.	09/25/1820
In this city, on Sunday morning, the 24th instant, at half past 1 o'clock, after a long and tedious complaint, which she bore with Christian fortitude and resignation to the last, Mrs. Rachel Decamp, consort of Mr. John Decamp, of this city.	09/25/1820
On Saturday, the 16th inst., at Oak Grove farm, Charles county, Md., about 50 years, George H. Spalding, Esq., Sheriff of said county. He was an honest man, and a warm hearted and faithful friend; a pious and benevolent Christian; an affectionate husband; a fond father and a kind master. His family and numerous friends and acquaintances have great cause to deplore this dispensation of Providence, in taking from them a kind protector and worthy member of society.	09/25/1820
On Monday evening last, by the Rev. Dr. S. K. Jennings, Mr. William Kenner, to Miss Elizabeth H. Tarr, both of this city.	09/26/1820
On Monday evening last, by the Rev. Mr. Bartow, Mr. Conrad Holdam, to Mrs. Frances Manroe, all of this city.	09/28/1820
Last evening, by the Rev. Dr. Roberts, Mr. John Knight, to Miss Sarah M'Laughlin, both of this city.	09/29/1820
On the 15th inst., at his farm near Cambridge, in the state of Ohio, Mr. John Heslip, formerly and for many years, a respectable mechanic of this city, aged about 69 years.	09/29/1820

Marriage and Death Notices	Date
On Saturday evening last, by the Rev. Mr. Burgess, Mr. Thomas R. Lusby, to Miss Lucinda D. McKey, all of this city.	10/02/1820
At Philadelphia, Sept. 27th, after a long and tedious illness, Mrs. Elizabeth Lefaver, formerly of this city, widow of Mr. Nicholas Lefaver, deceased, aged 81 years.	10/03/1820
On Monday evening last, at Deer Park, Harford county, Md., by the Rev. Mr. O'Brien, Mr. Nicholas W. Luke, of Baltimore, to Miss Henrietta Maria, eldest daughter of Mr. Samuel Brown, formerly of Baltimore.	10/05/1820
On Tuesday evening, by the Rev. Dr. Wyatt, James Howard, Esq. to Miss Sophia G., daughter of Gen. Charles Ridgely, of Hampton.	10/05/1820
By the Rev. Dr. Glendy, on the 25th ult., Mr. William Powers, to Miss Jane Valentine.	10/05/1820
By the Rev. Dr. Glendy, on the 28th ult., Mr. Thomas Humes, to Miss Susanna Jackson, all of this city.	10/05/1820
Of a lingering and painful illness, Robert A. Compton, son of the late John Compton, in the fourth year of his age.	10/05/1820
Departed this transitory life, on Saturday evening last, after a short illness, which he bore with Christian fortitude, Mr. Joseph Despaux, in the 62nd year of his age. Mr. Despaux has been a long and respectable inhabitant of Fell's Point, for the last 28 years – he was an affectionate husband and kind father – he has left behind him a wife and a large family of children to deplore their irreparable loss.	10/05/1820
Departed this life, on Wednesday evening last, after a short, but painful illness, Mrs. Lucinda B. Walker, in the 70th year of her age.	10/06/1820
On the 4th inst., Col. Jos. Biays, in the 68th year of his age, long a respectable inhabitant of this city.	10/07/1820
On the 30th September last, Mrs. Ann Humphreys, wife of Capt. John Humphreys, Swan Creek, Kent county, aged about 65 years. She has left a disconsolate husband to mourn his irreparable loss.	10/07/1820
On Thursday evening last, by the Rev. Mr. Bartow, Capt. Thomas Griffen to Miss Susan Alexander, all of this city.	10/09/1820
Last evening, by the Rev. Dr. Roberts, Mr. James Geddes, to Miss Sarah	10/10/1820

Marriage and Death Notices	Date
Robinson, all of this city.	
In Talbot county, William Henry Banning, son of R. Banning, Esq., aged 20.	10/10/1820
On Thursday, the 28th ult., by the Rev. Mr. Samuel Rawley, Mr. Jacob C. Wilson, of Caroline county, to Miss Mary C. Smith, of Dorchester county.	10/11/1820
Last evening, David Goging, aged four months.	10/11/1820
Yesterday morning, after a long indisposition, Mrs. Charity Jenkins, widow of the late Michael Jenkins, of Long Green, Baltimore county, aged 77 years.	10/11/1820
On the 25th ult., after a lingering indisposition, in the 44th year of her age, Mrs. Elizabeth Colston, consort of Mr. Jesse Colston, of Dorchester county.	10/11/1820
At Philadelphia, after a long and distressing illness, Mrs. Lydia, wife of Thomas Wilson, formerly of Baltimore, and daughter of Samuel Oakford, of Southwark, in the 47th year of her age.	10/11/1820
On the 11th inst., by the Rev. Mr. Waugh, Capt. Jewet Allen to Mrs. Hannah Perley, both of this city.	10/12/1820
On Tuesday morning, in the 77th year of her age, Mrs. Jane Thomas, widow of Mr. Luke Thomas, late of the city of Baltimore. The deceased, thro' a long life, confined herself to a limited society, because there she could be useful; but she possessed and merited the confidence and esteem of those who knew her; the purity and excellency of her principles and her character were clearly proved by her patience and submission under a long, a severe, and an afflictive disease. In this world, however, she enjoyed a foretaste of that perfection of happiness which is promised the true in heart – she died at peace with her God.	10/12/1820
By the Rev. Dr. Glendy on Monday last, James Sloan, Esq., to Mrs. Harriet Norris, all of this city.	10/13/1820
On the 7th of September last, at St. Louis, Missouri Territory, after a short and painful illness of a bilious fever, in the 22nd year of his age, John William Ratien, second son of Richard Ratien, of Baltimore.	10/13/1820
On Monday evening last, by the Rev. Dr. Moranville, Mr. Capt. Francis Gallagher to Miss Mary Rynd, all of this city.	10/14/1820

Marriage and Death Notices	Date
On Thursday evening last, the 12th inst., by the Rev. Mr. Tidings, Henry W. Fitzhugh, of the U. S. army, to Miss Ellen O. Wilkins, eldest daughter of Dr. Henry Wilkins, of this city.	10/14/1820
On Thursday night, Mr. Samuel Sowers, long a respectable inhabitant of this city.	10/14/1820
On Sunday last, Mr. John Hanan, long a respectable inhabitant of this city.	10/14/1820
At Gettysburg, Pa., Mr. Frederick Ashbaugh to Miss Mary Ann B. Hall, recently of Baltimore.	10/16/1820
At Fredericktown, Mr. John Koontz to Miss Margaret Norris. Mr. Laurence Hogan to Miss Jane Maby.	10/16/1820
On Sunday evening last, by the Rev. Mr. Neale, Mr. John Kirkwood, to Miss Ann Dupuy, both of this city.	10/17/1820
On Tuesday evening, the 10th inst., by the Rev. Mr. McLean, the Rev. William Finney, of Harford county, Md., to Mrs. Margaret Miller, of Philadelphia.	10/17/1820
At Ellicott's Mills, on Thursday last, John Ellicott, a worthy member of the Society of Friends.	10/17/1820
On the 6th inst., Mrs. Sarah Dennis, consort of Robt. Dennis, Esq., of Dorchester county.	10/17/1820
On Tuesday evening, the 10th inst., by the Rev. Mr. Reach, Dr. Dorsey, of Anne Arundel county, to Miss Sarah M'Comas, of Harford county.	10/18/1820
At Hanover, Pa., Joshua Gosnell, Esq. to Miss Elizabeth Bailey, daughter of John Bailey, Esq., of Pikeville, Baltimore county, Md.	10/18/1820
On Sunday evening last, by the Rev. Mr. Reese, Mr. Enoch Lancaster, to Mrs. Mary Chrisfield.	10/18/1820
On Saturday, the 14th inst., by the Rev. Bishop Kemp, Mr. L. Lannay, Jr., to Miss Elizabeth V. Salve, both of this city.	10/18/1820
On Monday last, in the 25th year of her age, Miss Elizabeth Waters, of Rhode River, Ann Arundel county.	10/18/1820
In Talbot county, Md., Mrs. Mary Trippe, aged 70.	10/18/1820

Marriage and Death Notices	Date
On Tuesday evening, the 17th inst., by the Rev. Mr. Griston, Mr. Wm. Blackway, to Miss Harriot Young, all of Bear Hill, Baltimore county.	10/19/1820
On Tuesday evening, by the Rev. Mr. Hagerty, Mr. Thomas Curtain, to Miss Elizabeth Eldridge.	10/19/1820
On the 27th ult., in the 24th year of his age, after a short illness of seven days, Mr. Benjamin Branson, of Frederick county, a member of the Society of Friends.	10/19/1820
On Wednesday last, by the Rev. Mr. Burgess, Mr. Stryder, of Virginia, to Miss Harriet Powers, of this city.	10/20/1820
Last evening, by the Rev. Mr. Nevins, Mr. Robert Wilson, Jr., to Miss Elizabeth Kilty, all of this city.	10/20/1820
Last evening, by the Rev. Dr. Roberts, Mr. James Baldwin, of Harford county, to Miss Mary Hermitage, of this city.	10/20/1820
Last evening, by the Rev. Mr. Hargrove, Mr. Joseph Vonder Muhl, merchant, from the Havana, to Miss Catherine Shafer, of this city.	10/20/1820
On Thursday evening last, by the Rev. Mr. Swarmstedt, Mr. Joshua Rawlings, to Miss Ann Eliza Wright, all of this city.	10/21/1820
On Thursday evening last, by the Rev. Mr. Nevins, Mr. B. Wm. Hall, to Miss Ann Calhoun.	10/21/1820
On Thursday evening last, by the Rev. Mr. Nevins, Dr. Horace W. Waters, to Miss Alverda, daughter of Alexander Robinson, Esq., of this city.	10/21/1820
On Thursday evening last, by the Rev. Nelson Reed, Mr. W. R. Burneston, to Miss Matilda Edwards, all of this city.	10/21/1820
On Tuesday evening last, by the Rev. Dr. Glendy, Mr. Daniel Valentine, to Miss Araminta Valentine, all of this city.	10/21/1820
On the 15th inst., after a tedious illness, Mr. John Roy, aged 40, for many years a merchant of this city.	10/21/1820
Yesterday morning, in the 64th year of her age, of a lingering illness, Mrs. Elizabeth Neill, relict of Dr. John Neill, of Maryland.	10/21/1820
On Thursday evening last, by the Rev. Mr. Moranville, Mr. Peter Peduzi	10/24/1820

Marriage and Death Notices	Date
to Miss Catherine Harramon, all of this city.	
On Thursday evening last, in Georgetown, D. C., by the Rev. Mr. Davis, Mr. David Banes of Baltimore, to Miss Elizabeth Boon, of Georgetown.	10/24/1820
At Annapolis, on Thursday evening last, Mr. Westol Hohne to Miss Sophia Cross, all of that city.	10/24/1820
In Talbot county, Maj. William Caulk to Mrs. Artrige Stevens.	10/24/1820
In Talbot county, Mr. James Higgins. Mrs. Rachel Watts.	10/24/1820
At Denton, Md., Mr. Joseph Harrison, innkeeper. Dr. Robert Stevens.	10/24/1820
In Dorchester county, Mrs. Sarah Dennis, wife of Robert Dennis, Esq., in the 53rd year of her age.	10/24/1820
On Thursday, 12th inst., at St. Inegoes, St. Mary's county, after several days painful illness, Alexander Thompson.	10/24/1820
At Knoxville, Tennessee, on the 7th of this month, Mr. John Dickins, at the age of 36. Formerly of Baltimore. He was a dutiful son, a kind and affectionate brother, and a man of the most unblemished integrity.	10/24/1820
In Roxbury, on Thursday evening, by the Rev. Mr. Gray, Mr. Samuel Wyman, merchant, of Baltimore, to Miss Hannah D. Mayo.	10/25/1820
On Sunday evening last, by the Rev. D. E. Reese, Mr. Jacob Bromwell to Miss Eliza Gooden, all of this city.	10/25/1820
By the Rev. Dr. Glendy, on Monday last, Mr. Robert Davis, to Miss Elizabeth Gould.	10/25/1820
By the Rev. Dr. Glendy, on Monday last, Mr. Robert Moody, to Miss Sarah Gamble, all of this city.	10/25/1820
On Sunday morning, at his late residence in Baltimore county, Mr. George Lindenberger. Amidst the perplexities, the disappointments, and vices of life, few, very few indeed, are so uniformly affable, so inflexibly honest, and so constantly humane, as was the deceased. The loss society has sustained, will be his highest panegyric. In his family, he was as estimable as he was in society generally; there his virtues and his worth, were known and felt, by the liberal exercise of benevolence and humanity; and while he sympathized with the afflicted, relieved the distressed, and administered comfort to all around him, he remembered that he was rendering an acceptable service to God, that he was	10/25/1820

Marriage and Death Notices	Date
performing the will of Him, from whom he derived his feelings, and his principles.	
Dr. William Van Lear, of Washington county, Md., to Miss Susan Graham, of Bedford, Penn.	10/26/1820
On the 18th inst., at Portsmouth, N. H., by the Rev. Mr. Parker, Mr. Lewis Horton of Baltimore, to Miss Julia L. Sherburne, only daughter of the Hon. John S. Sherburne, of that place.	10/26/1820
In Harford county, Mr. Benjamin Tracy, to Miss Eleanor Thompson. Dr. Archibald Dorsey to Miss Sarah M'Comas. Mr. Shadrich Rutledge, Jr. to Miss Sarah Brindley.	10/26/1820
At Fredericktown, Mr. Wm. R. Elvin, to Miss Caroline Bogen.	10/26/1820
In the county of Albemarle, Va., Thomas Nelson, Esq., of Frederick, to Miss Mildred Nelson, daughter of the Hon. Hugh Nelson.	10/26/1820
On Wednesday evening last, by the Rev. Joseph Toy, Mr. Francis Smith, to Miss Susanna, only daughter of Isaac N. Toy, Esq., all of this city.	10/26/1820
At Fredericktown, after a short indisposition, Mr. Charles Sower, editor of the Star of Federalism.	10/26/1820
Suddenly, at St. Osyth, in Price George's county, Md., the seat of H. Webb, Esq., on the 19th inst., in the 70th year of her age, Mrs. Anna Hebb.	10/26/1820
On Tuesday evening, 24th, by the Rev. Dr. Roberts, Mr. Jesse Gudgeon to Miss Rachel Murphy, all of this city.	10/27/1820
On Wednesday evening last, by the Rev. Mr. Bartow, Mr. William Allen, to Miss Ann Roberts, all of this city.	10/27/1820
By the Rev. Dr. Glendy, on the evening of Thursday last, Mr. James Logan, to Miss Mary Johnson, all of this city.	10/27/18200
On Thursday evening last, by the Rev. Dr. Wyatt, Mr. Thomas Wilson, merchant, to Miss Hannah Holton, all of this city.	10/28/1820
By the Rev. Dr. Hagerthy, Mr. Jesse Williams, Miss Roedeah Chenea, both of this city.	10/28/1820

Marriage and Death Notices	Date
On Wednesday, the 25th inst., Mrs. Mary Jennings, wife of the Rev. Dr. S. K. Jennings, of this city. In her death, society has suffered the loss of an amiable companion, a tender mother, a sincere friend, free from all ostentation, and most beloved by those who had the happiness of knowing her the best.	10/28/1820
On Wednesday morning last, Mr. Pierson Nichols, in the 42nd year of his age. He was a native of Massachusetts, and late a respectable merchant of this city.	10/28/1820
On Thursday evening last, by the Rev. Dr. Roberts, Mr. John Carter to Miss Elizabeth Albright, all of this city.	10/30/1820
On Thursday Evening last, by the Rev. Mr. Hagerty, Mr. William Owens, merchant, to Miss Eliza Ann Stevens, all of this city.	10/30/1820
At 1 o'clock this morning, after an illness of 14 days, Mr. John Levering, of the house of John & Aaron Levering. His friends and acquaintances are invited to attend his funeral, at 4 o'clock this afternoon, from his dwelling, in Jefferson, or Conway street extended. The funeral will proceed on foot to the grave.	10/30/1820
On Saturday morning last, after a lingering illness, which he bore with Christian fortitude, Mr. Benjamin Garrison, in the 55th year of his age.	10/30/1820
At Hillsdale, on the 19th inst., Miss Susan Cook, much lamented by all her acquaintance. Her death was occasioned by her attempts to extricate herself from a chaise, in which she had been riding, after both reins had been broken by the driver's endeavors to hold the horse, and after the horse had run some distance. The velocity of the carriage being so great, that in jumping, although she at first struck the ground on her feet, she was instantly precipitated headlong to the earth, never to rise again.	10/30/1820
At New Orleans, after a short illness, Mr. Barthelemy Lafon, the Engineer, Geographer, and Architect, an old inhabitant of this place. His death is much lamented by a number of respectable citizens, who had known how to appreciate his talents and his heart.	10/31/1820
On Monday evening last, by the Rev. Dr. Roberts, Mr. John Woodland, of Kent County, to Miss Cassandra Divers, of this city.	11/01/1820
On Thursday evening last, by the Rev. E. J. Reese, Mr. Josiah Cobb to Miss Amelia Jane Foster, all of this city.	11/04/1820

Marriage and Death Notices	Date
On Thursday evening, by the Rev. Dr. Jennings, Mr. Amos Stout, to Miss Mary Covenhoven.	11/04/1820
On Sunday evening last, by the Rev. Dr. Roberts, Mr. Jonathan Truxel to Miss Deborah Starr, both of this city.	11/04/1820
On Sunday evening last, by the Rev. Mr. John Grobp, Mr. Abraham Lynn, to the amiable and accomplished Miss Eve Schwartz, both of Taney Town, Md.	11/04/1820
On Sunday morning last, after a long and painful illness, which she bore with unusual fortitude and resignation, Miss Elizabeth Brown, aged twenty four years.	11/04/1820
Last night, after a short and painful illness, which he bore with Christian fortitude, in the 28th year of his age, Charles Croxall, Esq., late one of the coroners of Baltimore county, and son of John Croxall, Esq., of this city. An aged father and mother, and four young sisters, survive to lament the loss of a dutiful son, an affectionate brother, and a worthy man.	11/04/1820
This morning, Mrs. Ann Shaw, relict of the late Rev. Dr. Shaw, of Marshfield, Mass., aged 63. The friends of the family are respectfully invited to attend her funeral, tomorrow, at 3 o'clock P. M.	11/04/1820
Departed this life, on Friday morning, October 27th, 1820, at her residence on Conococheague Manor, Washington county, Maryland, Mrs. Susanna Swearingen, relict of the late Col. Charles Swearingen, in the 82nd year of her age. Herself and her husband were the descendants of the oldest families in Maryland, in different parts of Virginia, in Kentucky, and Illinois. She was one of those virtuous and industrious women who are a crown to their husbands, a blessing to their families, and eminently useful to society; and her memory will long be dear to a very large connection of relatives and friends. Her mortal remains were on Saturday accompanied to the grave by a large and respectable company of friends and neighbors, and interred by the side of her deceased partner. Death has not long divided those who lived together so happily. *"Or ne'er to meet – or ne'er to part in peace."* An excellent sermon was delivered on the occasion by the Rev. Mr. Clay, from these words: *"For the great day of his wrath is come; and who shall be able to stand?"* Rev. vi. 17.	11/04/1820
On Tuesday evening last, by the Rev. Dr. Roberts, Mr. George King to Miss Sarah Jordan, all of this city.	11/04/1820

Marriage and Death Notices	Date
On Wednesday evening last, Mr. Hans Creevy, long a respectable Merchant of this city.	11/06/1820
Departed this transitory life, on the 31st Oct., in the 60th year of his age, after a long and painful illness, Capt. William Reeves.	11/06/1820
In Brimfield, Mass., Charles Prentiss, Esq., formerly distinguished for his literary productions in poetry and prose, and for his editorial labours at Washington and Baltimore.	11/06/1820
On Saturday evening last, 4th inst., after a long and severe illness, in the 38th year of her age, Mrs. Ann Prior, formerly of Newport, R. I., leaving three small children to lament their irreparable loss.	11/07/1820
At one o'clock, yesterday, Mr. William Jackson, Measurer, long a respectable resident of this city. His friends are invited to attend his funeral, at three o'clock, this afternoon; to proceed from his late dwelling, Holiday street.	11/08/1820
On Monday, the 7th inst., after a long indisposition, John Henry Purviance, Esq., aged 48, of the Department of State, where he had discharged responsible duties for several years.	11/08/1820
In Dorchester county, Md., Mr. John Brannoch, in the 35th year of his age.	11/08/1820
In Denton, Caroline county, Mrs. Elizabeth, consort of Joseph Richardson, Esq., in the 34th year of her age.	11/08/1820
In Easton, Md., Mr. Andrew Simmons. Mr. James Andrews. In Talbot county, Mr. Thomas Harden.	11/08/1820
On the 7th inst., by the Rev. Dr. Smith, Mr. John Sullivan, to Miss Christiana Boughan, both of this city.	11/09/1820
On Tuesday evening, the 7th inst., at Sassafras Neck, Cecil county, Md., by the Rt. Rev. Bishop Kemp, Mr. Franklin Betts, Bookseller, of Baltimore, to Mrs. Ann Davis, of the former place.	11/09/1820
On Thursday, the 26th October, Miss Mary Roberts, aged 13 years, daughter of Mr. Henry Roberts, of Charles county, Maryland; took fire in consequence of her frock coming in contact with some of the cinders, and before any assistance could be rendered was entirely burnt, and expired within thirteen hours after. Thus a young and blooming girl, in perfect health, was cut off by an untimely death.	11/09/1820

Marriage and Death Notices	Date
On Sunday morning, the 29th ult., Mrs. Elizabeth Roberts, mother of the above Miss Mary Roberts, after a few weeks illness.	11/09/1820
On Thursday morning, 9th inst., Robert Lowrey, Merchant Taylor, in the 35th year of his age.	11/10/1820
On Tuesday morning, the 7th inst., suddenly, Mrs. Ann, consort of Stephen Clark, for many years a respectable inhabitant of this city, aged 62 years.	11/10/1820
On Sunday evening last, the 5th inst., by the Rev. Dr. Jennings, Mr. David W. Wilson, to Miss Elizabeth Stewart, both of Baltimore county.	11/11/1820
On Tuesday evening last, Mr. Ignatius P. Lyles, of Montgomery County, Md., to Miss Emelia Claggett, daughter of Mr. Joseph Claggett, late of Anne Arundel County.	11/11/1820
On Wednesday evening last, by the Rev. Mr. Bartow, Mr. John Wells, to Miss Susan Croxford, all of this city.	11/11/1820
At York, by the Rev. Thomas Jackson, the Rev. William Jackson, of Baltimore, Md., to Miss Margaret Bryon, of that city.	11/11/1820
Last night, after a distressing illness, which she bore with uncommon resignation, Mrs. Ann Maria Sadler, in the 19th year of her age. Her friends have the assurance, from her last expressions, to believe that she rests in the arms of a blessed redeemer. She has left an infant child, an affectionate husband, and a tender mother, to deplore her early death.	11/11/1820
On Thursday evening last, by the Rev. Mr. Smith, Mr. David Coulter, of Queen Ann's county, Maryland, aged 81, to Mrs. Eleanor Sawyer, of this city, aged 80.	11/13/1820
On Tuesday evening last, by the Rev. Mr. Jefferson, Mr. John Chase, formerly of Chester, N. H., to Miss Eliza Dawes, of Montgomery county, Md.	11/13/1820
On Thursday evening last, by the Rev. Mr. Bartow, Mr. William Peck, to Miss Elizabeth Croney, of Fell's Point.	11/13/1820
On the evening of the 9th inst., by the Rev. D. E. Reese, Mr. George Frederick Miller, to Miss Hester Taylor, all of this city.	11/13/1820
In Prince George's county, Miss Eleanor Lee, daughter of Dr. Joseph Kent.	11/13/1820

Marriage and Death Notices	Date
On Sunday evening, the 5th inst., by the Rev. ____ Burgess, Mr. William J. Thompson, to Miss Eliza A. Crosby, all of this city.	11/14/1820
At Havre de Grace, on Thursday the 9th inst., by the Rev. Mr. William Stephenson, Mr. Joseph C. Carver, to Miss Motlener Peterman, both of Harford County.	11/14/1820
At her father's residence, on Saturday, the 11th inst., after a painful and lingering illness, which she bore with truly Christian fortitude and resignation, Miss Catherine Digges Sewell, eldest daughter of Robert D. Sewell, Esq., of Poplar Hill, Prince George's County, Maryland.	11/14/1820
On Sunday, the 12th inst., Mr. Hugh Burrows, aged 45 years, from County Down, Ireland, many years a citizen of this city. He has left a wife and three children to lament his loss.	11/15/1820
This day, the venerable and respected, Peter Holtz, Sr., a man long respected for his virtues, as a friend, a Patriot, and a benevolent member of society. His friends are requested to attend his funeral, tomorrow afternoon, at 3 o'clock.	11/16/1820
Yesterday morning, after a long and painful illness, Mrs. Catherine Isabella Buchanan, in the 38th year of her age.	11/16/1820
On Thursday morning, 9th inst., after a severe illness, in the 40th year of his age, Mr. Henry Allston, formerly of Baltimore, but for a long time a respectable inhabitant of St. Mary's County, Md. He has left a disconsolate widow and eight small children to deplore his loss. But why lament, departed friends, Or shake at death's alarms; Death's but the servant Jesus sends, To call us to his arms.	11/16/1820
At Woodstock, Virginia, on the 13th inst., on his way from Orleans to Baltimore, in the 23rd year of his age, Mr. William D. Young, son of the Rev. John Young, deceased, former Pastor of the Ass. Ref. Church, in Green Castle, Pennsylvania.	11/16/1820
On Thursday evening last, by the Rev. Mr. Birch, Mr. William J. Smith, to Miss Eliza C. Chambers, all of this city.	11/18/1820
Last evening, by the Rev. Daniel Reese, Mr. Lemuel S. Lenox to Miss Sarah Hornsby, all of this city.	11/18/1820
On Thursday evening last, by the Rev. Mr. Kurtz, Mr. Joseph Mettee to	11/18/1820

Marriage and Death Notices	Date
Miss Ann McDermot, all of this city.	
On Friday evening, 17th inst., after a long and painful illness, Capt. Thos. Moore, in the 74th year of his age, long a respectable citizen of Fell's Point. His friends and acquaintances are requested to attend his funeral tomorrow, Sunday evening, at 3 o'clock, from his late residence, Wilke street, Fell's Point.	11/18/1820
On Wednesday evening, the 15th inst., Mrs. Martha Disney, wife of Mr. James Disney, of this city, in the triumphs of faith, and with a joyous hope of a glorious resurrection, through the infinite merits of her Redeemer. For her, death had no sting, the grave no terror.	11/20/1820
At Avalon Iron Works, Baltimore county, Mr. John Dyke, in the 33rd year of his age, a native of Massachusetts, and for the last five years a resident of that county. He was a kind and affectionate husband and parent, and a valuable neighbor.	11/20/1820
In Easton, Md., Capt. James Nicholson.	11/20/1820
In Talbot county, Md., Mr. Henry M'Neal.	11/20/1820
On Sunday evening last, by the Rev. D. E. Reese, Mr. Robert Hervey to Mrs. Sarah Curtage, all of this city.	11/21/1820
On Sunday evening last, by the Rev. D. E. Reese, Mr. John G. Plummer, to Miss Hannah Johnson, all of this city.	11/21/1820
On Sunday evening last, by the Rev. D. E. Reese, Mr. Wm. D. Ball, to Miss Temperance Maydwell, all of this city.	11/21/1820
On Thursday evening last, by the Rev. T. J. Reis, Mr. John Berryman, to Miss Deborah Choate, all of this city.	11/21/1820
On Thursday evening last, by the Rt. Rev. Archbishop Mareschal, Dr. Elie Durand, to Miss Polymnia Rose, daughter of Edme Ducatel, of this place.	11/21/1820
On Tuesday, the 15th ult., at the seat of Mr. Thomas Chew, Harford county, Md., Mrs. Sarah, consort of Samuel Worthington, eldest daughter of Mr. Thomas Chew. Summoned hence in the bloom of years, surrounded with every blessing to make life desirable. Her character, during her short pilgrimage here, has been marked by all those soft, amiable, and engaging virtues, which diffuse peace and happiness in the domestic circle. A dutiful, fond daughter, affectionate wife, and tender mother, pious and resigned, her soul has, we hope,	11/21/1820

Marriage and Death Notices	Date
winged its way to the presence of him, in whom she placed her full trust, where those early graces, which were beginning to expand her, will be permitted to improve and flourish, forever in the presence of her Redeemer. Then cease to grieve, ye weeping friends, forbear! Her spirit lives, enlarg'd, in realms of bliss; The *"pure in heart,"* are God's peculiar care; he calls them hence to everlasting peace.	
On Sunday evening last, by the Rev. J. Healey, Mr. Abraham Todd, to Miss Elizabeth Hulse, all of this city.	11/22/1820
On Sunday evening last, by the Rev. Mr. Birch, Mr. Philip McGuire, to Miss Harriet Latschaw, all of this city.	11/22/1820
By the Rev. Dr. Glendy, on the 14th instant, Mr. Adam Virtue, to Miss Margaret Mungan, both of Baltimore county.	11/23/1820
By the Rev. Dr. Glendy, on Monday last, Mr. Elijah Clark, to Miss Elizabeth Thompson, both of this city.	11/23/1820
On Tuesday night, the 20th inst., after a long and painful illness, M. Louis A. Pise, in the 60th year of his age.	11/23/1820
Last evening, by the Rev. Mr. Healey, Mr. William W. Hilton, to Miss Catherine, eldest daughter of Capt. Anthony Gorton, all of this city.	11/24/1820
At Chestertown, on the evening of the 7th inst., by the Rev. Mr. Walker, Mr. Alexander W. Ringgold, to Miss Mary Ann Brown, elder daughter of Dr. Morgan Brown.	11/24/1820
At Hagerstown, Mr. Jacob Keisacker, to Miss Mary Ann Lose, of Franklin county, Pa. Mr. Daniel Schechter to Miss Mary Emmert. Mr. Adam Brewer to Miss Maria Johnson.	11/24/1820
By the Rev. Mr. Bartow, on Thursday evening last, Jacob Baltzell, Esq., merchant, to Miss Frances Buchanan, all of this city.	11/28/1820
At Samarang, (Java) 14th April, 1820, A. E. Soreman, of Baltimore, American Consul, to Mrs. Arabella Van Wickham.	11/28/1820
On the 16th inst., by the Rev. Mr. Nevins, Henry Hall, Esq., of Harford county, to Miss Charlotte Jane Ramsay, daughter of the late Col. Ramsay, of this city.	11/28/1820

Marriage and Death Notices	Date
At Fredericktown, the Rev. John Johns to Miss Juliana E. W. Johnson.	11/29/1820
At Washington, D. C., Mr. John Waters to Miss Dorothy Edmonston, daughter of Capt. Arch. Edmonston, of Prince George's county, Md.	11/29/1820
At Little Falls, Mr. John M'Ardle, aged 50. He was employed in blasting rocks, and was killed by an explosion. The accidents in the family of Mr. M. are very peculiar. He had lost seven sons, not one of whom died a natural death; five of them were drowned – and one, who was employed with his father, recently met his death in the same way.	11/29/1820
At Claibourne, Alabama, about the 25th Oct., Nicholas F. Horton, formerly of Baltimore. He was active, industrious, and intelligent, and by his exemplary life, had gained the esteem and respect by all who knew him. As he lived, so he died, in the full belief of a happy immortality.	11/29/1820
On Tuesday evening last, by the Rt. Rev. Bishop Kemp, Dr. R. W. Armstrong, to Miss Eliza R., second daughter of Elias Glenn, Esq., all of this city.	11/30/1820
Yesterday morning, at 8 o'clock, of a lingering illness, which he bore with Christian fortitude, Mr. John Ash, in the 36th year of his age.	11/30/1820
On the 22nd ult., Miss Mary Witmer, daughter of Mr. Henry Witmer, of Washington county, Md.	12/01/1820
On the 21st inst., at Ranelagh, the residence of W. G. Sanders, in Prince George's county, Dennis Magruder, Esq. to Miss Mary Ann Beard.	12/02/1820
On Thursday evening last, by the Rev. Mr. Bartow, Mr. Richard Shaw to Miss Sarah Ann Flemming, all of this city.	12/02/1820
At Centreville, Md., on Friday, the 24th ult., Mr. Zebulon Skinner, merchant of that place, of the firm of Skinner & Emory, after a very short illness. He was greatly respected for his correct deportment and Christian walk. He was about 23 years of age.	12/04/1820
At Mount Carmel, near Queen's Town, Md., on the 22nd ult., of a violent quinsey, Mrs. Hannah Massey, consort of Maj. James Massey, after suffering eight days of extreme pain, which she bore with Christian fortitude and resignation. She had been a member of the Methodist Church a number of years, and enjoyed great tranquility of soul and joy in believing.	12/04/1820

Marriage and Death Notices	Date
Departed his life, on the 14th ult., at the residence of Dr. Wm. Whitely, of Caroline County, Md., Mr. Henry Baynard, formerly of the City of Baltimore, in the twenty-eighth year of his age. His relatives and numerous acquaintances, will long deplore the loss of this amiable and exemplary young man. He bid farewell to this world of sorrow, rejoicing in his Savior.	12/04/1820
On Sunday evening last, by the Rev. Dr. Albert, Mr. Joshua German, to Miss Sarah W. Kersey, all of this city.	12/05/1820
On Tuesday evening, the 28th ult., by the Rev. Mr. Tidings, Mr. Benjamin Mead, of Annapolis, to Miss Louisa C. Rouselle, of this city.	12/05/1820
On Tuesday, the 28th ult., at the seat of John P. Paca, Esq., on Wye, in Queen Anne's county, by the Rev. Mr. Bain, Charles Carroll Tilghman, Esq., to Miss Mary Lloyd Tilghman, both of the same county.	12/05/1820
Yesterday morning, at nine o'clock, Mrs. Hull, consort of James Hull. Her friends and relations are invited to attend her funeral this afternoon at three o'clock.	12/05/1820
On the 12th November last, Mr. William Ward, in the 60th year of his age, after a long and painful illness, which he bore with Christian fortitude. Summoned hence, in the prime of years, surrounded with every blessing to make life desirable. His character during his pilgrimage here has been marked by all amiable and engaging qualities. Pious and resigned, as we hope, winged its way to the presence of Him, in whom he placed his full trust.	12/05/1820
Last evening, by the Rev. Mr. Healey, Mr. William Silcock, to Mrs. Hannah Schroder, all of this city.	12/07/1820
Departed this life, yesterday afternoon, Elizabeth Lancaster, wife of Joseph Lancaster. The friends and acquaintances of Joseph Lancaster are invited to attend her funeral, THIS AFTERNOON, at No. 43, Front street, Old Town, so as to leave the house at 3 o'clock.	12/07/1820
In this city, yesterday, about 3 o'clock P. M., Mr. Charles Miller, aged 63, for seven years past, *Clerk in the Office of the Baltimore Patriot*, and for several years before, *Clerk in the offices of the Baltimore Post*, and the *Sun*. He was suddenly attacked at dinner, the preceding day, with an apoplectic fit; all medical and other attention was unavailing; and he lingered, without consciousness, until the time of his decease. Few men have been more generally known, in this city, and by many from the counties, than Mr. Miller; and very few, in his humble and	12/08/1820

Marriage and Death Notices	Date
unostentatious line of life, more generally respected. Assiduous in business, and of unimpeached integrity, he added to these qualities an unassuming suavity and cheerfulness of manners, which made him many friends. His health and strength had been declining for some time; though the call, which summoned him to change worlds, was sudden and unexpected. Peace to his departed spirit and a tear to his memory!	
The 15th of September last, on Staten Island, after four days illness, of a bilious remittent, in the 56th year of his age, Mr. Bernard H. Cook, a resident of Baltimore county.	12/08/1820
At New York, Mr. Garrett Nelson, of Harford county, Maryland, to Miss Hannah Cole.	12/11/1820
On Tuesday evening last, by the Rev. Dr. Roberts, Mr. Samuel Tweedy, of Delaware, to Miss Ann Williams, of this city.	12/11/1820
On Thursday evening last, at Pikesville, by the Rev. Parson Peyton, Maj. Conrad Hook, to Miss Mary Decker, both of Baltimore county.	12/11/1820
On Tuesday, the 29th Nov., by the Rev. Mr. Carroll, Mr. Robert Manning, to Miss Ann Priscilla Gough, both of St. Mary's county.	12/11/1820
On Friday, 10th November, Mrs. Elizabeth Plater, Jr., in the 21st year of her age, after a painful illness, which she bore with Christian fortitude.	12/11/1820
At Chestertown, Md., on Tuesday, 5th inst., by the Rev. Mr. Martindale, Mr. Joseph Redue, to Emeline Comegys, all of that place.	12/12/1820
On Thursday last, by the Rev. Mr. Healey, Mr. John Boise Tyler, to Mrs. Charlotte Frizzell, both of Baltimore County.	12/12/1820
On the 9th instant, at Poplar Neck, Harford county, the residence of her father, Mr. Buckler Bond, in the 38th year of her age, Mrs. Rebecca Howard, consort of the late, Dr. Henry Howard, of this city. "Early, bright, transient, chaste, as morning dew, She sparkled, was exhal'd, and went to Heaven; Heaven gives the needful, but neglected call, What day, what hour, but knocks at human hearts, To wake the soul to sense of future scenes?"	12/13/1820
Last evening, by the Rev. Dr. Jennings, Mr. James Spencer, of St. Mary's County, to Miss Elizabeth Turner, of this city.	12/15/1820

Marriage and Death Notices	Date
At Hagerstown, Mr. Daniel Shriver, to Miss Elizabeth Grosh. Mr. George Brunner to Miss Elizabeth Faulkwell. Mr. Nathaniel Webb to Miss Harriet Allender. Mr. James Kendle to Miss Margaret Wherrett.	12/15/1820
On Thursday evening last, by the Rev. Dr. Roberts, Mr. Michael Cromwell, to Miss Elizabeth Weary, all of this city.	12/18/1820
On Thursday evening last, by the Rev. Mr. Birch, Mr. James B. Smith, to Louisa, daughter of Job Smith, Esq., all of this city.	12/18/1820
On Sunday evening last, by the Rev. D. E. Reese, Mr. William T. Schreck, to Miss Elizabeth Smith, both of this city.	12/18/1820
On Saturday, the 19th inst., at his seat in Harford county, in the seventy fifth year of his age, Josias William Dallam, Esq.	12/18/1820
On Thursday, the 7th inst., Mr. William K. Knotts, to Miss Mary Rich, both of Queen Ann's county.	12/19/1820
At Philadelphia, on the 14th inst., by the Rt. Rev. Bishop Conwell, Richard H. Bayard, Esq., to Miss Mary Sophia Carroll, daughter of Charles Carroll, Jr., Esq., of Baltimore.	12/19/1820
On Thursday, the 14th instant, while absent on a visit to his farm in Harford county, Mr. Samuel G. Griffith, in the 40th year of his age. His remains were yesterday brought to town, and deposited in the German Lutheran burial ground.	12/19/1820
On the 16th inst., after a long and distressing illness, which he bore with the fortitude and resignation of a Christian, Robert Sewell, Esq., of Poplar Hill, Prince George's county, Maryland.	12/19/1820
On Tuesday, the 5th inst., by the Rev. Mr. Walker, Mr. Beckington Scott, of Queen Ann's, to Miss Julian Miller, of Kent county.	12/20/1820
On the 17th inst., Capt. Matthias Rich, aged 64, a native of Massachusetts, and for a number of years, a resident of this city.	12/20/1820
Lately, in the alms-house, Hagar Waters, the colored woman, whose musical talents were so well known in this city. The singularity of her manners, her inoffensive disposition, and strict integrity of character, excited interest in all who knew her. She was at different times a professed member of the Roman Catholic, Presbyterian, Episcopal, Methodist, Quaker, and Baptist religions – and has gone, we hope, to a place where sectarian principles have no existence, and where the Christian finds a resting place, from the toils and vexations of this	12/20/1820

Marriage and Death Notices	Date
transitory veil of tears.	
On the 10th inst., Mrs. Dorcas, the widow of Mr. Archibald Young, late of Boston.	12/20/1820
On Tuesday evening last, by the Rev. Mr. Rich, Mr. Joshua C. Davis, to Miss Esther Jones, all of this city.	12/22/1820
On Thursday evening last, by the Rev. Mr. Tidings, Mr. Saml. Dryden, to Miss Ann Coburn, all of this city.	12/23/1820
On Thursday evening last, by the Rev. Mr. Kurtz, Mr. William Hahn, to Miss Susan Goff, all of this city.	12/23/1820
Yesterday morning, at 3 o'clock, after a lingering illness, Mr. John C. Steinbeck, long a respectable inhabitant of this city. His friends and acquaintances are respectfully invited to attend his funeral, this evening at 3 o'clock.	12/23/1820
On Tuesday, Dec. the 19th, Jacob Cromwell, Sr., of Baltimore county, in the 81st year of his age.	12/23/1820
At Fredericktown, Mr. John Shriver to Miss Julian Garver.	12/27/1820
In Talbot county, Md., Mr. Joseph L. Turner, Esq., to Mrs. Ann Abbott.	12/27/1820
Last Saturday evening, by the Rev. Bishop Kemp, Mr. Samuel Jennings, to Miss Eliza Dowdell, all of this city.	12/27/1820
By the Rev. Mr. Stevenson, on 21st inst., Saml. Bageley, Esq., to Miss Mary Smith, both of Deer Creek, Harford, Co.	12/27/1820
By the Rev. Dr. Glendy, on Monday evening last, Mr. David Manly, to Miss Mary Boyer Cross.	12/27/1820
By the Rev. Dr. Glendy, on Monday evening last, Mr. Robert Aitkin, Druggist, to Miss Eliza M, eldest daughter of Alexander Mitchell, Esq., all of this city.	12/27/1820
On Tuesday evening, by the Rev. Mr. Roberts, Mr. Edmund Gibson, to Miss Mary Gallagher, both of this city.	12/27/1820
At York Haven, on the 21st inst., by the Rev. Mr. A. Hemphill, Mr. Nicholas Baylies, of Baltimore, to Miss Susan Stone, of the former place.	12/27/1820 12/30/1820

Marriage and Death Notices	Date
Last evening, by the Rev. John Hargrove, Edward Hinkley, Esq., Attorney at Law, to Miss Hannah E., youngest daughter of the Rev. Mr. H., all of this city.	12/28/1820
On Saturday last, by the Rev. Mr. Bartow, Mr. Solomon H. Van Praag, to Miss Heister B. Swaab, all of this city.	12/29/1820
On Monday evening, by the Rev. Mr. Henshaw, Mr. Joseph Walker, to Miss Ellen Stacy, both of this city.	12/29/1820
At Cincinnati, (Ohio) the 4th Dec., by the Rt. Rev. Bishop Chase, the Rev. Samuel Johnson, Rector of Christ Church, to Miss Margaretta Elizabeth Wilson, formerly of this place.	12/29/1820
On Saturday, 23rd inst., in the 39th year of her age, Mrs. Ann Keener, consort of the late Jacob Keener, deceased.	12/29/1820
In Washington county, Md., Mr. Christopher Trovinger, in the 64th year of his age. Capt. Adam Ridenour.	12/29/1820
At Blakely, Alabama, on the 28th of November, after a lingering illness, Mrs. Lavinia Stoddard, in the 34 year of her age, wife of the late Dr. William Stoddard, and daughter of Mrs. J. Stone, of this city.	12/29/1820
In Raleigh, N. C., on the 21st inst., Alexander Lucas, Esq., the senior Editor of the Minerva. Mr. Lucas was a native of Pennsylvania, but had for several years been a resident of this place. He was in the prime of life, and has left a disconsolate widow and three young children to lament the loss of a most indulgent and tender husband and father. Mr. Lucas' colloquial talents and literary taste have been duly appreciated by all who knew him in the vigor of health and intellect; but for some time they have gradually declined. His death, however, was rather sudden and unexpected; "in the twinkling of an eye" he was changed, and slept to wake no more.	12/29/1820
Last evening, by the Rev. Mr. Waugh, Mr. George Farrell, to Miss Mary Ann Bailey, all of this city.	12/29/1820
This morning, at 1 o'clock, after a short, but painful illness, which he bore with the fortitude and resignation of the just, Maj. Jacob Steiger, late of the 39th Regiment off M. M., in the 55th year of his age. His friends and acquaintances are invited to attend his funeral, from his late dwelling in Franklin street, at 3 o'clock, tomorrow. He discharged the various relations he sustained in society, with a zeal and fidelity peculiar only to enlarged and elevated minds. Liberal himself, in his sentiments,	12/30/1820

Marriage and Death Notices	Date
his charity to those who differed from him was not restrained with any limits; believing that all "who fear the Lord, and work righteousness will be accepted of him." To his numerous and respectable family and friends, he has bequeathed the example of a virtuous and well spent life, a consciousness of which was his firmest support in the most trying moment, when it was announced to him, that all was done that could be done. This communication, so terrible to those, whose evil deeds have left them no hope, was received with that calmness and fortitude which bespoke a nobleness of soul, that had no fears for the change he was about to undergo.	
At Drakies' Plantation, Georgia, on the evening of the 24th ult., by the Rev. Mr. Cranston, John Eager Howard, Jun., Esq., of Baltimore, to Cornelia Annabella, second daughter of the late Hon. Jacob Read, of South Carolina.	01/01/1821 01/02/1821
On Saturday, 30th ult., Mrs. Mary Adreon, consort of George Adreon, after a painful and lingering illness, which she bore with Christian fortitude. She has left a husband and three children to deplore their irreparable loss. It may be said, with full confidence, that death and the grave were no terror or fear. She only smiled at them, as friendly messengers, to welcome her to that place, where she will join in with the companies of angels and archangels, and sing praises unto God and the Lamb forever.	01/02/1821
On Friday evening last, by the Rev. Mr. Bartow, Mr. Oliver Hanson, to Miss Mary Ann Murray, all of this city.	01/02/1821
At Baltimore, on Monday evening last, the 25th Dec., by the Rev. Mr. Henshaw, minister of the Episcopal Church, Mr. Joseph Walker, Jr., mathematical tutor in the Rev. Dr. Barry's Academy, and the son of Mr. Joseph Walker, Sr., teacher of the mathematics in Cherry-street, in Philadelphia, to Miss Stacey, daughter of Mr. Stacey, of Baltimore.	01/02/1821
By the Rev. Dr. Glendy, on the evening of Saturday last, Mr. James Smith, to Miss Mary Carr, both of Baltimore county.	01/03/1821
By the Rev. Mr. Grice, Mr. Samuel Hook, to Miss Sidney Riter, both of Baltimore county.	01/03/1821
On Tuesday evening last, by the Rev. Mr. Burch, Mr. Charles Nicholson, Jr., silversmith, to Miss Frances Turner, both of this city.	01/03/1821
Departed this life, on Saturday last, Mrs. Elizabeth Steever, in the 40th year of her age, after a severe and lingering sickness, under which	01/04/1821

Marriage and Death Notices	Date
affliction, she exhibited a pious example of Christian patience and fortitude.	
On Tuesday evening last, by the Rev. Mr. Moranville, Capt. A. P. Valangin, to Miss Wilhelmina Baartcheer, all of this city.	01/04/1821
On Tuesday evening last, by the Rev. Dr. Roberts, Mr. Isaac Hulse, youngest son of the late Caleb M. Hulse, Esq., of Long Island, New York, to Miss Amelia T., eldest daughter of the Rev. Dr. Roberts, of this city.	01/04/1821
In Talbot county, Md., Mr. Charles Goldsborough, Jr., to Caroline, daughter of Col. Jabez Caldwell, all of that county.	01/04/1821
Yesterday morning, January 5th, Mr. Samuel Biggert, aged 49 years.	01/05/1821
On Thursday evening last, by the Rev. Mr. Burch, Mr. James Allen, of this city, to Miss Eliza Taylor, of Baltimore county.	01/06/1821
In Harford county, Md., Charles A. Rumsey to Miss Caroline B. Howard. Mr. Thomas Martin to Miss Mary Grafton. Mr. Samuel Bayley to Miss Mary Smith. Mr. John Molton to Miss Mary Nevil. Mr. John Thompkins to Miss Ann Anderson. Mr. John Rogers to Miss Elizabeth Malone. Mr. Joseph Dulany to Miss Mary Ann Mitchell. Mr. Garsham Gerrell to Miss Rachel Spence. Mr. Hugh McKoen to Miss Hannah Mitchell.	01/06/1821
On the 12th Dec., H. H. Hawkins, Esq., merchant of Prince George's county, Md., to Margaret, eldest daughter of Ann W. Wood, of Charles county.	01/06/1821
On the 26th Dec. last, the Hon. Ebenezer Hunt, M. D., aged 76.	01/08/1821
At her residence, in Chestertown, Md., on the morning of the 27th Dec., Mrs. Elizabeth Chambers, relict of the late Gen. Benj. Chambers. It is a duty to exhibit for imitation, the virtues and piety of those, who seem designed by Providence, as peculiar lights to our path. During three years, and more, she was the victim of a painful and hopeless disease, and her sufferings have perhaps, never been surpassed – yet they were borne with a resignation, which can only flow from a settled conviction, that all inflictions are sent to us in mercy. Her piety was not of that bold character, which challenges a claim to heaven, but a calm and timid hope, often alarmed and depressed under the sense of the perfect purity, and the holiness of the God, "unto all hearts are open" – but as often cheered and animated by the recollection of a dying Saviour's love. Her	01/08/1821

Marriage and Death Notices	Date
greatest consolation consisted in hearing read to her, the gracious promises of the Gospel. So far from repining at the weight of her affliction, in the midst of hourly and agonizing pain, she thanked her God, who had given to her so many comforts, and such a season of preparation, that the ties which bound her to earth, were gradually and imperceptibly loosened – thus all things were made by her, to manifest the love and mercy of her Redeemer. Towards the close of the solemn scene, her aspirations for eternity became fervent and her friends daily witnessed her prayers for the coming of "Christ's messenger." One of the last articulate sounds she uttered, when asked *"what she would have?"* was *"Heaven!"* The writer of this feeble sketch of "the dying Christian," *knew her well*, and fears that 'twill be long ere the chasm her removal has caused will be supplied.	
On Thursday evening last, by the Rev. Mr. Waugh, Mr. John Quay, to Miss Sarah Watts, both of Fell's Point.	01/08/1821
Sunday afternoon, the 7th inst., in the 90th year of her age, Mrs. Barbary Tschudy, relict of the late Nicholas Tschudy, formerly a respectable merchant of Baltimore.	01/09/1821
On Thursday night last, at his residence near Baltimore, Mr. Caleb Arnest, aged sixty-two years.	01/09/1821
On the 4th inst., after a short illness, Mr. James J. Johnson, of this city, in the 42nd year of his age.	01/09/1821
Last evening, after an indisposition of a few hours, Mrs. Anna Magdalena Schwartz, aged 34 years.	01/09/1821
On Sunday evening, the 7th inst., by the Rev. Mr. Bartow, Capt. John Hill, to Mrs. Elizabeth Brown, all of this city.	01/09/1821
On Saturday evening last, by the Rev. Mr. Burges, James Powers, Esq., to Miss Sophia Stryder, of Virginia.	01/09/1821
In Talbot county, Maryland, Robbert Banning, Esq., to Miss Eliza E. Makin. Mr. James Cook to Miss Catherine Norris.	01/11/1821
By the Rev. Mr. Healey, Mr. Daniel Brewer, to Miss Anice Whitmore, all of this city.	01/12/1821
On Tuesday evening, by the Rev. Mr. Valiant, Mr. Wm. M'Pherson, of this city, to Miss Ann Scharf, of Baltimore county.	01/12/1821

Marriage and Death Notices	Date
Mr. George A. Barnes, to Miss Susan C. Phillips, all of Prince George's County, Maryland.	01/12/1821
On Thursday, the 28th of December last, at the house of Mr. George M. Elliott, near Hagerstown, in the 57th year of his age, Mr. Edward Green. He was formerly engaged in the Bay trade from Baltimore. He stated that he had a daughter of the Eastern Shore – for the information of whom, some of the public prints in Baltimore, will confer a favor by giving this an insertion.	01/13/1821
Died, yesterday morning at 6 o'clock, Mr. Adam Alexander, a Revolutionary Patriot, aged upwards of 75 years, well known as being in the employ of the Baltimore and Philadelphia theatres, for the last 28 years. His friends and acquaintance are respectfully requested to attend his funeral from his late dwelling, in Straight lane, near the Friends Meeting House, this evening at 3 o'clock.	01/18/1821
On Sunday evening last, by the Rev. Mr. Birch, Mr. Wm. H. Brown, to Miss Jane Shryack, all of this city.	01/18/1821
On Tuesday evening last, by the Rev. Dr. Roberts, Mr. Rezin S. Simpson, to Miss Jane Sleppy, both of this city.	01/18/1821
On the 9th inst., by the Rev. Mr. Keech, on Ladies Manor, Baltimore county, Mr. Shadrach Gilbert, to Miss Ann Anderson, of the former place.	01/18/1821
At Fredericktown, on the 8th inst., by the Rev. John Johns, Mr. Stuart Gaither, to Miss Margaret Schell, all of that place.	01/18/1821
At Cumberland, on Thursday evening, the 11th inst., by the Rev. J. C. Clay, Frederick Augustus Schley, Esq., to Miss Francina C. Lynn, daughter of David Lynn, Esq.	01/18/1821
Yesterday afternoon, in the 48th year of his age, Gen. Joseph Sterett, a gentleman and a soldier. *His friends are invited to join in the procession from his late residence, tomorrow morning, at 11 o'clock.*	01/19/1821
On the 14th inst. at his residence in Charles county, Capt. Philip Richard Tendall, aged 33.	01/19/1821
On Sunday evening, by the most Rev. Archbishop Mareschal, Mr. Henry Pike, to Miss Mary White, daughter of Mr. Abraham White, of this city.	01/19/1821

Marriage and Death Notices	Date
At Locust Grove, on Tuesday evening, the 16th inst., by the Rev. Nial, Mr. William H. Hall, to Miss Eliza M. Haword, all of Baltimore county.	01/19/1821
On the 18th inst., in Baltimore county, Mr. Samuel Swarts, in the 83rd year of his age. He was a man justly esteemed, and has left a numerous family to mourn his decease.	01/20/1821
Departed this transitory life, on Wednesday evening last, after a short, though painful illness, which he bore with Christian fortitude, Mr. Joshua Redman, aged about 18 years. *"Blessed are the dead who die in the Lord."*	01/20/1821
On Tuesday last, by the Rev. D. E. Reese, Mr. John Wilhelm, to Mrs. Ediff Pitts, both of Baltimore county.	01/20/1821
On Tuesday evening last, by the Rev. Mr. Moranville, Mr. Charles Frederick Eckel, to Miss Mary Ann O'Connor, all of this city.	01/20/1821
Yesterday morning, in the 38th year of her age, Mrs. Sarah Gallagher, wife of Michael Gallagher. She has left an affectionate husband and six young children to deplore her loss.	01/23/1821
By the Rev. Dr. Glendy, on the evening of Thursday last, Mr. John Hunter, to Miss Mary Ann Smiley, all of this city.	01/23/1821
On Thursday evening last, 18th inst., in Anne Arundel county, by the Rev. Mr. Welsh, Mr. Theodore Anderson, of Baltimore, to Miss Sarah Stevens, of the former place.	01/23/1821
On the 13th December last, in Richmond county, Georgia, Mr. James Bond, formerly of Maryland, but for many years past an inhabitant of that state; he has left a son and a number of relatives to lament for this unexpected call of Divine Providence.	01/24/1821
On Thursday evening last, by the Rev. Dr. Roberts, Mr. John Stinchcomb, to Miss Susan Sullivan, both of this city.	01/24/1821
On Thursday evening last, by the Rev. Dr. Jennings, Mr. Reuben M. Dorsey, to Miss Sarah D. Merriweather, both of Anne Arundel county.	01/24/1821
On Saturday evening last, after a short illness, Miss Ann Hyde, aged 18 years, daughter of Mr. Francis Hyde, of this city – loved, esteemed, and admired by all who knew her. This amiable young lady, who but for a few weeks since, we beheld in the full bloom of health, and enjoying the pleasing anticipation of many happy years – by the unsparing hand of death, is thus suddenly consigned to that eternal world, *from whose*	01/25/1821

Marriage and Death Notices	Date
bourne no traveler e'er returns – a solemn and affecting warning to her numerous friends, *to be also ready.* A large circle will long cherish the memory of one, they so justly, so highly prized, so sincerely loved. The writer of this will not attempt to delineate the grief, which this event has caused to her bereaved family – their feelings may be more easily conceived than described. May that merciful parent, who *"tempers the wind to the shorn lamb,"* give them consolation and comfort, under this severe dispensation of his providence – may they consider, that however inscrutable are his ways to man, yet that his severest trials are for their good. C. "Oh! What can charm or turn one thought from thee? "So dearly lov'd, so hard a destiny! "Where is that look, which could the heart unfold? "That heavenly smile, which all thy virtues told? "Where is that voice whose sympathizing tone? "Are they all buried with that angel form? "Where Hope no more can cheer, nor light can warm? "Breathe, sainted Anna! From thy holy rest, "Breathe that spirit, which inspired thy breast, "Be thou the still small voice, that whisp'ring near, "Shall teach submission from thy silent bier." ACG&T	
On Sunday morning last, by the Rev. Mr. Burgess, James Jenkins, Esq., to Miss Elizabeth Sweeney, all of this city.	01/25/1821
On Wednesday evening last, by the Rev. Mr. Burch, Mr. Samuel Pastorius, to Miss Eliza Goddard, all of this city.	01/26/1821
On Wednesday last, after a severe illness of two weeks, Miss Susan Williams, aged 18 years and 1 month, daughter of Mr. John Williams, of this city.	01/27/1821
In Washington City, on the 24th inst., Miss Elizabeth Carroll, of Montgomery county, Md., at an advanced stage of life.	01/27/1821
On Tuesday evening last, by the Rev. D. E. Reese, Mr. Edward Barret, to Miss Eliza Ensor.	01/27/1821
By the Rev. D. E. Reese, on the evening of Thursday last, Mr. Thomas Bussey, to Miss Ann Mass, all of this city.	01/27/1821
Last Thursday evening, by the Rev. J. M. Duncan, Mr. John Johnson, to Miss Priscilla S. Boyd, all of this city.	01/27/1821

Marriage and Death Notices	Date
On Thursday, the 18th inst., by the Rev. Mr. Allen, Mr. Richard W. M'Pherson, of Charles county, to Miss Helen E. Parker, of Prince George's county.	01/27/1821
At Cedar Grove, Charles county, Md., on the 14th inst., Capt. Philip Fendall, in the 33rd year of his age.	01/29/1821
On Tuesday evening, 23rd inst., Mr. Joseph Stewart, to Miss Elizabeth Webb, both of this city.	01/29/1821
On the 14th inst., by the Rev. Mr. Waugh, Mr. Samuel T. Glenn, to Mrs. Mary Kennedy, both of this city.	01/29/1821
At Annapolis, Mr. Joseph Allen to Miss Rebecca A. F. Tucker.	01/29/1821
On Sunday evening last, by the Rev. Dr. Kurtz, Mr. Deaderick Koster, to Miss Mary Ann Commons, both of this city.	01/31/1821
On Saturday, 27th inst., of an afflicting and protracted illness, which she bore with great piety and resignation, Mrs. Ann Maria Cooch, consort of Mr. Zebulon H. Cooch, in the 22nd year of her age. She was an ornament to her sex, and her amiable virtues attracted the admiration and esteem of all who knew her.	02/01/1821
Died, at his residence in Frederick county, on the 25th instant, Thomas Hawkins, Esq., in the 74th year of his age. In speaking of the virtues of our deceased fellow countrymen, we are at a loss to select the most prominent, by which he was characterized. He was no common man; and were his numerous excellencies pointed out, they would far exceed the circumscribed limits of a newspaper. In the possession of a large patrimonial estate, he was among the first to volunteer, as a private, and shoulder his musket, at an early period of our revolutionary conflict. At that trying time, when it was treason to resist the omnipotence of parliamentary legislation, Hawkins did not hesitate one moment to take the part of his country. From the most disinterested patriotism, he staked his all upon the contest – and that decision and energy, which so eminently marked his character throughout life, shown conspicuously at the period to which we allude. From some of his fellow soldiers, who fought by his side, we learn that his bosom was a stranger to fear, and in the battle's slaughter, he was always to be found in the foremost ranks of danger, amongst the bravest of the brave. After having served his country faithfully, in the field, he was again called on to promote the interest of his native state, in her legislative councils. For twenty years, he served alternately in the senate and	02/01/1821

76

Marriage and Death Notices	Date
house of delegates, and a charge of inconsistency was never alleged against him, all the severe political struggles, in which he was engaged. No man ever possessed higher civic virtues than the deceased. He was slow to form an opinion, but so clear was his judgment, than when he once took his stand, no considerations of self interest or the suggestions of a timid, time serving policy, could drive him from that purpose. Although often solicited, he was never known to receive any appointment or trust, except from the people. A republican from principle, he disdained the trappings and distinctions, which grow out of aristocratic institutions, and a poor man and a prince, would have been entertained on an equal footing at his plain and hospitable board. In his immediate neighborhood, the objects of his charity were in full proportion to his ample and affluent means, and many a tear already flows from the dreadful stroke which has irreparably bereaved them of their kind and affectionate benefactor. He was emphatically the widow's friend, and the poor man's stay – and it may be sincerely and truly said, that he lived not for himself, but for others. In a life longer that that which is generally allotted to man, he has left much to endear his memory to us, and nothing wherewith to reproach his reputation. To his children, he has left that which excels all worldly inheritance, a bright example of a well-spent life, a character untarnished and without reproach.	
At Somerset, Pennsylvania, Mr. Joseph Smith, Editor of the Western Herald, Cumberland, Maryland, to Miss Maria L. Boyer, of the former place.	02/02/1821
At the Oak-Grove, Charles county, Maryland, Mr. Edward I. Hamilton, to Miss Maria E. Spalding, daughter of Mr. George H. Spalding, deceased.	02/02/1821
Departed this life, on the 2nd inst., Mrs. Ann Martin, consort of Dr. S. B. Martin. Her friends and acquaintances are invited to attend her funeral, this afternoon at 3 o'clock, from her late dwelling, in Alisanna street.	02/03/1821
In Baltimore, on Tuesday evening last, by the Rev. Joseph Shane, Mr. David Daugherty, Jr., Printer, to Miss Elizabeth W. Johnson, both of Wilmington, Delaware.	02/03/1821
At New Orleans, on 31st December last, Joseph Saul, Esq., of that city, to Miss Mary Meroney, of Baltimore.	02/05/1821 02/06/1821
Departed this life, yesterday afternoon, Mr. Joseph Wallace, merchant, in the 52nd year of his age. His friends and acquaintances are invited to attend his funeral, from his late dwelling, in south Eutaw street, on	02/06/1821

Marriage and Death Notices	Date
Wednesday morning, at 11 o'clock.	
On Saturday evening last, by the Rev. Dr. Roberts, Mr. John Whitney to Miss Lydia Ann Hatch, all of this city.	02/06/1821
On Saturday evening, by the Rev. Mr. Helfenstein, Mr. Martin Bowers, Jr., to Miss Margaret Browning, all of this city.	02/07/1821
On Tuesday evening last, by the Rev. Dr. Roberts, Mr. W. Quynn, of Georgetown, D. C., to Miss Margaret Branson, of this city.	02/08/1821
On Tuesday evening last, by the Rev. Mr. Tidings, Mr. Joseph Hohne, of Annapolis, to Miss Ann Howard, of this city.	02/08/1821
By the Rev. Dr. Glendy, on Monday last, Mr. Henry Butler to Miss Margaret Henderson, both of Baltimore county.	02/08/1821
At Philadelphia, Mr. Wm. G. Latimer, of Baltimore, to Miss Mary Collins, daughter of Benj. Collins, of that city.	02/08/1821
On Wednesday, the 24th ult., by the Rev. Mr. Goforth, Mr. James E. Mahan, to Miss Margaret Whan, all of Cecil county.	02/08/1821
At Fredericktown, on Thursday evening last, Mr. Evan Hopkins, to Miss Nancy Patterson, both of that place.	02/08/1821
On Tuesday night last, after a short illness, Mr. James Black, in the 60th year of his age, for many years a respectable inhabitant of this city.	02/09/1821
At Annapolis, on Tuesday night, after a lingering illness, Thomas H. Bowie, Esq., Attorney at Law, and late Register of Chancery.	02/09/1821
Last evening, by the Rev. Dr. Roberts, Mr. Anthony Nagle, to Miss Eleanor Robinson, all of this city.	02/09/1821
Last evening, by the Rev. Mr. Hargrove, Capt. William Hubbard, to Miss Sarah Baker, all of this city.	02/09/1821
Last evening, by the Rev. E. J. Reis, Capt. James Holmes, to Miss Priscilla Lewis, both of this city.	02/09/1821
On Sunday evening, the 4th inst., by the Rev. Mr. Hood, the Rev. Dr. Samuel K. Jennings, of this city, to Mrs. Hannah Owings, of Anne Arundel county.	02/09/1821

78

Marriage and Death Notices	Date
Last evening, Capt. Wm. N. Williams, in the 51st year of his age, and for the last 22 years a respectable ship master out of this port. Few men possessed more amiable and estimable qualities than did the deceased. The tears of a bereaved family bespeak the estimation and affection in which he was held by them. Like the element upon which Capt. Williams spent most of his life, his fortune was varied – Now sailing before a fair and gentle breeze; anon, tossed by storms and countercurrents. But as the elements found him at all times skillful to manage his barque, when their sport, so he was not less prepared for the assaults of adversity. He therefore viewed death as a friend, and, like a man whose treasure is in another and a better world, he left his hold on this without a pang or a struggle.	02/10/1821
On the 22nd ult., at his late residence near Denton, in Caroline county, Henry Driver, Esq., a gentleman highly respected by those who knew him.	02/10/1821
On Thursday evening last, by the Rev. Mr. Sparks, Mr. Aquila B. Murray, to Miss Florence M. Fowler.	02/10/1821
On Tuesday, the 6th inst., by the Rev. Mr. O'Brien, Mr. Clement Butler, to Miss Isabella Street, both of Harford county.	02/10/1821
On Thursday evening last, at the residence of Dr. Street, by the Rev. Mr. Rockwell, Mr. Thomas Johnson, of Baltimore county, to Miss Martha Jarrett, of Harford county.	02/10/1821
On Saturday morning last, Mr. Jacob Foltz, in the 34th year of his age.	02/12/1821
On Tuesday morning last, by the Rev. Mr. Nevins, David P. Polk, Esq., of Washington city, to Miss Letitia Jane Stewart, of this city.	02/12/1821
On Saturday evening, by the Rev. Mr. Smith, Mr. William A. Dubernard, to Miss Mary Aime, daughter of Mr. Simon Rhodes, all of this city.	02/12/1821
On Thursday last, by the Rev. Mr. Grace, Mr. Horace Knight, to Miss Catherine Gambrill, all of Baltimore county.	02/12/1821
On Tuesday evening last, by the Rev. Mr. Limb, Capt. John Johnson, of Hancock, Md., to Miss Isabella M'Clanahan, of Franklin county, Pa.	02/12/1821
On the 12th inst., Mr. George Ludden, aged 22 years.	02/13/1821
Near Charlotte Hall, Md., at the residence of Mrs. Mary Sothoron, on the 16th January, Nell Courcey, a negro woman, aged 130. She had been	02/15/1821

Marriage and Death Notices	Date
deaf and totally blind for the last 16 years of her life, but enjoyed uninterrupted health, till a very few days before her dissolution. Also, at the residence of the late John Chapellier, Sarah, aged 105. Both these old women were born in St. Mary's county, where their births are on record, and where they are generally known.	
Near Lewis-town, in Talbot county, on the 25th ult., after a short illness, Mrs. Prudence Slaughter, consort of Mr. Wm. Slaughter, aged 36 years.	02/15/1821 02/20/1821
In Georgetown, D. C., at Linthicum's Hotel, suddenly, Mr. Benjamin Blagge, a native of Boston, and for many years past, a merchant in Baltimore and Georgetown. He has left a wife and one child to lament his death.	02/16/1821
On Tuesday evening, the 13th inst., by the Rev. John Duncan, Mr. John M'Pherson, to Miss Elizabeth M'Kennell, all of this city.	02/16/1821
At his late residence, near New Market, in Frederick county, Maryland, on the evening of the 7th inst., the Rev. John Pitts, long an itinerant minister in the Methodist Episcopal Church, leaving a widow with six children to bemoan their irreparable bereavement. This obituary notice will be read with no common concern, for the deceased was no ordinary man. His great abilities as a minister, his ardent zeal, his unaffected piety, the sweet complacency of his manner, together with his abundant and successful labours in the vineyard of his Lord, will long be remembered throughout the wide sphere of his ministerial labours, while thousands who have been edified by his preaching and his piety, will feel the fondest and most endearing recollections, awakened by the intelligence, that he no longer walks before them, to guide their steps in this vale of tears. This eminent servant of God was called to the ministry in early life, and in this arduous service he continued to devote all his powers, both of body and mind, counting not his life dear unto himself, so that he might win Christ, and promote the interests of his kingdom – until utterly broken down by incessant toil, he obtained a superannuated relation to the connexion, and settled with his family in Frederick county. His numerous friends, and particularly those who own him as their father in the gospel, will derive no small consolation, from the assurance, that during the long and unusually severe affliction, which ultimately put an end to all that was mortal in him, he found in the doctrines he had so long and so faithfully preached, all that support and comfort, which he so often declared, that they and they only were calculated to afford. From this perennial spring, the waters of divine consolation ever overflowed his soul, sweetening all his sufferings, and giving him to rejoice, with a joy which is unspeakable, and full of glory. The sacred conscience, the philosophic stoic, like the idiot, may meet	02/20/1820

Marriage and Death Notices	Date
death with indifference, with apathy, but it is the Christian's privilege, alone, to die triumphantly. Our brother's victory was complete, his triumph unexpressly glorious, made perfect through suffering, and the design of his affliction accomplished. He whose voice the winds and seas obey, rebuked the fierce destroyer, and this eminent saint fell asleep in Jesus, without a sigh or groan. He taught us how to live – and O! too high A price for knowledge – taught us how to die.	
On the 18th February, Mr. Isaac Wheeler, in the 60th year of his age, and long a respectable inhabitant of Baltimore, regretted by his friends and relations. *Requiescat in peace.*	02/20/1821
At his residence, near Lower Marlborough, Calvert county, Md., on the 13th inst., Thomas Gantt, after a short illness of four days. He has left a wife, two small children, and a numerous circle of friends and acquaintances to deplore their early loss.	02/20/1821
At Denton, Mrs. Rachel Rhodes, aged 60 years.	02/20/1821
In Talbot county, Mr. William Ozman, after a short illness.	02/20/1821
A short time since, at his residence in Prince George's county, Md., Mr. Francis Tolson, Jr., in the 34th year of his age.	02/20/1821
On Sunday evening last, by the Rev. Mr. Henshaw, Mr. William Summers, to Miss Sophia Ewington, all of this city.	02/20/1821
Early this morning, of a lingering illness, Miss Frances Emily Dance, late of the island of Jamaica.	02/21/1821
By the Rev. Dr. Glendy, on Thursday last, Mr. John M'Clestal, to Miss Elizabeth Lorman, all of this city.	02/21/1821
On the 18th inst., by the Rev. Mr. Murphy, Mr. David Middleton, of Charles county, to Miss Ann, only daughter of Benjamin Gwynn, Esq., of Prince George's County, Md.	02/21/1821
On Tuesday morning, the 20th inst., Mrs. Martha Goodding, in the 67th year of her age, after a short, but painful illness, which she bore with Christian fortitude. Having long been familiar with death, she viewed him not as the King of Terrors, but as the welcome messenger of peace. Thus have her children been bereaved of an affectionate parent, and of her acquaintances of her Christian example. "She died in Jesus, and is bless'd,	02/22/1821

Marriage and Death Notices	Date
How sweet her slumbers are, From suffering and from pain releas'd, And freed from every snare."	
At Philadelphia, on Saturday, the 17th instant, Mr. Samuel M'Kean, formerly of the firm of Barclay & M'Kean, of this city.	02/22/1821
At Cambridge, Ms. Widow Catherine Wenden, aged 94. She was the grand daughter of Gov. Saltonstall, of Connecticut, who was a descendant of Sir Richard Saltonstall, one of the emigrants from England, who settled at Boston.	02/22/1821
On the 21st inst., of a lingering pulmonary affection, Miss Mary Tunis, of this city, in the 23rd year of her age. In those trying moments, when earth is fading from the view, and a boundless eternity is opening upon the sight, she gave decisive evidence that her life had not been spent in vain. Supported by a confidence in her Redeemer, she waited with Christian patience and resignation, the arrival of the king of terrors, and breathed her last in the full hope and confidence of a blessed immortality.	02/22/1821
On Tuesday evening, by the Rev. Dr. Kurtz, Mr. William Loney, to Miss Rebecca Tryer, both of Baltimore.	02/23/1821
On the 18th inst., by the Rev. Mr. Tidings, Mr. Alexander Reaney, to Miss Eleanor Benowra, daughter of Mr. J. W. Carroll, all of this city.	02/24/1821
On Thursday evening last, by the Rev. Mr. Bartow, Capt. John Jones, to Miss Elizabeth Dashield Story, all of this city.	02/24/1821
In Washington county, Capt. John Johnson, of Hancock, Md., to Miss Isabella M'Lenahan, of Franklin county, Penn. Marmaduke W. Boyd, Esq. to Miss Susan Hogmire. Mr. John Crowell to Miss Nancy Stinemetz.	02/24/1821
On Friday morning last, Mrs. Clara Farrell, in the 67th year of her age, after a short, but painful illness, which she bore with Christian fortitude and resignation. She viewed death, not as the King of Terrors, but as the messenger of peace. She has left behind her a numerous circle of friends and relatives to mourn their irreparable loss.	02/26/1821
At his father's residence, in Queen Ann's county, on Tuesday, the 15th inst., Samuel Thomas Hopper, eldest child of Daniel C. Hopper, Esq., in the thirteenth year of his age.	02/26/1821

Marriage and Death Notices	Date
In Talbot county, Capt. Wm. Mackey.	02/26/1821
In Harford county, Mr. Jacob Hoke to Miss Eliza Spangler, of York, Pa. Mr. Oliver Gallup to Miss Pamela Ann Halloway. Mr. Stephen Boyd to Miss Eliza C. Stump. Mr. Reuben H. Davis to Miss May A. Hays. Mr. Daniel R. Waters to Miss Sarah Ruff.	02/26/1821
On Tuesday, the 6th inst., in Calvert county, Fayette Gibson, Esq., of Talbot, to Miss Mary Clagett, daughter of John Chew, Esq., of the former place.	02/26/1821
In Talbot county, Mr. James Catrup to Miss Mary Harden. Mr. Wm. Watts to Miss Catherine Saulsbury. Mr. James Dawson to Miss Nancy Kinnamont.	02/26/1821
Suddenly, yesterday morning, at Barnum's Hotel, William Bowden, Esq., of Petersburg, Virginia. Every person who had the pleasure of his acquaintance will regret his death, for he was an honest, upright man, an excellent member of society, an affectionate husband, and a tender father.	02/27/1821
On Sunday evening last, by the Rev. Mr. Bartow, Mr. Andrew T. Leaken, to Miss Hannah W. Trimble, all of this city.	02/27/1821
Departed this life, on Friday last, Mrs. Hannah Fisher, in the 52nd year of her age, after a long and distressful illness, which she bore with Christian fortitude and resignation. She has left an afflicted family, with a large circle of relations and friends, to deplore their loss. But, this loss is her infinite gain; for, having fought the good fight, having finished her course, having kept the faith, she died in the full assurance of a blissful immortality through the merits of her Redeemer.	02/28/1821
Last evening, by the Rev. Dr. Glendy, Mr. Thomas G. Peachy, to Miss Frances Andrews, daughter of the Rev. Mr. Andrews, all of this city.	02/28/1821
On the 6th ultimo, the honorable, generous, and beloved Col. Thomas Carvill, of Kent county, in the 50th year of his age. He was most beloved by those who knew him best; and his friends who surrounded him in his sick and dying hours have every reasonable hope, that his soul has winged its way to the mansions of eternal bliss. In his humane and benevolent disposition, he was equaled by few, and excelled by none, for he always fed the hungry, clothed the naked, and took the stranger in! He was a kind and affectionate husband, and a tender father. He has left an affectionate and disconsolate widow, and six dutiful children to bewail their irreparable loss. But, "Blessed are the	03/01/1821

83

Marriage and Death Notices	Date
dead that die in the Lord, for they rest from their labors. "	
Yesterday morning, in the 43rd year of his age, Mr. George Foss, Jr. His friends and acquaintances are respectfully invited to attend his funeral, from his late residence, at 3 o'clock, P. M., today.	03/02/1821
At Easton, Mrs. Catherine Tomlinson. Capt. William Mackay, in the 64th year of his age.	03/02/1821
On Thursday evening last, by the Rev. Mr. Glendy, Mr. Pearly P. B. Chamberlain, of Strafford, Vermont, to Miss Ann Read, of Baltimore.	03/02/1821
On the 22nd of February, by the Rev. Mr. Sewell, at the residence of Mr. Wm. Pryor, Eastern Shore of Md., Mr. Ebenezer Massey, to Miss Emily Ann Massey, both of Kent county, Md.	03/02/1821
On Tuesday evening last, by the Rev. Mr. Nevins, Mr. Joseph Cummins, Merchant of Mifflintown, Pa., to Miss Jane H., daughter of the late Joseph Knox, Esq., of that place.	03/02/1821
On Tuesday evening, the 20th ult., by the Rev. Mr. Austin, Dr. Edward Gill, to Miss Ellen Caroline, daughter of Hickman Johnson, Esq., of Baltimore county.	03/02/1821
At Annapolis, Mr. William Glover to Miss Mary Ann Beard. Mr. James White to Miss Eliza Sifton.	03/02/1821
On Tuesday evening last, by the Rev. Mr. Kurtz, Mr. Jacob Rupp, to Miss Elizabeth M. Richards, both of Baltimore county.	03/02/1821 03/03/1821
On Sunday last, in St. Mary's county, Md., Mr. Jason Jenkins, formerly of this city. In company with his wife and brother-in-law, he was returning from a neighbor's, where they had been on a visit, when his horse threw him with so much violence, that he survived it but a few hours.	03/03/1821
In Charles county, Md., on the 18th ult., after a short and painful illness, Mrs. E. A. Brawner, wife of Mr. Robert Brawner.	03/03/1821
By the Rev. Mr. Grice, Mr. Philip Beckley to Miss Rebecca Schoate.	03/03/1821
In Harford county, Mr. Israel Day to Miss Mary Baker. Mr. Cooper Boyd to Milcha Taylor. Mr. Nathan Lytle to Miss Sarah Wadsworth.	03/03/1821
On the evening of the 20th inst., in Georgetown, Kent county, Maryland, by the Rev. Rich. D. Hall, the Rev. Purnell Fletcher Smith, Rector of	03/03/1821

Marriage and Death Notices	Date
Shrewsbury Parish, to the amiable Miss Mary Wright Everitt, daughter of the late Benjamin Everitt, Esq., of Georgetown Cross Roads, Kent, Md.	
On Sunday morning, after a lingering illness, Mrs. Catherine Pringle, consort of Mr. Mark U. Pringle. Her friends are invited to attend her funeral, this afternoon, at 3 o'clock, from her late residence.	03/05/1821
On the 3rd inst., Mrs. Ann Markland, in the 23rd year of her age, consort of Mr. Jas. Markland, of this city.	03/05/1821
On the morning of the 27th ult., of a rapid decline, Miss Laura M. Schreiber, in the 16th year of her age.	03/05/1821
On Thursday morning, the 22nd ult., after a lingering illness of about six years, Mrs. Ann Hopper, wife of Mr. Thomas W. Hopper, of Queen Ann's county, in the 33rd year of her age.	03/05/1821
On Thursday evening, the 22nd ult., by the Rev. Joseph M'Elroy, Capt. William Savory, formerly of Baltimore, to Miss Phoebe, youngest daughter of Mr. Lawrence Mullenix, of St. Clair Township.	03/06/1821
On Sunday evening last, by the Rev. D. E. Reese, Mr. Isaiah Peters, to Miss Eliza Mills, all of this city.	03/06/1821
On the morning of the 2nd inst., Mrs. Mary P. M'Cannon, wife of James M'Cannon, in the 22nd year of her age.	03/07/1821
On Friday last, in the 82nd year of her age, Mrs. Frances Purviance, relict of the late Robert Purviance, Esq., of this city. There are duties, which, usually termed melancholy, it is not paradoxical to say, are sometimes attended with pleasure in their performance. A duty of this kind, "pleasant yet mournful to the soul," exists, when the heart of affection labors to pourtray the virtues of a beloved, lost object; and friendship, suffering her grief awhile to merge in higher considerations, holds out to the admiration and imitation of men, those who do honor human nature in *this* world, and are heirs of immortality in the *next*. It is our misfortune, indeed, to be so much the creatures of pomp and circumstances, as rarely to have our attention arrested, but by the proud career, or lowly fall, of those who act the most conspicuous parts in the drama of life. But when we reflect, that such exalted destinies are allotted to comparatively *few*; while the *mass* of mankind may look up to them with admiration, but never can expect to follow in the same bright path: and when we also reflect, there are other characters which every one may fill, generally, indeed, considered as subordinate, but in	03/08/1821

fact of the most real importance; in perfect characters of this kind, therefore, we should seek models for our own imitation. In order to find them, the shades of domestic privacy should be pierced, and the spot far excluded from the glare and sunshine of the world. We should take a sketch of those who move in "calm majesty" through the scenes of "still, retired life," which they adorn by their accomplishments and beautify by their virtues. Absolute perfect, it has been said, *is not the lot of man below*, but there are minor degrees of it, to which a few specimens of exalted humanity have sometimes aspired; and among this number, who have reached the point of attainable excellence, the lamented subject of the present obituary, is justly entitled to a distinguished rank. If we were allowed to dwell on any particular feature of her character, where all the features were beautiful, we would advert to a prominent one; and that was, the charitable disposition, with which she was super eminently endowed. She possessed not only that charity which consists of *alms giving*, and which knew no other bounds save those necessarily imposed by the range of its objects, but charity in the more exalted scriptural sense of the term; a disposition which, through a sacred regard to the feelings of others, overlooking their defects, never permitted itself to indulge, in the slightest degree, in any remark, which might convey a pang to sensibility, or cast a stigma on reputation. Born of one of the most respectable families in the north of Ireland, and educated in affluence from her situation, she was, in her youth, obliged to mingle more in the gay world, than was, perhaps, congenial to her natural disposition; but a sufficient conformity with the mandates of fashion, was never suffered to degenerate into a servile compliance; and the *accomplishments* of the *lady* were never allowed to obscure the *virtues* of the *Christian*. To some these observations may wear the appearance of extravagant panegyric, but those who were acquainted with the subject of them, must, in candor, acknowledge they were dictated by the heart of sincerity, and that the interests of truth have not been sacrificed on the altar of adulation. The closing scene of such a life, it is almost needless to add, was in perfect harmony and unison with all that preceded it. Her pilgrimage had been quite as long and chequered as that of any of the children of men; and that equanimity which had borne her up in many a trying hour, did not desert her at the final catastrophe: death had no terrors for her, the tenor of whose whole existence had been but a preparation to meet his alarms. So calm and serene was the transition of her immortal soul, from its earthly tabernacle, to its resting place in the skies, that even after all signs of life were gone, the spirit seemed still to linger about its wonted tenement, and the twilight of setting mortality, was but the harbinger of the rising of the glorious sun eternity.

Marriage and Death Notices	Date
At her residence, Prospect Hill, near Queenstown, Mrs. Mary Griffin, consort of Capt. Greenbury Griffin, in the 48th year of her age.	03/08/1821
On Tuesday evening, by the Rev. Mr. Guest, Dr. William Willis, to Mary Ann, eldest daughter of Mr. John M'Clure, all of this city.	03/08/1821
On Wednesday evening last, by the Rev. Mr. Bartow, Mr. Samuel Dennet, to Eliza Connor, all of this city.	03/09/1821
On Tuesday evening, the 6th inst., by the Rev. Bishop Kemp, Mr. William Crawford, to Miss Ann Maria Churchman, all of this city.	03/09/1821
On Wednesday evening last, by the Rev. Mr. Gibson, Mr. Robert Crawford, merchant, of Newberg, N. Y., to Miss Margaret, eldest daughter of Capt. Alexander P. Grigg, of this city.	03/09/1821
At St. Bartholomews, on the 7th of February last, Mr. John Turenne, formerly a resident of Baltimore.	03/10/1821
On Thursday evening last, by the Rev. Dr. Kurtz, Mr. H. Kehlenbeck, to Miss Maria Zode, all of this city.	03/10/1821
On Thursday evening last, by the Rev. Mr. Bartow, Mr. George W. Ellis, to Miss Sarah James, both of this city.	03/10/1821
On Thursday evening last, by the Rev. Dr. Roberts, Mr. John Law, to Miss Ann Ringgold, all of this city.	03/12/1821
In Harford county, Mr. David Atkinson to Miss Sarah Spencer. Mr. Robert Ramsay to Miss Jane Whiteford. Mr. William Kimble to Miss Jemima Stephenson. Mr. Mifflin Beaumont to Miss Mary Lake.	03/12/1821
On Saturday, 10th inst., in the 40th year of her age, Mrs. Mary Rogers, consort of Mr. Elisha Rogers, merchant, of this city leaving a disconsolate husband and seven sons to mourn her decease. In the death of this amiable woman, society has sustained a loss which her acquaintance will long deplore. She possessed a warm and generous heart, feeling a lively interest, wherever she could be useful to her fellow creatures. As she lived, she died, a Christian, in the hope that her soul would be received into immortal glory.	03/13/1821
Died, on Monday, the 12th instant, Miss Maria, daughter of Mr. Matthew W. Simmons, of this city, aged 17 years. In the premature death of this amiable young lady, surviving friends are made to feel the uncertainty of earthly joys and prospects, However excellent or much beloved, Death, with remorseless grasp, snatches	03/15/1821

Marriage and Death Notices	Date
away, with greedy preference, those whose loss is most severely felt! But it is solacing thought to her pious parents and all her friends that they are not left to "sorrow as those who have no hope." A degree of patience, that would have done honor to the most distinguished philosopher, and which was maintained without failure under an affliction protracted for many months, had given rise to hopes that her departure would be tranquil, and that her spirit would be triumphant at the closing scene. And lo! With a peaceful heart, washed in the blood of the lamb! With a mind serene and happy in God! And with her eyes fixed on the bright mansions of the blessed, she took her flight, whilst yet her tongue had scarcely ceased to proclaim, It is Heaven! It is Heaven!! Oh yes, know I know it is Heaven!!!	
On Friday, the 9th inst., after an illness of near five months, which he bore with Christian fortitude, in the 39th year of his age, Mr. Stephen P. Rose, of Baltimore county. For honesty and integrity few equaled and none surpassed him.	03/16/1821
At Riverside, near Bladensburg, Mrs. Rosalie Eugenia Calvert, wife of George Calvert, Esq., and daughter of Mr. Henry Joseph Steer, of Antwerp, in the 44th year of her age. In the death of this excellent lady, her family, her friends, and society, have sustained an irreparable loss; for, in the discharge of every social and domestic duty, she lived upright, in the fear of God, and in charity with all the world. If intrinsic benevolence, moral rectitude, and exemplary piety, could not ward off the early stroke, well may we conclude, that Heaven designs the virtuous soul for nobler purposes than the fleeting engagements of sublunary change.	03/16/1821
At Lexington, Ken., on the 16th ult., Mr. Henry Johnson, a stranger in that place, who said he was from Maryland. His friends may obtain further information of his effects, by applying to Mr. James M'Connell, innkeeper, Lexington, Ky., at whose house he died.	03/16/1821
On Tuesday evening last, by the Rev. Dr. Jennings, Mr. Daniel Powles, to Miss Julian Miller, both of this city.	03/16/1821
On the 4th inst., at his residence in Chestertown, Eastern Shore of Maryland, Bedingfield Hands, Esq., after a long period of ill health, borne with true Christian fortitude, and fully sensible of his approaching end, he meekly resigned his soul into the hands of his Creator, deeply lamented, and sincerely esteemed by all who had the pleasure of knowing him. To a most excellent heart, and an uncommon mind, he joined all the modesty inseparable from the genuine worth and high literary acquirements. And, if unimpeached integrity; sincere piety;	03/17/1821

Marriage and Death Notices	Date
gentleness of manners; and a character of many virtues, without *one* vice to dim their lustre – can claim the regret of the virtuous and the wise, in him were all united.	
On Thursday evening last, by the Rev. Dr. Jennings, Mr. Robert Robinson, Merchant, to Miss Jane G. Smith, all of this city.	03/17/1821
On Monday evening last, by the Rev. Mr. Waugh, Capt. James Withington, to Miss Margaret M. Morrow, all of this city.	03/17/1821
On Thursday evening last, by the Rev. Dr. Roberts, Mr. Henry Smith, to Miss Sarah Hutchins, all of this city.	03/20/1821
Yesterday morning, in the 38th year of his age, Mr. Robert A. Welch, leaving a mother and numerous other relatives to lament his loss.	03/21/1821
At St. Jago de Cuba, on the 17th ult., Mr. Joseph Boddily, aged 20 years. Mr. B. was a native of Newburyport, Mass., but of late a resident of Baltimore.	03/21/1821
At Fredericktown, Mr. Charles Lewis, of Loudon county, Va., to Miss Ann M. Hoffman, daughter of John Hoffman, Esq., of Frederick county.	03/21/1821
In this city, on the 19th of this month, Patrick Henry Emmerson, Esq., of Calvert county, only son of the Hon. Peter Emmerson, Esq., after a wasting illness of many months, aged 21.	03/21/1821
On Tuesday evening, by the Rev. Mr. Toy, Mr. George C. Addison, to Miss Susanna Harvey, both of this city.	03/22/1821
Suddenly, at Philadelphia, on Sunday afternoon, the 18th instant, in the 67th year of his age, Mr. John Dover, one of the few surviving officers of our Revolutionary war.	03/22/1821
At Easton, Mrs. Mary Goldsborough, widow of Dr. Howes Goldsborough, of Cambridge.	03/23/1821
At Charleston, S. C., after a protracted illness, Robert Wilson, M. D., in the 51st year of his age.	03/23/1821
On the 20th inst., Patrick Henry Emmerson, of this city, son of the Hon. Peter Emmerson, Senator of Maryland, in the 21st year of his age. That fell destroyer of our unhappy race, the consumption, thus early seized its victim, and has deprived the father of the fond hope of his declining years, and rendered the partner of his bosom, inconsolable for his loss. Although thus bright with the beams of early youth, the features of his	03/23/1821

Marriage and Death Notices	Date
character were distinct, defined, and luminous. A strong and vigorous native genius, was improved and fostered by culture, and softened by all the sensibilities of the heart – while the lamp of life was quivering in the socket, he was solaced by Christian hope, and the world that was gradually stealing from his vision, seemed but a preparatory process for the enjoyment of glories more enduring. If we are asked, whence this dying youth derived this consolation, let us answer in the works of his favorite bard, an extract of which was found deposited in the volume, in the hand writing of the deceased: "Believe and shew the reason of a man, Believe and taste the pleasures of a God Believe and look the triumph on the tomb." Young men, the deceased addresses you; he speaks, the grave is not my prison house; it is not even the abode of my rest. I have believed and "now my immortal spirit looks indeed with triumph on the tomb."	
Departed this transitory life, on Monday, 19th inst., Mrs. Rose Jandine, in the 98th year of her age. She was respected by all who knew her, she possessed a benevolent heart, and was eminently blessed with that Christian Charity which vaunteth not itself – resentment had no seat in her bosom; but whoever inflicted an injury on her, was forgiven – her heart was ever open to sympathise with the widow, and her fostering hand was on all occasions extended to the Orphan. She was born of one of the most respectable families of Canada, and was a member of the Holy Catholic and Apostolic Church. She expired without a groan, being consoled with the cheery promise of her Savior, "Blessed are the merciful, for they shall obtain mercy; blessed are the clean of heart, for they shall see God." *Matthew, chap. 5, 7 and 8 verse.*	03/24/1821
On Friday, the 16th inst., at his residence in Baltimore county, Mr. Thomas Worthington, aged 82 years, justly esteemed for his virtue and piety.	03/24/1821
On Tuesday evening last, by the Rev. Mr. Fectig, Mr. George Price, of Washington county, to Miss Elizabeth Zimmerman, of this city.	03/24/1821
At Frankham, Charles county, Md., Mr. John R. Evans, to Miss Catherine Brawner.	03/24/1821
On Thursday evening, by the Rev. Mr. Duncan, Mr. Robert Campbell, to Miss Eliza Ann Moore, both of this city.	03/26/1821
By the Rev. Dr. Glendy, on the 4th inst., Mr. Owen Elder, to Miss Juliet Ann Jones, both of Anne Arundel county.	03/26/1821

Marriage and Death Notices	Date
By the Rev. Dr. Glendy, on Thursday evening last, Mr. Archibald Campbell, to Miss Eliza Ann Moore, both of this city.	03/27/1821
By the Rev. Dr. Glendy, on Tuesday evening last, Mr. William Litchfield Hammond, merchant, to Miss Maria, third daughter of the late Dr. Andrew Aitkin, all of this city.	03/29/1821
On Sunday evening last, by the Rev. Mr. Healey, Mr. Hugh Roberts, to Miss Caroline Halfpenny, all of this city.	03/30/1821
By the Rev. Mr. Healey, last evening, Mr. Robert Walker, to Miss Mary Stevenson, all of this city.	03/30/1821
On Thursday evening last, by the Rev. Dr. Roberts, Mr. David G. Davenport, to Miss Susan Green, all of this city.	03/30/1821
At Philadelphia, Mr. William Stuckert, to Miss Amelia C., daughter of Mr. John Martiacq, of Baltimore.	03/30/1821
Yesterday morning, of a lingering complaint, Mr. Alexander Irvine, in the 70th year of his age – he was for many years a respectable merchant of this city. His friends and acquaintances are respectfully invited to attend his funeral, from his late residence, corner of Howard and Fayette sts., at ten o'clock, tomorrow morning, the 4th instant.	04/03/1821
On Tuesday, 15th March last, at the residence of Col. John Fitzhugh, in the 26th year of his age, Capt. Alexander M'Kim Andrew, formerly of the United States' Navy. Every attention which friendship and humanity could dictate, was paid by Col. Fitzhugh & gentlemen in the neighborhood, particularly Capt. John Chew, at whose house Capt. Andrew resided the greater part of the winter, to Capt. Andrew during his illness, & it will be consolatory to his friends and relatives to learn that Capt. Andrew died quite composed and resigned, without a struggle – that his dear departed spirit may have taken its flight to join those of his sainted parents in eternal bliss is the ardent prayer and fervent wish of one who loved him most affectionately.	04/03/1821
In Talbot county, Md., Mrs. Rebecca Harris, in the 28th year of her age, consort of Mr. Jno. Harris. Also, Mrs. Mary Catrup, consort of Mr. James C.	04/03/1821
On Sunday last, at Sandy Mount, by the Rev. Mr. Garretson, Mr. John Stocksdale, of Baltimore county, to Miss Sarah A. Kurtz, of this city.	04/03/1821
On the morning of the 19th ult., after a lingering illness, Mrs. Elizabeth	04/04/1821

Marriage and Death Notices	Date
Dagen, wife of Mr. John Dagen, merchant, of New Windsor, Md.	
On Monday last, Mr. Luke Work, of this city, in the 21st year of his age.	04/05/1821
On the 30th of last month, after a few days illness, in the bloom of life, Mrs. Ann Louisa Edmonson, consort of Mr. Thomas A. Edmonson, of this city. She left one child 17 months old, and her husband, and relations, and numerous friends, to lament their loss.	04/06/1821
In this city, on Tuesday morning, 3rd inst., by the Rev. Mr. Samuel Davis, Dr. William Hammond, to Miss Rachel Warfield, both of Anne Arundel county.	04/06/1821
Last evening, by the Rev. Dr. Glendy, Mr. John H. Bell, to Miss Catherine Kirk, all of this city.	04/07/1821
On Friday, the 6th inst., after a tedious and painful illness, Mrs. Ann Gray, in the 71st year of her age.	04/09/1821
By the Rev. Dr. Glendy, on the evening of Thursday last, Mr. John C. Clarke, merchant in this city, to Miss Frances M., second daughter of the late Samuel Patterson Wallace, Esq., of Cecil county.	04/09/1821
On Thursday evening last, by Bishop Kemp, Mr. Alfred V. Clagett, to Miss Fanny Caroline, daughter of Hezekiah Clagett, Esq.	04/09/1821
5th inst., at the U. S. Naval Hospital, at Gosport, Midshipman James L. Nowland, of the U. S. ship John Adams – aged 17 years. Mr. Nowland was a native of Baltimore, and justly admired and esteemed by his brother officers, and all who had the pleasure of his acquaintance.	04/10/1821
On the 23rd ult., Samuel Thomas, Esq., at his residence, in Queen Ann's County, Md., in the 79th year of his age.	04/10/1821
In Talbot county, Mrs. Rebecca Perry, relict of the late Tristram Perry.	04/10/1821
William Thomas, Esq., of Easton.	04/10/1821
In Caroline county, Mr. Greenbury Toole, in the 31st year of his age.	04/10/1821
On the 20th ult., by the Rev. Mr. Poteet, Mr. Edward Parish, to Miss Clemmency Hughes, both of this city.	04/10/1821
On Saturday last, by the Rev. Mr. Bartow, Capt. Christopher Prestwick, to Miss Mary Alexander, all of Millar's Island, Baltimore county.	04/10/1821

Marriage and Death Notices	Date
On Thursday evening last, by the Rev. Dr. Wyatt, John S. Gittings, Esq., to Ellina, daughter of Wm. R. Smith, Esq., all of this city.	04/11/1821
On Tuesday evening last, by the Rev. E. J. Reis, Mr. Warren Carter, of Virginia, to Miss Maria Margaret, eldest daughter of James Carnighan, Esq., of this city.	04/12/1821
On Tuesday evening last, by the Rev. Dr. Jennings, Mr. Jacob Rogers, to Miss Belinda Johns, both of this city.	04/12/1821
By the Rev. Mr. Gist, on the evening of Tuesday last, Mr. Louis Shipley, to Miss Elizabeth, daughter of the late John Mackelfresh, Esq., of Reisterstown.	04/12/1821
On Thursday evening, 12th inst., by the Rev. Mr. Samuel Davis, Dr. Robert C. Shelmerdine, to Miss Eliza Quail, all of this city.	04/13/1821
Last evening, by the Rev. Dr. Roberts, Mr. George Adreon, of this city, to Miss Phebe P. Pearson, of Harford county.	04/13/1821
On Thursday evening last, by the Rev. Mr. Tidings, Mr. Henry B. M'Coy, to Miss Ann Maria Shipley.	04/13/1821
Yesterday, at Friends Meeting House, O. T., Thomas J. Hull to Harriet Ford, both of this city.	04/13/1821
On Wednesday evening last, by the Rev. Mr. Bartow, Mr. Thomas Brook, to Miss Hannah Lee, all of this city.	04/13/1821
At New York, on Tuesday morning last, by the Rev. Dr. Romeyn, Mr. Charles G. Robb, of Baltimore, to Miss Sarah E. S. M'Clenachen, of the former city.	04/13/1821
Yesterday, at nine o'clock, A. M., Mr. Jesse Morgan, Jr., in the 39th year of his age. Friends and acquaintance are respectfully invited to attend his funeral, this evening, at 4 o'clock, from his late residence, George street, Old Town.	04/14/1821
Departed this life, on the 13th inst., in the 52nd year of his age, Mr. Jacob Mainster, long a respectable inhabitant of this city.	04/14/1821
On the 5th instant, by the Rev. Mr. Guest, Mr. Lewis Demoiny, to Miss Mary Jane Gosse, all of this city.	04/14/1821
In Anne Arundel county, on Thursday evening last, by the Rev. Mr. Welsh, Mr. Elias Brewer, of Baltimore, to Miss Ann, second daughter	04/14/1821

Marriage and Death Notices	Date
of Edward Pumphrey, Esq., of the former place.	
Near Denton, Caroline county, Mr. Christopher Pratt, in the 60th year of his age.	04/16/1821
On the 15th inst., by the Rev. Mr. Helfenstein, Mr. Frederick Eree, to Miss Sarah Smith, both of this city.	04/17/1821
By the Rev. Mr. Helfenstein, on the 12th inst., Mr. John P. W. Amelung, to Miss Ann Snyder, all of this city.	04/17/1821
On the morning of the 10th ult., after a lingering illness, Mrs. Charlotte Spencer, in the 31st year of her age, consort of Mr. Abel Spencer, Jr.	04/18/1821
Last evening, by the Rev. Dr. Roberts, Capt. Joseph Hook, of this city, to Miss Ann Channells, of Baltimore county.	04/18/1821
It is with no ordinary regret that we consign to obituary notice, the name of Dr. James Orrick, who departed from this, we hope and believe, for a better world, on the 13th inst., in the 32nd year of his age, after a painful and lingering pulmonary complaint. Few are descended to the grave more beloved and respected – few have been more esteemed and successful in the profession, of which he was a member. He had a very extensive practice, and was always ready to relieve the distresses of others. No appeal was ever made to his sympathy in vain. A disconsolate widow and four helpless children, by this melancholy dispensation of Providence, are left to mourn the irreparable loss they have sustained. Convinced from the slow, but obstinate progress of his disease, that medical skill could only administer palliative remedies, and that his malady must finally terminate in dissolution, he reposed all his hopes in the mediation of his Savior, and left this world of sorrow, in the triumphant hope of a glorious immortality. *Baltimore county, April 4th, 1821.*	04/19/1821
On Tuesday evening last, by the Rev. Mr. Bartow, Mr. Joseph Stewart, to Miss Ann Shapey, all of this city.	04/19/1821
On Saturday evening last, by the Rev. Mr. Healey, Mr. George Grimsditch, to Miss Hannah Goodwin, both of this city.	04/19/1821
On Tuesday evening last, by the Rev. Dr. Kurtz, Mr. Sebastian Konig, to Miss Catherine Utt, both of this city.	04/19/1821
On the 29th March, Henry Koontz, aged 94 years. This venerable German came to Frederick county, Md., at 22 years of age. By trade a	04/20/1821

Marriage and Death Notices	Date
blacksmith; by his industry and frugality, he was soon enabled to purchase a small farm, on Pipe Creek, where he has resided fifty seven years, has raised ten children, most of whom he lived to see respectably established, with the families, in his own neighborhood, on farms he provided for them. Temperate in his habits, cheerful and amiable in his disposition, his health was good almost without interruption, until within weeks of his death; his mind and memory sound and clear to the last. His large German Bible, his friend and guide through life, was his comfort in death. He lived in all good conscience, and so peaceably with all men, that he could assert he never had a quarrel or dispute with any man, never sued or was sued by any man. His neighbors all testify to his good report, and venerate his memory. Mr. Koontz has left with his six surviving children, 110 grand children, and more than 135 great grand children, all respectable inhabitants of Frederick county.	
On Tuesday evening, by the Rev. Mr. Henshaw, Mr. W. M'Neir, of Annapolis, to Miss Mary Maccubbin, of this city.	04/20/1821
Last evening, by the Rev. Mr. Shane, Mr. George Painter, to Miss Elizabeth Leggitt, both of this city.	04/21/1821
On Thursday evening last, by the Rev. Abner Neal, Mr. Luther Davis, to Mary Ann, daughter of John T. Keppler, Esq., all of this city.	04/21/1821
In Charleston, S. C., on Thursday, the 12th inst., by the Rev. Frederick Dalcho, James Creighton, Esq., of Baltimore, Md., to Ann, daughter of the late Gen. John M'Pherson, of that city.	04/21/1821
On the 19th inst., Mrs. Elizabeth Johns, in the 73rd year of her age.	04/23/1821
On Thursday, 12th inst., Mrs. Deliah Chenoweth, in the 79th year of her age. The deceased was for many years a worthy member of the Baptist Church in this city. Her affliction was long and tedious, but possessing a tranquil mind, she was enabled to rejoice *"with those that do rejoice."* Her piety was tested by an upright walk and Godly conversation. It pleased her Maker to touch her with the hand of affliction. But her happy spirit was wafted from the shores of time to eternity by that same being, who has prepared a place for those that *"love him and keep his commandments."* She has left behind her, numerous friends and relations to deplore the loss of a valuable and worthy friend – but it may be said, that their loss was her eternal gain.	04/23/1821
In the midst of Life, we are in Death. Of which the following is a melancholy demonstration. Mr. Samuel King, a highly respected resident of Elk Ridge, left his home on Monday last in good health, on a	04/23/1821

95

Marriage and Death Notices	Date
journey to the Potomac, for the purpose of getting fish, as is usual for farmers at this season, whilst the boatmen were in the act of delivering him the fish, his horses took fright and attempted to runaway. Mr. King, in attempting to stop them, was thrown against a pole, or oar, that perforated his bowels, which terminated his life, after suffering extreme pain in about twenty-four hours. He has left a numerous family, as well as a large circle of friends and acquaintances, to whom he was much beloved, to deplore his loss.	
On Sunday evening last, by the Rev. John Healey, Mr. James Richardson, to Miss Charlotte Talbott, both of Baltimore county.	04/24/1821
By the Rev. Mr. Valiant, Mr. Benjamin Knight to Miss Margaret Stone, of Baltimore county.	04/25/1821
On Sunday evening last, by the Rev. Mr. Moranville, Mr. John Alexander, to Miss Mary Ann Williamson, all of this city.	04/25/1821
In Fredericktown, of a pulmonary complaint, Mr. Jonathan W. Dustin, in the 28th year of his age. The deceased was a native of New Hampshire, but for the last six years had been a resident of that county.	04/26/1821
On the 9th inst., Mrs. Ann Stone, aged 32 years, wife of the Rev. William M. Stone, Rector of Stepney Parish, Somerset county, Maryland.	04/26/1821
In Frederick county, Md., Mr. Jonathan Getzendanner, to Miss Elizabeth Deer. Mr. Enos Hedge to Miss Catherine Scholl.	04/26/1821
On Tuesday, 17th inst., Mr. John Price, Jr., Queen Ann's county, to the amiable Miss Ann Maria, eldest daughter of Mrs. Martha Wilson, of Talbot county.	04/26/1821
On Monday evening, by the Rev. Mr. Wyatt, Mr. James Thomas, to Miss Isabella Dean, all of this city.	04/27/1821
On Tuesday night last, 24th inst., after a long and painful illness, which he bore with great fortitude, Mr. Louis Francis Leloup, aged 46 and 23 days. Mr. Leloup was a native of Paris and for many years filled the office of Consul of France in several of the sea port towns in the U. States, and particularly in this city, which he at last chose as the place of his permanent residence. He had the misfortune of losing his eye sight some years ago, which obliged him to resign his public office. It falls perhaps to the lot of few men to have a larger number of friends than Mr. Leloup possessed, and the number of persons who attended his	04/28/1821

Marriage and Death Notices	Date
remains to the grave, proved how much he was esteemed. He has left a family and many relations to mourn their irreparable loss.	
On Tuesday morning, 24th inst., Mrs. Sarah Carnan, wife of Mr. Robert North Carnan, of Baltimore county.	04/28/1821
On Saturday, 28th April, of but a few hours illness, from the bursting of a blood vessel in the stomach, Mr. John W. Beall. At his usual hour, he was up and about, at 5 in the evening, the subject of the tomb – he has left a wife and five small children, with a numerous circle of relations and friends to deplore his premature loss. What a lesson to mortals! How short the passage from life and health to the grave. His friends and acquaintance are invited to attend his funeral, at 4 o'clock this afternoon, from his late dwelling, Coffee House Hotel, South street.	04/30/1821
In Harford county, Mrs. Margaret Shultz, relict of the late Mr. John Shultz.	04/30/1821
At his father's, near Belle-Air, Mr. Daniel Scott, aged about 23.	04/30/1821
In Centreville, Mrs. Harriet Ridgaway, consort of the Rev. James Ridgaway, in the 31st year of her age.	04/30/1821
In Talbot county, Margaret Stuart, consort of Mr. A. Stuart.	04/30/1821
On Sunday evening last, by the Rev. Dr. Roberts, Mr. Jacob Fox, to Miss Eliza Harper, all of this city.	04/30/1821
On Thursday evening last, by the Rev. Mr. Moranville, Mr. Thomas Peters to Miss Agnes Peduzi.	04/30/1821
On the 26th April inst., Mr. Notley L. Adams to Miss Eliza A. H. Davidson, both of Upper Marlboro, Prince George's county.	04/30/1821
In Hartford county, Mr. Edward G. Mitchell to Miss Margaret Williams, of Cecil. Mr. Amos Anderson to Miss Ann Gilbert. Mr. Abraham Amos to Miss Elizabeth Rigdon.	04/30/1821
By the Rev. Mr. Luckey, Mr. Saml. Hughes to Miss Elizabeth Wadsworth, both of Baltimore county.	04/30/1821
At Philadelphia, on Thursday evening, by the Rt. Rev. Bishop White, Mr. Daniel B. Bicknell, merchant, of Baltimore, to Miss Ellen, daughter of Anthony Chardron, Esq., of that city.	04/30/1821

Marriage and Death Notices	Date
In Salisbury, E. S. Maryland, by the Rev. Wm. Stone, on Wednesday evening, the 18th April, Cathell Humphreys, M. D., to Miss Leah Walker, all of that place.	05/01/1821
At sea, Mr. Thomas Brazier, aged 25, formerly of Boston.	05/02/1821
By the Rev. Dr. Glendy, on the evening of yesterday, Capt. Thomas Coward, Jr., to Miss Margaret, fourth daughter of Hamilton Graham, Esq., all of this city.	05/02/1821
Last evening, by the Rev. Mr. Gibson, Mr. Samuel Lyon, to Miss Margaret Kirkland, all of this city.	05/02/1821
On Tuesday evening last, by the Rev. Mr. Tidings, Mr. Samuel Mather, to Miss Ann Cooper, both of this city.	05/02/1821
Last evening, by the Rev. Dr. Roberts, Mr. Edward D. Burke, to Miss Mary C. Gilmore.	05/02/1821
Last evening, by the Rev. S. G. Roszel, Dr. Samuel K. Jennings, Jr., to Miss Elizabeth H. Owings, both of this city.	05/02/1821
At Easton, Md., Mr. William M. Wainer, to Miss Susan Webb, both of that town.	05/02/1821
On Tuesday evening, 22nd, by the Rev. Mr. Walker, Mr. P. H. Feddiman, to Miss Elizabeth Ann, eldest daughter of Judge Earle, all of Queen Ann's county, Maryland.	05/02/1821
On Tuesday last, by the Rev. Mr. Jackson, Thomas Blandy, Esq., Merchant, of Madeira, to Miss Frances P. S., daughter of the late Joseph Dallam, of Harford county.	05/02/1821
On Tuesday evening, by the Rev. Dr. Kurtz, Mr. John Smith, to Miss Margaret Cutcher, both of this city.	05/03/1821
At Mr. Jacob Moots, near Hagerstown, Md., Mr. John King, of New Brunswick, N. J., a pedlar of Essences.	05/04/1821
On Tuesday evening last, by the Rev. Mr. Whitfield, Mr. Charles M'Manus, to Miss Elizabeth Buchanan, both of this city.	05/04/1821
On Thursday evening last, by the Rev. Mr. Valiant, Mr. William Benett, to Miss Ann Robinson, both of this place.	05/04/1821

Marriage and Death Notices	Date
By the Rev. Dr. Glendy, on the evening of yesterday, Mt. Thomas Osburne, to Miss Martha L. Munn, both of Baltimore county.	05/04/1821
On the 1st inst., Mr. William Harvey, of Prince George's county, to Miss Elizabeth, daughter of Lancroft Wilson, Esq., of the District of Columbia.	05/04/1821
On Sunday evening last, by the Rev. Dr. Roberts, Mr. Charles Rhinchart, to Miss Sarah Ann Curry, all of this city.	05/05/1821
On Thursday evening last, by the Rev. Mr. Bartow, Mr. Charles Argust, to Miss Helena Hance, all of this city.	05/05/1821
At Greenfield, his residence, near this city, on the 3rd inst., Thomas Worthington, Esq., aged 82 years.	05/07/1821
In St. Mary's county, Maryland, Mrs. Sarah S. Hebb, consort of James Hebb, Esq., after a lingering illness.	05/07/1821
In Talbot county, Mr. Perry Ward Steuart, aged 54 years.	05/07/1821
On Thursday evening, by the Rev. Dr. Roberts, Mr. William Brown, to Miss Mary Camper, both of Baltimore county.	05/07/1821
At Easton, Md., Mr. William M. Warner to Miss Susan Webb. Mr. John Jump to Miss Elizabeth Martindale.	05/07/1821
In Kent county, on the 26th ult., Dr. Henry Page, in the fiftieth year of his age. The subject of this obituary evinced at a very early period of his life, a srong propensity for the medical profession, and after having obtained a degree from Washington College, a school of great repute at that time, was permitted by an indulgent father to commence the sudy of the healing art. Formed by nature for intense application, glowing with a holy ambition for acquirement of knowledge, gifted with a memory peculiarly retentive, and endowed with a clear and penetrating judgement – he established at an early stage of his medical career a reputation among the inhabitants of Kent seldom equaled and never surpassed. His mild, amiable, and dignified deportment, his easiness of access – his love of honor, justice, charity, and religion, commanded the respect and acquired the esteem of all classes of his fellow-men. His extraordinary success in the healing art, but was the well-earned harvest of minute and continual observation, profound reflection, and great personal and mental labor. But in his ardent devotion to the medical profession, he was not insensible to paramount obligations – he was tremblingly alive to the calls of religion, and obeyed her sacred	05/09/1821

Marriage and Death Notices	Date
mandates with cheerfulness and humility. Whenever disease appeared in so stuborn a shape as to defy his every effort and baffle all his skill, he could calm the spirit of his expiring patient t the comforts of our holy religion. "At his controul, "Despair and anguish fled the struggled soul, "Comfort came down the trembling wretch to raise, "And his last faultering accents whispered praise." If at the commencement, or during the progress of the fatal disease, which terminated his earthly career, he expressed a wish to sojourn a little longer in this "veil of tears," that wish originated in the fullness of his benevolent heart. As a philanthropist, he felt that if restored to health he would continue to dispense comforts and blessings to the needy and afflicted; and as a father and husband, he knew that his services and example were of infinite importance to his family; but when the fatal summons, which called him from this earth arrived; he resigned his soul in the hands of his God without a pang, and gave to those, who were assembled around his death bed, a bright example of the benign influence of religion in the moments of dissolution. His death was a consoling evidence of a well spent life. In this melancholy dispensation, his family has been deprived of a tender husband and an indulgent and affectionate father – his friends of a virtuous and able counsellor – the medical profession has been deprived of one of its brightest ornaments, and the poor of a generous benefactor. The tears and unaffected sorrow of a large concourse of people who followed him to the *"narrow house,"* which contains his *"tabernacle of clay,"* speak his best, his proudest eulogy. The writer of this feeble tribute of respect to the memory of the deceased, can never cease to mourn the irreparable loss of his earliest friend and kindest benefactor. "He taught us how to live, and ah! too high, "A price for learning, taught us how to die."	
On Monday evening last, by the Rev. Mr. Bartow, Mr. William Davis to Mrs. Rebecca Neril, all of this city.	05/09/1821
At Richmond, Vir., suddenly, Mr. Samuel Payne, aged 63 years. Soon after the close of the Revolution – in which he took an active share in the ranks of his countrymen, was with Pulaski at Savannah; and at the capture of Charleston was severely wounded in its defense, a volunteer in the army – Mr. Payne fixed his abode in Richmond, and has ever since remained a worthy member among us.	05/09/1821
In Orange county, North Carolina, on the 11th ultimo, Daniel May, in the 99th year of his age. He has had 16 children, 187 grand children, and	05/19/1821

Marriage and Death Notices	Date
84 great grandchildren, making the total number of his descendants 287.	
At Cambridge, Md., Master Thomas Muse, the eldest son of Dr. Joseph E. Muse, of that town, in the thirteenth year of his age.	05/10/1821
At the residence of her great grand son, Mr. Evan Webb, on Little Pipe Creek, Mrs. Mary Meredith, aged 100 years, 11 months, and 26 days; the whole of her descendants are upwards of 300.	05/10/1821
In Fredericktown, Mr. Frederick Marckey to Miss Elizabeth Gill. Mr. Lewis Remsberg to Miss Charlotte Steiner.	05/10/1821
At Annapolis, on Saturday night last, after a lingering illness, Mrs. Mary Hurst, consort of Mr. Bennett Hurst, of that city.	05/11/1821
Of a pulmonary complaint, on the 30th of March last, on board the brig Gen. Jackson, on the passage from Savannah to St. Thomas, Mr. Malcom McEwen Wetmore, aged 24, son of the late Prosper Wetmore, formerly of New York.	05/12/1821
On Tuesday evening, 10th inst., by the Rev. Dr. Jennings, Mr. Samuel B. Fowler, to Miss Louisa Ann Hardester, all of this city.	05/12/1821
On Tuesday evening, 10th inst., by the Rev. Mr. Tidings, Mr. George Dowdle, of York, Penn., to Miss Nancy, second daughter of Mr. Jacob Wall, of this city.	05/12/1821
On Sunday evening last, by the Rev. Mr. Prester, Mr. George Streibell, to Miss Mary Fillinger, all of this city.	05/16/1821
By the Rev. Dr. Glendy, on the evening of yesterday, Mr. Robert Pocock, to Miss Jane Johnson, both of Baltimore county.	05/16/1821
At Oak Grove, on Tuesday evening, the 8th inst., by the Rev. Francis Neale, Dr. George W. Jameson, to Miss Henrietta, daughter of the late George H. Spalding, Esq., all of Charles county, Md.	05/16/1821
On Wednesday night last, of an affection of the liver and lungs, Mr. Wm. Nevitt Bailey, aged 22 years, son of Thos. Bailey, Esq.	05/18/1821
On Sunday morning last, Mr. John Hobby, aged 31 years. The deceased was a native of Massachusetts, and for the last six years, a resident of this city. His disease, which was pulmonary, and confined him to his house for several months, he sustained with great patience and fortitude, and awaited the approach of death with the resignation and hope of a	05/18/1821

Marriage and Death Notices	Date
Christian.	
Last evening, by the Rev. Mr. Bartow, Mr. Enoch Cook, of Baltimore, to Miss Jane Catherine Ryan, of Cork, Ireland.	05/18/1821
At Friends Meeting House, Lombard street, on the 16th inst., Israel Price, Merchant, of this city, to Jane, only daughter of Isaac Trimble, of Baltimore county.	05/19/1821
On Tuesday evening, the 15th inst., by the Rev. Mr. Nevins, Henry Carroll, Esq. to Miss Mary B. Sterrett, daughter of Samuel Sterrett, Esq.	05/19/1821
At New Orleans, on Wednesday, the 18th April, Mr. Thomas Jefferson Burke, belonging to the ship Armata, of this port.	05/21/1821
On Thursday evening last, by the Rev. Dr. Jennings, Mr. John Lawrence, to Miss Rebecca Randall, all of this city.	05/21/1821
At St. Jago de Cuba, on the 29th of March, 1821, Capt. Nathaniel Tileston, of Boston, to the amiable Miss Adeline Duplante, of Baltimore.	05/21/1821 05/28/1821
Suddenly, on Saturday evening last, in the 57th year of his age, Mr. James M'Culley, a native of Ireland, but for a long time past a respectable inhabitant of this city.	05/22/1821
Yesterday morning, Mary Waterhouse, in the 16th year of her age. Like that flower which is destroyed by the untimely frost, she was cut off ere nature had fairly reached maturity, by a rapid consumption. She was young, blooming, and gay; but her youth and gaiety were dedicated to innocence and virtue. She had judiciously formed a small circle of acquaintance, consequently her attachments to the fleeting pleasures of this life were few; and those few she resigned with Christian fortitude, before she was summoned to the grave.	05/23/1821
At Fredericktown, after a lingering and distressing illness, Mrs. Elizabeth Elliott, wife of the Rev. Mr. Elliott, of that place.	05/23/1821
On Saturday last, by the Rev. Mr. Henshaw, Maj. George Keyser, to Miss Henriann F. Walter, all of this city.	05/23/1821
On Thursday evening last, by the Rev. Bishop Kemp, Mr. Francis Cressott, to Mrs. Louisa Braderhous, all of this city.	05/23/1821
At Fredericktown, on Thursday evening last, Col. Stephen Steiner, to	05/23/1821

Marriage and Death Notices	Date
Mrs. Elizabeth Bausman, both of that town.	
At Belvidere, on Tuesday afternoon, Juliana Elizabeth, wife of John M'Henry, Esq., and eldest daughter of Col. John E. Howard. Her eulogy is written in the hearts of all who knew her.	05/24/1821
At Washington City, of a pulmonary affection, Mr. John Boyce, aged about twenty-four years.	05/25/1821
At Hagerstown, after a lingering pulmonary illness, in the 27th year of his age, Mr. John W. Miller, merchant.	05/25/1821
Mr. Robert Kursey, of Prince George's co., to Miss Catherine McKenney, only daughter of the late James McKenney, of Washington.	05/25/1821
At Hagerstown, Mr. Samuel Nennemacher, to Miss Elizabeth Bragonier. Mr. Jacob A. Brewer to Miss Harriet Welsh.	05/25/1821
On Thursday evening last, by the Rev. Asa Shin, Mr. Jesse Lee to Miss Eliza, second daughter of George Millemon, Esq., all of this city.	05/26/1821
On Thursday evening last, by the Rev. Asa Shin, Mr. Jesse Lee Hiss, to Miss Eliza, second daughter of George Millemoo, Esq., all of this city.	05/28/1821
On Thursday evening last, by the Rev. Mr. Kurtz, Mr. James W. Smithers, of Virginia, to Miss Beulah, only daughter of Jesse Brown, Esq., of this city.	05/28/1821
On Friday, the 25th inst., in the 47th year of his age, Mr. Samuel Burns, for many years a respectable inhabitant of this city. The deceased has left a widow and four children, together with a number of relations and acquaintances, to lament their irreparable loss and has left them a full and sufficient testimony on an everlasting inheritance of a better world.	05/28/1821 05/29/1821
On Tuesday evening last, Thomas G. Armstrong, aged 37 years, of that disease "Consumption," which hurries so many in the bloom of youth and manhood, to an untimely grave. He had the happy art, which few indeed possess, of retaining to the last the various friendships he had formed through life; he had that also about him, which made his company always agreeable and desirable. But the best of all was that, although his affliction was of the most distressing kind, he realized that, which *even* makes a *death bed* comfortable. That "death is not the worst of evils" that when there is a blooming prospect of immortality, and eternal life, men may even look with *triumph* on the tomb.	05/28/1821 05/29/1821

Marriage and Death Notices	Date
On the 22nd inst., Rebecca B. Butler, in the full enjoyment of the comforts of the Gospel.	05/30/1821
On Tuesday, 22nd inst., Mary, widow of Dickinson Gorsuch, after a painful and lingering complaint, in the 54th year of her age. Her eulogy is printed in the hearts of all by whom she was known.	05/30/1821
On Tuesday evening last, by the Rev. Dr. Roberts, Mr. Garner Betterton to Miss Rachel M. Kinsey.	05/31/1821
In the *Isle of Bourbon*, the Rev. John Pasquiet, formerly President of St. Mary's College, of Baltimore.	06/01/1821
By the Rev. Dr. Glendy, on the evening of Thursday last, Mr. William M'Kee, merchant, to Miss Ann, third daughter of Harmanus Alricks, Esq., all of this city.	06/01/1821
On the 17th inst., by the Rev. Mr. Magraw, Samuel Nesbitt, Jr., Esq., Merchant, of Port Deposit, to Miss Hariott Lyons, of Harford county.	06/01/1821
On the 3rd of May, at Eddyville, Ken., of the scalds he received on board the steam boat Gen. Robertson, as heretofore noticed, Mr. Henry Bailey, of this city, aged 28 years. The deceased was an amiable man, much esteemed by the acquaintance he had made during his short residence among us.	06/02/1821
On the 9th of July, 1820, on the Arkansas river, Jacob H. Gatch, a young man employed as a boatman of the Mission Family, destined to Union among the Osages. Superintendents of the Mission in their journal observe – "He was a youth, amiable and faithful, and not entirely destitute of thoughtfulness. His fever, in its progress, assumed much of the typhus character. He was closely attended by our physician, but his disease proved unyielding. He shipped at Pittsburgh, but he had come from some place near Baltimore, where, he said, his widowed mother now lives. We sincerely mourn the loss of this youth. We also feel for a mother, who must, sooner or later, hear that this day her son was interred on the banks of the Arkansas, about one hundred miles from its mouth."	06/02/1821
On Tuesday evening last, by the Rev. Dr. Roberts, Mr. Thomas Hunter, to Miss Sarah Burland, both of this city.	06/02/1821
At Blenheim, on Thursday evening last, by the Rev. Mr. M'Elheney, Mr. Edward Prill, of this city, to Matilda H., second daughter of Larkin	06/02/1821

Marriage and Death Notices	Date
H. Smith, of Baltimore county.	
On Thursday evening, by the Rev. Mr. Valiant, Mr. Charles Sandsbury, to Miss Mary Cooper, all of this city.	06/02/1821
On Thursday evening, by the Rev. Mr. Valiant, Mr. William Danyer, to Miss Elizabeth Sliver, all of this city.	06/02/1821
On Thursday evening, by the Rev. Dr. John Welsh, Mr. Nicholas Speaks, to Miss Ann Maria Duncan, all of this city.	06/02/1821
On the 24th inst., by the Rev. William M. Stone, the Rev. John Forman, of Georgetown, Del., to Mrs. Elizabeth Richards, of Worcester county, Md.	06/02/1821
On Sunday, the 20th inst., at Waterloo, the seat of Needham L. Washington, Esq., King George's county, Va., by the Rev. Mr. Thornton, Otho W. Callis, Esq., of Prince George's county, Md., to Miss Jane Ashton Alexander, fourth daughter of Col. Gerrard Alexander, of Prince William county, Va.	06/02/1821
At Easton, Md., Mr. Benjamin Denny, Sr., to Miss Mary Ann Rhodes. Mr. Thomas Sylvester to Miss Lydia Collison.	06/04/1821
On the 31st ult., after a lingering illness, which he bore with Christian fortitude, Mr. George Solomon, in the 33rd year of his age – he has left a wife and four small children to lament his loss.	06/05/1821
List of persons who died on board the U. S. frigate Congress, on her voyage to India. Robert Campfer, alias Emmerson, seaman, a native of England, 15th April 1819, of fever; James Rogers, marine, of Lancashire, May 15, of intemperance; John Davis, armorer, of Ireland, June 19, drowned; Robert Ellis, carpenter, of do., August 18, do; Wm. Jackson, seaman, of do., Oct. 8, of dysentery; Wm. Manning, seaman, of N. York, Oct. 13, consumption; Wm. Craige, alias Calbertson, seaman, of Maryland, Nov. 1, do; Martin Van Orden, blacksmith, of New York, Nov. 7, dysentery; Jeduthan Hammond, marine, of Massachusets, Dec 12, do; John Johnson, seaman, of Wales, Dec. 15, do; John Comiskey, marine of Pennsylvania, Dec 21, do; James Carey, ord. seaman, of Massachusetts, Dec. 26, consumption; Geo. Andrews, seaman, of Ireland, Jan. 15, 1820, drowned; Patrick O'Rourke, marine, of do., Feb. 14, suicide; Tho's. Walker, 2nd gunner, of Scotland, March 11, dysentery; Henry C. Neal, sergeant marines, of Maryland, March 28, do; Josh Foxcraft, alias Bison, seaman, of Maine, March 31, do; Miles Wells, marine, of Virginia, April 21, do; Wm. Currie, marine, of	06/06/1821

Marriage and Death Notices	Date
Pennsylvania, April 27, do; Samuel Lewis, seaman, of Wales, May 28, do; Tho's. Quay, seaman, of Isle of Man, June 8, do; Henry Simmons, alias James Augustus Usher, musician, of Dublin, June 10; do; John Fagan, seaman, of Ireland, June 24th, do; Richard J. Appleby, ord. seaman, of New York, June 30, do; Henry Jones, blacksmith, of Md., July 4, scurvy; Joshua G. Garrison, ord. seaman, of Barney, same day, dysentery; Wm. Brown, seaman, of Poland, August 2, mortification of from bruises; John Miller, seaman, of Ireland, Oct. 25, dysentery; J. M'Kenney, seaman, of Hudson, 81, fever; O. M'Aulister, ord. seaman, of Philad., Nov. 9, do; Robt. Dunn, gunner's mate, of Ireland, Dec. 3, cholera morbus; Thos. Jones, qr. gunner, of Boston, Dec. 4, do; Jacob Hawkes, carpenter, of N. Jersey, Dec. 5, do; John Wister, seaman, of Penn., same day, do; James Penn, seaman, of N. Carolina, same day, do; Joseph Pickens, boatswain, of Mass., Dec. 6, do; John Block, seaman, of Scotland, same day, do; John Adams, do., of do., same day, do; John White, cook, of Ireland, same day, do; James ___ker, ord. seaman, of N. York, Dec. 8, do; E. Reynolds, do., of Boson, do., do; Jos. Russell, seaman, of N. Yarmouth, (Eng.) do., do; Geo. Sewel, do., of Rockland, do., do; John Ma___son, of N. York, do., do; Charles Lewis, do., of Wales, Dec. 9, fell from aloft; T. Nutterval, do., of Baltimore, Dec. 15, cholera morbus; John Gunn, marine, of Virginia, Dec. 15, do; Jos. S. Starr, passenger, of Connecticut, Dec. 16, do; James Rice, marine, of Va., Dec. 18, consumption; Ransom Hall, do., of Vermont, do., cholera morbus; John Thomas, seaman, of France, do; Wm. Bradley, ord. seaman, do., do; Lemuel Scott, do., of Conn., Dec. 21, do; J. Brown, seaman, of Ipswich, Eng., Dec. 25, do; William Dailey, marine, of Providence, R. I., Dec. 28, bleeding; Wm. Arnold, seaman, of Bristol, Eng., January 1, 1821, cholera morbus; David Day, marine, American, Jan. 5, consumption; S. Jones, do., of Va., Jan. 17, do; T. Jones, alias W. Philips, bugler, of Lancashire, Jan. 21, fever; J. Wilington, alias Lawrence Waillen, marine, of Ireland, Feb. 10, intemperance.	
At Norfolk, Mr. James Henry, aged 40 years, late of Baltimore. Mrs. Clarissa Crocker, consort of Capt. D. W. Crocker. At his residence, in Rockbridge county, Va., aged 73 years, Gen. Andrew Moore, late Marshall of the United States, for the Eastern District of Virginia. At New Orleans, on the 10th ult., James Entwistle, of the Theatre.	06/06/1821
On Tuesday evening last, by the Rev. Mr. Smith, Dr. John Frazier, to Miss Caroline Simmons, all of Kent county, Md.	06/06/1821
At Montevideo, 17th Feb. last, Capt. William Stiles, aged 33, of the ship Balloon, of Baltimore. He was highly appreciated for his excellent qualities, and every respect was paid to his remains at their interment, in	06/08/1821

Marriage and Death Notices	Date
a foreign land.	
In Kent county, E. S. Md., on Sunday evening last, William Downy, aged 99.	06/08/1821
On Tuesday evening last, by the Rev. Mr. Duncan, Mr. David Hayes, to Miss Mary Garrett, all of this city.	06/08/1821
In Kent county, E. S., Md., by the Rev. Wm. Dodson, Mr. Henry Webb, to Miss Mary Benton, of Pine Neck.	06/08/1821
In Harford county, Mr. John Kennedy, to Miss Hetty Carman.	06/08/1821
At Liverpool, in England, in January last, Mr. William Smith, who was for many years an inhabitant of Baltimore, where he was much esteemed by those who best knew him.	06/09/1821
On Thursday morning last, by the Rev. Mr. Bartow, Capt. John J. Gatchell, to Miss Jane G. Davis, all of this city.	06/09/1821
On Thursday evening last, by the Rev. Mr. Bartow, Mr. Samuel Horves, to Miss Sarah Griffen, both of this city.	06/09/1821
On Sunday evening, May 27, Mr. James Wilson, of Washington City, to Miss Maria Sophia W. Marks, of Baltimore.	06/09/1821
At St. Croix, on the 10th of April, much regretted by his acquaintance, as he had in a residence of several months conciliated general esteem, Mr. Thomas H. Pryce, late of this city. To a widowed mother, to whom the aid of this her only child, was essentially important, the loss is peculiarly afflicting. His complaint was the fever incident to the climate; and his illness of very short duration.	06/11/1821
On Thursday evening last, Mrs. Rebecca Amoss, aged 27 years, consort of Wm. H. Amoss, after a severe illness, which she bore with that patience which becometh the Christian, whose whole hope and dependence is centered on the Redeemer, Jesus Christ. She has left a husband, three small children, and a numerous circle of relations and friends to mourn their loss.	06/12/1821
Yesterday, by the Rev. Mr. Henshaw, Gabriel Winter, Esq., of Natchez, to Catherine, daughter of Henry Cliffe, Esq., of this city.	06/12/1821
By the Rev. Dr. Glendy, on the 4th inst., Mr. Samuel H. Hatch, to Miss Sarah Good, all of this city.	06/12/1821

Marriage and Death Notices	Date
On Monday, the 11th instant, Alexander Clagett, Esq., in the 77th year of his age, after a long and protracted illness, which he bore with patience and great Christian fortitude; placing his hopes and dependence on our blessed Redeemer, Jesus Christ. Mr. Clagett was a native of Montgomery county, in this state, and settled at an early period in Washington county, and was sheriff of that county for 3 years. During the memorable event which secured our Independence, his great zeal in the cause of his country; his great exertion in keeping up the sinking credit of this state – obtained for him the thanks of his countrymen, and particularly of the Executive of Maryland. He moved to this city in the Spring of 1818, where he has since resided, till the tomb has closed upon him forever.	06/13/1821
At Cape Haytien, on the 10th ultimo, after an illness of three days, Samuel H. Harris, of Baltimore, aged 26. He was sincerely beloved by all who knew him, and his early departure is deeply regretted by the many friends he has left behind him.	06/13/1821
On Sunday last, in the 49th year of her age, Mrs. Margaret Donnelly, after a severe illness, which she bore with the patience and resignation of a Christian.	06/14/1821
Yesterday morning, at Friends' Meeting, Lombard street, Elijah Goldsmith to Mary M. Proctor.	06/14/1821
Tuesday evening last, by the Rev. Mr. Nevins, Edward G. Williams, Esq., of Washington county, to Miss Ann Gilmor, daughter of William Gilmor, Esq., of this city.	06/14/1821
At Coquimbo, in Chili, on 4th Dec. last, after a short, but severe illness, John C. Pawson, commander of the ship Chesapeake, of this port, aged 32 years and 6 months. It is not often that society mourns the loss of such a man as Capt. Pawson. He was honest, intelligent, enterprising, and brave – firm in the performance of his duties, but mild and amiable in his deportment. Few men that ever lived, more happily united in themselves the character of the gentleman, the merchant, and the seaman – whatever belonged to either was familiar to him. Though he was only in his 33rd year when he died, he had performed many of the longest, and of course the most confidential voyages made from Baltimore, having sole charge of several of our best ships and their cargoes, composed of the richest productions of China and the East Indies. He served his time to the sea in this port by indenture to that wealthy and enterprising merchant, John Donnell, Esq., in whose employ he continually remained to the day of his death, and whose confidence he entirely possessed. He has left a wife and child, and a	06/15/1821

Marriage and Death Notices	Date
long list of friends, to deplore his untimely decease.	
On Wednesday, 13th inst., Mrs. Mary Sinclair, consort of Mr. John Sinclair, after a long and painful illness, which she bore with Christian fortitude; and triumphantly yielded her virtuous spirit to the bosom of the blessed Redeemer.	06/15/1821
At New Orleans, on the 17th ult., Mr. James Bennett, in the 46th year of his age, a native of Maryland.	06/15/1821
In New Orleans, on the 7th March last, Mr. John R. Holliday, Esq., formerly of Baltimore, to Mrs. Davis, of Baton Rouge.	06/15/1821
At Hagerstown, Mr. John Cameron, of Shepherdstown, to Miss Maria M'Fall, of the former place.	06/15/1821
On Monday last, Mrs. Rebecca Stansbury, wife of Maj. William Stansbury.	06/16/1821
On Saturday last, Mr. Walter F. Athey, aged 38.	06/16/1821
Death of Mrs. Alsop. We are sorry to learn that Mrs. Alsop, the daughter of the celebrated Mrs. Jordan, died suddenly yesterday morning. Her death is attributed to taking too much laudanum by mistake; she had been sick for several days previous to this unfortunate occurrence. *National Advocate, 15th inst.*	06/16/1821
On Tuesday morning last, the 12th inst., by the Rev. Mr. Henshaw, Edward Griffith, Esq., of Harford county, to Miss Mary Ann, only daughter of Mr. Wm. Wetherall, of this city.	06/16/1821
On Sunday evening last, by the Rev. Mr. Valiant, Mr. James Ratcliff, to Miss Mary Ann Brawner, all of this city.	06/16/1821
On Thursday evening, by the Rev. Mr. Valiant, Mr. Abraham Hickman, to Miss Theodocius Ficklin, all of this city.	06/16/1821
On Thursday evening last, by the Rev. S. K. Jennings, Mr. George Pouder, of this city, to Miss Catherine A. Stine, of Harrisburg, Pennsylvania.	06/16/1821
On the 16th inst., after an illness of 3 days, Mr. Edward Jones, formerly of Portsmouth, N. H., much respected by all who knew him, and much beloved by those who knew him best. The deceased was amiable in his disposition, combining dignity, and urbanity in his manners, and had	06/18/1821

Marriage and Death Notices	Date
formed a character worthy of example.	
On Wednesday, the 14th inst., after a severe illness, which he bore with Christian fortitude, the Rev. Hamilton Jefferson, in the 53rd year of his age leaving a disconsolate widow and children to mourn their irreparable loss.	06/18/1821
In Harford county, Md., Mr. Thomas Turner.	06/18/1821
On the 12th inst., Mrs. Mary Ann Brown, consort of Col. James Brown, near Churchill, Queen Anne's county.	06/18/1821
On Tuesday last, by the Rev. Dr. Roberts, Mr. Reuben Brown, to Miss Rebecca Oram, all of this city.	06/18/1821
In Talbot county, Mr. Laban Littleton, to Miss Rebecca Matthews.	06/18/1821
In Kentucky, Mr. Daniel R. Southard, merchant, of Louisville, to Miss Anna Maria Coale, formerly of Baltimore.	06/19/1821
Yesterday morning, after a few days illness, Mr. Wynbert T. Mohler, in the 21st year of his age.	06/20/1821
On Wednesday evening, the 22nd ult., at his residence on Big Sand, Claiborne county, Mississippi, Mr. Reuben Davis, formerly of Maryland.	06/20/1821
In Charles county, Md., 12th inst., beloved by all who knew her, Mrs. Eliza Dyer, wife of Mr. Horatio Dyer, of Prince Georges County, she has left a disconsolate husband and a little daughter to lament their early and irreparable loss.	06/20/1821
On Thursday evening last, by the Rev. Mr. Grice, Mr. Thomas Ritter, Jr., to Miss Sidney Bell, both of Baltimore county.	06/22/1821
At New Orleans, Mr. James Flower, of Feliciana, to Miss Lucy Griffith, late of Baltimore.	06/22/1821
On Wednesday, the 13th instant, at his residence, near Reisterstown, Baltimore county, Mr. Andrew Cockey.	06/23/1821
On Thursday evening last, by the Rev. Mr. Tidings, Mr. Daniel W. B. Carroll, to Miss Lucy Ann Mainster, all of this city.	06/23/1821
On Tuesday, the 19th instant, Miss Susanna Sophia Simmonds, daughter of Mr. Matthew W. Simmonds, of this city, aged 22 years. In noticing	06/23/1821

Marriage and Death Notices	Date
this second visitation of a family so truly worthy of our highest esteem, we are made doubly sensitive to that important revelation, "Whom the Lord loveth, he chasteneth." A few months only have elapsed, since their friends were called to condole with them, the loss of the lovely Maria! What a bereavement was there! Yet by a death the most triumphant, God in his infinite goodness, has provided the only satisfactory solace for a wound so deep and lacerating to the hearts of her fond parents. The awful messenger has been stripped of all his terrors, and his victim happily admitted into Abraham's bosom. The solemn dedication of a tender father and the sincere devotion of a fond mother, had been approved? All acknowledged the rightful auhority of the King Eternal – all hearts bowed in deep submission, and said, it is the Lord! "Let his will be done on Earth as it is in Heaven." "The Lord giveth and the Lord taketh away, and blessed be the name of the Lord." Thus, the all bountiful Saviour, elevates his children to the mansions of rest, and prepares surviving friends to consent with the pius King, who said of his deceased infant, "I shall go to him, but he shall not return to me." It was not the will of Heaven, that Maria should dwell in the realms of bliss, and Susanna continue still to languish in her afflictions. Taught by God in the same successful school, she had acquired an equal portion of the meekness of wisdom in tribulation. She too had learned patience; in patience experience; in experience hope; and hope did not disappoint her. The love of God was shed abroad in her heart by the Holy Ghost which was given unto her!! The Lord was pleased therefore to say *"it is enough,"* Let her too come up higher, and lo! sweetly as babes sleep, she went to rest!! The scene so closed is mournful, but in mourning for these lovely sisters, we do not mourn, like those who have no hope. Blessed immortality, bright beam of the sun of righteousness, how splendidly dost thou illuminate the mansions of the dead, who die in the Lord! Let us all endeavor to be found watching when the Son of Man cometh.	
On Thursday morning, 21st inst., at 4 o'clock A. M., in the 29th year of his age, Mr. Michael Carroll. He has left a disconsolate wife and three children to mourn the loss of an affectionate husband and a kind parent. His death was occasioned by a fall from the basement of the Washington Monument. He has, for the last two or three years, been a worthy industrious attendant, well known for his good conduct and sober habits. Mrs. Carroll and relations return their sincere thanks to the citizens, for tendering their kind services, in time of serious distress. She is a worthy woman; and deserves the contributions of the humane and benevolent. Her dwelling is in Mill street, near the south end of the jail.	06/23/1821

Marriage and Death Notices	Date
On Friday evening last, by the Rev. D. E. Reese, Mr. William Cole, to Mrs. Mary Vaner, all of this city.	06/26/1821
On Sunday evening last, by the Rev. Mr. Valiant, Mr. John Connely, to Miss Elizabeth Shaw, all of this city.	06/26/1821
On Tuesday evening last, by the Rev. Mr. Finley, Mr. Thomas A. Loney, to Miss Martha, daughter of Robert Wilson, of this city.	06/27/1821
Last evening, by the Rev. Dr. Roberts, Peter Webb, Esq., of Talbot county, to Miss Elizabeth Dickinson, of this city.	06/27/1821
On Sunday evening last, by the Rev. Mr. Bartow, Mr. Peter Olding, to Mrs. Mary Ann Cloyne, all of this city.	06/27/1821
Yesterday, in the 26th year of his age, after a lingering illness, William Smith, nephew of Dr. Sinclair, late of Baltimore College.	06/27/1821
In Virginia, in March last, Mr. Francis Grasse, formerly of this city.	06/29/1821
On Thursday evening last, by the Rev. J. P. K. Henshaw, Edward H. Harris, Esq., to Miss Catherine Brunner, second daughter of Mr. Andrew Brunner, all of this city.	06/29/1821
In Kent county, Md., on the 21st inst., Capt. John Humphreys, to Miss Martha Blackestone.	06/29/1821
On Sunday, the 1st inst., at Aetna powderworks, Baltimore county, by the Rev. Mr. Welsh, Mr. Owen Carroll to Miss Mary Compton.	06/29/1821
On Saturday evening last, by the Rev. Mr. Bartow, Mr. James Sevey, to Miss Jane Boyd, all of this city.	07/03/1821
On Thursday evening last, by the Rev. Mr. Roszel, Mr. Edward Thompson, to Miss Elizabeth Casle, all of this city.	07/03/1821
Departed this life, last evening, John D. Detken, a native of Bremen, aged 22, after an illness of four days. He had resided in this country only eighteen or twenty months; but, during this short period, had by his amiable deportment and gentlemanly manner, gained many friends. He was brave, generous, and virtuous – that he was the first, he proved when but a youth, by exchanging the comforts of ease and opulence, for the deprivations and fatigues of a camp, in the defense of his country; surely, the noblest test. That he was the second and the last, his many and sorrowing friends can most amply testify. In short, to draw his character in the most simple manner, he was what Pope so beautifully	07/03/1821

Marriage and Death Notices	Date
and concisely describes as "the noblest work of God, an honest man." Leara, O! Ye youth, by the short summons this amiable young man has received, how important the consideration – "That in the midst of life, we are in death!" But a few days ago, he was in the bloom of life and health, and now where is he? Surrounded by the gloom and silence of the grave. Oh! May we all be as well prepared at that awful hour as he appeared to be. He has left a father and a large family of brothers and sisters to deplore him, cut off just as he had attained the age of manhood. Yet, the whole tenor of his short life has been such, that they may surely enjoy the hope, that he has been transferred from this vale of pain and incertaintude, to those realms of eternal bliss, where no grief can enter. A trifling tribute from one who knew him. B.	
Wednesday morning, by the Rev. Bishop Kemp, Jehu Chandler, Esq., Editor of the Maryland Republican, at Annapolis, to Miss Eliza C. Inloes, of this place.	07/05/1821
On Sunday evening last, by the Rev. John Healey, Mr. Jacob Miller, to Miss Catherine Bankard, all of this city.	07/05/1821
Yesterday Morning, with the composure resulting from a philosophic, well spent life, Mr. Samuel Sherburne, son of the late consul of the United States at Nantes, in France. This amiable young man, thus snatched away in his twenty-fourth year, was distinguished among his acquaintance for many virtues. His manliness of temper and independence of disposition, were happily blended with politeness and urbanity; his beneficence was active, but not ostentatious; his accomplishments and learning were various and profound, untinged with pedantry, and unalloyed by arrogance. Exemplary in his deportment, zealous in the discharge of the trusts reposed in him, charitable and sympathetic, Mr. S. carries to the grave, the cordial regret of all who knew him. He experienced, in his last hours, the anxious tenderness and unwaried assiduity of the worthy lady with whom he lived.	07/05/1821
Last evening, by the Rev. John Healey, Mr. James Wood, to Miss Dorcas Daste, both of this city.	07/05/1821
Yesterday morning, after a short illness, Mr. James Neilson. His friends are invited to attend his funeral, at 4 o'clock, this afternoon, from his residence, Holiday street.	07/06/1821

Marriage and Death Notices	Dates
On Tuesday evening, the 3rd instant, Mr. Peter Shane, in the 68th year of his age, long a respectable inhabitant of this place.	07/06/1821
Last evening, by the Rev. Mr. Finley, Mr. William Acy, of Columbia, to Miss Mary Ann Gardiner, of this city.	07/06/1821
Last evening, by the Rev. Dr. Glendy, Alexander Washington Reeder, Esq., of St. Mary's county, to Miss Ann Williams, daughter of the late Andrew Hanna, of this city.	07/06/1821
At Woodbury, the residence of John Leigh, Esq., on Wednesday evening last, by the Rev. Mr. Monnelly, Mr. Philip Greenwell, to Miss Susana Cabbeen, all of St. Mary's county.	07/06/1821 07/18/1821
On the 1st inst., Mr. Robert Watson, aged 42 years, after a long and painful illness, which he bore with great fortitude. He was a virtuous and useful citizen, exemplary in all the relations of life. He has left a widow and three infant children to mourn this irreparable bereavement.	07/07/1821
On Friday, 29th ult., Mrs. Elizabeth Bankson, in the 68th year of her age. Her best eulogy is in the hearts of all who knew her.	07/07/1821
Yesterday, about two o'clock in the afternoon, John W. Wilson, merchant of this city, in the 51st year of his age. He was a most affectionate husband and father – as well as a kind, obliging friend and neighbour.	07/07/1821
At his father's residence, near Bell-Air, Md., on Saturday, 30th inst., of a malignant fever, Elias Ellicott Amos, in his 22nd year.	07/07/1821
On the 28th ult., by the Rev. Alfred Helfenstein, Mr. John Ristor, to Miss Susanna Steivers, both of this city.	07/07/1821
By the Rev. Albert Helfenstein, on Tuesday last, Mr. Valentine Hoffman, of Philadelphia, to Miss Mary Brunner, of this city.	07/07/1821
Last evening, in the 21st year of his age, John C. Clapham, an estimable youth and only son.	07/09/1821
On Saturday last, by the Rev. Nelson Reid, Mr. Jesse Hollingsworth Willis, of Frederick county, Md., to Miss Ann Winchester, only daughter of the late Judge Winchester, of this city.	07/09/1821
At Easton, Md., on Wednesday, the 27th inst., by the Rev. Mr. Bayne, Mr. John Brown, of (Sol.) Caroline county, to Miss Nannette, daughter	07/10/1820

Marriage and Death Notices	Dates
of Mr. George Martin, Esq., of Easton.	
On Sunday morning, the 8th instant, in his 30th year, William Douglass, of the house of R. H. & W. Douglass, of this city. Enterprise, talent, and inflexible integrity, had already raised him to a commercial rank, to which few attain at any age. His modest and unassuming manners, secured the willing respect of all; the manly and social virtues of his nature, commanded among his intimate friends the most cordial and sincere affection. The pride and honest boast of his fond and beloved relatives, his every prospect, on the one hand, presented wealth and honor – his every anticipation, on the other, friendship and sincerest affection. From numerous relatives, and still more numerous friends; from prospects so brilliant and honorable, he has been untimely torn. "Child of mortality," well may'st "thou mourn" – well may "thine eyes be red with weeping."	07/10/1821
In Talbot county, on Monday, the 18th of June, Mrs. Mary Rathell, in the 51st year of her age, consort of Mr. Parrott Rathell.	07/10/1821
On Tuesday evening last, by the Rev. E. J. Reis, Mr. Stephen Highland, of Chestertown, Eastern Shore of Maryland, to Miss Hester Wright, of this city.	07/10/1821
In Havana, Mr. Charles Pollard, printer, formerly of Boston, aged 29.	07/11/1821
Near Batavia, Solomon Rutter, commander of the ship William, of Baltimore – one of the oldest and most respectable ship masters of this port. He has left a large family and circle of friends to cherish his memory, and who know how to feel and appreciate his loss.	07/11/1821
Yesterday morning, after a severe illness, Peter Kampf, a native of Germany. His loss is deeply felt by those who knew and appreciated his integrity and amiable deportment.	07/11/1821
OBITUARY. He death of the aged and infirm, although they be greatly beloved and respected, although hey be followed to the grave by a long and melancholy train of friends and acquaintances, makes no half so strong and lasing an impression on the human soul, as that of the young and vigorous. When a young man is suddenly cut off by the relentless hand of death, and especially when he has, during the brief period of his existence, gained he affections of his acquaintance and excited expectations of future worth, then it is, that he young and the old, he gay and the thoughtful, are induced to reflect seriously upon the melancholy occurence. The young and the gay, in particular, who have been the associates of his worldly pleasures are irresistibly compelled to pause	07/11/1821

Marriage and Death Notices	Dates
for awhile in their giddy career, and to drop a few tears to his memory. The impression caused by the unhappy event, is often very deep and productive of the most poignant anguish. But ah! too soon does a fresh succession of enjoyments dispel the clouds of grief, and obliterate every remembrance of him, that was once their friend and companion. These remarks have occurred on a mournful occasion; the death of Mr. John C. Clapham, who terminated his mortal career on Sunday night last, in the 21st year of his age. Seldom has the death of one so young, excited such unfeigned sorrow in the hearts of his friends and acquaintances. Indeed, there were few young men of his age that were more generally esteemed, or more deservedly beloved. His disposition was so amiable and so obliging, his manners so pleasing and so unassuming, his deportment so correct, and his character so well formed, that he was entirely adapted to win the affections of all who knew him. And that he did win those affections is amply testified by the deep and heart-felt sympathy which is manifested for his early and unexpected fate. When we see a tender interest excited in the minds of many, who have been comparatively strangers to him, we can only *imagine* what must be the unspeakable anguish of those to whom he stood in the nearer relation of family connexion; but theirs is a sacred grief and we must not intrude upon it. When we behold one so young and so amiable as he was, cut off thus suddenly, in the midst of a pleasurable existence, from those by whom he was so tenderly beloved, cut off from that society which he fairly promised to adorn, we are naturally led to hink of he uncertainty of life, and he instability of all earthly enjoyments. And to those, who have been his companions, who have long been accustomed to meet him in the daily walks of life, and in the scenes of gaiety and festivity so usually frequented by the youthful, this event should act as a solemn warning. Let us only reflect, that not long since, we saw him in the full enjoyment of life, and youth, and health. Two short and fleeting weeks have not yet intervened, *and now where is he?* Consigned to the dark and lonely and silent tomb, he shall there abide, until the awful trump of the general resurrection shall burst the iron slumber of the grave, and summon forth the dead to receive their final doom at the bar of their God and their Redeemer. AC&G	
On Sunday, 8th inst., Capt. Nicholas Eaverson, of a dropsy, in the 66th year of his age, and for many years a respectable citizen of the city of Baltimore, and a firm man of '75.	07/12/1821
10th instant, Joseph, aged 16, second son of Mr. Walter Simpson.	07/12/1821
By the Rev. Dr. Glendy, on the 29th ult., Mr. John Cathcart to Miss Agnes Rankin, both of this city.	07/12/1821

Marriage and Death Notices	Dates
By the Rev. Dr. Glendy, on Friday last, Alexander Wilson, Esq., to Miss Mary Willis, both natives of Ireland.	07/12/1821
Yesterday morning, in the 17th year of his age, William T. Wilson, son of the late John T. Wilson.	07/13/1821
About 1 o'clock, on Sunday, the 8th instant, Miss Mary Leatherberry, after 3 weeks severe affliction, which she bore with Christian meekness, fortitude, and resignation, looking beyond the bounds of time, in full assurance of a blessed immortality and eternal life.	07/13/1821
On Wednesday last, in the 26th year of his age, Michael O'Riley, a native of Ireland, but for several years past, a resident of this city.	07/13/1821
On Sunday evening last, by the Rev. Dr. Kurtz, Mr. Charles Amey, to Miss Margaret Mills, all of this city.	07/13/1821
Yesterday morning, by the Rev. Dr. Roberts, Thomas Irwin, Jr., Esq., of Alexandria, D. C., to Miss Eleanor, eldest daughter of the late Nathan Tyson, Esq., of this city.	07/13/1821
Last evening, by the Rev. Mr. Helfenstein, Mr. George Heidelback, to Miss Louisa, daughter of Mr. F. Focke, both of this city.	07/13/1821
Departed this life, the 7th inst., Henry, the eldest son of Capt. Thorndick Chase, aged 16 years and 3 month, of the fatal disease which lately made its appearance on Smith's wharf. He suffered only four days and a half, during which time, he gave full assurance to his distressed parents, of his reliance on the mercy and acceptance of his redeemer; while the sympathizing regrets of all those who had known him remains, of the strongest proof of the virtues and real worth, which had even at so tender an age, been remarkable in him.	07/14/1821
On Thursday evening last, by the Rev. Mr. Bartow, Mr. Thomas Ellis, to Mrs. Jane Henderson, all of this city.	07/14/1821
On Thursday evening last, by the Rev. Dr. Roberts, Mr. Thos. Parsons, to Miss Elizabeth Waltham, all of this city.	07/14/1821
On Thursday, the 12th inst., by the Rev. Mr. Tidings, Mr. Seth Stone, to Miss Martha Clap, all of this city.	07/14/1821
Was drowned, on the evening of the 13th inst., Miss Elizabeth Moody, in the 20th year of her age, respected and beloved by all who knew her, for her amiable deportment and mental qualifications. The death of this young lady has left a void in the circle of her acquaintance not easily to	07/18/1821

Marriage and Death Notices	Dates
be filled; and her affectionate relatives have sustained an irreparable deprivation. Yet, while they deplore her loss, let them trust that she is enjoying happiness, in another and a better world.	
In Fredericktown, Md., Dr. Thomas Spinger to Miss Mary Keller.	07/18/1821
The subject of this notice, Miss Elizabeth Murray, was a native of Northumberland county, Virginia, whence she had lately come to visit her friends in Baltimore. On the evening of the 13th inst., while engaged in a party of pleasure, she was unfortunately drowned, with her young companions, Miss Moody and Miss Stanley. If piety, charity, and amiableness of disposition claim respect – the memory of Miss Murray will long be held in pleasing recollection.	07/21/1821
By the Rev. Dr. Glendy, on the evening of Thursday last, Dr. William Sheppard Woodside, to Miss Rachel Beatty, all of this city.	07/21/1821
Yesterday, by the Rev. Dr. Jennings, Thomas H. Harland, to Miss Eleanor Merryman, both of Baltimore county.	07/21/1821
On Thursday evening last, by the Rev. Mr. Duncan, Mr. John Russell, to Miss Susan Welsh, both of this city.	07/21/1821 07/23/1821
Departed this sublunary scene, for "another and a better world," at 2 o'clock, on Saturday evening last, Samuel Cole, Esq., aged 47 years. The deceased passed through life with honor and sterling integrity, enjoying the confidence, and esteem of all who had the pleasure of his acquaintance – and it is believed who has descended to the tomb, without leaving a solitary enemy. But a few days since, we beheld him in the full flow of soul – pleasure beaming in his eyes and health glowing in his countenance. Alas! How changed. No more shall the generous hand of friendship be ardently compressed by him – no more the heart of wife or children bound in his society. As a philanthropist, he was pre-eminent. His benevolence was of that diffusive and all pervading character, that distress, no matter in what form, found alleviation under his enlivening influence.	07/23/1821
In Kent county, on Monday morning, the 16th inst., Mrs. Amelia Sophia Charlotte, wife of Thomas Hynson, Esq., in the 40th year of her age. She has left a husband and six children to lament their heavy, their irreparable loss, as well as a very numerous circle of relatives and friends, to mingle in the regret at this afflicting dispensation. She was a most affectionate wife, an indulgent mother, a kind mistress, and good neighbor. It may indeed be truly said of the deceased, that such was the mildness and purity of her life and conversation, that she made or left	07/23/1821

Marriage and Death Notices	Dates
any enemies. Although her affliction was most severe, she sustained it with Christian patience and fortitude. Persuaded that she was entirely resigned to the will of Him who knoweth and searcheth the secrets of all hearts, in the surest confidence of his unbounded goodness and mercy, and that through the merits and pardoning grace of a blessed Redeemer, she should find happiness and life eternal at the right hand of God. Bouyed above the fear of death, with this most consolatory reflection, she resigned her last breath. The above imperfect tribute of respect is offered by one, who had the happiness to be acquainted with the deceased, from a very early period of her life to the last; and who very sincerely joins in the general sorrow of her friends.	
On Thursday evening, 19th inst., by the Rev. Mr. Duncan, Mr. George Robinson, to Miss Maria Settin, both of this city.	07/23/1821
On the 15th instant, Mr. Ebenezer Chermon, to Miss Catherine Tidings, both of Severn.	07/23/1821
On Tuesday, July 4th, by the Rev. Mr. De Le Ree, Mr. Joseph Levant, to Miss Catherine Brugnon, all of this city.	07/25/1821
On Tuesday evening last, by the Rev. Mr. Bartow, Capt. Richard Bucking, to Mrs. Elizabeth Feldhousen, all of this city.	07/26/1821
On Wednesday, July 25th, by the Rev. Mr. Welsh, Mr. John Etherington, to Miss Susan C. Smith, all of this city.	07/27/1821
At St. Augustine, E. F., on Thursday evening, June 28· by the Rev. Father Crosby, Mr. Ede Van Evour, of New York, to Miss Eliza Edes, of Baltimore, Md.	07/30/1821
At King's Creek, John Parrott, son of Mr. Aaron Parrott, late of Talbot county, deceased, in the 23rd year of his age.	07/31/1821
In Talbot county, on the 27th inst., Mrs. Caulk, wife of Mr. Daniel Caulk, after a lingering illness.	07/31/1821
Mr. Solomon Plummer, of Easton.	07/31/1821
On Saturday evening last, by the Rev. Dr. Roberts, Mr. Walter L. Biscoe, of St. Mary's, Md., to Miss Rebecca Patrick, of this city.	07/31/1821
In Talbot county, Mr. Joseph Turner, to Miss Margaret Loveday.	07/31/1821
In Harford county, on Thursday, the 19th inst., by the Rev. Mr. Park, Mr. Henry Fullard, aged 73 years, to the amiable Miss Elizabeth Cox, aged	07/31/1821

Marriage and Death Notices	Dates
28, both of Harford.	
On the 2_th ult., by the Rev. Mr. Anger, Mr. Henry Pye, of Port Tobacco, to Miss Sarah Boon, of Bean Town, Charles County, Maryland.	08/01/1821
At Philadelphia, Mr. Thomas S. R. Fassitt, of Maryland, to Mary Ann, daughter of Thos. Fassett, Esq., of that city.	08/01/1821
On Tuesday evening last, by the Rev. Mr. Greenfield, Mr. August J. Brockemiller, of this city, to Miss Rebecca Stansbury, of Baltimore county.	08/02/1821
On Wednesday evening, the 1st August, George Carnaghan.	08/03/1821
On Saturday last, after a lingering illness, Mrs. Arby Worthington, in the sixtieth year of her age.	08/03/1821
Departed this life in Annapolis, at 8 o'clock, on Wednesday evening, 1st of August, Miss Ann Maria, youngest daughter of Baltzer Schaffer, Esq., of this city, in the 16th year of her age. She left home on the 30th of June last, on a visit to her acquaintances, and on the 25th July, was seized with the bilious fever, which terminated her earthly career. She has left behind her an indulgent father and mother, and numerous friends and relations, to mourn their irreparable loss. "How chang'd! that heart is cold, Her bosom rests within the earth, And mem'ry's dirge hath fondly told, Of all her sweetness, all her worth. Unsparing death! Must then the young, The innocent in heart and tongue, The lov'd, the loving and the gay, Aye, be the first to fall thy prey? Alas! that mild unchiding breast, Is in the icy grave compressed - And the dull earth-worm riots now, Upon the smooth and marble brow."	08/03/1821
Last evening, by the Rev. Mr. Hargrove, Mr. Thomas H. Thomas, of this city, to Miss Mary Ann George, of Charleston, S. C.	08/03/1821
On the 31st of July, Mrs. Deborah Cochran, relict of the late William Cochran, merchant of this city, in the fifty first year of her age.	08/04/1821

Marriage and Death Notices	Dates
On Thursday evening last, by the Rev. Samuel Davis, Mr. Thomas Watkins, to Miss Elizabeth Ann Warfield, all of this city.	08/04/1821
This morning, in St. Paul's Church, by the Rt. Rev. Bishop Kemp, Mr. James Colles, of New Orleans, to Miss Hannah Augusta Wetmore, of this city.	08/04/1821 08/06/1821
On Thursday evening last, by the Rev. Dr. George Roberts, Mr. William Royston, to Miss Ellen Fuller, all of Baltimore county.	08/06/1821
By the Rev. Dr. Glendy, on Saturday last, Moses Ruth, Esq. to Miss Susannah O. Bagely, all of this city.	08/06/1821
On Wednesday aft., after a short illness, which she sustained with a truly Christian fortitude, Mrs. Abby Kerr, wife of Capt. Archibald Kerr, of this city, in the 47th year of her age. In all the relative and Christian duties of wife, mother, and neighbor, she was exemplary – to her distressed partner and dear children the bereavement is irreparable, and by her numerous friends and neighbors, she is deeply lamented.	08/07/1821
Suddenly, on Saturday evening, the 4th inst., Mr. H. Elliott, aged about 65 years, who has left a wife and two children to mourn their irreparable loss. He was a kind, affectionate husband, father, and friend; and it may be emphatically said of him, that he was among the noblest works of God, *"an honest man."*	08/07/1821
On Friday last, Mr. Patrick M'Cabe, in the 48th year of his age, of a lingering complaint, a native of the Parish and county of Monaghan, Ireland. He has left here an orphan child, bereft of a father and mother.	08/07/1821
On Sunday evening last, by the Rev. Dr. Roberts, Mr. Laurence O'Laughlan to Miss Mary Ann Hixley, all of this city.	08/07/1821
On the 8th of July last, by the Most Rev. Archbishop Mareschal, Graeme Keith Spence, Esq., of Portsmouth, New Hampshire, to Miss Susan S. Randall, of this city.	08/08/1821
On Wednesday evening, by the Rev. Dr. Kurtz, Mr. James Duyer, of the Eastern Shore of Maryland, to Miss Elizabeth Dorney, of this city.	08/09/1821
On Wednesday last, Mr. Jonathan Edwards, of this city, a worthy and respectable citizen.	08/10/1821
At Washington, Mr. John D. Emack, Jr., to Miss Mary Ann Van Horn, daughter of the late Archibald Van Horn, Esq., of Md.	08/10/1821

Marriage and Death Notices	Dates
At his residence, on Pennsylvania Avenue, this morning, of a lingering illness, Mr. Henry Myers, aged 45 years. His friends are invited to attend his funeral, tomorrow, at 3 o'clock P. M.	08/14/1821
On Sunday evening last, after a tedious and lingering illness, John J. B. M'Gibbon, aged 21 years.	08/14/1821
On the 9th inst., in the 43rd year of his age, after a distressing illness, borne with patient resignation, William Shippen Willing, Esq., late merchant of Philadelphia.	08/14/1821
At Easton, Md. on the 3rd inst., Mr. Thomas Cooper, after a lingering illness.	08/14/1821
On Thursday evening last, by the Rev. Dr. Roberts, Mr. William R. Carver, to Miss Elizabeth Fusselbaugh, all of this city.	08/14/1821
On Monday, the 6th inst., after a lingering and distressing illness, Mrs. Anne O. Gibson, relict of the late John Gibson, Esq., of Magothy.	08/17/1821
By the Rev. Dr. Glendy, on Tuesday last, Mr. John Cazier, of the state of Delaware, to Miss Elizabeth Powell, of this city.	08/17/1821
At Hagerstown, on Monday, the 6th inst., by the Rev. Mr. Buchanan, Mr. _____ Haslett, of Baltimore, to Miss Eliza Hughes, of that town.	08/17/1821
On Thursday evening last, by the Rev. Mr. M'Cann, Mr. Joseph Virlander, to Miss Julian M'Gloshe, all of this city.	08/18/1821
On Sunday last, at 9 o'clock, A. M., by the Rev. Abner Neal, Mr. Jesse Leatherwood, to Miss Ann Leatherwood, both of Anne Arundel county, Md.	08/21/1821
On Monday evening, 13th inst., by the Rev. Mr. Valiant, Mr. James Wardell, to Miss Mary Ann Mankelly.	08/21/1821
On Thursday evening, by the Rev. Mr. Valiant, Mr. William Williams, to Miss Elizabeth Williams, all of this city.	08/21/1821
Last evening, at 10 o'clock, in the 72nd year of his age, Gen. John Swan, an officer of the Revolution. His friends are invited to attend his funeral, tomorrow morning, at 8 o'clock, from his late dwelling.	08/22/1821
Near Middletown, Md., on the 9th inst., after a short, but painful illness, Mr. George Motter, in the 56th year of his age.	08/22/1821

Marriage and Death Notices	Dates
At his late residence, near St. Michaels, Md., after a short illness, Mr. John Rolle, in the 68th year of his age.	08/22/1821
In Dorchester county, on Sunday, Aug. 12th, after a lingering illness, Mrs. Deborah Rawleigh, consort of Mr. Stephen Rawleigh, aged 26 years.	08/22/1821
On board the steam boat Paragon, at Blue River Island, on the River Ohio, Mr. Isaac Tyson.	08/22/1821
On Sunday evening last, by the Rev. Dr. Roberts, Mr. Joseph H. Ball, to Miss Ann Eliza Strebeck, all of this city.	08/22/1821
At Wood Lawn, Prince George's county, Md., on the 9th inst., by the Rev. Ethan Allen, Capt. W. C. Beard, of the U. S. army, to Miss Matilda H. Jones.	08/22/1821
On the 20th instant, in Prince George's Co., Md., at the residence of Mr. Henry Culvere, Mrs. Eleanor Beall, widow of the late James A. Beall, Esq.	08/23/1821
On Tuesday evening last, by the Rev. Mr. Tidings, Mr. John W. Burns, to Miss Ann Barker, all of this city.	08/23/1821
In this city, on Wednesday last, Mr. Salem Willard, formerly of Boston, aged 36.	08/24/1821
In Baltimore county, on Friday, 17th inst., Jonathan Stone, formerly of Watertown, Ms., aged 33 years.	08/24/1821
In Easton, Md., Mr. Peter Denny, in the 64th year of his age.	08/24/1821
In Fayetteville, North Carolina, on Wednesday, 25th ult., Mr. James Powers, a native of Maryland. He was a Lieutenant in the Revolutionary War, under Gen. Greene; was in the battles of Guilford, Eutaw Spring, and several others, and was discharged in consequence of having been severely wounded.	08/24/1821
In Hagerstown, Miss Mary Pottenger, daughter of Dr. Pottenger, formerly of Prince George's county. Capt. Henry Ridenour, in the 75th year of his age. Mrs. Magdalen Hofleich, in the 42nd year of her age.	08/24/1821
On Saturday, the 11th inst., at his father's residence, in Eastern neck, Md., Mr. James W. Ringgold, of Kent county, Md., in the 24th year of his age, leaving a wife and infant daughter, a father, mother, and numerous other near and affectionate relatives to lament their loss, and	08/24/1821

Marriage and Death Notices	Dates
his early end.	
Lately, in Chestertown, Peregrine Bantham, aged about 61 years. He enlisted a soldier in the 5th Maryland Regiment, at an early period of the war of the Revolution, while he was yet very young, and served in the Maryland line, until the end of the war. He was always an orderly and gallant soldier. The writer of this article knew him well, having served in the same corps, and an eye witness to his deportment, now offers this humble tribute of respect to his memory. He served again in the war against the Indians, under Gen. Wayne, and last of all, in the late war in the militia of Ohio. Having served in three wars, he has now gone to mingle with his kindred spirits where strife and war cease.	08/24/1821
At New Orleans, Capt. W. Boyd. Mr. G. W. Robinson. Reuben Johnson, from Massachusetts. John Elder, a stranger. Goodwin, from Maine.	08/25/1821
On Thursday evening last, by the Rev. Mr. Shane, Mr. John Crisall, to Hester Carter, all of this city.	08/25/1821
On the 25th inst., after a long and painful illness, in the fiftieth year of her age, Madame Charlotte Dunan, wife of Dr. Dunan. This happy pair had lived together 25 years in conjugal love and reciprocal affection: but he who holds the destinies of men under his control, was pleased to put an end to their union – no medical skill could save her from the grave – neither could the unremitted attention of a tender husband and numerous friends snatch her from the arms of death. But, she was resigned to her fate – No murmur was permitted to escape her lips during a long affliction – she seemed as though she had never lost sight of this solemn and important truth, that man is born to die. She is gone where the wicked cease from troubling, and where the weary are at rest." – and has left behind a disconsolate partner, grateful offspring, numerous friends, and indigent poor, to lament the loss of their benefactress.	08/27/1821
The annunciation of the death of Charles Wirgman will be received with surprise, by many who were unacquainted with his sudden illness, and with heartfelt regret by all of his fellow-citizens. He departed this transitory life, yesterday, at a few minutes past 12 o'clock, having been ill only since the preceding Thursday night. His disease was a highly malignant fever, contracted at the Point; where a too close attention to his mercantile concerns had frequently taken him within the last few days. The deceased was conspicuous for the rare combination of those attributes of character, which make the death of such a man a cause of general regret. In his business, systematic, punctual, and indefatigable – in his intercourse with society, the polished gentleman and amiable	08/27/1821

Marriage and Death Notices	Dates
citizen, and in the domestic retirement of his family, the affectionate husband and kind father. His well known worth had placed him in the Chair of the Right Worshipful Grand Master of the Grand Lodge of Maryland, where he presided with *honor to himself* and *profit to the Craft*.	
On Sunday afternoon, about 3 o'clock, in the sixty-first year of his age, Jesse Tyson, a member of the society of friends, and for many years a respectable merchant of this city. His relatives and friends are invited to attend his funeral, from his late dwelling, this afternoon, at 4 o'clock, without further invitation.	08/27/1821
On the 24th inst., Mrs. Hester H. Von Kappf, daughter of Mr. Henry Didier, and consort of Mr. B. J. Von Kappf, merchant of this city.	08/27/1821
Yesterday morning, at 7 o'clock, Lucretia Wilson, consort of the late John W. Wilson. Her relations and friends are invited to attend the funeral, from her late residence, on the Falls' road, three miles from town, tomorrow morning at 9 o'clock, without further notice.	08/27/1821
On Friday morning, Mrs. Judith De Garis, and on Saturday morning, Mrs. Mary Smith, both of the prevailing disease – natives of Guernsey.	08/27/1821
In Easton, Md. on the 21st inst., Mr. James Nabb, Jr., son of James Nabb, Esq., aged 22 years. Rarely does it become our painful duty to record a death which has thrown such a gloom over the society in which he moved, as that of this amiable young man. Just arrived at an age when the development of the mind takes place, his friends witnessed the most flattering portraiture of a valuable member of society in that of Mr. Nabb. His remarkable filial affection, the suavity and urbanity of his manners, the evenness of his temper, and mildness of disposition, joined to an eager and ardent thirst after the knowledge of the profession he had chosen, justified the most sanguine hope of his family and numerous friends, and now render doubly distressing the loss they have sustained. A friend, who knew him well, pays this slight tribute to his memory, and tho' his clay cold corpse reposes in the silent dust, and 'soon will his tomb be hid, and the rank grass cover his grave" yet long shall the sweet remembrance of hours passed in his company with D.	08/27/1821
On Sunday morning, of dysentery, Mr. Wm. Alcock, of this city, universally respected.	08/28/1821
On Sunday evening last, Miss Jane Bond, in the 20th year of her age.	08/28/1821

Marriage and Death Notices	Dates
In Talbot county, Mr. Raymond Morris. Capt. John Seth.	08/28/1821
In Caroline county, Philemon Plummer.	08/28/1821
At Norfolk, on board the sloop Abeona, of New London, between sunset on Monday evening, and daylight yesterday morning, Mr. _____ Lucas, mate of said sloop. The captain being sick at lodgings, no person was on board the vessel with him. It is known only, that he appeared unwell on Monday evening, about dark, and went into the cabin, where he was found dead yesterday morning, siting on the floor, with his head leaning on his hand. We learn that he has a family in Baltimore.	08/28/1821
With the most painful feeling of deep felt sorrow, it becomes our melancholy duty, to announce the untimely death of Mr. James Ringould, Jr., who departed this life on the 11th inst., in the 24th year of his age, at the residence of his father, in Kent county, universally beloved and regretted.	08/28/1821
On Sunday evening, the 26th inst., by the Rev. Dr. Kurtz, Mr. D. Frost, to Miss Mary Ann Troutwine, both of this city.	08/28/1821
At Matanzas, on the 20th July, of a malignant fever, Capt. Jeremiah Russel, late of the schooner Rebecca Ann, of Baltimore.	08/29/1821
On Tuesday afternoon last, three miles from Baltimore, on the Frederick road, after a short and painful illness, Miss Mary Ann Baartscheer, in the 15th year of her age, second daughter of Mr. Wm. Baartscheer, of this city.	08/30/1821
On the 7th inst., at the house of John Comegys, Esq., in Sassafras Neck, Cecil, Miss Mary Davis, of Annapolis, daughter of the late Mr. Naylor Davis, of Prince George's county, in the fortieth year of her age.	08/30/1821
At Fredericktown, Mrs. Charlotte Birely, wife of Mr. Valentine Birely, and daughter of Mr. Francis Mantz, of that place.	08/30/1821
At Oak Hill, Randolph county, Illinois, on the 24th ult., Mr. John Ringgold, merchant, of Bellville, to Miss Elizabeth L. Sprigg, both formerly of Maryland.	08/30/1821
On the 22nd instant, Howell Powell, a very respectable native of Talbot county, Maryland, in the 91st year of his age. [There seems to be a great mortality at present on the Eastern Shore of Maryland.]	08/31/1821
At Oakley, within the limits of the city, on Thursday last, Mr. Levi Peirce, Esq., aged 52, and about two hours after, his wife, both of a	09/01/1821

Marriage and Death Notices	Dates
bilious fever. They were both interred in the same grave yesterday. Mr. Peirce was formerly of Boston, but for many years past, a highly respectable citizen of Baltimore. This sudden departure of both father and mother is an incalculable loss to a numerous young family.	
At Dedham, Mass., Elizabeth Mary, wife of Nicholas Murray, late of Baltimore, aged 39.	09/01/1821
Last evening, by the Rev. Mr. Healey, Mr. James B. Scott to Miss Mary W. Woodson, of Virginia.	09/01/1821
On Thursday evening last, by the Rev. Dr. Jennings, Mr. William A. Woodall, to Miss Sarah Cruse, both of this city.	09/01/1821
At Canton, Thursday last, by the Rev. Mr. Bartow, Mr. William Brown, to Miss Ann Maria Smith, all of this city.	09/01/1821
On the 1st inst., Mr. James Johns, in the 34th year of his age, a respectable mechanic of this city.	09/03/1821
At White Haven, in Dorchester county, Levin Richardson, Esq., to Miss Elizabeth, daughter of James Busick, Esq.	09/03/1821
At Greencastle, Pa., Mr. George Strause, of Hagerstown, to Miss Ellen Cromwell, of Baltimore.	09/03/1821
At Hagerstown, Mr. George W. Sands to Miss Maria Cronise. Mr. Jeremiah Leggett to Miss Mary Easterby.	09/03/1821
On Saturday last, Mary Jane, the infant daughter of Capt. John Wightman, aged 18 months.	09/04/1821
It is with deep and heart felt regret, that we have to subscribe upon the funeral obelisk the name of John S. Young. From this sublunary vale, he departed for a better world on the 1st inst. of a rheumatic affection of the head. It being his particular request, the "First Baltimore Sharpshooters," a company he once honored in command, and a detachment of the rifle battalion, under martial insignia, attended his obsequies. Thus ended his mortal pilgrimage. In life possessing an acute sensibility of soul, a mind quick to conceive, and strong in its impulse to every good and honorable action.	09/04/1821
On the 28th ult., after a short illness, at the seat of his father in Prince George's county, John Duvall, Jr., in the 16th year of his age.	09/04/1821

Marriage and Death Notices	Dates
On Saturday morning, by the Rev. Mr. Wyatt, Augustus Thorndyke, Esq., of Boston, to Henrietta, third daughter of Dr. James Steuart, of this city.	09/04/1821
In the Lord, on Friday, August 31st, after an illness of 8 months, Rev. Mr. John L. Phrow, formerly a member of the Methodist Society. Mr. Phrow was a native of Charleston, and had lived 11 years in this city; the exemplary piety of that worthy citizen could not but be noticed with gratitude to God, by his Christian friends. He was a loving husband and a kind parent; he was a faithful friend, and an honest man.	09/05/1821
Suddenly yesterday evening, Mr. William Lovell, Jr., of this city.	09/05/1821
At a period of life, when his character had acquired the utmost stability, his example unusual influence, and his estate the most prosperous condition – when society regarded him with respectful confidence, and his friends with cordial affection, Captain David Warfield, has been called from the possession of such enjoyment, into the eternal world. He died on Saturday, September 1st. We presume not to challenge for him the favorable judgments of heaven, and to him our eulogium would be unavailing. But, if the merchant of stern integrity, the intelligent and warm friend, the manly defender of his country, and the unostentatious but devout Christian, he accepted through redeeming mercy, we are well assured that his transition is a happy one. If these characters be important to society, and entitled to its regard, Capt. Warfield will be long and sincerely lamented. Throughout a long, and often distressing, decline, his gentleness and patience, his firmness and equanimity, never forsook him. And his last hours were employed in acts of the most humble, and impassioned devotion. While to the eye and ear, the melancholy symptoms of approaching dissolution were most apparent; and after it was apprehended that the power of speech had failed him, he was asked by a friend, solicitous for a renewed evidence of his Christian tranquility, if he could express in one word the ground of his confidence and hope. Summoning all his remaining energy, lifting again those eyes soon to open upon the world of spirits, he slowly and firmly pronounced, "I trust in God, through the merits of Jesus Christ." He spoke no more. But he has left to his friends an example to be honored and imitated – to society, the expression of a principle, precious in life, inestimable in death.	09/05/1821
On Monday last, universally regretted, Mr. Aaron Levering, merchant of this city. He left an affectionate wife and five children to lament their irreparable loss.	09/05/1821

Marriage and Death Notices	Dates
On the 29th ultimo, Thomas Palmer, a native of Pennsylvania, for many years a respectable farmer in the vicinity of Baltimore. He had but a few weeks since moved with his family, to reside near the head of the tide on Patapsco, where he was soon seized with a bilious fever; which, in a few days, terminated his earthly career, in the forty-ninth year of his age. Thomas Palmer was an honest man; and much respected as a kind and amiable neighbor. He has left an interesting family, deeply afflicted with a sense of their loss.	09/05/1821
On the 30th ult., Miss Margaret Murdock, in the 20th year of her age. Her mild and amiable disposition renders her much and deservedly regretted by those who knew her.	09/05/1821
Last evening, by the Rev. Mr. Gibson, Mr. Leonard Kernan, to Miss Elizabeth Lowry, all of this city.	09/05/1821
On Saturday evening last, by the Rev. Mr. Bartow, Mr. Thomas Charles Philips, to Miss Mary Brown, all of this city.	09/05/1821
On Monday evening last, by the Rev. Dr. Jennings, Mr. Joseph Loane, to Miss Sarah B. Davis, both of this city.	09/05/1821
On the 4th inst., after a short illness, of the nervous fever, Mr. John Siemers, a native of Germany – he lived respected and died regretted.	09/06/1821
At Carracoa, 7th Aug., Wm. Bolster, a native of Harford county, Md., late mate of the sch. George Washington.	09/06/1821
On Saturday evening last, by the Rev. Mr. Shinn, Mr. Francis Alfred Lorre, to Miss Ann Elizabeth Towson, all of this city.	09/06/1821
Wednesday evening, at Bolton, in the 25th year of her age, Mary Jane, wife of Mr. Thomas Byrum Grundy, and daughter of the late Dr. Bend. Her bereaved husband and three small children have sustained an irreparable loss.	09/07/1821
In Harford county, on Sunday night last, in the 37th year of his age, Mr. James Stirling, eldest son of the late James Stirling, Esq.	09/07/1821
On the 3rd inst., in Charles county, Horatio C. M'Eldery, Esq., of a bilious fever.	09/07/1821
Last evening, by the Rev. Mr. John Snyder, Mr. Wm. Marfield, to Miss Sarah, third daughter of Peter Fowble, Esq., all of this city.	09/07/1821

Marriage and Death Notices	Dates
On Wednesday evening last, by the Rev. Mr. Duncan, Rev. Thomas M. Armstrong, of Chambersburg, to Miss Ellen Campbell, of this city.	09/07/1821
On Thursday night, the 30th ult., at Philadelphia, in the 64th year of his age, of a lingering disease, Col. John F. Mercer, of West River, Md. At a very early age, Col. Mercer took up arms in the defense of his country, and after the close of the war, was sent from Virginia, his native state, as a Delegate to the Old Congress; in which, though one of its youngest members, he was highly respected. On his marriage, he removed to Maryland, where he commenced the practice of the law; but, he was soon appointed by the Legislature of Maryland, a Member of the Convention, which framed our present Constitution, and took a considerable part in the discussion of that body. Some years after, he was chosen a Member of the House of Representatives, from the Congressional District of Maryland; and, after a short interval, and the public voice raised him to the arduous and distinguished station of Governor of the State, and having honorably and impartially fulfilled this duty, he returned to the enjoyments of private life, till he was elected a Member of the House of Delegates in the General Assembly of Maryland – the last public station which he filled. Until increasing and alarming infirmities induced him to visit Philadelphia, for the purpose of consulting Dr. Physick, he continued to reside in the midst of his affectionate family, in elegant hospitality to his friends, in the full enjoyment of his taste for classical literature, in the active dispensation of judicious charities and kindness to those of his neighbours who wanted assistance and relief, and in increasing and securing the respect and love of all who knew him. His remains were, on Saturday morning, deposited in the churchyard of St. Peter's, attended by a number of the respectable citizens of Philadelphia.	09/08/1821
By the Rev. Dr. Glendy, on the 22nd ultimo, Mr. George Brown, to Miss Sarah Condle, all of this city.	09/08/1821
Last Friday evening, at 6 o'clock, Dr. Richard Sex Kingsmore, aged 42 years, a native of England, and long a resident of this city.	09/11/1821
At Norfolk, on the 6th inst., Mr. William G. Barry, hatter, a native of Baltimore.	09/11/1821
At Great Yeomico, Virg., August 2nd, Mr. George Jones, aged 40 years, recently a resident of Baltimore.	09/11/1821
On Friday last, after a short, but painful illness, Mrs. Sarah Stinchcomb, consort of Mr. A. D. Stinchcomb, merchant of this city.	09/12/1821

Marriage and Death Notices	Dates
Died, at Calverton, on Monday morning, 10th inst., Mary Matilda Presbury, daughter of the late George G. Presbury, after a painful and protracted illness of more than two years. Death is at all times an awful visitant, but when youth, and beauty, and innocence, are his victims, we view his ravages with feelings of peculiar poignancy. In the present instance, however, whilst we deplore the premature dissolution of this amiable and interesting young lady, and deeply sympathize with her widowed mother and only sister, in their sad bereavement, we find a delightful consolation in the belief, that her beatified spirit, now associated with angels and celestials, has escaped from a world of sorrow, and suffering, and distress, to regions of eternal and everlasting bliss. Her unusual patience and fortitude, during the sufferings of a lingering and trying consumption – and her confident expressions of hope through the Saviour of the world, until the last moments of her earthly existence, are consoling testimonials to her friends that her immortal soul has winged its flightg to that world where sickness and sufferings are not known. Such instances should not be suffered to pass unnoticed and unimproved, but those who are left behind should be reminded that themselves must soon be called upon to meet this last and most important of human trials, they should examine the state of their own souls, and inquire whether or not they are also ready.	09/12/1821
On Thursday evening last, by the Rev. Mr. Tidings, Mr. Wm. R. Jones, to Miss Jemima Carum, all of this city.	09/12/1821
On the 20th ult., by the Rev. Mr. Dashiell, Mr. John King, to Miss Mary Ann Rice, all of this city.	09/12/1821
On Friday, the 7th instant, in the 69th year of her age, Mrs. Susanna Ireland, widow of the late Edward Ireland, Esq.	09/13/1821
On Friday evening last, the 8th instant, Mrs. Mary Goldthwait, relict of the late Samuel Goldthwait, Esq., in the 58th year of her age, after a lingering illness of many months – throughout which time, with a perfect knowledge of her approaching dissolution, she manifested the greatest resignation to the will of her Heavenly Father, and died in peace and goodwill to all mankind. Her remains were interred in the family burial ground in Garrison Forrest.	09/13/1821
On board the schr. Eagle, on her passage to St. Thomas, Mr. William Reyburn, aged 19 years. Mr. R. was a native of Limerick, Ireland. He had just reached that period of life when a development of character seems to mark the destiny of men. His life has been short, but	09/13/1821

Marriage and Death Notices	Dates
sufficiently long to impress with sorrow, all who knew him. Though in the foaming wave his body sleeps, There is a power that still controls the deeps; Whether he slumbers in the wave or hill, Almighty mercy is his guardian still.	
On Tuesday evening last, by the Rev. Mr. Duncan, Mr. David Kizer, of Baltimore, to Miss Rachel Crawford, daughter of James Crawford, Esq., of Delaware.	09/13/1821
At Alexandria, on Thursday evening last, Thomas John, Esq., of Prince George's county, Maryland, to Miss Anna Maria Seaton, of the former place.	09/13/1821
On Wednesday, the 5th instant, after a short illness, in the 69th year of his age, Capt. Edward Mattingly, an officer of the Revolution. Early in life, he entered the tented field, in defense of our rights, and in the eventful struggle, aided to establish American liberty. He has since lived in retirement, at his residence in St. Mary's county, and it is but right to pronounce upon his memory, the testimony which exalts him to "the noblest work of God" – He was an "honest man."	09/15/1821
On Monday evening, the 10th inst., after a short illness of seven days, Mrs. Evelina, widow of the late Henry Gore, and daughter of Stephen Whalen, near West Friendship, Anne Arundel county, Md. She has left an only son, and a numerous circle of relatives and acquaintances to mourn her irreparable loss.	09/15/1821
In Philadelphia, on the 13th inst., by the Rev. Mr. Ely, Mr. James Watts, of Baltimore, to Miss Rebecca Michael, of the former place.	09/15/1821
On Tuesday evening, the 11th inst., by the Rev. Mr. Henshaw, Robert Riddell, Esq., to Miss Rebecca Amanda Dalrymple, both of this city.	09/15/1821
Last evening, by the Rev. Dr. Jennings, Mr. John Holland, to Miss Jane Ester Finn, all of this city.	09/15/1821
Last evening, by the Rev. Dr. Jennings, Mr. James W. Channell, of this city, to Miss Mary Creamer, of the state of Virginia.	09/15/1821
On Sunday morning, 16th inst., after a short illness, Mr. Eli Munn, formerly of the town of Munson, Mass., and for some years past a respectable teacher in this city.	09/17/1821
On Monday, 10th inst., of a lingering illness, which he bore with	09/17/1821

Marriage and Death Notices	Dates
exemplary fortitude and Christian resignation, Capt. William Fleetwood, aged 40 years, long a respectable ship master out of the port of Baltimore. His last moments were devoted to his Savior and his God, who manifestly gave him an unshakable confidence of his acceptance. He has left a widow to lament the loss of a tender and affectionate husband. Rest from your toils thou son of man, Calmly submit to a Creator's will, Thou knowest thy life is but a span, Thoul't rise above these scenes of ill.	
On the 8th inst., in Richmond county, Va., where she was a few months on a visit, Mrs. Burke, wife of Mr. William Burke, late of this city. It is a painful duty to record the demise of one to whom a husband, three young children, a father, and friends, looked up to for happiness and peace; never did they meet her without experiencing those advantages, and now bereft of her, they can only condole themselves with the pleasing hope, that she is gone to receive a return for those blessings administered to all.	09/17/1821
In Montgomery county, Md., Eliza Painter, wife of John Painter, of that place. We sincerely sympathize with the husband of this afflicting bereavement. No premonitory sickness, no throbs of fiery pain, or cold graduations of decay, gave to the afflicted survivor, intelligence that he was soon to receive, so awful a disposition of Divine Providence. He awoke in the morning and his wife was speechless, and before the sun had shed his last rays, she was cold and lifeless. There is something in such bereavement, more afflicting than death itself – the apoplexy strikes usually but one blow, and the silver chord is loosened, the golden bowl is broke, surviving friends are transported to the grave-yard, they hardly know by what means.	09/17/1821
In the state of Mississippi, on the 6th off August last, Mrs. Elizabeth Norwood, formerly of Baltimore, and daughter of Mrs. Elizabeth Smith, of Baltimore county. By this affective bereavement, the church is deprived of an ornament, the husband of a kind and affectionate consort, and a son of a tender parent; she saw the advance of the king of terrors, supported by faith – she grasped his clay cold hand, and fell asleep in the humble hope of a blessed immortality.	09/18/1821
On Sunday evening last, by the Rev. D. E. Reese, Mr. Frederick Woolf, to Miss Sarah Spedding, all of this city.	09/18/1821
On Thursday evening last, by the Rev. Dr. Glendy, Mr. Philip P. Eckle,	09/18/1821

Marriage and Death Notices	Dates
to Mrs. Mary Crummer, both of this city.	
Last evening, by the Rev. Dr. Roberts, Mr. William Gooding, to Miss Sophia Hutson, both of this city.	09/19/1821
On Tuesday evening, the 18th inst., by the Rev. Mr. Wyatt, Mr. John Pindell, to Miss Charlotte Grimes, both of this city.	09/19/1821
On Friday night, the 14th inst., in the 24th year of her age, much lamented by all who had the pleasure of her acquaintance, Rebecca Prill, after a tedious illness of upwards of two years, which she bore with a patience and resignation never surpassed. In this afflictive dispensation of Divine Providence; this mournful change, from life unto death, how much do the surviving relations and friends of this lady, find cause, seriously to meditate upon the unsubstantial vanities of time, and the real necessity of a due preparation for the all important, invaluable concerns of eternity. It was only the other day, she was in the full enjoyment of youth and bloom and surrounded with worldly interest, common to all of us; and yet now, alas, she is numbered among the silent dead. How humbling to human pride, is such a mournful reality; what a religious and moral lesson does it offer to the gay and the thoughtless. Language is inadequate to do justice to her worth – the hear can only feel it.	09/20/1821
Yesterday, Andrew Price, Esq., for a long time an officer of the county court, deputy in the clerk's office, and a justice of the peace. His knowledge of business enabled him to be very useful in the different offices he filled; and his benevolence was such that he omitted no opportunity of relieving his fellow creatures in distress, whenever he had power to serve them.	09/20/1821
On Wednesday evening, Sept. 19th, after a short illness, in the 51st year of his age, Mr. John Myers, for many years a respectable merchant of this city. He has left an affectionate widow and a numerous circle of friends to lament his loss. It may be truly said he lived and died an honest man, respected and beloved by all who knew him.	09/20/1821
On the 6th inst., in Baltimore county, Hannah Ann Bull, after an illness of 12 days.	09/20/1821
At Hanover, Penn., on the 17th inst., in the 22nd year of her age, Susan, second daughter of Mr. David Forney, of this city. An illness, protracted five years, afforded her an opportunity of testing the truth of that religion, which is the only sure refuge in the day of trouble. Her animated conversation and cheerful deportment, engaged the affection	09/20/1821

Marriage and Death Notices	Dates
of an extensive circle of acquaintances, while her unassuming piety, and the unmurmuring resignation with which she bore her affliction, commanded their sympathy and respect. For some hours previous to her dissolution, she manifested not only an unshaken fortitude, but triumph over the king of terrors, which the full assurance of Christian faith can alone afford. While she exhorted an agonizing mother and weeping friends, not "to sorrow as those without hope," she could exclaim, "I will pass through the valley and shadow of death and fear no evil, thy rod and thy staff shall comfort me." *"He mourns the dead, who lives as they desire."* May her surviving relatives apply to the source, whence her consolation was derived, and they shall not be disappointed. A short space and they shall be re-united, to part no more. A.	
On Sunday evening last, by the Rev. Abner Neal, Mr. Joseph Edmundson, to Miss Susannah G. Hitchcock.	09/20/1821
On Tuesday evening last, by the Rev. Mr. Burgess, Mr. Robert H. Dowson, to Miss Ann Agness, only daughter of Mr. John Deloughery, all of this city.	09/20/1821
On Wednesday evening last, by the Rev. Mr. Finley, Mr. Joshua Fort, to Miss Ann Maria Sands, all of this city.	09/20/1821
On Tuesday evening, the 18th inst., by the Rev. Mr. Wyatt, Jacob G. Davies, Esq., to Mary, youngest daughter of Solomon Betts, Esq.	09/20/1821
On Thursday, the 18th inst., in Queen Ann's county, Mrs. Helen Jones, wife of Mr. Talbot Jones, merchant, of this city. The death of this lady has made a blank which cannot easily be filled up. A numerous family mourn the loss of one of the best wives and mothers – the poor, one of their most active and liberal benefactors – and the church, one of its most zealous and exemplary members. Following the impulse of maternal affection, accompanied by William, her second son, a most amiable and promising youth, she visited the Eastern Shore to watch over the sickbed of a younger child; but by the mysterious dispensation of Him, who wisely and graciously "orders all things," not according to human hopes and expectations, but "according to the counsel of his own will," the object of their solicitude has been spared, while William and his mother have been hurried to a common grave. A numerous circle of acquaintances and friends sympathize with the bereaved family in their sorrows, and unite with them in pouring fourth those tears which affection sheds over the memory of departed worth. "But I would not have you to be ignorant, brethren, concerning them which are asleep, that ye sorrow not even as those which have no hope.	09/20/1921

Marriage and Death Notices	Dates
For, if we believe that Jesus died and rose again, even so them also which sleep in Jesus will God bring with him. Wherefore comfort one another with these words." 1 Thess. 4 ch. 13, 14 and 18 verses.	
At Middle Ridge, Patuxent, Anne Arundel county, Md., on Saturday evening, the 8th inst., after a short and tedious illness, which she sustained with Christian fortitude, Mrs. Rachel I., relict of Capt. James H. Marriott, aged 47 years. Her mild and amiable character had procured her the respect and esteem of all who knew her. She has descended o the grave, honored and lamented, her memory embalmed wih the tears and consecrated to the affecions of many! Her family now plunged in comfortless despair, looked forweard with the most pleasing associations to the enjoymen of years of happiness in her society, and contemplated with delight, the virtues her instrucions would inculcate. As a wife, she was always tender and affectionate; as a mother, deeply impressed with the responsibility attached to her; she performed the principal functions of her situation, in a manner that assured the love of her children, and attracted the admiration of all around her – as a mistress, conspicuous for the exercise of her humanity towards the race of people Providence had provided to her care. Her afflicted family, and all those who had an opporunity of knowing the benevolent feelings of her heart, will long and sincerely regret her loss; itl is however a source of consolation to them to reflect, that although she is removed, her example still may be imitated, enjoining the practice of those irresistible virtues which never fail to engage the affections of mankind. Her last words were, "O what a land I shall inherit." J. W.	09/21/1821
By the Rev. Dr. Glendy, on Thursday last, Mr. John Gardner, to Miss Margaret Blakely, all of this city.	09/22/1821
On Thursday, the 20th inst., Mr. Elias Parks, son of Mr. Maybury Parks, aged 21 years and 7 months.	09/24/1821
On Tuesday, the 7th August, Dr. George W. Pratt, to Miss Susan Keene, both of Caroline county.	09/24/1821
On Tuesday morning, the 25th instant, after a short, but painful illness, which he bore with Christian fortitude, Mr. George Fishwick, in the 22nd year of his age – much lamented by all who knew him.	09/26/1821
On the 20th inst., after a short, but painful illness, in the 64th year of her age, Mrs. Sabina Groff. In life beloved, in death lamented.	09/26/1821
On Tuesday evening, the 25th inst., in the 20th year of her age, Mrs. Mary Ann Thomas, wife of Mr. T. H. Thomas, after the short, but	09/26/1821

Marriage and Death Notices	Dates
painful illness of 36 hours.	
On Thursday evening last, by the Rev. Mr. Larkin, Capt. Isaac Martin, to Miss Ann Dawson, both of this city.	09/26/1821
Suddenly, this morning, Mr. William Diffenderffer, eldest son of Mr. Peter Diffenderffer, aged 33 years. His friends and acquaintances are respectfully invited to attend his funeral, tomorrow morning, at 9 o'clock.	09/27/1821
On Friday evening last, after a long and severe indisposition, Mr. Wendel Michael, long a resident of this city.	09/27/1821
On the 20th inst., at her father's residence, near Washington city, after an illness of five days, Elizabeth Porter, daughter of Commodore David Porter, in the 14th year of her age.	09/27/1821
On Tuesday evening last, by the Rev. Dr. Kurtz, Mr. James A. Willick, to Miss Mary McCullough, all of this city.	09/27/1821
On Tuesday evening last, by the Rev. Mr. Nevins, Mr. George Y. Kelso, to Miss Ellen Rich, daughter of the late Capt. Matthias Rich.	09/28/1821
On Sunday evening last, by the Rev. D. E. Reese, Mr. Amos Davis, to Miss Sarah Payne, both of this city.	09/28/1821
On Thursday evening last, by the Rev. Robert Lusk, of Chambersburg, Pa., Rev. John Gibson, to Elizabeth, second daughter of H. G. Jamison, all of this city.	09/29/1821
On Thursday evening last, by the Rev. Mr. Larkin, Capt. Thomas L. Howell, to Miss Ann Eliza Townsend, all of this city.	09/29/1821
In Baltimore county, on the 27th inst., by the Rev. Mr. Guest, Mr. Charles Ridgely Watts, to Miss Mary Johnson.	09/29/1821
By the Rev. Dr. Glendy, on the evening of Friday, Mr. John Platt, to Miss Mary Gillmore, all of this city.	10/01/1821
On Tuesday evening last, by the Rev. Mr. Smith, Mr. James B. Berry, to Miss Ann Maria Appleby.	10/01/1821
Departed this transitory life, last night, after an illness of 10 days, which she bore with Christian fortitude and perfect resignation to the Divine will, Mrs. Sarah McDonald, consort of Gen. Wm. McDonald, in the 63rd year of her age. Her friends and acquaintances are respectfully invited	10/03/1821

Marriage and Death Notices	Dates
to attend her funeral, from her late dwelling, this afternoon, at four o'clock.	
In Frederick county, Miss Jane Beall, youngest daughter of Mr. Elisha Beall, of that county.	10/03/1821
Yesterday morning, after a short illness, Mr. John Sinclair, a native of Ireland, aged 45 years.	10/04/1821
Departed this life, on Wednesday, the 26th ult., at Milford, Del., Susan, wife of Mr. James Mowbray, formerly of this city, after a severe illness of eight days, which she bore with that fortitude and resignation, which always mark the death-bed of a true Christian.	10/04/1821
On the 3rd inst., Mr. Walter D. Belt, son of Tobias J. Belt.	10/05/1821
Yesterday morning, in the 21st year of his age, after a short illness, Mr. John Dillihunt, Jr., son of Mr. J. Dillehunt, currier, of this city.	10/05/1821
On Wednesday evening, the 3rd inst., after a short illness, contracted on the Eastern Shore, Maryland, Mr. John H. Samuels, of the 32nd year of his age. His memory will be long cherished by those who formed the circle of his acquaintance.	10/05/1821
On the 21st ult., at Mount Ararat, in Cecil county, Catherine Davidson, wife of George Davidson, Esq., in the 36th year of her age. Possessing, in an eminent degree, all the qualities necessary to render her inestimably precious and useful to her husband and children, and endeared connexions, no pen can describe, nor hearts except their own, conceive the loss they have sustained. Her illness was lingering and peculiar distressing; but such was her patience, resignation, and humble confidence in Divine goodness, that her sorrowing relatives have the consolation to believe, that the pure and glorified spirit reposes in the mansions "of rest, in a house not made with hands, eternal in the heavens."	10/05/1821
On Thursday morning, by the Rev. Mr. Bartow, Mr. George Ulrich, of the U. S. navy, to Mrs. Hannah Schneemann, both of this city.	10/05/1821
In Washington county, Md., Mr. G. C. Hamilton, to Miss Amelia Iseminger, both of Funkstown. Mr. Henry Grash to Miss Prudence M. Leggett. Mr. John Bragonier to Miss Susan Cook.	10/05/1821
A very deplorable of the effects of ungovernable human passion, occurred last evening, in Bond street, Fell's Point. A mate of a vessel,	10/06/1821

Marriage and Death Notices	Dates
by name Thomson, had paid his addresses to a young lady, named Hamilton, and it was understood they were contracted. After a conversation with her, as she sat sewing, he blew out her brains with a pistol, and attempted the same outrage upon himself, by firing another, by which he severely wounded himself in the head. He is now in jail, and awaits the investigation of the law. He had prepared himself for the act, by dividing a bullet in halves, and loading the two pistols with the several parts.	
On the 5th inst., Mr. Arthur Cradock, in the 39th year of his age.	10/06/1821
On the 2nd October, at a very advanced age, Mr. John O'Brien, a native of Ireland, but for many years, a useful, upright, and worthy citizen of Washington.	10/06/1821
Last evening, by the Rt. Rev. Bishop Kemp, John C. Delprat, Esq., to Sophia, second daughter of Dr. James Stewart.	10/06/1821
HORRID MURDER! A coroner's inquest was held in Bond st., F. P., at the house of M. John Hamilton, on Friday night, between 9 and 10 o'clock, by Lambert Thomas, Esq., over the body of Miss Ann Hamilton, aged about 15 years. The verdict of the jury was, that *"She came to her death by a pistol ball shot at her by Joseph Thompson, first mate of the hermaphrodite brig Leopard, the ball entering her head behind the right ear, and penetrating into the brain."* As far as the circumstances of this distressing affair have come to our knowledge, I appears that he father of he young lady, about seven o'clock in the evening, came home – he passed through the parlor, in which Thompson and the young lady were sitting. A short time afterwards, while the faher and moher were above stairs, they heard heir daughter cry out, *"My God! Thompson is going to shoot me!"* Alarmed at the expression, they were in the act of descending the stairs, when the report of a pistol was heared – and the mother, who came down first, received her daughter in her arms at the bottom. She was found shot in the head, as stated in the verdict above, and instantly expired. Before the father could pass by his wife and daughter, Thompson had raised another pisol to his own (Thompson's) head, and discharged it. He instantly fell on the floor, but from the after report of the surgeon, who extracted the ball from his head, we learn that the deed was not followed by the mortal consequences intended. Thompson was soon placed in the watch-house, and on Saurday commited to the gaol. The cause which led to the commission of this dreadful act, we understand to be briefly this – Thompson, who boarded in the house, had evinced an affection for the young lady, which was not, it is said, reciprocated on her part; and under the suspicion that she was more	10/08/1821

Marriage and Death Notices	Dates
favorably disposed towards another, he determined to destroy both her life and his own. Since the murder, he has maintained an obstinate silence on all questions put to him. *American*	
Died, on the 6th inst., at his country residence, near Germantown, the venerable Commodore Murray, the senior officer of the Navy of the United States. To the urbanity of a gentleman, he added all the social and religious attributes of a good citizen and sincere Christian.	10/08/1821
On Thursday evening, by the Rev. Dr. Jennings, Capt. David Griffith, to Miss Rebecca James, both of this city.	10/08/1821
On Monday last, by the Rev. Dr. Kurtz, Mr. George F. Womrath, of Philadelphia, to Miss Henrietta, daughter of the late Dr. Herwig, of this city.	10/08/1821
On the 7th inst., after a short illness, Mrs. Eve Ann, consort of Mr. Lewis Kalbfus, Sr., in the 54th year of her age. She was a loving wife and an affectionate mother, and will live in the affections of those who knew her. She has left a disconsolate husband and nine children to mourn their irreparable loss.	10/09/1821
By the Rev. Mr. Sparks, on the 6th inst., John D. Godman, M. D., Prof. of Surgery, in the Medical Institution at Cincinnati, Ohio, to Miss Angelica, daughter of Rembrandt Peale, Esq., of this city.	10/09/1821
On Monday evening, the 1st inst., time closed and eternity dawned upon George Hoffman, having entered a short distance upon the second period of existence – having passed the boundaries of childhood, and not yet entered those of middle age – he was snatched from us at a period of peculiar promise.	10/10/1821
In Frederick county, M. John Dall, in the 46th year of his age. Mrs. Catherine Scholl, in the 46th year of her age. Mr. Adam Shook, in the 71st year of his age. Mr. Peter Bruner, in the 96th year of his age. Miss Susanna Smith, in the 59th year of her age. Mr. Jacob Malambre.	10/10/1821
On the 11th August, at his seat in Chariton county, Missouri, Col. Samuel Williams, a member of the Missouri Legislature. Col. Williams was a native of Maryland – leaving his place of nativity, became a resident of Virginia, from whence he emigrated to Missouri, about two or three years ago.	10/10/1821
On Thursday evening, by the Rev. Mr. Matthews, Mr. James P. Loudon,	10/10/1821

Marriage and Death Notices	Dates
to Miss Harriet M'Donnel, all of this city.	
Last evening, by the Rev. Mr. Gist, George W. Nabb, Esq., of Easton, to Miss Elizabeth D., daughter of Dr. Henry Wilkins, of this city.	10/10/1821
In Talbot county, Capt. David Robinson, of Baltimore, to Miss Margaret S. Lowery, of Talbot. Mr. Michael Winkind to Miss Henrietta Plummer. Mr. William Mullikin, of Caroline county, to Mrs. Mary Brown, of Talbot.	10/10/1821
At the house of Mr. John E. Wall, York st., Mr. Thomas Prendergast, a native of Ireland, after a very tedious and severe illness, which he bore with a patience and resignation seldom equaled, but which in him was only in conformity with his general character and disposition.	10/11/1821
Departed this life, in the 52nd year of her age, Mrs. Marthew M'Clean, consort of Mr. Chas. M'Clean	10/11/1821
Yesterday morning, at 3 o'clock, at Annapolis, the Hon. William Kilty, Chancellor of the State of Maryland, in the 64th year of his age.	10/11/1821
Departed this life, at Mr. Hebert's, on Sunday morning last, of the prevailing fever, Miss Harriet Lenox, of a respectable family and connexions in Baltimore, aged 18 years and seven months. Her family and friends will long lament her loss, to whom she was particularly endeared by the suavity of her temper, obliging disposition, and easy, unaffected manners. She died as sincerely regretted, as she had lived beloved, by all who had the pleasure of her acquaintance. *Norfolk Beacon.*	10/11/1821
Died, on Thursday night, after a very short illness, of malignant fever, Mr. Willis Holt, Printer, of this Borough, but more recently, a Grocer. A young man of good character, and very respectable connexions, who only a few months since had formed a matrimonial connexion, and promised himself much happiness and length of days – but, alas! He has fallen the victim to the indiscretion of moving back into the infected district, before there existed any just cause for the belief, that it had been restored to a more salubrious state.	10/11/1821
At 4 o'clock, this morning, of the prevailing disease, after a short, but severe illness of six days, Mrs. Elizabeth Jury, aged 36 years. She has left a sister and two sons, with a numerous circle of acquaintances to lament her irreparable loss.	10/12/1821

Marriage and Death Notices	Dates
On the 8th inst., in Cecil county, Md., after a short illness, Mr. James Evans, aged 26 years, fourth son of Capt. John Evans, of Robert. He was esteemed and respected by all who knew him. His memory will be long cherished by his mourning friends and relations.	10/12/1821
On the 16th ult., in Frederick county, Independent Gist, eldest son of Gen. M. Gist.	10/12/1821
At Hagerstown, Mrs. Mary Oldwine, in the 57th year of her age. Miss Theresa Gruber, in the 23rd year of her age. Mr. Samuel Beecher, merchant, at an advanced age.	10/12/1821
At Dr. Warfield's, in Anne Arundel county, after a very short and severe illness, aged about 24 years, Mr. Mifflin Thomas, of Kent county, Eastern Shore, Maryland, and late a resident of this city.	10/13/1821
Last Tuesday evening, by the Rev. Mr. Wyatt, Mr. Dan'l Anderson, to Miss Eliza Haskins, all of this city.	10/13/1821
On Thursday evening last, by the Rev. Mr. Valiant, Mr. Charles Hopkins, to Miss Juliana Ferguson, all of this city.	10/13/1821
On the 9th inst., at 12 o'clock A. M., after a severe illness of about 14 days, which he bore with Christian fortitude and resignation, Col. Joshua F. Cockey, in the 57th year of his age. In the last struggles of dissolving nature, he could exclaim, Thy will Lord, and not mine be done. He has left a widow and nine children, together with a wide and extensive circle of relatives and friends to regret and deplore their loss.	10/15/1821
Yesterday morning, Mr. John Price.	10/15/1821
On Thursday evening last, by the Rev. Mr. Henshaw, Mr. William Brundige, merchant, to Miss Rosetta, only daughter of the late James Usher, Esq., all of this city.	10/15/1821
On Sunday evening last, by the Rev. Dr. Jennings, Mr. Thomas Eton, to Miss Ellen Jennings, all of this city.	10/15/1821
On Thursday evening last, by the Rev. J. Guest, the Rev. James Taylor, of Alleghany county, to Miss Meranda Benney, of Baltimore county.	10/15/1821
On Thursday evening last, by the Rev. Mr. Valiant, Mr. Miskimones, to Miss Mary Barton, all of this city.	10/15/1821
Yesterday morning, Mr. Isaac Burneston, merchant, of this city. His remembrance will long be cherished by his fellow citizens, for his mild	10/16/1821

Marriage and Death Notices	Dates
and affectionate manners. He was a correct merchant, an upright man, and devout Christian.	
In Easton, on Thursday last, Thomas Scott Bullitt, late a resident of Baltimore, and younger son of Thomas J. Bullitt, Esq. In the death of this promising young man, his acquaintance have sustained an irreparable loss, and a pang has been afflicted upon his relatives and friends, which time may assuage, but can never remove.	10/16/1821
On Thursday evening last, by the Rev. Mr. Moranville, Mr. Michael Dunn, to Miss Bridget Haslin, all of this city.	10/16/1821
On Sunday evening last, by the Rev. Mr. Bartow, Mr. Timothy Kelly, of North Carolina, to Mrs. Elizabeth Fletcher, of this city.	10/17/1821
"How oft death's solemn knell alarms our ear, *How many friends, on all sides, disappear!* *Snatched from earth's pleasures, to the rueful tomb,* *Mindless, perhaps, of their eternal home;* *Almighty Being! Ere from time we fly,* *Teach us life's greatest lesson, how to die."* Departed this life, on the evening of the 17th inst., in the 39th year of his age, William H. Windstanly, long a respectable merchant of this city. During a peculiarly painful, distressing, and lingering illness, which he sustained with the patience of a Job, his mind was serene and resigned to the will of his Heavenly Redeemer. Besides an affectionate and tender wife and many friends, who lament his death, he has left a family of little children, whose tender age will doubly experience the loss of an attentive and kind parent.	10/18/1821
On Sunday last, at her residence, near Westminster, in the 69th year of her age, Mrs. Mary Winchester, relict of the late William Winchester, Esq., of this city.	10/18/1821
On the 12th inst., by the Rev. Mr. Helfenstein, Mr. Reese Williams, to Miss Ellen Davis, of Baltimore county.	10/18/1821
On the 12th inst., by the Rev. Mr. Helfenstein, Mr. Martin Tschudy, to Miss Elizabeth Price.	10/18/1821
On the 3rd inst., by the Rev. Mr. Piper, Mr. Jacob Erhardt, of York county, Pa., to Miss Ann Patterson, of this place.	10/18/1821
In Harford county, on Tuesday evening, the 9th inst., by the Rev. Mr.	10/18/1821

Marriage and Death Notices	Dates
Richardson, Mr. Jesse Hollingsworth, to Miss Gulielma Maria Spice.	
On the 14th inst., Mrs. Keller, the wife of George Keller, of Fell's Point. She has been, for upwards of twelve months lingering with the consumption, and died with the same disease.	10/19/1821
At Snowhill, on the 8th inst., Mr. James Taylor, a respectable inhabitant of that place.	10/19/1821
On Tuesday evening, at the Roman Catholic Church, by the Rev. Roger Smith, Mr. Bartholomew Cronigin, of this place, to Miss Frances Lohary, of Harford county.	10/19/1821
On Tuesday evening last, by the Rev. Dr. Roberts, Samuel Dorsey, Esq., of Baltimore county, to Miss Mary, eldest daughter of Wm. Wilkins, Jr., of this city.	10/19/1821
Yesterday, in the 45th year of her age, Mrs. Elizabeth Geddis, a native of Ireland, relict of the late Capt. David Geddis, formerly of this city.	10/20/1821
On Tuesday evening last, Mrs. Eleanor Gardner, late relict of Mr. George Gardner leaving a disconsolate husband and six small children to mourn her irreparable loss.	10/20/1821
On the 12th inst., Gen. John Ross Key, an officer of the Revolution, and a respectable inhabitant of Frederick county, in the State of Md.	10/20/1821
On Friday, 19th ult., Dr. Thomas Cradock, in the 70th year of his age, long a Practitioner in Baltimore county.	10/20/1821
At Centreville, Maryland, on the 13th inst., Miss Ann Faulkner, aged 17 – a young lady whose virtues and qualifications had gained the respect of her acquaintance, and the affection of her friends. Those who mourn her should not mourn as those, who will not be comforted. To be taken from this world, at an age before trouble could have deeply invaded repose, in the purity of youth, and the glow of hope, is indeed apparently distressing – but religion affords the high consolation, that the departed profits by the change, and that it is only on their own account, that the survivors should lament the loss of her society, and the blasting of their expectations.	10/20/1821
On Thursday afternoon, the 27th ult., Master Class Ringelds, of a fever which is at present prevalent.	10/20/1821
On Thursday evening, by the Rev. Mr. Nevins, Mr. Robert Lyon, Jr., to	10/20/1821

Marriage and Death Notices	Dates
Miss Mary C. Latimer.	
In Kent county, E. S., Md., on Tuesday evening, 9th inst., by the Rev. Mr. Smith, Mr. James Hodges, to Miss Mary Ringgold, both of that county.	10/20/1821
On Saturday last, at 6 o'clock P. M., of a pulmonary complaint, Mr. Theodore C. Proebsting, in the 40th year of his age. His friends and acquaintance are respectfully invited to attend his funeral, from his late dwelling, at 3 o'clock, this afternoon.	10/22/1821
Yesterday, Mrs. Hannah Foster, in the 42nd year of her age, wife of Benjamin W. Foster, of this city. The funeral will take place this afternoon, at 2 o'clock – friends and acquaintance are requested to attend.	10/22/1821
On the 20th inst., Mr. Richard Waddington, aged about 27 years. He passed those years in humble life; but was one of those whose conduct proves, "That an honest man is the noblest work of the Creator." The deceased was a member of the Franklin Lodge of Independent Odd Fellows, and his remains were respectfully followed to their long home, by a numerous band of his brothers of the Washington and Franklin Lodges. "The Lord giveth and the Lord taketh away, and blessed be the name of the Lord."	10/22/1821
On Thursday, the 4th inst., by the Rev. Geo. Luckey, Mr. John Rutledge, to Miss Belina Bull, both of Baltimore county.	10/22/1821
On Tuesday last, at his residence, near Baltimore, Mr. Joseph Auguste Larouraudais, in his 55th year. This gentleman was formerly a rich planter in the island of St. Domingo, and resided for the last thirty years in this country, much beloved by his friends and respected by all who knew him.	10/23/1821
On the 11th inst., by the Rev. Mr. Tidings, Mr. Jonathan Hayworth, to Miss Mary Ann Randall, both of this city.	10/23/1821
On Sunday evening last, by the Rev. Dr. Roberts, Mr. Levi Robb, to Miss Elizabeth Forney, all of this city.	10/23/1821 10/24/1821
Yesterday morning, Mrs. Margaret McPherson, in the 38th year of her age, wife of Mr. Jonas McPherson, of this city.	10/24/1821
On Monday, the 22nd inst., after a short, but painful illness, which he	10/24/1821

Marriage and Death Notices	Dates
bore with Christian fortitude, Mr. Silas Penniman, of Baltimore, in the 43rd year of his age, formerly a merchant of Boston, in which character he was respected and honored by all who knew him. Such is life, a fleeting shadow, For man's illusion given.	
In Talbot county, on Thursday morning last, after a short, but painful illness, Miss Mary Ann Mullikin, in the 18th year of her age.	10/24/1821
On the 10th inst., at her residence, near Snow Hill, Md., Mrs. Sophia Tarr, after a short, but severe illness, in the 71st year of her age leaving an only daughter, with many relatives, to mourn their irreparable loss.	10/24/1821
On Saturday, the 20th inst., near Westminster, Frederick county, of a bilious fever, Mrs. Elizabeth Reese, consort of Mr. Andrew Reese. She was esteemed and respected by all who were acquainted with her.	10/24/1821
On Tuesday evening last, by the Rev. John M. Duncan, Mr. Robert Beveridge, merchant, to Miss Anna Maria, daughter of Mr. David Forney.	10/26/1821
On Monday last, the 22nd inst., after a short illness, John Spicknall, Sr., in the 74th year of his age. He was a native of Calvert county, Md., but for the last ten or twelve years resided in this city. Blest with a constitution uncommonly strong, he arrived at an age attained but by a few, but notwithstanding which he fell at length beneath the stroke of the common enemy. Reader, prepare to follow him, for "in such an hour ye think not, the Son of Man cometh."	10/26/1827
At Annapolis, Mr. John L. Levely, formerly of Baltimore.	10/26/1827
Mr. Hezekiah Dunn, of Baltimore, aged 32.	10/26/1827
At Joshua Crump's, in the city of Richmond, on Tuesday, the 16th inst., James Lorman, aged 19 or 20 years, lately of Pittsburgh, and last from the city of Baltimore.	10/26/1827
On Thursday evening last, by the Rev. Mr. Whitfield, Mr. Philip Prehol, to Miss Ann M. Britton, all of this city.	10/27/1821
On Tuesday evening last, by the Rev. John Hagerty, Mr. James Malone, of New York, to Miss Mary Ann Johnson, of Annapolis, Maryland.	10/27/1821
On Thursday evening last, by the Rev. Mr. Nevins, Mr. William H. Murray, Esq., to Miss Isabella Maria Stirling, daughter of the late James	10/27/1821

Marriage and Death Notices	Dates
Stirling, Esq., of this city.	
On Saturday morning last, by the Rev. Mr. Whitfield, Mr. Lewis Webb, to Miss Elizabeth Devouroux, both of this city.	10/29/1821
On Wednesday evening, the 24th inst., at Charleston, Va., by the Rev. Mr. Bryan, Mr. Samuel F. Merrett, merchant of Baltimore, to Mary Elizabeth, youngest daughter of the late George Hite, Esq., of the former place.	10/29/1821
On Saturday evening last, by the Rev. Dr. Roberts, Mr. James Wilson to Miss Elizabeth Jones, all of Baltimore county.	10/29/1821
On Thursday evening last, by the Rev. Mr. Hinkle, Mr. Henry Allen, to Miss Sarah Willis, both of this city.	10/29/1821
On Thursday evening last, by the Rev. Dr. Roberts, Mr. Joseph Ruddock, of this city, to Miss Rebecca, daughter of D. S. Stellwagen, Esq., U. S. N., Philadelphia.	10/29/1821
On Monday evening last, by the Rt. Rev. Bishop Kemp, William Stewart, Esq., to Charlotte, daughter of the Hon. Wm. Pinkney.	10/31/1821
Last evening, by the Rev. Mr. Burgess, Lt. William H. Mann, U. S. Army, to Miss Marian S. M'Keane, of this city.	10/31/1821
At the residence of his brother, in Baltimore, on the evening of the 25th inst., after a few days illness, Thomas Bunyie, in the 22nd year of his age.	11/01/1821
In Frederick county, John Woodrow, Esq., formerly surveyor of that county. Mr. Edward Eastburn, aged 19 years. Mr. John Ecker, in the 75th year of his age.	11/01/1821
On the 26th ult., in Worcester county, Md., James Direckson, Esq., to Miss Henrietta Purnell, daughter of Littleton Purnell, Esq.	11/01/1821
At Fredericktown, Mr. David B. Devitt to Miss Agnes Mantz.	11/01/1821
In Talbot county, Mr. Thomas Martin to Miss Elizabeth Ruth. Mr. Lobert Covey to Miss Mary Vinton.	11/01/1821
"Heaven gives us friends to bless the present scene, *"Removes them, to prepare us for the next."* Died at the U. S. Navy Yard, Gosport, on the afternoon of the 19th instant, Mr. John J. Burke, of this city, in the 22nd year of his age. This	11/01/1821I

Marriage and Death Notices	Dates
in the midst of happiness and in the bloom of youth, has this young gentleman terminated his mortal career. As a son, he was affectionate – as a brother, he was tender – as a friend, he was sincere – and as a companion, he was amiable. His noble and generous disposition, his moral and intellectual accomplishment, and the suavity of his manners, particularly endeared him to those who had the pleasure of knowing him. In the true faith of a Christian, he expired, and, as such, we hope, his soul has winged its flight to the dwellings of eternal bliss. "To honor's dictates, proudly true, Of noble and exalted mind, He practiced all the good he knew, And left a spotless name behind."	
In Washington county, Md., Mr. John Ankeney, in the 23rd year of his age. Mrs. Amelia Boteler. Mr. Abraham Rowland. Mr. Elijah Leisure. Mr. David Westenberger. Miss Elizabeth Whitney, of Hagerstown. Joseph Keller, Esq., formerly of the Hagerstown bar.	11/02/1821
On Thursday morning last, by the Rev. Dr. Jennings, George Mr. Austen, to Caroline, daughter of Geo. Milleman, Esq.	11/04/1821
At his residence, in Queen Ann's county, at an advanced age, Joseph George, Esq.	11/05/1821
Last evening, by the Rev. Mr. Hinkle, Mr. James West, to Miss Elizabeth West, both of this city.	11/05/1821
On Thursday night, the 1st November, of a consumption, Mrs. Elizabeth Talbot, wife of Mr. Edward Talbot, in the 27th year of her age, and although she filled all the relaions of life as an affectionate wife – tender mother – faithful friend – and kind neighbor, with propriety well worthy of imitation; yet, how she met the King of Terrors, is of far greater importance – and the writer of this is happy, to have it in his power to say, that although the cares and concerns of maturity, and the married life, had in a painful degree, interrupted her attention to, and her ardent concern about the religion of Jesus; which it was believed by herself, and her friends, she was made a partaker of when very young – yet that gracious Godwho never leaves a good work of grace unfinished, was pleased on the near approach of death, to revive in her soul, an earnest concern about her state, which made her exceedingly anxious after the word of instruction and comfort; and it is confidently hoped that he who comforts all that mourn, that he who despiseth not the sighing of the needy, who hath promised that their hearts shall live who seek God, was pleased to grant her the desire of her heart, and shew himself so gracious, as to enable her to break out in a believing admiration of "a	11/06/1821

148

Marriage and Death Notices	Dates
precious Jesus, as the chiefest of ten thousand," "and altogether lovely," and call upon all about her to celebrate his praise, in which she attempted to join, but Hosannahs languish'd on her dying tongue. This was but a few hours before her spirit departed from her enfeebled tabernacle, to be with Christ, where immortal vigor forever excludes incapacity to praise. Her departure took place on her wedding night, from which we may learn the fleeting and uncertain nature of all earthly felicity. We may also learn from this brief narrative to admire the great faithfulness of God. He is indeed, "abundant in goodness" "and in truth, forgiving iniquity, transgression, and sin." Your hearts shall live that seek God. Live, when the harden'd sinner dies, Live, when the earth, and sea, and skies, Shall burn, and vanish at his word, E'en then, they'll live, who seek the Lord!	
Departed this life, on Sunday evening, the 4th inst., Mr. William Bruff, of this city, in the 45th year of his age.	11/06/1821
Died at St. Augustine, East Florida, of the sickness prevalent at that place, on the 10th ult., Mrs. Eliza Ann Evour, and on the 15th ult., Mr. Richard W. Edes, daughter and son of Mr. Peter Edes, of this city, and formerly of Maine. The Rev. Divine, who communicated the afflicting intelligence to the distressed parents and relatives of the deceased in this city, observes "Amidst your sorrows, it will be a solace to you when you learn, that your children departed this life in the strong and comfortable hope of Salvation through a Redeemer. They also left behind them a good name amongst their numerous neighbors and the character of useful citizens. Their loss is much lamented by the people here; and we consider the death of Mr. Edes, in particular, as a public calamity. He had just established a printing office, which bid fair to be useful to the inhabitants as well as beneficial to himself." Mr. Edes was proprietor and editor of the Florida Gazette.	11/06/1821
At the residence of L. Miller, Esq., at Elkton, Md., Miss Caroline M. Favier, of this city. Possessing the qualifications calculated to endear her to society, the loss of this amiable young lady has left a void in the hearts of her acquaintance which can never be filled. Our dearest friends are given us by our Maker, to sweeten the cup of bitterness below, and this said hath he cometh to demand the loan of nature, in an hour we know not. Then let us like Caroline be ready to *"meet the Master when he calleth."* In the possession of that religion, which prepares our souls for the presence of our God, she beheld death as but the commencement of her joys, and left her tenement of clay, but to	11/07/1821

Marriage and Death Notices	Dates
receive from her Savior, the welcome of *"Well done, good and faithful servant, enter unto the joy of the Lord."*	
At New Orleans, John Baker, of Baltimore, aged 22.	11/07/1821
Last evening, by the Rev. Mr. Henshaw, Mr. David G. M'Coy, to Miss Eliza H., daughter of Richard H. Jones, Esq., all of this city.	11/07/1821
Last evening, by the Rev. Greenbury Ridgely, Mr. Archibald Campbell, of Morristown, N. J., to Miss Sarah Goldsmith, of this city.	11/07/1821
In Talbot county, Mr. William Slaughter to Miss Ann Dudley.	11/07/1821
In Montgomery county, Mr. John A. Howard to Miss Louisa S. Jamison.	11/07/1821
Suddenly, about three miles from Hagerstown, Mr. Joseph Kellar, in the 36 year of his age.	11/08/1821
In Williams-Port, Mr. Edmund H. Turner, a worthy and useful citizen of that place.	11/08/1821
By the Rev. Dr. Glendy, on the evening of Saturday last, Mr. John Corvine, to Miss Elizabeth Mumma, all of this city.	11/08/1821
Mr. Henry Firey, Jr. to Miss Martha Miller, both of Washington county.	11/08/1821
At Funkstown, Mr. Jacob Geiger, of the state of Kentucky, to Miss Eliza Geiger, of the city of Baltimore.	11/08/1821
This morning, at 1 o'clock, after a painful illness, which she bore with Christian fortitude, Mrs. Ann Fifer, in the 66th year of her age. Her friends and acquaintance are invited to attend her funeral, from her late dwelling, No. 103 Green street, Old Town, tomorrow afternoon, at 2 o'clock.	11/10/1821
By the Rev. Dr. Glendy, on the evening of Wednesday last, Mr. John Irvine, of Cecil county, to Miss Elizabeth Laudsberry, of this city.	11/10/1821
On Thursday evening, by the Rev. Dr. Roberts, Mr. Joseph Stevens, merchant, to Miss Caroline Barnes, all of this city.	11/10/1821
On Thursday morning last, by the Rev. Dr. Jennings, Mr. Orville Carpenter, to Miss Ann Hassan, both of this city.	11/10/1821
On Tuesday evening, by the Rev. Mr. Bartow, Mr. Martin Peterson, to	11/10/1821

Marriage and Death Notices	Dates
Miss Catherine Pope, both of this city.	11/12/1821
On Thursday morning last, at his farm, on South River, after a short, but severe illness, Richard Mackubin, Esq., of Anne Arundel county, in the 59th year of his age.	11/14/1821
In Fredericktown, Md., Miss Mary Carlin, in the 26th year of her age, after an illness of three weeks. Mr. William Birely, a worthy, honest, and useful citizen.	11/14/1821
Very suddenly, on Wednesday evening last, Mr. John Remsberg, of Frederick county. Mr. Remsberg was, to all appearance, in his usual health, and while speaking to his wife was struck dead, before he had completed the sentence on his lips!	11/14/1821
On Wednesday last, at his residence, in Denton, Md., Mr. Alexander Maxwell, at an advanced age.	11/14/1821
In Talbot county, very suddenly, Mr. Henry Casson.	11/14/1821
Last evening, by the Rev. Asa Shinn, Mr. James Williams, to Miss Mary M., eldest daughter of Mr. Jacob Myers, all of this city.	11/14/1821
On Tuesday evening last, by the Rev. Mr. Henshaw, at "Pilgrims Choice" near Baltimore, Mr. William Lippincott, merchant of Philadelphia, to Mrs. Christiana Barnes, daughter of William Pechin, Esq., of the former place.	11/14/1821
In Talbot county, Md., Mr. John Fleming, to Mrs. Jane Delehay. Mr. Woolman Porter to Miss Sally Hoxter. Mr. William Blake to Mrs. Elizabeth Harden.	11/14/1821
On Tuesday, the 2nd inst., in the 57th year of his age, the Rev. John Weems, late Rector of Port Tobacco Parish, Md., in which he was an officiating minister of the Protestant Episcopal Church, more than thirty years.	11/15/1821
On the 23rd ult., at Richmond, on his way from Baltimore to Augusta, Sidney H. Burrough, Esq., formerly of Providence, R. I.	11/16/1821
On Thursday evening last, by the Rev. Mr. Tidings, Mr. Alexander Gaddess, of Virginia, to Miss Mary Ann, eldest daughter of Mr. John Weatwood, of this city.	11/16/1821
On Wednesday evening last, by the Rev. Mr. Tidings, Mr. George	11/16/1821

Marriage and Death Notices	Dates
Beatty, to Miss Sarah Hussey, all of this city.	
Last evening, by the Rev. Mr. Smith, Mr. George S. Boarman, of Charles county, to Miss Rebecca, first daughter of Mr. Ignatius Boarman, of this city.	11/16/1821
On Thursday, the 15th inst., William H. Woods, late of Wm. & A. H. Woods, aged 27 years. He has left a disconsolate wife and 4 children to lament his loss.	11/17/1821
In Baltimore, on the 16th inst., of an apoplectic fit, Mr. Francis Cressot, in the 40th year of his age.	11/17/1821
On the 12th inst., at the residence of Isaac Duckett, Esq., of Prince George's county, his only daughter, Mrs. Eliza Contee, the wife of John Contee, Esq. The untimely death of so amiable a member of society, will long be felt in the circle of her friends, and sincerely lamented even by those least acquainted with her. Delicate in her form, affectionate in her disposition, and prudent in every action, all who knew her were her friends. Few parents and husbands have had more reason to mourn over the fall of their hopes, than those who stood in that endearing relation with the deceased. She has left four children surviving her.	11/17/1821
On Thursday evening last, by the Rev. Mr. Healey, Mr. Alexander Sterrett, to Miss Rosanna Ellis, all of this city.	11/17/1821
Last evening, by the Rev. Dr. Roberts, Mr. William Clarke, to Miss Isabella Winchester.	11/19/1821
On Wednesday evening last, at Evergreen, by the Rt. Rev. Bishop Kemp, the Rev. Charles Austin, to Ann, daughter of William Buckler, Esq., both of Baltimore county.	11/20/1821
On the 19th inst., Charlotte Williams, aged six years, daughter of Mr. Benjamin Williams, of Gay street, Bridge Hotel.	11/22/1821
On Sunday, 18th inst., Capt. Samuel Pour, for many years a respectable inhabitant of this city.	11/22/1821
On Tuesday evening last, by the Rev. Mr. P. Smith, Mr. Frederick Gustavus Briscoe, to Mrs. Jemima Blackstone, both of Kent county, Md.	11/22/1821
At Easton, Md., Mr. Charles M. Bromwell to Mrs. Pamela F. M'Ginnis.	11/22/1821

Marriage and Death Notices	Dates
On Wednesday, the 21st inst., in the 66th year of her age, Mrs. Wilhelmina Hunt, late consort of Samuel C. Hunt, Esq., of Baltimore county leaving a numerous circle of relatives, friends, and acquaintance, to mourn their irreparable loss.	11/23/1/21
On the 10th inst., in the 60th year of his age, Mr. Henry Boswell, Collector of the Customs, at the port of Nottingham, P. George's county, after a long and painful illness, which he bore with Christian fortitude.	11/23/1/21
On Saturday last, in the 25th year of his age, Mr. William Cheston, a young gentleman, greatly beloved by all who had the pleasure of his acquaintance. Thus have we seen the fairest prospects of the young and the fondest hopes of a parent blasted – and thus, the holy bond of friendship severed. Long will acquaintance mourn their loss – oft will friendship drop a tear to his memory.	11/23/1821
At his residence, in Charles county, Md., on the 14th inst., Capt. Thomas Jenkins, aged 71. His early life was devoted to the sea, and during our Revolutionary struggle, he had the misfortune to be captured by the enemy, and lay nine months a prisoner at New York, on board the memorable old Jersey; there after suffering all the horrors of disease and want, he was sent on shore to die of a malignant fever, contracted on board the prison-ship, but, by the aid of a strong constitution, and the protecting hand of Providence, was restored to health and his friends. Several years after this he married, and raised a numerous family of children, six sons and two daughters. To the characteristic bluntness and rough manners of a sailor, he united the most rigid principles of probity, with the finest feelings of humanity. Respected and esteemed by his neighbors, revered and beloved by his children, and numerous relatives, he died lamented by all, but by none more than the poor of his neighborhood, who can with sorrowful truth say, we have lost a friend. This is no panegyric, it is simply the truth, and known to be such by the whole circle of his friends.	11/23/1821
At sea, on his passage from Virginia, the 20th of Aug., Capt. Wallace, of the ship Sibson, 6 days after sailing.	11/23/1821
On Tuesday evening last, by the Rev. Mr. Tidings, Mr. John Myers, to Miss Catherine Finn, daughter of Mr. Wm. Finn, all of this city.	11/23/1821
On Sunday morning last, by the Rev. Dr. Roberts, Mr. Zebulon Hewit, of Elkton, Md., to Miss Mary Evang, of this place.	11/23/1821

Marriage and Death Notices	Dates
In Hagerstown, Mr. Jacob Freize, to Miss Harriet Bubb. Mr. David Nyeswander to Miss Susan Slooker. Mr. Henry Gower to Miss Elizabeth Kelly.	11/23/1821
On Tuesday, the 20th, by the Rev. Mr. Allen, at Abington, Harford county, Mr. Ebenezer N. Allen, to Miss Alicia Marvina Monks, both of that county.	11/23/1821
At Edwardsville, Ill., on the 23rd ult., Mr. George Pogue, of Baltimore, in the 23rd year of his age, late of the firm R. & H. Pogue.	11/24/1821
At Mobile, on the 20th ult., Dr. Edward Pannel, in the 34th year of his age, a native of Baltimore.	11/24/1821
At New Market, Frederick county, Mr. Francis D. Wayman, in the 24th year of his age.	11/24/1821
Near Charlestown, Va., Mr. Leonard Jamison, late of Frederick county, Md.	11/24/1821
On Monday, the 19th inst., at his seat, at Notley Hall, Prince George's county, Md., Dr. Wm. A. Dangerfield. His spirit has fled to another region, where virtue like his can alone find their just reward.	11/24/1821
On Thursday evening last, by the Rev. Mr. Dashiell, Mr. Joseph G. Moore, to Miss Margaret Aller, all of this place.	11/24/1821
On Thursday evening last, by the Rev. Mr. Helfenstein, Mr. William Wall, to Miss Hannah Gover.	11/24/1821
In Harford county, Md., Mrs. Sarah, wife of Mr. Samuel Bevard, aged about 28 years. On the same day, an infant child of the deceased. Also, on the same day, Mrs. Sarah, wife of Mr. John Wright, and mother of the deceased, Mrs. Bevard, aged about 68 years. The day following, the three bodies were conveyed in the same hearse to a neighboring burying ground, and all deposited in the same grave.	11/24/1824
Mr. Athel Stuart, aged about 43 years, of Talbot county.	11/26/1821
In Cumana Roads, 23rd Sept., Capt. James Barnes, of the Columbian brig of war Vancedor, a native of Baltimore. He was buried with military honors, and a notice was published by Gen. Bermudez, that his family would be provided for by the government.	11/26/1821
On the 18th of August, at Granite place, near Aberdeen, Scotland,	11/26/1821

Marriage and Death Notices	Dates
William Duger, Esq., late of Baltimore.	
Mr. Charles M. Bromwell to Mrs. Pamela F. M'Ginney, all of Talbot county.	11/26/1821
At Boston, by the Rev. Mr. Peirpont, Mr. Christopher Johnson, of Baltimore, to Miss Eliza Gates, formerly of Baltimore.	11/26/1821
At Cambridge, Dorchester county, Md., Benjamin W. Lecompte, Esq., in the 35th year of his age, for several years, a leading federal member of the House of Delegates, generally esteemed as a man of talent, and a good citizen and Christian.	11/27/1821
At Chancellor's Point, Talbot county, Mrs. Mary Ross.	11/29/1821
By the Rev. Dr. Glendy, on the evening of Tuesday last, Mr. Hance Warley, to Miss Eve Barton, all of this city.	11/29/1821
On Saturday evening last, by the Rev. Mr. Healey, Thomas Radford to Miss Grace Davidson, all of this city.	11/29/1821
On the 28th inst., Eleanor, wife of Isaac Atkinson, of this city, in the 45th year of her age, after a lingering illness, which she bore with patience and resignation.	11/30/1821
At the Island of St. Thomas, in the beginning of Nov. last, Mr. Henry L. Maund, of Alexandria, Va., in the 23rd year of his age.	12/01/1821
At Havana, on the 13th November, after an illness of two days, Capt. Job D. Porter, of the schooner Gen. Jackson, of this port. Capt. Porter was a native of Salem, Mass. And had, by his urbanity of manners, gained the estimation of all who knew him. He has left a wife and several children to mourn the loss of a kind husband and affectionate father.	12/01/1821
At Batavia, India, Mr. J. L. Bessell, Mr. Charles Stout, and Mr. Thomas Mason, all of Salem; Mr. Thomas Davis, Jr., of Beverly.	12/01/1821
Departed this life, in St. Mary's county, on the 5th November, Miss Alice Keech, in the morning and bloom of her days. Short, though extremely painful and excrutiating was the illness which terminated her earthly career. Her sufferings were supported with that Christian fortitude and patient resignation which characterize the meek and humble followers of the lamb. She had been convinced for some years of the vanity and transitory nature of all sublunary enjoyments and had yielded herself willingly to the free and sovereign grace of God. In her life, she manifested many of those graces which evidence the devout	12/01/1821

Marriage and Death Notices	Dates
Christian; and in her death she experienced the sweet consolations of religion, and evinced that faith and hope which animates the souls of the just, and enables them to triumph in the awful hour when suffering nature is breathing its last. These few remarks are made by one who well knew her worth, and wishes to pay a just tribute of respect to her memory. Alhough he does not expect that those who frequent the busy haunts of life will be arrested in their awful course, by a short obituary notice, yet he cannot neglect this most favorable opportunity to warn the thoughtless, the young, and the gay; and he humbly hopes that her youthful companions in particular will be admonished to imitate her repentance, her piety, and her virtues. While her memory is fondly cherished by her afflicted relatives and mourning friends, may her virtues become the ornament of many a female character, and her death be made effectual to the awakening, conversion, and salvation of many a soul.	
On Thursday evening last, by the Rev. John M. Duncan, Mr. Alexander K. M'Daniel, to Elizabeth, only daughter of Mr. Joshua Evans, all of this city.	12/01/1821
In Harford county, Md., Mr. Henry Whittemore, to Miss Mary Bell. Mr. Thomas T. Bond to Miss Mary Ann Bond. In Abingdon, Mr. Ralph Clark to Miss Eliza C. Monks.	12/01/1821
On the 25th inst., at her father's house in Georgetown, Miss Sally Ford, aged about 20. I feel no other interest than as a common Christian in saying that my eyes never before saw a more interesting vision. She was Nun of the order of Emmittsburg, and trained in her assimilated virtues under the auspices of the accomplished, fatherly, and tender superior of the order, Mr. Du Bois. If any one ever found a nearer way to the throne of grace, it must be, we may naturally conclude, by some secret tract – some hidden or concealed way, which only the swift messengers of Heaven are allowed to travel. *Geo. Metrop.*	12/03/1821
On Sunday evening last, by the Rev. Mr. Kurtz, Mr. Henry Claridge, of Baltimore, to Miss Margaret Rutter, late of Lancaster, Pa.	12/03/1821
In Montgomery, by the Rev. A. H. Dashiell, Mr. Zadock Cook, to Miss Rebecca D. Magruder, daughter of the late D. Z. Magruder.	12/03/1821
On Sunday morning last, after a short, but painful illness, Mrs. Selina Bangs, consort of Mr. John Bangs. Her exemplary Christian life, and her unassuming deportment, had endeared her to a large circle of acquaintance, who will long deplore her loss.	12/04/1821

Marriage and Death Notices	Dates
At Patterson, New Jersey, by the Rev. Mr. Fisher, Mr. James Richards to Miss Henrietta Maria Robinson, eldest daughter of the late Wm. Robinson, of this city.	12/04/1821
On Friday evening last, by the Rev. Mr. Henshaw, Mr. William Hamilton, of Edinburg, Scotland, to Miss Mary Clayton, of this city.	12/05/1821
On Tuesday evening last, by the Rev. Dr. Glendy, Robert S. Hollins, Esq., to Cordelia Margaret, daughter of Cumberland Dugan, Esq., all of this city.	12/05/1821 12/08/1821
At Easton, Md., Mr. John G. Thomas, of Talbot county, to Miss Mary E. Dimond, of Queen Ann's county.	12/05/1821 12/11/1821
On Sunday, the 2nd inst., in the 21st year of her age, Anne Handy, consort of Wm. Handy. During her long and painful illness, she manifested the most perfect resignation to the will of her Heavenly Father. She was endeared to all who had the pleasure of her acquaintance, by her mild and amiable disposition. She has left a numerous circle of relatives and friends to mourn her loss.	12/06/1821
At Elk Ridge, Anne Arundel county, on Tuesday evening, the 4th inst., by the Rev. Dr. Adalot, Geo. S. Stockett, Esq., to Christiana, second daughter of John Thompson, Esq.	12/08/1821
At Hagerstown, Dr. John J. Hays, of Washington county, to Miss Sophia B. Pottenger, late of Prince George's county.	12/08/1821
In Washington county, Md., Mr. John Daniel to Miss Catherine Hose.	12/08/1821
At New Orleans, on the 15th November, in the 23rd year of his age, Dr. Charles Sloan, youngest son of James Sloan, Esq., of this city.	12/11/1821
Mr. Hugh S. Hamilton to Miss Mary Sherwood, both of Talbot county. Joseph K. Neale to Eliza Jenkinson, both of Talbot county. Mr. John H. Loveday to Miss Ann Pearson, both of Easton.	12/11/1821
Last evening, very suddenly, Gen. Richard K. Heath.	12/12/1821
The friends and acquaintance of Mr. Claude Jollie are particularly invited to attend his funeral, this afternoon, at 3 o'clock, from his late residence, in South Charles street.	12/12/1821
On the 3rd inst., by the Rev. Dr. Jennings, Mr. John Stiver to Miss Sarah Norris, both of this city.	12/12/1821

Marriage and Death Notices	Dates
In Fredericktown, Dr. William M. B. Wilson, to Miss Martha Wootten, of Montgomery county, Md.	12/12/1821
On the 23rd ult., at Cedar Grove, in Kent county, in the 30th year of her age, Mrs. Mary Ann Eliza Cruickshank, consort of D. Robert Cruickshank, after a long and painful sickness, which she bore with a truly Christian patience and resignation – an irreparable loss to a tender husband and five small children, and much lamented by a numerous acquaintance.	12/13/1821
Yesterday morning, in St. Peter's Church, by the Rev. Mr. Henshaw, the Rev. Ethan Allen, of Prince Geo. County, to Miss Elizabeth Griffith, of this city.	12/13/1821
This morning, about 2 o'clock, John Mitchell, aged 65 years, long a respectable merchant of this city. His friends and acquaintance are respectfully invited to attend his funeral, to meet at his late dwelling, corner of Pratt & Sharp streets, at 10 o'clock, tomorrow morning, the 15th inst. The interment will be in the country burying ground, two miles distant.	12/14/1821
By the Rev. Dr. Glendy, on the evening of Thursday last, Mr. Richard Barnes to Miss Maria Lee, all of this city.	12/14/1821
On Saturday evening last, by the Rev. Mr. Patterson, David Morrison, Esq., to Miss Harriet M'Intosh, both of this city.	12/14/1821
Early on Friday morning, Mr. John Stacy, aged about 54 years, a native of Manchester, Eng., and for several years employed in the Warren Manufacturing Company store, of this city.	12/15/1821
On Thursday evening last, by the Rev. Mr. Bartow, Mr. John Halbert, to Miss Mary Ann Downey, all of this city.	12/15/1821
At 10 o'clock, on Saturday evening last, Mrs. Mary Channell, in the 20th year of her age, much lamented and regretted by all who with whom she was acquainted.	12/17/1821
At Annapolis, on Saturday evening last, Thomas Rogers, Esq., Chief Clerk of the Senate of Maryland, and late Collector of Taxes for the city of Baltimore.	12/17/1821
Last evening, by the Rev. Mr. Larkin, Capt. John Von Rosson, to Miss Ann Eliza Button, all of this city.	12/17/1821

Marriage and Death Notices	Dates
In Harford county, Mr. James Fisher to Miss Janella Boyd. Mr. Thomas Montgomery to Miss Jane Howe.	12/17/1821
At his residence, in Bank street, Fell's Point, aged 60 years, Capt. Isaac Murphy, long a respectable inhabitant of this city. His disease was that of the most afflicting and trying nature, which he sustained with that perfect resignation to the Divine will, which is ever characteristic of the Christian.	12/18/1821
On Sunday evening, Martha Jenkins, in the 24th year of her age, consort of Felix Jenkins, of this city.	12/18/1821
On Sunday evening last, by the Rev. Mr. Moranville, Mr. Patrick Connelly to Miss Ann Christe, both of this city.	12/18/1821
Yesterday morning, after a long and tedious illness, which he bore with Christian fortitude, Mr. Erasmus Cannon, in the 22nd year of his age, formerly of Mercer county, Pennsylvania.	12/19/1821
On Saturday last, Mrs. Patsey Fitch, relict of the Hon. Thomas Fitch. Under the afflicting circumstances of the present epidemic, it is impossible for pen to do justice to the characteristic qualities of this good Christian, who died as such, overwhelmed by the grief which the loss, within two months, of her husband, and three young and interesting children had occasioned.	12/19/1821
On Thursday, of the same family, John G. Bird, Esq., United States' District Attorney for this Province. In hopes of saving his aunt and her children, by his tender care of them, he became himself a victim to the fatal epidemic. The loss of his promising talents and amiable qualities is a source of universal regret.	12/19/1821
On the 12th inst., of the yellow fever, John F. Davidson, of the 4th regiment, United States Artillery. His correct deportment as an officer and a gentleman had greatly endeared him to his brother officers, and to the inhabitants of this place. His untimely death is a matter of universal regret.	12/19/1821
On the 16th, Dr. Charles Nesbit M'Coskry, Assistant Surgeon at this port. He died a victim to his own humanity, devotion to his professional duties, and unremitted attention to the sick. By his death, the Medical Department is deprived of one of its brightest ornaments, and the army one of its most valuable officers.	12/19/1821

Marriage and Death Notices	Dates
On the 7th, Mr. Obediah Dickinson, of the firm of Dickinson & Hanson, a native of Boston, Mass, aged 26 years.	12/19/1821
On the 15th, Mr. Benjamin Hamlen, aged 29 years, a native of Ireland.	12/19/1821
At Savannah, 5th inst., Mr. Robert M. Goodwin, of Baltimore, to Miss Elizabeth, only daughter of Wm. Taylor, Esq., of Savannah.	12/19/1821
By the Rev. Dr. Glendy, on the evening of Tuesday last, Capt. Stephen H. Moore, Judge of the Orphan's Court, to Miss Jane Helm, all of this city.	12/20/1821
In Kent county, on the 12th ult., by the Rev. Mr. Waters, Mr. William Camp, Jr., of this city, to Miss Augusta, daughter of John Beck, Esq., of the former place.	12/20/1821
On Wednesday morning, 19th inst., John Wilhelm, in the 42nd year of his age.	12/21/1821
Last evening, by the Rev. Dr. Jennings, Mr. Joshua Sindall, to Miss Catherine Doughaday, all of this city.	12/21/1821
At Mount Pleasant Hall, Baltimore county, by the Rev. Mr. Rohen, Elisha Plummer, of the society of Friends, to Mary Kittlewell, both of that place.	12/21/1821
At Smith-point, Charles county, Md., on the 14th inst., Mrs. Sally Greer, consort of Maj. Alexander Greer, in the 63rd year of her age.	12/23/1821
Last evening, by the Rev. Richard Tidings, Mr. John Sneavely, to Miss Elizabeth Hatten, all of this city.	12/23/1821
Last evening, by the Rev. E. J. Reis, Mr. Greenbury Baxter, to Miss Rebecca Clark, both of this city.	12/23/1821
In Queen Ann's county, on Tuesday, the 18th inst., by the Rev. James Moynihan, Mr. John B. Tate, to Miss Caroline Matilda Hobbs, both of said county.	12/23/1821
At Bremont, on the 27th ult., Josias Hawkins, Esq., to Caroline Ashton, third daughter of the late James Clerklee, both of Charles county, Md.	12/23/1821
On Thursday evening, 20th inst., Mr. Peter Bond, in the 55th year of his age, long a respectable inhabitant of this city.	12/26/1821

Marriage and Death Notices	Dates
In Harford county, Mr. Samuel Baxter to Miss Rebecca Robinson. Mr. John Thompson to Miss Hannah Hope. Mr. Jacob James to Miss Mary Bailey.	12/26/1821
By the Rev. Mr. Helfenstein, Dr. John Baltzell, of Frederick, to Miss Ruth, youngest daughter of the late Charles Ridgely, of William.	12/27/1821
By the Rev. Mr. Helfenstein, on Thursday evening last, Mr. Henry Hook, to Miss Susan Weaver.	12/27/1821
On the 16th inst., Mr. Stephen Le Compt, to Miss Ann J. Dixon, both of Dorchester county.	12/27/1821
In Talbot county, Mr. Henry Townsend, to Miss Elizabeth Cox.	12/27/1821
At Hagerstown, Mr. William W. Allender, to Miss Mary Marker. Mr. George W. Kerfoot to Miss Maria Seifert.	12/27/1821
At Samarang, in the East Indies, Mr. John James, of Baltimore, in the bloom of youth, aged 19. His parents were thus deprived of a dutiful son, and divested of the hope of his future welfare and usefulness; and his brothers and sisters bereaved of a true friend and brother.	12/28/1821
On Thursday evening last, by the Rev. Mr. Bartow, Capt. Alexander Donoho, of this city, to Miss Mary Breerwood, of Dorchester county.	12/28/1821
At Batavia, on the 5th of September last, after a distressing illness of nine hours, of the prevailing epidemic, Capt. Robert Cook, of this city, in the 52nd year of his age. The very general expression of regret and sorrow which accompanied the news of his mournful event is the best evidence of the high estimation in which he was held by the community at large. He was esteemed generally as a consumate navigator, a complete master of his profession, and regarded as a citizen of most upright principle, and of unbending integrity of character. He thus acquired the confidence as well as the esteem of the merchants of this city. He was a man of great simplicity of manners, and of pure republican principles; and though immediately descended from a family of no little rank in his native country, he conceived it as a matter of so little importance, that it was never communicated to his most intimate friends, until rendered necessary for the benefit of his children. But it was in private that the character of this estimable man could be only appreciated. There he was known as an accomplished scholar; and singular as it may appear in a man of business, as a student of intense application. As the best of husbands, the tender father, and the kind and attentive neighbor; and what now alone consoles his deeply afflicted	12/29/1821

Marriage and Death Notices	Dates
family, as the consciencious Christian, shunning all parade of his religious feelings, but firmly and deeply grounded in the Faith of Jesus Christ, and resting all his hopes of Salvation on Him alone.	
At Weston, District of Columbia, the residence of Thos. L. McKenney, at 5 o'clock, on the afternoon of the 25th inst., Mrs. Hannah Burneston, of Chester-Town, Eastern Shore of Maryland, in the 68th year of her age.	12/29/1821
At his residence, in Prince George's county, Mr. Jacob Waters, in the 78th year of his age, leaving a number of friends and relatives to mourn his death.	12/29/1821
By the Rev. Dr. Glendy, on the evening of Thursday last, Mr. Thomas Alford, to Miss Alice Ann Langley, all of this city.	12/29/1821
On his passage home, from the West Indies, Charles R. Steever, in the 18th year of his age.	12/31/1821
On Saturday evening last, Mrs. Mary Chambers, of Bridge street, Old Town, after a short sickness, during which the amiable virtues that had adorned the days of health and enjoyment, together with a hope of "another and a better world," supported her till the soul took its flight, and left to a bereaved husband and three children, only a breathless corpse – and the sympathy of surviving friends; many of whom followed her remains to their long home. The deceased was in the bloom of life, and had but about eight weeks ago, with her children, left her native land to join her husband in this country.	12/31/1821
Departed this transitory life, we hope for a blessed immortality, on Saturday, the 8th inst., after a few days of severe sickness and suffering, Mr. George S. Baker, aged 34 years, leaving a wife and 6 children, a mother, brothers and sisters, and numerous friends, who all tenderly loved him, to mourn his early removal, and their deep and lasting bereavement. In the death of Mr. Baker, our city has lost one of its worthiest citizens, for whether we view him as a merchant, a son, a father, a relative, or friend, we may safely say, he was most excellent, uniformly kind in his temper, obliging in his manners, and correct in all his deportment.	12/31/1821
On the evening of the 24th inst., Thomas Peters, Esq., for many years a respectable inhabitant of this city. He was one of those heroes who fought and bled for our liberty and independence, and at the battle of Trenton, he distinguished himself in particular. His spirit has fled to the mansions of his fathers. He was a native of Philadelphia, and brother to	12/31/1821

Marriage and Death Notices	Dates
the accomplished Judge Peters, of that city. A large family and an extensive circle of friends and acquaintance deplore their loss.	
By the Rev. Mr. Bartow, Mr. Anthony Despeaux, to Miss Catherine Ann Beard, both of this place.	12/31/1821
By the Rev. Mr. Valiant, Mr. Joseph C. Almacost, of Baltimore county, to Miss Priscilla Williams, of this city.	12/31/1821
On Thursday evening last, by the Rev. Mr. Gist, Mr. Stephen Griffith to Miss Teresa Hennick, eldest daughter of Maj. George Hennick, all of Baltimore county.	01/01/1822
On Thursday evening last, by the Rev. Mr. Healey, Mr. John Wright, to Mrs. Elizabeth Reed, all of Baltimore county.	01/02/1822
Last evening, by the Rev. Dr. Roberts, Wm. P. Watkins, to Miss Harriet, daughter of Mr. Vachel Burgess, of this city.	01/02/1822
On Monday last, Mrs. Joanna Sherwood, consort of Samuel Sherwood, in the 19th year of her age, of a lingering disease. She bore her affliction, with all that Christian fortitude and godliness that characterizes a saint departing this life. She has left a disconsolate husband and an infant to deplore their irreparable loss. *"For me to live in Christ, but to die is gain."*	01/02/1822
In Prince George's county, Md., on the 10th ult., Capt. Thomas Brooke, in the 46th year of his age. His friendly hospitality and charity for the neighboring poor will be duly felt and appreciated by all who knew him.	01/02/1822
On the 19th of November, at New Orleans, Mrs. Thompson, wife of Capt. Thompson. And, on the 22nd, Capt. Thomas Thompson, of the brig Unity, of Baltimore, which arrived here from France, on the first of November, and in a few days the worthy Capt. and his amiable consort, were attacked by a Bilious Fever, which has deprived a son and a daughter of their affectionate parents, and Society of their generous and affectionate friendship.	01/02/1822
By the Rev. Dr. Glendy, on the evening of Tuesday last, Mr. William Hamilton, Merchant, to Miss Eliza McCausland, all of this city.	01/03/1822
On Tuesday evening, Mr. Jacob Welsh, of Adam, in the 35th year of his age.	01/03/1822
In Adams county, Penn., on the 23rd December, Mr. John Fisher, of	01/03/1822

Marriage and Death Notices	Dates
Baltimore.	
On Thursday evening, by the Rev. John Valiant, Mr. David Atkinson, to Miss Ann Jones, all of this city.	01/05/1822
Mr. John Ridout, of Horace, of Queen Anns county, to Miss Anna R. Seth, daughter of the late Dr. Wm. E. Seth, of Talbot.	01/05/1822
On Friday evening, the 4th inst., after a lingering illness, in the 27th year of his age, Richard Rogers, late of Marsh Market, Baltimore. He has left a wife and daughter to lament the loss of an affectionate husband and tender parent. His friends and acquaintance are requested to attend his funeral, at his mother's residence, No. 37 Marsh Market, tomorrow afternoon, at 4 o'clock.	01/05/1822
At Annapolis, Thursday evening last, by the Rev. Mr. Davis, Capt. David M. Miles to Miss Elizabeth Harrison, all of this city.	01/07/1822
On Wednesday, the 2nd January, Mr. Charles Faulac, aged 23 years, after a lingering and tedious illness, which he bore with patience and fortitude.	01/07/1822
By the Rev. Mr. Henshaw, John A. Robinson, Esq., Counsellor at Law, to Mrs. Elizabeth H. Stakes, of Ranges Lodge, Harford county.	01/08/1822
At the residence of Reuben Stump, Esq., in Harford county, on Thursday evening last, by the Rev. Wm. Stevenson, William Wilson, Esq., to Mrs. Rachel Price, all of the same place.	01/08/1822
In Harford county, Mr. William Styles to Miss Hannah Carter. Mr. William Mowberry to Miss Elizabeth Adams. Mr. Benjamin Wakeland to Miss Mary Ann Bay. Mr. Ford Barnes to Miss Mary Ann Osborn.	01/08/1822
In Talbot county, Mr. Robert Delahy to Miss Sally Stevens. Mr. Richard H. Locker to Miss Hessey Ridgeway, both of Prince George's county, Md.	01/08/1822
In Hagerstown, Mr. William W. Allender to Miss Mary Marker. Mr. George W. Kerfoot to Miss Maria Selfort. Mr. Jonathan Reidenaur to Miss Eleanora Reidenaur. Mr. George Bowman to Miss Mary E. Fiery.	01/08/1822
In Frederick county, Mrs. Sophia Higgins. Mr. Christopher Hyter.	01/08/1822
In Talbot county, Mrs. Mary Valiant. Miss Ann Hambleton.	01/08/1822

Marriage and Death Notices	Dates
In Hagerstown, in the 18th year of his age, Mr. Edward B. Y. Shippen, son of the late John Shippen, Esq., of Penn.	01/08/1822
Last evening, by the Rev. Dr. Glendy, Mr. Samuel K. White, merchant, to Miss Mary, daughter of Mr. Daniel Hoffman, all of this city.	01/09/1822
At his residence, in Baltimore county, on the 25th ult., Col. Beale Owings, aged 47 years. He was a worthy and respectable citizen, and highly esteemed by his friends and neighbors.	01/09/1822
At 9 o'clock, Dec. 29, near Richmond, Mrs. Frances Ann Giles, consort of W. B. Giles.	01/09/1822
On Tuesday evening last, by the Rev. Wm. Nevins, William L. Gill, Esq. to Elizabeth Ann, daughter of the late David C. Stewart, Esq., all of this city.	01/10/1822
On Tuesday evening last, by the Rev. Dr. Glendy, Mr. John Morel to Miss Anna Diehl, all of this city.	01/10/1822
In Talbot county, Mr. John Graham to Miss Mary Harrison. Mr. Jesse Mullikin to Miss Lydia Brown.	01/11/1822
In Princess Ann, Somerset county, Mr. John H. Adams, in the 26th year of his age, a gentleman universally regretted.	01/11/1822
On Saturday last, of a pulmonary complaint, Mr. Ephraim R. Robinson, aged 23 years and 7 months. Society has experienced a heavy loss in the death of this truly amiable young man, who in his journey to a far and better country has left an amiable wife and a numerous circle of relations and friends, to mourn their irreparable loss.	01/11/1822
In Princess Ann, Somerset county, Mr. John H. Adams, in the 26th year of his age, a gentleman universally regretted.	01/11/1822
On Thursday evening last, by the Rev. Mr. Bartow, Doct. Wm. H. Clendenen to Miss Jane Dashiell, all of this city.	01/12/1822
In Fredericktown, on Wednesday night last, Dr. G. J. Schneider, a native of Germany; who lately immigrated to this country. A great part of his life was spent in active military service in the late Wars of Europe; and the wounds which he received in the army rendered him infirm and subject to frequent attacks of sickness; and were very probably the remote, if not the immediate cause of his death.	01/11/1822

Marriage and Death Notices	Date
On Thursday evening last, by the Rev. Mr. Bartow, Mr. Jas. Renno to Miss Catherine Smith, both of this city.	01/12/1822
In Worcester county, Maryland, on Wednesday, 2nd Jan., by the Rev. John Forman, Mr. Edwin Forman to Miss Mary B. Richards, only daughter of the late John Richards, Esq.	01/12/1822
On the 2nd inst., at Druid Hill, his country residence, near this city, Col. Nicholas Rogers, in the 68th year of his age.	01/12/1822
Yesterday, Mr. Robert Gilmor, Sr., Esq., an old and respectable merchant, in the 74th year of his age. By an industrious attention to his concerns, and a very correct private demeanor, Mr. Gilmor had acquired a high standing among his commercial fellow citizens, and with the rest of the community. The friends and acquaintance of the deceased are invited to attend his funeral, this afternoon, at 3 o'clock, from his late dwelling, in Water street.	01/15/1822
On Saturday last, in the 14th year of her age, Agnes Sarah Cunningham, the only child of John Cunningham, Esq., late of this city, deceased.	01/15/1822
On the 23rd ult., at Turner's Creek, Kent county, Md., after a lingering illness, which he bore with Christian resignation, Dr. Robert Maguire, eldest son of Mr. Hugh Maguire, of this city.	01/15/1822
Last evening, by the Rt. Rev. Bishop Kemp, Samuel H. Moale, Esq., to Eleanor, only daughter of Thomas Gittings, Esq., all of this city.	01/16/1822
On Tuesday evening, the 8th inst., by the Rev. Alfred Griffith, the Rev. Dennis H. Battee, of Anne Arundel county, to Miss Elizabeth, daughter of the Rev. Joshua Jones, of Frederick county.	01/16/1822
On Tuesday evening, the 1st of January, at Charlestown, Jefferson county, Va., Andrew Kennedy, Esq., formerly of Baltimore, to Miss Mary Ann R. Lane, of the former place.	01/16/1822
In Limerick, Ireland, on the 6th February last, by the Rt. Rev. Bishop, of Limerick, Dr. Elliot O'Donnell, of Baltimore, to Sarah, youngest daughter of Dr. Vize, of the former place.	01/16/1822
Between 3 and 9 o'clock yesterday morning, Mr. Richardson Steuart, in the 76th year of his age. He has long been a useful, benevolent, and much esteemed citizen of Baltimore.	01/16/1822
____ yesterday, George G. Presbury, Esq., in the 85th year of his age. His friends and acquaintances are invited to attend his funeral, this	01/16/1822

Marriage and Death Notices	Date
afternoon, at 3 o'clock, from his late dwelling house, in Gay street.	
On Tuesday evening last, by the Rev. Mr. Keetch, Mr. James Street, of Harford county, Md., to Miss Margaretta Miles, of this place.	01/17/1822
In Easton, Md., Mr. Bennett Tomlinson to Miss Ann Vickars, daughter of Capt. Clement Vickars.	01/17/1822
In Talbot county, Mr. Nicholas Thomas, Esq., to Miss Jane Goldsborough, daughter of James Goldsborough, Esq.	01/17/1822
In Dorchester county, Mr. John Brohawn, to Miss Susan Matilda Robson.	01/17/1822
At her residence, near Centreville, Queen Anne's county, Md., Mrs. Henrietta Maria Earl, consort of Thomas C. Earl, Esq.	01/17/1822
At Snow Hill, Worcester county, Md., on Sunday evening, the 6th inst., after a long and afflicting indisposition, Mrs. Mary Ann Rice, widow of Capt. George Rice, in the 49th year of her age.	01/17/1822
_____, at Upper Marlborough, Prince Geo's. county, on Saturday last, of an inflammation of the brain, Richard K. Seath, of the house of Seath & Hodges, of said place.	01/17/1822
By the Rev. Dr. Glendy, on the evening of Tuesday last, Mr. Daniel Todd, merchant, to Miss Ellen Howard, all of this city.	01/18/1822
On Tuesday evening, by the Rev. Mr. Richards, Mr. Andrew Collins, of Baltimore, to Miss Mara Ann, only daughter of Mr. Ephraim Stansbury, late of Baltimore county.	01/18/1822
On Thursday evening last, by the Rev. Mr. Smith, Mr. Joseph Klunk, of St. Louis, Missouri state, to Miss Maria R. Bradenbaugh, of the city of Baltimore.	01/18/1822
On Wednesday last, of a long and painful illness, which she bore with Christian fortitude, Miss Elizabeth Lee, in the 19th year of her age. She has left an amiable family, and a numerous circle of relations and friends to mourn their irreparable loss.	01/18/1822
On the 13th inst., at the Red Lyon Mills, Queen Ann's county, Mrs. Action Tscudy, wife of Mr. Wimbert Tscudy.	01/18/1822
On the 24th December, at her residence, in Kent county, near	01/18/1822

Marriage and Death Notices	Date
Chestertown, Mrs. Susanna Perkins.	
On Thursday evening last, by the Rt. Rev. Bishop Kemp, Mr. William T. Morgan, of Annapolis, to Miss Eleanor Robertson, of this city.	01/19/1822
In Hartford county, Mr. James Fisher to Miss Elizabeth Albert. Mr. James Spicer to Miss Susan M. Paul. Mr. Joshua Davis to Miss Margaret Mishlinmon.	01/19/1822
At Hagerstown, Jan. 12th, 1822, Peter Bazlin, a man of colour, formerly the servant of Col. John Rea, of Savannah, aged upwards of *one hundred and ten years*. He perfectly recollected the war in which the colonies were engaged with the Yamasees, Cherokees, Creeks, and other Indian nations, which ended in 1720. And was employed in assisting to erect forts on the river Savanna before the arrival from England of Gen. Oglethorpe, on the side of Yomacraw, an Indian village.	01/19/1822
In this city, Mr. Bennett Biscoe to Miss Catherine Shirley.	01/21/1822
On Saturday morning, at the residence of Col. James Hindman, Wm. Hindman, Esq., of Talbot county, Md., aged 79.	01/21/1822
At the Head of Sassafras, in Kent county, on the 13th inst., after an illness of ten days, Miss Susan Hall, aged 17, daughter of Cuthbert Hull, Esq., of Chestertown. Possessing an amiable disposition and a refined mind, she was much respected, and is extremely lamented by all who knew her. Cut off in the vigor of life and the bloom of youth, society, in the death of this amiable lady, has sustained an irreparable loss, but it is a pleasing consolation that she died happy in the Lord. A short time before her death, she raised her hands toward Heaven and exclaimed "Glory to God!" These were her last words, when her pure and immortal soul forsook its tenement of clay and escorted, it is hoped, by angels, winged its flight to ethereal climes, to dwell in mansions of eternal rest. Grace to her, on earth was given, To die triumphant, and ascend to Heaven.	
On Thursday evening last, by the Rev. Thos. Leaman, Mr. Charles Grimes, to Miss Jane Leaman, both of this city.	01/22/1822
On the 9th inst., Dr. John Ruan, of Rockland, Cecil county, Md., to Miss Susan Rodman, daughter of William Rodman, Esq., of Flushing, Buck's county, Pennsylvania.	01/22/1822

Marriage and Death Notices	Date
Yesterday morning, Miss Susan Norris, aged 44, the pattern of piety.	01/22/1822
Yesterday afternoon, Capt. David Wilson, a respectable inhabitant of this city. His friends, acquaintances, and Masonic brethren are requested to attend his funeral, this afternoon, at 3 o'clock, from his dwelling, in Straight lane, near the Friends' Meeting House, Old Town.	01/23/1822
On Monday night last, at 10 o'clock, Mrs. Juliana Sharp, consort of Mr. Andrew Sharp, in the 52nd year of her age.	01/23/1822
On Sunday evening last, after a protracted illness, and great suffering, which was borne with exemplary patience, in the 72nd year of her age, Mrs. Martha Ensor, leaving a large circle of relations and friends to lament her loss.	01/23/1822
On the 8th inst., Mr. Samuel O. Moale, Esq., to Eliza, only daughter of the late Col. Beale Owings, all of Baltimore county.	01/24/1822
Last evening, by the Rev. Dr. Roberts, Wesley Cowles, Esq., of Warrenton, Virginia, to Miss Elizabeth, eldest daughter of Mr. Geo. Earnest, merchant, of this city.	01/24/1822
On the 21st inst., at the residence of Charles S. Sewell, Esq., of Harford, Maryland, Mrs. Cornelia Southern, aged 62 years. A woman of exemplary piety, and whose affability of manners, and sound understanding, secured the esteem and respect of all who were acquainted with her. She died in the full assurance of that bliss they have who die in the *Lord*.	01/25/1822
By the Rev. Dr. Roberts, Mr. Rowland Rogers to Miss Ellen Endly, all of this city.	01/26/1822
On Thursday last, by the Rev. E. J. Reis, Mr. William G. Cook to Miss Emily Murphy.	01/26/1822
On the 24th inst., by the Rev. Mr. Keech, Mr. John King, to Miss Henrietta Day, both of Baltimore county.	01/26/1822
Last evening, by the Rev. J. Allen, Mr. Wm. Hayes, to Miss Mary Ann Benney, both of this city.	01/28/1822
At Annapolis, on Thursday evening last, by the Rev. Mr. Hammond, Mr. Charles Boon to Miss Elizabeth Hancock.	01/28/1822
At his residence, on Sunday evening, the 27th inst., Mr. Jacob Laudenslager, in the 50th year of his age. His disease was lingering and	01/28/1822

Marriage and Death Notices	Date
protracted, and he bore it with the courage of the man, and the fortitude of a Christian. As a father, husband, and citizen, the deceased was tender, affectionate, and patriotic, and has left a numerous family, and an extensive circle of friends, to deplore his loss. His friends and acquaintance are invited to attend his funeral, on Tuesday, the 29th, at 3 o'clock. A&C	
On Thursday, 24th inst., at his residence in Baltimore county, after a short, but severe illness, which he bore with Christian fortitude, Mr. Thomas C. Brown, in the 32nd year of his age. He has left an amiable family and a numerous circle of relations and friends to mourn their irreparable loss.	01/28/1822
On the 26th inst., after a sickness of __ days, with the small pox, Daniel Preston, aged about 22 years. It appears he was a native of Virginia, near the town of Richmond. His relations, or others concerned, may be informed of the particulars respecting him on application to William Monchton, house joiner, at the intersection of Baltimore street and Market street.	01/29/1822
On Sunday evening last, by the Rev. Mr. Toy, Mr. William Durham to Miss Clarissa Robinson, all of this city.	01/30/1822
On Friday night last, after a long and distressing illness, which she bore with exemplary fortitude and resignation, Mrs. Elizabeth Hanson, aged 28 years, leaving a husband and two young children, with relatives and friends to mourn her exit, and in whose memory her many virtues will long live.	01/30/1822
On Tuesday evening last, by the Rev. Mr. Healey, Mr. John Griffith to Mrs. Mary Gooding, all of Baltimore county.	01/31/1822
At Paterson, New Jersey, on Sunday, the 27th Jan. inst., in the 24th year of her age, Mrs. Susan Travers, consort of John Travers, Esq., and daughter of Samuel Moale, Esq., of this city.	01/31/1822
At Fredericktown, Mr. Richare Colgate, in the 76th year of his age.	01/31/1822
On Thursday evening last, by the Rev. D. E. Reis, Mr. Jacob P. Winn, of Philadelphia, to Mrs. Susan Ebby, of Newburg, New York.	02/04/1822
On Thursday evening last, by the Rev. E. J. Reis, Mr. John Stains, to Miss Mary C. Key, all of this city.	02/04/1822
On Saturday evening, on the 26th ult., by the Rev. Albert Helfenstein,	02/04/1822

Marriage and Death Notices	Date
Mr. Philip Augustus Saundoz, of Philadelphia, to Miss Mary Ann Barquet, of Baltimore.	
At New Orleans, Mr. John Lowery Donaldson to Miss Harriet Griffith, both of Baltimore.	02/04/1822
By the Rev. Dr. Glendy, on the evening of Thursday last, Mr. William Knox to Miss Rachel Patterson, all of this city.	02/05/1822
On the 24th Jan., 1822, Mrs. Mary Ann, late consort of George W. Bayly, aged 23 years and 4 months, leaving a husband and two small children to deplore an irreparable loss. Mrs. Bayly was a subject of tedious and protracted affliction, which she bore with much patience and submission. It is true, previous to her late illness, she was not a professor of experimental religion; but always manifested a respect for the Christian institutions. The education and pious examples given her, had their influence, for she was considered moral in a distinguished point of view, and much endeared to all of her numerous relatives & friends. Some weeks previous to her decease, the religion of Jesus Christ, in all its importance and necessity, came home with due weight upon her mind, which excited much ardor and fervency in her prayers, until she was enabled by faith to lay hold on a crucified Saviour, and rejoice in the Divine favor. During the last week of her probationary state, her mind was calm and stayed upon God as the object of her hope, praised the Lord much, and gave satisfactory testimony to all around, that her soul was happy, and was now willing to die, in order to gain the felicities of Heaven. Sometime previous to this, great concern bore upon her mind for her children, and she felt some reluctance to leave them; but aided by the comforts of God's love shed abroad in the heart, and realizing the happy prospects of an eternal world of felicity, she was able to resign both herself and family into the hands of the Disposer of events. She died in peace, with the full assurance of hope of sharing in the inheritance of the Saints at God's right hand. Emphatically may we say then, *"Blessed are the dead which die in the Lord."*	02/05/1822
On first day, the 3rd inst., in the 77th year of her age, Mary Gray, a respectable member of the society of friends. Funeral to take place this day, at 3 o'clock, from her late dwelling, corner of Eutaw and Saratoga st.	02/05/1822
At Annapolis, in the 55th year of her age, Mrs. Catherine Mackubin, widow of the late Richard Mackubin, Esq.	02/05/1822
Near Berlin, Md., on Wednesday evening, the 16th inst., by the Rev. Mr. Balch, Mr. Thomas Weaver to Miss Margaret Mitchell, of the former	02/06/1822

Marriage and Death Notices	Date
place.	
On Sunday evening last, by the Rev. Dr. Jennings, Mr. George Ketsall, to Miss Elizabeth Rundles, all of this city.	02/07/1822
At Port Deposit, on the evening of Thursday, the 31st ult., by the Rev. Mr. Magraw, Mr. Joel Chamberlain, of the state of New York, to Miss Eleanor Kerr, of the former place.	02/07/1822
In Fredericktown, Mr. Lawrence Doyle to Miss Sarah Gordon.	02/07/1822
On Monday, the 4th inst., Dr. Charles Hintze, in the 68th year of his age, an old and respectable citizen of this city.	02/07/1822
After a severe indisposition, of about two weeks, Mr. Walter Jenkins, late merchant, of this city, in the 45th year of his age.	02/08/1822
On Wednesday morning, after a short illness, Anna Robinson, daughter of Mr. Henry Robing, aged 5 years. The loss of a lovely and interesting child is one of the severest afflictions assigned to the lot of humanity – yet this afflicting trial is not permitted without a corresponding consolation, as we are assured in the words of Divine truth, that "Of such are the kingdom of Heaven."	02/08/1822
At sea, on board the ship Wabash, of this port, on the 24th ult., after a lingering illness, Mr. Henry Ring, a native of the island of Guernsey, in the 26th year of his age. The deceased, although in a foreign clime, was loved and esteemed by all who knew him, and has left a large circle of friends and acquaintance to lament his irreparable loss.	02/08/1822
At her residence, Horton Lodge, near Epsom, in the 84th year of her age, Hon. Louisa Browning, widow of John Browning, Esq., of the same place. She was the eldest daughter and only surviving child of the late Rt. Hon. Charles Calvert, Lord Baltimore, and sister to Fred. Calvert, who was the last Lord Baltimore. *London paper of Nov.*	02/08/1822
By the Rev. Dr. Glendy, on Thursday last, Mr. Bennet H. Barnes, to Miss Eliza Mack, all of this city.	02/09/1822
Last evening, by the Rev. E. J. Reis, Mr. Samuel Shauck, to Miss Catherine Revell, both of this city.	02/09/1822
On the 1st inst., Mr. Aquilla Brown, of Harford county, to Miss Elizabeth Barnes, of this city.	02/09/1822

Marriage and Death Notices	Date
In Talbot county, Mr. William James to Miss Elizabeth Brown. Mr. William Faulkner, of Queen Ann's, to Miss Charlotte Stichberry, of Talbot county.	02/09/1822
At Cambridge, Md., Martin Luther Wright, Esq., of Dorchester, to Miss Mary Wall, of Cambridge.	02/09/1822
This morning, between the hours of 10 and 11 o'clock, Mrs. Susan H. Westley, after a long and severe illness. Her surviving friends will be consoled to know, that she died almost without a sigh, and with the comfortable assurance of salvation, thro' the merits of the Redeemer. The friends of the deceased are invited to attend the funeral tomorrow, at 4 o'clock.	02/09/1822
At her residence, near Belle Air, of a short, but malignant illness, Miss Clarissa Norris.	02/09/1822
At Queen Ann's county, Md., Charles B. Hobbs, postmaster of that place, after a short and severe illness, aged 22.	02/09/1822
At her late residence, in Queen Ann's county, on the 16th ult., after a short illness, Mrs. Anna Maria Blake.	02/09/1822
Departed this life, yesterday morning, after a lingering illness, Hannah Tyson, consort of the late George Tyson, of this city, in the 33rd year of her age. Her friends and acquaintances are respectfully invited to attend the funeral, this afternoon, at 3 o'clock, from her late dwelling, at the corner of Hanover and Pratt streets.	02/11/1822
Was washed overboard, from the ship Wabash, of this port, on the 4th of January, Mr. John Holdruff, seaman, a native of Rhode Island, aged 19 years.	02/11/1822
On Saturday evening last, by the Rev. Mr. Bartow, Mr. David Nicoll, to Mrs. Mary Ann Cornell, all of this city.	02/12/1822
At Denton, Caroline county, Md., Mr. Robert T. Keene, to Miss Margaret Ann Young.	02/12/1822
At Greensborough, Caroline county, Md., John Hardester, to Mrs. Mary Ann Tool.	02/12/1822
Between 4 and 5 o'clock, yesterday morning, after a long and painful illness, which she bore with Christian fortitude, Mrs. Fanny H., consort of Thomas G. Peachy, in the 24th year of her age.	02/12/1822

Marriage and Death Notices	Date
On the 2nd February, Rev. Townsend Dade, at his seat in Montgomery county, Md., in the 80th year of his age, after a lingering illness, which he bore with Christian patience.	02/12/1822
At Charleston, S. C., on the 1st inst., States Gist, Esq., in the 36th year of his age, youngest son of the late Gen. Mordecai Gist, of Maryland.	02/12/1822
In Washington, DC, Mr. James Odd, to Miss Ann Hickey, both of Charles county, Md.	02/13/1822
On Tuesday, the 5th inst., at 10 o'clock, P. M., Mrs. Maria, late consort of Thomas McCormick, aged 28 years, 4 months, and 25 days, leaving a husband and two children to bemoan their loss. As a daughter, she had been very respectful and obedient to her parents. As a wife, affectionate to her husband. As a mother, tender & careful to the children. When, at the age of nine years, she embraced the religion of Jesus Christ, and became a member of the Methodist Episcopal Church, in which she lived in full and acceptable membership until her decease. Having made a business of religion, she was not disappointed in that buoyance and comfort, which it is calculated to inspire. Death, to her, was now completely disarmed of all its terrors. The idea of eternity presented no gloom to her mind, but under the full assurance of the divine favor, daily welcomed her approaching dissolution. And, having her mind singly fixed upon the recompense of reward, rejoiced and exulted in the praises of God, calling upon others to join in the angelic theme.	02/13/1822
Early this morning, at the residence of Mr. Brian Byrne, on the Hookstown road, after a short illness, Mr. John Byrne, a native of Ireland, in the 40th year of his age. The deceased was a man of sterling honor and integrity. He met death with Christian fortitude and a perfect resignation to the will of Divine Providence. AGCT	02/14/1822
By the Rev. Dr. Glendy, on the evening of Thursday last, Mr. Barney Donoho, to Miss Bridget O'Reily, all of this city.	02/15/1822
On Wednesday, the 13th inst., by the Rev. Mr. Moranville, Samuel G. Colwell, Esq., to Miss Catherine Donnelly, all of this city.	02/15/1822
At Easton, Md., Dr. John Rodgers to Maria Kerr. Mr. Nicholas Layton to Mrs. Sophia Warner.	02/15/1822
On Thursday evening last, by the Rev. Mr. Lankin, Mr. Reuben Sewell to Miss Mary Ann Blades, all of this city.	02/16/1822

Marriage and Death Notices	Date
On Thursday evening last, by the Rev. Mr. Henshaw, Mr. George White, of St. Mary's county, to Miss Ann E., daughter of Capt. Jno. H. Holmes, of Baltimore.	02/16/1822
In Harford county, Mr. William B. Bateman to Miss Sarah Brickhead.	02/16/1822
On Thursday last, after a painful illness of about five weeks, Miss Eliza, youngest daughter of Mr. William Smith, aged seventeen years and nine month – which illness she bore with Christian fortitude, fully assured that her immortal soul would be wafted on wings of Seraphs, to that rest where sin and sorrow shall reach her no more.	02/16/1822
At Aux Cayes, on the 10th January, Mr. Charles Schwartze, son of Dr. A. J. Schwartze, of this city.	02/16/1822
At the residence of Mr. Wm. Beam, Baltimore county, on Saturday last, in the ninth year of his age, Theodore C., son of Joshua Brown, Esq., of Charleston, South Carolina. His decease was occasioned by a fall from a wagon, and was instantaneous. The amiable and promising youth was sent the last summer to receive his education at the Garrison forest academy; but it has pleased Him, whose ways, though mysterious, we know to be right, thus suddenly to remove him from this world to a better. Suffer little children to come unto me, said the holy messenger of God, for such is the kingdom of Heaven. May his afflicted parents, when they hear of this bereavement, have those Christian feelings which shall lead them to say with the patriarch Job, the Lord gave, the Lord hath taken away – blessed be the name of the Lord.	02/16/1822
On Thursday evening last, by the Rev. Mr. Haskins, Mr. George Jacobs, of Prince George's county, to Charlotte, eldest daughter of James H. Marriott, Esq., of Anne Arundel county.	02/18/1822
At Friends' Meeting House, on the Little Falls of Gunpowder, on Thursday, the 14th inst., William Lee Amoss, of Harford county, to Abigail, youngest daughter of Jonas Garret, Esq., of Baltimore county.	02/19/1822
Alexander Hemsley, Esq., of the Eastern Shore of Maryland, to Miss Elizabeth, second daughter of Frances West, Esq., of Philadelphia.	02/19/1822
Yesterday morning, after a short illness, Mrs. Polymnie R. Durand, daughter of Dr. Edme Ducatel, of this city. In the demise of this young, amiable, and accomplished woman, a severe blow is inflicted at once on her aged, loving parents, her affectionate husband, her family, and acquaintance. The friends of the deceased are invited to attend the funeral from her father's residence, this afternoon, at half past three	02/19/1822

Marriage and Death Notices	Date
o'clock.	
On the 17th, by the Rev. Mr. Tidings, Mr. John P. Brotherton, of Harrisburg, to Miss Louisa Bodensick, of this city.	02/20/1822
On Tuesday evening, by the Rev. Daniel P. Reese, Mr. John Paul, to Miss Maria Warfield, both of this city.	02/21/1822
By the Rev. Mr. Carberry, on Thursday, the 14th inst., Mr. John Hatton, to Miss Catherine Armstrong, of St. Mary's county.	02/21/1822
On Monday evening last, in Harford county, by the Rev. Mr. William Stevenson, Mr. Peter Wilson, of this city, to Miss Adeline Miller, of the former place.	02/22/1822
On the 6th inst., by the Rev. Dr. Roberts, Mr. Henry G. Jacobsen, to Mrs. Maria E. Thomsen, both of this city.	02/22/1822
On Tuesday evening, by the Rev. Mr. Finley, Mr. John Juden, of Jackson, Missouri, to Miss Eliza S. Moore, of this city.	02/22/1822
On Thursday evening last, by the Rt. Rev. Bishop Kemp, Mr. John Pouge, to Miss Margaret, second daughter of Robert Cary Long, Esq.	02/22/1822
On Saturday last, in the 36th year of his age, Mr. Wm. Lafferty, leaving a disconsolate wife and six children to bemoan their irreparable loss.	02/22/1822
On Monday morning last, at 7 o'clock, Mrs. Elizabeth Ritchards, aged 66 years.	02/22/1822
At Rockville, Md., Mr. John Adams, aged 38.	02/22/1822
In Frederick county, Miss Susan Kemp. Mr. Jonas Whitmore. Mr. Thomas Hoffman.	02/22/1822
In Wheeling, Va., on the 31st ult., Col. John Houston, formerly of Fredericktown, Md.	02/22/1822
On Thursday evening last, by the Rev. Dr. Jennings, Mr. Jno. Coulson, to Miss Elizabeth Warner.	02/23/1822
On the 17th inst., Miss Julianna Simmonds, daughter of Mr. M. W. Simmonds, of this city, aged 20 years. The decease of this truly amiable and much lamented young lady is the third instance of the fatal power of pulmonary disease which has occurred in this worthy family, within the last twelve months. The ravages of death under circumstances of any	02/23/1822

kind are necessarily distressing to surviving friends; but, when the stroke is reiterated in such rapid succession, how awfully severe! Before the opening wound began to heal, a second stroke had made the dread incision more deep and wide; and when all soothing time, by the kindly influence with which he heals distress, had imperceptibly began to smooth the face of grief, with now and then a solemn smile, though mingled still with tears, the ruthless monster made a third unerring blow, and lo! a triple wound, with threefold anguish, bleeds afresh!

Under afflictions so rarely equaled, what but the hope of the Christian, could save a tender parent, or an affectionate brother or sister, or loving friend from the horrid pangs of a broken heart? Blessed be God! "His word is truth – whom the Lord loveth he chasteneth." All these lovely fair ones, died in triumphant hope of joys eternal! Not in the transient constacies of a sickly imagination; but in the firm assurances of faith; tried by the fire of affliction long and patiently endured. Nothing on earth could equal the sublime consolations, which Julianna and her amiable mother again and again enjoyed, in heavenly converse, respecting their everlasting home! So familiar were these solemn themes, when Death was throwing his icy arms around this lovely victim, her Godly mother weeping by her bed, said, "My dear, you will now very soon, stand before the bar of God," "Well" replied the dying saint, "I am glad to hear that, I should rejoice to be there his very night." Examine yourself faithfully continued the mother. "Perhaps you are glad at the thought of leaving your pains and suffering here." "Thus" said Julianna, "I have sufficiently done." "I am willing to suffer all that my God sees fit to inflict upon me;" "And yet I am glad." Her mother filled with solemn but submissive grief; bowed before the Lord, and supplicated in her behalf, a peaceful and a silent death.

This done, returning to her dying daughter, whose vision was beginning to fail; "Why" said Julianna, do all of you "appear so large?" "Why so changed" said she? "The change, my dear" said her mother, is not in us; it is in you. "Your ideas are changed." "Well" said she, "is this dying?" "Yes" said her mother, "This is dying!" "Glory," "Glory," said she, and in a few minutes sweetly breathed her last, clapping her glad wings, with accompanying angels took her flight from earth, and with her happy sisters, entered upon the enjoyment of the bliss of Heaven! How easy then it is to die, if God be with us in that trying hour! Methinks, dear Julianna, now looks down in pity, upon all that mourn for her, and says, "My dear, my loving friends, weep not for me, but hear my warning voice which loudly speaks, Be ye also ready!"

In Wavertree, Eng., Miss Mary Dexter, daughter of the late Hon. Samuel Dexter, of Boston.	02/23/1822

Marriage and Death Notices	Date
Last evening, by the Rev. Dr. Roberts, Mr. John McCleskey, to Miss Mary Hall, all of this city.	02/25/1822
On the 5th inst., Mrs. Elizabeth H. Jennings, consort of Dr. Samuel K. Jennings, Jr., after a lingering and very painful illness. Her patience under her affliction – her deep submission to the will of Heaven – her hearty surrender of all that is dear on earth, when summoned to leave the world, were evidences of the sterling value of the religion which she professed.	02/25/1822
After a few hours illness yesterday, Capt. Ellis, of the schr. Maine, of Bristol, Maine. In consequence, the flags in the harbor are at half mast.	02/25/1822
On Sunday evening last, by the Rev. Mr. Wyatt, Mr. Thomas Finlay, to Miss Elizabeth Hall, all of this city.	02/26/1822
In Harford county, Mr. Robert W. Holland to Miss Eliza Bond. Mr. John Wadsworth to Miss Margaret Klinefelter. Mr. William Vansant to Miss Ann Hill. Mr. John Muckelwee to Miss Rosanna Morrison, of Cecil. Mr. H. Heaton to Miss Jane Campbell. Mr. David Troutner to Miss Frances Davis.	02/26/1822
On Saturday morning, the 23rd inst., in this city, of a protracted and painful disease, Mr. Joseph Young, in his seventy-eighth year.	02/26/1822
On Saturday last, 23rd inst., at his late dwelling, in South Charles street, Mr. Paul Bigeo, in the 96th year of his age. The deceased was a native of Canada, and emigrated to this country in consequence of the surrender of that colony to the British arms, in the year 1759, and for sixty-two years past that he resided here, maintained a character of strictest integrity.	02/27/1822
Suddenly, on Sunday morning last, Catherine, daughter of Mr. Benjamin Macher, in the 14th year of her age.	02/27/1822
On Tuesday evening last, by the Rev. Mr. Bartow, Capt. George C. Thompson, to Miss Catherine Thomson, all of this city.	02/28/1822
On the 27th inst., Mr. Archibald Campbell, of Baltimore county, four miles out, on the Georgetown road. All his friends and acquaintances are particularly invited to attend, tomorrow morning, at Mr. Joseph M'Kelding's, head of Pratt street, when they will find conveyance out.	02/28/1822
At St. Barts, Capt. John Cock, of the sch'nr Dick, of this port.	03/01/1822

Marriage and Death Notices	Date
On Tuesday evening last, by the Rev. Mr. M'Cann, Mr. John P. E. Stanley, to Ann, youngest daughter of the late Mr. Jas. M'Cannon, of this city.	03/02/1822
On Thursday evening last, by the Rev. Dr. Jennings, Capt. Charles G. Snow, to Miss Cinthia Wight, all of this city.	03/02/1822
On Tuesday evening last, the 26th ult., in the 17th year of her age, Miss Lydia Presstman, daughter of the late Wm. Presstman, Esq., of this city.	03/02/1822
After a short illness, at Plinlimmon, Baltimore county, on the 26th inst., full of years, in the blissful hope of a glorious resurrection to eternal life through the merits and atonement of his crucified Saviour, Richard Owen, aged 77.	03/02/1822
On Sunday evening last, by the Rev. Mr. Bartow, Mr. Andrew Murgrave, to Miss Mary Ann Gardner, both of this city.	03/04/1822
On Thursday evening last, by the Rev. E. J. Reis, Capt. Edward Kelly, to Mrs. Eliza Riddle.	03/04/1822
OBITUARY – On the 23rd ult., terminated the earthly pilgrimage of Paul Bigeo, of this city, in the 93rd year of his age. He was remarked by those who had long been intimately acquainted with him, to have lived a pious, inoffensive, and upright life, endeavoring to *experience a conscience void of offense* both *to God and man.* He was one of those persecuted *Acadians*, termed *"French Neutrals,"* who were dispossessed of their property by the tyrannical government of Great Britain, when *Nova Scotia* was taken from the French inhabitants, who were cruelly forced away from their own happy country and every enjoyment that was near and dear to them, except with what was allowed in the decree proclaimed by *Capt. Murray* by express orders from *Governor Lawrence*, in the following words after they had been convened in their Chapel or worship house, for the purpose – 418 of their best men were assembled, without their having any previous intimation of the object, or sentence, to be then passed upon them. "That it is peremptorily his majesty's orders that the whole French inhabitants of these districts be removed, and I am, through his majesty's goodness, directed to allow you liberty to carry off your money and household goods, as many as you can, without discommoding the vessel you go in." They were accordingly crowded on board to that degree, that no room was left to admit of the indulgence granted "to carry with them their household goods" and transported to different places of the then British	03/05/1822

179

Marriage and Death Notices	Date
colonies in America, and a considerable number of them, *men, women, and children*, landed on the shores of the Chesapeake bay, about the year 1756, and left in a destitute situation, to seek a subsistence in a foreign clime, amongst strangers, with whose language they were totally unacquainted. It appears that Mr. Bigeo was amongst those of his countrymen shipped to Philadelphia, or in the Delaware, where he was landed, but soon after emigrated to this place, and fixed a residence amongst some of those above mentioned, who had commenced building of huts to dwell in at the head of the Basin, afterwards known as *Frenchtown*, now South Charles street. They being of a *harmless, peaceable disposition*, and of *orderly deportment*, soon gained the esteem and good will of the respectable part of the community they were amongst, which continued to be the case during their lives – their offspring not being very numerous, and some of them being removed to different parts, and the hand of time having reduced a great number of the first settlers, the race has nearly become extinct in this city. {The long obituary includes the address delivered to them by their clergyman upon their departure from Nova Scotia, as quoted from *New Travels Through North America*, by Abbe Claude Robin.} The cruel and unfeeling requisition aforementioned, he who is now with others deceased heard with astonishment, but was compelled to a compliance, however painful and distressing it must have been to them, as it is well known, that scarce any nation or sect of people in the world are more attached to each other and their country, than the *Acadians*. And the parting advice which was impressed upon him by their pious and affectionate pastor, he strictly adhered to the remainder of his life, which enabled him to meet the solemn and awful messenger wih great composure and sincerity of mind, having been favored with a foresight of his dissolution for some time previous to its taking place.	
In Somerset county, Md., on the 26th Feb'y, Mr. Edward North, aged twenty-one, to Mrs. Russell Dunn, aged seventy, both of said county.	03/05/1822 03/21/1822
By the Rev. Albert Helfenstein, last Thursday, Mr. George Merrica, to Catherine Mininger, both of this city.	03/06/1822
On Tuesday evening last, by the Rev. Mr. Wyatt, Mr. Stephen Marsh, to Mrs. Elenora Owings, all of this city.	03/07/1822
On Tuesday last, after two days severe indisposition, William Mackenheimer, of John, in the 23rd year of his age, much regretted – being much esteemed by his relations and acquaintance.	03/07/1822

Marriage and Death Notices	Date
At St. Thomas, Mr. Philip Wiley, mariner, supposed to belong to the port of Baltimore. He had lately arrived at that place from Rio Janeiro, after having been absent several years in the Pacific Ocean. His effects, together with a small sum of money, are in the hands of Messrs. Balestier, Bailey, and Clark, Merchants, at St. Thomas, which will be delivered to any person authorised to receive them. For further information, please apply to Perkins & Saltonstall, No. 81, Bowley's wharf.	03/07/1822
Last evening, by the Rev. Mr. Kurtz, Charles Kurstendorf, to Miss Jane Foye, both of this city.	03/08/1822
Yesterday morning, at his residence near Ellicott's Mills, Dr. William P. Matthews, formerly of this city.	03/09/1822
In Cecil county, Maryland, on the 5th inst., William Whann, late of Georgetown, D. C.	03/09/1822
At Hagerstown, after an illness of a few days, William Kreps, Esq., Post master at that place, in the 51st year of his age.	03/09/1822
At his residence, at the head of Long Green, Baltimore county, on Sunday night, the 3rd inst., Mr. Joseph Gorsuch, in the 32nd year of his age. His death was occasioned by being thrown from his horse.	03/09/1822
In this city, on Friday evening last, Mr. Elijah B. Watson, aged 44, a native of Hartford county, in this state.	03/11/1822
Last Sunday evening, after a short, but painful illness, which he bore with Christian fortitude and resignation, and a full confidence in the merits of his Redeemer, Mr. James Hannan, for many years a respectable inhabitant of this city.	03/12/1822
At Pamunky, in Charles county, Md., on the 2nd of Dec. last, Mr. John Rowe, Sr., aged 73 years.	03/12/1822
On Sunday evening last, by the Rev. Dr. Kurtz, Mr. Philip Maul, to Miss Amelia Biddle, all of this city.	03/13/1822
On Tuesday morning last, by the Rev. Mr. Henshaw, Mr. James M. Smith, of Virginia, to Miss Elizabeth, daughter of Eli Hewitt, Esq., of Baltimore.	03/13/1822
On Tuesday evening last, by the Rev. Mr. Kurtz, Mr. Thomas S. Lamden, to Miss Ann Jones, all of this city. On the same evening, by the same, in the same house, in the same hour, Mr. Louis Chasteau to	03/15/1822

Marriage and Death Notices	Date
Miss Mary M'Connell, of the same city.	
On Wednesday morning, Mrs. Martha Booth, wife of Mr. Joseph Booth, Inn-keeper, Light street.	03/15/1822
On Monday evening last, by the Rev. Mr. Bartow, Mr. William Anderson, to Miss Mary Louisa Chapey, all of this city.	03/16/1822
Suddenly, at Montrose, Penn., Mrs. Sarah Horton, formerly of Baltimore, in the 69th year of her age.	03/16/1822
On Thursday evening last, by the Rev. Mr. Pyfer, Mr. Thomas Mahannah, to Miss Rebecca Mewshaw, both of this city.	03/18/1822
On Thursday evening last, by the Rev. Mr. Tidings, Mr. Edward Oursler, to Miss Susan Wilson, both of Baltimore county.	03/18/1822
On his passage, from Batavia to Baltimore, on the 13th of Dec. last, Mr. Davis Burke, Jr., aged 25 years.	03/18/1822
On Thursday, the 14th inst., at Hollow Rock, near the town of Westminster, Frederick county, Mr. Andrew Reese, after a lingering illness, which he bore with Christian fortitude, in the sixty third year of his age. He was a man much esteemed and respected by all who knew him; and his relatives and friends may well say that they have sustained an irreparable loss, and he was one of the noblest works of God, *an honest man.*	03/18/1822
On Sunday evening last, by the Rev. Mr. M'Cann, Mr. Jesse Carter, to Miss Catherine Krepps, all of this city.	03/20/1822
On the 16th inst., of a pulmonary complaint, at her father's residence, in Pitt street, Mrs. Ann Dew, in the 33rd year of her age. She was formerly the wife of Mr. Baruch Williams, a man of whom it is difficult to speak, even at this period, without emotion. When we take a retrospect of the short, but eventful, life of his young woman, torn from an infant family, the last child of her aged parents; who in the course of a few years followed to the same melancholy spot, five daughters and three grand children, we must view it as one of those awful mysteries which we cannot contemplate without astonishment, but will nevertheless be revealed hereafter. The writer of this knew well the value of the deceased, and offers this short obituary as a tribute of respect to her memory.	03/20/1822
On Saturday last, at Monkton Mills, in Baltimore county, John Gwinn,	03/20/1822

Marriage and Death Notices	Date
Jr., in the forty fourth year of his age.	
At Washington, 19th inst., at Dr. Ewell's, on Capitol Hill, the Hon. Robert Wright, member of Congress from Maryland, to Elizabeth Harriot. Youngest daughter of the late Andrew Robertson, of Virginia.	03/21/1822
Last evening, by the Rev. Alexander McCaine, Dr. Samuel B. Martin, to Miss Ruth Dorsey Hawkins, both of this city.	03/22/1822
On Sunday evening last, by the Rev. Mr. Bartow, Mr. Richard Summers to Miss Ann Wherrett, all of this city.	03/22/1822
On Thursday, the 7th March, by the Rev. Mr. Waters, Upton Welsh, Esq., of Anne Arundel county, to Miss Mary, daughter of Wm. Shipley, Esq., late of said county.	03/22/1822
On Sunday evening last, by the Rev. Samuel Williams, Mr. Peregrine Love, to Miss Levina Owens, all of this city.	03/22/1822
On the 16th inst., of a pulmonary complaint, Mrs. Ann Dew, consort of Mr. James C. Dew, in the 33rd year of her age. Religion supported her under her afflictions, and her last words were "I am going to God, which is far better for me." O glorious hope to her surviving friends – 'tis like the bread on the waters, it will be remembered for many days. Her advice to her friends were, "O prepare to meet me in Heaven – do not suffer yourselves to be led away by the allurements of this world, for it is full of deception, and no real happiness to be found in it – but in our blessed Saviour there is all happiness; and if you will only ask aright. He will bestow his bountiful blessings on you."	03/22/1822
On Monday morning, the 18th inst., Mrs. Mary Yagers, in the 55th year of her age.	03/22/1822
On Wednesday, the 13th inst., in Baltimore county, Mr. Abraham Cole, Sr., in his ninety-fifth year. He was born in Baltimore county, about 15 miles from Baltimore; and lived where he breathed his last, about seventy years. A few years past, he has been deprived of his sight, and in a measure his hearing; but under these deprivations he exercised the genuine Christian patience and viewed his approaching end with calm resignation and as an event that would end all his troubles. He has fought the good fight; he has finished his course; he kept the faith; and is now gone to receive the welcome approbation, "Come though good and faithful servant, into the joy of the Lord."	03/22/1822

Marriage and Death Notices	Date
At Augusta, Georgia, on he 8th inst., after a short but violent illness, Mr. James Fennell, of the Augusta Theatre.	03/22/1822
On Wednesday last, Mr. John Hignat, an old and respected inhabitant of this city.	03/23/1822
On Thursday evening last, by the Rev. Mr. Hinkle, Mr. Sydenham Marsh, to Miss Sarah Stretch, all of this city.	03/25/1822
At the Salt Works, in the Forks of Gunpowder, on Thursday, the 21st inst., by the Rev. Mr. Keech, Capt. Ishmael Day to Miss Charity Johnson, both of Baltimore county.	03/25/1822
Mr. Jacob Basford, of Prince George's county, Md., to Mrs. Sarah Paterson, of Alexandria.	03/26/1822
On the 18th inst., by the Rev. Mr. Bartow, Mr. John C. A. Seidel, to Miss Ann Otto, all of this city.	03/26/1822
Miss Ann Hyatt, daughter of Mr. Seth Hyatt, Sr., of Prince George's county, Md.	03/26/1822
Last evening, by the Rev. Mr. Bartow, Mr. George W. Burke, to Miss Rebecca Bier, all of this city.	03/27/1822
On Thursday, the 21st inst., by the Rev. Mr. Henshaw, Mr. Joseph B. Tenison, to Miss Catherine Goldsmith, both of this city.	03/27/1822
On the 12th inst., Mr. James Sangston to Miss Catherine Maria Whiteley, both of Caroline county.	03/27/1822
In Dorchester county, Mr. Joseph S. Hooper to Miss Ann Hodson.	03/27/1822
In Salisbury, Mr. Samuel E. Moore, of Somerset county, to Miss Elizabeth Ann H. D. Vance, of Worcester county.	03/27/1822
In Talbot county, Md., Mr. Samuel Ward, to Miss Ellen Mackey. Mr. John Dewlin to Miss Ann Price.	03/27/1822
On Saturday, the 16th inst., after a long and painful sickness, Philip Tevis, in the 24th year of his age.	03/27/1822
On Monday last, in the 20th year of his age, Amos James, Jr., after a most painful and distressing disease of seventeen days duration.	03/27/1822

Marriage and Death Notices	Date
On Wednesday, 13th inst., Mr. Jacob F. Waters, a very respectable planter of Prince George's County.	03/27/1822
At his residence, after a lingering illness, Mr. James Evans, Sr., a respectable inhabitant of Somerset county for nearly 60 years.	03/27/1822
On Sunday, the 10th inst., Mr. Jeremiah Rhodes, of Caroline county, after a short illness, in his 51st year.	03/27/1822
In Talbot county, Mr. Henry Allen. Mrs. Henrietta M. Hayward, consort of Col. Wm. Hayward.	03/27/1822
On Tuesday evening last, by the Rev. Mr. Hagarty, Mr. Oswald Bayly, to Miss Elizabeth McLaughlin, all of this city.	03/28/1822
On Tuesday morning, by the Rev. E. J. Reis, M. Peter Wilson, to Mary W., eldest daughter of Nixon Wilson, Esq., all of this city.	03/28/1822
On Sunday last, in the 39th year of her age, Mrs. Margaret Walters, consort of Benj. Walters.	03/28/1822
Last evening, in the full assurance of the mercy of his Heavenly Father, Mr. William Charlton. His friends and acquaintance are invited to attend his funeral, this afternoon, at four o'clock, from his late residence, in Eutaw, between Lexington and Saratoga streets.	03/28/1822
By the Rev. Dr. Glendy, on the evening of Monday last, Mr. John Jones, to Miss Anna Jackson, all of this city.	03/29/1822
At Annapolis, Mr. Thomas G. Waters, to Miss Ann E. Beard, head of South river.	03/29/1822
At Washington county, Md., Mr. John Steinmetz to Miss Susan Myers. Mr. Samuel Murcan to Miss Margaret Brunner. Mr. Jacob W. Mealy to Miss Rebecca Gerhart. Mr. Andrew Shenefelt to Miss Sarah A. Louiza Bra__nan. Mr. Daniel Miller to Miss Rachel Houser. Mr. Solomon Thornburg to Miss Mary Lefeber. Mr. Michael Crissman to Miss Harriet Davis. Mr. William Smith to Miss Margaret Downey. Mr. John Newcomer to Miss Catherine Knafe. Mr. Henry Fishaugh to Miss Margaret Flora. Mr. Abijah Smith to Miss Catherine Trovinger.	03/29/1822
On the morning of the 27th inst., of a pulmonary complaint, John Spitler Smith, in the 39th year of his age, eldest son of George C. Smith, of this city.	03/30/1822

Marriage and Death Notices	Date
On Thursday evening last, by the Rev. Mr. Snyder, Mr. Henry B. Williams to Miss Rachel Kelly, all of this city.	04/01/1822
At Snow-hill, Md., Mrs. Elizabeth, the amiable consort of Maj. Tar.	04/01/1822
At Easton, Mr. William Nelson. Miss Mary Patton.	04/01/1822
At Philadelphia, on the 29th inst., in the 55th year of his age, Mr. John Durang, late of the Baltimore Theatre.	04/01/1822
The moral career of Elizabeth Bosley, consort of Caleb Bosley, Esq., closed on the 29th ult., at her residence in Baltimore county, leaving a large circle of relations and acquaintance to mourn their irreparable loss.	04/01/1822
In Winchester, on the 26th ult., Mrs. Mary J. Peyton, consort of John S. Peyton, Esq., and daughter of John Carrere, Esq., of this city, in the 24th year of her age. {Her name is Mary Josephine Peyton, her husband is Major John S. Peyton, and her place of death is Winchester, Va. in the second notice.}	04/01/1822 04/06/1822
On Thursday evening last, by the Rev. Dr. Roberts, Mr. David Jones, to Miss Ann Patterson, all of this city.	04/02/1822
At Philadelphia, Mr. William W. Neilson, of Baltimore, to Miss Sarah Helena, daughter of the late Nalbro Frazier, of the former city.	04/02/1822
On Friday, the 29th ult., Mr. Edward Sandell, a native of Bradford, Wiltshire, Eng., aged 41 years. Mr. S. had been confined for about 5 weeks immediately preceding his death, during which he manifested that patience and resignation which are the unerring marks of a noble mind. If ingenuousness of mind, frankness of manners, benevolence of heart, especially to the distressed emigrants from his native country, can constitute maturity, he was indeed ripe for the sickle. But virtues and vices are equally disregarded by the fiat of mysterious fate.	04/02/1822
On Monday evening last, by the Rev. Mr. Hagerty, Mr. William Davis Hoffman, to Miss Susannah Hoffman, all of this city.	04/03/1822
At Upper Marlborough, the 28th inst., after a short, but severe illness of ten days, in the 25th year of his age, Thomas Hodges, Jr., a respectable merchant of that place, of the firm John & Thomas Hodges. Cut off in the bloom of life, his death will be lamented by his numerous relatives and friends, and by all who knew him. "He is gone, but not lost."	04/03/1822
In Washington county, Mr. Jacob Good to Miss Sarah Stover. Mr. Darius Simpkins to Miss Roena Kadle. Mr. Jacob Hawken, of St.	04/04/1822

Marriage and Death Notices	Date
Louis, to Miss Catherine Allison.	
Extraordinary Case of Dropsy. Died, on Sunday last, Mrs. Leroy, a French lady, aged twenty seven years, after having been tapped seventy-six times, by Dr. Chatard, in the space of two years and five months. The quantity of water obtained by the several operations, amounts to eight hundred and seventy one quarts, by measure. The deceased informed the doctor, the first time he saw her, that she had already been tapped three times in Philadelphia, by Dr. Matthieu.	04/04/1822
At Hagerstown, Miss Elizabeth Harry, daughter of the late Jacob Harry, in the 36th year of her age.	04/04/1822
On Wednesday evening last, by the Rev. Mr. Healey, Mr. Jacob Carman, to Miss Rebecca G. Vaughn, all of this city.	04/05/1822
Last evening, by the Rev. Mr. Dashiell, Mr. Edward Griffith, to Miss Evelina Moore, all of this city.	04/05/1822
On Tuesday evening, the 26th ult., after a short and severe illness, which she bore with Christian fortitude, Miss Susan Dutton, aged 19 years. In the death of this young lady, society had been deprived of one of its brightest ornaments. Amidst the bloom of health and beauty, suddenly was she snatched from the numerous circle of her family and friends, and consigned to the cold, the silent, the solemn mansion of the dead. Long will her memory be cherished by all those, who had the pleasure of her acquaintance.	04/05/1822
Departed this life, on the 3rd inst., Mrs. Jane Phoenix, consort of Thomas Phoenix, Esq., after enduring the keenest pangs of affliction, with a degree of fortitude rarely equaled. In the demise of this amiable woman, society mourns the loss of a useful member; her brothers and sisters the sweet companion of their childhood, and the tender friend of riper years; her husband, the partner of his love torn from his bosom in the morning of life – leaving, to console his widowed heart, three tender pledges of their mutual affections – Alas! too young to be sensible of their irreparable loss. "By nature form'd for pure connubial bliss, Her soul consenting, gave the plighted hand; But, Ah! design'd for noble joys above, A gentle Seraph cnt the silken band, Calm in that hour, when firmest nature fails, She look'd from earth, with heav'n directed flight, And upward borne on faith's triumphant sails,	04/05/1822

Marriage and Death Notices	Date
The saint ascending, sought the realms of light!"	
Lately, at his residence, in Kent county, Maryland, William Spencer, Esq., President of the Senate, of this state.	04/05/1822
On Friday last, in the 22nd year of her age, of a lingering illness, Mrs. Mary Logan, consort of Mr. John Logan.	04/08/1822
At Cragg's ferry, Anne Arundel county, on Wednesday, the 3rd inst., in the 35th year of his age, Mr. George Craggs, after a short, but painful illness.	04/08/1822
Last evening, by the Rev. Mr. Bartow, Mr. Thomas C. Goodrich, to Miss Mary Lee, both of this city.	04/10/1822
In Hagerstown, Mr. Joseph Eakle to Miss Catherine Kauffman. Mr. Jacob Gould to Miss Sarah Stover. Mr. Darius Simpkins to Miss Roena Kadle. Mr. Jacob Hawken, of St. Louis, to Miss Catherine Allison, of Hagerstown.	04/10/1822
In Hagerstown, Miss Elizabeth Harvey. Mr. John Kinkade, in the 30th year of his age. Edward Boteler, Esq., of Washington county.	04/10/1822
Yesterday morning, at Friends Meeting House, Lombard street, William Little to Elizabeth, daughter of Amos James. Also, John M. Foulk, to Ann, daughter of Robert Sinclair, all of this city.	04/11/1822
On the 26th of March, at Pemberton, West River, Mrs. Ann Fitzhugh Steuart, the consort of Dr. Charles C. Steuart, after a painful illness of 9 days. She was exemplary in the duties of wife, mother, friend, and neighbor. Her loss is irreparable to her husband and four small children, and her death severely felt by numerous friends and family connexions.	04/11/1822
In Washington city, the 9th inst., Henry M. Wilson, aged about 40 years, son of John Wilson, of Henry, of Prince George's county, Md., a man of uncommon powers of mind, and great inventive genius.	04/11/1822
On Wednesday evening last, by the Rev. Mr. Bartow, Mr. Edward Taylor to Miss Mary Henderson, all of this city.	04/12/1822
On Tuesday evening last, by the Rt. Rev. Bishop Kemp, William Potts, Esq., of this city, to Miss Jane Alexander, of Alleghany county, Md.	04/12/1822
On Tuesday evening last, by the Rev. Mr. Dashiell, Mr. Patrick Murphy, to Miss Ann Hughes, all of this city.	04/12/1822

Marriage and Death Notices	Date
By the Rev. Dr. Wyatt, on Tuesday evening, 9th inst., Darley, the Seat of Henry Nicols, Esq., Jas. C. Gittings, Esq., of Long Green, to Miss Rebecca Nicols Smith, all of Baltimore county.	04/12/1822
At Annapolis, on Saturday last, Capt. John T. Barber, in the 51st year of his age.	04/12/1822
Yesterday morning, at 5 o'clock, George William Vance, aged eight months, son of Capt. Thomas Vance – the croup was his disease, by which he was taken at 5 o'clock, Thursday evening.	04/13/1822
On Thursday evening last, by the Rev. Mr. Moranville, Mr. James Dougherty, to Miss Bridget Dougherty, both of this city.	04/15/1822
At Harford, Md., Mr. Wm. Carr, Jr., to Miss Hannah Forwood. Mr. Stephen Gorsuch, to Miss Rachel Gorsuch, of Baltimore county. Capt. John B. Bayless to Miss Eliza Day, of Baltimore county. Mr. Abraham Wilson to Miss Jane Ramsay, of York county, Pa.	04/15/1822
On Sunday Morning, in the 72nd year of his age, Samuel Vincent, Esq., for many years a valuable resident of this city.	04/15/1822
On Thursday evening, by the Rev. Mr. Tidings, Mr. John H. Bates, to Miss Sarah Allen, both of this city.	04/16/1822
On Sunday, the 7th inst., by the Rev. Mr. Hawskins, Mr. Zachariah Baldwin, to Miss Mary Ann Meeks, both of Prince George's county, Maryland.	04/16/1822
Suddenly, yesterday, in the 65th year of his age, Mr. Michael Grub, long a respectable citizen of this place. His friends and acquaintance are invited to attend his funeral, from his late dwelling, in Park lane, nearly opposite to Mr. John Matthews' Morocco Factory, at 4 o'clock, this afternoon.	04/16/1822
On the 13th inst., in the 74th year of his age, James Buchanan, Esq., of this city. The deceased was for twenty or thirty years one of the most opulent merchants in Baltimore. During this brilliant and fascinating period of his life, he was the abode of hospitality, and every stranger guest received a cordial welcome to his table. He shared the bounties of Divine Providence with his fellow men, freely and munificently. At length, in the decline of his life, those golden visions vanished, and darkness and dejection oppressed his setting day. But amidst all the wreck of his earthly hopes, his heart was still the mansion, and the last retreat of his benevolence. He maintained the kindliness of the father	04/17/1822

Marriage and Death Notices	Date
and the friend. Death, which had often visited his mansion, and whose ruthless hand tore away the blossoms of his parental hopes, he was enabled at last to meet with the resignation of a Christian.	
On Tuesday evening last, by the Rev. Dr. Roberts, Mr. Richard Phillips, to Miss Sarah Ashman, both of this city.	04/18/1822
On Tuesday morning last, with an inflammation on the breast, John Myers Liddle, aged three years and two months, son of the late Capt. Michael and Matilda Liddle, who is yet left to lament his early demise. *"Early, bright, transient, chaste as morning dew,* *"He sparkled, was exhal'd, and went to Heaven."*	04/18/1822
In Easton, Md., Mr. Joseph Parrott.	04/18/1822
At Friend's Meeting House, Lombard st., on the 17th inst., Joseph Trimble, of Baltimore county, to Ann Cheyney, formerly of Delaware county, Pennsylvania.	04/19/1822
At Washington, Del., on Thursday, the 5th inst., by the Rev. Samuel R. Green, Mr. John Wise, of Baltimore, to Miss Elizabeth Hope.	04/19/1822
On Sunday morning last, Sam'l Vincent, aged 71 years. He was born in London, emigrated to this country, previous to the revolution, and zealously espoused the cause of independence. He was a man of learning and information, which he devoted to the service of the public and his friends with great industry, until the year eighteen hundred fourteen, when his powers of usefulness were prostrated by a visitation of paralysis. He remained in this situation, an helpless object of commiseration, until it pleased God, in his mercy, to call him from an existence of much bodily pain and suffering, which he had labored under nearly eight years. Mr. Vincent was a patron of justice and truth, which were the basis of his private and public transactions. In private life – in health and affliction – in business and retirement, those who knew him best have declared, that they never met with his superior in solid virtue and undeviating integrity. His religious principles were ostensively *Trinitarian* – his morality proverbial, and his truth exact. He was a man of universal charity and benevolence; and extended his means of relief to *those in distress from their own indiscretions.* In prosperity, he was modest and unassuming, in adversity, patient and resigned. In a word, if we look to his general conduct, it was most honorable – if to his domestic life, it was provident, affectionate, and indulgent, almost to a fault. He spared no pains, nor expense, in the education of his children, and lived to see them comfortably settled in life, and well disposed to console and cherish their widowed mother in	04/19/1822

Marriage and Death Notices	Date
her declining years.	
On the 9th inst., at his residence, 4 miles from Hagerstown, Mr. Jacob Rohrer, in the 76th year of his age.	04/19/1822
On Thursday evening last, by the Rev. Mr. Henshaw, Mr. John R. Keech, of Baltimore county, to Miss Susan P., second daughter of the late Judge Scott, of this city.	04/20/1822
Last evening, by the Rev. Mr. McCain, Mr. William Few, late of Baltimore, to Miss Susan Ritchie, daughter of the late Wm. Ritchie, Esq., of Fredericktown, Md.	04/20/1822
On Tuesday, the 16th inst., Dr. Calistus Lancaster, to Miss Adeline Posey, all of Charles county, Md.	04/20/1822
On Tuesday evening last, Mr. C Tschoertner, chemist, a native of Silesia, Germany, and within this four years, a resident of this city, in the 39th year of his age.	04/20/1822
On Thursday evening, the 8th inst., by the Rev. Mr. Richards, Thomas Ferguson, Esq., to Caroline, daughter of George Heide, Esq., all of this city.	04/201822
On Saturday, the 20th inst., of a severe and protracted illness, Sarah, the wife of Dr. Thomas Hamilton, of this city.	04/22/1822
At Norfolk, Harrison Allmand, Esq., in the 65th year of his age.	04/22/1822
Lately, at Genoa, of pulmonary consumption, in the 29th year of his age, Dr. Edward Barton, a gentleman widely known and greatly esteemed. He received his elementary instruction in letters, at Wethersfield, Connecticut, under the Abbe Tisserand, and completed his education at the college of St. Mary's, Baltimore.	04/22/1822
On Thursday, by the Rev. Mr. Joubert, Mr. Aime Prevost, to Miss Julia Servary, both of Baltimore.	04/23/1822
On Sunday last, by the Rev. Mr. Tidings, Mr. Benjamin Franklin, of Baltimore, to Miss Sarah Leddon, of Philadelphia.	04/23/1822
At Fredericktown, on Thursday morning last, the Rev. Samuel Knox, of Baltimore, to Miss Zeruah M'Cleery, of that place.	04/23/1822
On Monday evening last, by the Rev. Mr. Bartow, Mr. William Warren,	04/24/1822

Marriage and Death Notices	Date
to Miss Ann Boyd, all of this city.	
On Monday evening last, by the Rev. Mr. Hinkle, Mr. Daniel Stansbury, of Patapsco Neck, to Miss Mary Ann, eldest daughter of Mr. Wm. Goodman, of Annapolis.	04/24/1822
On Tuesday morning, in St. Peter's Church, by the Rev. Mr. Whitefield, Mr. John Jones, to Miss Margaret McDermott, all of this city.	04/24/1822
On Tuesday, the 23rd inst., by the Rt. Rev. Bishop Kemp, James Bosley, Esq., to Elizabeth Nicholson Noel, eldest daughter of the late Dr. Perry E. Noel.	04/24/1822
On Tuesday morning, the 22nd inst., in the 21st year of her age, Miss Mary Hickly, the only daughter of Mr. Sebastian Hickly, an old and respectable inhabitant of this city, after a painful illness of about five weeks, which she bore with uncommon Christian patience, and resignation to the will of God.	04/24/1822 04/25/1822
In Talbot county, Md., Mr. Robert Dawson to Miss Susan Harrison.	04/25/1822
On the 23rd inst., Mr. Adam Riley.	04/25/1822
At Easton, Md. Miss Ann Kennard, daughter of the late Owen Kennard.	04/25/1822
Departed this life, on the 31st ult., Mr. Samuel Smith, of Patapsco Neck, in his 82nd year. He was a man universally esteemed, and one of God's noblest works, an honest man. He was born, resided, died, and was buried on the same plantation.	04/25/1822
On Tuesday evening last, by the Rev. Mr. Finley, Mr. Israel McNulty, to Miss Ann Grant, all of this city.	04/26/1822
On the 16th inst., at the residence of Col. Learned, in Paca street, Mrs. Lydia Gates, relict of the late Maj. Lemuel Gates, of the U. S. Army, in the 60th year of her age. Few persons have passed through the vicissitudes of life with such fortitude, and none have lived with more respect. Possessing a mind of superior strength and activity, she pursued the objects of duty with zeal and perseverance. Kind, benevolent, charitable, and upright, in her feelings and principles, through life she was endeared to her family and friends, as an affectionate mother, and an interesting companion. During a long and severe sickness, borne with the most heroic fortitude, she looked upon its termination with that perfect composure, which shewed a mind prepared for the event, and died as a Christian should die, with	04/27/1822

Marriage and Death Notices	Date
unshaken confidence and joyous hope for a blissful immortality beyond the grave. To the last period of her existence, her intellect was clear and lucid, and she passed into eternity like one who drops to rest to wake in a morning of glory.	
On Wednesday, 25th inst., James Kennedy, on his birthday, having completed the 63rd year of his age. His sufferings were protracted and acute, and of a complicated nature, being an assemblage of afflictions scarcely paralleled. During the whole time of his afflictions, he manifested Christian resignation to the will of God, and resigned his breath with the consoling hope of eternal salvation, through the merits of Jesus Christ.	04/27/1822
At Hereford, in Baltimore county, on Tuesday last, the 23rd inst., after a short illness, Mrs. Martha Gwynn, wife of Mr. John R. Gwynn, of Baltimore county, in the 21st year of her age - by her death, a disconsolate husband has been suddenly deprived of an amiable and affectionate wife, esteemed by all who knew her, under circumstances peculiarly distressing – one short month saw her in full bloom of health – a mother and a corpse.	04/27/1822
On Sunday, 7th inst., at Princess Anne, Somerset county, Md., by the Rev. Mr. Samuel Grace, Mr. John V. Pinter, to Miss Leah W., youngest daughter of Mr. Azedock Long.	04/29/1822
On the 18th inst., after a lingering illness, Mrs. Mary Donnelly, in the 56th year of her age. The deceased was a native of Ireland, and through life a member of the Roman Catholic Church, in the faith of which she happily lived and triumphantly died. She bore a long and painful confinement, without a murmur, and received with the most perfect tranquility the fiat which removed her from earth; calmly resigning all things into the hands of that God, with whom she hoped to dwell forever.	04/29/1822
Last evening, by the Rev. Mr. Bartow, Mr. Emanuel D. Smith, to Miss Jane Elizabeth Ann Bouzee, both of this city.	04/30/1822
On Saturday last, the 7th inst., Mr. Obediah Mathewson, merchant, of this city, and a native of Rhode Island, in the 29th year of his age.	04/30/1822
On Tuesday evening last, by the Rev. J. M. Duncan, Mr. Jonathan Rogers, to Miss Maria Smith, both of this city.	05/01/1822
On Tuesday, the 16th ult., by the Rev. Wm. Armstrong, Dr. Samuel Turner, of Loudon county, Va., to Miss Amanda M. Williams, of	05/02/1822

Marriage and Death Notices	Date
Montgomery county, Md.	
In Frederick county, on Thursday last, Mr. Elie Graff, to Miss Amanda Biggs, both of that city.	05/02/1822
On Tuesday evening, Mrs. Isabella Alexander, in the 77th year of her age.	05/02/1822
Lately, at Lisbon, of pulmonary consumption, in the 29th year of his age, Dr. Edward Barton, a gentleman widely known and greatly esteemed in this city. He received his elementary instruction in letters, at Weathersfield, Connecticut, under the Abbe Fiserand, and completed his education at the college of St. Mary's Balimore. His class mates loved him for his excellent qualities of temper and heart, and admired for his talents and application. On quitting the college he studied medicine in Philadelphia; took his degree with reputation; and then visited Paris, London, and Edinburg, in order to qualify himself further for usefulness and eminence in his profession. During a residence of two years in Europe, his assiduity and progress corresponded with those of his early life, and he left upon the minds of several of the most distinguished European professors, the same deep impressions in his favor, which were common to the faculty and to all of his acquaintance at home. On his return to Philadelphia, he was chosen one of the physicians of the dispensary, of the Asylum of the Deaf and Dumb, and of the St. George's Society. By the uniform rectitude and sedateness of his deportment, and an unostentatious display of zeal, knowledge, and judgement, he was daily fortifying himself in the respect and confidence of his fellow ciizens, and acquiring business and credit as a practitioner, when he was seized wih the malady to which he fell a vicim. Under the advice of his friends, he vainly sought a cure, first by travel in the northern states, and an intermission of his professional labours, and then by seeking a milder climate and new scenes across the Atlanttic. No one of his age had carried abroad more emphatic testimony to his merits; his situation and manners excited the sympathy & obtained the best offices, of the strangers among whom he expired; and the intelligence of his demise produced in his former inmates a strong sensation of grief and regret, though his condition on his embarkation was such as nearly to extinguish all hope of his recovery. *National Gazette (Philadelphia)*	05/02/1822
On Thursday evening last, by the Rt. Rev. Bishop Kemp, Richard Dorsey, Esq., to Mrs. Elizabeth Sherlock, both of this city.	05/04/1822
On Thursday evening last, by the Rev. Mr. Linthicum, Mr. James	05/04/1822

Marriage and Death Notices	Date
Peregoy, of this city, to Miss Mary Price, of Anne Arundel county.	
At Bellevue, on Thursday evening last, by the Rev. Mr. Henshaw, Mr. Andrew Aldridge, merchant, to Miss Ann Maria C. Hughes, both of this city.	05/04/1822
In Baltimore county, Mr. Caleb Hunt to Miss Ann Curtis.	05/04/1822
In Harford county, Mr. Caleb Pue, Esq. to Miss Harriet Bond. Mr. Joseph Whitson to Mrs. Elizabeth M'Faddon. Mr. John Miller, of Pennsylvania, to Miss Mary Ryland, of Harford. Mr. John Bevard, of Harford, to Miss Margaret Pool, of York, Pa.	05/04/1822
Yesterday afternoon, after a short and severe illness, Mrs. Elizabeth, wife of Mr. John Redgraves, and only daughter of Mr. Henry Hoffman. The friends and acquaintances of the family are invited to attend her funeral, from her father's dwelling, in Paca street, at 4 o'clock, this afternoon.	05/04/1822
At his residence, in Prince George's County, Maryland, on Saturday morning last, Capt. Henry Hill, aged about 73. He entered the service of his country during the Revolutionary War, as a captain in the Maryland Militia, and was at the battle of Germantown. He was distinguished for all those social and domestic virtues, which characterize the honest man and pious Christian.	05/04/1822
In Harford county, Mr. Samuel Doherty, in the 83rd year of his age.	05/04/1822
On Friday evening last, by the Rev. Mr. Moranville, Mr. Thomas Clark, to Mrs. Morris, of Fell's Point.	05/07/1822
On Saturday morning last, by the Rev. Jno. M. Duncan, Mr. Benjamin Harrison, merchant, to Miss Mary Ann Haubert, both of this city.	05/07/1822
At Judge Earle's, the residence of her Uncle, Queen Ann's county, Eastern Shore, of Maryland, on the 22nd of April, Mrs. Maria H. Harris, wife of Turbutt Harris, in the 33rd year of her age.	05/07/1822
Last evening, by the Rev. Mr. Beir, Mr. John P. Howard, to Miss Henrietta Beckwith, all of this city.	05/08/1822
On the 30th ult., Josiah Brown, in the 57th year of his age, a member of the Society of Friends, and for upwards of thirty years past, a respectable and worthy citizen of the city of Baltimore. He possessed, in an eminent degree, the characteristics of a noble mind – open, generous, and humane – yet steadfast and persevering in the discharge	05/08/1822

Marriage and Death Notices	Date
of his known duties towards society. His loss is deeply regretted by his family, his friends, and acquaintance.	
After a lingering illness, which he bore with Christian fortitude, Maj. John M. Kane. His friends are invited to attend his funeral, from his late dwelling, in Aisquith street, O. T., at 7 o'clock.	05/08/1822
At his residence, in Frederick county, of a lingering illness, which he bore with Christian resignation, Upton Hammond, in the 43rd year of his age.	05/08/1822
On Friday, the 25th April, near Emittsburg, John Heugh, Esq., of Georgetown, District of Columbia.	05/08/1822
On Tuesday evening last, by the Rev. Mr. Bartow, Mr. James Jones, to Miss Justina W. Schaeler, all of this city.	05/09/1822
On Tuesday evening last, by the Rev. Mr. Bester, Mr. William Amey, to Miss Elizabeth Reither, all of this city.	05/09/1822
On Tuesday, the 7th inst., of a pulmonary complaint, at Powhatan, Mrs. Anne, consort of Mr. Hall Wilson, aged 33 years, leaving a distressed husband and four helpless infants to lament their irreparable loss.	05/09/1822
In Philadelphia, on Thursday, 9th inst., by the Rev. Dr. Helmuth, Mr. Michael Warner, Jr., of Baltimore, to Miss Caroline, youngest daughter of George Krebs, Esq., of the former place.	05/10/1822
In Queen Ann's county, on the 7th inst., by the Rev. Mr. Moynihan, Richard C. Hall, of Prince George's county, Md., to Miss Mary C. Hall, daughter of Richard Hall, Esq., of Queen Ann's county.	05/10/1822
On Tuesday evening past, by the Rev. Jared Sparks, Mr. John Hastings, to Mary A., youngest daughter of Thomas Sweeting, Esq., all of this city.	05/11/1822
On Thursday evening, the 9th inst., by the Rev. Dr. Kurtz, Mr. John Fisher, of this city, to Miss Elizabeth Taben, from Bremen, Germany.	05/11/1822
On the 8th inst., after a short, but painful illness, of only 4 days, Mr. John Price Rose, in the 37th year of his age, long a respectable inhabitant of this city – he has left a disconsolate wife, four children, and a large circle of relatives, to mourn their irreparable loss. *"In the midst of life, we are in death."*	05/11/1822

Marriage and Death Notices	Date
By the Rev. Dr. George Roberts, on Sunday last, Jacob G. Crumwell to Miss Elizabeth Hilton, all of this place.	05/13/1822
On Tuesday evening, the 14th inst., by the Rev. Mr. M'Cann, Mr. Robert Wiley, to Mrs. Mary Ann Cragin, both of this city.	05/15/1822
On the 13th inst., Miss Susanna Walker, daughter of Charles Walker, of Baltimore county.	05/15/1822
Yesterday morning, of a pulmonary disease, in the 28th year of her age, Miss Christiana Kurtz. Her friends and acquaintance are respectfully invited to attend her funeral, from the residence of her mother, in German street, between Howard and Liberty streets, at 4 o'clock, this afternoon.	05/15/1822
Yesterday noon, Isabella Entwisle, youngest daughter of Mr. M. Blakeley, of this city.	05/15/1822
On Wednesday, 5th inst., at her residence in Somerset county, Mrs. Mary S. Winder, relict of the late Gen. Levin Winder. Those who knew the amiable and polished manners of this most estimable lady – her devoted and exemplary attention to her children, will, with sincerity of heart, condole with them under this most afflicting bereavement.	05/15/1822
On Tuesday evening last, by the Rt. Rev. Bishop Kemp, Henry B. Chew, of Philadelphia, to Harriet, daughter of Gen. Charles Ridgely, of Hampton.	05/16/1822
On the 14th inst., after a short, but severe illness, which she bore with Christian fortitude, Miss Catherine Belts, in the 22nd year of her age. The deceased was an amiable and dutiful child, and has left a numerous circle of friends and relations to lament their irreparable loss.	05/16/1822
Yesterday, at twelve o'clock, after a long and painful illness, which he bore with the most exemplary fortitude, Dr. John Welsh, 47 years of age. If a life of charity and Christian virtues entitles us to regard, the deceased merited it fully. His friends and relatives are particularly invited to attend his funeral, from his late dwelling, in North Frederick street, two doors from Market street, on Friday morning, at 8 o'clock precisely.	05/16/1822
On Wednesday, the 1st inst., at his residence, in Westminster, Md., Dr. George Colegate, in the 39th year of his age. In the death of Dr. Colegate, his wife and three infant children mourn an irreparable loss. The village of Westminster is deprived of one of its best citizens, and	05/16/1822

Marriage and Death Notices	Date
the district of country through which he extended his professional labours, has lost a skillful and valuable Physician.	
At sea, on the 7th February last, on board the ship Voltaire, whilst on his passage from Batavia to Amsterdam, Capt. Daniel MacPherson, late of Philadelphia.	05/16/1822
In Cambridge, Dorchester county, on the 2nd inst., aged 36 years, after a very short illness of a few hours, Mrs. Mary E. Le Compte, relict of the late Benjamin W. Lecompte, Esq. In the space of six months, society has been bereaved of two of its brightest ornaments, and has been called to deplore a loss hitherto unexampled. Never did the shaft of death produce so deep and wide spread affliction. The best encomium upon the deceased would be a simple recital of her virtues. She was universally acknowledged to possess and practice all those mild, amiable, and unobtrusive virtues which constitute the highest excellence of female character. Frugality, industry, benevolence, charity to the poor without ostentation or misguided profusion, sweetness and serenity of temper, humility and an unaffected conversation and deportment; rendered her the best and tenderest of wives, the most affectionate and devoted mother, the kind mistress, and sincere friend. For many years, she was a sincere and humble believer in the Christian religion. Her piety was ardent, yet meek; and all its heartfelt consolations disarmed death of all its terrors, save the recollection of a young and tender offspring, who in the very morning of their days, are deprived of the best of parents. To the ken of earthly beings, this last stroke of death would appear ruthless and severe; but it is not for mortals to arraign the dispensations of Providence, to murmur and repine. Let those who mourn her loss, also profit by the example which the virtuous tenor of her whole life exhibited, and the impressive lesson which her sudden death ought forcibly to inculcate.	05/16/1822
On the 25th ult., after a very short illness, at her late residence in Queen Ann's county, Mrs. Sarah B. Finley, consort of George Finley, Esq., in the 30th year of her age – deeply lamented by an afflicted husband, and a numerous and affectionate connexion.	05/16/1822
Tuesday evening last, by the Rev. Dr. Gray, Dr. James Bain, to Miss Mary Ann Donnelly, both of this city.	05/17/1822
On the 11th inst., by the Rev. Dr. Jennings, Mr. John Hill, druggist, Pratt street, to Miss Sarah Brown, both of this city.	05/17/1822
At Green-Castle, Pa., the Rev. John Lind, Pastor of the Associate Reformed Church of Hagerstown, to Miss Margaretta St. Clair C.	05/17/1822

Marriage and Death Notices	Date
Young, daughter of the late Rev. John Young.	
On Thursday morning, the 9th inst., after a protracted illness, Mrs. Rebecca Burnham, in the 63rd year of her age.	05/17/1822
At Reisterstown, Baltimore County, on the 26th April last, Miss Nancy Mercer, in the 66th year of her age, after a short, but painful illness, which she bore with the resignation of a Christian.	05/17/1822
At the Retreat, Charles county, Md., on the 14th inst., Daniel of St. Thomas Jenifer, Esq., after a severe illness of four weeks, leaving a wife, to whom he had been married less than six months.	05/17/1822
On Thursday evening last, in St. Peter's Church, by the Rev. Mr. Henshaw, Randle H. Moale, Esq., of this city, to Miss Elizabeth S. Peck, daughter of Nicholas Peck, Esq., of Bristol, R. I.	05/18/1822
In Fredericktown, Mr. Worthington Johnson, to Miss Mary J. F. Potts, daughter of the late Richard Potts.	05/20/1822
In Talbot county, Mr. John R. Plater, Esq., of St. Mary's county, to Miss Matilda Edmonson, of Easton, Md.	05/20/1822
On the 17th inst., Sarah, widow of the late David Whalen, and eldest daughter of the late Zachariah Macubbin.	05/20/1822
On Thursday last, the 16th inst., in the 23rd year of her age, Mrs. Sarah Young, wife of Mr. Wm. Young, of this city.	05/20/1822
In Calvert county, Md., Mrs. Mary Clare, relict of the late Mr. John Clare.	05/20/1822
At Centreville, after a very long and distressing illness, Mrs. Rebecca E. Hopper, wife of Philemon B. Hopper, Esq., in the 29th year of her age.	05/20/1822
At her residence, in Queen Ann's county, Mrs. Sarah R. Finley, Esq., in the 30th year of her age.	05/20/1822
In Easton, Md., Miss Sarah Price, in the 23rd year of her age. Mrs. Rebecca Colston, consort of Saml. Colson, Esq.	05/20/1822
On Thursday evening, at St. Peter's Church, by the Rev. J. Whitfield, Mr. James Duke, to Mrs. Cecelia Heaps, all of this city.	05/21/1822
By the Rev. Jehu Finlay, on the 20th inst., James Carnighan, Esq., to	05/21/1822

Marriage and Death Notices	Date
Mrs. Brook, all of this city.	
At St. Augustine, East Florida, on the 24th of April, Capt. Thomas B. Bennett, in the 43rd year of his age, and for many years, a respectable ship master out of the port of Baltimore. He was a sincere friend, and affectionate husband, and a kind father. The morning of his life was bright, his meridian clear, and his evening cloudy. "It seemed as if misfortune had marked him for her own."	05/21/1822
In Miledgeville, Geo., on the 5th inst., Thomas P. Carnes, Esq., in the 60th year of his age. He was a native of Maryland; of considerable eminence as a lawyer; presided in the Superior Court of the state of Georgia for many years, was afterwards a Representative in Congress, and repeatedly elected to both branches of the Legislature of that state. "The evening of his life was as dark as its meridian had been serene. It seemed as if misfortune had marked him for her own.	05/21/1822
On the 16th inst., at Friends Meeting House, in Old Town, William Trimble to Mary Brown, both of this city.	05/22/1822
On the 21st inst., at the residence of G. Melvin, Esq., by the Rev. Dr. Kurtz, Thomas Yarrell, Esq., to Miss Augusta, daughter of the late John Hubly, Esq., of the city of Lancaster.	05/22/1822
On Monday morning, William H. Brown, eldest son of Stewart Brown, of this city, in the 24th year of his age.	05/22/1822
On Sunday evening, after a long and distressing illness, Mrs. Matilda Hill, wife of George Hill, in the 25th year of her age. She has left an affectionate husband and children, another brilliant evidence of the mercy of God, and unbounded love of Jesus Christ; in her last moments, her only wish was to 'go'; "the door is open and I am invited to go in."	05/22/1822
On Tuesday evening last, by the Rev. Mr. Henshaw, Mr. Benjamin B. Beale, of Washington city, to Miss Caroline Matilda, youngest daughter of George Warner, Esq., of this city.	05/23/1822
At Philadelphia, Mr. William Taylor, of Baltimore, to Miss Rebecca Sanderson.	05/23/1822
On Wednesday evening last, by the Rt. Rev. Bishop Kemp, Lt. Joseph M. Baxley, U. S. A., to Mrs. Mary Horre, of this city.	05/24/1822
At Hagerstown, Mr. John M. May, to Miss Maria S. W. Kendal. Mr. Alexander Kennedy to Miss Susan Booth.	05/24/1822

Marriage and Death Notices	Date
At his residence, near Salisbury, on Thursday, the 16th of May, at the hour of eight in the evening, Mr. Thomas Byrd, in the 69th year of his age, leaving behind him a disconsolate widow and three endearing children to bemoan their irreparable loss. Mr. Byrd has passed his life in industry, sobriety, and economy – he was one of those whose conduct has proved *"an honest man is the noblest work of God."* In his death, the indigent have lost a good friend, and society a valuable member, but we can only say "The Lord gave, and the Lord hath taken away, and blessed be the name of the Lord." Mr. Byrd's illness was short, but powerful; under all his deprivations, he appeared to exercise a genuine Christian fortitude, and to view his approaching end with calm resignation, as an event that would end all his troubles. "He has fought the good fight, he has finished his course," and is now gone, we hope, to receive the welcome approbation of "Come thou good and faithful servant, enter into the joys of thy Lord. Y. Z.	05/24/1822
On Thursday evening last, by the Rev. Mr. Bartow, Mr. Jacob Laudeman, to Miss Eleanor Harrison, all of this city.	05/25/1822
In Harford county, on Thursday evening last, by the Rev. Dr. Glendy, Mr. Charles D. W. Johnson, of Fredericktown, to Miss Eliza McConkey, of Harford county.	05/25/1822
On the 21st inst., after a short, but severe illness, Mrs. Rebecca Page, consort of John Page, Esq., in the 38th year of her age – her bereaved husband and five small children have sustained an irreparable loss. Such a bereavement very seldom happens to the human family.	05/25/1822
On Tuesday evening last, by the Rev. Mr. Helfenstein, Mr. Charles F. Wasmus, to Miss Euphenia Pein, both of this city.	05/28/1822
Yesterday evening, by the Rev. Mr. Helfenstein, Mr. Valentine Lutz, to Miss Christiana Hedrick, of Baltimore county.	05/28/1822
This morning, Mrs. Ann Guthrow, in the 80th year of her age. Her friends and acquaintances are invited to attend her funeral, at 8 o'clock, tomorrow morning, from her late dwelling, in South Charles street.	05/28/1822
On the night of the 26th instant, Mrs. Elizabeth Dumest, in the 61st year of her age.	05/29/1822
On the Coast of Africa, Capt. Andrew Smith, of Baltimore.	05/29/1822
On Monday evening last, by the Rev. Mr. Smith, Mr. Thomas C.	05/30/1822

Marriage and Death Notices	Date
Dunlevy, to Miss Keziah Askew, all of this city.	
Last evening, by the Rev. Mr. Smith, Mr. Jacob Crawford, of Delaware, to Miss Frances Ducheman, of this city.	05/31/1822
After a severe and protracted illness, William Cathell, in the 34th year of his age. His Masonic brethren are requested to meet at Washington Lodge Room, at half past 4 o'clock, to assist at his funeral; and his friends generally are invited to attend the funeral from his house in Old Town, at 5 o'clock, this afternoon. Friday morning, May 31st.	05/31/1822
In Pensacola, W. F., where he had gone for the benefit of his health, John V. D. Vorhees, M. D., health physician for the above port.	05/31/1822
On Thursday evening last, by the Rev. Mr. Bartow, Mr. William Pate, to Miss Mary Greaves, all of this city.	06/01/1822
On Tuesday evening last, by the Rev. Bryan, in Frederick county, Mr. Brian Philpot, of Baltimore county, to Miss Harriet W. Belt, of Frederick county.	06/01/1822
In Charles county, Md., on Tuesday, the 21st ult., Mrs. Eleanor P. Digges, the much respected consort of Francis Digges, Esq.	06/01/1822
On the 27th ult., at her residence, in Baltimore county, Mrs. Catherine Little, in the 70th year of her age, much respected by her relations and neighbors.	06/01/1822
On Saturday evening last, by the Rev. Mr. Baer, Capt. William C. Deal, to Miss Elizabeth F. E. Reese, all of this city.	06/03/1822
On Thursday evening last, by the Rev. Mr. Hagerty, Mr. Peter Voinard, of New York, to Miss Casandra Inloes, of this city.	06/03/1822
On Tuesday last, James Massey, Esq., to Mrs. Frances Kennard, both of Queen's Ann's county.	06/03/1822
Last evening, after a short illness, Mr. Thomas Long, aged 67. Of him, it may be emphatically said, that he was an honest man, "the noblest work of God."	06/03/1822
By the Rev. Dr. Glendy, on the 15th ult., Mr. James Arnold, to Mrs. Nancy McKee.	06/04/1822
By the Rev. Dr. Glendy, on the evening of Thursday last, Mr. James	06/04/1822

Marriage and Death Notices	Date
Reside, to Miss Ann Crozier, all of this city.	
On Thursday evening last, by the Rev. Mr. McCormick, Mr. George Bailly, to Miss Ann Marie Browning.	06/04/1822
On Thursday evening last, by the Rev. Mr. Hinkle, Mr. Thomas Dougherty, to Miss Jane Robinson, all of this city.	06/06/1822
On Tuesday evening last, by the Rev. Mr. Hinkle, Mr. Joseph T. Beeman, to Miss Mary Corner, all of this city.	06/06/1822
On Tuesday, the 4th inst., Mr. John Bradenbaugh, an old and respectable citizen, in the 81st year of his age, venerated and beloved by all who knew him.	06/08/1822
At Salem, Mr. Benjamin C. Rhodes, merchant, of Baltimore, to Miss Mary Luscomb, of that town.	06/10/1822
On Saturday last, at the United States Arsenal in Baltimore county, Mrs. Hannah Hopkins, wife of Maj. David Hopkins, and daughter of the late Stephen Arnold, Esq., of Rhode Island.	06/10/1822
On the 10th inst., at his residence in St. Mary's County, Md., Mr. Lewis Fenwick, in the 49th year of his age.	06/10/1822
By the Rev. Dr. Kurtz, Mr. Richard D. Scrivener, to Miss Margaret Ann League, all of this city.	06/11/1822
On Saturday last, in Harford county, at the seat of Dr. Davis, in the 20th year of her age, Miss Adeline Elizabeth Hynson, third daughter of the late Ringgold Hynson, Esq., of Kent county. If beauty, innocence, and worth were sureties for life, then had we not to record this obituary.	06/12/1822
In Easton, Md., on Wednesday evening last, Mr. Joseph Hussey, after a lingering illness.	06/12/1822
By the Rev. John Valiant, on Tuesday morning last, Mr. John Pyle, to Miss Elizabeth Ecoff, of Baltimore county.	06/13/1822
On the evening of Tuesday last, by the Rev. John Valiant, Mr. Wm. Green, to Miss Eliza Duvall, of Baltimore city.	06/13/1822
Departed this transitory scene, on the evening of Tuesday last, Mrs. Sophia Taylor, consort of James Taylor, in the 57th year of her age, after an illness of six months, which she bore with Christian fortitude. Her life was an example of industry, charity, hospitality, benevolence,	06/13/1822

Marriage and Death Notices	Date
friendship, and love. In her death, it may be truly said, her family has suffered an irreparable loss, and society is deprived of one of its brightest ornaments – she was an affectionate mother and loving friend. She lived beloved, and died lamented. Let her many virtues be engraved on the hearts of a numerous acquaintance, and her connexions be consoled with the assurance that she has gone to another and a better world – and closed a life in full confidence of the abundant mercy of God.	
"In the midst of life, we are in death." *Obituary.* Died, on the 9th inst., George W. Moore, Esq., in the 45th year of his age, long a respectable inhabitant of Baltimore, and for upwards of twenty-two years held an important office under the Corporation; he has left behind him an aged mother, a loving wife, with a large family, and a numerous circle of relations and friends to lament their irreparable loss. Farewell dear friend, thou art from a tender hearted mother, a loving family, an intimate friend*, and a troublesome world removed, by whom your friendship shall long be esteemed, and your memory loved. H. *The author.	06/13/1822
At Abingdon, the 31st ult., Mrs. Leah Farrow, aged 101 years and six months. She was born at Higham, in Dec. 1720, and has lived more than one half the time elapsed since our forefathers landed at Plymouth.	06/13/1822
In Salem, Mrs. Ward, widow of the late Samuel Ward, Esq., aged 72. In consequence of an alarm occasioned by a heavy clap of thunder, about 11 o'clock, she fell into a convulsive fit, and expired.	06/13/1822
On Thursday last, by the Rev. Mr. Valiant, Mr. Thomas Floray, to Miss Elizabeth Pine, all of this city.	06/15/1822
On Thursday evening last, by the Rt. Rev. Bishop Kemp, Mr. Jonas M'Pherson, to Mrs. Ann Alcock, all of this city.	06/15/1822
Early this morning, Mr. Lewis O'Connor, a native of Ireland, in the 38th year of his age, after a long and painful illness, which he bore with Christian fortitude and resignation. His friends and acquaintances are respectfully invited to attend his funeral, tomorrow afternoon, at 3 o'clock, from his late dwelling, corner of Pitt and Temple streets.	06/15/1822
At Cape Coast Castle, Africa, Mr. Isaac Blanchard, supercargo of the brig Pedlar, of this port.	06/17/1822
On Sunday, 16th June, by the Rev. Mr. Hinkle, Mr. John F. De Valengin,	06/18/1822

Marriage and Death Notices	Date
to Miss Mary Ann Haley, all of this city.	
On Saturday evening, 15th inst., by the Rev. Mr. Gibson, Mr. Peter Bruce, to Miss Elizabeth Downing, both of this city.	06/18/1822
Last evening, by the Rev. E. J. Reis, Mr. James Boding, to Mary E. Foder, both of this city.	06/18/1822
On Saturday last, at 10 o'clock in the evening, Mr. Frederick Focke, in the 50th year of his age, for many years a respectable citizen of Baltimore.	06/18/1822
By the Rev. Dr. Glendy, on the evening of Thursday last, Mr. James White to Miss Sarah Winrod, all of this city.	06/19/1822
At Friends Meeting, in Le Roy Ville, Jefferson county, New York, George J. Knight, of Brownville, formerly of this city, to Abi Brown, daughter of Clary Brown, and niece to Maj. Gen. Brown.	06/19/1822
On Tuesday evening last, by the Rev. Mr. Kurtz, Mr. Joseph Arng, of Georgetown, D. C., to Miss Caroline Henrietta Von Weisensee, niece to Charles G. Boehm, of this city.	06/20/1822
This morning, after a painful illness, John Elliott Simpson, in the 20th year of his age. His friends and acquaintances are invited to attend his funeral, this afternoon, at 4 o'clock, from his late dwelling, Liberty st., O. T.	06/20/1822
On Monday morning last, Mr. Lavallin Barry, in the 53rd year of his age. The deceased was, for many years, an officer of the Bank of Baltimore, and while there his conduct insured him the regard and friendship of his fellow citizens. The high confidence and esteem he enjoyed, and the many virtues emanating from a well spent life, may well insure him the appellation of God's noblest work, 'an honest man.' After a short illness of four days, he was summoned to that "bourne from whence no traveler returns," leaving a wife and six children to mourn their irreparable bereavement. Alas! how uncertain and futile is life – It was but four days – four little days ago, and we beheld the deceased, high in health and spirits, surrounded by his family and friends, and blessed with every endearment that could render life valuable and happy. But ah! The sad reverse – almost without warning, from a tender wife and affectionate children, he has been suddenly torn by the rude hand of death and severed from them forever. Vanity of vanities, said the inspired writer, all is vanity. When our most valuable friends are thus torn from us, we may well exclaim,	06/20/1822

Marriage and Death Notices	Date
Why should we toil for triumphs of an hour, Why should we seek for wealth or soar for fame, Earth's highest station ends in the "here he lies," And dust to dust concludes her noblest song.	
By the Rev. Dr. Glendy, on the evening of Tuesday last, Mr. James Hughy to Miss Isabella Gamble, all of this city.	06/21/1822
On Tuesday morning last, by the Rev. Dr. Roberts, Mr. Jesse W. Cook, of Pennsylvania, to Miss Elizabeth S. Johns, daughter of Mr. Hosea Johns, of this city.	06/26/1822
In this city, on the 24th inst., Sarah Prince, daughter of John W. Osgood, Esq., aged two years.	06/26/1822
On Sunday evening, the 23rd inst., Mrs. Prudence Gough, relict of Harry Dorsey Gough, late of Perry hall, Baltimore county, in the 69th year of her age.	06/27/1822
Last evening, by the Rev. Mr. Baer, Mr. Charles Williams, to Mrs. Sarah Hubbard, all of this city.	06/28/1822
At 7 o'clock P. M., on Friday, the 28th inst., in the 16th year of her age, Miss Mary Olcott Barry, daughter of the Rev. Dr. Barry.	06/29/1822
On Friday evening, by the Rev. J. M. Duncan, Mr. William Primrose, to Miss Jane Russell, all of this city.	07/01/1822
At Bel Air, Prince George's county, on Thursday, 27th June, by the Rev. Mr. Shaw, William Woodville, Esq., to Elizabeth, eldest daughter of Benj. Ogle, Esq.	07/01/1822
On Thursday last, by the Rev. Mr. Valiant, Dr. Julius C. Mann, to Miss Prudence Thomas, all of this city.	07/02/1822
On Thursday last, by the Rev. Mr. Valiant, Mr. Vincent Leary, to Miss Margaret Harvey, all of this city.	07/02/1822
At Salem, by the Rev. Mr. Brazer, Mr. Nathaniel W. Osgood to Miss Mary B. Archer. Mr. Daniel Millet, Jr. to Miss Mary Caldwell.	07/02/1822
On Thursday evening, the 4th July, by the Rev. Dr. Glendy, Mr. Joseph Michard, to Miss Eloise Bentalou Sanger, niece to Col. Paul Bentalou, Marshall of the District of Maryland.	07/05/1822

Marriage and Death Notices	Date
On Wednesday morning, at his residence, Mulberry street, Mr. Daniel Conner. He was, for nearly thirty years, a resident of this city, and in all the relative duties of life, could not be surpassed; a fond father, a kind husband, a sincere friend, one of whom the tale of sorrow- could not be told without a falling tear of sympathy – it may be well said, the stranger's father and the widow's friend.	07/05/1822
At Berry Hill, the residence of Richard Gittings, Esq., on the 30th ult., after a short, but severe indisposition, Mr. James Gittings, in the 31st year of his age.	07/05/1822
At Germantown, Penn., in the 55th year of his age, Daniel Thomas, a member of the society of Friends.	07/05/1822
On Saturday last, much regretted by all who knew him, in the 30th year of his age, Joseph H. Causten, son of Mr. Isaac Causten, of this city, of a protracted illness, originating from that fatal disease, yellow fever, contracted in the West Indies.	07/05/1822
At Washington City, Mrs. Catherine Walker Brent, wife of Col. Wm. Brent.	07/05/1822
At New York, Mr. Timothy Burn, printer.	07/05/1822
Died, on Wednesday, the 19th ult., in Kent county, Frederick Worrell, Esq. This young gentleman had but just been admitted to the bar and enjoyed a prospect as rich and extensive, as popularity and acknowledged talents could present. His amiable temper, his soft and winning manners, his wit and colloquial excellence, rendered him the favorite of all who knew him. But it was not his disposition and deportment alone, that distinguished him. His mind was active, powerful and capacious, and for his years enriched almost beyond example, with the learning of the law, and its auxillary sciences. He was an affectionate and dutiful relative, a sincere and generous friend, a man of truth and talents, calculated not only to become eminently useful to society. But also a splendid ornament to his profession. He was bound to life, by more than ordinary ties, and is followed to the tomb with more than ordinary grief.	07/05/1822
On Tuesday evening last, by the Rev. Mr. Helfenstein, Mr. William Adams, to Miss Catherine Schaeffer, both of this city.	07/06/1822
On Tuesday evening last, by the Rev. Mr. Helfenstein, Mr. Mark Thurall, to Miss Catherine Sames, both of this city.	07/06/1822

Marriage and Death Notices	Date
On Thursday, 4th July, by the Rev. Mr. McCann, Mr. Jeremiah W. Harrison, of New Haven, Connecticut, to Miss Margaret Baker, of this city.	07/06/1822
On Tuesday evening last, by the Rev. Mr. Hagerty, Mr. Joshua Dabbs, to Miss Ann King, both of Baltimore county.	07/06/1822
Departed this life, on the 30th June, 1822, James Humphrey Neale, only son of John G. Neale, of this city, in the 6th year of his age.	07/06/1822
At Fredericktown, Mr. John D. Smith, to Miss Christiana Gomer.	07/07/1822
On Monday morning, the 8th inst., by the Rev. Mr. McCaine, John P. Harris, Esq., to Miss Ann Eliza Prill, all of this city.	07/09/1822
On Sunday evening, the 7th inst., by the Rev. Mr. Moranville, Mr. Edward Wells, to Miss Mary Ann Burke, all of this city.	07/09/1822
On Friday evening, by the Rev. J. M. Duncan, Mr. William Primrose, to Miss Jane Russell, both of this city.	07/09/1822
On Thursday evening, by the Rev. Mr. Baer, Mr. Charles Williams, to Mrs. Sarah Hubbard, both of this city.	07/09/1822
In Talbot county, at Friends Meeting house, Isaac Jenkinson, to Eliza Ann, daughter of James Neal.	07/09/1822
On the 4th inst., at Evergreen, the seat of Greenbury Goldsborough, Esq., by the Rev. Mr. Bayne, John G. Johnson, Esq., of Baltimore, to Ariana Frisby, youngest daughter of the late Andrew Price, Esq., of the above city.	07/09/1822
At the country seat of her father, Charles Bohn, Esq., Mrs. Margaret Cross, on the 6th inst., of a lingering pulmonary disease, in the 25th year of her age. By the death of this lady, a father has been bereaved of his only remaining child – a husband and two infant children are left to lament a loss irreparable. In the full possession of her mind, she was resigned to the will of her Redeemer – she prayed that if such were the will of God, that she might be removed from her state of suffering. In peace with the world, and surrounded by a numerous circle of relatives and friends, she died in the full assurance of a happy eternity – leaving a void in the affections of those, who best knew her worth, which can never be filled up. But they mourn not, as those "who mourn without hope."	07/10/1822

Marriage and Death Notices	Date
On the 2nd inst., in Leonard Town, St. Mary's County, at the residence of his uncle, Enoch J. Millard, Esq., after a severe illness, which confined him for some weeks in Baltimore, William J. Brooke, in the 21st year of his age. He was a young gentleman warm in his attachments, frank in his deportment, generous, humane, and charitable; his death is much regretted by his friends and numerous acquaintance.	07/10/1822
Last evening, by the Rev. Mr. Healey, Mr. Thomas Kay, to Miss Ann Wright, both of Baltimore county.	07/11/1822
On his passage from the West Indies to Baltimore, Capt. Alexander Adams, long a respectable inhabitant of this city. Possessing all of the characterisics of a gentleman, ogether with hose refinements, acquired by an extensive intercourse with the world, he was in an eminent degree calculated to ornament society. He enjoyed a quality of disposition scarcely equaled – he was mild, affable, and pleasing to all, and was by all beloved – his deportment was such as to command respect and admiration. Possessed neither of selfishness nor avarice – he was highly gifted wih liberality and generosity. He was one of those who during the late war with Great Britain exerted themselves in their country's cause. It will not be forgotten that he was a contributor to the honor of our national flag. Capt. Adams will long be regretted, as the fond husband, the idolizing parent, the sincere friend, the enterprizing and worthy citizen. The arms of an affectionate family were in vain outstretched to receive him, he was alas! clasped in those of death – their sweet and delighted anticipations, together with those of expecting friends, were dashed at once by the dreadful realization. The husband, the parent, the friend was no more. Grief now holds her empire o'er those countenances so lately lighted up with joy; and that mansion whose inmates were blest with every hope of bliss below, is now converted into the house of mourning. May they find consolation in the precepts of our holy Religion, for the irreparable deprivation which they have sustained. AGT E.	07/11/1822
On Monday last, Mrs. Catherine Shryack, in the 78th year of her age.	07/11/1822
In Norwich, state of Vermont, on the 20th June last, Samuel White, aged 100 years, 8 months, and 10 days.	07/11/1822
Last evening, by the Rev. E. J. Reis, Mr. David B. Small, to Miss Eliza Edes, both of this city.	07/12/1822
In Zanesville, Ohio, by the Rev. Mr. Hinkle, Moses D. Brooke, formerly of this city, to Miss Eliza McFadden, of the former place.	07/12/1822

Marriage and Death Notices	Date
By the Rev. Dr. Glendy, on the 4th inst., Mr. John Jamieson, to Miss Sarah Dove, of Baltimore county.	07/13/1822
By the Rev. Dr. Glendy, on the evening of Tuesday last, Capt. Daniel James, to Mrs. Maria Thomas, of this city.	07/13/1822
By the Rev. Dr. Glendy, on Thursday last, Mr. Isaac Stallings, to Miss Ann Clarke, of Baltimore county.	07/13/1822
On Friday last, in consequence of a fall from the roof of a house, during the late fire on McElderry's wharf, Stephen Davis, a native of Shropshire, England.	07/13/1822
In Philadelphia, on Tuesday, the 9th inst., on her way to Baltimore, from New Orleans, where she had resided the last three years, Mrs. Margaret Lewis, relict of Charles Lewis, late of this city.	07/13/1822
On Thursday evening last, by the Rev. Mr. Healey, Mr. James Baker, to Miss Ann Thompson, all of this city.	07/15/1822
On Monday, 8th inst., at the residence of her father's, by the Rev. Mr. Stone, Mr. Thomas Horsey, of Salisbury, Somerset county, Md., to Miss Sarah, daughter of the Hon. Judge Cooper, of Delaware.	07/15/1822
At Annapolis, on Thursday evening last, by the Rev. Mr. Ryland, Ramsay Waters, Esq., to Miss Ann, sister of Gen. Wm. H. Marriot.	07/15/1822
In Centreville, Md., Mrs. Elizabeth Dawson, consort of Thomas Dawson, in the 32nd year of her age.	07/15/1822
At Clifton Factory, in St. Mary's county, on the 5th inst., after a short illness, Walter L. Briscoe, in the thirty first year of his age. In his early death, society has lost a promising member, his parents, a dutiful son, his acquaintances, an agreeable companion, and his youthful and interesting consort, a tender and affectionate husband.	07/15/1822
In Cambridge, Mr. Levi Frisbie, Prof. of Natural Religion, Moral Philosophy, and Civil Polity, in the University, aged 38.	07/15/1822
At his residence in Dorchester county, Capt. Thomas F. Hill, in the 39th year of his age, after a severe illness of two weeks.	07/15/1822 07/19/1822
On Saturday evening last, by the Rev. Mr. Toy, Mr. Peter Wells, to Miss Elizabeth Gray.	07/16/1822

Marriage and Death Notices	Date
On Saturday evening last, by the Rev. Mr. Toy, Mr. Hugh Daugherty, to Miss Mary Ann Sablas, all of this city.	07/16/1822
Yesterday, at 12 o'clock, Mr. John M'Cristall, in the 42nd year of his age.	07/16/1822
Yesterday, in the 35th year of his age, Mr. Lewis Labome. His friends and acquaintance are requested to attend his funeral, this afternoon, at 3 o'clock, from his late residence, in Harrison street.	07/16/1822
In this city, after a short illness, Miss Elizabeth Jones, aged 18. Her death was caused by incautious bathing in cold water, when heated by exercise.	07/16/1822
At Snow Hill, Md., on Wednesday, 26th ult., by the Rev. Mr. Judah, Severn E. Parker, Esq., of Northampton county, Va., to Miss Catherine Purnell, of the former place.	07/17/1822
On Tuesday evening last, by the Rt. Rev. Bishop Kemp, Elisha Riggs, Esq., to Mary Ann, eldest daughter of Joseph Karrick, Esq., both of this city.	07/18/1822
On Wednesday evening, by the Rev. Mr. Sparks, Osmond C. Tiffany, Esq., to Miss Ann C., daughter of the late Rev. William Shaw, of Marshfield, Mass.	07/18/1822
On Thursday evening last, by the Rev. Mr. Kurtz, Mr. John Williams, to Miss Juliana Crawford, both of this city.	07/19/1822
In Easton, Md., Mr. Isaac Chambers, to Miss Henrietta Chamberlaine.	07/19/1822
In Talbot county, Md., Mr. John Grace, to Miss Mary Ann Morgan.	07/19/1822
Yesterday morning, Mrs. Elizabeth Hay, consort of Mr. Jacob Hay, aged 57 years, of a pulmonary disease, which she bore with Christian resignation.	07/19/1822
Yesterday morning, 18th inst., in the 63rd year of his age, Mr. William Dykes, a native of Scotland, but, for the last 35 years, a resident of Baltimore. He was "an honest man."	07/19/1822
At Easton, Md., Mrs. Elizabeth Merchant.	07/19/1822
In Talbot county, Md., Mr. James M'Neale.	07/19/1822

Marriage and Death Notices	Date
Mrs. Harriet Weeks, consort of Mr. James Weeks, of Queen Ann's county.	07/19/1822
On Thursday evening last, after an illness of five days, Mrs. Elizabeth Wilson, consort of David W. Wilson.	07/22/1822
"In the midst of life, we are in death." Departed this transitory life, on Saturday last, 20th inst., Mr. William Wood, in the 22nd year of his age. In the death of this young man, society is bereft of an honest, upright member.	07/22/1822
On the 21st instant, Mrs. Mary Coulter, consort of Dr. John Coulter, aged 56 years. If piety and purity; if mere excellence and feminine worth; if the love and veneration; if the gratitude and admiration of all who were nearly and dearly connected with her, could have rescued from the day of death, Mrs. Mary Coulter would have still survived. But yet she is gone! The beloved wife and darling mother is gone to happier climes. Be it is so. Heaven's will be done. In her as daughter, sister, wife, mother, Christian, friend, were happily blended a flowing humanity, and a tender benevolence. She was sincerely faithful and politely obliging. In all her affections warm and animated; affable, friendly, and communicative. She was intelligent, yet not assuming; humble, yet not mean; familiar, yet not loquatious; religious, yet not gloomy nor ostentatious. Her aged mother, tottering on the brink of the grave, can bear testimony, that in all the gentle offices, and winning attentions of filial affection, she was rarely equaled. Blessed with a husband, tender and affectionate, and a numerous and lovely family; to them melting kindness was the law of her life, and to yield them consummate felicity, her highest pleasure. Thus happy beyond expression, in contributing to their happiness, no wonder anguish should wound the hearts, and the briny tears of sorrow gall the cheeks, and the sable weeds of woe be the garb of that husband, widowed of the best of wives, and those children bereaved of the dearest and best of mothers. "Blessed are the dead that die in the Lord." "There remaineth a rest for the people of God."	07/24/1822
On Monday, the 15th inst., at Upper Marlborough, Mrs. Sarah Beanes, consort of Wm. Beanes, of that place, in the 72nd year of her age. Few persons have died more justly and more generally lamented by all who knew her than this amiable lady. She was truly an affectionate and tender wife, a sincere friend, a kind neighbor, a gentle mistress, a good Christian, and to sum up all, one of the best of women.	07/25/1822

Marriage and Death Notices	Date
Died, in Paris, on the 7th of May last, in the 23rd year of his age, Mr. Charles A. Morton, eldest son of the late Mr. Nathaniel Morton, of this city. It is due to the character which this estimable young man sustained in life, and it will be grateful to the feelings of those who survive, to lament over his premature fate, that something more should be said of him, than that he lived and is dead. When a youth, whom a generous enthusiasm in his profession, had impelled to leave his native shores for the greater opporunities of a foreign country, who had seen and studied the specimens of ancient art, and having completed his preparatory course, was on the eve of returning to the bosom of an anxious family, and to the hope of professional fame and emolument in his own country, is suddenly summoned away to another world, just as he has qualified himself to act with credit and usefulness in this, it is an event of too frequent occurrence, and of too little general interest to arrest the attention and the sympathy of the great and busy world; but the little circle of hearts, through which it has struck the sensation of sorrow, and around which it has drawn the curtain of mourning, may be indulged in giving this measure of publicity to their private grief, and in using as their text, for commenting on human vanity, the event which has brought the doctrine home in its most affecting application to themselves. It is at the tomb of youth, who fall full of hope and promise, that pity and grief unite to draw forth the deepest tears that nature has to weep, and here it is as the heart may be permitted in the first moment of its bereavement, to utter itself in the pathetic complaint of inspiration, "wherefore hast thou made man in vain?" But it should silence the voice of complaining, and justify the ways of God to man, that the gospel has brought immortaliy to light, and disclosed a theatre, on which those that are dead to this world live, and find yet a nobler field for the employment of their imperishable faculties; and it may sustain and comfort the heart of the bereaved, that he, who in the day of his humiliation, stopped the bier that bore tthe widow's son, and restored him alive to his mourning mother, will, on another day, come in glory to the grave, and silence the voice of universal lamintation, by returning to every weeping Rachel, her first born child.	07/25/1822
On Thursday evening, the 8th inst., by the Rev. Mr. Nind, Dr. Edward Veazey, to Miss Eliza Fox, both of Cecil county, Md.	07/26/1822
On Tuesday last, on South River, by the Rev. Dr. Davis, Thomas H. Hall, Esq., Register of Wills, to Miss Mary Watkins.	07/26/1822
On Tuesday last, near the head of South River, by the Rev. Mr. Watkins, Mr. Theodore Williams, to Miss Caroline Gover.	07/26/1822

Marriage and Death Notices	Date
July 22nd, Mrs. Elizabeth D. McDowell, aged 56 years, daughter of the late Mrs. Providence Lane, of this place.	07/26/1822
On the 21st inst., 77th year of his age, Mr. Charles Torrance, an old and respectable resident of this city.	07/26/1822
On Wednesday evening last, Mrs. Elizabeth McQuinn, aged 63 years. The poor has lost a friend and society one of its brightest ornaments.	07/26/1822
At Annapolis, Mr. Henry Duvall, in the 43rd year of his age, one of the judges of the Orphans' Court of Anne Arundel county.	07/26/1822
At Washington city, Mrs. Mary Sewall, relict of Robert Sewell, Esq., of Poplar Hill, Maryland, and youngest daughter of William Brent, Esq., of Richland, Virginia.	07/26/1822
On Thursday evening last, by the Rev. Mr. Shinn, Mr. Daniel Pentz, to Miss Julian, daughter of Mr. Jacob Daily, all of this city.	07/27/1822
On Tuesday evening last, by the Rev. Mr. Hinkle, Mr. John Bangs to Mary Ann, daughter of James McComes, Esq.	07/27/1822
Yesterday evening, Mr. William Cockey, son of Thomas Cockey, aged 26 years. His friends and acquaintance are requested to attend his funeral, at 6 o'clock, tomorrow morning, from his father's dwelling, Jones' street, Old Town.	07/27/1822
At Elk Ridge, on Wednesday morning last, after a very painful and long, protracted illness, Mrs. Catherine Welling, consort of Mr. Wm. Welling, and daughter of the late Wm. Winchester, Esq., of this city.	07/27/1822
On the 22nd, at his residence, in Dedham, Dr. Nathaniel Ames, in the 82nd year of his age.	07/27/1822
On Sunday evening, by the Rev. Mr. Hinkley, Mr. Samuel Taylor, to Miss Catherine Mugers, both of this city.	07/29/1822
In Talbot county, the Rev. John Collins, itinerant minister of the Methodist Episcopal Church, to Miss Sarah Bradford, of Worcester county.	07/29/1822
With heart-felt sorrow, we record the death of Dr. George Thum, of this city, and late of Philadelphia. This amiable and excellent man breathed his last yesterday morning, after a lingering illness of six weeks, occasioned by his great exertions at the late fire at M'Elderry's wharf. He was in his twenty-eighth year. An affectionate wife, two infant	07/29/1822

Marriage and Death Notices	Date
children, and a large and respectable circle of relations and relatives and friends, bemoan his loss. The writer of this knew the doctor well; he has often witnessed the benevolent exercise of his professional talents for the relief of the suffering and poor. His extensive acquirements, and his mind and amiable manners, made him an useful and agreeable associate. His fortitude and resignation throughout his life; but particularly in his illness, were truly remarkable. The author of this saw him but a few hours before he expired – and as he grasped his hand, which the chill of death made cold and moist, he conversed with calmness and resignation. He is now relieved from his pains, and we trust his spirit rests, in the society of "good men made perfect."	
On Saturday evening last, Mrs. Martha M. Young, consort of the late Capt. John S. Young, in the 40th year of her age.	07/29/1822
On the 26th inst., Midshipman Wilson C. Purviance, U. S. navy, of Baltimore, Md., aged 21 years.	07/29/1822
In Dorchester county, Henry Hamilton.	07/29/1822
In Talbot county, at a very advanced age, Mr. Thomas Bullen.	07/29/1822
This morning, after a short indisposition, at his residence, on the York Road, Col. James Byas.	07/30/1822
Departed this life, at Vincennes, Indiana, on the 2nd inst., Mrs. Mary Ann I'Anson, consort of Richard M. I'Anson, and daughter of Capt. John Snyder, of this city, aged 26 years. A consumption of the lungs, fatal in its termination, as it was painful in its progress, had fixed its relentless hold upon her, and in the bloom of life she has been summoned away, leaving her distressed and anxious parents, a disconsolate and truly affectionate husband, and two infant children, to bewail their irreparable loss. She was truly, truly an example of filial piety and conjugal affection, and died perfectly resigned to the will of her Heavenly Father. Z.	07/30/1822
Last evening, by the Rev. Dr. Roberts, Mr. James Lawrenson, to Miss Eliza Jane Smiley, all of this city.	07/31/1822
After a lingering illness, Mrs. Sarah, consort of James Nabb, Esq., of Talbot county.	07/31/1822
At Pittsburgh, on the 13th inst., Mr. Nicholas Hart, a native of Rhode Island, but for nearly 20 years an inhabitant of Baltimore; he was a soldier of the Revolution, and steadily maintained those principles	07/31/1822

Marriage and Death Notices	Date
throughout his life, which actuated our fathers in their struggle for independence.	
On Sunday evening, at the chapel of St. John, by the Rev. John William Beschter, Dr. John Peckochock, to Miss Beule Malvina Kennedy, both of this city.	08/01/1822
On Tuesday, 30th ult., Miss Sophia Bernard, after a painful and lingering illness, which she bore with the most heroic fortitude. She looked upon its termination with that perfect composure which shewed a mind prepared for the event, and died as a Christian should die, with unshaken confidence and joyous hope of blissful immortality beyond the grave. Thus has society been deprived of one who was kind, benevolent, charitable, and upright in her feelings and principles. Through life she was endeared to her family as an affectionate daughter and sister, and to her friends as an interesting and agreeable companion.	08/01/1822
On Sunday morning, after a short, but most trying illness, Abraham B., eldest son of Mr. Abraham R. Williams, of this city. The deceased was in the 19th year of his age; and possessed in an abundant measure all that vigour of body and sprightfulness of disposition, which generally belong to the spring of life. But, in respect of his understanding, few of his age were endowed with superior faculties, which were at once invigorated by assiduous contemplation, and refined by the lighter graces of learning. The deep and distressful sorrow of his parents, his brothers and sisters, and the heartfelt regret of his many acquaintances, but too truly attest the amiable qualities of his mind, his good nature, and warm affections. In his expiring agonies, he showed the serene resignation to the will of Heaven, which can result only from a peaceful conscience and a Christian faith. His youth necessarily implies that he had but few opportunities of distinguishing himself by acting in the great theatre of the world; but he lived long enough notwithstanding, to deserve that he should not sink into a silent grave unnoticed; whilst the more domestic and private virtues that adorned his character will ever make his name dear to the remembrance of his afflicted friends. ATC S	08/01/1822
At Fountain Rock, on Sunday morning last, after a short illness, in the sixteenth year of his age, Master Edward Lloyd Ringold, son of Gen. Samuel Ringold, of Washington county. He was a very promising youth, and bid fair to be an ornament to society and to his country – he has fallen at a period of life when hope promises much, and renders such an affliction peculiarly severe to relatives and friends – but he will long live in their affectionate remembrance.	08/01/1822

Marriage and Death Notices	Date
At the village of Queen Ann, Prince George's county, Md., on Friday, 26th of July, Mr. Richard T. Currier, in the 25th year of his age. He was a native of Newburyport, Massachusetts, where his relations reside. The printers of Boston and Newburyport are requested to publish the above for the information of his friends.	08/01/1822
On Thursday evening last, by the Rev. Daniel Stansbury, Mr. William R. Gwinn, to Miss Hennah J. Evans, both of this city.	08/02/1822
At Annapolis, Mr. Alexander Todd to Mrs. Margaret Mace.	08/02/1822
"An honest man's the noblest work of God." Died, on the 26th ultimo, in the 26th year of his age, Mr. William Cockey, son of Thomas Cockey, and late one of the constables of this city. It is due to the character, which this toung man sustained in youth and more especially as a public officer, to say something more of him than that he is dead – he lived an ornament to his profession, assiduous and punctual, to the trust reposed in him, and withal humane, tender, and obliging; and it would be a great consolation to the citizens of Baltimore if all of his profession would follow his example. Honesty and sobriety were the true traits of his character. His aged father tottering on the brink of the grave, can bear testimony, that in all the gentle offices of filial affection, he was rarely equaled; and elderly mother and aged grand-mother, together with sisters and brothers, have to deplore the loss of a dutiful son and an affectionate brother. At the tomb of youths, where pity and grief unite to draw forth the deepest tear, may the heart be permitted in the bereavement, to utter "wherefore hast thou made man in vain." But it may sustain and comfort the heart of the bereaved that he who is dead, died an honest man. Well might the inspired penman say, "in the midst of life we are in death." But we, his friends and acquaintances, ere left to mourn, but not as those without hope. "Our wasting lives grow shorter still, As days and months increase; And ev'ry beating pulse we tell Leaves but the number less. The year rolls round, and steals away The breath that first it gave; Whatever we do, wherever we be, We're traveling to the grave."	08/02/1822
Yesterday morning, after a short, but severe illness, George Smith, gilder, of this city, leaving a wife and five children to lament his loss. The deceased has been a resident of Baltimore for upwards of thirty years; to those who knew him, it can be justly said, he was an honest	08/02/1822

Marriage and Death Notices	Date
man; that in all his avocations through life, he has done unto others as he would wish to have been done by.	
In Queen Ann's county, Eastern Shore, Md., Mr. Solomon Wright.	08/02/1822
On the 30th of July last, by the Rev. Mr. Finney, John Whitaker, Esq., to Miss Harriet Myers, of Havre de Grace, Harford county, Md.	08/05/1822
Departed this life, on the 3rd inst., Mrs. Ann Ricaud, consort of Mr. Thomas P. Ricaud, of this city. In the relations of daughter, wife, mother, friend, and neighbor, she was dutiful, affection, sincere, and kind. And that which gave a finishing stroke to her amiable character, was her heartfelt experience and devout practice of Christianity: This blessed religion afforded her real happiness amidst the troubles and cares of life. And, during her long continued illness, and at the hour of death, the Almighty Savior, in whom she trusted, crowned her with resignation, peace, and a glorious triumph.	08/05/1822
On Saturday evening last, Mr. Solomon W. Winchester, a naïve of Portland, Me., in the 31st year of his age leaving a wife and three small children to bemoan their loss. The deceased had been employed for a number of years in the Federal Republican Office, during which time his deportment and conduct were uniformly such as to secure him the affection of his fellow workmen and sincere respect of his employer. The traits of character for which the deceased was remarkable, were, in particular, honesty and active benevolence. Altho' not gifted with riches, yet a portion of his earnings were given to those who stood in need. Nothing could induce him to swerve from his duty. His honesty and integrity were of that cast which make a man truly respectable, altho' he be poor. He was a valuable and useful member of society, because he performed all the duties of his station with punctuality and integrity. His remains were followed to the grave by a number of relatives and friends, as well as by a very respectable number of "Odd Fellows," of which order he was an useful and valuable member.	08/05/1822
At the residence of his sister, of the village of Towson Town, Baltimore county, on Friday evening last, Mr. John C. Ridgely, son of C. Ridgely, of W., in the 33rd year of his age. His faith and constancy surmounted his lingering and painful disease, and full of Christian resignation, he closed his eyes on this world, in the humble hope of a better.	08/06/1822
Last evening, by the Rev. Mr. Gibson, Capt. Stephen Smith, to Miss Mary Ann M'Laughlin, both of this city.	08/08/1822

Marriage and Death Notices	Date
In Talbot county, Mr. Peter Tarr to Miss Margaret Hopkins.	08/08/1822
In Talbot county, at the residence of Jas. Nabb, Esq., Mrs. Frances Parrott.	08/08/1822
Last evening, by the Rev. Mr. James M'Cann, Mr. Samuel Rooker, to Miss Mary Ann, eldest daughter of Mr. Joseph Oldham.	08/09/1822
Mrs. Sarah Craig, wife of Capt. James Craig. Mrs. Craig was a native of Virginia, and, with her husband, removed to, and has resided in Baltimore more than twenty years past. It was only a few weeks ago, that her friends saw her recover from a tedious and severe indisposition, and they confidently hoped to enjoy her society a long time to come; but her heavenly father had determined otherwise, and, after a few moments' illness, called her hence of Monday last. Mrs. Craig's deportment in life was that of benevolent and pious character, which procures the love and respect of others, and warrants the belief that she was not taken unprepared, though unapprised of her approaching dissolution; but, on the contrary, will secure to her, and all those who imitate her example, a happy reward in that world to which all are bound, and where the deeds of the good do follow them.	08/09/1822
By the Rev. Dr. Glendy, on the 31st ultimo, Mr. Robert Loughridge, to Miss Catherine McCurdy, all of this city.	08/10/1822
On Sunday evening last, by the Rt. Rev. Bishop Kemp, Mr. John L. Dubois, of New York, to Miss Arabella M'Dowell.	08/10/1822
In Harford county, Md., Mr. John Ward, to Miss Rebecca White. Mr. Jonathan Ward to Miss Mary White.	08/10/1822
Yesterday, Sunday, after a severe illness, Mr. William L. Schmidt, merchant, of this city, aged 43 years. By the death of this worthy and highly respectable citizen, society has sustained a serious loss – his eulogy is written on the hearts of all who knew him.	08/12/1822
On the 7th inst., George F. Janney, a respectable member of the Society of Friends. Eulogy is needless; yet it is due to the memory of the deceased, to say, he was a man of unblemished life and conversation, and a useful member of the society to which he belonged.	08/12/1822
On the 9th inst., Mr. Nicholas M. Monsarrat, eldest son of Capt. David Monsarrat, of this city, aged 17 years and 7 months.	08/12/1822
Departed this life, on the 10th inst., after a long and painful illness,	08/12/1822

Marriage and Death Notices	Date
which she bore with Christian fortitude and resignation, Amelia, the wife of Nathaniel Lock, in the 52nd year of her age, leaving a husband, six children, and a numerous circle of acquaintances, to lament their irreparable loss.	
In Frederick County, Md., on the 8th inst., in the 36th year of his age, Mr. Thomas Kernan, of Baltimore County. He was a worthy citizen and a pious Christian and has left a numerous circle of relations and friends to deplore his loss.	08/12/1822
On the 14th inst., in Baltimore county, Mrs. Nancy Stansbury, aged 32 years, consort of Gen. Tobias E. Stansbury. She had long been afflicted with a pulmonary disease, which terminated but with her life. Her early departure from time to eternity is a source of real grief for her husband, children, connexions, and friends, but they have great consolation, in a well grounded belief, from her resignation to the Divine will, that she now rests in peace with the "just made perfect."	08/15/1822
On Friday last, near Baltimore, Mrs. Rogers, wife of Lloyd N. Rogers, and daughter of Thomas Law, Esq., of Washington city. Youth, beauty, accomplishment, and goodness, have suddenly descended to the grave. The house of gaiety has turned into a house of mourning. Her fond husband was absent, and, with all his hopes of happiness dashed at once from him forever, will return and feel all the pangs of a distressed parent on beholding his lovely children. "Who now their infant steps shall guide, "Now she, alas, is gone?" Let not man rely upon worldly blessings. Happy are they who are called earliest from this transitory scene; those who linger behind have only to lament over those who sink into the grave, and to have their affections lacerated, one by one, till nature signs the glad release. We refrain from an obituary eulogium: those who knew Mrs. Rogers feel more than we could express.	08/15/1822
On the 8th inst., after a few days illness, at Norwich, on Four Mile Creek, his late residence, near Richmond, Va., Thomas Amoss, of William, a native of Harford county, Md., and for many years a resident of this city, in the 36th year of his age, leaving a wife and one child and an extensive circle of relations and acquaintance to mourn their loss. He was a kind and affectionate husband and father, a warm friend, and an honest member of society; he will long be remembered by those who had the opportunity to test his many virtues.	08/16/1822
On Friday evening last, by the Rev. Mr. Hagerty, Mr. Elias Merryman,	08/19/1822

Marriage and Death Notices	Date
to Miss Susan Lavely, all of this city.	
At York, Penn., on the 18th inst., Mr. Michael Carney, formerly of Baltimore, and late of New Orleans, where his family now reside.	08/19/1822
On Thursday evening last, by the Rev. Mr. Helfenstein, Mr. Luke Kiersted, to Miss Catherine S. Myer, both of this city.	08/22/1822
On the 5th inst., at Little York, Penn., Jacob Miller, father of Mr. Jacob Miller, of this city, at the advanced age of 93 years, during which long period he resided in the same neighborhood. He was followed to his grave by a large number of friends, among whom were several surpassing him in years. It may be truly said of this venerable man that he was placed in the cradle of the grave, if it may be so expressed – his coffin – as unimpeached with crime as when he was first placed in the cradle as an infant.	08/23/1822
In this city, on Thursday morning last, after a short illness, Miss Mary Lawrence, aged about eighty years. She was a pious Christian, and a member of the Methodist Society for upwards of forty years.	08/23/1822
At Annapolis, on Sunday night last, in 27th year of his age, Mr. Wrightson Bryan, merchant.	08/23/1822
On Friday, the 16th inst., at Providence, R. I., John J. C. Oldfield, Esq., late of this City.	08/23/1822
In Anne Arundel county, on Thursday, the 15th inst., Mr. Edwin Gott, after an illness of sixteen days, in the 29th year of his age leaving behind him a disconsolate wife, to whom he had been wedded only 4 months and eight days.	08/23/1822
Departed this life, on the 15th inst., in the 11th year of his age, at Manor Vale, the seat of Judge Dorsey, George Henry Hern Emory, son of Gideon Emory, deceased. The sudden and unexpected death of this interesting and affectionate youth, who had accompanied his mother, from Centreville, to pay her usual affectionate visits, to her relatives on this shore, should admonish parents not to fix, too deeply, their affections on things of time and sense – and, that they should always be prepared to part with their children, when, according to the ways of Providence, hey are required of them.	08/23/1822
At Lexington, in the state of Kentucky, Thomas Dougherty, Esq., of this city, who was, at the time of his death, Clerk of the House of Representatives of the U. States, the duties of which station he had filled	08/24/1822

Marriage and Death Notices	Date
for eight years, with uncommon correctness and fidelity. As a man, he was justly and generally esteemed. Honesty in his heart, truth on his lips, there was no guile in him. He was a most affectionate husband and father, and a sincere friend. We shall long and seriously lament the loss of so worthy a citizen. *Nat. Int.*	
On Wednesday evening, the 21st instant, after a short, but painful illness, Mrs. Mary Albridge, formerly of Nantucket, in the 54th year of her age.	08/24/1822
At Port au Prince, on the 24th of July last, Mr. Benjamin Perkins, of Baltimore. The deceased has left a disconsolate widow, and a number of relations and acquaintance to deplore his loss.	08/24/1822
Yesterday morning, Miss Elizabeth Young, aged about 70 years.	08/26/1822
It has become our painful task to report the death of Dr. George Brown. He died on Saturday last, and his remains were interred yesterday morning. Dr. Brown was so universally known and respected, that it seems almost superfluous to repeat the many virtues which he possessed, and which gave additional lustre to his profession. He was a practicing physician in this city for thirty-eight years. (for many years, and until his death, he had associated with him, our amiable and valuable citizen, Dr. Colin Mackenzie.) In point of medical skill, and in general knowledge, he was among the first of the many eminent physicians of which Baltimore so justly boasts. As a gentleman, he was remarkable for the politeness and urbanity of his manners, and as a citizen, he was an ornament to society. His general demeanor was such that, we believe we are warranted in saying, that he died without a single enemy – his death is a subject of great and general regret, and his memory will be cherished by thousands who have been restored to health by his skill, and by many more who have enjoyed his acquaintance and benevolence. The doctor was in his 68th year at the time of his death – his mental faculties remained unimpaired to the last moment. Convinced that his long life had been a useful one, feeling the approach of those bodily infirmities incident to old age, and filled with that faith that marks the Christian, he desired to live no longer – the hope of changing this life care and vicissitude for a blissful eternity, filled the aged and venerable man with cheerfulness; in which happy state of mind his soul took its flight to that "bourne whence no traveler returns."	08/26/1822
On the 24th, a Newcastle, Del., by the Rev. J. E. Latta, Mr. David Martin, to Miss Sinners, both of this city.	08/27/1822

Marriage and Death Notices	Date
In Kent county, Md., Mr. David Webb, to Mrs. Whithington, both of Kent. This gentleman has been married seven times, and had six wives, having been married to one twice, in consequence of a mistake made by the minister, in her first name. He is a stout, hearty looking man, weighing upwards of 200 pounds, and about 50 years of age.	08/27/1822
On the morning of Friday, the 23rd inst., at his dwelling, in Philpott street, Fell's Point, after a short illness, in the 46th year of his age, Maurice Leahy, cooper. Persevering industry, probity, regularity of deportment, and benevolence of disposition, were conspicuous traits in the character of the deceased. On the same day, took place the death of his only son, a promising boy, in the eighth year of his age. The widow bewails the death of an affectionate and provident husband, and his two remaining children will deplore the loss of an attentive, kind, and indulgent parent.	08/27/1822
In New Market, Dorchester county, Capt. Thomas Troth, after a short illness.	08/27/1822
In Talbot county, Mrs. Ann, consort of Mr. Haley Moffit, after a short illness.	08/27/1822
In Matthews County, Va., Mr. Edmund P. Benson, late of the city of Baltimore, to Miss Mary Repass.	08/28/1822
On Tuesday last, Miss Ann M. Levering, in the 19th year of her age, the eldest daughter of Mr. Nathan Levering, of this city. In the full flush of youth, while life was brightened by all its fascinations, while the present was brilliant with happiness, and brighter and lovelier hues glittered on the clouds of the future; while seated in the very bosom of domestic felicity, The spoiler came, and in an evil hour, With hurried hand, he snatched this beautiful flower; Surviving mourners, dry your weeping eyes, It blooms more splendid in its native skies.	08/28/1822
Departed his transitory life, on the 13th inst., in St. Mary's County, Mrs. Margaret Barber, wife of Col. Tho. Barber, of this city, in the 48th year of her age, of a severe illness, which she bore with Christian resignation to the will of her Heavenly Father; leaving a disconsolate husband and a numerous circle of relatives and friends to bemoan their bereavement.	08/28/1822
On Tuesday evening, 27th inst., by the Rt. Rev. Bishop Kemp, Mr. Charles Green, to Miss Eleanor Charlotte, daughter of J. M. Bennett, of	08/29/1822

Marriage and Death Notices	Date
this city.	
On the 26th August, Mrs. Harriet Shinnick, consort of Mr. Jacob, in the 48th year of her age, after a short, but painful illness.	08/29/1822
In Talbot county, Md., in the 62nd year of her age, Mrs. Ann, consort of Mr. Samuel Jackson. Mr. John Battee, after a lingering illness.	08/29/1822
In Washington county, Md., Mr. Cyrus R. Sanders, printer, aged 26 years.	08/29/1822
Departed this life, at 3 o'clock A. M., on the 28th inst., at the residence of Capt. J. Snyder, of this city, Miss Eleanor J. Dashiell, aged 18 years. In recording the death of this truly amiable young lady, it is in vain the arguments of cold philosophy are brought forward to enable us to restrain the sympathetic tear; and we feel compelled to heave an heartfelt sigh to the memory of one whom we loved so much. Endowed with every accomplishment calculated to adorn polite society, and possessed of every trait requisite to charachterise the affecionate sister and the sincere and valuable friend, she lived respected and beloved. Eleanor was an orphan, and though no tear of maternal affection was shed over her ripening years, or anxious solicitude felt for her in a paternal bosom, "the flowret was not left to blossom in a barren soil, but was watered with the refreshing dews of disinterested friendship" – and to her "New grace from other worlds are given." The poet may tune his harp and sing - "Virtue succeeds to virtue, friend to friend, "And where the hero bled the hero blooms, "Spreading his laurels on the parent tomb;" But the friends of Eleanor feel but too forcibly, that such a friend when lost, is lost forever here. That eye which but four short days since sparkled with beauty, and that cheek which was adorned wih the rosey tint of health, is now reposing in the silent dust, and the place that knew her then will know her no more! But while we mourn our irreparable loss, we are not destitute of that hope which is the best gift of Heaven to the bereaved bosom, "the sweet anicipation of again embracing her where friendship knows no alloy, and where kindred spirits meet to part no more."	08/30/1822
On Monday evening last, the 26th inst., at 4 o'clock, at the residence of Elijah Robinson, Esq., of Baltimore county, Mrs. Martha Randall, consort of Col. Beale Randall, of this city.	08/30/1822

Marriage and Death Notices	Date
On his farm, at West River, Md., John Johns, Esq., in the 64th year of his age.	08/30/1822
At Hagerstown, Mrs. Amelia Ragan, in the 34th year of her age, the relict of the late Col. John Ragan.	08/30/1822
At Norfolk, Midshipman Henry Zantzinger, recently attached to the U. S. ship Hornet, a young officer of great promise. His illness was of but a few days.	08/30/1822
By the Rev. Mr. Helfenstein, Mr. John R. Guynn, to Miss Ann Merryman, both of Baltimore county.	08/31/1822
On Monday evening, 26th inst., by the Rev. Mr. Smyth, Mr. Robert T. Jacobs, to Miss Mary C. Seth, both of Queen Ann's county.	08/31/1822
On Saturday evening, August 31st, by the Rev. Dr. Smyth, Mr. Thomas Gorman, of New York, to Mrs. Burke, of this city.	09/03/1822
On Sunday evening last, by the Rev. Mr. Melshimer, Mr. Peter Johnson, of Baltimore, to Miss Wilhelmina Reichart, of Hanover.	09/03/1822
On the 31st inst., Mrs. Susan Higinbotham, wife of Thomas Higinbotham, of this city.	09/03/1822
On Saturday, the 31st August, the Misses Eliza and Cornelia Pise; one 14 and the other 11 years of age – young ladies of esteemed value. What renders this a more than unusual affliction, was, the sudden demise of one sister, which produced the death of the other, who had been laboring under a severe sickness, all in the course of one hour; thus completing the affection they had formed here as sisters – and one grave received them both, rendering their love indissoluble, we hope, hereafter.	09/03/1822
Departed this life, on the 21st of August, at Mount Prospect, Anne Arundel County, in the 44th year of his age, Dr. William T. Graham, formerly a resident of this city, after an illness of only six days. In the life and death of his truly amiable man, the viscissitudes of this varying and uncertain world, are indeed exemplified; few are the persons that pass through a scene more chequered, and more perhaps ever bore the frowns of fortune, with more composure, or displayed more magnammity in the trying moments of accumulating misfortunes – at one period of his life, fortune smiled on him, and bestowed with a liberal hand her favors – at that time we behold him the poor man's friend, the widow's comfort, and the orphan's protector; but suddenly	09/03/1822

Marriage and Death Notices	Date
fortune changed, yet he received the shock with courageous firmness, nor shrunk not from the perils that surrounded him, but still struggled against his difficulties. Yet alas! alas, he was cut off in the vigour and prime of life, in an hour when least expected or looked for; snatched from the arms of a weeping wife and blooming offspring, and summoned to quit scenes and objects near and dear to his bosom. Well indeed may we exclaim, "time, how short; eternity, how long." And now gentle spirit, peace to thy shade – no more shall the bosom throb with anguish, or thy heart feel sorrow and trouble in this world; for we trust thou art now at rest, reposing in the bosom of thy God.	
On Thursday evening last, by the Rev. Mr. Shane, Mr. William Smith, of Anne Arundel county, to Miss Alice Williams, of this city.	09/04/1822
On the 2nd instant, Mr. Levi Hollingsworth, Esq., aged 58, merchant of this city, and formerly a member of the Senate of Maryland.	09/04/1822
In Clarke County, Alabama, Mr. William Raborg, formerly of Baltimore.	09/04/1822
On Monday evening, the 2nd inst., by the Rev. Alexander McCain, Dr. Thomas L. Murphy, to Miss Ann Caroline, second daughter of Jonathan Harrison, Esq., both of this city.	09/05/1822
On Wednesday, the 28th ult., at the seat of John Jolliffe, Esq., Lt. William S. Newton, of the U. States' Army, to Miss Mary, eldest daughter of Mr. Robert McCandless, of Walnut Grove, Frederick County, Virginia.	09/05/1822
On Tuesday morning, after a wearied and protracted illness, Mrs. Susan Hoban, consort of Capt. James Hoban, of this city. Words can feebly essay the pious worth of this lady.	09/05/1822
On Monday, the 2nd inst., of a short but painful illness, Capt. Daniel Mandels, late master of the Bremen brig Washoamkiet.	09/05/1822
At Edgefield Court House, South Carolina, Dr. John Baptist Labourde, in the 21st year of his age, formerly a student of the Medical University of Baltimore.	09/05/1822
At Elkridge, on the 2nd inst., Abegail Atkinson, of a cancer in the breast.	09/05/1822
At the residence of his father, in Dorchester County, Md., Mr. Aquilla, third son of Col. John Jones, in the 27th year of his age.	09/05/1822

Marriage and Death Notices	Date
At Augusta, Geo., 21st ult., Mr. James Nagle, aged 24 years, a native of Baltimore, but for several years past a resident of that place.	09/05/1822
On Thursday evening last, by the Rev. Dr. Jennings, Capt. James Phillips, Jr., to Miss Eleanor Jennings, all of this city.	09/06/1822
At Pleasant Plains, Md., Miss Louisa Mayer, in the bloom of youth.	09/06/1822
At Annapolis, Mrs. Lydia Dodson, in the 92nd year of her age.	09/06/1822
At Hagerstown, Md., the Rev. Colin M'Farquhar. Mr. Jacob Cordiman and Mr. John Leypold.	09/06/1822
By the Rev. Dr. Glendy, on the 29th ult., Mr. Jeremiah Twomay, to Mrs. Margaret Lavary.	09/07/1822
By the Rev. Dr. Glendy, on the evening of Thursday last, Mr. Thomas Thompson, to Miss Jane Prouell, all of this city.	09/07/1822
On Thursday evening, by the Rev. Mr. McCann, Mr. John Pool, to Miss Ruth Angelina Howard, all of this city.	09/07/1822
On Wednesday morning, the 4th inst., by the Rev. Mr. Duncan, Mr. James Wilks, Jr., to Miss Mary Kimmel, eldest daughter of Michael Kimmel, of this city.	09/07/1822
On the 3rd inst., by the Rev. Mr. Johns, Maj. Daniel Hughes, to Miss Elizabeth Potts, of Frederick.	09/07/1822
On Thursday evening last, by the Rev. Mr. Hinkle, Mr. Rodney Manly, to Miss Mary Ann Moor, both of this city.	09/09/1822
On Sunday night last, by the Rev. Mr. Bartow, Mr. William Clarke, to Miss Anne Cullum, all of this city.	09/10/1822
On Saturday evening last, Mr. Jeremiah Gatchell, aged about 42 years, leaving an affectionate wife and two small children to mourn an irreparable loss. He was a native of Pennsylvania, and for the last ten years, steward of that excellent and extensive establishment, the Baltimore Hospital, the duty of which he performed with unsurpassed vigilance, tenderness, and skill. He was a kind husband, indulgent parent, obliging neighbor, sincere friend, and an honest man. In this important public station, he enjoyed the entire confidence and respect with all of whom he had to do, as manager of the institution or patients under his care. His death is sincerely deplored by all who knew him, and it is a general as well as a private misfortune. The Philadelphia	09/10/1822

Marriage and Death Notices	Date
papers will please copy the above.	
In Sunday, the 1st inst., at her residence in Charles County, Md., after a short, but painful illness, Mrs. Rebecca Childs, consort of Saml. Childs and daughter of Jacob Myers, Esq., of this city.	09/10/1822
At Easton, Md., Mrs. Ann Maria Scull, consort of the Rev. Joseph Scull, of that town – and Mr. James Ninde, at an advanced age.	09/10/1822
In Talbot county, Capt. Aldern Maynard.	09/10/1822
On Thursday evening last, by the Rev. Mr. Allen, Mr. Basil Owens, of Anne Arundel County, to Miss Ellen A. Griffith, of Montgomery County.	09/11/1822
Last evening, by the Rev. Mr. Baer, Mr. Caleb Turner, to Miss Margaret Johnson, all of this city.	09/11/1822
On the 4th ult., aged 16, Miss Margaret Calhoon M'Coull, third daughter of Mr. Robert M'Coull, of this city, departed this life of a short illness, which she bore with Christian fortitude and resignation. She rested on the finished work of the Lord Jesus, the Rock of Ages, for the remission of her sins and eternal glory.	09/11/1822
At Upper Marlbro', Prince Georges, on the 1st inst., Mrs. Margaret Shortt, aged 39, consort of Mr. John Shortt; and on the same night, Mrs. Charlotte Vernon, both late of Baltimore.	09/11/1822
On Monday, the 1st inst., at Chestertown, Kent County, Maryland, in the 26th year of his age, Dr. William I. Clarke, son of Mr. Samuel Clarke, of Philadelphia, after a short, but severe illness. This truly amiable and interesting young man settled himself in Kent County during the last winter, for the purpose of attending to the practice of medicine. By the urbanity of his manners, his amiable deportment, and the prompt attention to the calls of his profession, he invariably acquired the confidence, and insured the affectionate esteem of all who had occasion for his professional services. To the poor within the limits of his practice, although gratuitous, his attention was not less devoted than to the most wealthy, thus evincing the philanthropy of his nature. To the amiable qualities of the heart, in him were united the valuable properties of the mind. In a public point of view, the death of this valuable man is severely felt and deeply lamented; and in the more intimate social connexions of life this dispensation of Providence is a most serious affliction. His aged parents are doomed to deplore the loss of a dutiful and affectionate son. He has left a young and affectionate wife to	09/11/1822

Marriage and Death Notices	Date
lament the dissolution of the strongest tie in nature. Her grief is intense, just at the period when fortune seemed propitious, and the brightest prospect for a permanent and happy settlement in life was opening, did the king of terrors pointed his dart and cut the thread of life; at one sad stroke crushing the fondest anticipations, and spreading the dark cloud of doom where lately was to be seen the brightest sunshine of joyous hope. He created, and secured to himself, sincere and devoted friends, in a land to which he was but recently an entire stranger. Truly may it be said, twas but to know him to esteem him. Those who knew him best, loved him most.	
Last evening, by the Rt. Rev. Bishop Kemp, Mr. Thomas George Gutch, to Miss Maria Randolph Claiborne, all of this place.	09/13/1822
On Tuesday evening last, by the Rev. Mr. Helfenstein, Mr. Joseph Entler, to Miss Sarah, youngest daughter of the late Nicholas Hopkins.	09/13/1822
Last evening, by the Rev. Dr. Glendy, Mr. James Shuter, to Miss Sarah Espey, both of this city.	09/13/1822
On Thursday evening, by the Rev. Mr. Helfenstein, Mr. John Christopher Helmton, to Miss Eliza Garrison, all of this city.	09/13/1822
Departed this transitory life, on Wednesday evening last, after a long protracted illness, which he bore with Christian fortitude and resignation, Mr. John Gould, a native of England, in the 64th year of his age. The writer of this imperfect sketch is well aware of how stale newspaper eulogium has become, but feels justified in saying that the deceased possessed in an eminent degree, virtues, and qualities, which are seldom to be found – his heart was ever ready to relieve the wants of the distressed – humanity and benevolence were the inmates of his bosom – and he was that which is the noblest work of God, an honest man.	09/13/1822
Departed this transitory state of existence, on Wednesday night last, in the 75th year of his age, Henry Didier, Esq., a native of France, but long a citizen of this Country, having emigrated to America previous to the revolutionary war. He was a strenuous supporter of the rights of man, and a warm admirer of our political institutions. In his several relations of husband, father, and friend, he had few *equals*, no *superiors*. Mr. Didier was one of the first receivers of the *Heavenly doctrines of the New Jerusalem* in this city; and to the graceful politeness peculiar to his native country, was added the most unbounded hospitality; and a heart *open as day to melting charity*. For nearly thirty years past, he labored under a most afflicting disorder; yet always meekly resigned to the will	09/14/1822

Marriage and Death Notices	Date
of his Heavenly Father. In a word, this good man lived, loved and respected by all who knew him, and his bereaved family will, and must long lament his loss.	
On Thursday last, the 12th Sept., after a short illness, Mrs. Mary Fenton, aged thirty-four years. She was much beloved by all who had the pleasure of her acquaintance.	09/14/1822
On Thursday, the 12th inst., Master Edward L. Pise, aged five years. Thus has it pleased Divine Providence to take one more, making in all three children from one family in the space of 12 days.	09/14/1822
On the 10th inst., Miss Helen Ann Livers, youngest daughter of the late Anthony Livers, aged 15 years and 4 months.	09/14/1822
At Annapolis, Mr. Gilbert Murdock, in the 69th year of his age. Also, Mr. James Smith, after a short illness.	09/14/1822
On Tuesday evening last, by the Rev. Mr. Baer, Mr. George Holding, to Miss Rachael Leig, both of this city.	09/16/1822
In Fredericktown, Md., Mr. Thomas J. Grahame, to Miss Caroline Johnson, youngest daughter of the late Col. Baker Johnson. Dr. Lloyd Dorsey to Miss Rebecca Ann L. Torrance, daughter of James Torrance, Esq., of that county.	09/16/1822
On Sunday, the 15th inst., after a short, but severe illness, Col. John H. Rogers, in the 37th year of his age. This is again one of the striking examples of the uncertainty of human life; it were but as yesterday that the deceased appeared to be in the full bloom of health, enjoying all the comforts that an affectionate and amiable family could afford, but alas, in a few short fleeting hours the cold hand of death extinguished the lamp of life, depriving a disconsolate and fond wife of her best friend, and a large family of children of a tender parent. But let the widow and orphans recollect, it was done by the unerring hand of God, the father of the widow and the orphan, and that although they are deprived of his presence here, there is yet consolation in the hope, that he has changed this world of woe for one of eternal bliss. "Death wounds to cure, we fall, we rise, we reign, Spring from our fetters, fasten in the skies, Where blooming Eden withers in our sight, Nor to be thought on but with tide of joy."	09/16/1822
On the tenth instant, at Chalk Hill, near Union Town, Pennsylvania, Mr. William Cole, of this city, in the fifty-eighth year of his age. He was a	09/16/1822

Marriage and Death Notices	Date
native of England, but for nearly thirty years he has resided in the United States, the last twenty-five of where he has been a citizen of Baltimore, which he has been well known and highly esteemed as a respectable merchant. In private life, Mr. Cole was an affectionate husband, a kind father, and a faithful friend – his death will be severely felt by his intimate friends – to his family, the loss will be irreparable.	
On Thursday morning last, at Gettysburg, Pa., Lt. J. W. Sherburne, of the U. S. Navy, to Miss Louisa Myers, of this city.	09/17/1822
After a short illness, on the 13th inst., at his residence near this city, Ebenezer Finley, Esq. We are accustomed to regard the death of the youthful, with feelings of disappointed anticipation – the death of the aged wih a deeper and more hallowed sorrow. The prospective influence of immature virtue, upon the best interests of society, it at once lost to our hope, when the buoyant spirit of youth, wings its flights to a higher and a better world; but when the old and respectable after the completion of the dearest views of humanity, yield to the inevitable destiny all that is mortal, we mourn the irreparable loss of those, from whom life has already realized permanent advantages. The long train of useful services to the community in which he resided – the expansive benevolence of heart – the circle of whose activity knew but the limits of enlarged philanthropy – the domesic charities of soul in the exercise of its affections – the fervent adherence to the religious denomination to which he belonged, and among whom he held a patriarchal station; these constitute the motives of unfeigned grief inspired to the event, which is our melancholy task to record. Balimore may mourn the departure of one of her most valuable citizens to the mansions of eternal repose of one, whose history is identified with her most prosperous institutions. Domestic affection may mourn the privation of him, who, in the estimable and intelligent family he reared, has left the most unequivocal testimony of the faithful discharge of her most responsible duties. Public gratitude mingles is tears wih domestic affliction.	09/17/1822
At Washington, after an illness of two weeks, the Rev. Saml. Davis, Minister of the Methodist Episcopal Church, aged about 28 years. On the 14th inst., George Page, son of John Page, Esq., with the Cholera Infantum, aged 11 months.	09/17/1822
At Pensacola, 10th August, of the yellow fever, Capt. Robert Gerrish, a native of Salem, Mass.	09/17/1822
Communication. Truly may it be said, "In the midst of life, we are in death." *Obituary.* Died on the 15th inst., Mr. Elisha Cook, in the 46th year of his age, long a respectable inhabitant of Baltimore, after a severe	09/17/1822

Marriage and Death Notices	Date
illness of eight days, which he bore with true Christian fortitude, resigning his immortal spirit to the mercy of his God, from whom he received it, and with the full hope of enjoying, the "mansion of the just man made perfect." He has left behind him brothers and sisters, as well as a numerous circle of relations and friends, to lament their irreparable loss. J. G. M.	
On Thursday evening last, 12th inst., by the Rt. Rev. Bishop Kemp, Mr. Ezekiel C. Wysham, to Miss Isabella Selman, both of this city.	09/18/1822
On Thursday evening last, by the Rev. Mr. Goforth, Samuel McMullan, Esq., to Miss Eliza Taylor, of Port Deposit.	09/18/1822
On Saturday evening last, by the Rev. Mr. Barry, Mr. John Phifer, to Miss Alesy Catherell, both of this city.	09/18/1822
On the 13th inst., Mr. Joseph S. Williams, after a painful sickness, which he bore with truly Christian resignation, in the esteem of all who knew him leaving a disconsolate wife and five small children, to lament a good father and friend. May he rest in peace.	09/18/1822
Departed this life, on Monday night last, 16th inst., James Edward Shinn, second son of Rev. Asa Shinn, aged about 9 years, after a painful illness of 9 days.	09/18/1822
Near Easton, Talbot County, Md., on the 13th inst., Miss Ann, daughter of John Edmonson, Esq. In the death of this amiable, young lady, her parents are bereaved of an only and affectionate child, her friends deprived of a sprightly and intelligent companion, and society of one of its brightest ornaments. T.	09/18/1822
At Chestertown, Kent county, Md., on the 11th inst., Mrs. Sarah Clarke, widow of the late Dr. William I. Clarke. She was remarkable for her pity and all the virtues which adorn the female character; and has left behind her numerous friends whose affection for her memory time cannot obliterate. Her soul was too pure for this world and, in the prime of her womanhood, left the mortal body and winged its way to heaven. Angels beheld her ripe for joys to come, And called, by God's command, their sister home.	09/18/1822
On Wednesday morning last, of bilious fever, taken on the Eastern Shore, where she had been with her mother on a short visit to her friends, Sarah Jane Cummins, infant daughter of E. H. Cummins, Esq., of this city.	09/19/1822

Marriage and Death Notices	Date
Departed this life, on Wednesday, on 11th inst., at his residence in Baltimore county, John Royston, Sr., Esq., in the 60th year of his age, after a short, but severe illness, which he bore with Christian fortitude and resignation. The deceased was, for upwards of twenty years, a respectable member of the Methodist Society; he died as he had lived, a bright example of the influence of that religion which disarms death of all its terrors, and inspires the most perfect assurance of a blessed immortality; to him, "death was swallowed up in victory," and he exclaimed a short time before his death, "I feel prepared to die." How soothing a reflection for his numerous mourning relatives and friends to know that he had left this earthly tabernacle for "an inheritance which faded not away." In the separate relations of husband, father, and friend, he was tender, affectionate, and sincere. He lived to rear a numerous offspring, and see them ripen to maturity, which afforded in a great degree to sooth the evening of his life, and to take his departure in peace – his memory is engraven on the hearts of those who knew him, and which time can never erase. "Let me die the death of the righteous, that my end may be like unto his."	09/19/1822
On the 12th inst., after a painful illness of 19 days, which she bore with patience and fortitude, worthy of herself, Mrs. Susan Gable, consort of Jno. Gable, in the 30th year of her age. She has left a disconsolate husband and an extensive circle of relations and friends, to bemoan her untimely end. At Quantico Mills, Somerset county, Dr. James, post master, at that place. At Easton, Md., Mrs. Rebecca Austin. Mrs. Mary Robinson. And, in Talbot county, Mr. Joseph James. At Taney Town, on Friday, the 16th inst., Dr. Joseph Sim Smith, a patriot of '76 and an officer of the Revolution. In Frederick Town, Mr. Henry McBleery, Jr. At his residence, near New Market, Frederick county, Mr. James Adams, a respectable farmer, in the 55th year of his age. In Virginia, Spencer Roane, Esq., one of the Judges of the court of appeals.	09/19/1822
On Friday morning last, after a short illness, at his residence, in Cecil county, the Rev. William Nind, Rector of St. Stephens Parish. The deceased was in the 45th year of his age – an humble, faithful minister of the gospel, universally beloved and respected by all who knew him, and greatly regretted by those o'er who Providence had placed him in the pastoral charge. Scarcely had the grave closed over the remains of this aged and reverend father, ere he is also called to give an account of his stewardship. A wife and six children are left to mourn the loss of one of the best husbands, and most affectionate parents; but having been taught by precept and example to say, "thy will be done," will we trust, through grace be enabled to bear this heavy affliction with becoming resignation and to mourn, but "not as those without hope," having this	09/19/1822

Marriage and Death Notices	Date
consolation, that their loss is his eternal gain.	
Departed this life, at Pinckneyville, Mississippi, on the 20th ult., Mr. Benjamin Robinson, formerly of Baltimore, after a short illness of two days, of yellow fever.	09/19/1822
Last evening, by the Rev. Mr. Bartow, Mr. Alexander Allan, to Miss Adeline, daughter of Capt. Peter Davy, both of this city.	09/20/1820
By the Rev. John Finlay, on the 12th Sept., Nathan B. Hammond, Esq., of Baltimore county, to Miss Mary Ann King, of this city.	09/20/1822
By the Rev. John Finlay, on the 18th Sept., Mr. Thomas Matthews, to Mrs. Margaret Davis, of Baltimore county.	09/20/1822
At Annapolis, on Sunday night last, Mr. Jehu Chandler, editor of the Maryland Republican, aged 38 years.	09/20/1822
On Monday morning last, near South River, Mr. John Davidson, carpenter and joiner, of Baltimore. He had been at Work for sometime on the bridge now erecting on that river.	09/20/1822
Died, on Wednesday Morning, the 18th inst., at Spring Grove, the residence of her uncle, Jacob Myers, Esq., Miss Elizabeth Warren, aged 22 years, after a very severe attack of the Bilious Fever, which fatal disease she contracted, while performing the tender offices of a friend, at the bed of a dying cousin, who has but a few short days preceded her departure to that world of spirits, where they shall meet to enjoy an uninterrupted scene of joy and happiness. She had commenced early to run the race which was set before her, and has thus in her youthful career been called forth by the Divine Providence. A striking instance of the proof of that saying, "In the midst of life, we are in Death;" as it is but a very short time since, she was enjoying in the full flow of health and spirit, the society of a numerous circle of youthful friends, but she has left them for an exchange of better worlds above, she has gone. "To where her blessed Jesus reigns in Heavens unmeasured space, to spend a vast Eternity in pleasures and in praise."	09/20/1822
On Thursday evening last, by the Rev. Dr. Roberts, Mr. Levin P. Clark, to Miss Fbanes Kelly, all of this city.	09/21/1822
On Thursday evening last, by the Rev. Dr. Glendy, Dr. Robert Dorsey, of Edward, of Baltimore county, to Miss Susan, eldest daughter of Jas.	09/21/1822

Marriage and Death Notices	Date
Beatty, Esq., of this city.	
Yesterday, after a short illness, in the 86th year of his age, Mr. John A. Groc. His friends and acquaintance are invited to attend his funeral, this afternoon, at 3 o'clock, from his late dwelling, in South Charles street.	09/21/1822
Yesterday morning, after a short, but painful illness, Mr. James Beachem, printer, aged 22 years.	09/21/1822
On Sunday evening last, by the Rev. Mr. Valiant, Mr. Joseph Adams to Miss Mary Grant, formerly of Harford.	09/23/1822
On Sunday morning last, after a short illness, Miss Emily Williams, in the 16th year of her age. It is but a few days since, that we beheld the deceased in the fullest enjoyment of health, when suddenly she has been called away from this world of sorrow, we hope for another and a better. She has left an affectionate mother and sister, and a numerous circle of relatives and friends, to cherish her remembrance and recollect, with the most lively regret, her early and lamented death.	09/23/1822
At the Magazine Station, on Charleston Neck, on the 11th instant, after an illness of five days, Samuel Doolittle, a native of Connecticut, aged 30 years.	09/23/1822
On Sunday evening last, by the Rev. Mr. Bartow, Mr. Elijah Thurlkeld, of Washington, to Miss Harriet Cullum, of this city.	09/24/1822
On Tuesday evening last, by the Rev. Mr. Valiant, Mr. Edward Chairs, to Miss Deborah Peirce, all of this city.	09/24/1822
On Wednesday morning, by the Rev. Mr. Valiant, Mr. John Anderson Earl, to Miss Martha York, of Baltimore county.	09/24/1822
On Sunday evening last, by the Rev. Mr. Valiant, Mt. Thomas Robertson, to Miss Elizabeth Howard, both of this city.	09/24/1822
On Sunday evening last, by the Rev. Dr. Jennings, Capt. William Bate, of the Columbian schr. _____, to Miss Eliza Beatty, of this city.	09/24/1822
On Sunday evening last, by the Rev. Mr. Valiant, Mr. Joseph Adams, to Miss Mary Grant, formerly of Harford.	09/24/1822
On Monday evening, by the Rev. Dr. Roberts, Mr. Christian Zell, to Miss Mary Anne Bader, all of this city.	09/24/1822

Marriage and Death Notices	Date
On Tuesday, the 17th inst., by the Rev. Mr. Finney, Mr. John Creswell, of Port Deposit, Md., to Miss Rebecca E., daughter of Mr. Jonathan Webb, of Penn.	09/24/1822
At the residence of Daniel C. Hopper, Esq., Queen Ann's, the 2nd inst., by the Rev. James Smith, of Baltimore, Philemon B. Hopper, attorney at law, Centreville, to Miss Margaret Ann, eldest daughter of Mr. Richard Thomas, late of Queen Ann's county.	09/24/1822
On Thursday, the 19th inst., in the 15th year of his age, Master Nicholas J. R. Wellmore, only son of William Wellmore, of this city.	09/24/1822
Yesterday morning, after an illness of nine days, Mr. Willaim Downing, in the 35th year of his age. He was formely of Boston, but for the last twelve years a resident of Baltimore.	09/24/1822
On Monday evening, at St. Mary's Church, by Rev. Mr. Wheeler, Felix Jenkins, Esq., to Miss Frances H. Wheeler, all of this city.	09/25/1822
Departed this life, on the 20th inst., Jacob Myers, Esq., in the 64th year of his age. Mr. Myers was the third member of his family who, in the short space of three weeks, have been hurried to the silent grave by the bilious remittent fever. The deceased was one among our oldest and best citizens, having been for more than 40 years past engaged in an extensive mercantile business in this city. He obtained generally the confisewnce and esteem of all all who knew him; and those who knew him most can best appreciate his value; as a merchant, a husband, a father, and a friend; he was truly excellent; he had always a feeling heart and a ready hand to help the distressed, even beyond his power; he reverenced the Sabbath day and taught, by example, his large and growing family, that to fear the Lord and keep his Commandments, is the true felicity of man, and this brought him peace at the last and trying hour; and while his family loved him living and mourn him dead; they do not mourn as those without hope, for in his last moments the Christian principle, and the pain and parting agony they felt, was lessened when they saw the chamber where the good man meets his fate; it is a priviledge beyond the common walks of life. "For God sustained him in his final hour, "His final hour was brings glory to his God."	09/25/1822
Departed this life, on the 23rd of September, Miss Ann Nicholson, in the 45th year of her age, a native of Westmoreland county, England.	09/25/1822
Departed this transitory life, after a few days illness, which she bore with Christian fortitude, in the 20th year of her age, Miss Margaret West,	09/25/1822

Marriage and Death Notices	Date
daughter of James West, Sr., of this city.	
On Monday night last, 22nd inst., of a painful illness, Miss Frances Jane Wickes, in the 21st year of her age.	09/25/1822
Yesterday afternoon, in the 48th year of his age, Mr. Andrew Dalck, a native of Germany, and a long resident of this city. His friends and acquaintances are invited to his funeral, to take place this afternoon, at 3 o'clock, from his late dwelling, in Pearl street.	09/25/1822
On the 6th inst., at Port-au-Prince, in the 25th year of his age, John Angell, a young gentleman of amiable disposition and correct deportment. It is the fourth son of his widowed mother has parted with, to meet no more; they constituted all of the family of the late James Angell of this city – and having at different periods gone to sea, never returned.	09/25/1822
By the Rev. Dr. Glendy, on the evening of Monday last, Mr. James Wallace, to Miss Elizabeth Love, all of this city.	09/28/1822
By the Rev. Dr. Glendy, on the evening of Thursday last, Mr. James Ensor, to Miss Sarah Duhurst, all of this city.	09/28/1822
On Thursday, the 26th inst., by the Rev. John R. Keech, of Harford County, Mr. John Franklin, to Miss Rachel Ridgely Lux, both of this city.	09/28/1822
On Tuesday evening last, by the Rev. Mr. Valiant, Mr. David Owings, of Cecil county, to Miss Provy Brian, of this city.	09/28/1822
On Tuesday evening last, by the Rev. Mr. Valiant, Mr. John F. Fisher, to Miss Sarah Ann Booth, of this city.	09/28/1822
On Thursday evening, by the Rev. Mr. Valiant, Mr. John F. Fisher, to Miss Sarah Lane, all of this city.	09/28/1822
On Thursday evening, by the Rev. Mr. Soule, Mr. George Crook, to Miss Elizabeth, only daughter of Capt. William Buck, both of this city.	09/28/1822
On Thursday evening, by the Rev. Dr. Roberts, Mr. John Peake, to Miss Juliana Todhunter, both of this city.	09/28/1822
On Monday last, in the 45th year of his age, Mr. Henry Heyman Barnard, a native of Hamburg, for the last six years of his life a resident of this city.	09/28/1822

Marriage and Death Notices	Date
In Pensacola, on the 23 ult., Mr. John Coppinger Conner, in the 23rd year of his age, eldest son of the late Daniel Conner, of this city. He had filled the office of Chief Clerk to the Legislative Council, previous to his falling victim to the prevailing disease. It is but justice to the deceased to state, that the feelings of regret for his loss are universal among those who knew him.	09/28/1822
At Elkton, Md., on the 14th inst., Mrs. Catherine Andrews, wife of Mr. Eleazer P. Andrews, aged sixty-four years. Also, at the same place, on the 25th, Mr. Eleazer P. Andrews, aged sixty-six years, for many years a respectable inhabitant of the town of Preston, Connecticut.	09/28/1822
Departed this transitory life, on Friday morning last, after a short and severe illness, which she bore with the fortitude of an expiring Christian, Mrs. Elizabeth Dutton, widow of the late John Dutton, deceased, in the 48th year of her age. In the demise of this truly amiable woman, her family have to lament the loss of an affectionate and tender mother, whose many virtues will not be forgotten soon, and whose memory exists in all the poignancy of grief. It has been but a short time since, that they were deprived of a young and affectionate sister by the ruthless messenger of death, when now it has been their misfortune to lose a valuable and highly esteemed mother, whose loss is irreparable. But while they lament the loss of such beloved and valuable friends, they should not mourn as those that have no hope, but be consoled in the belief, that they left this world, in the religion of Jesus Church, which they so well adorned, for another and a better – and it should be borne in mind, by surviving friends that "in the midst of life we are in death;" and that for the accomplishment of so great a charge as we have to keep. *Be ye also ready.* This feeble tribute of respect is written by one, who, not possessing genius to eulogize sincerely sympathies with them in the loss they have sustained. A. G.	09/30/1822
At St. Louis, Missouri, on Saturday, August 31st, Mr. Otis Tiffany, merchant, from Baltimore, Md.	09/30/1822
In Anne Arundel county, on the 9th of September, of a short illness, Mr. Samuel Hopkins, aged 46 years, leaving a widow and six children to deplore the loss of an affectionate husband and fond father. For the last ten years of his life, he faithfully discharged the duties of Supervisor of the Fredericktown Turnpike Road, and was invariably distinguished for his fidelity and unbending integrity.	10/03/1822
On Sunday morning, at his residence, on Hampstead Hill, in the 35th year of his age, Mr. William Codd, leaving an affectionate wife and four small children to mourn his irreparable loss. In the death of this man, it	10/03/1822

Marriage and Death Notices	Date
may be truly said his wife is bereaved of an affectionate husband, and his children of a tender parent.	
On Thursday evening last, on the 26th ult., after a short and painful illness, Mrs. Helena Argust, wife of Mr. Charles, of this city, aged about 40 years.	10/03/1822
At Port Tobacco, Charles county, Md., on Thursday, the 26th ult., after a short illness, Mr. George Snodgrass. This young gentleman was a native of Lancaster county, Pa., and, although a short time a resident of the former place, he died much regretted and lamented by all who knew him.	10/03/1822
At Philadelphia, in the 26th year of his age, after a short, but severe illness, Dr. J. Russel Smith.	10/03/1822
By the Rev. Mr. Hinkle, Mr. John Davis, to Miss Frances Ann Easley, all of this city.	10/05/1822
On Thursday last, by the Rev. Dr. Jennings, Mr. Jeremiah Ducker, to Miss Juliana Fisher, both of Baltimore county.	10/05/1822
On Thursday evening, by the Rev. Dr. Roberts, Mr. Joseph L. Donoven, to Miss Caroline Soulsby, all of this city.	10/05/1822
On Tuesday evening last, by the Rev. Mr. Lemmon, Caleb D. Owings, Esq., of Baltimore county, to Miss Eleanor R. Edwards, of this city.	10/05/1822
On Tuesday evening last, by the Rev. J. P. H. Henshaw, Mr. John Quarly Hewlett, to Miss Mary Ann, second daughter of Richard H. Jones, Esq., all of this city.	10/05/1822
On the 29th ult., in the 34th year of his age, Mr. Patrick Nicholson, of Fell's Point, after a short and painful illness of four days and a half, which he bore with Christian resignation to the will of his God, and in his last moments, expressed these words: "Live, Jesus, live, and let it be my happy lot to die for love and thee."	10/05/1822
On Thursday afternoon, between 1 and 2 o'clock, John Frailey, son of Leonard Frailey, in the 7th year of his age.	10/05/1822
On board the Columbian brig Camelion, of and for Laguyra, on the 26th of September, Mr. David Manly, of Baltimore, of a wound received by the explosion of a pistol whilst in the act of loading.	10/05/1822

Marriage and Death Notices	Date
On Monday last, Mr. John Hayes, aged 65 years, a Custom House Officer, and old and respectable inhabitant of this city. He has left three children to lament the loss of a worthy parent.	10/05/1822
On Friday morning last, the 4th inst., after a short, but painful illness, which she bore with Christian fortitude, Mrs. Mary Williamson, consort of Mr. John Williamson, of this city, aged 50 years. Her Christian virtues, it is impossible to describe; too much cannot be said. As a wife, mother, and friend, she was amiable, gentle, and affectionate. In her, the family has lost a treasure that can never be replaced. But a few weeks past, we beheld her in the bloom of health, administering balm to the sick and distressed; but alas, she has now descended to the grave, the common lot of all, and is now happy in the arms of her Savior.	10/05/1822
Aug. 20th, at Point Coupee, Louisiana, in the 37th year of his age, Mr. John C. Young, formerly of this city.	10/05/1822
Died, at Hampton, the country seat of Gen. Ridgely, universally lamented, Mrs. Gough Ridgely, the wife of John Ridgely, Esq., and the only daughter of James Carrol, Esq. The amiable deportment and exemplary piety of this excellent lady endeared to all who had the pleasure of her acquaintance. Her death has created a void that will not soon be filled – still there is left to her surviving friends, the consolation that her bright spirit has been called from a world of trouble to rest forever in the bosom of her Creator.	10/05/1822
The desolating pestilence which has for some time past pervaded almost every section of our state has in its progress proved unusually fatal. With deep regret, we add to the number of its victims, the name of Miss Sally Mann, formerly of this city, Annapolis, who died on the 19th ult., in Charles county, at the residence of her brother, the Rev. Charles Mann.	10/05/1822
On Thursday evening last, after a long and painful illness, Mr. Thomas Leaman, in the 68th year of his age.	10/05/1825
On Friday morning last, after an illness of one day, Mr. James West, in the 25th year of his age, leaving a disconsolate wife and one child to lament the loss of an affectionate husband and a kind parent.	10/07/1822
Last evening, in this city, Mr. John Callaghan, in the sixty-first year of his age. He has long resided in this city, was a native of Ireland, and an intelligent, honest man. He pursued a course of useful industry, until infirmities came upon him, which have ended in his demise, in the hope of a joyful resurrection. His friends and acquaintance are respectfully	10/07/1822

Marriage and Death Notices	Date
invited to attend his funeral, this evening, at four o'clock, from his late dwelling, in South street.	
In this city, yesterday, between one and two o'clock, of typhus fever, Mr. William Baker, merchant, of White Stone, Lancaster county, Virginia.	10/07/1822
At City Point, Capt. Langdon, of the ship Trajan.	10/07/1822
On the 7th inst., at Mercersburg, Col. John McHenry, late of this city.	10/09/1822
On board the brig Alonzo, on his passage from Havana to Baltimore, Pliny D. Hamilton, eldest son of Capt. Pliny Hamilton, of this city, in the 19th year of his age. In the death of this truly amiable young man, a worthy and grief-oppressed father has to mourn the loss of a dutiful and affectionate son, and his friends and acquaintances the loss of an amiable and beloved companion. Just ripening into manhood, and about realizing the fondest wishes of his parents and friends, he has been summoned to the cold and silent tomb, and has left his aged father and disconsolate brother and sister, to mourn their irreparable loss.	10/09/1822
On Thursday evening last, by the Rev. Mr. Soule, Mr. William Hardy, to Miss Ann Dines, all of this city.	10/10/1822
This morning, at 3 o'clock, after a severe illness, William Litle, in the 26th year of his age. His friends and connexions are respectfully invited to attend his funeral, from his late dwelling, corner of Camden and Eutaw streets, this afternoon, at half past 4 o'clock, without further notice.	10/10/1822
On Sunday, the 28th ultimo, Mrs. Sarah P. Weathers, aged 33 years and 3 months, after a long and tedious illness, which she bore with Christian fortitude and resignation, to the will of her heavenly father, leaving four small children and a numerous circle of friends and acquaintance to lament their irreparable loss.	10/10/1822
In Easton, Md., Mr. Joseph Dawson, in the 65th year of his age.	10/10/1822
At her residence, Sweet Prospect, on Church Creek, Dorchester county, Md., Mrs. Elizabeth, consort of the late Thos. Colston, Esq., in the 64th year of her age.	10/10/1822
In Cambridge, Md., Miss Elizabeth E. Waters.	10/10/1822
At his residence, near Brookvill, Maryland, on Thursday, the 3rd inst., after a severe illness of eleven days, contracted on his late laborious	10/11/1822

241

Marriage and Death Notices	Date
survey and examination of the Potomac river, Thomas Moore, for several years past the principal Engineer of the Board of Public Works, of Virginia – in which capacity, he had given very great satisfaction both to the Board and the state at large.	
On Thursday evening last, by the Rev. Dr. Roberts, Capt. Walter R. Gallaway, to Miss Elizabeth Haubert, both of this city.	10/12/1822
In Harford county, Mr. Joseph Adams, to Miss Mary Grant, both of Baltimore.	10/12/1822
On Tuesday evening last, after a short, but excruciating illness, which he bore with Christian fortitude and resignation, James, eldest son of Capt. William Dimond, in the 17th year of his age. This is another striking instance of the uncertainty of life, and the awful responsibility that devolves upon us to prepare for the change. But a few short days have elapsed since we beheld this promising youth in fullness of health and vigor, advancing towards manhood. Scarcely had he shed the tear of affection over the grave of a younger Brother, when suddenly the rude messenger of death summoned him to accompany him. Thus have his disconsolate parents have been hastily deprived of the objects of their most anxious wishes and expectations, in one short week.	10/12/1822
Died, at Old Point Comfort, on Monday night last, at a very advanced age, Capt. Thomas Dulton, naval store keeper, at Gosport Dock Yard.	10/12/1822
On Monday, the 30th September, after an illness of five days, Mr. Richard Sappington, in the 26th year of his age.	10/12/1822
On Thursday evening, the 3rd inst., at Fredericktown, Md., the Rev. Francis Malleve, S. J., aged 52 years, and for the last 13 years Pastor of the Roman Catholic Congregation of that town, as also of the adjoining congregations of the county.	10/12/1822
At Harford county, Md., Mrs. Sarah Guyton, in the 86th year of her age.	10/12/1822
On Sunday evening, the 6th inst., at Southampton, St. Mary's county, by the Rev. Mr. Mitchell, Mr. Thomas B. Kelly, to Miss Rebecca G. S. Key, daughter of the late Philip Key, Jr., Esq., of St. Mary's.	10/14/1822
Departed this life, on the 16th ult., near St. Louis, Missouri, Mrs. Mary A. Hamtramck, wife of Mr. John H. Hamtramck, and daughter of David Williamson, of this city.	10/14/1822
Departed this life, on the 16th ult., at Fruithill, Northumberland county,	10/14/1822

Marriage and Death Notices	Date
Virginia, in the 20th year of her age, Elizabeth, consort of Mr. James M. Smith, esq., and only daughter of Mr. Eli Hewitt, of this city. Painful is the task to announce to her relatives and friends their afflicting bereavement. She left them but a short time since buoyant with hope and expectation; but now, how sad the reverse.	
On Thursday evening last, the 10th inst., by the Rev. Dr. Roberts, Mr. Thomas Jarrett to Miss Ann Young, both of this city.	10/15/1822
On Thursday evening last, by the Rev. Mr. Valiant, Mr. Luther Wright, to Miss Emily Lusbz.	10/15/1822
By the Rev. Mr. Valiant, on Sunday evening, Mr. Israel Robinson, to Miss Ann Parmer.	10/15/1822
On the 3rd inst., in the 21st year of her age, after a short and severe illness, Miss Sarah Price.	10/15/1822
On Saturday evening, the 12th inst., Dr. Harrison Dixon, aged 36 years, 4 months, and 3 days. He was born in Caroline county, E. S. Maryland, practiced physic for some years in Dorchester county, and had been living in Baltimore for a few years before his death, engaged in merchandise.	10/15/1822
At Church Hill, Md., Ebenezer Price, Esq., late of Baltimore.	10/15/1822
On Tuesday evening last, by the Rev. Mr. Shinn, Mr. Andrew Adgate to Miss Elizabeth O., daughter of Owen Dorsey, Esq., both of this city.	10/17/1822
On Tuesday evening last, by the Rev. Mr. Helfenstein, Mr. Charles Morgan, to Miss Mary B. Griffith, both of this city.	10/17/1822
At Hayes, in Montgomery county, Md., on Thursday, the 10th inst., William Laird, Esq., of Georgetown, D. C., to Helen Dunlop, daughter of James Dunlop, Esq.	10/17/1822
At Annapolis, Benjamin Gaither, Esq., to Miss Catherine Ridgely.	10/18/1822
Departed this life, on the 8th inst., at Havre de Grace, Harford county, Mrs. Sarah Day, a member of the Society of Friends, in the 73rd year of her age.	10/18/1822
At New Orleans, 17th ult., Madame, the widow Zacharie, formerly of Baltimore, distinguished for her piety, humility, and charity.	10/18/1822

Marriage and Death Notices	Date
In Cambridge, on the Eastern Shore of Md., Mrs. Mary Cook, wife of Thomas Cook, in the 19th year of her age, of a short and severe illness, which she bore with Christian fortitude and resignation to the will of God.	10/18/1822
On the 6th inst., Mr. Alexander Widney, of this city, aged 38 years, after a short and severe illness – likewise a daughter and son, buried in one week.	10/18/1822
At Annapolis, Mrs. Elizabeth Foxcroft, in the 53rd year of her age.	10/18/1822
OBITUARY. In these afflicting times, when every day reveals to us some new source of sorrow, it becomes our painful duty to add to the melancholy number of the dead, the name of Mrs. Anna Maria Winter, consort of Joseph S. Winter, Esq., of New Orleans, who expired yesterday morning in the 23rd year of her age. Mrs. Winter was the eldest daughter of the late Mr. Levi Pierce, of Baltimore. With a mind highly cultivated – a heart which was the abode of every affection – an amenity of manners which always accompanied purity – she lived the idol of her family and friends and an example all should wish to imitate. In her was a rare combination of all qualities which command admiration and esteem; in her breast, the bright flame of benevolence and charity burned without ceasing; the misfortunes of others were her own, and her whole life was one continued act of devotion to virtue and her God. Religion was part of her nature; it gladdened her happy hours, and soothed her in agony and death.	10/18/1822
On Tuesday evening last, by the Rev. Mr. Bartow, Capt. Richard Reardon, to Miss Sarah Cooper, all of this city.	10/19/1822
On Thursday evening last, by the Rev. Mr. Bartow, Mr. John L. Boyd, of this city, to Miss Temperance Ann Holmes, of Baltimore county.	10/19/1822
Last evening, by the Rev. Mr. Henshaw, Mr. Thomas Wilson Harris, of Calvert county, to Miss Louisa Ann Larsh, of this city.	10/19/1822
At Alexandria, Louisiana, 6th Sept., Mr. John C. Bankson, aged 24, recently of Baltimore.	10/19/1822
Recently, on the Eastern Shore of Maryland, Kent county, Mr. Thomas Bixby, aged 24 years, formerly of Litchfield, of the state of N. Hampshire.	10/19/1822
On Tuesday evening last, by the Rev. Mr. Beschter, Mr. Mathias Benzinger, to Miss Mary Catherine Crey, eldest daughter of Mr.	10/21/1822

244

Marriage and Death Notices	Date
Frederick Crey.	
At Mount Pleasant, Linganore, on Thursday last, by the Rev. James L. Higgins, Anthony Kimmel, Esq., of this city, to Miss Sidney Ann, only daughter of Maj. Danl. James, of Frederick county.	10/21/1822
Brig. Gen. John E. Howard, Jr., the eldest son of our Revolutionary veteran of that name, is no more – he died a few days since, at Mercersburg, Pennsylvania, of the fatal malady so prevalent at that place. He attended his brother-in-law, the lamented Col. McHenry, to the fatal spot, and both of these individuals, the pride and ornament of their native city, expired at that place. The subject of our present sympathy was peculiarly qualified to adorn any sphere, either public or private. In the hour of invasion, he stood forth our undaunted defender, in private life superadded to all those confiding qualities that render friendship so dear, he inherited from nature what we venture to call, the urbanity of the heart; there was no studied smile, no disciplined courtesy; the stranger in his company, found himself at home; he seemed to meet on common ground, and scarcely to entertain a suspicion that they had not long been acquainted. *Chronicle.*	10/21/1822
On Thursday evening last, by the Rev. John Finley, Edward Austen, to Mary Davis Brown.	10/22/1822
On Wednesday evening, 16th, by the Rt. Rev. Bishop Kemp, Mr. Joel Brag, of Ostego county, state of N. York, to Mrs. Margaret Bennett, of Baltimore.	10/22/1822
On the 11th inst., after a short illness, in this city, Francis Farrell, aged 42, a Student of divinity. About 5 months antecedent to his death, he arrived here from St. Louis, in the state of Missouri, where he had been latterly studying. He was originally from Dublin, in Ireland. In this terrestrial sphere, he has received his final lecture; and is now gone to other regions to receive the result of his researches, and learn the realities in the ethereal temple of the All Intelligent.	10/22/1822
Yesterday, of a severe illness, which he bore with Christian fortitude, in the fifty-fifth year of his age, Hoops Chamberlain, leaving a widow and two children to bemoan their irreparable loss.	10/22/1822
In Baltimore county, on the 18th, John G. Walker, Esq., member of the Levy Court, in the _6th year of his age.	10/22/1822
On the 11th Sept. last, near Rock Hall, Kent County, John C. Hynson, Esq., aged 53 years. There are few men "whose void will be more	10/22/1822

Marriage and Death Notices	Date
severely felt than the deceased; his kind and benevolent disposition, pleasing address, and hospitable character, had endeared him to all who knew him." After a severe and distressing illness of several months, he *realized "a long devotion"* to the service of his Savior; and although he has left a widow and a number of children to deplore his loss, yet they have comfort in knowing that he now reaps the reward of a life well spent.	
On the 7th inst., at the same place, Mrs. Mary Burton, aged 88 years. She was born in England, and at an early age became a resident of this state, and was long a member of Mr. John C. Hynson's family.	10/22/1822
On the 12th inst., Mr. William H. Ringgold, one of the late elected members of the General Assembly of this state, from Kent county.	10/22/1822
In this place, on the 20th inst., Capt. Isaac Martin, of the schr. Enterprize, of Lubec, Maine.	10/22/1822
On Monday last, at his residence, at Nottingham, P. George's county, Dr. Reverdy Gheselin, in the 60th year of his age. Few men have lived more respected, or died more regretted. He served many years in the Executive Councils of this state.	10/22/1822
At the U. S. Navy Hospital, at Gosport, Va., on the 15th, after a short illness, Mr. Charles Ghequire, of the U. S. marine corps, a native of Maryland.	10/22/1822
Last evening, by the Rev. Dr. Kurtz, Mr. Richard Ball, of Anne Arundel county, to Miss Ann Elizabeth Krise, of Frederick county.	10/23/1822
On the 10th ult., at Louisville, Ky., Daniel R. Southard, Esq., merchant of that place, to Miss Elizabeth Young, formerly of this place.	10/23/1822
At Richland Mills, York county, Penn., on Sunday, the 6th inst., in the 37th year of his age, Mr. Charles Walsh, formerly of this city. The kind and amiable disposition of the deceased had much endeared him to his friends and relatives, who dearly regret his early and unexpected death.	10/23/1822
At the same place, on Tuesday, the 8th inst., in the 79th year of her age, Mrs. Anna Maria Walsh, relict of Mr. Jacob Walsh, formerly of this city. A long life passed in the active and conscientious discharge of moral and religious duties had fully ripened her for the tomb, and her death, which to her relatives and friends is a most severe and afflicting loss, we humbly, but confidently trust is to be accounted as great gain to	10/23/1822

246

Marriage and Death Notices	Date
her.	
At Newton, Mass., Mr. Joseph Parker, of Baltimore, to Miss Hope Grafton, only daughter of the Rev. Joseph Grafton.	10/24/1822
Last evening, of a lingering pulmonic disease, Mr. Mark Carroll, in the 36th year of his age.	10/24/1822
On the 20th ult., Madame Maria Ann Gilles, in the 71st year of her age. The deceased was born at Paris, and emigrated to this city but a few years past. In this country, her advanced age and retired habits limited the use of her estimable worth and virtue to the select circle who enjoyed the advantage of her acquaintance; and the example of her piety, patience, and resignation, in a land of strangers, in trial and affliction, can afford the only consolation to those who, with her bereaved family, mourn their irreparable loss.	10/24/1822
On the 16th inst., time closed on Elizabeth, consort of Mr. Joel Morgan, of this city, in the 48th year of her age, after a long and lingering illness, borne as becomes the Christian.	10/24/1822
Last evening, by the Rev. Mr. Henshaw, William H. Barroll, Esq., of Chestertown, to Rebecca, eldest daughter of Edward Johnson, Esq., mayor elect of Baltimore.	10/25/1822
At Annapolis, Mr. William Parsons, of the District of Columbia, to Miss Sarah Miller, of Annapolis.	10/25/1822
In Washington county, Md., Mr. Henry Lidy, to Mrs. Ridenour. Mr. Wm. Schleigh to Miss Elizabeth Spangler.	10/25/1822
On Wednesday, 16th inst., after a severe illness of six weeks and three days, Mr. James Traies, aged 27 years, a native of Crediton, Devon, England. AG&C	10/25/1822
On the 22nd inst., at Oxford, the residence of Mrs. Edwards, Miss Mary Butler, after a long and painful illness, which she bore with the most Christian resignation to the All-wise Disposer of events. Her many amiable qualities, her correct deportment thro' life, combined with her exemplary piety, endeared her to a very respectable circle of friends. The loss of her cheering society will long be sensibly felt by all who knew her best.	10/25/1822
At Havana, on the 13th inst., on board the brig Canada, John Moore, eldest son of the late Capt. Thomas Moore, aged 18 years.	10/26/1822

Marriage and Death Notices	Date
On Tuesday last, after a short and severe illness, Miss Margaret Hammond, in the 69th year of her age.	10/26/1822
At St. Jago de Cuba, on the 2nd of last month, of the fever, Capt. Winthrop Farrin, in the 28th year of his age, formerly of Brunswick. He has left a wife and two children to lament the loss of an affectionate husband and father; and a number of respectable relations and friends to mourn the loss of a kind friend and a good and honest man. The writer of those knows well how to esteem the memory of her departed friend. "Blessed are ye that die in the Lord."	10/26/1822
On the last of Aug., of the fever, in the same place, Mr. George Stride, a native of London.	10/26/1822
On board the U. S. ship Peacock, on the 28th of September, Midshipman Christopher Lowndes, of apoplexy, and native of Maryland. And on the 7th inst., Lt. Thomas H. Bowyer, a native of Virginia, after a few days sickness. The Navy is deprived of the services of two very promising officers, in the death of Lt. Bowyer and Mr. Lowndes, who bid fair to be ornament to the country.	10/26/1822
On Thursday last, by the Rev. Mr. Young, Mr. Charles Bowers, to Miss Ibby Massay, both of this city.	10/28/1822
On Tuesday evening last, by the Rev. Mr. Bartow, Mr. Augustus Vallette, to Miss Emily Jane Quim, all of this city.	10/28/1822
On Sunday evening last, in Trinity Church, by the Rev. Mr. Bartow, Mr. John Barrett, to Mrs. Elizabeth Lowe, all of this city.	10/28/1822
On Friday morning last, Mrs. Ann Welsh, relict of the late Dr. Robert Welsh, of South River, Anne Arundel county, in the 64th year of her age.	10/28/1822
On Thursday afternoon, the 24th inst., at Brookland Wood, the seat of Richard Caton, Esq., Robert Patterson, in the 42nd year of his age. A man whose public and private worth need no recommendation for those who knew him.	10/28/1822
At her late dwelling, in Calvert county, on Thursday, 17th inst., Barbara Wilkinson, relict of Gen. Joseph Wilkinson.	10/28/1822
At Fredericktown, Md., Mr. Henry Koontz, Sr., in the 87th year of his age.	10/28/1822
At Germantown, Nicholas Antoine Poulletiere, aged 62, an emigrant from Paris in the reign of terror under Robespierre, and who, ever since,	10/28/1822

Marriage and Death Notices	Date
has lived in retirement, principally supported by numerous friends, a blessing that honest poverty never wants.	
By the Rev. Dr. Glendy, on the evening of Thursday last, Mr. Alexander Maydwell, to Miss Sarah Peters, all of this city.	10/28/1822 10/28/1822
On Thursday evening, the 24th inst., Mr. Daniel Cheston, in the 69th year of his age, long a respectable inhabitant of this city.	10/29/1822
In Upper Marlboro', on the 26th inst., Mr. John Shortt, late of this city.	10/29/1822
At Centreville, Queen Anns County, on Wednesday, the 23rd inst., George Washington Massey, aged 22 years, student at law.	10/29/1822
Last evening, by the Rev. Mr. Healey, Mr. John Slater, to Miss Naomi Thomas, all of this city.	10/30/1822
On the evening of Tuesday, the 22nd inst., by the Rev. Mr. Magraw, Mr. Robert McMaster, to Miss Martha Tagart, all of Cecil county, Maryland.	10/30/1822
This morning, at 7 o'clock, after a lingering illness, which he bore with Christian resignation, Mr. Joseph Mather, aged about 48 years. His friends are invited to attend his remains to the grave, at 9 o'clock, tomorrow morning, from his late dwelling, in Fish Market space.	10/30/1822
Yesterday afternoon, Mr. Isaac Edmondson, long a respectable merchant of this city. His friends and acquaintances are respectively invited to attend his funeral, this afternoon, at 3 o'clock, from his late dwelling, No. 74 Market street.	10/30/1822
On Monday morning last, of a short, but painful illness, master John West, in the 17th year of his age. This is the third death in the family within five weeks.	10/30/1822
Yesterday evening, at 5 o'clock, Christian Simon Konig, Esq., Consul of the Netherlands, &c. His friends and acquaintance are invited to attend his funeral, which will take place this afternoon, at 3 o'clock, from his late dwelling, No. 194 Market street.	11/01/1822
At Washington county, Md., Mr. George H. Reynolds, in the 24th year of his age.	11/01/1822
At Augusta, Georgia, on the 17th inst., Mr. Oliver Miller, a native of Hagerstown, Md., in the 24th year of his age.	11/01/1822

Marriage and Death Notices	Date
On Thursday evening last, by the Rev. Mr. Bidderson, Mr. Henry Bullen, to Miss Rachel Garey, all of this city.	11/02/1822
In Harford county, Md., Mrs. Mary Worthington, wife of Dr. Worthington, in the 28th year of her age. At Deer Creeks, same county, Isaac Coale, a member of the Society of Friends, in the 58th year of his age. At Harper's Ferry, Va., Capt. Nicholas Write, in the 75th year of his age, formerly of Fredericktown, Md.	11/02/1822
On Last Tuesday evening, by the Rev. Mr. Duncan, Mr. John C. Smith, to Miss Mary Ann Taylor, all of this city.	11/04/1822
On Tuesday evening, 29th ult., at Retirement Farm, Jefferson county, Va., by the Rev. Mr. Mahons, Mr. John Piet, of Baltimore, to Miss Susan Catherine, eldest daughter of the late Richard McSherry, Esq.	11/04/1822
On Thursday, 24th ult., at Rose Cottage, Accomac county, Virginia, by the Rev. William Lee, Richard Saltonstall, Esq., of Baltimore, to Margaret Ann, daughter of the late Geo. Savage, Esq., of Northampton.	11/04/1822
In Somerset county, Eastern Shore of Maryland, on Thursday, the 11th ult., by the Rev. White, Mr. William Sudler, to Miss Elizabeth T. Curtis, daughter of the late Capt. Wm. Curtis, all of said county.	11/04/1822
On the 18th of September last, in Jefferson county, Kentucky, Corilla, consort of Henry Dorsey, Esq., after two weeks of severe illness of the prevailing fever, at that place. The early piety of the deceased, her regular Christian life, her strong marked affection as a wife and mother, and lastly her patience and resignation during her illness, was an example worthy of imitation. "Let me die the death of the righteous and let my last end be like theirs."	11/04/1822
October 31st, in the 22nd year of her age, Mrs. Achsah Marvin, wife of Mr. Clar Marvin, after a painful illness of five weeks, which she bore with Christian patience and resignation. Having embraced religion in early life, she was enabled in the hour of death to lean her breast on her beloved, and breathe her life out sweetly there.	11/04/1822
At Bladensburg, Md., after a short illness, Mr. Henry T. Tilley, aged about 28 years.	11/04/1822
On the 2nd inst., in the 24th year of her age, Mrs. Mary Ann Schade, consort of Mr. Martin G. Schade. In the demise of this lady, we have to lament the loss of a beautiful daughter, an affectionate wife, and a kind	11/05/1822

Marriage and Death Notices	Date
and charitable neighbor.	
On the 3rd of Oct., in New Orleans, Mr. Henry Seaton, late of Baltimore, after a painful illness of 4 days.	11/05/1822
Last evening, by the Rev. Mr. Duncan, Gen. William H. Marriott, of Annapolis, to Jane, daughter of John M'Kim, Jr., Esq., of this city.	11/06/1822
On Tuesday evening last, by the Rev. Dr. Jennings, Mr. Ezekiel C. Johnson, to Miss Susan M. Fry, all of this city.	11/07/1822
On Thursday evening last, by the Rev. Mr. Hamilton, Mr. John Coates, to Miss Lucretia Corum, both of this city.	11/07/1822
On Tuesday evening last, by the Rev. Mr. Soule, Mr. James R. Preston, of Harford, to Miss Eliza Ann Johnson, of Anne Arundel county.	11/08/1822
At Hagerstown, Mr. George Coler to Miss Catherine Martin.	11/08/1822
At New Orleans, on the 21st of September, in the 25th year of his age, of the prevailing fever, after 4 days illness, Mr. John Devereaux, late of Worcester County, Maryland.	11/08/1822
At Hagerstown, Mrs. Catherine Houser, in the 20th year of her age.	11/08/1822
At Deerfield, Cumberland county, N. J., on the 23rd ult., after a severe illness of two weeks, John Mayhew, Esq.	11/08/1822
At New Orleans, on the 1st of October, of the prevailing epidemic, Capt. Reuben West, master of the ship Washington, of New York. After a lingering illness, Capt. Thomas Rodney, of Kent Island, Md. Mr. Peyton Roach, of Virginia, deeply regretted both by relations and friends.	11/08/1822
At Port Tobacco, Charles county, Md., on the 2nd inst., after a severe illness, which she bore with Christian fortitude, Miss Catherine, daughter of the late John Laidler, Esq., of Charles county.	11/08/1822
On Thursday evening last, by the Rev. Mr. Bartow, Mr. James E. Miller, of Annapolis, to Miss Louisa Bray, of this city.	11/09/1822
At Dumfries, Pa., on Sunday evening last, by the Rev. George Lemmon, the Rev. Stephen William Prestman, of Baltimore, to Ann, youngest daughter of the late Timothy Brundige, Esq.	11/09/1822 11/09/1822

Marriage and Death Notices	Date
On Thursday evening last, by the Rev. William Hamilton, Mr. Robert B. Varnum, to Miss Ann W. Todd, all of this city.	11/11/1822
On Thursday evening, after a lingering illness, which she bore with the resignation of a Christian, whose hopes were fixed on a happier and better world, Mrs. Eliza Towers, widow of Capt. John Towers. Having finished the portion of time allowed her by Divine Providence, and having upon all occasions, carefully attended to the duties of her religion; with perfect calmness and a full confidence in the merits of her Redeemer, she resigned herself into the arms of her Creator. She has left a tender and affectionate neice, whom she always regarded as her child, and who in return always considered her as her mother; and with filial solicitude and trembling anxiety administered to her wants and soothed her in her last moments. The reflection, that after a life well spent, her soul has been received into the kingdom of the blessed, is the only thing that can support her on this trying occasions and console her for her loss.	11/11/1822
At Easton, Mr. Gardner Bayley, to Miss Elizabeth Coward.	11/12/1820
Yesterday afternoon, at the residence of her son-in-law, Capt. Haliard, of the U. S. Navy, Mrs. Martha, wife of James Mackubin, Esq., of Anne Arundel county, in the sixty-fourth year of her age.	11/12/1822
On Monday evening last, by the Rev. Mr. Bartow, Mr. James Kinch, to Mrs. Bridget T. Martin, of this city.	11/13/1822
On Monday evening last, by the Rev. Mr. Bartow, Capt. Hezekiah Hall, of Westerly, Rhode Island, to Miss Jane Smith, all of this city.	11/13/1822
By the Rev. Dr. Glendy, on Monday last, Joshua B. Stearns, Esq., of Salem, to Miss Louisa H. King, of this city.	11/14/1822
By the Rev. Dr. Glendy, on the evening of Tuesday last, Mr. Thomas Vickory, to Miss Mary Ann Graham, all of this city.	11/14/1822
On the 12th inst., by the Rev. Mr. Nevins, Mr. Stephen S. Wilson to Ann Somerville, eldest daughter of Col. David Harris.	11/14/1822
At New Orleans, of yellow fever, Littleton Joynes, late of Philadelphia, supercargo and first officer of the schr. Time, Tucker, of Baltimore.	11/14/1822
On Thursday, the 1st inst., by the Rev. Edmund J. Reis, Mr. James M'Cormick, to Miss Ann Ellis.	11/15/1822

Marriage and Death Notices	Date
By the Rev. Edmund J. Reis, on Wednesday last, Mr. Edward Talbot, to Miss Rachel Kelly, all of this city.	11/15/1822
Last evening, by the Rev. D. E. Reese, Mr. Jacob G. Hardister, to Miss Mary Ann Austin, all of this city.	11/15/1822
At Hagerstown, Mr. Samuel Smith to Miss Mary Howard.	11/15/1822
Early yesterday morning, in the 72nd year of her age, Mrs. Mary B. Smith, relict of Mr. Thoroughgood Smith, formerly Mayor, and long a respectable merchant of this city. She was one amongst the many melancholy examples of worldly vicissitudes, presented to the contemplation, as if to humble pride and chasten character. Long accustomed to the smiles of prosperity, she has passed the greater part of her life in affluence; but, though her declining years were unfortunate, she submitted to the Divine Will with meekness and Christian resignation.	11/15/1822
On Thursday evening, the 7th inst., by the Rev. Mr. Valiant, Mr. James Wilson, to Miss Harriet Chenowith, all of Harford county.	11/16/1822
On Tuesday evening last, by the Rev. Mr. Soule, John Glenn, Esq., to Henrietta Rebecca, daughter of William Wilkins, Esq.	11/16/1822
On Wednesday evening, the 30th ult., at Shepherd's-town, Va., by the Rev. Thomas Kenerly, Mr. Asbury Jarett, merchant of Baltimore, to Miss Eliza Sophronia Lefevre, daughter of Mr. John Lefevre, of White Post, Frederick co., Va.	11/16/1822
On Tuesday evening, Nov. 5th, by the Rev. Mr. Redman, Mr. John O'Ferrall, of Morgan county, Va., to Miss Eliza Humrickhouse, daughter of Mr. Peter Humrickhouse, of Hagerstown, Md.	11/16/1822
On the 13th inst., in Georgetown, D. C., by the Rev. Mr. McIlvaine, the Rev. William Nevins, of Baltimore, to Miss Mary Lloyd, second daughter of the late P. E. Key, Esq.	11/18/1822
On Thursday last, by the Rev. Dr. Roberts, Mr. James Gray, to Miss Wilhelmina Jones, all of this city.	11/18/1822
In Harford county, Md., Mr. James Bond Preston, of Harford, to Miss Eliza Ann Johnson, of Anne Arundel county. Mr. Aqilla Hall to Miss Catherine Amos. Mr. James Manaham to Miss Ann Maria Brown.	11/18/1822
In Frederick county, Md., Mr. Bazil Norris, Merchant, to Miss Jane Charlton. Mr. Randolph Campbell to Miss Mary Butterworth. Mr.	11/18/1822

Marriage and Death Notices	Date
William T. Davis to Miss Mary Shire.	
Yesterday morning, in the 35th year of his age, William E. Williams, son of the late Gen. Otho H. Williams. He left an interesting family and a large circle of friends to mourn his early death.	11/18/1822
Last evening, by the Rev. John Hargrove, the Rev. Robert Elliott, of Washington, D. C., to Elizabeth, daughter of the late Daniel Lamott, Esq., of this city.	11/20/1822
On the evening of Thursday last, by the Rev. D. E. Reese, Mr. Jacob G. Hardester, to Miss Mary Austen, all of this city.	11/20/1822
By the Rev. Dr. Glendy, on the evening of Thursday last, Mr. James Murphy, to Miss Ellen Davis, all of this city.	11/21/1822
On Sunday last, by the Rev. Dr. Kurtz, Mr. Carsten Torney, to Miss Charlotte Caroline Kotman, both of this city.	11/21/1822
At Richmond, Va., on Sunday evening, the 17th inst., by the Rev. Philip Courtney, Mr. Alexander Cushman, of the firm of Cushman & Campbell, merchants, to Miss Jane Ramsay, formerly of Baltimore.	11/22/1822
On Saturday, the 16th inst., Mr. James C. Dew, in the 38th year of his age.	11/22/1822
In Talbot County, Maryland, Col. Perry Spencer.	11/22/1822
Thursday evening, by the Rt. Rev. Bishop Kemp, Charles R. Carroll, Esq., to Rebecca Ann, eldest daughter of Dr. Pue.	11/23/1822
On Thursday evening, 21st inst., by the Rev. Mr. Kurtz, Mr. William Connaway, to Miss Elizabeth Bowers, all of this city.	11/23/1822
On Sunday, the 17th Nov., at Mount Pleasant, Montgomery county, where she had gone for the benefit of her health, Ann Boyd, in the 29th year of her age.	11/23/1822
On Thursday evening last, by the Rev. Mr. M'Ilhany, Mr. Richard Croxall, of this city, to Miss Deborah, daughter of the late James Gittings, Esq., of Long Green.	11/25/1822
In Harford county, Md., Mr. David Tucker to Miss Sarah Carter.	11/25/1822
On Thursday, the 12th inst., Mr. Edward B. Hardcastle, of Denton, Md.,	11/25/1822

Marriage and Death Notices	Date
to Miss Mary Ann Lockwood, of Whiteleysburg, Del.	
On Sunday morning, the 24th inst., William Camp, Sr., Esq., in the 49th year of his age. His friends and Masonic brethren are requested to attend his funeral, which will be conducted in Masonic order, from his late dwelling, at 3 o'clock, this afternoon.	11/25/1822
Yesterday morning, Mrs. Ann Laty, consort Mr. Joseph Laty, Sr., in the 48th year of her age.	11/25/1822
On Wednesday morning last, Dr. Joseph Hall, of Anne Arundel county, in the 45th year of his age, after a short, but severe illness.	11/25/1822
In Harford county, Md., Mr. John Kirkwood, aged 60. Mr. Thomas C. Street, in the 23rd year of his age.	11/25/1822
In Washington city, Mrs. Ann Elbertina Middleton, in the 19th year of her age, wife of Arthur Middleton, Esq.	11/25/1822
On Tuesday evening last, by the Rev. Mr. Austen, Dr. John D. Readel, of Baltimore, to Miss Martha Worthington, daughter of Walter Worthington, Esq., of Baltimore county.	11/26/1822
On Thursday evening, 21st inst., by the Rev. Dr. Jennings, Capt. William French, to Miss Lucy Ann Cully, all of this city.	11/26/1822
On the 23rd inst., after a long and painful illness, Mr. Thomas M. Meech, in the 38th year of his age.	11/26/1822
In Baltimore, yesterday morning, at 8 o'clock, by the Rev. John R. Keech, Mr. Daniel M. Conn, to Miss Emily B. Kenley, all of Harford county.	11/27/1822
At West River, Md., on Thursday last, Mr. James Islehart, to Miss Nancy, daughter of Osborn Harwood, Esq., of Anne Arundel county.	11/27/1822
On the 26th inst., Rebecca Page, daughter of John Page, Esq., in the fourth year of her age.	11/27/1822
At West River, on Thursday last, the 21st inst., Mrs. Battee, wife of the Rev. Dennis Battee, of that place.	11/27/1822
At Annapolis, on Sunday evening last, the 24th inst., Mr. Edmund Briz, of Anne Arundel county.	11/27/1822

Marriage and Death Notices	Date
On Monday evening last, by the Rev. Dr. Glendy, Mr. Thomas White, to Miss Maria Druggon, both of this city.	11/28/1822
At Philadelphia, the 20th inst., by the Rev. Dr. Collins, Mr. Charles Piper, of that place, to Caroline Augusta, youngest daughter of Mr. John Martiacq, of Baltimore.	11/28/1822
On Sunday evening last, Mr. Samuel Harris, Printer, of Washington city, in the 22nd year of his age.	11/28/1822
On Tuesday, the 26th inst., in the 64th year of her age, Mrs. Elizabeth Curson, relict of the late Richard Curson, Jr., Esq., and daughter of Mrs. Ellen Moale.	11/29/1/22
Last evening, by the Rev. Mr. Henshaw, John C. Van Wyck, Esq., to Sidney J., daughter of Judge McMechen.	11/29/1822
Last evening, by the Rev. Dr. Glendy, Mr. George Gillingham, Jr., to Miss Sarah, daughter of Mr. James Haslett, of this city.	11/29/1822
On Monday last, by the Rev. Dr. Kurtz, Mr. Godfrey Sanders, to Mrs. Hannah Foster, all of this city.	11/29/1822
On the evening of Tuesday, the 19th inst., by the Rev. Mr. Magraw, Mr. John Moore, to Miss Jane, eldest daughter of the late Joseph Barnes, all of Cecil county.	11/29/1822
On Thursday evening last, by the Rev. Mr. McCann, Mr. Daniel A. Ellis, to Miss Ann Taylor, both of this city.	11/30/1822
On the 11th Sept. last, of a bilious fever, on his passage from Philadelphia to Alvarado, Mr. James C. Neilson, late of Baltimore.	11/30/1822
On Monday, the 25th inst., after a severe illness of five days, at his residence in Madison county, Virginia, Marcus Dennison, formerly of this city, aged 39 years. He has left an amiable wife to bewail his loss.	11/30/1822
Yesterday morning, after a lingering illness, Mr. William Spear, about 30 years of age.	11/30/1822
At the Theological Seminary at Princeton, N. J., Mr. William G. Krebs, in the 21st year of his age.	11/30/1822
On Sunday morning, the 17th instant, Mr. Robert Johnson, in the 56th year of his age. He was a native of Harford county, and for the last four	11/30/1822 12/02/1822

Marriage and Death Notices	Date
or five years a resident of this city.	
On the 28th inst., by the Rev. Mr. Millsimer, Mr. Benjamin Deford, of this city, to Miss Harriet Boeugher, of Abbetstown, Pa.	12/02/1822
On Thursday evening, 28th inst., in the 30th year of his age, Mr. William Armat, merchant of this city.	12/02/1822
On the morning of the 30th November, Mrs. Shinah Etting, at the advanced age of 78 years. The deceased has been about forty years a resident of Baltimore – she needs no eulogy, the affection of all who knew her speaks more than praise.	12/02/1822
On Saturday last, aged 25, Susan T., wife of Charles Mayer, Esq., and daughter of Henry Pratt, Esq., of Philadelphia. The virtues of departed relatives and friends are often magnified by the affection of their survivors; and obituary notices sometimes present but a feeble likeness of their originals. With rigid truth, however, it may be said of this lady, that her character was strongly marked by an uncommon purity of heart; by a mind of an excellent order, highly cultivated; a fancy playful and innocent; a benevolence truly admirable; and domestic virtues which endeared her to all around her. She contracted the disease, which proved fatal, whilst engaged in an act of kindness to others; and has left a husband and two infant children, who must ever, with her friends, deeply deplore her loss.	12/02/1822
On Saturday last, by the Rev. Mr. Smith, Dr. Hugh O'Brien, to Mrs. Cassandra Broadfoot, both of this city.	12/06/1822
In Washington county, Md., Mr. John Ringer to Miss Mary Witmer.	12/06/1822
On the 17th of November, at his residence, in Newmarket, Dorchester county, Maryland, Mr. Abraham Ross, long a respectable inhabitant of that County.	12/06/1822
In Washington County, Md., Mr. Cyrus Sanders, at an advanced age. Mrs. Mary Thornburg, wife of Mr. S. Thornburg, of Hagerstown. Mrs. Eliza L. Elliott, consort of Mr. G. M. E.	12/06/1822
On Thursday evening last, by the Rev. Mr. Duncan, Mr. James Martin, Esq., to Mrs. Susannah Lee, both of this city.	12/07/1822
Last evening, in the 30th year of his age, Thomas Vance, of the firm John & Thomas Vance, booksellers, of this city. His friends are requested to attend his funeral, from his late residence, No. 178 Market	12/07/1822

Marriage and Death Notices	Date
street, at half past 8 o'clock, tomorrow morning.	
In Talbot county, Md., Mr. Francis Councell to Miss Sophia Turbutt.	12/09/1822
Yesterday morning, 8th inst., between 4 and 5 o'clock, John B. Elliott. His friends are requested to attend his funeral, from his late residence, Straight lane, O. T., at half past 2 o'clock, this afternoon.	12/09/1822
On Saturday evening, after a short, but painful illness, which he bore with Christian fortitude, Maj. White Young, late of the United States Army. Though a stranger from the urbanity of his manners, he was much respected by all who knew him. His friends in Mount Holly or Charleston, S. C., will hear of his papers by addressing a line to J. Mareschal, 71 Pratt street, Baltimore.	12/09/1822
In Talbot county, Md., Mrs. Hester Rigby.	12/09/1822
In Centreville, Md., Mrs. Alley Boardley Harper, in the 30th year of her age, wife of Dr. Harper.	12/09/1822
At his residence, near Woodsboro', Md., Mr. Charles Copeland.	12/09/1822
In Fredericktown, Mrs. Margaret Weigle, in the 59th year of her age.	12/09/1822
On Friday evening last, by the Rev. Mr. Young, Mr. Benjamin Lynch, to Miss Cassandra Rollins, all of this city.	12/10/1822
On Wednesday evening last, by the Rev. Mr. Bartow, Mr. George Hamilton, to Miss Mary Boyd, all of this city.	12/10/1822
On Sunday evening last, by the Rev. Mr. Bartow, Mr. James Carnes, of Philadelphia, to Miss Cashman Jane Dupree.	12/10/1822
Yesterday morning, 9th Dec., at 8 o'clock, Mrs. Margaret Ann Scrivener, aged 19 years, wife of Rich'd D. Scrivener, and daughter of the late Reuben A. League, of this city.	12/10/1822
Yesterday, George Hogarthe, Esq.	12/10/1822
At Bremen, on the 17th Sept., H. D. Wichelhausen, Esq., formerly of this city, to Miss Ann Henrietta, daughter of Dr. and Prof. Ahasverus, of Bremen.	12/12/1822
On Monday, the 9th instant, of a pulmonary disease, Mrs. Elizabeth, consort of Thomas Bruscup – she has left an affectionate husband and six small children to bemoan their irreparable loss; but they do not	12/12/1822

Marriage and Death Notices	Date
sorrow as those who have no hope; she gave them satisfactory assurance that she was going to Christ, which is far better!	
By the Rev. Dr. Glendy, on the evening of Tuesday last, Mr. Robert Ferguson, to Miss Mary Caughy, all of this city.	12/13/1822
At Hagerstown, Md., Mr. Valentine Wachtel to Miss Margaret Bovey. Mr. Isaac Hildebrandt to Miss Elizabeth Wolfersberger.	12/13/1822
At his late residence, in Lexington street, on the morning of the 5th instant, Mr. William Winchester, formerly of Brooklin, in Massachusetts, in the 36th year of his age. In the character of Mr. Winchester, those traits which form the truly worthy man were closely associated. In those pursuits which were renedered necessary for the provision of his family, he was unwearied; so much so, that while living his means were ample, and by his death his family were not deprived of a comfortable competency. He was mild in his manners, and truly affectionate in his family. During a severe illness of a pulmonary description, which confined him to his bed near two months, he was cheerful and perfectly resigned to the will of Providence as to the final recovery of his health; and when death became certain, he left no doubts in the minds of his friends respecing the brightness of his prospects in passing from this world to that from which no traveler returns.	12/13/1822
At New York, on Thursday last, of consumption, Jacob Dyckman, M. D., late Health Commissioner of that city.	12/13/1822
On Thursday morning last, about 4 o'clock, after a long and painful illness, which he bore with Christian fortitude and resignation, Capt. John Kennedy, long a respectable inhabitant of this city.	12/14/1822
On Thursday morning, 12th inst., William Cooke, Jr., in the 17th year of his age, eldest son of Mr. Wm. Cooke.	12/14/1822
On the 15th December, by the Rev. Mr. Hinkle, Mr. William H. Watts, to Miss Jemima Cannon, all of this city.	12/16/1822
On Thursday evening last, by the Rev. Mr. Onell, Mr. Benjamin McCeney, late of the firm of Hutchins & McCeney, of this city, to Caroline, daughter of Benjamin Owens, Esq., of West River, Md.	12/16/1822
On Thursday, the 12th inst., at his residence, Mr. John Cretzer, after a short and severe illness, which he bore with Christian fortitude leaving a wife and four small children and numerous friends to lament his loss,	12/16/1822

Marriage and Death Notices	Date
aged forty-one.	
On Tuesday evening, the 10th inst., by the Rev. Wm. Finney, Mr. Henry S. Styles, to Miss Ann, daughter of Mr. John Megredy, all of Cecil county.	12/17/1822
On the 12th inst., by the Rev. Mr. McCormick, Mr. Joseph Soper, to Miss Priscilla Pope, both of Prince George's County, Maryland.	12/17/1822
On Thursday evening last, by the Rev. Mr. Styer, Mr. Lemuel Beck, to Miss Susanna Hall, both of Prince George's County, Md.	12/17/1822
At Philadelphia, on Saturday last, Mr. John Sperry.	12/17/1822
On Saturday, the 15th inst., at his residence, in Baltimore county, Mr. Henry E. Bayly, in the 44th year of his age.	12/17/1822
On Tuesday evening last, by the Rev. J. P. K. Henshaw, Mr. William H. Beatty, merchant, to Miss Mary M. Stocket, both of this city.	12/18/1822
On Sunday evening last, by the Rev. Daniel Hitt, the Rev. Andrew Hemphill, of Virginia, to Mrs. Ruth A. Green, of this city.	12/18/1822
At New Orleans, 14th ult., Mr. Samuel H. Woods, of New Jersey, much regretted. He arrived here a few weeks previous, from New York, and resided about a mile from, but occasionally visited the city. Nov. 8 to 14, Mr. Jeremiah Miller, formerly of Stillwater, N. Y.; Thos. Jugall, of New York; Peter Willard and John Roufase, of Massachusetts; Robert Blasden, of Boston; John Jack and Neil Green, of Philadelphia.	12/18/1822
This morning, 19th instant, Mr. William Barker, of the firm Wm. Barker & Son, Iron Founderers, after a short, but painful illness, which he bore with Christian fortitude. He has left a large family behind him to deplore his loss. His friends are requested to attend his funeral, tomorrow afternoon, at three o'clock, from his late residence, in Mulberry street.	12/19/1822
In Hillsborough, Md., James G. Seth, Esq.	12/19/1822
In Easton, Md., Mrs. Maria Clayland.	12/19/1822
In Talbot county, Md., Mr. Wm. Wainer.	12/19/1822
Last evening, by the Rev. Edmund J. Reis, Mr. James Heden, to Miss Catherine S. Headinger, both of this city.	12/20/1822

Marriage and Death Notices	Date
At Hagerstown, Mr. John Newcomer to Miss Catherine Newcomer. Mr. John Stockslager to Miss Regina Slenker.	12/20/1822
At Hancock, Md., Mr. Jacob Brossius, in the 78th year of his age.	12/20/1822
Near Boonsborough, Mr. Bartholomew Booth, son of J. Booth, Esq.	12/20/1822
At Philadelphia, Jeremiah Warder, in the 79th year of his age.	12/20/1822
On Thursday evening last, by the Rev. Mr. Bartow, Mr. Thomas W. Belt, to Miss Louisa Ann Heever, all of this city.	12/21/1822
By the Rev. Dr. Glendy, on Monday last, Mr. John Short, to Miss Maria Mills, all of this city.	12/21/1822
By the Rev. Dr. Glendy, on the evening of Thursday last, Mr. Hugh Bolton, to Miss Maria Louisa Bankson, all of this city.	12/21/1822
On Tuesday, the 3rd inst., by the Rev. Thomas Smith, James Blackiston, Esq., to Miss Mary Ann Hatcheson, both of Kent county, Md.	12/21/1822
At St. Jago de Cuba, on the 26th November last, of the yellow fever, Mr. William Morgan, of this city, in the 23rd year of his age. The deceased had gone to that place for the purpose of entering into business, but he has been thus prematurely cut off in the vigor of life and usefulness.	12/23/1822
This morning, by the Rev. Mr. Healey, Mr. Samuel Cockey, to Miss Sarah Ford, all of Baltimore County.	12/24/1822
On Thursday evening last, by the Rev. Mr. Soule, Mr. Arthur L. Johnson, to Miss Margaret, youngest daughter of Job Smith, Sr., Esq., all of this city.	12/24/1822
In Frederick county, Md., Mr. Micah Keepers, to Miss Susan Stevens. Mr. Samuel Kessler to Miss Mary Ann Stonebraker.	12/24/1822
On the 23rd inst., in the 37th year of his age, Capt. Steven Pindell, after a short and painful illness of 48 hours.	12/24/1822
In St. Mary's county, Md., on the 13th Nov. last, Augustus H. M. Conkling, aged 33, late lieutenant commandant U. States Navy. He distinguished himself during the late war, particularly when having the command of the Tigress in the Battle on Lake Erie.	12/24/1822
Last evening, by the Rev. Mr. Hinkley, Mr. Edward Coleman, to Miss	12/26/1822

Marriage and Death Notices	Date
Sally Hughes, all of this city.	
Last evening, by the Rev. Mr. Healey, Mr. Henry Holt, to Miss Ann Richardson, all of Baltimore county.	12/26/1822
Suddenly, this morning, Mr. Hamilton McDowell, aged 53 years. His friends and acquaintance are invited to attend his funeral, tomorrow morning, at 10 o'clock, from his late dwelling, in Liberty street, Old Town.	12/27/1822
On Thursday morning, 19th inst., in the 9th year of his age, at Montalcino, the residence of Mr. Edward Goodwin, Frederick Price, second son of the late Frederick Price, Esq.	12/28/1822
On Tuesday evening last, by the Rev. Joshua Soule, Mr. Thomas G. Hill, to Miss Martha Ann Bryant, all of this city,	12/28/1822
By the Rev. Dr. Glendy, on Thursday last, Mr. William Adrean, to Miss Susan Forsyth, all of this city.	12/28/1822
On Wednesday evening last, by the Rev. George B. Schaffer, Mr. John H. W. Hawkins, to Miss Rachel Thompson, all of this city.	12/28/1822
On Wednesday evening, the 25th inst., by the Most Rev. Archbishop Mareschal, Henry N. Gilles, Esq., to Miss Clara Ann Faulac, all of this city.	12/28/1822
On Thursday last, by the Rev. Dr. Jennings, Mr. William J. Smith, to Miss Lavinia S. Lenox, both of this city.	12/28/1822
On Thursday evening last, Dec. 26th, by the Rev. Mr. Soule, Mr. Robert McKage, of Alexandria, D. C., to Miss Elizabeth Lewis, of Baltimore.	12/28/1822
On Thursday evening last, by the Rev. Mr. Healey, Mr. James Newbury, to Miss Clarissa Blizzard, all of this city.	12/28/1822
At Freedom, on Thursday, 19th inst., by the Rev. Mr. Selby, Mr. Hardress Young to Miss Ruth Davis, both of Baltimore county.	12/28/1822
At Salt Creek, Spanish Maine, on the 11th June last, in the 19th year of his age, Mr. Colin Mackenzie, youngest son of Mr. George Mackenzie, of this city.	12/28/1822
This morning, at 9 o'clock, after nineteen hours illness, in the 28th year of his age, Mr. David Robinson, U. S. Public Store keeper, universally regretted. His urbanity and attention endeared him to a large circle of	12/28/1822

Marriage and Death Notices	Date
friends and acquaintance, who will long cherish his memory, in proud remembrance of scenes past and gone; but to his aged and surviving parents and connections it will be a consolation to reflect that he died as he lived, a truly honest man. His friends and acquaintance are requested to attend his remains from his father's dwelling in George street, O. T., on Sunday, at 4 o'clock, P. M. W.	
On Monday last, Mrs. Jones, at an advanced age. Her death was occasioned by her clothes catching fire while busied about the hearth, and so complete was the work of Death, that ten minutes had not elapsed from the time that her family left her employed in her usual avocations, until they returned and found her a corpse. She was a native of North Wales, and has left a numerous family, among whom an aged husband and several grand-children who mourn at her loss as they respected her living.	12/28/1822
By the Rev. Mr. Reynolds, on Tuesday evening last, 17th inst., Mr. Aquilla Turner, of Bryantown, to Miss Catherina Ann, only daughter of Mr. Joseph Baker, all of Charles county, Md.	01/01/1823
On Thursday evening last, by the Rev. Mr. Griffiths, the Rev. John Davis, to Miss Phoebe Webster, daughter of Richard Webster, of Harford county.	01/01/1823
On Sunday evening last, by the Rev. Mr. Dashiell, Mr. Julius De St. Ceran, to Miss Anna Livingston, of this city.	01/01/1823
On Sunday evening last, by the Rev. Mr. J. Barber, Mr. Edwin S. Tarr, to Miss Eugenia Pendleton, of Hagerstown.	01/02/1823
On Wednesday evening last, by the Rev. Dr. Roberts, Mr. Joseph Yager, to Miss Letitia Hilton, all of this city.	01/03/1823
On Tuesday evening, 21st inst., by the Rev. Mr. Rouin, Mr. Levi Merryman, to Mary, eldest daughter of Charles Jessop, Esq., both of Baltimore County.	01/03/1823
At Annapolis, Mr. Peregrine Ringgold, to Miss Mary Clarke Coe.	01/03/1823
At his residence, in St. Mary's County, John F. Ford, Esq., the youngest son of the late Joseph Ford, Esq.	01/03/1823
In Anne Arundel county, Capt. Benjamin Franklin, much regretted.	01/03/1823
On the 26th ult., aged 26 years, Mrs. Louisa Warfield, of Anne Arundel	01/03/1823

Marriage and Death Notices	Date
county.	
On Sunday evening last, by the Rev. Mr. Bartow, Mr. Bennet Cooper, to Miss Ann Saybles, all of this city.	01/04/1823
On Monday evening last, by the Rev. Mr. Hinkle, Capt. Abraham Curtis, to Miss Mary C. Atkinson, all of this city.	01/04/1823
On the evening of Tuesday last, by the Rev. Mr. Hinkle, Mr. Nathaniel Sewell, to Miss Ann Eliza Atkinson, all of this city.	01/04/1823
On Friday evening, by the Rev. Mr. Healey, Mr. John Foster, of Mathews County, Va., to Ann Seward, of Dorchester County, Maryland.	01/04/1823
On the 26th ult., by the Rev. Mr. Guest, Mr. Aquila Wilmot, to Miss Sarah Hamilton, both of Baltimore County.	01/04/1823
On the evening of the 31st ult., by the Rev. Mr. Guest, Mr. Solomon Stocksdale, to Miss Dolly B. Cockey, both of Baltimore County.	01/04/1823
On the evening of the 3rd inst., by the Rev. Mr. Guest, Mr. Samuel Cornelius, of Gettysburg, Pa., to Miss Dorothy Guest, of Baltimore city.	01/04/1823
On Friday morning, by the Rev. Mr. Stansbury, Mr. James Gordon, to Miss Catherine Winn, of this city.	01/06/1823
At West River, Anne Arundel county, on Thursday evening, 2nd inst., by the Rev. Mr. Horrel, Dr. John Ridout, of Hagerstown, to Miss Prudence Gough Owings, daughter of the late Samuel Owings, of Stephen, of Baltimore.	01/06/1823
In Talbot county, Mr. John W. Hopkins, to Miss Hester Hopkin. Mr. Hugh Auld, of Baltimore, to Miss Sophia Keithley, of that county.	01/06/1823
In Dorchester county, Mr. Wm. H. Applegarth, Esq. to Miss Matilda Phipps.	01/06/1823
Yesterday, the 5th inst., at 1 o'clock, Eliza H., wife of Nelson Norris, and the daughter of the late Col. Charles Carnan, of Baltimore county, in the 33rd year of her age. Her friends and acquaintance are invited to attend her funeral, from her late dwelling, corner of Lombard and Eutaw streets, tomorrow morning, the 7th inst., at 8 o'clock.	01/06/1823
On Friday evening last, in the 57th year of his age, Mr. John Norwood. He was regretted by all who knew him.	01/06/1823

Marriage and Death Notices	Date
In Talbot county, Mr. Thomas Dudley. Maj. W. Haskins, of Caroline county. In Dorchester county, Mrs. Mary Ennalls.	01/06/1823
On Monday morning, James Armstrong, Esq., in the 68th year of his age, long a respectable merchant of this place.	01/07/1823
On Thursday evening last, by the Rev. Mr. Valiant, Mr. Jesse Davis, to Miss Sarah Reed, all of this city.	01/09/1823
By the Rev. Mr. Valiant, on Saturday last, Mr. George Winsall, to Miss Jane Ball, of Baltimore county.	01/09/1823
On Sunday evening last, by the Rev. John Chalmers, Mr. Nathan Hoskinson, of Montgomery county, to Mrs. Elizabeth Hall, of Prince George's county, Md.	01/09/1823
In Talbot county, Mr. Beachman Corset. Mrs. Ann Howell, wife of the late Howell Powell. Mr. Henry Morgan.	01/09/1823
On Wednesday evening last, by the Rev. Dr. Moranville, Mr. Patrick Scott, to Miss Mary Elizabeth Calf, all of this city.	01/10/1823
By the Rev. Dr. Glendy, on Saturday evening last, Mr. Alexander J. Bouldin, to Miss Susan Hutton, all of this city.	01/11/1823
By the Rev. Dr. Glendy, on Thursday last, Mr. George King, to Miss Eliza Walker, all of this city.	01/11/1823
On Thursday evening last, by the Rev. Mr. Bartow, Capt. James Manley, to Miss Elizabeth Fish, all of this city.	01/11/1823
On Thursday evening, Michael Sanderson, in the 57th year of his age. Mr. Sanderson was a native of England, but has resided many years in this city; he was successful and respected as a merchant, distinguished for probity and punctuality – he was a kind friend and obliging neighbor – and his benevolence rendered comfortable many who would otherwise have often experienced distress.	01/11/1823
Last evening, by the Rev. Edmund J. Reis, Mr. Andrew Robinson, to Miss Elizabeth Wilson, both of this city.	01/13/1823
On Saturday evening last, after a short illness, Capt. Cornelius Wagner, in the 32nd year of his age. He was a native of Amsterdam, and late commander of the brig Dick, of this port.	01/14/1823

265

Marriage and Death Notices	Date
On Friday, 10th inst., about 11 o'clock, Mr. Edward Gott, of Baltimore county, in the 63rd year of his age.	01/14/1823
Last evening, by the Rev. Mr. Duncan, Mr. James P. Smith, to Miss Susanna Sent, all of this city.	01/15/1823
At New Market, Dorchester county, Md., on the evening of the 30th ult., by the Rev. Mr. Charles Reed, Mr. Thomas Parrott to Miss Sarah R. Sullivan, both of that place.	01/15/1823
At Easton, Md., Mr. Henry Newcomb, to Miss Eleanor, daughter of Mr. John Councell, both of that county.	01/15/1823
At Easton, Md., Mr. Henry Townsend to Miss Mahaly Delahay.	01/15/1823
On Monday, the 13th inst., after a painful and lingering illness, Miss Sarah M. Daley, in her 29th year. She was calculated by her amiable disposition and her affable manners, to obtain the esteem of all who had the happiness of an acquaintance with her; but in a close and intimate friendship alone, could the superiority of her mind and the excellency of her heart be properly appreciated, or thoroughly discovered.	01/15/1823
Yesterday morning, after a long and painful illness, which she bore with Christian fortitude and resignation, Miss Marcella Jennings, in the 21st year of her age. Her friends and acquaintances are respectfully invited to attend her funeral, this afternoon, at 3 o'clock, at her late residence, in Mulberry street.	01/16/1823
On the morning of the 29th December, Mrs. Jane Woods, in the 73rd year of her age. Mrs. Woods was a native of the state of Delaware, but for the last twelve years of her life, a resident of this city. Her life presented many variegated scenes through which she passed, occasionally plucking the rose and the thorn with the same degree of indifference, believing that all things here below is "vanity and vexation of spirit." Amidst the most trying affliction, which confined her to the house for five years, and to her bed a great portion of that time, she steadfastly depended on the Great Disposer of all events, for support, anxiously awaiting her dissolution.	01/16/1823
Last evening, by the Rev. Roger Smith, Mr. James S. Cremen, to Miss Henrietta Ann Eisler, all of this city.	01/17/1823
On Thursday evening, by the Rev. Mr. Roberts, Mr. David Baker, to Miss Sarah King, of this city.	01/17/1823

Marriage and Death Notices	Date
At West River, Anne Arundel County, Mr. John Sellman, to Miss Elizabeth Selby.	01/17/1823
At Hagerstown, Mr. David Morrison, to Miss Amelia Dillman, daughter of Mr. Dillman, both of that place.	01/17/1823
At Philadelphia, Mr. John H. Lusby, Esq., of Elkton, to Miss Mary C. Hartley, of Maryland.	01/17/1823
By the Rev. Dr. Glendy, on Wednesday last, Mr. John L. Burgen to Miss Catherine Lughman, all of this city.	01/18/1823
On Thursday evening last, by the Rev. Mr. Smith, Mr. Samuel J. Lea, to Mrs. Susanna T. Maglennin, all of this city.	01/18/1823
On Thursday evening last, by the Rev. Dr. Jennings, Mr. Joseph D. Paul, to Miss Lydia Ann Yeiser, all of this city.	01/18/1823
Last night, by the Rev. John Hargrove, Mr. William Hinkley, to Miss Mary Ann Pidgeon, all of this city.	01/20/1823
On Tuesday last, by the Rev. Francis Neale, Mr. David D. Floyd, merchant, of Baltimore, to Miss Sarah Semmes, of Rose Hill, Charles county.	01/20/1823
On Thursday evening, 19th ult., by the Rev. Mr. Pifer, Mr. Henry Watson, to Mrs. Elizabeth McGowan, all of this city.	01/20/1823
On Saturday morning, in the 48th year of his age, Andrew Ellicott, a member of the Society of Friends.	01/20/1823
On Monday evening last, Mr. Benjamin Strider, formerly of Smithfield, where he was interred, and of late, an inhabitant of Winchester. Through all the vicissitudes of life, he was beloved by all who knew him – seemed the most true friendship, with whomsoever contracted – a strict adherent to the Methodist Church – and till his last, continued to shew forth the warmest zeal for Christianity; and triumphantly, in the hour of his dissolution, firmly relied on the "Strong arm of Omnipotence." He has left a numerous circle of friends and acquaintance to lament his loss.	01/21/1823
Last evening, by the Rev. Mr. Finlay, Mr. James Reyburn, to Miss Eleanora Stewart, eldest daughter of the late Capt. James C. Stewart.	01/22/1823
Last evening, by the Rev. E. J. Reis, Mr. Joshua Walker, to Miss Mary	01/24/1823

Marriage and Death Notices	Date
C. Raborg, all of this city.	
In Washington city, on Thursday evening, the 16th inst., Lt. William I. Belt, of the United States' Navy, to Miss Ellen U. Bowie, daughter of the late John Bowie, Esq., of Prince George's county, Md.	01/24/1823
On Thursday evening, the 16th inst., at Rockville, Montgomery county, by the Rev. Thomas G. Allen, Mr. James Stuttson, of Baltimore, to Miss Amelia Musgrove, daughter of Maj. Musgrove, of Montgomery county.	01/24/1823
On the 1st of January, 1823, by the Rev. Dr. Jennings, Mr. Hudson Hayward, of New York, to Miss Elizabeth Mother, of this city.	01/25/1823
On Thursday evening last, by the Rev. Mr. Smith, Mr. P. Gaffney, to Miss Eliza Byrne, second daughter of Mr. Bernard Byrne, all of this city.	01/25/1823
On Thursday evening last, by the Rev. Mr. Baer, Mr. Josiah Bosworth, to Miss Mary Truscott, all of Washington city.	01/28/1823
Yesterday morning, after a short illness, Mrs. Dorothy Pfeiffer, wife of the Rev. Henry H. Pfeiffer. Her friends and acquaintances are requested to attend her funeral, this afternoon, at 3 o'clock, from the corner of Lee and Sharp sts.	01/28/1823
On Thursday evening last, at his residence on Long Green, Baltimore county, Francis Haughey, Esq., in the 50th year of his age, formerly of New Castle county, Delaware. Also, on Friday morning last, at the same place, Mrs. Sarah Thompson, relict of Mr. Richard Thompson, formerly of Cecil County, Md., in the 73rd year of her age.	01/28/1823
Last evening, by the Rev. Mr. Hinkle, Mr. Jacob Skilman, to Miss Elizabeth Clackner, all of this city.	01/31/1823
At Portland, Maine, Mr. Thomas B. Parsons, of Baltimore, to Miss Elizabeth Street.	01/31/1823
In the city of Lancaster, on Wednesday, by the Rev. Mr. Muhlenburg, Leonard Kimball, Esq., of this city, to Sarah Yeates, daughter of the Hon. Charles Smith, L. L. D.	01/31/1823
At Washington city, suddenly, on Tuesday evening last, while attending Divine Service in Dr. Laurie's Church, Col. Thomas Bowie, of Bladensburg.	01/31/1823

Marriage and Death Notices	Date
At Philadelphia, on Tuesday morning last, Mr. Frederick Rheinboth, Mr. James McCully, Mr. Thomas Huston.	01/31/1823
On the 30th inst., by the Rev. William J. Beschter, Mr. Mathias Steigers, to Miss Mary Ann Gross, all of this city.	02/01/1823
In Charles county, Md., on the 28th inst., by the Rev. Mr. Mann, Dr. Robert Crain, Jr., to Miss Mary Wood, daughter of the late Dr. Gerard Wood, all of said county.	02/01/1823
Recently, at Havana, Richard W. Ganettson, Esq., of Baltimore, aged about 34 years. He was amiable and intelligent, loved and respected by all who knew him.	02/01/1823
Died, in this city, on Thursday last, Gen. Humbert, formerly a brigadier in the army of the French Republic, and a resident of this town during the last nine years. This man has held a place in the history of more than one century. About the beginning of the French revolution, he entered the army as a private soldier. Favored with a good person and distinguished by much personal bravery, he obtained the rank of brigadier general, after 5 or 6 years service. In Aug., 1798, he landed on the south of Ireland, at the head of 1,000 men, and after some rapid movements, he attacked the English Gen. Lake, and put him and his army to an ignominious flight, although he had only 800 French troops of the line and 1,000 Irish peasants, to oppose 3 or 4,000 British regulars. Some time after, he commanded a division of Massena's army when Suwarooff was repulsed in Switzerland. Napoleon Bonaparte, refusing to employ him, he came to the United States, and was authorized to raise a volunteer legion in this city during the invasion. He was always to be found at every sortie from Gen. Jackson's lines, and where danger most threatened. The deceased was certainly a man of good natural parts, although illiterate. Latterly, years and misfortunes have weighed both on his mind and body. Under such circumstances, death should be welcome to the hero who had so often looked him in the face on the field of battle and of victory. *Louisiana Gazette of Jan. 4.*	02/01/1823
At Columbus, Ohio, the 15th ult., in the 24th year of his age, Samuel Mincher, a native of Baltimore leaving an aged mother and a large circle of relations and friends to deplore his untimely end. His natural disposition, probity, morality, and genuine worth were excelled by few. His death was occasioned by the fall of a piece of timber, while assisting to upset a boat.	02/03/1823
On the 30th ult., Mrs. Mary Wells, in the 74th year of her age, after a	02/03/1823

Marriage and Death Notices	Date
lingering illness, which she bore with Christian fortitude.	
In this city, on Wednesday, the 15th inst., of pulmonary consumption, Capt. James H. Ballard, of the U. S. 4th Regt. of Artillery. Capt. Ballard was a native of Massachusetts. During the late war with Great Britain, he served with distinguished reputation in the rifle corps on the northern frontier, and was subsequently an Aid de Camp to Gen. Miller. His remains were interred with military and masonic honors on the Glacis of Fort St. Mark. *East Florida Herald.*	02/03/1823
At Fredericktown, Frederick S. Nelson, aged 20, son of the late Gen. Roger Nelson.	02/04/1823
Yesterday, at 2 o'clock, Mr. Francis Waddle. His friends and acquaintances are requested to attend his funeral, from his late residence, near Pratt street bridge, at 3 o'clock, this evening.	02/05/1823
On Monday, the 27th January, 1823, Mr. Samuel Shaw, late of the firm McHenry & Shaw, aged 29 years, and for many years a respectable merchant of this city – he was scrupulously honest and correct in all his transactions.	02/05/1823
On Tuesday evening last, by the Rev. Mr. Bartow, Mr. Patrick Dillon, to Miss Elizabeth Reese, all of this city.	02/06/1823
At Long Green, Baltimore county, 2nd inst., by the Rev. Mr. Poteet, Mr. Samuel Watkins to Miss Emeline, eldest daughter of Mr. John Davis.	02/06/1823
On Tuesday evening last, by the Rev. E. J. Reis, Mr. Columbus E. Cook, to Miss Catherine Grafflin.	02/07/1823
On Thursday evening last, by the Rev. Dr. Glendy, Mr. William H. Freeman, to Mary Pue, daughter of Mr. Edward H. Dorsey.	02/08/1823
On Thursday evening last, by the Rev. John M. Duncan, Mr. Asahel Weston, to Miss Ann, daughter of the late Jonathan Alder, Esq.	02/08/1823
On Thursday evening last, in Anne Arundel county, by the Rev. George B. Schaeffer, Mr. R. Stewart, to Miss Ann, second daughter of Henry Evans, Esq., both of said county.	02/08/1823
At Washington, Mr. Saml. Hills, to Mrs. Eudocia Gird, daughter of the late Maj. Richard Dorsey, of this city, both of Alexandria.	02/08/1823
At Belle Air, Md., Mr. Samuel Smith to Miss Laura Graham.	02/08/1823

Marriage and Death Notices	Date
At Philadelphia, Miss Elizabeth M'Farland; Mrs. Ann Cavenaugh. At New York, Mrs. Mary Ann Stevens. At Norfolk, Mrs. Elizabeth Dwyer. In Queen Annes' Co., Mrs. Ann Keirn.	02/08/1823
On Thursday evening last, by the Rev. Dr. Roberts, Mr. William H. Miller, to Miss Mary Ann S. Ward, eldest daughter of William Ward, of Anne Arundel county.	02/10/1823
Last Thursday evening, at Col. Jameson's, by the Rev. Mr. Garrettson, Mr. Elias Jordan, of Baltimore County, to Miss Sophia Medairy, of this city.	02/10/1823
Suddenly, on Friday morning, the 7th inst., at his residence, in Charles street, Hammond Dorsey, Esq., of this city, aged 29 years. His remains were interred on Saturday morning in the family burial ground, at Belmont, with every suitable mark of respect. Mr. Dorsey has left a numerous circle of friends, whose affections had been riveted by the sensibility, disinterestedness, and frankness uniformly displayed in his life.	02/10/1823
Suddenly, at his residence, in George street, on Wednesday last, Mr. Samuel Frey, aged 57. In this dispensation of providence, his family has suffered an irreparable loss, and society is deprived of an useful and worthy citizen. He died as he lived, respected by all who knew him.	02/10/1823
At Charleston, on Thursday last, on board the brig Rachel & Sally, Capt. Noes, from Havana, Master Obed Swain, aged 14 years, a native of Baltimore.	02/10/1823
Mrs. Elizabeth Pryse, on the 8th instant, aged 44 years. She was a native of Frederick county, and an industrious, deserving, and amiable woman. She had no enemies while living and many friends remain to regret her departure.	02/11/1823
On the 9th inst., Mrs. Nancey McCubbey, a native of Ireland, but for some years past, a respectable inhabitant of this city. She has a family to mourn their irreparable loss; left few enemies, but many friends – and died with the assurance of partaking of the blessings of a better world, through the atoning blood of her Redeemer.	02/11/1823
At Chestertown, on the 23rd January, Mrs. Eve Hall, consort of Cuthbert Hall, Esq., in the 57th year of her age. The deceased had for many years been afflicted with a pulmonary disease, which she bore with the fortitude of a Christian. She had long lived a pious life, and was a respectable member of the Methodist Episcopal Church, when she was	02/11/1823

271

Marriage and Death Notices	Date
called from her temporary abode, to an eternal residence in the Kingdom of Heaven. It is a pleasing consolation to her family and friends, and although she is dead to the world, she is alive in Christ. A few minutes before her death, she observed "The Lord was about taking her to himself," and with this aspiration, fell asleep in the arms of her Savior	
Died, this morning, in the 58th year of her age, Mrs. Sarah Lemmon, relict of the late Joshua Lemmon. Her friends and acquaintances are requested to attend her funeral, without further invitation, from her late dwelling, in Goodman street, tomorrow morning, the 12th inst., at nine o'clock.	02/11/1823
On Thursday evening last, by the Rev. Dr. Wyatt, Mr. Thomas Curtin, to Miss Margaret Green, both of this city.	02/12/1823
Last evening, by the Rev. Mr. Shane, Mr. Joseph Coram, to Miss Hester Reed, all of this city.	02/13/1823
At Friends Meeting House, Lombard street, on the 12th inst., John Smith, merchant, to Eliza Proctor, both of this city.	02/13/1823
In Trieste, in Oct. last, Mr. John Stewart, of Scotland, to Mrs. Ellen I. Wright, of Baltimore, daughter of Judge Benjamin Nicholson.	02/13/1823
On Tuesday evening, 28th ult., near Rock Hall, Kent County, Maryland, Mr. Frederick G. Ringgold, to Miss Ann E. Bradshaw.	02/13/1823
On Tuesday evening, 28th ult., at Sportsman's Hall, near Queen's town, Maryland, Mr. Edmund Wright Pratt, to Miss Catherine Augusta, eldest daughter of William Ringgold, Esq.	02/13/1823
On Monday evening last, Mr. James Trimble, in the 41st year of his age, son of William Trimble, Sr., late of Baltimore.	02/13/1823
Yesterday, in the 56th year of his age, Mr. Adam Denmead, a native of Ireland, and long a respectable citizen of Baltimore. He was an affectionate husband and kind father. In his death, society has to lament, the loss of a useful and honest citizen, humanity, an amiable and charitable man, and religion a sincere and zealous friend. The friends of the deceased are invited to attend his funeral, from his late dwelling, in Green street, Old Town, on Sunday afternoon, 16th inst., at 3 o'clock.	02/14/1823
By the Rev. Dr. Glendy, on the evening of Thursday last, Mr. Theodore Kimmel, to Miss Elizabeth Hicks, all of this city.	02/15/1823

Marriage and Death Notices	Date
Yesterday morning, Mary Hoffman, daughter of Hugh Birckhead, aged 3 years and 3 months.	02/15/1823
At New York, Mr. Benjamin Clapp, to Miss Mary Catherine, daughter of the late John Herman Behn, Esq., of Baltimore.	02/17/1823
On Sunday morning, 16th inst., about half past 2 o'clock, Mr. Russell Kilbourne.	02/17/1823
On Sunday evening last, by the Rev. Mr. Bartow, Mr. William Stuart, to Miss Mary Ferris, both of this city.	02/18/1823
On Thursday evening last, in the 79th year of his age, Mr. Wm. Etchberger, Sr., a native of Germany, but for many years a respectable inhabitant of this city. In his demise, we have to lament the loss of a kind neighbor, and an affectionate and indulgent parent.	02/18/1823
On Friday morning, 14th inst., Miss Mary Maxwell, a resident of this city. Her friends may humbly hope the intense sufferings she sustained through a series of years, in the full confidence in the merits of her Redeemer, have prepared her an entrance into that world of bliss, where pain and sorrow are known no more. Thy spirit disengaged from mortal clay, Sought the bright regions of eternal day; Hastened through realms of light, its Lord to meet, And now rests tranquil at its Savior's feet.	02/18/1823
On Tuesday last, after a long and painful illness, Mrs. Ruth Widney, consort of the late Alexander Widney.	02/18/1823
At New York, Mr. Edwin Jesup, of Con., to Miss Mary Ann, daughter of the late James Bryden, Esq., of Baltimore.	02/19/1823
OBITUARY. This morning, in the 42nd year of his age, paid the last debt of nature, William Hopkins of this city, a worthy member of the Society of Friends. Endeared to a large circle of acquaintance by his truly Christian virtues, and called to the regions of immortality, in the meridian of life, his death will be greatly lamented. His friends and acquaintance are respectfully invited to attend his funeral, at 3 o'clock, tomorrow afternoon, to meet at No. 80 Pratt street. ATC	02/20/1823
At Louisville, Ken., Thomas Prather, Esq., late President of the Branch Bank at that place. Near Louisville, Col. Samuel Oldham, at an advanced age. At Shippingsport, on his return from New Orleans, Mr.	02/20/1823

Marriage and Death Notices	Date
Robert M'Connell.	
This morning, at 3 o'clock, Mrs. Catherine Ann, wife of George Pouder, in the 22nd year of her age. Her friends and acquaintance are respectfully invited to attend her funeral, tomorrow, the 22nd inst., at 2 o'clock, from her late dwelling, in North Howard street.	02/21/1823
At Annapolis, aged 55, wife of Jonathan Pinkney, Esq., Cashier of the Farmers Bank of Maryland. At the south side of South River, much regretted, Col. Joseph Watkins.	02/21/1823
At Boston, Mrs. Lucy M., aged 38, wife of Dr. William Ingalls.	02/21/1823
On Thursday evening last, by the Rev. Mr. Hamilton, Mr. John Boyd, to Miss Elizabeth King, both of this city.	02/22/1823
Yesterday, after a very short illness, Mrs. Mary Woodyear, wife of Edward G. Woodyear, Esq., of Baltimore county, in the 60th year of her age, after having faithfully discharged the respective duties of wife, mother, and neighbor.	02/22/1823
At Calcutta, Mr. Samuel Ropes, son of the late Capt. George Ropes, of Salem, aged 21.	02/22/1823
At Fredericktown, Mr. John Collins to Miss Miranda Henry.	02/25/1823
On Thursday evening last, at Evandale, Lancaster Co., Pa., by the Rev. Joseph Clarkson, J. J. Hodgewerff, Esq., of this city, to Elizabeth, youngest daughter of the late Samuel Evans, Esq.	02/25/1823
At Fredericktown, Mr. John Collins to Miss Miranda Henry.	02/25/1823
In Thomastown, Mr. Darius Brewster, aged 60, to Miss Sally Fales, aged 40.	02/25/1823
Yesterday, Mr. Samuel Brazer, Jr., aged 40. Funeral from his late residence, in South street, this afternoon, at 4 o'clock, which his friends are respectfully invited to attend.	02/25/1823
At Philadelphia, Mr. John Napp, of Baltimore, to Miss Susanna, 2nd daughter of Mr. Robert Desilver.	02/27/1823
On the morning of the 25th, James Calhoun Buchanan, in the 24th year of his age, second son of James A. Buchanan, Esq., of this city.	02/27/1823

Marriage and Death Notices	Date
This morning, Mr. David Wentworth Boisseau. His friends and pupils are respectfully invited to attend his funeral, which will proceed on foot, from his late dwelling, 132 Baltimore street, precisely at 10 o'clock, tomorrow morning, 28th inst.	02/27/1823
On the 25th inst., in the 64th year of her age, Mrs. Eleanora Schaeffer, consort of Mr. Baltzer Schaeffer, of this city. Few mothers have been so ardently attached and devoted to her children than her, to whose memory we now pay the last respect. She was the mother of ten children, seven of whom she raised, who presented to her arms thirty-three grand children, thirty of whom are now living. Thus, after seeing around her a growing and affectionate family, and, in the course of Divine Providence, much affliction, she breathed out her soul in joyful anticipation, at rest, which remains for the people of God, where sorrow and sighing are known no more. "Blessed are the dead, which die in the Lord, from henceforth: yea, saith the Spirit, that they may rest from their labors; and their works do follow them." Revelations, 14th chap., 18th verse.	02/28/1823
On Saturday, the 22nd inst., Frederick county, Big Pipe creek, Md., Mr. Henry Groff, in the 64th year of his age. He was a patriot of the Revolution and for a number of years past, Printer's joiner, of this city, and respected by all who had the pleasure of his acquaintance.	02/28/1823
On Monday evening, after a short and severe illness, aged six years and six months, Elizabeth Sarah, daughter of R. L. Colt. "The Lord gave, and the Lord hath taken away, and blested be his holy name."	02/28/1823
In Baltimore county, on Friday evening last, 21st inst., Miss Harriet Gallop, in the 17th year of her age, youngest daughter of Gilbert Gallop, formerly of Harford county.	02/28/1823
At New York, Mrs. Elizabeth R. Fash. At Schenectady, N. Y., David Mumford, Esq. At Chambersburg, Pa., Peter S. Dechert, Esq.	02/28/1823
OBITUARY. Departed this life, on the 24th inst., in the 40th year of his age, Samuel Brazer, Jr., Esq., for many years assistant editor of the Baltimore Patriot. In noticing the death of Mr. Brazer, it is not the purpose of the writer to launch into fulsome panegyrics, or to call in the aid of metaphor to embellish his virtues or his talents; or to take from the silence of the tomb the foibles of human nature, but to pay a just tribute to one whose goodness of heart, and whose extensive acquirements entitle his memory at least to the sympathy of humanity, and the admiration of the friends of literature and of science. Mr. Brazer was born in Worcester, Massachusetts, and at an early age	02/28/1823

Marriage and Death Notices	Date
commenced the study of the law, for which arduous profession he was duly qualified, and prosecuted for a short period, with the most flattering prospects of wealth and fame. But the political situation of the country at that period called forth the energies of his mind, and the energetic support he yielded the Republican cause, against the misdirected zeal of factionists, and the ebulitions of party as manifested in the columns of the Worcester Ægis, of which he became the editor, are testimonials to his head and heart. From that period to the time of his decease he has been more or less connected with some political or literary publication, which he conducted with ability and industry; and well was he entitled to the appelation of "*a veteran in the cause of Republicanism and humanity.*" In the political writings of Mr. Brazer, there is not only an intimate knowledge of the relations of our country and the subjects discussed, but an avoidance of personality manifesting an enmity of erroneous "principles, not men." And when called on to raise his voice in the cause of suffering virtue, there was a pathos and feeling that aroused every latent energy of the soul. As a poet he had some claims to celebrity; as a dramatic critic, few equals; and in him the arts have lost an enthusiastic admirer and an able advocate; harmless and inoffensive in his manners; with principles untrammeled by dictation or a bending of the knee to assumptive power, he passed through this weary pilgrimage without enemies, but endeared to mankind. O. B.	
At Albany, N. Y., George Webster, Esq., one of the Editors of the Albany Daily Advertiser, aged 61 years. Mr. W. was one of the founders of that paper, about forty years ago.	02/28/1823
On Thursday last, by the Rev. Mr. Dodson, Mr. John L. Ringgold, to Miss Mary Rollinson, both of Harrisburg, Kent county.	03/01/1823
On Friday evening last, by the Rev. Mr. Bartow, Mr. J. B. M. Letournau, to Miss Lucretia, eldest daughter of Peter Galt, Esq.	03/01/1823
At Albany, N. Y., Mr. Alexander S. Bunker, to Miss Almira Bushnell, of Baltimore.	03/01/1823
At the residence of William H. Penn, Laidler's ferry, Md., Mr. Benjamin T. Williamson, of Richmond, to Miss Ann B. Meaux, of King William county, Va.	03/01/1823
On Tuesday last, Mrs. Mary N. Beall, aged 24, consort of Richard B. Beall, and eldest daughter of the late Andrew Hanna, of this city.	03/01/1823

Marriage and Death Notices	Date
On Sunday, 23rd inst., after a short, but painful illness, Mr. Joseph Osborne, Sr., in the 56th year of his age. He has left a family & numerous circle of friends to lament his loss.	03/01/1823
On the 23rd inst., in the 76th year of his age, John Brown, a native of England, and for the last 30 years a resident of this city.	03/01/1823
At Calcutta, aboard the ship Adonis, of New York, on the 6th Sept. last, Capt. Benjamin Halsted, after an illness of ten hours; also, Cornelius Dodd, Benjamin Bloomer, and John Smith, seamen – all cholera morbus. Some others of the crew had been ill, but were on the recovery.	03/01/1823
At Woodgrove, Va., Mr. William King, a patriot of '76. At Leesburg, Va., Mrs. Jane Carr, Mr. Samuel Frank, Mr. William Woody, Sr. At Petersburg, Mrs. Stainback. At Savannah, Benjamin Burnon, Esq. At Cincinnati, John N. Robins. At Annapolis, Mrs. Isabella Plains. At New York, Mr. William Sickles, Mr. Samuel Wall, Mr. John Daily, Mr. Wm. N. Massaneau, Mr. Theodorus Van Wyck. At Boston, Mrs. Desire Leach. At Germantown, Mrs. Margaret Beck. At Boston, Mrs. Isabella Luke. At Salem, Capt. Solomon F. Gould. At Savannah, Mr. William Starr, Jr., of the firm Hall, Hoyt & Co.	03/01/1823
On board the brig of war Gen. Bolivar, in the port of Carthagena, S. A., on the 24th October last, after an illness of four days, Richard Cockey, Esq., in the 42nd year of his age, formerly a merchant of this city, and son of the Hon. Joshua Cockey, of Frederick county, Md. At Philadelphia, Mr. William Chamberlain. At and near Easton, Md., Miss Frances Ann Hopper, Mrs. Ann Harwood, Mr. James Faulkner, Mr. Jesse Kirby, Mr. Levin Meginney, Mr. Richard Edgar. At Denton, Md., Mrs. Rachel Rhodes. At Cincinnati, Ohio, Mr. John Newton Robins, aged 26, late of Hartford, Con.	03/01/1823
On Thursday evening last, by the Rev. Dr. Roberts, Mr. William Wallace, to Miss Catherine S. Cochrane, all of this city.	03/03/1823
At Bellefield, Prince George's county, Md., on Tuesday evening last, by the Rev. Mr. Gilliss, Barruch Mullikin, Esq., of Baltimore, to Miss Sophia M., daughter of Benjamin Oden, Esq., of the former place.	03/03/1823
At Easton, Md., Mr. Joseph K. Travers, to Miss Priscilla B. Smith. Capt. Thomas C. Dawson to Miss Harriet Linthicum.	03/03/1823
On Saturday, the 14th ult., Mrs. Sarah Horsey, wife of Thomas Horsey, at the residence of her father, the Hon. William H. Cooper, near Laurel, Sussex County, Delaware. This mournful bereavement is truly	03/04/1823

Marriage and Death Notices	Date
afflicting to husband and father. She had become a wife only a few months since, and was the only remaining child of her father. Distinguished as well for her accomplishments as sweetness of disposition, dearly beloved by her friends and acquaintance, she has been cut down in the very bloom of her life, deeply regretted by all who knew her.	
Near Easton, Md., Mr. George Jenkins. At Cambridge, Md., Dr. Washington M. Craig. At Hillsboro', Mr. Jacob Dyott. At Charleston, Mrs. Mary C. Gregorie.	03/04/1823
On Monday evening last, by the Rev. Mr. Bartow, Mr. Rowland Robinson, to Miss Sarah Searley, all of this city.	03/05/1823
Last evening, by the Rev. Mr. Soule, Darius Clagett, Esq., of Georgetown, D. C., to Providene D., second daughter of John Brice, Esq., of this city.	03/05/1823
On the 11th of February last, by the Rev. Mr. James Heron, Mr. Levin W. Deshardon, to Miss Elizabeth Davis, all of Salisbury, Md.	03/05/1823
On Tuesday evening, Feb. 25th, by the Rev. Mr. De La Ree, Maj. John Stitcher to Miss Elenor Colegate, of Frederick county.	03/06/1823
On Friday, the 28th ult., in the 62nd year of his age, Mr. Tristram Bowdle, a respectable citizen of Talbot county. He has left a family exquisitely sensible of their loss. On the morning of the 28th ult., George Norbury, a worthy member of the Society of Friends.	03/07/1823
At the port of Tampico, Dec. 22nd, after a short illness, Capt. John Coleman, formerly of Nantucket, late of Baltimore. At Wilmington, Del., William Robinson, a member of the Society of Friends. At New York, Mrs. Margaret Roach. At Boston, Miss Elizabeth Call Perkins, Miss Sarah Austin, Miss Antoinette, Mrs. Susan Richardson. At Nantucket, widow Ruth Garner, aged 89, leaving a posterity of 100, 10 children, 34 grand children, 40 great grand children, and 16 of the 4th generation.	03/07/1823
At Lancaster, Pa., Eliza M. J. Rogers, Mary Catherine Thompson, Adam Kurtz. At Strasburgh, Mr. Andrew Diffenbaugh.	03/07/1823
OBITUARY. Died on the 1st inst., near Queens Town, Queen Ann's county, of this state, G. W. T. Wright, second son of Governor Wright, leaving a widow and several young children to deplore a loss, which to them, it may be truly said, is irreparable; for what can avail the	03/07/1823

attentions of friends, however devoted and kind, when the wife is bereft of the guidance and faithful counsels of the *Husband*, in whom she confided every thought – when children are left without a *Father* to protect their infancy, and to instruct them in the ways of wisdom and virtue? It was in this light that death approached the deceased in this most terrible aspect, pointing to his family whom he was about to leave, exposed like the fragile vine when lightning blasts the oak on which it twined for shelter, from the "peltings of the pitiless storm." The deceased was endowed by nature with talents of the first order, and these had been cultivated by study and embellished with classical attainments under the tuition of Bishop Madison of Virginia. Thus had he been qualified to shine with splendor in the councils of his country, if a natural disposition for retirement, and an exquisite sensibility, aggravated by feeble health, had not withheld him from public pursuits. A qualiy for which the deceased may be said to have been remarkable, was a *never failing* adherence, even to minuteness, to the dictates of the most refined sense of honor and propriety, in his intercourse with the world – always exacting it himself, he treated with scrupulous respect the feelings of others; observing in this particular not the slightest difference between the rich and the poor, the humble and the exalted. His character was marked by another trait – where he *professed friendship*, he was always ready to prove it by *any sacrifice*. Common as is the world, even to abuse, with him, there was ever something inviolably sacred, even as his own honour, in the very sound of *friend* – it was a title he rarely bestowed, but when he did, it was known to convey a pledge, for the redemption of which life and fortune would be given if necessary. His last moments, with all their afflicting circumstances of bodily pain and domestic grief, were met with becoming composure and self-possession. The selection of friends to bear him to his grave, the designation of a minister to perform the funeral service, and a message to an absent friend, were among the last instructions to his afflicted relatives – the closing efforts of exhausted nature.

	Date
On Thursday evening last, by the Rev. Mr. Helfenstein, Mr. Henry Conn, Jr., of Marrietta, Lancaster county, Pennsylvania, to Miss Catherine Wilhelm, of Baltimore county.	03/08/1823
On Thursday evening last, by the Rev. Mr. Hamilton, Capt. Thomas Kennedy, to Miss Ellen F. Barker.	03/08/1823
At Hagerstown, Mr. David Rickenbaugh, to Miss Margaret Sprecker. Mr. Jacob Cassell to Miss Sophia Lambert.	03/08/1823

Marriage and Death Notices	Date
This morning, after a painful and lingering illness of 8 months, in the 22nd year of his age, Mr. Christopher Crofts, a native of the county of Cork, Ireland.	03/08/1823
On the 27th ult., at Emmittsburg, Capt. Richard Williams, for many years a respectable ship master, out of the port of Baltimore.	03/08/1823
Departed this life, on Saturday afternoon, after a long and painful disease, which she bore with Christian fortitude, Mrs. Catherine Brown, in the 34th year of her age, consort of Mr. Charles Brown. She has left an afflicted husband with seven children, and a large circle of connections, to deplore her death.	03/10/1823
Last evening, by the Rev. Dr. Roberts, Mr. Jacob Adams, to Miss Jane Marsden, all of this city.	03/11/1823
On Saturday, 22nd February, by the Rev. John Valiant, Mr. Elias Winks, to Miss Catherine Newcarric, both of this city.	03/11/1823
At Camden, state of Delaware, on Thursday evening last, by the Rev. Mr. Torbert, the Rev. Wm. Prettyman, of Baltimore, to Miss Eliza Barrett, of the former place.	03/11/1823
On Tuesday evening last, the 4th inst., by the Rev. Mr. McIlhainey, Mr. Richard McGaw, of Baltimore county, to Sarah Ann, eldest daughter of John Slade, of Harford county.	03/11/1823
Yesterday morning, after a short, but painful illness, Mr. John T. Bibb, in the 27th year of his age, a native of Virginia. The friends and acquaintance of Mr. John T. Bibb are requested to attend his funeral, from the residence of Mr. Austin Woolfolk, this evening at 3 o'clock.	03/11/1823
On Tuesday, the 4th instant, by the Rev. Mr. Healey, Mr. Richard Bean, to Miss Elizabeth Richardson, all of this city.	03/12/1823
"Blessed are the dead who die in the Lord; even so saith the spirit, for they rest from their labors, and their works do follow them." Departed this transitory life, on Sunday evening last, Mrs. Abigail Sullivan, in the 74th year of her age. To pronounce a panegyric on her would be to say she lived and died a Christian. Never was there a more affectionate and tender friend, or one who possessed more amiable qualities, or who was more respected and beloved by all that knew her, than was the deceased; she was a kind and benevolent neighbor and a sincere friend. But one short day before her death, the hope of her friends were buoyed up by the expectation of her being restored to	03/12/1823

Marriage and Death Notices	Date
health, from an illness which, for some ttime, she had been laboring under! But alas! such is the uncertainty of life, the fondest expectations were suddenly blasted, and on the following day they beheld her a lifeless corpse! Long will her memory be cherished with esteem by her numerous acquaintance, and from the minds of her bereaved family, her irreparable loss cannot be erased – yet will they not greive as those without hope, for blessed are the dead that die in the Lord, surely they rest in the arms of Jesus, the Redeemer of all.	
On Tuesday evening, by the Rev. Mr. Shinn, Rev. Thomas McCormic to Miss Eliza Martin, niece of Luther Martin, Esq.	03/14/1823
On Saturday last, after a long and protracted illness, Mrs. Frances Latorunau, in the 56th year of her age.	03/14/1823
On Thursday evening last, by the Rev. Mr. Bartow, Mr. Wm. M'Causland, to Mrs. Mary Frow, all of this city.	03/15/1823
On Monday, the 10th inst., at Port Deposit, Cecil county, after a long and painful illness, Mrs. Elizabeth Creswell, consort of the late Col. John Creswell, in the 63rd year of her age; may her departed spirit experience a joyful reception into the mansions of eternal bliss.	03/15/1823
At New Orleans, 24th ult., Mr. William Eichberger, aged 24, formerly of Baltimore.	03/15/1823
Yesterday morning, at 1 o'clock, in the 73rd year of his age, Mr. Henry Messonier, a native of Switzerland, and for upwards of forty years past a respectable merchant, of this place.	03/15/1823
On Thursday evening, the 6th inst., by the Rev. Mr. Valiant, Mr. Philemon Merryman to Miss Maria Wilson.	03/17/1823
By the Rev. Mr. Valiant, on the evening of the 13th inst., Mr. John Porter to Miss Mary Arthur, all of this city.	03/17/1823
Off Cape Horn, 19th September, Thomas Rogers, aged 19, of Baltimore. He fell from the mizen top of the ship Corinthian, on her passage to Lima. He was formerly a carrier of the Baltimore Patriot.	03/18/1823
At Washington, after a short illness, Mr. William Felch, for many years a Clerk in the First Auditor's and Comptroller's Office; a man highly esteemed, and whose death is much regretted by all who knew him.	03/19/1823
Last evening, Mr. Loudon L. Townsend, of the firm of Edward J. Coale & Co., aged 22 years. His friends are invited to attend his funeral,	03/19/1823

Marriage and Death Notices	Date
tomorrow morning, at 10 o'clock.	
On the 6th inst., in the 25th year of her age, of a lingering pulmonary complaint, Hannah Wilson, consort of Thomas Wilson, of this city.	03/20/1823
At Charleston, S. C., on the 24th of February last, Capt. William J. Stafford, late of Baltimore.	03/20/1823
At Washington, on Tuesday, at 1 o'clock, in the 66th year of his age, departed this life, the Hon. Brockholst Livingston, one of the Associate Justices of the Supreme Court of the United States. This distinguished citizen has long occupied a conspicuous place in the public eye, and his talents and worth are too well known to require an obituary notice. On the bench of the state of New York, and since, on that of the supreme court of the U. States, the public have long acknowledged in him the learned and independent Judge, the finished gentleman, and truly benelovent man. It is some consolation to his family and friends that he has sunk into the grave at a good old age, crowned with honors, and wept by all who knew him. To his afflicted family, his loss is irreparable.	03/20/1823
On Wednesday evening, the 19th inst., by the Rev. Mr. Hinkle, Mr. Joshua Maxwell, to Miss Mary Ann, eldest daughter of Wm. Davy, all of this city.	03/21/1823
On Kent Island, Mr. James Dunn, of Annapolis, to Miss Elizabeth Phenix.	03/21/1823
In Jefferson county, Va., Dr. Scollay, to Miss Harriet Lowndes, formerly of Annapolis.	03/21/1823
On the morning of Wednesday last, Mr. John Croxall, in the 62nd year of his age. Mr. Croxall was an old and respectable resident of this city, and enjoyed the esteem of all who knew him. To his family, he was particularly endeared by all those ties which bind the husband to the wife, the father to his children; for he was the best of husbands, the tenderest of parents; his loss will be long deplored.	03/21/1823
On the 19th inst., of a lingering complaint, in her 27th year, Maria Hertzog, wife of J. F. Hertzog. Her friends and acquaintance are invited to attend her funeral, this afternoon, at three o'clock, from her late dwelling, South Charles street.	03/21/1823
At Annapolis, at an advanced age, Mrs. Rachel Nicholls, and Rachel	03/21/1823

Marriage and Death Notices	Date
Ann, aged six years, daughter of Washington G. Tuck, Esq.	
At Philadelphia, on Sunday evening last, after a short, but severe illness, Mr. William Howard, of Baltimore, in the 48th year of his age, where he has left many friends to mourn his loss.	03/21/1823
At Washington, Indiana, James Nash, Esq., a native of Massachusetts, and formerly Attorney at Law, in New York. At Louisville, Ken., on the 22nd ult., the Rev. Daniel Smith, aged 33, a native of Vermont. At Port Royal, Martinique, Feb. 8, Capt. M'Cormick, of schr. Lucy, of New York.	03/21/1823
In England, Adm., Kempe, aged 80. He assisted at the siege of Quebec, and accompanied Cooke and Furneaux round the world.	03/21/1823
Last night, Henry Craig, Esq., in the 56th year of his age. His friends and acquaintance are requested to attend his funeral, tomorrow, Sunday morning, at 9 o'clock, from his late dwelling, in Queen street.	03/22/1823
Lost overboard, from the ship Ophelia, on the 22nd Dec., on her passage from Europe to Boston, Henry Orne, aged 19, son of Capt. Josiah Orne, of Salem.	03/22/1823
Departed this life, on the 18th inst., at his seat on Elk Ridge, in Anne Arundel county, after a long and severe illness, Thomas Worthington, Esq., of Nicholas, in the 69th year of his age; one of the most distinguished and respectable citizens of his native county, Anne Arundel; he has left a numerous circle of relatives and friends to lament the loss they have sustained by the death of this truly amiable man.	03/22/1823
Departed this life on Tuesday, the 18th inst., Mr. Loudon L. Townsend, of the firm of Edward J. Coale & Co., aged 22 years. In the death of this truly amiable young man, society has to mourn an invaluable member, whose virtues and goodness endeared him to all who had the happiness of his acquaintance. But a few days since, he was in the full vigour of youth, with prospects as bright as the most sanguine wish of a parent could have desired, loved with an enthusiastic ardor by every friend, possessing the most unlimited confidence and friendship of every acquaintance. But all the strength of youth – all the prosperity and success attending unwearied industry and distinguished talents – all the attachments of friends – and all the confidence of acquaintance, could not stay the messenger of death. Feeling somewhat indisposed, he retired to his couch – none entertained an idea, that from that couch he was to rise no more! The disease progressed rapidly – he bore it with resignation and fortitude, entertaining a belief, differently too from the	03/22/1823

283

Marriage and Death Notices	Date
opinion of his friends, that it would (as he emphatically expressed himself to a young friend) "terminate his earthly career. A strong constitution enabled him to bear much – but it could not answer as a bulwark against the progress of the disease – his time grew short – the lamp of life glimmered faintly – and in the agonies of death a smile of pleasure played about his features, which spoke what utterance could not – "O grave, where is thy victory? O death, where is thy sting?" and in a few moments he sunk into the arms of death as if he was in a sweet and refreshing slumber – To an absent father there is this consolation – that in his absence there was one who watched him with a father's care – and one whose solicitude and attention appeared as if it was prompted by an affection that could only emanate from a father's heart.	
Henry Messonnier, who died here the 14th inst., was born in Neufchatel, one of the Swiss Cantons, in the year 1750. Having received an education to fit him for the counting house, he went to Nantz, and was there employed in a respectable commercial establishment, when the American Revolution commenced. From this port were fitted out some of the first vessels to bring supplies, which were so essential to the success of that cause, in which our patriotic fathers were engaged; and among the rest, one which was commanded by the brave Capt. Cottineau, with whom our departed friend arrived at New Bern, North Carolina, in the year 1778.	03/22/1823

Henry Messonnier, who died here the 14th inst., was born in Neufchatel, one of the Swiss Cantons, in the year 1750. Having received an education to fit him for the counting house, he went to Nantz, and was there employed in a respectable commercial establishment, when the American Revolution commenced. From this port were fitted out some of the first vessels to bring supplies, which were so essential to the success of that cause, in which our patriotic fathers were engaged; and among the rest, one which was commanded by the brave Capt. Cottineau, with whom our departed friend arrived at New Bern, North Carolina, in the year 1778.

That part of the country offered fewer temptations to the spirit of commerce by which he was actuated, and Mr. Messonnier became a merchant of Baltimore the same year; his modest demeanor, his informed understanding, and his constant assiduity at once procured him the confidence and friendship of the citizens. At that time, the number of our inhabitants was so limited, that it may be truly said he enjoyed the confidence and friendship of every body; and it may be said of equal truth, and as much as an individual could be known in a larger population, he continued to enjoy them under all the vicissitudes of fortune, to the hour of his death. To say that Mr. M. was a man of integrity is not enough, it was sterling, stern integrity, and such that made him hold the deceiver or cheat, in absolute abhorrence and detestation.

In 1781, he married Elizabeth, the beautiful and the accomplished daughter of the late Dr. Charles F. Wisenthal; and about the close of the war of independence, he entered into partnership with Mr. Zollickoffer; but they were unfortunate in trade, as were many others at the same period; in consequence of importations and sales on credit, without the aid of banking institutions, or indeed of any efficient system of national government or trade. These circumstances induced him to accept of the office of Chancellor to the Chevalier D'Anmour, then his Most Christian Majesty's Consul for Virginia and Maryland, and who must be

Marriage and Death Notices	Date

remembered yet by many of our citizens, as well for his personal dignity of manners as his fidelity to that alliance which subsisted between the Sovereign and the United States. In 1787, Mrs. Messonnier died, without issue, and her husband remained a widower throughout the remainder of his life. But the Revolution in France terminated the official duites of Mr. D'Anmour, and Mr. Messonnier again applied himself to commerce, under auspices so favorable, that his capital became extensive in a short time. The events which were so disastrous to the French Colonies, were propitious to him, in proportion to that confidence he enjoyed, particularly amongst the unfortunate fugitives from St. Domingo; but this also made it a duty with him to extend similar or additional marks of friendship on France and Frenchmen, and he found his circumstances so embarrassed on that account, that he visited Paris in 1799, where his generous character was appreciated, and from whence he returned in 1800, with an ample fortune. He continued to be actively employed in commerce until the commencement of the last war, upon the same liberal principles he had always practiced, and about that time was made a director of the Farmers' and Merchants' Bank, rather against his will; for then feeling the approach of age, after a life of almost uninterrupted health, he thought it essential to put his affairs here in order and wait patiently the dispensations of providence in the enjoyment of the society of those friends whom he cherished, and by whom he was beloved. His acts of charity, and benevolence, together with some instances of misdplaced confidence, perhaps were sufficient to reduce his means, but the knowledge of the fact produced no remorse or chagrin, & after disposing of a part of what he still possessed, in tokens of friendship to those who were not related to him; he bestowed the residue on his brother's and sister's children. In his person, Mr. M. was a little above the middle stature, inclined to corpulency, and attentive to his appearance when abroad. He never acquired as much ease in speaking our language as the French, and on this account he took but little part in our politics or our amusements, but rather reserved – sometimes distant and cold in appearance, even when his heart was agitated by the warmest feelings of humanity; and always unassuming, he justified the character which the world bestows on the faithful Swiss. He was an honest man.

If the growth of Baltimore has been a public benefit, and that growth had its rise in the commercial enterprize of its citizens, then is the memory of Henry Messonnier entitled to the respect of this public, for he came to the place when it contained but about 6,000 souls, & he has terminated a most active mercantile life, now there is a population of 60,000. Yes, though he was not born amongst us; though originally, he did not bring a fortune to us, we are indebted to him, as well as to many others who have gone before him to the silent tomb. Let us discharge a

Marriage and Death Notices	Date
part of that debt, not only by wriing and reading an obituary notice of the man, but by imitating the examples of sobriety, justice, punctuality, moderation, and generosity, by which he was distinguished during 45 years of his residence in Baltimore. O. B.	
On Sunday evening last, by the Rev. Mr. Valiant, Mr. Thomas Newton, to Miss Ann Bryan, all of this city.	03/24/1823
On the 16th inst., by the Rev. Dr. Roberts, Mr. James P. M'Eleget, to Miss Elenora M. Holbrook, both of this city.	03/24/1823
OBITUARY. Departed this transitory life, suddenly, on Saturday night last, in the 22nd year of his age, Mr. George Wheeler. He has been afflicted with a pulmonary disease for a long time, though, on Saturday evening, he retired to bed, much better than he had been for a week previous. Between 11 and 12 o'clock, he was conscience of the approach of death, and was prepared to meet him as a welcome messenger – he commenced exhorting his friends who stood around him, and enquired if he should meet them in Heaven. He was a young man universally beloved and respected by all who had the pleasure of his acquaintance – he embraced the religion of Jesus Christ in early life; and was a useful member of the Sabbath school attached to the Methodist Episcopal Church, who followed his last remains, with great respect, to his long home. He has left a large number of relations and a large circle of friends to mourn their irreparable loss. But their loss is his infinite gain – then dry up your tears and say, the Lord gave and the lord taketh away – blessed be the name of the Lord. The last words he was perceived to utter were, Lord Jesus receive my spirit for I am thine.	03/25/1823
On Sunday, the 23rd inst., after a short illness, Mrs. Elizabeth, consort of Thomas Cooper, in the 70th year of her age. She manifested in her illness as she did through life, that placid serenity and resignation to the will of her Redeemer, which was indicative of her Christian character. She has engaged a state of mortality on earth, for an immortality of bliss, at God's right hand. "Blessed are the dead, who die in the Lord, from henceforth, yea, saith the spirit that they may rest from their labors, and their works do follow them."	03/25/1823
On Sunday, at Monkton Mills, in Baltimore County, John Gwynn, father of the Editor of the Federal Gazette, in the 75th year of his age.	03/25/1823
On Wednesday evening last, after a long suffering, of a pulmonary complaint, Mrs. Sarah Grimes, in the 37th year of her age leaving a husband and five children to lament their loss.	03/25/1823

Marriage and Death Notices	Date
On the 20th inst., Don Carlos Hall, aged 44 years. His exemplary life has gained him the esteem and regard of a numerous acquaintance, by whom he lived beloved, and died regretted.	03/25/1823
Yesterday, about 1 o'clock, of a lingering illness, Capt. Abraham Eagleston, in the 29th year of his age.	03/26/1823
On Monday morning, Emily Jane, eldest daughter of Mr. Thomas Byrom Grundy, in the seventh year of her age.	03/26/1823
At Annapolis, Mrs. Sarah Sands, consort of Joseph Sands. At Washington city, Mrs. Tasset, wife of Nicholas Tasset. At Bellefield, Benjamin Oden, Jr. At Norfolk, Capt. James Davis.	03/27/1823
By the Rev. Dr. Glendy, on the 23rd inst., Mr. James Phillips, to Miss Rachel Hared, all of this city.	03/28/1823
On Tuesday evening last, by the Rev. Mr. Nevins, Mr. Charles Crook, Jr., to Miss Sarah Ann Brown.	03/28/1823
In Baltimore county, on Tuesday, the 25th inst., by the Rev. Mr. Shote, Mr. Luke Ensor, of this city, to Miss Rachel Ensor, of the former place.	03/28/1823
Yesterday morning, suddenly, Mary Stewart, eldest daughter of the late David Stewart, Esq.	03/28/1823
At Panama, on the 17th January last, Capt. John Brown, of the schooner Freemason, late a respectable ship maser of this port leaving a widow and orphan to deplore his untimely end. For him, no eulogy is necessary his memory will long be revered by his numerous friends. May he who has promised to be a husband to the widow, and a father to the fatherless, cover them with his protecting arms, and give them consolation under such a trial.	03/28/1823
On the 13th ult., in the state of Alabama, Dr. Robert Gantt, formerly of Calvert county, Md.	03/28/1823
At Savannah, on the 15th inst., of a consumption, J. C. Mulvey, Esq., his Catholic Majesty's Vice Consul, aged 29 years.	03/28/1823
Early yesterday morning, at her residence, on Deer Creek, Harford county, Mary Mifflin, at the advanced age of 81 years. A respectable member and highly esteemed minister of the Society of Friends.	03/29/1823
At Philadelphia, by the Rev. Thomas S. Birch, Mr. William S. Dillingham, of Baltimore, to Miss Julia, only daughter of Dr. D.	03/31/1823

Marriage and Death Notices	Date
Harrington, of that city.	
On Sunday evening last, by the Rev. Mr. Hinkle, Mr. James M'Guire, to Miss Ann Curtain, both of this city.	04/01/1823
Yesterday morning, of an inflammatory complaint, Mr. Samuel Cutcher, in the 32nd year of his age.	04/01/1823
At Honduras, 12th ult., Capt. Benjamin Shaw, of Portland.	04/01/1823
On Monday evening last, by the Rev. Mr. Stansbury, Mr. Charles Mercer, to Miss Marian Randall, all of this city.	04/02/1823
On the 1st inst., by the Rev. Mr. Sarr, Mr. Richard C. Busteau, to Miss Prudence Chambers, both of this city.	04/02/1823
At Wilmington, Del., Mr. George Bush, to Miss Mary Jane Jackson, of Baltimore.	04/02/1823
On Tuesday evening last, by the Rev. Mr. Finlay, Dr. Richard G. Banks, of Virginia, to Miss Matilda Eliza, daughter of Andrew Dewees, Esq., of this city.	04/02/1823 04/10/1823 04/11/1823
On Sunday evening last, by the Rev. Mr. Smith, Mr. Hilery Elder, to Mrs. Catherine Hines, both of this city.	04/03/1823
Last evening, by the Rev. Dr. Jennings, Mr. George Appold to Miss Catherine, eldest daughter of the Rev. D. E. Reese, both of this city.	04/04/1823
At Mount Hope, on Thursday evening, by the Rev. Mr. Henshaw, Thomas G. Rutter, to Miss Louisa Rutter, both of this city.	04/05/1823
In Alexandria, on the 3rd inst., Mr. Arthur T. Urie, of Baltimore, to Mrs. Elizabeth Howard, of Alexandria.	04/08/1823
In Frederick County, Maryland, on last Thursday afternoon, by the Rev. Mr. Zollickoffer, Mr. John Gallion, to Miss Elizabeth Brown, both of said county.	04/08/1823
Died, at her residence, in Baltimore county, on the 2nd inst., Mrs. Rachel Wyse, aged 51.	04/08/1823
By the Rev. Mr. Gibson, on Tuesday evening, John Hassen, to Miss Mary McCoy, all of this city.	04/09/1823

Marriage and Death Notices	Date
On Monday evening, by the Rev. Mr. Henshaw, Dr. Peter Porsher, of Charleston, S. C., to Miss Mary Ann Hyatt, of this city.	04/09/1823
Last evening, by the Rev. Mr. Moranville, Mr. Thomas Bean, of St. Mary's, to Catherine, youngest daughter of Mr. Edward Hagthrop, of this city.	04/09/1823
On Saturday last, at his residence, in Baltimore county, in the 85th year of his age, Simon Perine, a Major in the Revolutionary war – much respected and esteemed by all who know him.	04/09/1823
On the night of the 4th, Franklin Madison, aged six months, and on the 5th instant, Samuel Thomas Worthington, aged two years and three months; the only children of Capt. Thomas Hook, of Frederick county. The former was but three days sick; the latter only six days. Thus, in so short a period, were their affectionate parents bereft of those lovely infants.	04/09/1823
Departed this life, on the morning of the 7th inst., between the hours of 12 and 1 o'clock, Mrs. Mary, consort of Mr. Isaac Reynolds, in the 36th year of her age. She was truly an affectionate wife, a tender parent, a dutiful daughter, kind sister, and sincere friend. But the greatest consolation to her relatives and friends is that she died a sincere and pious Christian. We may confidently say, that however much her death be lamented by her family and friends, their loss is indeed her gain.	04/09/1823
Died, on Tuesday afternoon, in the 38th year of her age, Mrs. Susan Levering, wife of Nathan Levering, Esq. In recording this afflicting dispensation of Divine Providence, by which an amiable family, numerous relatives, and a large circle of friends, have been bereaved of an ornament and blessing, yet it must afford no small consolation to them, as it dose to the writer of this (who had an opportunity of knowing her well) to know that the whole tenor of her life was marked by a faithful discharge of all the social, religious, and domesic duties. Exemplary in her conduct and pleasing in her manners, she endeared herself to all who were acquainted with her – and it can truly be said that she set an example such as all should follow. In her last moments she showed that confidence and composure which few have witnessed – and only a few minutes before her departure from this world, called her children to the bedside, kissed, and then bid them farewell. In the foundation and subsequent patronage of that Christian institution, the Union Female Sabbath School, of which she was treasurer, and a member of almost all the female charitable societies, she showed forth that zeal and munificence which becomes a true Christian – and we may be permitted humbly to hope both by her works and faith, that she was	04/09/1823

Marriage and Death Notices	Date
prepared to meet her Redeemer. J. S.	
Died, on Wednesday last, after a severe and lingering disease, Mrs. Susan Rose, consort of William Rose, in the 47th year of her age. The deceased was a native of Leicestershire, Eng., and for many years a respectable resident of this city. As wife, a mother, and a Christian, she gave every assurance that death, to her, was but a transition from the sorrows and affliction of this life, to the blessed immortality of a future state. Calm and collected under a painful illness, she looked upon the "King of terrors" as a soothing minister sent to her relief – and seemed only to regret that the fortitude and resignation she evinced on a bed of suffering could not be communicated to her relatives and friends. Her remains were interred in the Friends' Burial Ground, Old Town, on Thursday last, agreeably to her express desire; and were followed to the narrow house appointed for all the living by those whose "grief passeth show."	04/09/1823
Died, on the evening of Thursday last, Clarissa Pierce, aged 15 years. The death of this young lady is an event peculiarly calculated to awaken the grief of her connections and acquaintance. Her engaging manners, amiable disposition, sweetness of temper, her innocent and excellent character, had endeared her, with no common tie to the esteem and love of her friends. Their hopes were raised high; but it has pleased God to disappoint them all. The destroyer came; the flower has been cut off its bloom; it is withered in the grave; and the shades of death have settled on the fair prospects which the fond anticipations of friendship had clothed with brightness and joy. The spirit is fled from the earth; it is no more seen, nor heard, nor known in its mortal form; but it still dwells in the recollections of many, who weep for its departure; its remembrance is cherished in the affections of numerous friends, and affords solace to hearts of sympathy and sadness; nor will the day come when its deep traces shall be worn out.	04/09/1823
Died, in Baltimore county, on Wednesday, the 26th ult., Mrs. Elizabeth Ward, in the seventy-third year of her age, formerly of Harford county.	04/09/1823
On Tuesday evening last, at the Cathedral, by the Rt. Rev. Bishop Mareschal, Capt. John Aloysius Durkee, to Miss Adeline Wheeler, all of this city.	04/10/1823
On Tuesday evening last, by the Rev. Mr. Hall, Mr. James Poteete, of Harford county, to Mrs. Margaret L. Chapman, of this city.	04/10/1823
On Tuesday evening last, by the Rev. Mr. Duncan, Mr. John Millar, to	04/10/1823

Marriage and Death Notices	Date
Miss Anna Maria, daughter of Capt. Thomas Boyle, all of this city.	
On Thursday evening last, by the Rev. Mr. Valiant, Mr. William Moffitt, to Miss Louisa Perry.	04/10/1823
By the Rev. Mr. Valiant, on Tuesday evening last, the Rev. Stuart Redman, of Talbot county, to Miss Mary Hynson, of Baltimore.	04/10/1823
In Baltimore County, on Sunday, the 6th instant, Andrew Guinsberger, in the 19th year of his age. He has left a mother and a few friends to lament their loss.	04/10/1823
On Saturday evening last, by the Rev. Mr. McCormick, Mr. George Holtzman, to Miss Margaret H. Deaver.	04/11/1/23
On Tuesday, the 8th inst., by the Rev. Mr. Duncan, Mr. John Rose, to Miss Narcissa Jerusha, daughter of Col. Solomon R. Hall, all of this city.	04/11/1823
Last evening, by the Rev. Mr. Healey, Mr. Robert Crown, to Miss Susannah Philips, all of this city.	04/11/1823
On Thursday evening last, by the Rev. Mr. Hinkle, Mr. James Foulds, to Miss Elizabeth Ann, eldest daughter of Mr. Edward Hall, all of this city.	04/11/1823
On Thursday evening last, by the Rev. Mr. Helfenstein, Mr. Federal Earickson, to Miss Henrietta Magragh, both of this city.	04/12/1823
At Bellona Arsenal, Chesterfield county, Va., George Reardon, Esq., Sutler, at that post, late lieutenant in the army of the U. S. James Hanna, formerly of Baltimore, a soldier in the 3rd U. S. Reg. of Artillery.	04/12/1823
Yesterday morning, at Friends' Meeting House, Lombard st., William Ellis Coale to Hannah E. Carey, daughter of James Carey, of this city.	04/17/1823
On Thursday evening last, by the Rev. Dr. Roberts, Mr. Thomas Seabrooks, to Miss Elizabeth Ann Curtis, second daughter of David M. Curtis, late of New York.	04/17/1823
On Tuesday evening, by the Rev. Dr. Wyatt, Mr. Philip Sheerwood, to Miss Ann Ward, both of this city.	04/17/1823
Yesterday morning, by the Rev. Mr. Jubert, Mr. David Stuart, to Miss Mary Neal Burland, all of this city.	04/18/1823

Marriage and Death Notices	Date
At Charlottesville, Va., on the 6th inst., Mr. Peter Lemoine, of this city, in the 24th year of his age.	04/18/1823
On Thursday evening, by the Rev. Dr. Hurtz, Mr. Daniel Heddinger, to Miss Ann Elizabeth Crea, both of this city.	04/19/1823
On Thursday evening, at Charlesborough, by the Rev. Mr. Rockhold, Mr. Elisha Gorsuch, to Miss Hannah Gorsuch, both of Baltimore county.	04/19/1823
On Wednesday evening last, at Georgetown, D. C., by the Rev. Mr. Collins, Mr. John Patrick, of Baltimore, to Miss Maria H. W. Moore, eldest daughter of Mr. John Moore, of Georgetown.	04/21/1823
On the 15th inst., Mr. William Clark, of the District, to Miss Delia Kirby, of Prince George's county.	04/21/1823
In Frederick county, Md., on last Thursday afternoon, by the Rev. Mr. Zollickoffer, Mr. David Brown, to Miss Ann Maria Nicodemus, both of that county.	04/22/1823
On Saturday morning last, at 9 o'clock A.M., Mr. Charles Hammer, aged 42 years, and for the last eight years severely afflicted, and bore the disposition of Providence with Christian fortitude.	04/22/1823
Departed this life, on Sunday, the 20th inst., John Underwood, Sr., in the 56th year of his age, after a short, but painful disease.	04/22/1823
In Matthews county, Mrs. Ann Burton, aged upwards of 90 years.	04/22/1823
Yesterday, in the 23rd year of his age, Mr. Dines Chambers, a native of county Down, Ireland.	04/22/1823
On Sunday morning last, after a long and distressing illness, which he bore with Christian fortitude and resignation, Capt. Josias Jenkins, of Long Green, Baltimore county, aged 42 years, leaving a distressed widow and seven children to bemoan a loss which to them is irreparable, and to his numerous brothers and friends in this city, this affliction can be removed by time only.	04/22/1823
On Sunday evening last, by the Rev. Mr. Strawbridge, Mr. Caleb Merryman, Jr., to Miss Louisa Andrews, all of Baltimore Co.	04/23/1823
Last evening, by the Rev. Bishop Kemp, Mr. James C. Sellman, to Miss Eleanor Gould, daughter of Alexander Gould, all of this city.	04/23/1823

Marriage and Death Notices	Date
On Thursday evening last, at Elk Ridge, Anne Arundel County, by the Rev. Mr. Linthicum, Mr. James Clarke, to Miss Elizabeth, second daughter of Charles Feinour, Esq.	04/23/1823
In Havana, on the 8th inst., of yellow fever, aged about 14 years, Oliver Davis, son of the late Capt. Davis, of this city. He was a promising youth, and bid fair to be the comfort and support of his fond mother, who is thus, by the ruthless King of Terrors, bereft of a dutiful and beloved son, and left to mourn his early death. "There is another and a better world."	04/23/1823
Last evening, by the Rev. Mr. McCann, Mr. Henry Placide, to Miss Susan E. S. Daley, all of this city.	04/25/1823
On Tuesday evening last, by the Rev. Dr. Roberts, Mr. Joseph A. Scott, Jr., to Miss Mary A. Toner, of Baltimore county.	04/25/1823
Yesterday morning, suddenly, about 10 o'clock, John M'Quinn, Esq., in the 25th year of his age.	04/25/1823
Yesterday morning, Mr. David Davidson, in the 26th year of his age.	04/25/1823
Yesterday morning, at Calverton, Mr. Geo. Sampson.	04/25/1823
On Tuesday evening last, by the Rev. Dr. Jennings, Mr. Hugh Bay, to Miss Frances Ann Sanders, both of this city.	04/25/1823 04/26/1823
At Washington, Mr. Lund Washington, Sr., to Miss Sally, daughter of the late Mr. John Johnson, near Snow Hill, Worcester county, Maryland.	04/26/1823
In this city, at Dr. Horton's, on the 25th inst., after a short illness, Mr. John Elliott, of Queen Anne's county, in the 46th year of his age. Kind, indulgent, and affectionate as a husband and father – sincere in friendship, his loss will be long deplored by his numerous relatives and friends; but they have consolation in the soothing reflection that he departed in the firm hope and belief of a happy immortality.	04/26/1823
Departed this life, on the 23rd inst., Mrs. Ann Mary Atkinson, in the 84th year of her age, a native of Switzerland, and for the last forty years an inhabitant of this city.	04/26/1823
On Thursday evening last, by the Rev. Mr. Soule, Mr. William Joice, to Miss Sarah Ann Garish, both of this city.	04/28/1823
In Troy, N. Y., on the 21st inst., Col. Thomas Davis, aged 47.	04/29/1823

Marriage and Death Notices	Date
On Monday evening last, by the Rev. Dr. Jennings, Mr. John Mackelfresh, to Miss Mary L. Saunders, both of Baltimore county.	04/30/1823
On Monday evening last, by the Rev. Mr. Hemphill, Mr. Emanuel Kent Deaver to Miss Elizabeth Shiply, both of this city.	04/30/1823
At Annapolis, John Brewer, Esq., to Miss Ann, daughter of Francis Bealmear, Esq., of Anne Arundel County.	04/30/1823
On the 27th instant, Edward Peirce, of Baltimore county, in the 64th year of his age. The deceased served his country in the American revolution with honor to himself, and has been for the last thirty years a respectable farmer of this county.	04/30/1823
On Tuesday, 29th April, by the Rev. Mr. Grist, Mr. Abraham C. Cole, of this city, to Miss Eleanor, daughter of George Harryman, Esq., of Baltimore county.	05/01/1823
On Thursday evening, 1st May, by the Rev. John Tettier, Mr. Charles Steigers, to Miss Ellen Finn, all of this city.	05/02/1823
At Lancaster, Penn., Mr. Worthy H. Cunninham, of Conowingo, to Miss Mary Ann, daughter of Lewis Wernwerg, Esq.	05/02/1823
In Harford county, Md., Mr. Aquila Galloway to Mrs. Elizabeth Price. Mr. John Barcroft to Miss Elizabeth Bevard.	05/02/1823
Yesterday morning, at 10 o'clock, Mrs. Ellen Burton.	05/02/1823
In Harford county, Elizabeth, aged 26, wife of Mr. Jacob Ely. Ann, aged 24, wife of Mr. Thomas Ely. Miss Elizabeth Jeffrey, aged 16. She is the last of the little family of which she was a member. Mr. Mills and Mrs. Jeffrey, whose deaths have been recently announced, including Elizabeth, composed this family – all of whom, in the course of a few weeks, have descended to the tomb. Mrs. Elizabeth, wife of James G. Davis, Esq., of Belle Air. It is a melancholy fact that in less than two months, nearly one-fourth of the female heads of families in Belle Air have descended to the tomb; thus divesting the village of some of its brightest ornaments.	05/02/1823
On Thursday evening last, on Patapsco Neck, by the Rev. Mr. Bartow, Jonas Stansbury, Esq., to Keziah, daughter of Mr. Edw'd Bowen, all of that place.	05/03/1823
On Thursday evening last, by the Rev. Mr. Bartow, Mr. Frederick B. Minchin, to Miss Lydia, daughter of the late William Slater, all of this	05/03/1823

Marriage and Death Notices	Date
city.	
On Thursday evening last, by the Rev. Mr. Bartow, Mr. Charles Alteroff, to Miss Elizabeth Smith, all of this city.	05/03/1823
On Monday morning last, after a long and distressing illness, Mrs. Mary Gantz, aged 67 years, consort of Adam Gantz, Sr., of this city.	05/03/1823
On Friday evening, 2nd inst., in Baltimore county, Mrs. C. Carnan, wife of Col. Christopher Carnan. The friends and relatives of the deceased are informed that the funeral will take place on Sunday, 4th, at the residence of R. N. Carnan, Esq.	05/03/1823
On the 27th ultimo, by the Rt. Rev. Bishop Kemp, Mr. John R. Wier, to Miss Eliza, second daughter of Mr. Peter Fowble, all of this city.	05/06/1823
On Sunday evening, the 4th inst., by the Rev. Mr. Kearney, Mr. Eugene Fenton, to Mrs. Jane Nicholson, both of this city.	05/06/1823
On Thursday, the 24th of April, by the Rev. Mr. Stone, Mr. Littleton Waters, of Baltimore, to Miss Elizabeth Savage, of Dorchester county, Eastern Shore, Maryland.	05/06/1823
On Sunday morning, 4th inst., by the Rev. Dr. Jennings, Mr. William Clark, to Miss Elizabeth Simpson, both of Baltimore county.	05/06/1823
At Upper Marlborough, on Tuesday evening last, by the Rev. Mr. Summers, John Johnson, Jr., Esq., to Mary, second daughter of Trueman Tyler, Esq.	05/06/1823
Yesterday morning, at 3 o'clock, after a protracted illness, Mrs. Frances Frink, aged 62 years, late of Philadelphia.	05/06/1823
On Saturday morning last, after a few days illness, Miss Adeline Rebecca Barge, in the 18th year of her age.	05/06/1823
On Sunday evening last, 20th April, at his seat, near Oxford, in the county of Talbot, Eastern Shore of Maryland, AEt 65, John Leeds Bozman, Esq., a man highly respected in the society in which he lived, distinguished for his learning among learned men, a gentleman of urbane manners and refined sentiment. He was profoundly versed in the Science of the Law, and his mind was richly adorned and copiously stored with classical and miscellaneous literature. He will be handed down to future times as the first who successfully undertook to write a History of Maryland, and the world will long regret that he did not live	05/06/1823

Marriage and Death Notices	Date
to complete his excellent and important work. *U. S. Gazette.*	
On Sunday evening last, by the Rev. Mr. Valiant, Mr. Francis Hucorn, to Miss Maria Garrison, both of this city.	05/07/1823
Last evening, by the Rev. George Dashiell, Mr. Deter Barger, to Mrs. Sarah Athey, all of this city.	05/09/1823
On Thursday evening, at the Union Factory, by the Rev. Charles A. Davis, of Baltimore, Mr. Thomas Emhart, to Miss Margaret Low, both of Baltimore county.	05/10/1823
At his residence, Mount Carmel, near Port Tobacco, Md., on the 27th inst., aged 74 years, the Rev. Charles Neale, Superior of the Society of Jesus, in the United States, in which dignified station he had been appointed for the third time.	05/10/1823
On Thursday evening last, by the Rev. Mr. Conner, Mr. Joseph Boury, to Miss Mary Ann Higgins, all of this city.	05/12/1823
On the 10th inst., Dedrick Rabb, in the 52nd year of his age, an old resident of Fell's Point, and one of the noblest works of God, an honest man.	05/12/1823
On the 9th inst., in Baltimore county, about 3 o'clock P. M., in the 66th year of her age, Mrs. Sarah, consort of Mr. William Perine.	05/13/1823
Last evening, by the Rt. Rev. Bishop Kemp, Isaac Williams, Esq., of Somerset County, to Miss Virginia D. I. Polk, of this city.	05/14/1823
At Port-au-Prince, William H. Sinclair, Esq., merchant, of Baltimore, aged 24. Mr. James Bridges, seaman of sloop Charles, of Castine.	05/14/1823
On Friday, the 3rd inst., Mr. Thomas Stiff, in the 54th year of his age, an old and much respected resident of this city.	05/14/1823
On Sunday evening, 11th inst., by the Rev. Mr. Davis, Mr. George Knight, to Miss Catherine Brown, both of this city.	05/15/1823
OBITUARY. Departed this life, on the 11th April last, at the island of St. Thomas, whither he had gone for the benefit of his health, Henry Lamson, of this city, in the 37th year of his age. Mr. L. was a native of Havrehill, Mass., but for the past 12 years a resident of Baltimore. About two years since, he was attacked by pulmonary affection; on the appearance of which, yielded to medical advice, he abandoned all thoughts of business, and he gave himself up wholly to the recovery of	05/15/1823

Marriage and Death Notices	Date
his health. To effect this, he traveled for about a year in the United States. He then took a voyage to Europe and returned – lastly, being urged to try the West Indies, he sailed from this port late in December last. After passing some time at St. Jago de Cuba, Jamaica, Porto Rico, &c., he arrived at St. Thomas; where it pleased Almighty God to terminate his existence. Of the many individuals who are hourly swept into the grave by the unspairing hand of time, few indeed have fallen, around whose bier a large circle mourn, or over whose grave flow tears of deeper sorrow. Endeared to all who knew him, by the mildest and most amiable deportment, his death, while it has filled his immediate family with the most heart-felt anguish, has spread through the community a kindred sympathy. Of the life and character of Mr. L. little need be said. His public worth requires not the aid of eulogy to perpetuate its remembrance. Nor can his private life borrow lustre from panegyric. As a man, in the complicated and perplexing affairs of human life, he was prompt, liberal, and scrupulously just. As a husband, he was in the highest degree, devoted and affectionate. As a Christian, he was meek, humble, and sincere. An early and intimate acquaintance with the scriptures gave his character much of the gentleness of Christian forebearance. Satisfied himself, of the truth, efficacy, and power of the doctrines they inculcate, he permitted others to worship God, agreeably to the dictates of conscience. He had no sectarian bigotry – no dogmatic pertinacity – nor did his religion seek the applause of the world by its ostentation. His offerings at the throne of grace were those of a meek and humble spirit – his sacrifice was that of the heart! upon its alter, his devotion burned with pure and holy ardour; and we trust, its incense, while it ascended to the great 1 A. M., purified the innerman; and, filling the temple of the soul within, shed a halo of glory around the gloom of the grave!	
On the 14th inst., at the Friends' Meeting House, Lombard street, Thomas Mackenzie, to Tacy B. Norbury, of this city.	05/16/1823
At his residence, on Island Creek, Talbot county, Eastern Shore, Maryland, on the 7th instant., Mr. Anthony Ross, after a short, but severe illness of about 30 hours. In whom, society have to mourn the loss of a useful and worthy member.	05/16/1823
On Thursday evening last, by the Rt. Rev. Bishop Kemp, Mr. William Ramsey, to Miss Elizabeth Goodd, both of this city.	05/17/1823
On Tuesday, the 13th inst., John Worthington Dorsey, of Elkridge, Anne Arundel county, in the 73rd year of his age leaving a widow and five sons to mourn their loss. That the deceased was a charitable, humane, and upright man, a kind neighbor and fast friend, all who knew him will	05/17/1823

Marriage and Death Notices	Date
attest. That he was a brave man and zealous supporter of the rights and liberties of his country, those who served with him in our revolutionary war can bear witness.	
At Upper Marlborough, Prince George's County, Md., on the 13th inst., Mrs. Mary D. Lee, consort of Dr. Benjamin Lee, in the 26th year of her age. The deceased had labored under a long and tedious illness, which she bore to the last with great fortitude and resignation. She died leaving a husband and one child to deplore her loss, and universally regretted by her acquaintances.	05/17/1823
Last Thursday evening, by the Rev. John Hargrove, Mr. Aaron Stewart, to Mrs. Sarah Lovell, all of this city.	05/19/1823
In Georgetown, a few days ago, Dr. John M. Thomas, of Frederick county, Md., to Miss Catherine C. Turner, daughter of Thomas Turner, Esq.	05/19/1823
At New Orleans, 22nd ultimo, Dr. William Flood.	05/19/1823
Departed this life, at 5 o'clock, this morning, Mr. Wm. Sinclair, in the 60th year of his age, a native of Londonderry, Ireland. His friends and acquaintance are requested to attend his funeral, tomorrow morning, at 10 o'clock, from his late residence, corner of Exeter and Duke streets, O. T., without further invitation.	05/21/1823
Lately, in England, Mrs. Patterson, of Baltimore, Md., formerly Madame Jerome Bonaparte, to the young Earl of Cholmondely. And Edy Harvey, formerly Miss Caton, also of Baltimore, and relict of Col. Harvey, aid de Camp to the Duke of Wellington, to Lord Petre, nephew to the Duke of Norfolk. *Charleston Mercury.* [*Mrs. Patterson's friends here have received letters from her as late as the middle of March, when she was at Geneva, in Switzerland, and had no intention of going to England. The above announcement of marriages, therefore, is deemed incorrect.*] *Ed. Baltimore Patriot*	05/22/1823
By the Rev. Dr. Roberts, Mr. John J. Hederick, of this city, to Miss Mary Michael, of Philadelphia.	05/22/1823
At Washington, Mr. Wm. R. Lovelace to Miss Ann Whetmore, both of Prince George's county.	05/22/1823
In Talbot county, on Sunday last, after a short illness, James Nabb, Esq., late a member of the Executive Council of Maryland.	05/22/1823

298

Marriage and Death Notices	Date
At his residence, in Adams county, Mississippi, on the 8th March last, Dr. Daniel Rawlings, a native of Calvert County, Maryland. Dr. Rawlings left a large family to bewail his departure. He was cut off at an age, when a life of many years of usefulness to his family might have still been reasonably expected; he was eminent in his profession; his social and amiable qualities endeared him to a large circle of friends and acquaintance.	05/22/1823
Last evening, by the Rev. Mr. Helfenstein, John Diffenderffer, Esq., merchant, to Miss Catherine Rosalvah Cave, of Virginia.	05/23/1823
On Tuesday evening last, by the Rev. Dr. S. K. Jennings, Samuel Merritt to Rachel Smith.	05/24/1823
On the 17th inst., at his father's residence, in Kent County, John F. Keatting, late of this city, aged seventeen years. He was a youth of estimable moral qualities, and beloved by all who knew him.	05/24/1823
Last evening, by the Rev. D. E. Reese, Mr. Jacob Kneeland to Miss Sarah Short, all of this city.	05/26/1823
The 23rd instant, after a short, but painful illness, which she bore with Christian resignation, Mrs. Mary Casey, in the 56th year of her age, much regretted by an affectionate family and a large circle of friends and relatives, to whom she was most devoted. May she rest in peace. Amen.	05/26/1823
At Lexington, Ky., on the 29th ult., Mr. John Cole, late of this city, in the 29th year of his age.	05/26/1823
On Monday evening last, by the Rev. Mr. Bartow, Mr. Benjamin Lawson, to Miss Hannah Bliss, all of this city.	05/28/1823
On Friday morning, in the 17th year of his age, after a painful and lingering illness, which he bore with due resignation to the will of his Creator, Richard Coppinger Connor, youngest son of the late Daniel Conner, of this city.	05/28/1823
On Saturday morning, in the 40th year of her age, after a tedious and trying disease, which she endured with becoming calmness and perfect resignation to the will of God, Mrs. Ellen Prince, sister of the late Daniel Connor, of this city.	05/28/1823
On Sunday morning, the 18th inst., after a long and painful illness, Mrs. Sarah Alwood. She has left an affectionate mother and sister, and an	05/28/1823

Marriage and Death Notices	Date
amiable young daughter, to cherish her remembrance, and to mourn her early and lamented descent to the tomb!	
On Monday, the 26th inst., at Stockwood, upon Elkridge, by the Rev. Mr. Aydelott, John S. Matthews, Esq., to Miss Sophia A. Hall, daughter of the late Dr. Hall.	05/29/1823
On Tuesday, 27th inst., by the Rev. Dr. Aydelott, Richard Holmes, Esq., of Montgomery county, Maryland, to Miss Rebecca Emily, daughter of George F. Warfield, Esq., of this city.	05/29/1829
On Saturday, the 24th inst., by the Rev. Mr. Smaltz, Mr. Charles Pitcock, to Miss Elizabeth Spicer, both of Baltimore county.	05/30/1823
"Another Whig of the Revolution gone." Died suddenly, the 24th inst., after having apparently recovered from a severe illness of a few days continuance, Dr. John Coulter, of this city, in the 72nd year of his age. The character of this venerable patriot, is too well known to many of his fellow-citizens, to need newspaper panegyric. But, it too often happens that when old age approaches, mankind are prone either to disregard, or entirely forget, the worth of former times. Dr. Coulter was a native of Ireland, born in the county Down. At the age of six months, he emigrated to this country with his parents, who settled in Cecil county, in this state – about the age of 18 years, he commenced to study of medicine, under the auspices of the late venerable Dr. Henry Stevenson, and at 21, engaged in the arduous duties of his profession, associated with the same friend and patron. A few years subsequent to this period, the American Revolution began to dawn; and having zealously embraced the principles which animated the breast of every whig of that day, at the call of his country, abandoning private considerations, he entered as Surgeon on board a vessel of war. The cruise having ended and the war brought to a close, he returned again to his former pursuits. A party, however, having, at this critical moment, arisen, with views which were then considered hostile to the true interests of the country, Dr. Coulter and Dr. McHenry were selected by their fellow-citizens, as the only persons who could be found of weight and character, and at the same time possessing popularity, sufficient successfully to contend against two others, the most formidable in point of talent &c. from among the opposing party. Their triumph was complete; and the result of their labors, together with the rest of the members of the convention, terminated in the adoption of the present Constitution of Maryland. The reputation which the deceased had obtained at that time for capacity, integrity, and indeed for all the virtuous endowments which adorn the human mind, he maintained to the last hour of his life. As a master of the healing art, his success in the treatment of the desolating malady of	05/30/1823

Marriage and Death Notices	Date
the years 1794 and 1800 being ample testimony – as a man, he was beloved by all who knew him – as a husband, he was found indulgent and kind – as a father, he was affection itself – as a friend, he was sincere and unchangeable. Having completed his "three score years and ten," and too recently parted with the companion of his days, the partner of his griefs, the "prop of his declining years," he became anxious to take his final leave of this "vale of tears." His amiable and innocent children, alone occasioned him any concern. "When one by one, are ties are torn, "And friend from friend is snatched forlorn, "Oh ! How then sweet it is to die!"	
Near York Pa., on Friday evening last, Mr. Peter Spangler, son of the late Rudolph Spangler, Esq., in the 38th year of his age.	05/30/1823
On Thursday evening last, by the Rev. Mr. Guest, Capt. Robert Dutton, of this city, to Miss Mary Ann, youngest daughter of John Murray, Esq., of Baltimore county.	05/31/1823
On Thursday evening last, by the Rev. Dr. Roberts, Mr. Elisha Green, to Miss Ruth Royston, both of Baltimore county.	06/02/1823
On the 14th inst., at Snowhill, Eastern Shore of Maryland, by the Rev. Samuel Stratton, Edward D. Ingraham, Esq., of Philadelphia, to Miss Mary C., daughter of Ephraim K. Wilson, of the former place.	06/02/1823
Last evening, by the Rev. Mr. Henshaw, Mr. Edward Dorsey, to Miss Elizabeth Coulson, all of this city.	06/03/1823
On Tuesday, 27th May, by the Rev. Mr. Davis, Mr. Isaac Owens, to Miss Jane Steuart, all of this city.	06/03/1823
By the Rev. Dr. Glendy, on the first ult., Mr. William Boyd, to Miss Isabella Gant.	06/04/1823
By the Rev. Dr. Glendy, on the evening of Monday last, Mr. Samuel Sayre, to Miss Eleanor Betts, all of this city.	06/04/1823
On Sunday evening, 1st inst., by the Rev. Mr. M'Cormick, Mr. Thomas D. Wood, to Miss Sarah Ann Deaver.	06/04/1823
On Tuesday evening last, by the Rev. Mr. Guest, Mr. Joseph Headley, of Washington City, to Miss Eliza Newman, of this city.	06/04/1823
Last evening, by the Rev. Mr. Healey, Mr. James E. Searly, to Miss	06/05/1823

Marriage and Death Notices	Date
Eliza Dunham, both of this city.	
Last evening, by the Rev. Mr. Healey, Mr. William Ford, to Miss Catherine Richards, all of this city.	06/05/1823
By the Rev. Dr. Glendy, on the evening of Monday last, Mr. Henry Hazel, merchant of Georgetown, to Miss Jane Raymond, of this city.	06/06/1823
At Annapolis, Henry M. Steele, Esq., of Dorchester county, to Miss Maria Lloyd, second daughter of Francis S. Key, Esq., of the District of Columbia.	06/06/1823
Few men have left this mortal scene more deeply and justly lamented than Mr. John Oliver. He departed this life on Wednesday evening, the 4th instant, after a lingering and painful illness, which he bore with Christian patience. "Take him all in all, we shall seldom look upon his like again." Should virtue appear upon the earth in human form, it would be clothed nearly in the character of the deceased. In him was united genuine independence of mind, to warm and steady friendship and honourable and upright principles of moral action. These were exalted and seasoned by the mild influences of pure and rational religion, which enfused an amiable modesty into his demeanour and manners peculiarly pleasing and attractive. His friends and relations will long look back upon his past life with tears of affection and the poor will lift up their hands to bless his good deeds with grateful remembrance. The death of the good man excites many sensibilities, but the lustre of his worth shines when he is gone, and the sanctity of his example lives among posperity. "Mark the perfect man, and behold the upright, for the end of that man is peace." This much with propriety may be said of the deceased without adulation – to have said less, would not be justice to his memory.	06/06/1823
Departed this life, after a lingering illness, which she bore with truly Christian fortitude, Mrs. Mary Bond, aged 68 years, consort of Mr. Buckler D. Bond, of Harford county.	06/07/1823
Gen. Henry Livingston, was born Jan. 19, 1752, and died, at his residence, in the manor of Livingston, Monday, Mary 26, 1823.	06/07/1823
On Thursday evening last, by the Rev. Mr. Smith, Mr. John J. Wilson, Jr., to Miss Eliza Pool, both of this city.	06/09/1823

Marriage and Death Notices	Date
On Thursday evening last, by the Rev. Mr. J. P. K. Henshaw, Mr. G. W. Ridgely, merchant, to Miss Arrieta Ridgely Wellmore, both of this city.	06/09/1823
By the Rev. Dr. Glendy, on the evening of Thursday last, Mr. Frederick Young, to Mrs. Mary Clark.	06/10/1823
By the Rev. Dr. Glendy, on the evening of Thursday last, Mr. Richard Emmerson, to Mrs. Elizabeth Davies, all of this city.	06/10/1823
On Sunday evening last, by the Rev. Daniel Stansbury, Mr. Jesse Gosnell, to Miss Mary Wood, both of Baltimore county.	06/10/1823
In Columbia, Lancaster county, Pa., on the evening of the 5th inst., by the Rev. Mr. Boyer, Mr. Wm. Boggs, merchant, of Baltimore, to Miss Caroline Jeffries, of the former place.	06/10/1823
Last evening, by the Rev. Mr. M'Cain, Mr. Jonathan Fitch, to Miss Margaret, daughter of Mr. James H. Clarke, all of this city.	06/11/1823
On Monday evening, by the Rev. Mr. Smith, Mr. James C. Magauran, to Miss Elizabeth Cecelia, youngest daughter of the late Capt. Deagle.	06/12/1823
On Tuesday evening last, by the Rev. Dr. Wyatt, James Harwood, Esq., to Sarah, daughter of the Rt. Rev. Bishop Kemp.	06/12/1823
At New Orleans, on the 7th of May last, of an attack of the typhus fever, Mr. William Dimond, late commander of the brig Harriet, of this port, aged 52 years.	06/12/1823
In the borough of Erie, Pennsylvania, on the 19th of May, John Woodward, Esq., a captain of the Revolutionary war, and for many years transcribing clerk of the House of representatives of this State, aged 94 years.	06/12/1823
At Buenos Ayres, about the 1st of April last, Mr. James Wragg, mate of the ship Merchant, of New York.	06/13/1823
On Thursday evening last, by the Rev. Mr. Healey, Mr. Michael Wallace, to Miss Eliza Taylor, all of this city.	06/14/1823
In Quincy, Mass., on Monday last, Peter Boyleston Adams, Esq., aged 85.	06/14/1823
At Fredericktown, Mr. Robert B. Stevenson, to Miss Hannah Shriner. John H. Marshall, of Charles county, to Miss Harriet M., daughter of the	06/16/1823

Marriage and Death Notices	Date
late Richard Potts, Esq.	
On Thursday, the 12th inst., At Dougharagen manor, the residence of Hon. Charles Carroll, of Carrollton, Elizabeth Hyde Harper, the second daughter of Gen. Harper, of this city, in the fourteenth year of her age. Sweet as the fragrance of the rose, And ah! as transient as its bloom.	06/16/1823
At Springfield, on Friday morning, Ann, eldest daughter of Mr. John A. Brown, in the 7th year of her age.	06/16/1823
In Talbot county, Md., Miss Mary Enleston, in the 35th year of her age. Mr. Thomas Wade, formerly a commission merchant in Baltimore. Mr. Thomas Keyes. Mrs. Sarah Ennells. And Miss Elizabeth Norris.	06/16/1823
In Frederick county, Mr. John T. Norris, Mr. Richard Nokes, and George Creager, Esq.	06/16/1823
On Sunday evening, by the Rev. Mr. Moranville, Capt. F. A. Reynolds, to Miss Charity, youngest daughter of Wm. Baartscheer, Esq., all of this city.	06/17/1823
On Sunday evening, by the Rev. Dr. Jennings, Mr. Samuel Read, to Miss Sarah Grimes, both of Baltimore county.	06/17/1823
On Sunday morning last, by the Rev. Bishop Kemp, George A. Wells, Esq., to Susan McKeel, both of this place.	06/17/1823
On Sunday evening, by the Rev. Mr. Davis, of this city, Mr. Adam Rae, to Miss Elizabeth Murray, both of Baltimore county.	06/17/1823
On Sunday evening, by the Rev. Mr. Davis, Mr. John McCrone, to Miss Sarah Fox, of Baltimore county.	06/17/1823
In Petersburg, Va., on Monday evening, by the Rev. Mr. *Cannon*, of Baltimore, Mr. William Gustavus *Gun*, to the amiable and highly accomplished Miss Emily Maria Pistol, daughter of the late Capt. John T. *Pistol*, of that Borough.	06/17/1823
On the 14th inst., in the 44th year of his age, and of the 23rd of his residence in this city, universally regretted by almost all classes of society, Mr. James Daly, of Pratt street. To eulogize on the merits of the deceased to a discerning public is needless, it being manifest to many, that his purse has been open to the distressed, and his house the asylum of the shelterless. In him particularly had the emigrant, widow and orphan, a friend and benefactor. In a word, he was benevolent to all	06/17/1823

Marriage and Death Notices	Date
who in him sought relief. May he rest in peace. Amen.	
Last evening, by the Rev. Mr. Helfenstein, Mr. Thomas Maund, to Miss Metta H., daughter of Mr. Frederick Waesche, all of this city.	06/18/1823
On the 1st inst., Mr. Wm. Smith, of the firm Moore & Smith, of this city. It is thought superfluous to enter into any eulogium on the character of the deceased; as those who were acquainted with him knew his worth. Suffice it to say, that he was a warm friend and an honest man. His loss is deeply lamented by his relations and friends.	06/18/1823
This morning, by the Rev. Mr. Nevins, Capt. Robert. Leslie, to Miss Anna Maria Downes, all of this city.	06/19/1823
On Tuesday last, by the Rev. Dr. Roberts, Mr. Edward Somerville Tarr, to Miss Susannah R. B., daughter of Mr. Richard Diffenderffer, all of this city.	06/19/1823
On Tuesday evening last, by the Rev. Mr. Grice, Mr. William M. Risteau, to Miss Susan Wilson, all of Baltimore county.	06/19/1823
On Saturday morning last, in the 82nd year of her age, Mrs. Catherine Dickeson, consort of the late Capt. Brittingham Dickeson, of Fell's Point.	06/20/1823
On Thursday evening last, by the Rev. Mr. Kurtz, Mr. Peter W. Compario, to Miss Catherine Frederick, all of this city,	06/21/1823
On Thursday evening last, by the Rev. Mr. Valiant, Mr. Andrew Baker to Mrs. Elizabeth Phrow, all of this city.	06/21/1823
At Hamburg, Md., on 27th May last, by the Rev. Mr. Mitchell, Dr. John H. Briscoe, to Miss Mary H. Key, both of St. Mary's County.	06/21/1823
On Thursday evening last, by the Rev. Mr. Wells, Mr. John B. Potter, Jr., formerly of Alexandria, D. C., to Miss Elizabeth Redman, of this place.	06/23/1823
On the 16th inst., at Walnut Grove, Frederick Co., Maryland, Mrs. M. Perry, aged 83 years; respected, admired, and loved, by all who knew her.	06/23/1823
Departed this life, on the 22nd inst., Mary Tolly, aged 4 years, 1 month, and 15 days, eldest daughter of John T. H. Worthington, Esq., of Baltimore county.	06/24/1823

Marriage and Death Notices	Date
On Sunday evening last, by the Rev. Dr. Roberts, Mr. Henry W. Tilyard, to Miss Elizabeth Garrett, both of this city.	06/25/1823
Last evening, in the 79th year of his age, James Ogleby, Esq., many years a respectable merchant of this city. The friends and acquaintance of the deceased are invited to attend his funeral, this evening, at 5 o'clock, from No. 36 South street.	06/25/1823
On Tuesday evening last, by the Rev. Mr. Gibson, Mr. Andrew M'Causlin, to Miss Margaret Niccle, both of this city.	06/26/1823
At Washington City, on Thursday evening last, by the Rev. Mr. Addison, Thomas W. Morris, Esq., of Philadelphia, to Caroline Maria, eldest daughter of George Calvert, Esq., of Riversdale, Prince George's county, Maryland.	06/26/1823
Off the coast of California, the 4th of Oct. last, Capt. Obed Wyer, master of ship N. America, of Nantucket. In the Pacific Ocean, Capt. Arey, of ship Apollo, of Nantucket.	06/26/1823
In Columbia county, Geo., on the 7th inst., after a short, but severe illness, Dr. Thomas H. M. Fendall, and able and skillful Physician, a native of Maryland, and for many years a resident of the city of Augusta.	06/27/1823
Departed this life, this morning, after a short illness, Mr. Frederick W. Nagle, in the 23rd year of his age. His friends and acquaintance are requested to attend his funeral, tomorrow morning, at 9 o'clock, from his mother's dwelling, in Washington street.	06/28/1823
In Easton, Md., on Thursday, the 19th inst., Mr. William Hopkins, to Mrs. Elizabeth Edmonson.	07/01/1823
In Talbot county, Md., on Tuesday, the 17th inst., Mr. David Fountain, to Mrs. Sarah Harington.	07/01/1823
Yesterday morning, after a short, but painful illness, John Thomas, son of S. C. Leakin, Esq., aged 26 months.	07/01/1823
In Easton, Md., on Wednesday, the 18th inst., Mrs. Mary Smith, consort of Mr. Hopkins Smith. In Talbot county, Md., on the 18th inst., Mrs. Cain, consort of Mr. James Cain.	07/01/1823
OBITUARY – Is there a heart attuned to virtuous feeling, that can with the cold rules of philosophy contemplate the chasm made in society by the loss of those suddenly cut off in the flower of youth and beauty's	07/01/1823

Marriage and Death Notices	Date

bloom – can frail humanity gaze upon the victims of the fell monster, Death, and with stoic apathy view the wreck of human nature? No! Death even in his mildest form, with the aspect of slow and lingering disease, is appalling to our souls; but when he robs us of the young and beautiful – of those who have just set out in the morning of life, with bosoms buoyant with hope and expectation, and at one fell swoop with scarce an intimation of his purpose, destroys the bright visions of happiness – founded on virtuous principle, the sacred bonds of friendship and successful love – 'tis a calamity which lays prostrate the fortitude of man, and sets at naught the cold dictates of reason. What then must be the feelings, with which we announce the decease of Mr. William Armstrong, son of James Armstrong, Jr., Esq., in the 21st year of his age – the decease of one bound to us by the firmest ties of friendship, and whose many virtues endeared him to our hearts – and, who, as if on the yesterday, we greeted blest with health and happiness. But where now is our friend? The cold clod of the valley rests on that bosom that throbbed with manly virtue - the eye that beamed with pure benevolence is closed in the stilly sleep of death – the form that we so oft admired is now mouldering in the grave – and, the hand that ever sprung ready to meet our grasp lies palsied by its side. Few persons possessed in a more eminent degree the qualities which endear mankind to man than him who has departed to the "bourne from whence no traveler returns." To unaffected affability of manners, was joined a frank and generous disposition, and a heart tenderly alive to the dictates of humanity. As a son, none could be more zealously devoted to the interests of a parent – as a brother, he was kind and affectionate – as a friend, steadfast and firm – in short, in every feature of his character some qualification discovered itself to excite our admiration and esteem. May those who have sustained this heavy loss, take consolation in the assurance that a well spent life gives the hope of a blessed immortality beyond the grave; and, to his numerous young friends, may it be a beacon, warning them of the vanity of all earthly prospects, tho' now basking in the sunshine of fortune. But sacred be the sorrow of one who has most cause to mourn; may the power that tempers the wind to the shorn lamb, encircle her wih his arms and whisper peace and comfort to her bereaved soul.   J.

Last evening, by the Rt. Rev. Bishop Mareschal, Mr. Gideon Emory, to Caroline Mary, only daughter of Mr. John Walsh, all of this city.	07/02/1823
In Talbot county, on Tuesday, 24th instant, Mr. William Townsend, to Miss Anna Maria Benson.	07/02/1823
On the 25th inst., at his late residence, in Talbot county, Bay Side, Col. William Lambdin, after a lingering illness, in the 68th year of his age. In	07/02/1823

Marriage and Death Notices	Date
Cambridge, on Thursday, the 29th inst., Mr. Charles K. Bryan, in the 59th year of his age, long a worthy and respectable resident of that place.	
On Tuesday evening last, by the Rev. Dr. Wyatt, Mr. John R. Kelso, to Martha, second daughter of Ely Balderston, Esq., all of this city.	07/03/1823
On Wednesday, the 19th ult., by the Rev. William Monroe, at Pilgrim's Rest, the seat of Aaron Grigsby, Fauquier co., Va., Mr. William S. Williamson, of Baltimore, to Miss Eleanor H., second daughter of the late Henry Gerrard, Esq., of Kentucky.	07/03/1823
In Chestertown, Md., on the 14th ult., Mrs. Sarah Wilmer, aged 76 years and 8 days.	07/03/1823
Departed this life, on Thursday, the 26th inst., at Church-hill, after a severe illness of ten days, Thomas Crane, Esq., in the 50th year of his age. He has left a wife and seven small children to lament a loss to them irreparable; for it may be truly said of the deceased, that he was a most affectionate and tender husband, and an indulgent father. Aware of his approaching dissolution, he met the king of terrors with that degree of tranquility and resignation that bespeaks the upright man and true Christian. He was esteemed and beloved as friend and neighbor, and admired for the undeviating rectitude of his whole life. Rocked in the cradle of the revolution, imbibing and claiming its early principles, he was an inflexible patriot.	07/03/1823
Wednesday evening last, by the Rev. J. M. Duncan, Mr. McKeel Taylor Wise, to Miss Matilda Rogers, both of this city.	07/05/1823
On 27th ult., at Chesterfield, Queen Ann's county, Mr. Thos. Wright, son of Col. Thomas Wright, to Miss Rebecca P. Lux.	07/05/1823
Departed this life, last Thursday evening, after a lingering illness, Rachel Emmerson Lamb, wife of Isaac Lamb, merchant, of this city. The cheap panegyricks of newspapers, and the dignity of the present subject, forbid an indulgence by the writer, in a wish to record in many words, a high sense of the departed worth. The deceased was a minister of the Gospel, in the Society of Friends; of distinguished humility, and of corresponding benevolence and consistent life and character. A native of Kent county, Delaware.	07/05/1823
Departed this life, in May last, at St. Jago de Cuba, William, son of Edward Gott, late of Baltimore county, deceased, in the 24th year of his age.	07/05/1823

Marriage and Death Notices	Date
On Thursday evening last, by the Rev. Mr. Kennerley, Mr. Jacob Boston, to Miss Susannah Henrietta Hines, both of this city.	07/07/1823
On Saturday evening last, by the Rev. Mr. Shane, Mr. Frederick Davis to Miss Jane Johnston, all of this city.	07/07/1823
By the Rev. Dr. Glendy, on the evening of Thursday last, Dr. William W. Mason, of the Eastern Shore, to Miss Miranda Bradford, of this city.	07/08/1823
On the 6th inst., Francis Marion, son of Mr. John Dobbins, aged 3 years and eight months.	07/08/1823
Departed this transitory scene, on the 7th of last month, Dr. Richard C. Edgar, aged 33, of the United States Navy. He was in the ship Decoy, attached to Com. Porter's Squadron in the West Indies; was a native of this state, and has been in the service upwards of 16 years. By this dispensation of Providence, an affectionate wife has been deprived of a kind and indulgent husband, and a child of the parental affection of a good father; and numerous friends have been called to drop the sympathetic tears of friendship for the memory of one who had endeared himself to them by the faithful discharge of his public and private duties of life.	07/08/1823
At Pleasant Prospect, Prince George's county, Maryland, on the 3rd inst., Isaac Duckett, Esq., in the 71st year of his age. To those who have been acquainted with this gentleman, nothing need be said in commendation of his character. Through his whole life, he was distinguished by a peculiar mildness and gentleness of disposition, by unwavering integrity and uprightness in all his intercourse with the world, and by a constant kindness and urbanity of manners, which rendered him at once an object of reverence and love. To a character which, in the eyes of men, was always esteemed faultless, there were added, in the latter part of his life, the peculiar charms of religion; and from the period of this important era of his life, he literally spent his days in "doing good." It is, therefore, wih sincere regret, though arising only from a sense of their own deprivation, that his family and friends have regarded the departure of his spirit from its earthly abode. "We mourn, but, rather, that we are left behind."	07/09/1823
At Reisters Town, Baltimore county, on the 3rd inst., after a short illness, Mrs. Rebecca Staples, consort of Mr. William J. Staples, aged 56 years.	07/09/1823
Departed this life, on Tuesday last, after a short illness, Mr. Solomon Jennings, in the 39th year of his age, leaving a wife and child to deplore	07/10/1822

309

Marriage and Death Notices	Date
his loss.	
At Mount Tammany, on Saturday last, after a short illness, Matthew Van Lear, Esq., long a very respectable citizen of Washington county, Md., in the 69th year of his age.	07/10/1823
Last evening, by the Rev. Mr. Moranville, Mr. James Williamson, to Miss Bridget Elizabeth O'Brian, both of this city.	07/11/1823
On Thursday evening, by the Rev. Dr. Wyatt, Mr. John S. Linvill, to Mrs. Maria Linvill, all of this city.	07/12/1823
On Thursday evening, by the Rev. Dr. Glendy, Mr. Robert Howard, to Miss Phebe Ann Hayes, all of this city.	07/12/1823
On Thursday evening last, by the Rev. Mr. Soule, Mr. John Keence, Jr., to Miss Mary Ann, youngest daughter of Martin Bever, both of Baltimore county.	07/12/1823
On Tuesday evening, by the Most Rev. Archbishop Mareschal, Mr. John W. Smith, to Miss Louisa T. Marce.	07/17/1823
Departed this life, on the 15th inst., in the 62nd year of his age, after a painful and lingering sickness, which he bore with Christian fortitude and resignation, Samuel Byrnes, long a respectable merchant of this city, and a member of the religious society of Friends.	07/18/1823
On Thursday evening last, by the Rev. Mr. Snyder, Mr. John Ledley, to Miss Elizabeth Euler, both of this city.	07/19/1823
On Thursday evening last, by the Rev. Joseph Shane, Mr. Francis Rawlins, to Miss Nancy Stewart, all of Anne Arundel county.	07/19/1823
On Thursday evening last, by the Rev. Dr. Roberts, Mr. William S. Coath, to Miss Sarah Harriet Green, all of this city.	07/19/1823
In the Province of Texas, in January last, Mr. Peter L. White, formerly an industrious and respectable Mechanic, of this city leaving an aged mother, and a numerous circle of relatives and friends to deplore their irreparable loss.	07/22/1823
At sea, on the 28th of May last, on his passage from Mocha to Baltimore, after a long and painful illness, which he bore with Christian fortitude, Mr. John F. Paine, aged 23 years. He was a native of the island of Guernsey. He has left a large circle of friends and relations to mourn	07/23/1823

Marriage and Death Notices	Date
their irreparable loss.	
On Tuesday evening last, by the Rev. Dr. Glendy, Prentis Chubb, Esq., of Richmond, Virginia, to Miss Caroline Munroe, of this city.	07/24/1823
On Tuesday evening last, by the Rev. Mr. Nevins, Richard H. Douglass, Esq., to Letitia Grace, eldest daughter of the late Hugh McCurdy, Esq.	07/24/1823
On the 15th inst., at the residence of Mr. Joseph Van Lear, near William's port, by the Rev. John Lind, Col. Otho H. Williams, clerk of Washington county court, to Miss Eliza Van Lear, daughter of the late Maj. Wm. Van Lear.	07/25/1823
On Thursday evening last, by the Rev. Mr. Helfenstein, Mr. Herman Jordan, to Miss Maria Elizabeth Sanders, both of this city.	07/26/1823
On Thursday evening last, by the Rev. Mr. Healey, Mr. Henry Lauderman, to Mrs. Leonora Reiter, all of this city.	07/26/1823
On Tuesday, 22nd inst., after a very protracted illness, in the 27th year of her age, Mrs. Eliza Delcher, consort of Mr. John Delcher. She has left a bereaved husband and three small children; but the tenor of her short and useful life, gives to the grieving relatives and friends, who witnessed her bodily sufferings, for a long time past, the comforting assurance that her troubles now are over, and that her earthly trials were of short duration; because she was soon fitted for the awful and solemn change which has taken place. When vigorous life flowed in her veins, she did not forget her God; when she passed through the valley of the shadow of death, her God did not leave or forsake her, but enabled her, through faith in the redeemer, to maintain a successful conflict with the king of terrors, and exhibit to those who gathered round her deathbed scene, a bright example of resignation, piety, and hope, for "blessed are the pure in heart, for their's is the kingdom of Heaven."	07/28/1823
On Thursday, 24th inst., Mrs. Esther Elder, in the 60th year of her age.	07/28/1823
On the 27th inst., David Dupuy, son of Mr. John Dobbin, aged 2 years and 5 months.	07/29/1823
On Saturday morning, the 6th inst., Dr. Samuel L. P. Roberts, eldest son of the Rev. Dr. Roberts, of this city, aged 23 years and 7 months. O how uncertain is human life – 'twas but a few days since we saw him; then he was in perfect health; then he bid fair to live his three score years and ten. But he no longer holds a place among us – where is he? He, who was idolized by his family, has passed into the eternal world.	07/30/1823

311

Marriage and Death Notices	Date
Yes, when it was least expected, death suddenly deprived a father of his son, a mother of her hope, a wife of her husband, a babe of its father, before its infant tongue could lisp his name, and relations of the object of their affections. In the bloom of youth, he has been snatched by the ruthless hand of the destroyer from the fond embrace of her who loved him dearly. Well may it be said that his decease has made a wound which time itself can never heal. His conduct thro' out his sickness assures us that he has made a happy escape. This fact bouys up his friends and relations under their present affliction and distress. Reader, are you still out of the ark of safey? Take heed unto your steps, and hearken unto the exhortation of the Prophet, "Prepare to meet thy God." "Youth like the spring will soon be gone." For a proof of these words of the Poet, look around you; daily you behold one and another of your young friends and acquaintances dropping into eternity. Seeing, therefore, that your youth is not proof against death, permit me to exhort you "to work while it is called to-day, lest the night of death come upon you, when no man can work."	
On Tuesday evening last, by the Rev. John Reader Keitch, Dr. David Gittings, to Miss Julia Ann W., second daughter of Col. John Beale Howard, of Baltimore county.	07/31/1823
On Tuesday evening last, in Anne Arundel county, by the Rev. Mr. Welch, Mr. Nicholas Woodward, to Miss Sarah, eldest daughter of Richd. Gambrill, Esq.	07/31/1823
Departed this life on the 29th instant, Ann Catherine, youngest daughter of Jno. G. Neale, aged 17 months.	07/31/1823
On Thursday evening, by the Rev. Mr. Guest, Mr. John H. Browning, of this city, to Miss Margaretta Maranda Hunter, of Philadelphia.	08/01/1823
On Thursday evening last, by the Rev. Mr. Smith, Mr. Jacob Knipe to Miss Elizabeth Baudson, both of this city.	08/01/1823
On Thursday evening last, by the Rev. Mr. Uhlhorn, Mr. John P. Benson, to Miss Lydia Yoner, all of this city.	08/01/1823
On last Thursday afternoon, by the Rev. Dr. Elbert, Mr. Philip Bowen, to Miss Mary Ann, eldest daughter of Mr. Stephen Harryman, all of Patapsco Neck, Baltimore county.	08/01/1823
In the state of Illinois, on Thursday, the 26th of June last, Mr. Shadrick G. Bond, of Baltimore, to Miss Ann Maria Todd, of the former place.	08/01/1823

Marriage and Death Notices	Date
In Frederick county, Mr. Levi Hughes. In Philadelphia, Mr. Wm. Bartram, in the 85th year of his age. At Frankfort, Pa., Mr. Frederick Montmollin, aged 60 years, formerly of Philadelphia. At New Market, Va., Mrs. Eleanor Schmucker, wife of the Rev. Samuel S., formerly of York, Pa. Near Middleburg, Va., Mrs. W. Noland, wife of Lloyd Noland, Esq., in the 30th year of her age, daughter of the late Maj. Burr Powell. At Ellicott's Mills, Mrs. Augusta Denny. Near Sharpsburg, Dr. John J. Hays, aged about 25 years. In Washington county, Md., Mrs. Barbara Cellar, in the 65th year of her age. In Fredericktown, Mrs. Sophia Myers, consort of Mr. Wm. H. Myers, of the E. Shore of Md. In Dorchester county, Md., Col. John S. Macnamara, in the 68th year of his age. In Talbot county, Mrs. Susan Bowdle.	08/01/1823
On Thursday evening last, by the Rev. Mr. Helfenstein, Mr. William Russell, to Miss Mary Fouble, both of this city.	08/02/1823
On the 23rd ult., at his residence, near Belle Air, Harford county, in the 80th year of his age, Mr. Buckler J. Bond, long a respectable farmer of that county.	08/02/1823
By the Rev. W. E. Wyatt, on Saturday morning last, Mr. Levin Hall Dunkin, to Mrs. Matilda Liddle, eldest daughter of Capt. N. Myers, all of this city.	08/04/1823
On Wednesday morning, the 30th inst., after a short illness, in the 46th year of his age, Mr. Samuel Mullen, of this city.	08/04/1823
On the 28th July, Eliza Ann, daughter of Wade Hough, aged 6 years.	08/04/1823
At her residence, in Franklin street, on the 31st ult., Mrs. Amelia Zimmerman, wife of Mr. Jacob Zimmerman, in the 30th year of her age.	08/05/1823
On Monday evening last, by the Rev. Dr. Roberts, Mr. James S. Dykes, to Miss Ann Matilda Ford, both of this city.	08/06/1823
Last evening, by the Rev. Mr. Schroeder, Mr. William Schroeder, to Sophia, third daughter of the late Charles Ghequiere, Esq., both of this city.	08/06/1823
Last evening, by the Rev. Mr. Beschter, Mr. William Lambert, to Miss Elizabeth Boston, both of this city.	08/08/1823
On Monday evening last, by the Rev. Mr. Dashiell, Mr. John Rose, of Pennsylvania, to Mrs. Ann Danley, of this city.	08/08/1823

Marriage and Death Notices	Date
On Tuesday evening, by the Rev. Mr. Valiant, Mr. Edward P. Groom, Miss Eliza Garritee, of this city.	08/08/1823
On the 21st of July last, in Jeremie, island of St. Domingo, Mr. Francis Hoffman, late of Baltimore, in the 20th year of his age; a young gentleman highly esteemed by all who had the pleasure of his acquaintance.	08/09/1823
On the 6th inst., of the Dropsy, after a lingering illness of 12 months, Mr. Eben. Graves, aged 71 years. He was a native of Dedham, Mass., but for the last thirty years a resident of this city.	08/09/1823
On the 31st ult., near the borough of Hanover, Pa., Mrs. Magdalin Gitt, aged 101 years and 10 months.	08/09/1823
On Thursday evening last, by the Rev. Mr. Guest, Mr. William Pitt, to Miss Elizabeth Hubbard, both of this city.	08/11/1823
On Tuesday evening last, by the Rev. Mr. Nevins, John A. Brown, Esq., to Grace, daughter of the late Dr. George Brown, of this city.	08/11/1823
On Tuesday evening last, after a long and protracted illness, which he bore with Christian resignation, Mr. Robert D. Allen, in the 45th year of his age. He has left a wife and two children in sorrow and calamity, who deplore his retirement from this dismal world with unceasing tenderness and affection.	08/11/1823
At St. Thomas, on the 19th or 20th ultimo, Capt. D. M. Miller, of schnr. Topaz, of Baltimore.	08/11/1823
On Sunday evening last, by the Rev. Mr. Stansbury, Mr. J. Jones, Esq., to Miss Mary Elizabeth Eagle, all of this city.	08/12/1823
On Monday last, after a short, but sever illness, Miss Eliza Ann Mathiot, eldest daughter of George Mathiot, aged 15 years. "Christ called her to his peaceful breast, "And promised her eternal rest."	08/12/1823
On the afternoon of the 5th inst., Susanna, wife of George Harris, Sr., a member of the Society of Friends, in the 62nd year of her age.	08/13/1823
Last evening, in the 53rd year of his age, Mr. Peter Fowble. His friends and acquaintance are respectfully invited to attend his funeral, at 4 o'clock, this afternoon, from his dwelling, No. 120 North Howard street.	08/13/1823

Marriage and Death Notices	Date
At the house of his father, in Washington city, on the 24th of July, Mr. Basil W. Beall, of the Treasury Department, in the 27th year of his age. His complaint was a pulmonary affection, which formerly had threatened him, but for some time past, had left room for better hopes.	08/13/1823
On Tuesday evening last, by the Rev. Mr. Soule, Mr. James Robins, to Miss Elizabeth, eldest daughter of Mr. Henry Starr, all of this city.	08/14/1823
In Baltimore county, Dr. David S. Gittings, to Miss Julian W. Howard, second daughter of Col. John B. Howard.	08/14/1823
On Thursday, 14th, by the Rev. Mr. Guest, Mr. Samuel Smith to Miss Elizabeth Young, both of this city.	08/15/1823
On Thursday last, by the Rev. Dr. Jennings, Mr. Thomas Phenix, to Miss Martha Dawson, both of this place.	08/15/1823
Yesterday, Isabella Catherine, youngest daughter of Capt. Francis Forster, of this city.	08/15/1823
On the 14th inst., by the Rev. Dr. Kurtz, Mr. Jas. Buck, to Miss Louisa Margaret Simering, both of this city.	08/16/1823
On Saturday, the 9th inst., after several weeks illness, much and deservedly regretted, Miss Maria Craig, daughter of Thomas Craig, of Baltimore county.	08/16/1823
Yesterday morning, Thomas W. Cameraw, aged about 56 years. He was a descendant of Africa, and for many years carried on an extensive business in New York, where he was very generally known. He, among others, left this country for Sierra Leone, Africa, and after remaining there some time, returned to Baltimore.	08/16/1823
On last Sabbath morning, Mr. Wm. Dillehunt, at his residence, in Hagerstown, Washington county, in the fifty-eighth year of his age leaving a disconsolate widow and eight children to lament their irreparable loss. In life, he was an ornament to society, in death he will ever be remembered as the faithful friend, the affectionate husband, and the tender parent.	08/16/1823
On Friday morning, the 15th inst., after a painful illness of six weeks, Tench Tilghman, aged three years, two months, and twenty-eight days, only son of Mr. Matthew K. Stone, of this city.	08/18/1823
On Friday, the 15th inst., in the third year of his age, Joshua Brown,	08/18/1823

Marriage and Death Notices	Date
eldest child of Mr. M. P. Mitchell, of this city.	
A few days ago, at his residence, in Montgomery county, Maryland, Col. George Magruder, in the 27th year of his age. Col. Magruder was ill only 24 hours, having, during his whole life enjoyed a robust health. He was formerly, for many years, a resident of Georgetown, and commander of one of our regiments of Militia. He was, at the time of his death, one of the Judges of the Orphans' Court, of his native country, and enjoyed general esteem. He has left two daughters to lament his death.	08/18/1823
On Thursday morning, the 14th inst., Mr. Robert Brotherton, formerly of Green-castle, Pennsylvania, in the 32nd year of his age, of a long protracted illness, which he bore with Christian resignation.	08/18/1823
On the 11th inst., Sarah A. Hough, consort of Edward S. Hough, a member of the Society of Friends.	08/18/1823
At Carlisle, Pa., on Thursday, the 7th inst., after a short illness, Miss Emeline Hamilton, daughter of the late Judge Hamilton, aged 18 years. She died trusting in the mercy of her Redeemer, and looking joyfully to the hour when corruption shall put on incorruption, mortality immortality, and death be swallowed up in Victory.	08/18/1823
At Philadelphia, on the evening of the 15th inst., by the Rev. Dr. Abercrombie, Mr. Robert Hewitt, of Baltimore, to Miss Charlotte Hupfeld, of the former place.	08/20/1823
At Thomastown, Pa., on the 5th inst., of Typhus Fever, Mr. William Harr, of Baltimore, in the 24th year of his age. He was a young man much admired and esteemed by all who knew him, and has left a disconsolate mother, and a numerous circle of relations and friends, to lament this afflicting dispensation of Providence.	08/20/1823
On Wednesday last, 13th inst., at Havre de Grave, Harford county, after a short, but painful illness, Mr. Moses Carver, aged 35 years.	08/20/1823
On Tuesday, 19th inst., at 4 o'clock P. M., Mrs. Sarah Taylor, consort of Mr. Samuel Taylor, in the 30th year of her age. She is much regretted, and has left a numerous train of her acquaintance to mourn her irreparable loss.	08/22/1823
Departed this life, on the 12th inst., Mr. Peter Fowble, being 53 years, 2 months, and 12 days old, a native of the state of Maryland and county of Baltimore, and a long and respectable inhabitant of this city, and for	08/23/1823

Marriage and Death Notices	Date
many years an acceptable member of the late Rev. Mr. Otterbein's congregation. He was truly an honest man, moderate in all his deportment, and mild in his general demeanor. For many years an adherent to the principles of Christianity, and professor of Religion, in which profession he was generally approved of by those who were acquainted with him, for by the confidence of his brethren, he was raised to the office of an elder (or to the vestry) of the church to which he belonged. During his late and severe affliction, the efficiency of the doctrines of the gospel, and the power of religion upon his mind, were particularly demonstrated, for when his dissolution was seen approaching with rapidity, he was not affrighted from his hope in God, but having unlimited faith in Christ Jesus, he was enabled to possess himself in patience and resignation to the divine will, and speak of his acceptance of the Deity, and the prospect of eternal life, with the greatest assurance. And while in the agonies of death, surrounded by his affectionate family, accompanied by his pious Pastor and Christian brethren, he rejoiced with great joy, in expectation of the glories and felicities of the upper world – in this frame of mind, he closed his eyes to sleep in the arms of death. Thus lived and thus died this man of God. In reference to his case, may we quote this portion of God's word: "Blessed are the dead which die in the Lord from henceforth, yea, saith the spirit, that they may rest from their labors; and their works do follow them." A. G. P.	
Also, on Saturday, the 16th inst., in Accomack county, Va., Mr. Joseph M. Rowland, merchant, late of Baltimore.	08/23/1823
On Saturday evening last, by the Rev. Mr. Pipher, Mr. James Boyd to Mrs. Arraninta Gray, both of Baltimore county.	08/25/1823
On Thursday evening last, by the Rev. Mr. Valiant, Mr. Aquila Sparks, to Miss Sarah A. Merryman.	08/26/1823
On Tuesday, by the Rev. Mr. Valiant, Mr. John Brinkman to Miss Matilda Wadenbach.	08/26/1823
On Wednesday evening last, at the residence of his son Jacob, in Frederick county, Maryland, after a very severe illness of five days, in the 79th year of his age, Mr. George Poe, formerly of this city, much regretted by all of his friends and acquaintance.	08/26/1823
In Albany, suddenly, on the 21st inst., Mr. John Cook, state librarian and proprietor of the city reading rooms.	08/26/1823

317

Marriage and Death Notices	Date
In Columbia, S. C., on Wednesday evening, 13th inst., after an illness of about nine days, Mr. George Blackburn, formerly professor of Mathematics in the South Carolina College. Mr. Blackburn was one of the first Mathematicians of the age; he was a native of Ireland, where, in early life, he had received a very liberal education; and, after his immigration to this country, was employed in various seminaries of learning, as a teacher of mathematics. The peculiar facility he possessed of communicating knowledge to others, together with his extensive acquirements, enabled him to fill the various stations he from time to time held, with distinguished reputation as a teacher of that science. He taught in the male academy of this place up to the day of his last illness.	08/27/1823
On Tuesday, 24th inst., Mrs. Mary Mettee, late consort of Mr. Charles A. Mettee, in the 37th year of her age. She was a member of the Methodist Church and in the profession of religion 23 years. She was indeed a faithful companion, a tender mother, and kind friend. The vacuum occasioned by her death will not soon be filled up. She will long live in the recollection of those who knew her worth. In her life and death, the beauties and advantages of religion were exemplified, for throughout her life, she was unassuming, uniform and agreeable in her deportment, and in her departing moments triumphant. Then was she enabled to say she had peace with God and prospect of Heaven, and with these evidences present with her, without a struggle or groan breathed her last. It is then matter of consolation to the mournful family and connections to think that their loss is the infinite gain of their departed friend.	08/28/1823
At Pleasant Hill, near Port Tobacco, on the 16th inst., Miss Lucretia, daughter of Basil Spaulding, Esq., of Charles county, Md. In the death of this amiable and interesting young lady, society has lost a valuable member and her numerous relatives and affectionate companion.	08/28/1823
On Wednesday evening, by the Rev. Edwd. J. Reis, Mr. Francis Deluce Dungan, to Miss Catherine Reiman Peters, both of this city.	08/29/1823
On the 21st inst., after a short illness, Mr. William Wilkins, in the 87th year of his age.	08/29/1823
On the 31st July, at his plantation in St. Bartholomew's Parish, S. C., Capt. John Herbert Dent, of the U. States Navy, in the 42nd year of his age.	
At the Plaquemin Bend, near New Orleans, Lt. Horace C. Storey, an accomplished officer of the United States corps of Engineers.	08/29/1823

Marriage and Death Notices	Date
In Annapolis, on Friday night last, Mr. Telk Telkin, baker. He was a native of Germany, and came to this city from Baltimore.	08/29/1823
On Thursday evening last, by the Rev. Mr. Bartow, Mr. Christopher Abey to Mrs. Martha Morris.	08/30/1823
On Thursday evening last, by the Rev. Mr. Bartow, Mr. William Kirby, to Miss Mary Doxey, all of this city.	08/30/1823
On Thursday evening, by the Rev. Mr. Valiant, Mr. Charles Sprinkle, to Miss Pernon Sleeper, all of this city.	08/30/1823
On Thursday evening last, by the Rev. Mr. Uhlhorn, Mr. George Sauerhoff, to Mrs. Maria Elizabeth Kurdlefink Wildt, both of this city.	08/30/1823
Last evening, at Wester Ogle, Baltimore County, by the Rev. Mr. Henshaw, Mr. M. Rogers, of this city, to Mary Jane, daughter of Maj. Robert Lyon.	08/30/1823
On the 28th inst., Mr. Matthew W. Simmonds, of this city, in the 26th year of his age. In the death of Mr. Simmonds, a worthy family has sustained an irreparable loss, and the community is deprived of one of its important supports, the unwearied example of a persevering and conscientiously honest man. When it can be said in truth of a departed friend, that he strove with all his might, to do justly, to love mercy, and to walk humbly before his God, with becoming submission to the will of Heaven, let all who knew him say, it is enough. Infinite wisdom knows best when to take such men, from the toils and evils of this mortal life! "The Lord giveth and the Lord taketh away, and Blessed be the name of the Lord!"	08/30/1823
On the 6th inst., at Potts-grove, Pa., Mr. James Jackson, of Baltimore, in the 25th year of his age.	08/30/1823
On the 24th inst., Mary Jane, youngest daughter of D. G. Stansbury, in the second year of her age; being the second child her fond parents have been deprived of in less than one month.	08/30/1823
Departed this life, on the night of the 19th inst., at his farm, in Harford county, Dr. James Glasgow, in the 45th year of his age. Dr. Glasgow formerly resided several years in this city, where he was highly esteemed, as well for his medical knowledge as for his amiable manners – that same just estimation was entertained for him by a large circle of his neighbors in Harford, while those who most intimately knew him	08/30/1823

Marriage and Death Notices	Date
felt for him the sincerest attachment.	
On the 28th ult., in Friends' Meeting House, at Deer Creek, Dr. Ezra Gillingham, of Baltimore, to Mary E. Cole, daughter of the late Isaac Cole, of Harford county.	09/01/1823
On the evening of the 25th ult., by the Rev. Mr. Guest, John Robinson, to Eleanor Wheelan, all of this city.	09/01/1823
On the evening of Sunday last, Mr. Amos Chapman, in the 43rd year of his age. The deceased was a native of the town of Groton, Connecticut, but for a number of years a respectable inhabitant of this city.	09/01/1823
At Washington, Mrs. Martha Pratt, of that place, and lately of Baltimore, after a severe indisposition.	09/01/1823
By the Rev. Dr. Jennings, on Saturday, the 30th ult., John Shaffer to Ann Busly.	09/02/1823
By the Rev. Dr. Jennings, on the 31st ult., John Rose to Harriet Bennet.	09/02/1823
Yesterday, after a severe illness, Mr. Henry Green, in the 63rd year of his age. His friends and acquaintance are requested to attend his funeral, from his late dwelling, near Howard's Park, this afternoon, at 3 o'clock.	09/02/1823
On board the brig Oswego, June 26th, on her passage from Cape Mesurado to St. Jago, Richard B. Seaton, Esq., of Baltimore, late U. States assistant agent at Monrobia, aged 26 years.	09/02/1823
Departed this life, on Friday, the 23rd inst., Miss Amy Amanda Ware, second daughter of the Rev. Thomas Ware, of Chestertown, Md., aged 19 years and 9 months. She died with Christian fortitude, and now is realizing the blest promises of the gospel in heaven. Esteemed by all who were acquainted with her, admired by all who had the least connection of intimacy, panegyric is useless. She was a perfect model of purity and virtue. If ever religion exhibited its beauties in the countenance and actions of any human being, they were highly represented in Miss Ware. She lived a Christian, and died exalting in the same faith. To decorate this puerile obituary by lively imagination would be useless – the subject is too serious. On her death bed illness, she had all her intimate acquaintance assembled to bid them a final adieu. She administered her blessing to all by saying, "seek ye that religion which is in Jesus Christ, which will ensure you in that blessed abode a seat at his right hand, and a crown that will fadeth not away."	09/02/1823

Marriage and Death Notices	Date
Her parents, I regret to state, have lost an affectionate and pious daughter, her friends a religious associate, and society divested of one of its first ornaments. Irreparable is the loss, but such is the fate of mortal beings.	
On Monday evening, Capt. John H. Wood, of this city. His Masonic brethren are invited to attend his funeral. The procession will be formed at Washington Lodge, No. 3, this day, at 3 o'clock.	09/03/1823
On the 28th of June last, in St. Jago de Cuba, of the prevailing fever of that place, Mr. Henry J. W. Johnston, son of Mr. George Johnston, of Baltimore, in the 20th year of his age. Mr. Johnston was a youth of amiable manners, much esteemed by his acquaintances in this city, by whom his premature death is sincerely regretted.	09/03/1823
On Tuesday evening last, 2nd instant, by the Rev. Mr. Guest, Mr. Philip Boyer, of Tioga county, New York, to Miss Catherine Klinefelter, of this city.	09/04/1823
Last evening, Mr. William Parks, in the 61st year of his age, thirty-three years a resident of Fell's Point, and thirty-four years a member of the Methodist Society.	09/04/1823
On 24th Aug., at his country residence, in Roxborough, Mr. Wm. T. Stockton, of this city. Possessing a constitution unusually sound and healthful, it is believed, he scarcely knew sickness until the disease which has proved fatal to him, and so great were his bodily vigor and activity that his prowess in manly exercises was acknowledged by every competitor. Yet these are qualities of which the sad occasion would not invite us to speak were it no to impart to the reader a deep impression how true it is that "the race is not to the swift, nor he battle to he strong." If health scarcely interrupted, and extraordinary physical powers could give an assurance, the deceased had in an eminent degree, such assurance of length of years. But now, in the very meridian of his life, he is cut down – fallen 'ere time had scattered her earliest frost o'er his head, or bent his manly form! His heart was warm, open, frank, and generous; to this, his friends and neighbours bear their sorrowing testimony. Of his enterprize, the community have knowledge, and all who so knew him, will testify that he was honest and just in his dealings. His mind was sound, strong and quick, with an elevated independence and chivalrick spirit that challenged respect and attracted admiration. The loss of such a man in the mid-career of usefulness	09/04/1823
By the Rev. Mr. Higgins, on Tuesday evening last, Mr. Henry Stevenson, of Baltimore, to Miss Mary Owing, of Frederick county,	09/05/1823

Marriage and Death Notices	Date
Maryland.	
In this city, on Wednesday morning, in the 5th year of her age, Laura Ann, only daughter of Joseph T. Mitchell, of Kent county, Md.	09/05/1823
On Thursday evening last, at the Catholic Church, Saratoga street, by the Rev. Mr. Smith, Francis O'Neil, Esq., of Dublin, to the amiable Miss Olivia Mary Corey, of Philadelphia.	09/06/1823
On Thursday evening, the Rev. John Hagerty, in the 77th year of his age, who has been an acceptable minister in the Methodist Episcopal Church, nearly half a century. As a man, Mr. Hagerty was honest, frank, and courteous; as a Christian, ardent to his love to God and man; as a minister of the Gospel, laborious, useful, and persevering. To the close of his mortal career, he retained an unshaken confidence in God, and departed in full assurance of immortality and eternal life.	09/06/1823
On the 24th of Aug. last, at Dam Quarter, Somerset County, Md., Mrs. Mary Parks, aged 116 years and 5 month.	09/06/1823
On Friday, the 5th inst., Edward, youngest son of the late Edward Stiles, of this city.	09/08/1823
On the 24th inst., in the 28th year of her age, after a distressing illness of four days, Mrs. Maria Hammond, wife of Mr. Wm. L. Hammond, merchant, and third daughter of the late Dr. Andrew Aiken, of this city. Greatly endeared to her relatives and friends, by a most amiable disposition, her loss is afflicting to many, besides her surviving partner, to whose care she has left a tender pledge of mutual affection. May that Divine Being, who has thus suddenly removed the mother to the mansions of eternal rest, afford his all powerful protection to the bereaved and innocent infant and religious consolation to the lonely and afflicted parent.	09/08/1823
On Wednesday last, after a short, but severe illness, Mrs. Maria Chapman, wife of Amos Chapman, whom she only survived three days – the deceased was a native of Newport, Rhode Island, but her husband had lived a number of years in this city.	09/08/1823
In Alexandria, Louisiana, on the 30th July last, of the prevailing fever, Mr. George Rich, a native of Boston, and formerly a resident of this city.	09/08/1823
At Tammany's Mount, near Williamsport, on Thursday afternoon, August 21, after a few days sickness, Miss Mary Finley, daughter of the	09/08/1823

Marriage and Death Notices	Date
late Ebenezer Finley, Esq., of Baltimore.	
At Thompson's Island, Lt. R. M. Potter, of Philadelphia.	09/09/1823
On Sunday morning, after a short illness, John Wells, Esq., Counsellor at Law.	09/09/1823
On Tuesday morning last, by the Rev. W. E. Wyatt, Mr. George Evans, to Mrs. Emily Matthews, both of this city.	09/10/1823
On Tuesday evening last, by the Rev. Mr. Shane, Mr. John H. M'Fadon, to Miss Matilda Jones, all of this city.	09/10/1823
On Sunday evening, the 7th inst., after a short illness, which she bore with Christian patience and resignation, Mrs. Jane, wife of Mr. Wm. H. Richardson, of this city, in the 39th year of her age. In noting the death of this truly estimable woman, we cannot sufficiently express the deep anguish it has occasioned. A few days since, we beheld her in all the fullness of health, dispensing around the circle of her acquaintance, that happiness which always attends the virtuous and the good, and affording to her affectionate husband, from the rich treasures of her mind, all the felicity that mortals can enjoy, while by her example she was training up her youthful family, in the path of innocence and virtue. Though her sudden death has inflicted a deep wound in the hearts of her relations and friends, the change to her was we trust a blessed one; for, "Blessed are the dead who die in the Lord, from henceforth; Yea saih the spirit, that they may rest from their labours, and their works do follow them."	09/10/1823
On Wednesday, the 3rd inst., Mrs. Frances M. Garrison, of a protracted illness, which she bore with Christian fortitude.	09/10/1823
On Friday morning, September 5th, George P., eldest son of Charles Constable, in the 32nd year of his age.	09/10/1823
On the morning of the 21st Aug., at his residence, in Montgomery County, Md., Mr. Elijah Veirs, in the 64th year of his age. He expired in the arms of a friend, surrounded by his children. The deceased was a Christian and a strictly honest man. His virtues rendered him a citizen of high respectability, and his talents a most useful member of society. In the death of this individual, patriotism has lost a sterling friend, integrity a bright example, and Christianity a faithful advocate. To know him was to venerate him. None will contemplate his loss wihout regret; none will learn his death wihout a tear.	09/10/1823

Marriage and Death Notices	Date
Yesterday morning, at Friends Meeting, Elkridge, Anne Arundel County, Joshua W. Canby, of Baltimore county, to Esther E., eldest daughter of Joseph Lowens, Esq., of Elkridge.	09/11/1823
On Wednesday evening last, by the Rev. Mr. Valiant, Mr. Samuel E. Husband, to Miss Mary Ann Snowden, of Anne Arundel county.	09/11/1823
In Troy, N. Y., on Monday evening, 1st inst., Dr. Eli Burritt, in the 51st year of his age.	09/11/1823
In Bedford, Penn., on Sunday, a week, on his way to the west, Capt. William M. Littlejohn, of Cumberland, formerly of the U. S. army. His remains were interred with military honors.	09/11/1823
At New Orleans, Aug. 7, Capt. Welsh, of the ship Highlander.	09/11/1823
Last evening, by the Rev. Mr. Sparks, Mr. William Miles, merchant, to Miss Sarah Mickle, all of this city.	09/12/1823
On Tuesday evening last, by the Rt. Rev. Bishop Kemp, Mr. George Hayne, to Eliza, daughter of Mr. John Cole.	09/12/1823
Last evening, by the Rev. E. J. Reis, Mr. Wm. B. Shields, to Miss Eliza Jones, both of this city.	09/12/1823
On Monday, the 8th inst., at the residence of her father, Mr. William Gibson, Mrs. Harriet Crosdale, relict of the late Mr. George Crosdale – and, on Tuesday, the 9th, George, their son, in the 13th year of his age.	09/12/1823
On the 7th inst., Mrs. Mary Lansfield, in the 49th year of her age; a native of Ireland, and long a resident of this city.	09/12/1823
On Sunday last, Mrs. Mary Witman, consort of Mr. Geo. Witman.	09/12/1823
On the 4th inst., at Mount Erin, Henrico county, Va., Alexander Fulton, Esq., aged 49 years. He was a native of Ireland, whence he emigrated in early life to Baltimore and, for the last sixteen years, a resident of this place.	09/12/1823
At Louisville, on the 24th ult., Miss Sarah Heafer, late of Baltimore.	09/12/1823
On Thursday evening, by the Rev. Dr. Glendy, Capt. John Staples, to Miss Margaret Craig.	09/13/1823
On Thursday evening, the 28th ult., after a short, though painful illness, which he bore with Christian patience, the Hon. John Mooris, Chief	09/13/1823

324

Marriage and Death Notices	Date
Justice of the Orphans' Court of Harford county.	
At Frankfort, Ken., Joseph C. Breckenridge, Esq.	09/13/1823
On Wednesday evening last, by the Rev. Mr. Bartow, William H. Johnson, Esq., of Talbot county, Md., to Miss Ann Eliza Currie, of this city.	09/15/1823
On Tuesday morning, the 9th inst., after a short illness, Mrs. Ann Sweetser, consort of Seth Sweetser, in the 5th year of her age leaving a full assurance of her acceptance of God.	09/15/1823
At his seat, near this city, on the 14th inst., and in the 63rd year of his age, Dr. Anthony Mann. Dr. Mann was born at Marseilles, in France, and emigrated to Massachusetts, during the war of Independence, in which he served some time, as surgeon in a letter of marque, and of which he cherished the patriotic principles during his life. He settled in Baltimore, soon after the peace of 1783, and for many years kept an extensive drug store. He was uniformly just in his dealings in that capacity, and when retiring from business, he helped to improve the vicinity of this city, by introducing and cultivating, successfully, many valuable exotics, as well as fruits, as culinary and ornamental, but his universal benevolence and social disposition, will cause his memory to be more particularly cherished by those who had the pleasure of his acquaintance.	09/16/1823
On Sunday, the 7th inst., at his farm, in Baltimore county, after a short, but severe illness, which he bore with Christian fortitude and a mind perfectly resigned, Mr. Thomas Long, leaving a disconsolate wife and a numerous circle of friends and relations to deplore their loss.	09/16/1823
On the 13th inst., after a short illness, Mr. Robert M'Clellan, Jr., aged 18 years and 7 months.	09/16/1823
At St. Thomas, on the 30th of Aug., Mr. Francois, merchant, of the firm Francois & Co.	09/16/1823
At Norfolk, Mr. Levin B. Simmons, purser's steward of the U. S. ship Peacock; Mrs. Martha Oatest; Mrs. Sarah Shelton.	09/16/1823
On Tuesday, 16th inst., by the Rt. Rev. Bishop Kemp, Mr. Nicholas R. Merryman to Miss Ann Maria Gott.	09/17/1823
This morning, at 1 o'clock, in the 28th year of his age, John Marshall, first lieutenant of the revenue cutter Active, leaving a wife and 3	09/17/1823

Marriage and Death Notices	Date
children to lament his loss.	
On Friday last, the 12th inst., in the 21st year of her age, Mrs. Anna Eliza, wife of Mr. Matthew Pope Mitchell, of this city, and eldest daughter of Joshua Brown, Esq., of Charleston, S. C.	09/17/1823
On Monday, the 15th inst., Miss Maria Taylor, aged 24 years, eldest daughter of Mr. James Taylor, much regretted by all those who had the pleasure of her acquaintance.	09/18/1823
Near Piscataway, Prince George's County, Md., on the 12th inst., Mr. George Spalding, in the 25th year of his age.	09/18/1823
On Thursday, 18th inst., by the Rev. Mr. Soule, Mr. Henry Powel, to Miss Eleanor Fletcher, both of this city.	09/19/1823
On Monday morning, 15th inst., Benjamin Franklin Walker, son of William Walker, in the 17th year of his age, after a long affliction, which he bore with the greatest fortitude, and in his departing moments bore a full testimony to the merits of his Redeemer, praising God with his last breath.	09/19/1823
Departed this life, on the 17th instant, Mrs. Elizabeth Oliver, wife of Robert Oliver.	09/19/1823
Departed this life, on Tuesday, the 16th instant, after a long and painful illness, which he bore with Christian fortitude, Mr. John Cheston, of this city, in the 29th year of his age. It may well be said that he was a truly amiable young man.	09/19/1823
Departed this life, on Wednesday evening last, in the 13th year of his age, William Frederick Donaldson, son of James Lowry Donaldson, who fell in the defense of this city. He has left a disconsolate mother and a number of relatives to mourn his loss; but, he has gone to a world far better than this, to enjoy an unceasing and immortal bliss.	09/19/1823
On Wednesday last, of a distressing illness of 12 months, Mr. Zephaniah Cheney, in the 72nd year of his age, long a respectable inhabitant of this place.	09/20/1823
On Tuesday evening last, by the Rev. Mr. Smith, Mr. Simon Kemp, of this city, to Miss Ellen Dwyer.	09/22/1823
Yesterday morning, Miss Mary Ann Lawson, second daughter of Mr. Robert Lawson, of this city, aged 21 years.	09/22/1823

Marriage and Death Notices	Date
Departed this transitory life, on Saturday, the 20th instant, Miss Elizabeth Harris, in the 15th year of his age. In the death of this truly amiable and interesting young lady, her acquaintance and friends have to mourn the loss of a beloved and affectionate companion, and her bereaved and widowed mother, an affectionate and dutiful daughter.	09/22/1823
Of croup, on the 19th inst., near Downingtown, Pennsylvania, Andrew, son of the late Andrew Ellicott, of Baltimore, aged four years and three months.	09/23/1823
At Charlotte Hall, St. Mary's County, Md., on the morning of the 18th inst., Mr. Jason Haven Palmer, aged 21 youngest son of the Rev. Samuel Palmer, of Massachusetts.	09/23/1823
On Thursday evening last, by the Rev. Mr. Kurtz, Mr. John Keck, of Anne Arundel county, to Miss Elizabeth Tevis, of this city.	09/24/1823
On Tuesday evening last, by the Rev. Mr. Cook, Mr. Eaton R. Partridge, to Miss Susan S. Crook, all of this city.	09/24/1823
On the 17th inst., at Friends meeting, Still Pond, Kent county, Md., John E. Norris, of Baltimore, to Mary Ann, youngest daughter of the late Joab Alsten, of New Castle, Delaware.	09/24/1823
On Sunday, the 21st instant, after a protracted illness of twelve months, Elizabeth, youngest daughter of Mr. Hugh Maguire, of this city, aged 9 years.	09/24/1823
On Tuesday evening last, at Blenham, Baltimore county, by the Rev. Mr. M'Elhiney, Mr. William Owens, of West River, to Eleanor L., eldest daughter of Larkin H. Smith, Esq.	09/25/1823
Yesterday, at 4 o'clock, after a short illness, Capt. Joshua Beasman, of this city. The deceased had just returned from the west, where he contracted the prevailing fever, of which he died. He was a distinguished officer in the late war in the defense of Baltimore. He was a tender husband, an indulgent father, a sincere friend, and above all, he was the noblest work of God, an honest man.	09/25/1823
On the 6th instant, Miss Sarah Ann Jenkins, aged 17. And, on the 7th, Mrs. Martha Jenkins, aged 50, both of Georgetown, D. C.	09/25/1823
On Saturday, the 20th instant, Miss Eveline Cameron, eldest daughter of Mr. Hugh Cameron, in the twenty-first year of her age.	09/26/1823

Marriage and Death Notices	Date
On the 25th instant, after a short, but severe illness, which he bore with truly Christian fortitude, Mr. Reuben Burford, in the 23rd year of his age. His friends knew his worth and will lament his loss.	09/26/1823
In the Alms-House, Alexandria, on the 21st instant, Michael Steiber, generally called "Stever," baker, a native of Germany, about 80 years of age. He was a soldier in the army of Gen. Count Rochambeau.	09/26/1823
At New Orleans, on the 29th August, after a few days illness, Amos Henry McCoy, formerly of Baltimore, aged 22 years. Few have lived more beloved, or died more lamented.	09/26/1823
At St. Stephens, in Alabama, Mr. Henry S. Lee, a native of Baltimore, Md.	09/26/1823
The following persons died at New Orleans, from the 19th to the 25th of August: William Wallace, of Baltimore; B. M'Munday, of Ireland; Thomas Bryant, Philadelphia; Margaret West, N. York, a child; James Butler, Castine; James Pierre, N. York; Oliver Stebins, Massachusetts; Peter Young, Bremen.	09/26/1823
By the Rev. Dr. Glendy, Mr. August Bardet, a native of France, to Miss Margaret Craig, of Baltimore.	09/27/1823
On Thursday evening last, by the Rev. Mr. Greenfield, Mr. George Bishop to Miss Rebecca Fowler, daughter of Richard Fowler, Esq., all of Baltimore county.	09/27/1823
On Thursday evening, by the Rev. C. A. Davis, Capt. William Atkinson to Miss Catherine Fleming, all of this city.	09/27/1823
On Thursday evening last, by the Rev. Mr. Valiant, Mr. Samuel Guilfoy, to Miss Eleanor Holland, all of Baltimore county.	09/27/1823
On Saturday evening last, after a short illness, Miss Eliza Keaton Harris, youngest daughter of the late William Harris, of this city, in the sixteenth year of her age.	09/27/1823
On Thursday morning last, five days after his sister's departure, William Harris, in the 24th year of his age.	09/27/1823
At Philadelphia, on Thursday evening, 25th inst., Evan Poultney, of Baltimore, to Jane, daughter of the late Richard Tunis.	09/29/1823
On Tuesday, 23rd instant, Richard Mason, aged 46, a native of Birmingham, England, and long a respectable resident of this city. "Be	09/29/1823

Marriage and Death Notices	Date
ye also ready, for in the hour ye think not, the Son of Man cometh."	
In Washington, after an illness of ten days, the Rev. Louis R. Fechtig, an elder in the Methodist Episcopal Church, and at his death presiding elder of the Baltimore district. "Precious in the sight of the Lord is the death of his saints."	09/29/1823
On Saturday evening last, Mr. George Robertson, a native of Scotland, and late a merchant of this city. His friends will long deplore his loss.	09/30/1823
On Monday evening last, by the Rev. Chas. Cook, Mr. Philip S. Chappell, to Miss Mary Furlong, both of this city.	10/01/1823
On Sunday evening last, at the residence of his father, near Easton, Joseph Haskins, Jr., in the 23rd year of his age.	10/01/1823
At Locust Grove, the residence of Capt. John Beckett, in Calvert county, Maryland, in the 6th year of his age, Francis Peyton, eldest son of Craven T. Peyton, formerly of Alexandria.	10/01/1823
Last evening, by the Rt. Rev. Bishop Kemp, Maj. Christopher Vanderventer, of Washington, to Sally, daughter of Dr. Birckhead, of this city.	10/02/1823
On the 29th ultimo, after a short illness, at the residence of Ebenezer Stout, Esq., in Georgetown, D. C., Francis Hopkinson, formerly of this city.	10/02/1823
Last evening, by the Rev. Mr. Tournaire, Mr. James Boyle, to Mrs. Catherine Rogers, all of this city.	10/03/1823
At Washington city, on the 22nd ult., at the age of 84 years, Dr. William Steuart, for many years Health Officer of Baltimore, and late a surgeon in the army of the United States.	10/03/1823
On the 19th inst., at his seat in the county of Botetourt, Va., Col. Matthew Harvey. The deceased was a native of the state of Maryland.	10/03/1823
On Tuesday morning, at the seat of Mr. Maxwell, in Queen Ann County, Md., where he had gone on a visit to his mother, Mr. William Gibson, one of the Clerks in the department of the Treasury.	10/03/1823
On Sunday evening last, by the Rev. Mr. Greenfield, Mr. Hugh Smith, to Miss Elizabeth Bishop, daughter of Wm. Bishop, Esq., all of Baltimore county.	10/04/1823

Marriage and Death Notices	Date
Departed this life, last evening, after a distressing illness of several months, in the 34th year of her age, Mrs. Martha Hunter, wife of John Hunter, Esq., of Baltimore county, and second daughter of Mr. John Hillen, of this city, leaving a disconsolate husband and six children to deplore a bereavement to them irreparable.	10/04/1823
Died, on the 27th ultimo, Mrs. Mary Steiger, one of the first inhabitants of Baltimore, and, at the time of her death, probably one of the oldest natives of this country. She was born near York, Pennsylvania, in the year 1736, of parents who were among the first emigrants from Germany to the new world; and, in the year 1751, at the age of seventeen years, she came to this city, then containing only six dwellings, accompanied by her husband, Mr. Andrew Steiger, who is now in the recollection of hundreds of our citizens as an honest, industrious, enterprising inhabitant, and one who contributed more to the foundation of this city, in its infancy, than perhaps any other man. Mrs. Steiger survived her husband a number of years, and lived to see five generations, all descending from her by consanguinity. She lived respected and died lamented, at the advanced age of 88 years, 70 of which she had spent in this city.	10/06/1823
Died, in Hagerstown, on Monday last, after a short illness, Mr. Job Hunt, formerly a resident of this city, in the 39th year of his age – for many years, the deceased was a professed follower of Jesus Christ; and all who knew him can testify that in an eminent degree he adorned his profession by a Godly life. When convinced that his dissolution was fast approaching, in the triumphs of faith, he exclaimed, "I have fought a good fight, I have finished my course, I have kept the faith."	10/06/1823
Died, at Thompson's Town, Pa., on the 23rd ult., in the 16th year of his age, after a short illness, David M'Gary, son of Michael M'Garry, of this city. When such a youth as this is cut off from us, as it were, just as a bud blooming into full vigour, can it not, with the greatest propriety, be said, "in the midst of life, we are in death?" Therefore, let all, even those who are young, "prepare to meet their God."	10/06/1823
Died, at Cambridge, Dr. John Cropper, late Register of Wills, for Dorchester county.	10/06/1823
At Boston, after a short illness, Mrs. Elizabeth, wife of the Hon. Wm. Gray.	10/06/1823
On Thursday last, by the Rev. Mr. Rockwell, James Henderson, Esq., of Harford county, to Miss Sarah Hicks, daughter of the late Abraham	10/07/1823

Marriage and Death Notices	Date
Hicks, of Baltimore county.	
On Saturday, the 4th instant, by the Rev. L. Deluhol, Mr. Alfred Bujac, merchant, to Miss Ann Adele Turenne, both of this city.	10/07/1823
Last evening, by the Rev. Mr. Tournaire, Luke Whelan, to Mary O'Donnell, both of Fell's Point.	10/07/1823
On Sunday morning, after an illness of two weeks, Wm. Watson, in the sixth year of his age, second son of the late Robert Watson, of this city.	10/07/1823
At Chestertown, on the 6th inst., by the Rev. Mr. Smith, Dr. John Kearney Rodgers, of New York, to Miss Mary R. Nicholson, of Baltimore.	10/08/1823
On the 5th inst., by the Rev. Mr. Whitfield, Mr. James B. Lewis, to Miss Harriet Ann Russel, only daughter of Capt. Samuel Russel, all of this city.	10/08/1823
On Sunday evening last, by the Rev. Saml. Williams, Mr. Aaron Love, to Mrs. Lavina Love, all of this city.	10/08/1823
At his farm, in Anne Arundel county, Md., Mr. Joseph M'Ceney, Esq., formerly sheriff of that county.	10/08/1823
After a long and lingering illness, which she bore with fortitude becoming a Christian, Mrs. Caroline Milton Blake, wife of John S. Blake, Esq., of Church Hill, sheriff of Queen Ann's county. To an amiable disposition, she united an obliging temper, which had gained her the esteem of all who knew her. Her life was virtuous, and her death victorious. She has left a husband and three children to mourn her death.	10/08/1823
On Tuesday evening last, by the Rev. Mr. Duncan, Mr. Philip Turner, of St. Mary's county, Md., to Miss Sarah Ann, second daughter of Jonathan Manroe, of this city.	10/09/1823
In Talbot county, by the Rev. Mr. Scull, Mr. James P. Anderson, to Miss Susan Ann Hopkins, all of that county. By the Rev. Mr. Scull, Mr. Wm. Bullen, to Miss Eliza Ann Mears, all of that county.	10/09/1823
Last night, after an illness of four days, Mr. George Heidelbach. His friends and acquaintance are respectfully invited to attend his funeral, this afternoon, at 4 o'clock, from his late dwelling, in George street.	10/09/1823

Marriage and Death Notices	Date
On the 3rd inst., at the residence of Col. Joseph Harris, Saint Marys county, Maryland, after a short, but severe illness, William H. Landsdale, Esq., Post Master, at Leonardtown, and a principal clerk to Col. Harris, clerk of Saint Marys county court. In the prime of his life, was this meritorious young man cut off from a world in which he had led a life of the strictest morality. In his death, and only and affectionate sister is bereaved of the kindest of brothers, an aunt and many estimable relations of one whose affections were not excelled – with a heart made for friendship, his professions were sincere. Perfectly aware of his approaching end, he bore it with manly and resigned composure, which none can experience, save those who have a firm reliance in their Savior. His strict integrity and candid demeanor endeared him to all who knew him, and all lament his death.	10/09/1823
On Saturday, the 4th instant, Mrs. Elizabeth J. Courtenay, wife of Mr. Henry Courtenay.	10/10/1823
In Prince George's county, 8th instant, Mrs. Rebecca Crow, wife of Mr. Richard B. Crow.	10/10/1823
On the 2nd instant, after a short, but painful illness, Mary S. T. Reigart, in the 14th year of her age. She was kind and tender hearted, beloved by all who knew her, and sincerely regretted by her relaives and friends. In the death of this young female, who but a few days since was the very picture of health, we have another striking evidence of the uncertainty of life, and that God continually stands at the door knocking, admonishing us in language not to be misconceived, that we also should be ready, for we know not what hour we shall be called on to appear in the eternal world.	10/10/1823
At Philadelphia, Mr. George Daniel Reese, merchant, of Baltimore, to Miss Margaret K. Wartman, of that city.	10/11/1823
On Tuesday morning, at Sheppard's Town, Va., after an illness of eleven days, Mr. James S. Lane, a respectable merchant, of the firm Lane & Smiths, of this city.	10/11/1823
On Wednesday morning last, Mrs. Jane Stiff, consort of the late Thomas Stiff, in the 43rd year of her age, after an illness of thirteen days; resigned to meet her husband and daughter in another and a better world.	10/11/1823
Departed this life, on the 29th of September, 1823, at 8 o'clock A. M., in the 26th year of his age, at the residence of Alexander Maxwell, his step-father, in Queen Ann's County, William Gibson, a clerk in the Treasury	10/11/1823

Marriage and Death Notices	Date
Department, U. S. He had just returned from a long journey to the Indian trading houses in the west – he was taken with a violent liver complaint, which defied the utmost medical skill, and, in a few days, terminated his existence. He may be truly said to have died in the bosom of his family. A kind step-father, an affectionate pious mother, a devoted sister, and a kind brother, mingled their sympathies with his sufferings; nor did he sigh alone; and as the lamp of life was extinguished, a flame of united hallowed devotion accompanied his departing spirit to realms above, where, fond hope, we will indulge that hope, his sainted sister Elizabeth, with her dear little cherub Charles, met him and introduced him to scenes of endless joy, crowned with everlasting glory. He was the favorite of Mr. & J. Dallas, of never fading memory, who introduced him into the Treasury Department – and he died full in the confidence of Mr. Crawford. His friends, to whom he was known, will embalm his memory with the sacred tears of friendship.	
On Monday night last, by the Rev. Mr. Helfenstein, Capt. David H. White, to Mrs. Ann L. Laudenslager, all of this city.	10/14/1823
On the evening of the 11th inst., by the Rev. Mr. Parks, Mr. George Ruff, to Miss Cassandra Warfield, all of this city.	10/14/1823
On Sunday evening last, by the Rev. Dr. Jennings, Mr. James Scott, to Miss Martha Busey, both of this city.	10/14/1823
At Harrisburg, Penn., on Wednesday afternoon, the 8th inst., Mrs. Mary S. Snyder, consort of the late Gov. Snyder, aged 55 years.	10/14/1823
Last evening, by the Rev. Mr. Duncan, Dr. John P. Mackenzie, to Theresa A. M., daughter of John Carerre, Esq., both of this city.	10/15/1823
On the 9th inst., at his residence, at Harlem, much lamented, Joshua Wichersham, aged about 31 years – he was lately from the state of Pennsylvania, and engaged in the establishment of a nursery of good fruits, contiguous to this city; in which he had made considerable progress – his upright conduct through life endeared him to his acquaintance as an honest man, and his industry in the line of his profession promised fair to be of general utility to the community – his removal, therefore, at this early period, may be considered as a public loss, and a serious one to his afflicted widow and numerous connections.	10/15/1823

333

Marriage and Death Notices	Date
In this city, on Tuesday, Mr. George Weafer, in the 37th year of his age.	10/15/1823
At his residence, North East, Cecil county, Md., on Sunday morning, the 12th instant, Daniel Sheredine, Esq., in the 72nd year of his age. During his short but severe illness, he evinced the triumphs of a Christian, observing to a friend, "how intolerable would these pains be, was it not for the support derived from religion." For many years, he has been a highly esteemed member of the Methodist Society. Notwithstanding his advanced age, such was the vigor of his mind and firmness of constitution, the happy effects of habitual industry and the strictest temperance, that at no period of his life would his loss have been more deeply felt by his family, friends, and society at large. For upwards of 20 years, he has been highly distinguished as the firm supporter of democratic principles, and upon all warmly contested points in Cecil county, he has been selected as one of the democratic candidates; and such was the excellence of his private character, the warm attachment of a numerous circle of friends, and the gratitude of the poor and needy who had been relieved by his humanity and benevolence, that even party spirit lost its influence; the opposition to him was less active, and he was seldom, if ever, unsuccessful – he was sent to the last Legislator without opposition; and a few days before his death his fellow citizens by their votes confirmed upon him the same honorable distinction – but alas! for them his earthly labours are ended, their consolation must now be, that he is now receiving the glorious reward of "Well done thou good and faithful servant, enter thou unto the joy of thy Lord."	10/15/1823
Near Natchez, Capt. George Rearick, of Pittsburg, P., late master of the steamboat Dolphin. The Dolphin stopped a few hours at Natchez, bound to St. Louis, and the next day the fever carried off the captain, pilot, and several of the hands. Also, Capt. Embree, of steam boat Cincinnati, his clerk, and several of his hands – the boat having been detained a few hours at Natchez, communicated the fever on board.	10/15/1823
On Sunday evening last, by the Rev. Mr. Bartow, Mr. John Malone, to Mrs. Susannah Monroe, all of this city.	10/16/1823
On Sunday evening last, by the Rev. Mr. Bartow, Mr. John Dolan, to Mrs. Mary Johnson, both of this place.	10/16/1823
On Tuesday night last, by the Rev. Mr. Kurtz, Mr. Frederick Timmermann, to Mrs. Ann Catherine Marriott, both of this city.	10/16/1823
Yesterday morning, at Friends' Meeting House, Lombard street, James Moore, Jr., of Georgetown, D. C., to Esther Sinclair, Jr.	10/16/1823

Marriage and Death Notices	Date
Yesterday morning, at Friends' Meeting House, Lombard street, John Dukehart, Jr., to Ann P. Cornthwaite, both of this city.	10/16/1823
Last evening, by the Rev. Dr. John Glendy, Mr. Thomas Sayers, to Miss Winefred Preston, all of this city.	10/16/1823
By the Rev. Dr. Glendy, on the 4th inst., Mr. Edward Gready to Miss Mary Ann Jones.	10/17/1823
On Thursday evening, by the Rev. Dr. Jennings, Mr. William Barton, to Miss Ann Eliza Ives, both of this city.	10/17/1823
On Thursday, 16th inst., by the Rev. Mr. Guest, Mr. William S. Young, to Miss Mary Dutton, all of this city.	10/17/1823
In Somerset county, Eastern Shore of Maryland, on Tuesday evening, 23rd Sept., by the Rev. Mr. Laurenson, Mr. Freeborn Garretson, of New York, to Elizabeth H., second daughter of Mr. Francis H. Waters, of the former place.	10/17/1823
In Somerset county, Eastern Shore of Maryland, on Tuesday evening, 30th Sept., by the Rev. Mr. Laurenson, Mr. Henry Maddox, to Ann, second daughter of the late Mr. Wm. Turpin, all of said county.	10/17/1823
At Locust Grove, St. Mary's county, Md., on Friday morning, the 10th inst., Mrs. Frances Putnam Key, aged 37, wife of the late Philip Key, Jr., Esq., of said county.	10/17/1823
On Tuesday morning last, in the fifty-fifth year of his age, Mr. Jacob Wall, Sr., an old and respectable inhabitant of this city. The circumstances which attended his depar- were truly distressing. He had for a long time been confined; but, a few days before his death, there was apparently every prospect of recovery. Even one hour before the messenger of death called him hence, he was walking about, and the greatest hopes were entertained by his surrounding relatives and friends. Here we again see the uncertainty of life; and this should be an additional warning to the many we have, to be always ready when God summons.	10/17/1823
At Portsmouth, Va., on Thursday, the 9th inst., Midshipman James P. McCall, of the U. S. Navy. His remains were interred the day following with military honors.	10/17/1823
At New Orleans, on the 6th ult., Michel de Armas, Esq., Counsellor at Law, of that city.	10/17/1823

Marriage and Death Notices	Date
On the 11th ultimo, in Logan county, Ky., after a short illness, in the 72nd year of his age, Mr. Christopher Onndorff, formerly an inhabitant of Washington county, Md.	10/17/1823
The *Louisville (Ky.) Post* mentions the decease, in that town, of Mr. Owen Afflick, plaisterer, formerly of Baltimore. His death was occasioned by a wound received in a rencounter with Mr. James Wilson, of Louisville. Mr. Wilson has been arrested, and is now confined in jail.	10/20/1820
At Wheatland, Jefferson county, Va., on the 3rd inst., Dr. Charles C. Byrd, of Berryville, Frederick county, to Miss Jane C. F. Turner, second daughter of H. S. Turner, Esq., of Wheatland.	10/20/1823
Yesterday afternoon, at 4 o'clock, in the 70th year of his age, Col. John Mackenheimer, *a gallant soldier of the Revolution, and an honest man.* A further notice of this venerable patriot will appear hereafter. The body will leave his late residence, in Bridge street, this day, at 4 o'clock P. M., and, at his particular request, his friends who attend will form a procession on foot, to witness the interment of his remains.	10/20/1823
Last evening, in the 53rd year of his age, Mr. George Lawson, a native of the state of Delaware, but, for a long time past, a most highly esteemed and respectable inhabitant of this city. His friends and acquaintance are requested, without further invitation, to attend his funeral, from the residence of Capt. Graybell, in Market street, at 9 o'clock, tomorrow morning.	10/22/1823
Yesterday morning, in the 53rd year of his age, after a few days illness, Mr. Henry Altfather. His friends and acquaintance are respectfully invited to attend his funeral, this afternoon, at 3 o'clock, from his late dwelling, in Waggon alley.	10/22/1823
On Wednesday, the 15th inst., at the residence of Mr. James M. Cresap, Esq., in Alleghany county, Md., Mrs. Rebecca Young, in the 85th year of her age, long a respectable inhabitant of Baltimore county.	10/22/1823
At Norfolk, on Friday, the 17th instant, after a lingering illness of a pulmonary complaint, Gen. John C. Cohoon, in the 59th year of his age.	10/22/1823 10/23/1823
Yesterday, at Friends' Meeting House, Lombard st., John Ferris, of Wilmington, Del., to Mary Price, of this city.	10/23/1823
On Tuesday evening last, by the Rev. Mr. Hamilton, Mr. Emanuel K. J. Hand, to Miss Catherine S., youngest daughter of Dr. Samuel K.	10/23/1823

Marriage and Death Notices	Date
Jennings, all of this city.	
On Thursday evening last, by the Rev. Mr. Davis, Mr. John Showaker, to Miss Louisa, daughter of Mr. Michael Small, all of this city.	10/23/1823
Last night, at 8 o'clock, Mr. Casper Faks. His friends and acquaintances are invited to attend his funeral, at 4 o'clock, this afternoon, from his dwelling, No. 53 Water street.	10/23/1823
On the 16th inst., at his residence, near Chestertown, Kent county, Md., Mr. George Hanson, aged 61 years, a respectable farmer of that county.	10/23/1823
On Tuesday evening last, by the Rev. Mr. Valiant, Mr. Luther Amoss, to Miss Charlotte Palmer, all of Baltimore county.	10/24/1823
By the Rev. Mr. Valiant, on Thursday evening, Mr. Hugh Devalin, to Miss Sarah Working, all of this city.	10/24/1823
On the 9th inst., after a short, but severe illness, in the 23rd year of her age, Miss Rosella Ann, youngest daughter of Mr. James Middleton, of Charles county, Md.	10/24/1823
At Georgetown, in the 36th year of his age, Augustus Taney, Esq.	10/24/1823
On Thursday evening last, by the Rev. Mr. Cook, Mr. Charles B. Purnall, of Baltimore, to Miss Hannah Richards, of Baltimore county.	10/25/1823
At New Orleans, on the 22nd of September last, Mr. Benedict T. Vanpradelles, late of Baltimore, aged 22 years. His affectionate disposition and many amiable qualities justly endeared him to his relatives and numerous acquaintants.	10/25/1823
At Lewistown, Del., Mrs. Hannah White, wife of Dr. John White, and daughter of Daniel Rodney, Esq.	10/25/1823
At New Orleans, on the 27th ult., after a short illness, of yellow fever, Henry T. Beatty, Esq., editor of the New Orleans Iris. He was a son of Dr. Beatty, of Georgetown, D. C., and in the 30th year of his age.	10/27/1823
On Thursday evening last, by the Rev. Dr. Kurtz, Mr. John Boss, to Miss Harriet Little, all of this city.	10/27/1823
On the 27th Sept. last, at Port au Prince, St. Domingo, Mr. John Rudolph Schmeckpeper, in the 43rd year of his age. The deceased was a native of Germany, but for many years a respectable inhabitant of Baltimore. The pleasing assurance that there is another and a better world, affords the	10/28/1823

Marriage and Death Notices	Date
only true consolation to his widow and relatives, under this dispensation of Providence.	
Last night, by the Rev. Mr. Helfenstein, Mr. Arratus A. McGibbon to Miss Mary Ruth Lee Edes, both of this city.	10/29/1823
At Charleston, Kennah M'Cleod, late of Baltimore, aged about 58. A coroner's inquest gave a verdict that he came to his death by a fit.	10/30/1823
At Gonaives, Hayti, on the 16th ult., John J. Myer, Jr., a young man of singular worth.	10/31/1823
At Port au Prince, on the 7th inst., after a severe illness of 4 days, Mr. Peter Young, supercargo of the schooner Nancy Eleanor, of Baltimore.	10/31/1823
On the 30th Oct., by the Rev. Mr. Leidy, Mr. Lewis Wampler, to Miss Lydia, eldest daughter of Jacob Krouse, all of Westminster, Md.	11/01/1823
On the 29th inst., by the Rev. Solomon Sharp, Dr. Alfred L. Warner, of Baltimore, to Miss Ann, eldest daughter of Mr. Solomon Wiatt, of Philad.	11/01/1823
Last evening, by the Rev. Mr. Healey, Mr. William Finch to Miss Mary Ann Green, all of this city.	11/03/1823
On the 22nd, by the Rev. Mr. Stratton, Henry Franklin, Esq., to Miss Mary J. Purnell, both of Worcester county, Md.	11/03/1823
In Milledgeville, Geo., on the 19th ult., Mr. Cyrus B. Pritchard, a native of Maryland.	11/03/1823
On the 19th ultimo, Col. John Mackenheimer, who was born on the 22nd October, 1753, and consequently was within three days of being 70 years old. Our venerable friend entered the service of his country in 1775, as a private in the company commanded by the late respected Capt. Graybell, and joined the regiment commanded by Col. Honsaker, at Philadelphia, and crossed the Delaware, under Washington, when he surprised and captured the Hessians, and beat the enemy at Princetown, in which affairs, Mr. Mackenheimer acted so well that he was made a sergeant. He next fought in the battle of Brandywine, as an ensign, and we find that he was a lieutenant in command in the affair at Germantown. He left the regular service, some time after this, but performed occasional military duties to the close of the war. In 1794, he was commissioned as captain of the "Light Infantry Blues," attached to the 5th regiment of Maryland militia, for many years, the only uniform	11/04/1823

Marriage and Death Notices	Date
company in this state, and he belonged to it 20 years and upwards. This company volunteered its services at the time of the Western insurrection, and was selected by Washington for his life-guard at Cumberland. As he advanced in age, he at last gave up the command of his old associates, and accepted a majority in the 5th regiment, and was afterwards promoted to lieutenant colonel commandant, which he resigned several years ago, on account of increasing infirmities. He filled the office of City Councilman and other respectable places, conferred on him through the esteem of his fellow citizens. He was one of the oldest inhabitants of Baltimore, and always maintained the character of a kind neighbor and an honest man, not to be suspected of a mean or dishonorable action. He retained the surviving friends of his youth until the day of his death and, among them, is one who followed his track when crossing on the ice at Trenton, which track was marked with blood from his lacerated feet – and yet, with such as he, Washington conquered! The remains of Col. Mackenheimer were interred on the 20th, in presence of a large assemblage of his late friends and neighbours, who, at his particular request, followed the corpse in a procession on foot. His pall was borne by Mr. Stevens, governor of the state, and Mr. Johnson, mayor of Baltimore, Peter Diffenderffer and George Decker, Esq's., the first of whom had been a soldier with him in the revolution, and the latter for twenty years a member of the "Light Blues," and by William Steuart, late lieutenant colonel in the army of the United States, and one of the representatives elect of Baltimore, in the General Assembly of Maryland, and Col. G. H. Steuart, the present commander of the 5th regiment, the officers of which, soon after, had a meeting and unanimously resolved to wear crape for one month in testimony for their respect for the deceased.	
On Sunday last, by the Rev. Mr. Smith, Mr. John Bradenbaugh, to Miss Susan Denys, all of this city.	11/05/1823
On Thursday night last, Mrs. Mary Ann, wife of Mr. Henry Pike, of this city. In the brief, but severe illness which produced this heart rending bereavement to her afflicted relatives and friends, she evinced that patience under suffering, and that unshaken firmness at the conscience approach of death, which are only to be derived from the consoling influence of a well spent life and a truly religious mind. Although thus prematurely cut off in the bloom of youth, the remembrance of her virtues will ever be cherished in the hearts of those she has left behind.	11/05/1823
On the morning of the 4th inst., at one o'clock, Mrs. Rebecca R., wife of Mr. Joshua Tevis, of this city.	11/05/1823

Marriage and Death Notices	Date
On Friday last, Fanny W., daughter of the late John Dalrymple.	11/05/1823
On Thursday evening last, by the Rev. Mr. Rockhold, Mr. David Giles, to Miss Ann Lesourd, both of Baltimore county.	11/06/1823
In Lexington, Ky., on the 4th ult., Mr. Sanford Keen, proprietor of Keen's Inn.	11/06/1823
By the Rev. Mr. Nevins, on the 5th instant, William Edwards Mayhew, Esq., to Mrs. Maria Middleton Hobby, both of this city.	11/07/1823
At Plymouth, on board sch. King Solomon, Mr. Samuel Hathaway, of Baltimore.	11/07/1823
At Philadelphia, on Wednesday, 5th inst., Frederick G. Schaeffer, Esq., late editor of the Federal Republican and Baltimore Telegraph.	11/08/1823
Last Saturday, in the 50th year of his age, Mr. Hugh Patrick, formerly a merchant of this city.	11/10/1823
On Thursday last, by the Rev. Mr. Richardson, Mr. John Miller, aged upwards of 40 years, to Mrs. July Ann James, not quite 15, all of Harford county. But the marrow of the story is, that the above Parson married the above Miller to his first wife, about five years before this one was born; and she, although not 15 years of age, has now been united in the holy bands of matrimony no less than three times.	11/11/1823
On Friday evening, in the 66th year of her age, Mrs. Charlotte Irvine, relict of the late Alexander Irvine, of this city.	11/11/1823
On Saturday morning last, after a very protracted illness, which he bore with patient resignation, Mr. Joseph Taylor, in the 30th year of his age.	11/13/1823
In Pittsburgh, after a short illness, Mrs. Maria Poe, the amiable consort of George Poe, Esq., of that city.	11/13/1823
On Tuesday evening, the 11th inst., by the Rev. Mr. Wyatt, Samuel W. Smith, Esq., to Eleanor S., second daughter of John Donnell, Esq.	11/14/1823
On Thursday evening last, by the Rev. Bishop Kemp, Mr. Elias T. Griffin, to Miss Mary Ann E. Richards, both of this city.	11/15/1823
At Rock Hall, Md., on the 11th inst., Miss Rebecca Ringgold, of Chestertown.	11/15/1823

Marriage and Death Notices	Date
At New York, Tuesday morning, Benjamin F. Bourne, Esq., of the U. S. Navy.	11/15/1823
Last evening, by the Rev. Mr. Henshaw, Hugh Boyle, Esq., to Mrs. Agnes Owen, all of this city.	11/17/1823
A Panuco, in Mexico, on the 29th of July last, Austin Chapman, of this city, in the 22nd year of his age.	11/17/1823
On Sunday evening, by the Rev. Dr. Roberts, Mr. Hugh Holloson, to Miss Eliza Bowersox, all of this city.	11/18/1823
Last evening, by the Rev. Dr. Roberts, Mr. James P. Mulliken, to Miss Catherine Rankin, all of this city.	11/19/1823
On Thursday evening last, by the Rev. Mr. Valiant, Mr. Aquilla Miles, to Miss Elizabeth Hughes, both of Baltimore county.	11/20/1823
By the Rev. Mr. Valiant, on Tuesday evening last, Mr. Joseph M'Cubbin, to Miss Mary Ann Smith, all of this city.	11/20/1823
By the Rev. Mr. Valiant, on Tuesday evening last, Mr. George Briggs, to Miss Sarah Mathews, both of Pennsylvania.	11/20/1823
At Washington city, Mr. William Wilson, of Baltimore, to Miss Caroline, daughter of George Sandford, of that city.	11/21/1823
On Thursday evening last, by the Rev. Mr. Bartow, Mr. George Greggs, to Miss Lucretia Brown, all of this city.	11/22/1823
On Thursday evening last, by the Rev. Mr. Guest, Mr. Theophilus Brown, to Miss Mary Ann Stevens, both of this city.	11/22/1823
On Thursday evening, 20th inst., at Berry Hill, by the Rev. Mr. McIlhenny, Judson Claggett Duckett, Esq., to Elizabeth Ann, daughter of Richard Gittings, Esq.	11/24/1823
Deaths at Natchez, from the 10th to 15th of Oct., viz: Joseph Shillingslaw, William Hagerman, Charles Carre, Colton Rice, Mr. Blade, Miss Margaret Rice, Jacob R. Myers, Amis Rennels, Daniel Williams, and James Griffin.	11/24/1823
On Sunday evening last, by the Rev. Mr. Henshaw, Mr. John Redgrave, to Miss Susan Buchanan, all of this city.	11/25/1823

Marriage and Death Notices	Date
Last evening, by the Rev. Mr. Nevins, William T. Johnson, Esq., of Frederick county, Md., to Miss Dorothea, second daughter of Alexander Mactier, Esq., of this city.	11/26/1823
On Thursday evening, the 20th inst., by the Rev. Mr. Valiant, Mr. Samuel Thomas to Miss Harriet Hammond, both of Anne Arundel county.	11/26/1823
On Tuesday evening, by the Rev. Mr. Soule, Mr. William Carson, to Miss Sarah Jane James.	11/27/1823
On Sunday evening last, by the Rev. Mr. Guest, Mr. John Greves, to Miss Maria, eldest daughter of Capt. Samuel Ayers, all of this city.	11/27/1823
On Thursday last, by the Rev. Mr. Nevins, Mr. Joseph W. Stone, to Mrs. Ann Stone, all of Baltimore county.	11/27/1823
Last evening, by the Rev. Mr. Guest, Mr. Benjamin Hatcheson, to Miss Ann McMullin, all of this city.	11/28/1823
Last evening, by the Rev. E. J. Reis, Mr. Joseph J. Stewart, to Miss Eliza Birgan, both of Baltimore county.	11/28/1823
On Tuesday evening last, by the Rev. Mr. Bartow, Mr. James Field, to Miss Mary Bevans, all of this city.	11/28/1823
At Roxbury, Mass., Mr. Benjamin F. Copeland, of Boson, to Miss Julia F., daughter of the late Hon. Nathaniel Ruggles, of Roxbury.	11/28/1823
At Annapolis, Mrs. Hester, wife of the Hon. Jeremiah Townley Chase, of that city. All the various duties of life, of wife, mother, mistress, relation, and friend, the deceased fulfilled to the utmost.	11/28/1823
On Thursday evening last, by the Rev. Mr. Helfenstein, Mr. Martin G. Schade, to Miss Eliza Alberger, all of this city.	11/29/1823
On Thursday, 17th inst., on Elk Ridge, by the Rev. Mr. Wilson, Mr. Fielder Wilson, of Baltimore, to Miss Catherine Warfield, of the former place.	11/29/1823
On Wednesday, the 26th instant, at his residence in Baltimore county, Mr. Hugh Kerman, in the 78th year of his age.	11/29/1823
On Thursday evening last, by the Rev. Mr. Bartow, Mr. John McClure, of Harford county, to Miss Louisa Strutoff, of this city.	12/01/1823

Marriage and Death Notices	Date
On Saturday evening last, by the Rev. Dr. Glendy, Gen. William McDonald, to Miss Martha Webb, both of this city.	12/02/1823
Yesterday morning, by the Rev. Mr. Henshaw, Caleb Dorsey, Esq., of Anne Arundel county, to Elizabeth Hall, eldest daughter of Mrs. Elizabeth Dorsey.	12/04/1823
On Tuesday last, of a rapid pulmonary affection, in the 26th year of her age, Miss Anne Bond, daughter of the late Peter Bond, of this city.	12/04/1823
In the Havana, after a short illness, Mr. Thos. Duer, of this city, much beloved and respected by all who knew him.	12/04/1823
On the 27th ult., in the 65th year of her age, Mrs. Sarah Ann Beall, consort of Col. Wm. D. Beall, of Prince George's county, Md.	12/04/1823
On Tuesday evening last, by the Rev. Mr. Beschter, Mr. Jeremiah Green to Miss Susannah Catherine Gade, both of this city.	12/05/1823
On Tuesday evening last, by the Rev. Mr. Bartow, Mr. John O. H. Roberts, to Mrs. Mary Brown, of this city.	12/05/1823
On the 11th October last, by the Rev. Mr. Finlay, Mr. John M. Chandlee, of New York, to Sarah Maria, only daughter of the late Felix Kirk, of Norfolk.	12/05/1823
Last evening, by the Rev. Mr. Nevins, Andrew Ellicott, Esq., to Miss Emily Ann, youngest daughter of the late William M'Fadon, all of this city.	12/05/1823
On Thursday evening, 4th inst., by the Rev. Mr. Healey, Mr. James W. Keen, of Harford county, to Miss Anna Keen, of this city.	12/05/1823
At Springfield, in Clark's county, Ohio, on the 26th October last, Mr. Samuel S. Thomas, aged 23 years, formerly of Baltimore.	12/05/1823
In Baltimore County, at Mr. James A. M'Crearey's, George Beam, Jr., second son of the late Maj. George Beam, in the 37th year of his age.	12/05/1823
On Thursday evening last, by the Rev. Mr. Walton, Mr. Richard Mason to Miss Julia Ann Morrison, all of this city.	12/06/1823
On Saturday, 22nd ultimo, after a long and severe illness, Mrs. Elizabeth Pearce, consort of Philip Pearce, of Baltimore county, and daughter of the late Dickinson Gorsuch, of said county, in the 27th year of her age.	12/06/1823

Marriage and Death Notices	Date
On the 30th ult., at his residence, near Old Town, Allegany County, James M. Cresap, Esq.	12/06/1823
On Thursday evening last, by the Rev. John Allen, Ebenezer N. Allen, Esq., to Miss Mary Ann Billingslea, daughter of James Billingslea, both of Harford county.	12/08/1823
Yesterday morning, after a short illness, Mrs. Discretion Walker, in the 75th year of her age. Her friends are invited to attend the funeral, from her late dwelling, No. 87 North Howard street, tomorrow morning, Tuesday, at 8 o'clock.	12/08/1823
On the night of the 2nd inst., after an illness of five weeks, at the residence of her father, Thomas C. Shipley, Esq., near New Market, Mrs. Rachel Worthington, consort of Mr. Rezin H. Worthington, of Baltimore county, in the 18th year of her age. Mrs. Worthington was a lady of superior mental powers, had enjoyed the advantages of a finished education, and was adorned with all the virtues that give value to the female character.	12/09/1823
In the mouth of the Mississippi, on the 7th ult., on his return from a visit to Vera Cruz, Capt. Edward Fenno, of New Orleans – a gentleman who was the pride of his friends, and an ornament to the community in which he dwelt.	12/09/1823
At the Balize, Capt. Edward Fenno, of New Orleans.	12/09/1823
At Mount Jefferson, Baltimore county, on Tuesday evening, 9th inst., by the Rev. Dr. Glendy, Mr. Jacob Hoke, of Harford county, to Miss Ann, second daughter of the late Col. James Biays.	12/10/1823
At North Point, on Tuesday evening, 9th inst., by the Rev. Mr. Shane, Maj. Benjamin Wilson, Jr., to Miss Sarah Ann, second daughter of Lloyd Gooding, Esq., all of Baltimore county.	12/11/1823
At St. Jago de Cuba, on the 14th of October last, in the 21st year of his age, after a severe illness of four days, George Latimore Cathcart, eldest son of James L. Cathcart, Esq., late Consul of the United States to the States of Barbary, Madeira, and Cadiz. This unfortunate youth had made but three voyages to sea, for the attainment of the profession he had adopted; and during the third was promoted by his Captain (Stansbury, of Baltimore,) to be Chief Mate of the vessel under his command; in which station, with a prospect of promotion, he was called to expire on a foreign shore, without parent or relative to soothe his	12/11/1823

Marriage and Death Notices	Date
fleeting spirit.	
On Sunday last, at 1 o'clock, Capt. William Yeatman, of St. Mary's county.	12/11/1823
At sea, 20th November, on the passage from Rio Janeiro to Baltimore, Mr. Zine Robbins, of Weathersfield, Conn., mate of the brig Homer, Phillips, of this port – he has left a family and many relatives to lament their loss.	12/12/1823
On the 27th of October last, after a short, but severe illness, of nine hours, at his residence in Baltimore county, John Kerlinger, Esq., in the 47th year of his age.	12/12/1823
On Thursday evening last, by the Rev. J. P. K. Henshaw, Mr. Jacob Yundt, to Miss Bethiah, daughter of the late Capt. Wm. Barnes, all of this city.	12/13/1823
Last evening, by the Rev. Mr. Valiant, Mr. John Valiant, to Miss Sarah James Kelley, all of this city.	12/15/1823
On Thursday last, by the Rev. Dr. Wyatt, William H. Hanson, Esq., to Mrs. Elizabeth Fisher, both of this city.	12/15/1823
On Thursday evening, 4th inst., by the Rev. Mr. Valiant, Mr. Zephaniah Bailess, to Mrs. Sarah Pearce.	12/16/1823
By the Rev. Mr. Valiant, on Thursday evening last, Mr. Henry A. Johnson to Mrs. Ann Sewell, all of Anne Arundel county.	12/16/1823
By the Rev. Mr. Valiant, on Sunday evening last, Mr. John Delsher, to Miss Sarah Jane Kelly, all of this city.	12/16/1823
On Monday night, at 10 o'clock, Lloyd Buchanan, Esq., in the fiftieth year of his age.	12/17/1823
On the 16th inst., Mrs. Amelia Bremerman, consort of Mr. Harman Bremerman, in the 41st year of her age.	12/17/1823
Last evening, by the Rev. Dr. Jennings, Mr. Frederick Crabbs, of Frederick county, to Miss Matilda Todd, of this city.	12/18/1823
On Wednesday evening last, by the Rev. Mr. Valiant, Mr. William W. Wonn, to Miss Susanna Shade.	12/19/1823

Marriage and Death Notices	Date
On Thursday last, by the Rev. Dr. S. K. Jennings, Mr. Daniel Musgrave, to Mrs. Frances Taylor, all of this city.	12/20/1823
On the 16th inst., Mr. John Dent Ball, to Miss Chloe Ann Bryan, both of Prince George's county, Maryland.	12/20/1823
This morning, about 7 o'clock, John M. Bailey, Esq., Attorney at Law, of this city, in the 28th year of his age. His funeral will be attended from his dwelling, No. 13 Sharp st., at 10 o'clock, on Monday morning, where his friends, and the members of the Court and Bar, are invited to attend.	12/20/1823
Aboard the schr. Lorenzo, of this port, on her passage from St. Jago to Havana, Isaiah Saimer, seaman, on 14th November, a native of the Eastern Shore of Maryland. Also, aboard the same schr., on the 26th Oct., Edward West, seaman.	12/20/1823
Last evening, by the Rev. Mr. Shane, Mr. John Patterson, to Miss Harriet Boyer, all of this city.	12/22/1823
On Saturday last, Henry Chatard, eldest son of the Dr., aged 19 years, 6 months, and 15 days. It may be truly said of him, that he is sincerely regretted by all who knew him.	12/22/1823
On Monday evening last, by the Most Rev. Archbishop Mareschal, James C. Barry, of Alexandria, to Matilda, eldest daughter of Simon Wedge, of this city.	12/24/1823
On Monday evening last, by the Rev. Mr. Tessier, Mr. Jeremiah Harrison, to Mrs. Unity Maria Dooris, both of Talbot county, Eastern Shore, Maryland.	12/24/1823
On Sunday, the 14th inst., in the 16th year of her age, Miss Julia Ann Small, third daughter of Col. Jacob Small, and on Monday evening, the 15th inst., Miss Ann Maria Small, in the 18th year of her age, the second daughter of the same – thus have two of its brightest ornaments been torn from the bosom of an affectionate family, and consigned to the silent tomb.	12/24/1823
At New York, Mr. Albigence Heyward, of Boston, to Miss Mary Wetmore, of that city, both recently of this city.	12/26/1823
On Tuesday evening, 22nd inst., by the Rev. Dr. Wyatt, Mr. Henry S. Sanderson, to Miss Margaret Young.	12/27/1823

Marriage and Death Notices	Date
Last evening, by the Rev. Mr. Healey, Mr. Mark Miller, to Miss Sarah Gartside, both of Baltimore county.	12/27/1823
On Tuesday evening last, Mrs. Margaret Glenn, in the 82nd year of her age, formerly of Philadelphia, and for some years a respectable inhabitant of this city.	12/27/1823
On Wednesday evening last, by the Rev. Mr. Kennerly, Mr. Nicholas C. Brice, to Isabella, daughter of Alexander Russell, Esq., all of this city.	12/29/1823
On the 24th instant, at the residence of Stanislaus Hoxton, Esq., Prince George's county, Md., William Tolson, to Miss Mary Hoxton.	12/29/1823
On Sunday evening, the 21st inst., by the Rev. Mr. Valiant, Mr. Thomas Jenkins, to Miss Mary Paul.	12/30/1823
By the Rev. Mr. Valiant, on Sunday evening last, Mr. David Mummy, to Miss Julia Ann Taylor, all of Baltimore county.	12/30/1823
At Drumpoint, Calvert County, Md., on the 16th inst., by the Rev. Mr. Willis, Capt. John B. Toly, of Dorchester County, Md., to Elizabeth, first daughter of John Willoughby, Esq., of Calvert County, Md.	12/30/1823
Last evening, by the Rev. Mr. Guest, Mr. Edward Auld, to Miss Ann Catherine, eldest daughter of Mr. Levi Grimes, all of this city.	12/31/1823
At Chestertown, Kent county, Md., on the 15th ult., Charlotte Maria, youngest daughter of Dr. Wiesenthal, of the U. S. Navy.	01/03/1824
On Friday evening, by the Rev. Mr. Valiant, Mr. Nathan Ireland, to Mrs. Mary Young, all of this city.	01/05/1824
On Monday evening last, by the Rev. Dr. Roberts, Mr. Valentine Slaughter, to Miss Sophia Delpry, all of this city.	01/07/1824
On Tuesday, much regretted by his friends and acquaintances, about 10 o'clock, Mr. Joseph Lee Millard, in the 55th year of his age, a native of Bristol, England, but for many years a respectable inhabitant of Fell's Point, Baltimore. He has left several orphan grand children, to lament their loss, to whom he acted as a father.	01/07/1824
On Tuesday evening last, by the Rev. Dr. Wyatt, Mr. William F. Murdoch, merchant, to Miss Mary E., daughter of Mr. John Cole, all of this city.	01/08/1824

Marriage and Death Notices	Date
On Monday evening last, by the Rev. Abner Neal, Mr. Francis Fleetwood, to Miss Susan High, both of this city.	01/08/1824
On Monday evening, 8th Dec. last, by Hon. Thomas C. Scott, at the residence of Col. W. H. Overton, near Alexandria, Louisiana, Robert C. Hyson, Esq., merchant of that place, formerly of Baltimore, to Miss Harriet B. Overton, only daughter of Gen. Thomas Overton, of Tennessee.	01/08/1824
On Thursday, the 1st inst., at the seat of James Bosley, Esq., Baltimore county, by the Rev. Mr. Dorsey, Dr. John Lloyd Yates, to Maria Jane, second daughter of Mr. Henry Pennington, all of this city.	01/09/1824
Departed this life, on Friday, the 2nd inst., of a pulmonary complaint, James Carnighan, Jr., in the 22nd year of his age.	01/09/1824
On Thursday, 8th inst., at Mount Repose, by the Rev. Mr. Nevins, Philip T. Tyson, of Baltimore, to Rebecca, eldest daughter of John Skinner Webster.	01/13/1824
On Thursday last, by the Rev. Mr. Henshaw, Mr. Francis Dolphin, to Miss Henrietta Balden, both of this city.	01/14/1824
Last evening, by the Rev. Dr. Wyatt, Col. William Stansbury, to Rebecca, eldest daughter of the late Thomas Peters, Esq.	01/14/1824
Last evening by the Most Rev. Dr. Mareschal, Mr. Patrick Shannon, to Mary Harriet, daughter of the late Anthony Hermange, Esq.	01/14/1824
At West River, on Tuesday evening, the 6th inst., by the Rev. Mr. Gosnell, the Rev. Mr. Battee, to Miss Elizabeth Caroline Crandall, only daughter of Mrs. Hester Gosnell.	01/14/1824
On Tuesday evening last, by the Rev. Dr. Roberts, Mr. William Rowe, to Miss Eliza M., eldest daughter of William Bosley, Esq., all of this city.	01/15/1824
On Thursday last, by the Rev. Mr. Bartow, Capt. Joseph E. Jenney, to Miss Lenora Myers, both of this city.	01/17/1824
On Monday last, at Church-hill, Md., James Butcher, Esq., an officer of the Revolution, and recently a member of the Executive Council.	01/17/1824
On Sunday evening, 11th inst., at Chestertown, Kent County, Md., by the Rev. Thomas Ware, William Harris, Jr., Esq., to Miss Elizabeth	01/19/1824

Marriage and Death Notices	Date
Garnett, all of that place.	
Died, on the 17th inst., at his residence, in Baltimore County, Oliver Matthews, in the 103rd year of his age. He retained his faculties until near the close, when they, with his bodily strength were discovered to be on the decline, which evidently indicated his approaching dissolution, without any apparent disease, except what was brought on by the *hand of time*; he was one who had been blessed with a good constitution, was of a cheerful and active disposition, which continued with him during his long religious and useful life, in which he practiced great plainness amongst those of his contemporaries and uprightness of conduct, in his dealings amongst men was a principal feature in his character – and it is believed that the following language may with great propriety be adopted respecting him. "Thou shalt come to thy grave in a full age, like a shock of corn cometh in his season."	01/19/1824
Last evening, by the Rt. Rev. Archbishop Mareschal, Dr. Richard S. Steuart, to Maria Louisa, eldest daughter of the Chevalier de Bernabeu, Consul of his most Catholic Majesty, the King of Spain.	01/2/1824
On the 18th inst., by the Rev. Dr. Roberts, Mr. Joshua Cole, to Miss Elizabeth Joyce, all of this city.	01/20/1824
On Sunday evening, after a long and afflictive illness, Mrs. Sarah Welsh, consort of the late Jacob Welsh.	01/20/1824
At Washington, very suddenly, on Monday last, Mr. John Erskine, printer, aged about 40 years.	01/21/1824
On Thursday last, 15th inst., by the Rev. Dr. Glendy, Mr. Michael Sommers, to Miss Mary Ann Blyden, all of this city	01/22/1824
At New Orleans, on the 25th Dec., by the Rev. Mr. Hull, Mr. Lewis Phillips, to Miss Elizabeth Watts, of Baltimore, daughter of Capt. Thomas Watts, late of the U. S. Navy.	01/22/1824
On Thursday last, by the Rev. Dr. Glendy, Samuel Hunt, Esq., to Miss Ann, eldest daughter of the late Capt. John Murphy, all of this city.	01/22/1824
At Annapolis, after a short illness, Mr. Chas. C. Macubbin, assistant clerk to the Senate of Maryland.	01/22/1824
On Tuesday evening, by the Rt. Rev. Bishop Kemp, John P. Kennedy, Esq., to Mary, second daughter of Col. Tenant.	01/23/1824

Marriage and Death Notices	Date
On Tuesday evening last, by the Rev. Job Guest, Mr. Thomas Canon to Miss Harriet Tucker, all of this city.	01/23/1824
By the Rev. Dr. Glendy, on the 24th ult., Mr. John Matthewson, to Miss Emma Nelson.	01/23/1824
On the 15th inst., in the 52nd year of her age, Mrs. Ann Lassell, consort of Mr. Wm. C. Lassell, of Chestertown; the deceased had been for a long time sorely afflicted, but she bore her sufferings with Christian fortitude and resignation, and calmly resigned her spirit to the hands of him from whom she had received it. In her were united all the virtues of a dutiful daughter, a kind and affectionate wife, and a tender and indulgent mother. She has left a large circle of relations to mourn their irreparable loss, but who are consoled in the belief that her pure and immortal spirit is now at rest in the arms of her Redeemer.	01/23/1824
At Annapolis, on Tuesday morning last, much regretted, Mr. Charles C. Maccubbin, Assistant Clerk of the Senate. He was frank, generous, and friendly in disposition, and ever willing to contribute to the relief of the necessitous and unfortunate. His body was on Wednesday committed to the grave with masonic and military honors.	01/23/1824
On Tuesday evening, 20th inst., by the Rev. Mr. Gist, Mr. Worthington, of Baltimore county, to Mrs. Elizabeth Betts, third daughter of Mr. William Ball, Sr., of this city.	01/24/1824
OBITUARY. Departed this life, on the 12th inst., at his residence, in Church hill, Queen Ann's county, James Butcher, Esq., late a member of the executive council of Maryland, aged about 68 years. He was emphatically the noblest work of God - *an honest man.* When seventeen years of age, he embarked with enthusiasm into our revolutionary struggle, and the temperate flame of patriotism never glowed more steadily and unceasingly in the bosom of any man throughout the whole period of a long life than in his. He was long in the full enjoyment of public confidence, while his health permitted him to be in public life, and in *all the relations in life, whether public or private,* he was kind and punctiliously honorable, and perhaps no man ever died uniting the good opinion of all who knew him, of whatever politics, more completely than he did.	01/24/1824
Died, on Wednesday last, Dr. Thomas Hamilton, in the 60th year of his age. Dr. Hamilton was an elegant scholar and a polite gentleman; but he was chiefly esteemed for possessing, in an eminent degree, those amiable & valuable qualities which rendered him a delightful companion and a kind, safe, and useful friend. He was a native of	01/24/1824

Marriage and Death Notices	Date
Ireland, but had resided a number of years in Baltimore, where he had many and true friends, who will sincerely feel and regret the loss of a man of such talents and worth.	
On Thursday evening last, by the Rev. Mr. Carback, Mr. Cheany Hatton, to Miss Sarah Abercrombie, all of Baltimore county.	01/28/1824
On Thursday evening, by the Rev. Mr. Carback, Mr. William Wheaton, to Mrs. Eleanor Asher, both of Baltimore county.	01/28/1824
In Washington city, on Sunday night last, after a lingering illness, which he bore with singular fortitude and resignation, Mr. James Pettigreu, printer, aged 40 years.	01/28/1824
At Philadelphia, suddenly, Mr. James G. Chamberlain, formerly a respectable merchant of that city.	01/28/1824
At Elkton, on the 20th inst., by the Rev. Mr. Megraw, Mr. Alexander Millar, of this city, to Miss Amelia I. Coale, daughter of Wm. S. Coale, of Cecil county.	01/29/1824
At the bay of Baluxi, Mississippi, Cady La Fontaine, aged 137. He retained his faculties until the day of his death.	01/30/1824
On Thursday evening, Jan. 29th, by the Rev. John P. Peckworth, Mr. Benjamin Cromwell, to Miss Juliann Johnson, both of Baltimore county.	01/31/1824
On Thursday last, by the Rev. Mr. Kesley, Charles John Heart, merchant, of Baltimore, to Margaret, third daughter of James Halfpenny, of the same place.	01/31/1824
On Thursday last, by the Rev. E. J. Reis, Mr. James B. Preston, to Eleanor, daughter of Mr. William Cook, all of this city.	01/31/1824
On the 31st inst., Mr. Ignatius Hoover, in the 61st year of his age, an old and respectable citizen of this city. His friends and acquaintance are requested to attend his funeral, tomorrow afternoon, at 3 o'clock, from his late dwelling, on the old Georgetown road.	01/31/1824
On Wednesday evening last, by the Rev. Mr. McElheny, Dr. Thomas C. Risteau, to Miss Ann Boyd Courtney, only daughter of the late Hercules Courtney, Esq., all of Baltimore county.	02/02/1824
On Tuesday, the 20th of January, by the Rev. Dr. Roberts, Mr. Archibald Stewart, to Miss Matilda Hands Lock, second daughter of Nathaniel	02/02/1824

Marriage and Death Notices	Date
Lock, all of this city.	
Suddenly, on Saturday, noon, 31st ult., Mr. Nicholas Leake, aged 76, one among the first settlers of Baltimore town, and one of the oldest and most respectable inhabitants of Fell's Point. He participated in the great struggle for independence, in which he bore an honorable part in the fatigues and privations of the army with obedience and submission. Society has lost a useful member.	02/02/1824
By the Rev. Dr. Glendy, on the 23rd ult., Mr. John Rogers, to Miss Nancy Daffin, all of this city.	02/03/1824
By the Rev. Dr. Glendy, on Monday last, Mr. Henry M. Starr, to Miss Eliza Waters, all of this city.	02/03/1824
At Cotton Wood, near Natchez, Miss., on Thursday, 31st Dec., Mr. William A. Boughan, merchant of that place, and late of Baltimore, to Indiana, daughter of the late Judge McCaler.	02/03/1824
This morning, after an illness of 3 days, Mr. Derick Fahnestock, aged 49 years, long a resident and respectable merchant of this city. His numerous friends and acquaintance are respectfully invited to attend his funeral, tomorrow morning, at 10 o'clock, from his late dwelling, No. 15, North Howard street.	02/03/1824
On Tuesday evening, the 3rd inst., in the 62nd year of his age, Mr. James Cockey, of Edward. His relatives and friends are respectfully invited to attend his funeral, tomorrow, Feb. 5th, at 12 o'clock, A. M., from his late residence, in Jones street, O. T.	02/04/1824
On Tuesday evening last, by the Rev. Mr. Bartow, Mr. William James, to Miss Ann Allen, all of this city.	02/05/1824
At Westminster, Frederick county, on the 29th ult., by the Rev. Geo. Leidy, Mr. Jacob Reese, merchant, to Miss Eleanor Fisher, all of that place.	02/05/1824
On Tuesday evening last, by the Rev. Wm. Nevins, Dr. Patrick Macaulay, to Sarah, daughter of the late Joseph Thornburgh, all of this city.	02/06/1824
Yesterday, by the Rev. Dr. Kenley, Mr. Isaac Dryden, to Miss Elizabeth N. Thompson, only daughter of the late Mr. William Thompson, all of this city.	02/06/1824

Marriage and Death Notices	Date
On Thursday, the 29th ult., by the Rev. Mr. Allen, Mr. Thomas Camby to Miss Deborah, eldest daughter of Dr. Benjamin Duvall, all of Montgomery county, Md.	02/06/1824
On Monday last, the 2nd of February, Mr. John Parrish, carpenter, aged 55 years.	02/06/1824
On Wednesday evening, Mrs. Charity, wife of John H. Barney, Esq.	02/07/1824
On the evening of the 4th inst., of a very short illness, Mrs. Mary Taylor, in the 77th year of her age.	02/07/1824
On Thursday evening last, 5th Feb., by the Rev. Joshua Wells, Mr. Harry Fitch Turner, to Miss Rebecca Thomas, all of this city.	02/09/1824
On the 24th ult., Mrs. Elizabeth Cock, consort of the late Capt. John Cock, in the 42nd year of her age, much respected and lamented by all who knew her.	02/09/1824
At Louisville, Ken., Mr. Benjamin Crandall, coppersmith. Miss Eliza Barney, daughter of the late Com. Barney, aged 13.	02/09/1824
On Tuesday evening last, 3rd Feb., by the Rev. Mr. Choate, Mr. Luke Ensor, of this city, to Miss Eleanor Lemmon, of Baltimore county.	02/10/1824
At West River, Anne Arundel county, Md., Richard G. Watkins, Esq., to Lucretia Margaret, daughter of Col. Richard Harwood, of that county.	02/10/1824
On Tuesday last, after a short, but severe illness, Charles Dudley, youngest son of Mr. Dudley Poor.	02/10/1824
On the morning of the 8th inst., at his residence, near Baltimore, in the 48th year of his age, James Fulton, a native of Londonderry, and nearly the whole of the last thirty years, a respectable citizen of Baltimore.	02/10/1824
In Frederick, on Sunday, 8th inst., aged 33 years, Mrs. Matilda Auchincloss, daughter of Mr. James Inglis, of this city.	02/11/1824
On the 27th ult., in Accomack county, Va., by the Rev. Mr. Chase, Mr. John Rutter, of Baltimore, to Miss Mary U. Teackle.	02/12/1824
In Richmond, John Grantland, Esq., Attorney at Law; a gentleman of fine genius, extensive acquirements, and possessed of many valuable qualities.	02/12/1824

Marriage and Death Notices	Date
In Easton, on Wednesday night, 4th inst., after a short, but painful illness, Alexander Graham, eldest son of the editor of the Easton Gazette.	02/12/1824
At Harrisburg, Penn., 9th inst., Miss Elizabeth M'Call, formerly of Baltimore county, where her friends still reside.	02/13/1824
At Boston, Mrs. Elizabeth, wife of the Rev. Henry Ware, and eldest daughter of Dr. Benjamin Waterhouse, aged 31.	02/14/1824
On Thursday last, by the Rev. Dr. Jennings, Mr. Joshua Stinchcomb, to Miss Teresa Webster, all of this city.	02/16/1824
This morning, 16th of second month, in the 75th of his age, Elisha Tyson. The friends of the deceased are generally, *without further notice*, respectfully invited to attend his burial. The corpse to leave his late dwelling, on Sharp street, on fourth day, afternoon, the 8th inst., at three o'clock, precisely. The procession to be on foot, and the interment to take place in Friends burying ground, in the eastern end of the city.	02/16/1824
On Sunday last, by the Rt. Rev. Bishop Kemp, Mr. Robert Smiley, Jr., to Miss Elizabeth Welsh, both of this city.	02/17/1824
On Sunday evening last, by the Rev. Mr. Valiant, Mr. W. Gittings, to Miss Eliza Smith, both of this city.	02/17/1824
On Sunday evening last, by the Rev. Dr. Roberts, Mr. Thomas Norris, to Eliza, eldest daughter of John Ruckle, all of this city.	02/17/1824
On Sunday night last, in the 70th year of his age, Marmaduke Tilden, Esq., another of the Revolutionary characters who struggled for the independence of our country, and who has supported the character of an honest and upright man, and above all, that of a Christian.	02/17/1824
On Monday morning last, Mr. Charles William Augustus., eldest son of Mr. William Conway, merchant of this city, in the 26th year of his age, of a painful and lingering disease, which he bore for three years, with the greatest fortitude and resignation, after giving every manifestation of his joyful hope of being received into the bosom of his Father and his God.	02/17/1824
On Monday, 9th February, at 3 o'clock, Mr. Thomas Beasman, in his 74th year, after a lingering illness, which he bore with Christian fortitude, and was perfectly resigned to the will of God. He requested his friends not to weep for him – that he had a hope beyond the grave, as	02/17/1824

354

Marriage and Death Notices	Date
he had an advocate with the father, even Jesus Christ, the righteous.	
On the 11 inst., Mrs. Elizabeth Ward, in the 79th year of her age, formerly of Cecil county, but for many years a resident of this city. "Blessed are the dead which die in the Lord, from henceforth; yea saith the spirit, that they may rest from their labors; and their works do follow them."	02/17/1824
At Washington, on Saturday night, the 14th instant, in the 73rd year of his age, Richard O'Brien, Esq., late Consul General of the United States to the Barbary Powers. The character and history of this extraordinary man are too generally known to need any statement here. A mind of native vigor, and the most arden feeling, was in him still further strengthened by a series of adventures the most interesting and diversified. He was, in succession, an active and experienced seaman, a successful adventurer in the privateering exploits of the Revolution, a brave commander in the regular naval service, a captive slave in Algiers, Consul General to Barbary, member of the Pennsylvania Legislature, a worthy farmer, and lastly, an ardent party politician. His earthly scenes are now closed, and he has experienced his last and great change. The merit of his public services has been officially acknowledged by the successive Presidents; and will long be remembered by his country.	02/17/1824
Yesterday, the remains of the worthy and venerable Elisha Tyson were interred in the Friends burying ground in this city. A numerous concourse of relatives and friends attended his obsequies, together, it is supposed, with nearly four thousand people of color, who assembled to pay their last tribute of respect and gratitude to their deceased friend and patron. Mr. Tyson for many years had been the unvaried champion of oppressed humanity; and, whenever he discovered an attempt to violate the laws of his country in the cruel traffic of human flesh, his zeal was active and efficient. His feelings were alive to human suffering, and his sense of justice outweighed all considerations of favor and friendship. The spectacle was indeed truly impressive and solemn, and evinced a sense of gratitude in these children of misfortune, highly honorable to their character, which was manifested by a strict decorum and a high sense of the great loss they had sustained. *Telegraph.*	02/19/1824
On the 31st of December last, at her residence, near Versailles, Ripley county, Indiana, in the 27th year of her age, of a pulmonary complaint, Mrs. Henrietta Fisher, daughter of the late Mr. Henry Hupfild, of Philadelphia, leaving a husband and an infant son, together with a numerous circle of relatives and friends to lament her loss.	02/19/1824

Marriage and Death Notices	Date
Last evening, by the Rev. E. J. Reis, Mr. John R. Currie, to Miss Lydia Cole Webster, both of this city.	02/20/1824
On Thursday evening last, Mr. William D. Allen, in the 23rd year of his age. The members of Warren Lodge No. 51 and the masonic brethren generally, are invited to meet at the Masonic Hall, on Saturday evening, at 2 o'clock, for the purpose of attending his funeral.	02/20/1824
On board brigantine, John Dunscomb, on her passage from Kingston, Jam. to Turks Island, Mr. Charles Fair, a native of Baltimore. He has left a few dollars due him on account of wages, which will be paid to his legal representatives, on application to Capt. Seymour, on board, or to Messrs. J. Q. Aymar & Co., at Norfolk.	02/20/1824
On Thursday last, by the Rev. Dr. Jennings, Mr. John Thomas Barber, of Annapolis, to Miss Isabella Reaney, of this place.	02/21/1824
Last evening, by the Rev. Mr. Bartow, Dr. Marcellus Keene, to Miss Anna R. Horsey, all of this city.	02/23/1824
On Thursday last, by the Rev. Mr. Guest, Mr. Charles King, Jr., of Granville, Ohio, to Miss Louisa, daughter of Wm. Ball, Esq., of this city.	02/23/1824
This morning, of a pulmonary disease, Mr. Benjamin Stansbury, of Anne Arundel county, aged 35 years and 3 days, leaving to lament their irreparable loss, a disconsolate wife and four children. By the unexpected death of this man, the truth of that blessed saying of our Lord is made more than ever plain to us. "Be ye therefore also ready, for in such an hour as ye think not, the son of man cometh."	02/23/1824
On Saturday last, in the 63rd year of his age, Mr. Hugh Foy, Sr. Mr. Foy was formerly a merchant in the north of Ireland, very extensive in business, and possessed of considerable wealth. He met, however, with sad vicissitudes, which naturally rendered his temper hasty and irascible; but nothing ever befell him that could diminish the large benevolence of his heart. He has left in this city two sons to deplore his sudden dissolution.	02/23/1824
In this city, on Wednesday morning last, Mr. George I. Thornburg, in the 21st year of his age.	02/24/1824
On Sunday night last, after a few hours illness, Mr. James S. Dykes, in the 30th year of his age. "Blessed are the dead that die in the Lord, for	02/24/1824

Marriage and Death Notices	Date
they rest from their labours, and their works do follow them."	
Last evening, by the Rev. Mr. Stansbury, Mr. John R. Kemp, of Huntington, Pennsylvania, to Miss Ruth, youngest daughter of the late Capt. Joshua Beasman, of this city.	02/26/1824
On Tuesday evening last, by the Rev. Mr. Duncan, Mr. Samuel Moreton, Jr., of Baltimore county, to Miss Kezia Hubbal, of this place.	02/26/1824
On Tuesday evening last, by the Rev. Mr. Henshaw, Mr. William D. Nutt, merchant, of Alexandria, D. C., to Miss Pamela K. Andrew, of this city.	02/26/1824
On Tuesday morning, 24th inst., by the Rev. Dr. Deluhol, Mr. Thomas S. Hardy, of Prince George's county, to Eleanor A., only daughter of Capt. Pliny Hamilton, of this city.	02/27/1824
On the 21st inst., Miss Amelia Stansbury, of Baltimore county, in the 21st year of her age, after a short, but painful illness. Her friends have much reason to hope and believe that her soul has taken its flight to the mansions of everlasting rest.	02/27/1824
Departed this life, last evening, in the 88th year of her age, Margaret Fisher, long a respectable member of the Society of Friends, and for many years a resident of this city. Her friends and acquaintances are particularly invited to attend her funeral, from the late dwelling of William Starr, corner of Fell and Market streets, Fell's Point, at 10 o'clock, on seventh day morning, the 28th inst. *"Blessed are they who die in the Lord."*	02/27/1824
Departed this life, on the 22nd inst., Mrs. Mary Kramer, consort of Frederick A. Kramer, Esq., in the 54th year of her age – leaving a disconsolate husband and 3 amiable daughters to bemoan their irreparable bereavement of an affectionate wife and mother. "Best of thy sex, alas farewell! From this dark scene removed to shine, Where purest shades of mortals dwell, And virtue waits to welcome thine.	02/27/1824
In Washington, on the 11th inst., after a short illness, which he bore with Christian fortitude and resignation, Mrs. Amelia F. Wolfenden, relict of the late John Wolfenden, Esq., merchant, of Baltimore.	02/27/1824
On the 17th inst., in Prince George's county, Md., by the Rev. Mr. Tyng, John Contee, Esq., to Miss Ann Snowden, daughter of the late Richard	02/28/1824

Marriage and Death Notices	Date
Snowden, Esq., all of Prince George's county.	
Yesterday morning, after a severe illness, Col. Kennedy Long – long a respectable inhabitant of this city.	02/28/1824
Yesterday afternoon, of a protracted illness, John H., eldest son of Col. Jacob Small, in the 28th year of his age, having faithfully fulfilled the relationship of a dutiful son, affectionate brother, and sincere friend. In the death of this worthy young man, his afflicted parents have again to mourn the loss of a third one of their offspring, in the short space of three months – well may they explaim with the poet – "Insatiate archer! could not one suffice? Thy shaft flew thrice, and thrice our peace was slain; An thrice, e'er thrice yon moon had filled her horn."	02/28/1824
At his seat, in Anne Arundel county, yesterday morning, in the 69th year of his age, the Hon. Richard Ridgely, late an Associate Judge of the third Judicial District of Maryland. As a lawyer, Mr. Ridgely ranked high in the profession, and for many years occupied a prominent situation, as an advocate in the courts of this state. In times of peril and danger, during the revolutionary war, he took an active stand in support of those principles, the triumph of which, established the liberties of his country; and, he afterwards devoted a considerable portion of his life to public service, in the legislature of this his native state. As a judge, he was intelligent, firm, decided, and impartial; and, it is a source of consolation to his family and surviving relatives, to know, that in his last illness, he expressed his full and unequivocal believe in the doctrines of Christ, his Savior, and departed in the hope of a blessed immortality through his merits and mediation.	02/28/1824
Suddenly, on the 4th inst., John Cocky Robert Burly Boon, in the 84th year of his age; he was a citizen of Baltimore county, about six miles from the city, all his life.	02/28/1824
After a protracted illness, at his lodgings, in Washingon city, on Sunday last, the Hon. William Lee Ball, aged about 45, for several years past, and at the time of his death, a representative in Congress, from the state of Virginia. Mr. B. united to the social and amiable qualities which made him the delight of his friends, powers of intellect, which, though seldom called forth, were effective whenever exerted in his public station.	03/02/1824
On Thursday evening last, by the Rev. Mr. Smith, Mr. George C. Collins, Jr., to Miss Mary Vansant, all of this city.	03/02/1824

Marriage and Death Notices	Date
On Friday night last, at his residence in Washington city, after a long illness, Col. Constant Freeman, Auditor of the Treasury for the Navy Department, aged 67. Col. F. was an officer of the army during the whole of the Revolutionary war, and from its close down to the termination of the late war with Great Britain, when on the reduction of the Army, he was placed by the President in the responsible office which he filled at the time of his death.	03/02/1824
On the 10th ult., in Charleston, South Carolina, George Flagg, Esq., a native of Portsmouth, New Hampshire, but since the year 1776 a resident of the city in which he died. He was a patriot of the revolution, and one who devoted himself to the cause with ardor and zeal. He was one of those fifty-eight distinguished citizens of the republic who were torn from their families, borne into captivity, and confined in St. Augustine, in the year 1780.	03/02/1824
In Frederickton, New Brunswick, on the 9th inst., after two days illness, the Hon. Ward Chipman, President of the Providence, a native of Massachusetts, and brother to Mrs. Gray, of Boston, and Mrs. Blackler, of Marblehead, lately deceased. He has left only one child, a son, the inheritor of his father's talents and virtues, and now Speaker of the House of Assembly, of New Brunswick. Mr. Chipman's father, an eminent counsellor, died suddenly at Portland, many years since, of the same disorder, the gout in the stomach.	03/02/1824
Died at his late residence on Elkridge, on the morning of the 26th inst., the Hon. Richard Ridgely, an associate judge of the third judicial district of Maryland, in the 69th year of his age. Thus, after a long and painful illness, is closed the mortal existence of a man whose vigorous constitution, might have borne the weight of many years to come; and thus has passed from the earthly scene of his charities and labours, the affectionate parent, the indulgent master, the faithful friend, the kind neighbor, the able lawyer, and upright judge. This brief notice aims not at a delineation of the character of its subject; it is a hasty sketch of what may be usefully exhibited; a faithful record of what ought not to be concealed, and cannot be forgotton. The intellectual character of Judge Ridgely was known to be of a high order. To quick apprehension, a retentive memory, a judgment sound and discriminating, and an understanding acute, vigorous, and solid, was added a curiosity to enquire, patience in research, and labor of investigating, which led to a deep and accurate acquaintance with the principles and practice of law, and entitled his decision as a judge, to high respect and consideration; whilst his incessant and extensive reading, through a range, illuminated by moral, historical, and political scene, furnished not only resources and employment for his own mind,	03/02/1824

Marriage and Death Notices	Date

but whence he could afford amusement or improvement on the varied subjects of literary discussion. To the benevolence of his feelings, to his many kindnesses, there is an ample and not a silent testimony. The enumeration of the latter would form his most eloquent panegyric, and the tears of gratitude, which were often the only return of the widow and orphan, are the most affecting proof of that benevolence, which delighted in any relief it could afford. But it is the glory of the last scene which sheds that lustre upon his character and destiny; that dims the brightness of the most splendid acquirements, and casts in utter shadow, all human greatness. It is the glory of the "new man in Christ Jesus," who ransomed from sin and death, is renewed by the unction of the holy one with the love of God, shed abroad in his heart, and triumphant in the riches of his grace and the power of his spirit, longs to part and be with Christ. Such, in the plentitude of divine love, and the exhaustless riches of sovereign grace, was made the subject of this notice. In the 'eleventh hour' did God call his aged servant to this work and to this reward. Without the inrtervention of human means, but by the clear, powerful, and overwhelming testimony of the spirit to his own word, was the heart that had long been shut, opened to receive it. In all the might of its conviction, to lay hold on the only hope it offers to perishing sinners in the blood of the cross, to rejoice in the fullness of its consolations, and finally to exalt in the hope of its blessed, abundant, and everlasting happiness. It was the work of God – the happy Christian owned it – and in the spirit, and almost in the words of the psalmist, be he said, 'come all ye that fear God, and see what he hath done for my soul."

Let it only be remembered, that he, thus renewed, had spent a long life without reference to that awful futurity beyond the grave; that he inclined to that dismal philosophy, which denies to man peace in this life, and hope that in which is come; that during his severe and protracted illness, in the repeated prospect of immediate dissolution, though torured with distressing anxieties and fearful forebodings, in the pride and hardihood of unawakened mind, he maintained the utmost firmness and composure. But the power of God knows no resistance; and he who arrested the persecuting soul, erects this monument to his victorious grace. The deceased continued for several days, with his mind perfectly composed; never displaying more intellectual vigour, and never certainly such a concern for his own past life, as well as the immortal interests of his friends. Now enlightened, he wished to obviate any evil he might have occasioned, and repeatedly called upon his attending friends in the most solemn and affectionate manner "to testify" such were his words "his repentance deep and unfeigned, his sole hope and trust in the atoning merits of our Lord Jesus Christ; and of the mercy vouchsafed to his own soul through the mediator between

Marriage and Death Notices	Date

God and man." Then, after an interval of repose, on the night preceeding his dissolution, as if collecting his powers for one last great effort, during an hour and a half in eloquent, pathetic language, having exhorted his weeping firnds, and assured them of the nearing and brightening prospects of his eternal glory, he fell into a placid slumber, and a little after 8 o'clock in the morning, "he slept in Jesus."

Let the dying request of a public man, who has served the public faithfully and honorably, that his faith should be publicly known, be the apology of this lengthened notice. It is not to blazan a name – not to sound a trumpet of his righteousness and good deeds – not to make an ideal and vain parade of the triumphs of a spirit that we believe has gone to its glory; but in the face of the world to tell the gay voluptuary – the wretched infidel – the decent of this world's business or pleasures, or glories – and the man who hinks it decent to believe and profess religion, all of whom were probably in the circle of acquaintance and intercourse in which our departed friend moved – to tell them each and all, that they are in a lost and undone state, and that an old man, formerly estranged to God, in the last week of his life, found mercy in Christ Jesus, and died exalting in the hope of his glory. This feeble tribute is paid by one who was a witness to the last scenes of the deceased.

On the 1st inst., by the Rev. Dr. Bartow, Dr. Richard Bland, of Prince George county, Va., to Miss Adelina, daughter of Col. Robert Morton, of Somerset.	03/03/1824
Yesterday morning, after a long and painful illness, Margaret Dukehart, an old and respectable member of the Society of Friends, in the 82nd year of her age. In her domestic relations, she conducted herself with exemplary propriety. In the course of her life, she experienced sore bodily pains, and in the loss of relatives and friends, sore bereavements. But these trying dispensations of Divine Providence she bore with submissive patience, and under them exhibited great fortitude of mind. Her last illness was particularly distressing and the pains which she suffered were excruciating, yet she endured all with Christian patience, and while she bowed in silence to the will of God, gave the strongest possible evidence that she adored the hand that afflicted her. Her friends and acquaintance are respectfully requested to attend her funeral, on fifth day morning, at 11 o'clock, from her late dwelling, No. 100½ Market street.	03/03/1824
On the 20th of Feb., aged 33 years, Mrs. Susan M. Tharp, wife of Mr. George Tharp, of this city. She has left an affectionate husband and six small children, with a large circle of relatives and friends, to deplore	03/04/1824

Marriage and Death Notices	Date
their loss.	
On Thursday evening, by the Rev. Mr. Lee, Mr. Samuel Pinor, of this city, aged 70 years, to Mrs. Hannah Selby, of Snow Hill, aged 80 years.	03/06/1824
On Thursday evening last, by the Rev. Mr. Duncan, Mr. Samuel Barr, to Miss Eliza Thompson, all of this city.	03/06/1824
On the 4th inst., at the residence of Thos. Hillen, Esq., near this city, Mrs. Janett Wells, a native of Scotland, in the 82nd year of her age. She lived respected and died regretted by her numerous acquaintance. If universal benevolence, Christian charity, and firm faith in the death and merits of a crucified Redeemer, are virtues, which may claim a reward beyond the grave, her friends and relatives may indulge the pleasing hope, that she has exchanged the toils and troubles of this mortal life, for the joy and felicity of another which will never end.	03/06/1824
At Easton, Talbot county, Md., Peter S. Dickinson, Esq., aged 36. On Monday last, he was thrown from a gig, by which he sustained a fracture of the scull, and an injury of the breast, the effects of which he survived but a few hours.	03/06/1824
On Wednesday evening last, by the Rev. Mr. Bartow, Mr. Martin Vickart, to Miss Harriet Veldy, all of this city.	03/09/1824
On Sunday, the 7th inst., John Howard, son of Dr. Davidge, aged about two years and eight months.	03/09/1824
On the 1st of Sept., 1823, while descending the Mississippi River, in a boat, Mr. Joseph Murray, a native of Baltimore.	03/09/1824
On the 23rd ult., Mr. Corbin Preston, in the 65th year of his age, of a protracted illness, which he bore with Christian resignation and fortitude. His death his been regretted by all his friends and acquaintances. It may well be said that he was an honest and upright man.	03/09/1824
On 2nd March, in the 33rd year of her age, Mrs. Charlotte Hayner Done, wife of William Done, Esq., of Princess Ann, Somerset county; leaving an afflicted husband and three small children to lament their loss.	03/09/1824
At the United States Arsenal, near Baltimore, in the 75th year of his age, Maj. David Hopkins, a patriot and soldier of the revolution. He served in the army during the whole of the revolutionary war, and received honorable testimony from the Commander in Chief, Gen. Washington,	03/09/1824

Marriage and Death Notices	Date
of his ardor, zeal, and distinguished merit in that eventful contest.	
On Tuesday evening, by the Rev. Mr. Smith, Mr. Charles De Spada, to Miss Margaret Ann West, all of this city.	03/10/1824
By the Rev. Dr. Glendy, on Thursday last, Mr. John McCleary, to Miss Elizabeth McCleine, all of this city.	03/10/1824
By the Rev. Dr. Glendy, on Saturday last, Mr. James Kerr, to Miss Mary Ann McElroy, both of this city.	03/10/1824
Mr. Robert Norton to Miss Sarah Mullican, both of Prince George's county, Md.	03/10/1824
At Nottingham, Mr. Hewitt I. Morau, to Miss Susan Estep, both of Prince George's county, Md.	03/10/1824
At Easton, Md., on Monday last, Peter S. Dickinson, Esq., late Postmaster at the Trappe, in that county. Mr. Dickinson left home, on the above day, on horse back, for the purpose of transacting some business at St. Michaels, and having got thus far on his way engaged a sulkey, conceiving that the most pleasant mode of traveling, but not proceeded in it more than three hundred yards before his horse became unruly and making a plunge dashed him from his seat – he fell upon his head and expired a few hours afterwards – Mr. Dickinson was highly respected and has left a number of relatives and friends to lament his untimely end.	03/10/1824
On Thursday evening, the 4th, by the Rev. Dr. Wyatt, Mr. William S. Holmes, of Boston, to Susannah, second daughter of Mr. Martin Bowers, of this city.	03/11/1824
This morning, 11th inst., in the 24th year of his age, James W. Goodrick. His friends and acquaintance are respectfully invited to attend his funeral, at 10 o'clock, tomorrow morning, from his brother's dwelling, No. 60 Pratt street.	03/11/1824
On Tuesday evening, by the Rev. Mr. Nevins, James H. McCulloch, Jr., Esq., to Eliza, daughter of Alexander Mactier, Esq.	03/12/1824
On the 10th inst., by the Rev. Mr. Hargrove, Henry Chinowith, to Miss Louisa Hall, all of this city.	03/12/1824
On Sunday evening, 7th inst., after a long and painful disease, Mr. John Rich, fourth son of the late Capt. Mathias Rich, a native of Boston,	03/12/1824

Marriage and Death Notices	Date
Mass., aged 30 years.	
Yesterday evening, after a long and painful illness, James Anderson, Esq., formerly American Consul at several ports in Europe and the West Indies. His friends and acquaintance are invited to attend his funeral, from Mr. Barney's Hotel, in Light street, this evening, at 5 o'clock.	03/13/1824
Last evening, in the 53rd year of his age, Mr. Charles R. Green, auctioneer, leaving a wife and two children to lament their loss. His friends and acquaintance are requested to attend his funeral, this afternoon, at three o'clock, from his late dwelling, Swann street, Marsh Market.	03/13/1824
On Friday evening, in the 68th year of her age, Mrs. Elizabeth Beckley – her friends and acquaintances are respectfully invited to attend her funeral, from her late dwelling, South Howard street, at three o'clock, tomorrow afternoon.	03/13/1824
On Thursday evening, the 4th inst., by the Rev. Mr. Choate, Mr. John Devries, to Miss Sarah Ann King, both of Baltimore county.	03/15/1824
On Tuesday night last, at his seat, near Bladensburg, Prince George's County, William Bayly, Esq., in the 83rd year of his age, a Patriot of the Revolution.	03/16/1824
In Buenos Ayres, South America, Mr. Joseph Pierce, Jr., son of Joseph H. Pierce, Esq., of Boston, Massachusetts.	03/16/1824
Last evening, by the Rev. Mr. Bartow, Walter Price, Esq., to Eliza Ann, eldest daughter of Dr. Joseph Allender, all of this city.	03/17/1824
In Lansingburgh, N. Y., on the 23rd ult., Mrs. Mary Chubb, in the 63rd year of her age. She had been for some time afflicted with an increasing debility, and went down gradually to the grave. Her amiable deportment had endeared her to all her friends, and a numerous assembly testified their respect for departed worth, by attending her funeral solemnities. As a mother, she was kind and affectionate; as a friend, she was sincere, whose memory will be long dear to a numerous acquaintance and an affectionate but bereaved family. Her living and dying testimonies were in favor of the gospel.	03/17/1824
On Tuesday evening, by the Rt. Rev. Bishop Kemp, Nicholas Martin, Esq., of Talbot county, to Miss Sarah G. Stuart, of this city.	03/19/1824
On Thursday evening last, by the Rev. Mr. Kurtz, Mr. George Hoover,	03/19/1824

Marriage and Death Notices	Date
to Miss Elizabeth Hann, both of this city.	
On Thursday evening, 18th inst., by the Rev. John P. Peckworth, Mr. Darius Wheeler, to Miss Mary Moody, all of this city.	03/20/1824
On Sunday evening last, by the Rev. Mr. Guest, Mr. Nicholas Burtow, to Mrs. Mary Lawrence, both of this city.	03/20/1824
On Thursday evening last, by the Rev. Mr. Hinkle, the Rev. Jacob Lakin, to Miss Louisa, daughter of the late Capt. Dimond, deceased, of Fell's Point.	03/20/1824
On Tuesday evening last, by the Rev. Mr. Bartow, Capt. Edmund Gardner, to Miss Ann, eldest daughter of Benjamin Baker, both of Baltimore.	03/20/1824
In Boston, Mrs. Susanna Rowson, aged 62, consort of William Rowson, and formerly of the Baltimore Theatre. Mrs. Rowson was distinguished for her talents, virtues, and intelligence, and was the writer of several popular novels, approved school books, and articles in prose and poetry, in aid of charitable institutions.	03/20/1824
Last evening, by the Rev. Mr. Snyder, Mr. George Kraft, to Miss Eve Ann, daughter of Lewis Kalbfus, all of this city.	03/24/1824
On Sunday evening last, by the Rev. Mr. Soule, Mr. James G. Neale, to Miss Mary Ann Ruth, both of this city.	03/24/1824
On the 23rd inst., Mrs. Elliott, widow of the late Hartman Elliott, aged 62 years. Her friends and acquaintance are respectfully invited to attend her funeral, from her late dwelling, No. 20, South Howard street, this day, at 4 o'clock, P. M.	03/24/1824
On Wednesday, 17th of March, aged 13 years, Albertina, daughter of Albert Seekamp, Esq., late of this city. Seldom are the tenderest sympathies of friendship more justly due to sorrowing parents and grieving relations – seldom does the grave close over one so beloved in life, so lamented in death!	03/25/1824
On Wednesday evening last, by the Rev. Bishop Kemp, Mr. Frederick P. Belford, to Miss Elizabeth Rooley, all of this city.	03/27/1824
By the Rev. Mr. Uhlhorn, Mr. John Martin, to Miss Elizabeth Hollman, both of this city.	03/27/1824

Marriage and Death Notices	Date
On Thursday evening, the 25th, by the Rev. Mr. Greenwood, Mr. William Whitfield, to Miss Mary Stacey, both of Baltimore.	03/29/1824
This morning, the venerable William Wilson, President of the Bank of Baltimore, and long a distinguished and successful merchant of this city.	03/30/1824
On Sunday evening last, by the Rev. Mr. Ely, Mr. Jacob Kaylor, to Miss Elizabeth Fossett, eldest daughter of John Fossett, all of this city.	03/31/1824
On Thursday evening last, by the Rev. Dr. Jennings, Richard Jennings Anderson, to Elizabeth Rawlings, both of this place.	03/31/1824
Suddenly, in New Bedford, on the 23rd ult., Mary Tyson, consort of George Tyson, of this city. Mildness, simplicity, generosity, and benevolence were conspicuous embellishments in the radient character of the deceased.	03/31/1824
The friends and acquaintance of the late William Wilson, Esq., President of the Bank of Baltimore, are respectfully invited to attend his funeral, tomorrow, Thursday, afternoon, at 3 o'clock, without further invitation. A Ship Master respectfully suggests to the masters of vessels to hoist their flags at half mast tomorrow, Thursday, as a mark of respect to the late William Wilson, Esq.	03/31/1824
On Tuesday evening, by the Rev. Mr. Nevins, Mr. John A. Bentz, merchant, to Miss Caroline Jane Henderson, both of this city.	04/01/1824
On Tuesday evening, by the Rev. Mr. Evans, Mr. John A. Bentz, to Miss Caroline Jane Henderson, both of this city.	04/01/1824
On Thursday evening last, by the Rev. Mr. Kearny, Mr. David Sindall, to Miss Jane Conway, both of Baltimore county.	04/02/1824
On the 28th ultimo, aged near 77 years, Isaac Trimble, a respected member of the society of friends.	04/02/1824
After a protracted illness, which he bore with unexampled fortitude, Mr. William Hall, in the 45th year of his age.	04/03/1824
At Watertown, Con., Col. Abner Bradley, aged 71. He was a volunteer in the expedition at the northward under Arnold and Allen, and was present at the taking of Ticonderoga. When the British troops came into Connecticut, and burnt Danbury, he again volunteered in the American service, and was wounded on the retreat of the enemy at Compo.	04/03/1824

Marriage and Death Notices	Date
At Oakley, on Wednesday evening last, by the Rev. Mr. McElheny, Mr. Richard Emory, to Ann, daughter of Archibald Gittings, Esq., of Baltimore county.	04/05/1824
On Thursday evening last, by the Rev. Dr. Roberts, Mr. William Crook, to Catherine Theresa, only daughter of the late Mr. Wm. Casey, of this city.	04/05/1824
DEATH WARRANT. The Sheriff of Baltimore has received the warrant for the execution of *Rebecca Preston*, alias Scott, convicted at the recent term of the City Court, of the murder of her child. Her execution is to take place on Friday, 23rd inst.	04/05/1824
This morning, about 11 o'clock, Edward Evatt, in the 46th year of his age. His friends and acquaintance are respectfully invited to attend his funeral, tomorrow afternoon, at half past 3 o'clock, from his late dwelling, in Light street.	04/05/1824
On Saturday last, by the Rev. D. Deluhol, T. J. Bizouard, to Miss Elizabeth Lebon, both of this city.	04/06/1824
Last evening, by the Rev. Dr. Roberts, Mr. Tristram Bowdle, to Miss Elizabeth Trimble, all of this city.	04/06/1824
On Thursday morning, 1st April, after a brief indisposition, Miss Margaret Dorsey, of this city.	04/06/1824
On Sunday evening last, by the Rev. Mr. Bartow, Capt. John C. G. Dechamp, to Mrs. Eliza Porter, all of this city.	04/07/1824
On Thursday evening last, by the Rev. Mr. Guest, Mr. Roswell P. Fish, to Miss Ellen Clark, daughter of Capt. Alexander Clark, all of this city.	04/07/1824
Last evening, by the Rev. Dr. Wyatt, Mr. Richard Mackall, of Calvert county, to Miss Elizabeth, eldest daughter of Col. John Broome, of this city.	04/07/1824
In this city, on the 2nd inst., at the residence of her son in law, Elisha Tyson, Sarah T. Morris, wife of Thomas Morris, of Philadelphia.	04/07/1824
At Albany, Mrs. Sarah Buel, wife of Elias Buel, and mother of J. Buel, late editopr of the Albany Argus, in the 86th year of her age.	04/09/1824
In Portland, Hon. Mathew Cobb, aged 67. For many years a merchant of eminent integrity and benevolence.	04/09/1824

Marriage and Death Notices	Date
In Poland, Maine, 26th Feb., Miss Anna Hall, aged 17. The cause of the sudden exit of this young lady, to the mansion of the dead, is totally unknown, and therefore peculiarly distressing. After the other members of the family had retired to bed, she went to the outer door of the house, and exclaimed, "a fox, a fox." A young man hearing her cry, leaped from his bed, and instantly resorted to the place from whence the scream arose, and found her whom he expected to meet in the full exercise of life's faculties, *a cold lifeless corpse!* occupying a situation 10 or 15 feet from the door, where she stood before.	04/09/1824
On Sunday, 28th ult., after a lingering illness of six months, which he bore with Christian fortitude, Robert Dennis, Esq., of Dorchester county, E. S., Md., in the 73rd year of his age.	04/09/1824
On Thursday evening, by the Rev. Mr. Valiant, Mr. James Bromefield, to Mrs. Mary Ann Reeves, both of this city.	04/10/1824
On Sunday evening last, by the Rev. Dr. Roberts, Mr. Charles Myers, of this city, to Miss Ann Norwood, of Baltimore county.	04/10/1824
On Thursday last, in St. Margaret's Westminster Parish, Anne Arundel county, by the Rev. George B. Schaffer, Mr. John Hall, to Miss Mary, second daughter of the late Henry Hall Dorsey, Esq., all of said county.	04/10/1824
On the 30th ultimo, William Wilson, the venerable President of the Bank of Baltimore. The deceased exhibited in the various relations and uniform tenor of a long and useful life, an example worthy of the highest respect, and pregnant with salutary suggestions alike to the poor and the rich. The former may have learned by his successes, what may be amassed, both of character and fortune, from a laudacle ambition to acquire both by persevering industry and fair dealing; and the latter may have seen in his mild deportment, and numerous charities, how possible it is to enjoy and diffuse the blessings of wealth unassociated with avarice, pomp, and vanity. Few men ever more nearly fulfilled the wise injunction to "know thyself" – for he never aspired to stations of power beyond the compass of his abilities, and was ever less eager to acquire influence, than to use what he justly possessed for the good of society. All the numerous trusts both public and private, commited to his keeping, were discharged with a spotless integrity, which like the confidence it inspired in his fellow ciizens, had no limits or interruption. That he was deeply impressed with the benign doctrines of the Christian religion, he gave the best of all proofs – a constant adherence to the principles, and a daily *practice of the virtues they inculcate.* We are not in the habit of inserting obituary notices, but in this case we have sought to gratify our own feelings, bearing testimony in this way to the	04/10/1824

Marriage and Death Notices	Date
honorable character, the benevolence, and the public spirited and useful actions, of a man to whom this city is deeply indebted, not so much for the prosperity which his enterprise so essentially served to argument, as for the moral influence of a life which teaches propriety that dillegence and rectitude are the true paths to independence and usefulness, and qualify those who practice them, at the close of their mortal career to exclaim triumphantly Oh! death! where is thy sing? Oh! grave! where is thy victory? *American Farmer.*	
At Copenhagen, Jan. 7th, the First Minister of State and for Foreign Affairs, his Excellency Niels De Rosenkrantz, having been Ambassador during a long series of years at Warsaw, Petersburg, Berlin, Paris, and other courts. He was in the year 1810 appointed to the Department of Foreign Affairs, which he fulfilled till his death, and was invested with numerous of the most illustrious orders of knighthood. He was born in 1757, and married, in 1790, the Princess Barbara Wiasemska. He belonged to one of the most ancient noble families of Denmark, and his character and private life were as exemplary as his public was distinguished for talents, zeal, and moral rectitude.	04/10/1824
On the 22nd Feb., after a long, but painful illness, Mr. William Danskin, formerly sailmaker on Bowly's wharf, in this city, in the 43rd year of his age.	04/12/1824
Another Revolutionary Hero Gone. Died, at his residence, in Anne Arundel county, on the 30th ult., Capt. Vachel Burgis, in the 68th year of his age, a gallant soldier of the revolutionary army, attached for seven years to the Maryland line; he evinced a bold and heroic spirit, in the several actions in which that corps was engaged – he particularly distinguished himself, and obtained the eulogies of his commanding officers at Guilford Court House, Eutaw Springs, and in the unfortunate battle at Camden, under Baron de Kalb. His heroism as a soldier, in achieving independence and liberty he so long lived to enjoy, found an accompanying lustre in his virtues, as a citizen and a man. He was upright in his dealings, hospitable, cheerful and kind hearted, intelligent in conversation, pious in his life, and deeply lamented in his death by a numerous family, and a large circle of friends.	04/12/1824
On Thursday last, 8th instant, by the Most Rev. Archbishop Mareschal, Frederick H. A. Barker, Esq., to Miss Harriet A. Randall, daughter of the late Capt. Thomas Randall, of the Revolutionary Army.	04/13/1824

Marriage and Death Notices	Date
On Thursday evening last, by the Rev. Dr. Roberts, Mr. Henry D. Rice, to Miss Eliza Pritchard, both of this city.	04/13/1824
At Biddeford, Maine, on the morning of the 6th instant, of a paralytic affection, the Hon. George Thacher, late one of the Justices of the Supreme Judicial Court of this Commonwealth aged 70.	04/13/1824
On Tuesday evening last, by the Rev. Joseph Shane, Mr. Archibald Wincks, to Miss Sarah Chapman, all of this city.	04/14/1824
On Sunday, April 11, at Washington city, Mr. S. Drake Bryant, Jr., son of the proprietor of the Kentucky Theatre, to Miss Ann Fisher, eldest daughter of Mr. Palmer Fisher, Tragedian, of the Baltimore and Washington Theatres.	04/14/1824
Departed this life, on the 12th inst., after an illness of four days, of the cramp cholic, James Madison Tinges, eldest son of the late Chas. Tinges, of this city, in the 12th year of his age.	04/15/1824
Drowned, at Newcastle, Capt. Nathaniel Lear, aged 53. It is a singular fact, that out of five brothers, four have come to their end by drowning.	04/15/1824
On Thursday evening last, by the Rev. Dr. Roberts, Mr. Samuel McElwee, to Miss Elizabeth Elliott, both of this city.	04/16/1824
On Tuesday evening last, by the Rev. Mr. Henshaw, Vachel W. Randall, Esq., of Hagerstown, Md., to Miss Jane Clagett, of the city of Baltimore.	04/16/1824
At Friends meeting house, Lombard street, on the 14th inst., Asa Jones, of York county, Pennsylvania, to Hannah, second daughter of Wm. Riley, of this city.	04/16/1824
On the 7th inst., Dr. William W. Walls. He was distinguished by his talents as a physician, by his urbanity as a gentleman, and by his deportment as a Christian.	04/16/1824
At Boston, Abial Winship, Esq., aged 55, for many years a respectable merchant of that city.	04/16/1824
On the 13th inst., by the Rev. Dr. Roberts, Mr. Greenbury Kilmon, of Dorset, to Miss Ann Murray, of Baltimore county.	04/17/1824
On Thursday evening last, by the Rev. Dr. Roberts, Mr. Kloudsberry Kirby, of Baltimore county, to Miss Sophia Sands, of this city.	04/17/1824

Marriage and Death Notices	Date
On Sunday evening, 18th inst., by the Rev. John P. Peckworth, Mr. John King, to Miss Mary McQuiller, all of this city.	04/19/1824
On Thursday evening last, by the Rev. Mr. Grice, James Jessop, Esq., to Mrs. Ann Pearse, both of Baltimore county.	04/19/1824
On Thursday evening last, by the Rev. Mr. Bartow, Mr. William Dickson, to Miss Elizabeth Allen, both of this city.	04/19/1824
On Wednesday evening, 31st ult., by the Rev. Mr. Healey, Mr. John McClasky, to Miss Sarah Gibbins, both of Baltimore county.	04/22/1824
On Tuesday evening last, by the Rev. Mr. Healey, Mr. Henry Schofield to Miss Ellen Fisher, all of the same county.	04/22/1824
On Thursday evening last, by the Rt. Rev. Bishop Kemp, James Gallatin, Esq., eldest son of the Hon. Albert Gallatin, to Miss Josephine Mary, daughter of Louis Pascault, Esq., of this city.	04/23/1824
Last evening, by the Rev. Mr. Healey, Mr. Thomas C. Bosley, to Miss Elizabeth Wheeler, all of this city.	04/23/1824
On the 10th of Aprill, at his residence, in St. Mary's county, Charles Chilton, Esq., in the 69th year of his age. He was a patriot of the revolution, and was Purser on board the Virginia Frigate, when she was captured by the British fleet. He was a member of the State Convention, when she ratified the Federal Constitution, and an associate judge of St. Mary's county, when he was appointed by Gen. Washington, about 35 years ago, "surveyor of the Port of Town Creek," which he held until his death, notwithstanding the violent conflicts of party feeling while in office; yet he was always a decided federalist, and among the last men in the world that would ever succumb to those in power. He has left a chasm in his neighborhood that no human being can fill, unless they lived as he did, and did as he did. He lived and died a batchelor, though he lived not alone; for he was daily visited by the poor, the maimed, the halt, the blind, as well as by the rich, and they never left his dwelling, without leaving a blessing behind them. He seemed to live for others and not himself, and of all men the writer of this notice ever knew, he surely was, most emphatically, the poor man's friend.	04/23/1824
On Tuesday evening, last by the Rev. Mr. Bartow, Mr. John Robert to Miss Sarah Gallaway, all of this city.	04/24/1824
At Reisterstown, on the 17th of April, after a long and painful illness, which he bore with Christian fortitude, Mr. William Steeples, in the 69th	04/24/1824

371

Marriage and Death Notices	Date
year of his age.	
On Thursday evening last, by the Rev. Mr. Smith, Mr. John McGirr, to Miss Mary Sharkey, both of this city.	04/26/1824
At Baltimore, on Friday morning, 23rd inst., by the Rev. Mr. Valiant, Mr. Ezra Bourne, of Fayetteville, to Miss Jane P. Gibsen, daughter of William Gibsen, merchant, of Philadelphia.	04/26/1824
On the 18th inst., by the Rev. Mr. Ballentine, of Philadelphia, Mr. John F. Cassell, Surgeons Instrument maker, of this city, to Miss Ann M. Toy, of Philadelphia.	04/26/1824
In the full triumphs of the Christian faith, on the morning of the 22nd inst., Capt. William Howell, long a respectable inhabitant of this city. We are well aware that obituary eulogies have become so common as almost to destroy the effects for which they are intended. But there is no subject from which instruction can better be derived than the sudden demise of those, whose path was as the shining light that shineth more and more unto the perfect day; and whose presence reflected the rays of peace and joy around upon the society in which they moved. The subject of these observations was one in whose actions shone with brightest lustre the various beauties which adorn the Christian character. In life, by example he encouraged the pursuit of virtue; by precept, the excitement of emulation; and not a few can bear testimony, that through the walks of life he conscienciously fulfilled the divine command. "Do unto others as you would they should do unto you." Suavity of disposition, candour of sentiment, and force of expression accompanied, wherever he went, and such was his plainness and simplicity of manners, that he requested no mourning should be worn for him at his decease. The seeds of the religion of Jesus Christ were sown in his heart in the moring of life, they strengthened with his years, and when age had matured them, he went down to the grave as a shock of corn full ripe. The evening of his life was unobscured by a single cloud, and his sun sunk below the horizon, but to rise with renewed speldour in another and a better world. T.	04/26/1824
On the 25th inst., by the Rev. Mr. Smith, Mr. Sebastian Nussear, to Mrs. Elizabeth Dohm, all of this city.	04/27/1824
On Tuesday evening last, by the Rev. Mr. Henshaw, Mr. Thomas Cooper, to Mrs. Elizabeth Leonard, all of this city.	04/27/1824
On the 21st instant, Mrs. Mary Ann Emack, consort of Mr. John D. Emack, near Bladensburg, in the 21st year of her age, of a consumption,	04/27/1824

Marriage and Death Notices	Date
which she bore with a truly Christian resignation.	
On Tuesday night, 27th inst., by the Rev. Dr. Waters, Mr. Frederick M. Diffenderffer, merchant, to Miss Elizabeth B. Crawford, all of this city.	04/28/1824
On Tuesday, the 13th inst., by the Rev. Mr. Findlay, Mr. Henry Mentzel, to Miss Salina Morris Crocker, both of this city.	04/28/1824
On Tuesday evening, the 27th inst., by the Rev. Mr. Soule, Maj. Gen. Tobias E. Stansbury, Speaker of the House of Delegates of the state of Maryland, to Mrs. Ann D. Steinebeck, of this city.	04/29/1824
On Tuesday evening, by the Rev. J. Valiant, Mr. Jabob M'Intire, to Miss Mary M'Guire	04/29/1824
On Tuesday evening, by the Rev. J. Valiant., Mr. Thomas Hardy, to Miss Emily Augusta Bennett.	04/29/1824
Last evening, by the Rev. Mr. Henshaw, Mr. J. Mullen, to Miss Sarah Paine, of this city.	04/30/1824
On Monday morning, Mrs. Margaret, wife of Mr. Jacob Walsh.	04/30/1824
On Thursday evening, by the Rev. John Finley, Charles Slingluff, merchant, of this place, to Eliza U., eldest daughter of Daniel Haines, deceased, of Pipe Creek, Frederick county.	05/01/1824
At Washington, on Wednesday, 28th April, by the Rev. Mr. Hawley, Dr. Gerard H. Snowden, of Birmingham House, Anne Arundel county, Maryland, to Miss Arabella Orr, youngest daughter of the late Hugh Montgomery Stuart, of Virginia.	05/04/1824
At Havana, on the 30th day of March last, Col. Gerard Wilson, of this city.	05/04/1824
At her residence, in Baltimore county, on Thursday morning last, after a protracted illness, of a pulmonary affection, which she bore with fortitude and resignation, Mrs. Catherine Amos, in the 37th year of her age, leaving six children to bemoan their irreparable loss. Oft will fond remembrance call to mind the goodness and the virtue of this amiable and affectionate lady, and long will her death be lamented by her numerous relatives and friends, to whom she was truly dear, and the only consolation that can now sooth their troubled spirits, is, that her loss must be her infinite gain, that when her hour was at hand she was well prepared for the great and awful change, having fought a good fight, having finished her course; having kept the faith, imparts every	05/04/1824

Marriage and Death Notices	Date
copmfortable assurance that her happy soul has winged its way to the mansions of eternal bliss, for "blessed are the dead who die in the Lord."	
Departed this life, on the 21st of April, in her 33rd year, Mrs. Margaret, wife of Mr. William Walter, of this city, leaving a husband inconsolable, several children to regret their maternal loss, and a numerous circle of acquaintance, who derive consolation in the hope hat she has exchanged a world replete with trouble for one wherein we are assured that the righteous shall receive a crown immortal. "Too bright alas! for mortal flame, Her gentle spirit fled to Heaven."	05/05/1824
On Sunday evening last, by the Rev. Mr. Soule, Mr. John Brown, to Miss Elizabeth Clark, all of this city.	05/06/1824
On Tuesday evening last, by the Rev. Mr. Scofield, Mr. Hosea Johns, to Miss Elizabeth Cooper, all of this city.	05/06/1824
On Monday evening last, by the Rev. Mr. Bartow, Mr. John Smith, to Miss Ann Hornamer, all of this city.	05/06/1824
On Thursday evening last, by the Rev. Mr. Kurtz, Mr. Lewis Weiss, to Miss Catherine Eiselin, both of this city.	05/06/1824
At Philadelphia, on Thursday, 27th ult., by the Rev. Mr. Demme, Mr. Peter Sauerwine, Jr., merchant, of Baltimore, to Miss Mary Ann Rich, of Philadelphia.	05/07/1824
Last evening, by the Rev. Mr. Guest, Capt. Clother Allen, to Miss Dorcas, only daughter of J. W. Winslow, Esq., all of this city.	05/07/1824
Last evening, by the Rev. Mr. Guest, Mr. Gelear B. Hawkins, of Baltimore county, to Miss Elizabeth Smith, of this city.	05/07/1824
On Sunday evening last, by the Rt. Rev. Bishop Kemp, Mr. William Dundas, of Virginia, to Miss Mary Hesselius, of this place.	05/11/1824
By the Rev. Mr. Guest, on Thursday evening last, Mr. Christian Hildebrand, of York, Pa., to Miss Elizabeth, daughter of Michael Klinefelter, of this city.	05/11/1824
Last evening, at St. Peter's Church, by the Rev. Dr. Whitfield, Mr. George Savage, to Miss Susanna Agnes Chamillon, daughter of Joseph Chamillon, both of this city.	05/12/1824

Marriage and Death Notices	Date
Died on Monday, at 2 o'clock P. M., after a protracted and painful illness of 14 weeks, which she bore with Christian fortitude and resignation to the will of her Creator, Mrs. Elizabeth, consort of John I. Gross, leaving a disconsolate husband and two children to lament her departure. May she rest in peace. Amen!	05/12/1824
On Tuesday evening, by the Most Rev. Mareschal, Archbishop of Baltimore, Julius T. Ducatel, Esq., to Joanna, daughter of Robert Barry, Esq., of this city.	05/13/1824
On Tuesday evening, by the Rt. Rev. Bishop Kemp, Mr. Samuel Hoffman, to Elizabeth, eldest daughter of the late Richardson Curson, Jr., Esq.	05/13/1824
On Tuesday evening, by the Rev. Mr. Martland, Mr. John Dobson, to Miss Mary Ann Powel, all of this city.	05/13/1824
On Tuesday evening last, by the Rev. Mr. Guest, Mr. Elijah Bond, of Frederick county, to Miss Mary Ann Gott, of Baltimore county.	05/14/1824
Last evening, by the Rev. Mr. Bartow, Mr. James Creagh, to Miss Elizabeth, eldest daughter of Mr. George Gardiner, of Fell's Point.	05/15/1824
On Sunday evening last, by the Rev. Dr. Waters, Mr. William Johnson, of this city, to Maria M., youngest daughter of the late John Louis Kreider, Esq., of Philadelphia.	05/15/1824
On Tuesday last, in the 24th year of her age, Catherine, daughter of Henry Evans, Esq., of Anne Arundel county.	05/15/1824
On Friday evening, the 7th inst., Mr. William Rusk, formerly of Philadelphia, in the 59th year of his age, lamented by all who knew him.	05/15/1824
On Wicomico, on Thursday, 22nd ult., by the Rev. Mr. M. Stone, Dr. J. Yellott Dashiell, to Miss Ann G., youngest daughter of the late Wm. Cottman, of Somerset county.	05/17/1824
Last Thursday, 13th inst., by the Rev. Dr. Wyatt, Mr. Jacob Parish, to Miss Eliza Young, both of this city.	05/18/1824
Last evening, by the Rev. Dr. Damphoux, Mr. Louis J. Ghequiere, to Catherine C., only daughter of the late William Meredith, Esq., all of this city.	05/19/1824
On Tuesday evening, 18th inst., by the Rev. Mr. Henshaw, Mr. William H. Stump, of Harford, to Miss Mary Jane, daughter of Jacob G. Smith,	05/19/1824

Marriage and Death Notices	Date
Esq., of this city.	
By the Rev. Dr. Roberts, Mr. John M'Kay, to Miss Margaret Adams, both of this city.	05/19/1824
On Tuesday evening, 18th inst., by the Rev. Mr. Henshaw, the Rev. F. W. P. Greenwood, of Boston, to Miss Maria, youngest daughter of the late Dr. Goodwin, of this city.	05/19/1824
On Tuesday evening last, by the Rev. John Valiant, Mr. Leonard Keplinger, to Miss Sarah James, both of this city.	05/20/1824
On Tuesday evening last, by the Rev. Dr. Roberts, Mr. Joseph Kirby, to Mrs. Maria Dent, all of this city.	05/20/1824
This morning, by the Rev. Mr. Henshaw, Mr. C. N. Sweeny, to Miss Martha Wilson.	05/20/1824
On Thursday, the 20th inst., by the Rev. Mr. Bartow, William Armstead, second son of the Hon. Judge McMechen, to Mary, daughter of the late George Kennard.	05/21/1824
On Tuesday, 18th inst., by the Rev. Mr. Bartow, Mr. Joseph H. Rowe, to Miss Sarah Jane Halfpenny, all of this city.	05/21/1824
On Tuesday evening last, by the Rev. Mr. Martindale, Mr. William High, to Miss Susannah Randel, all of this city.	05/21/1824
Last evening, by the Rev. Mr. Guest, Capt. James Winch, of Philadelphia, to Miss Adeline Margerum, of this city.	05/21/1824
Last evening, by the Rev. Mr. Healey, Mr. Isaac Anderson, to Miss Elizabeth Williams, all of this city.	05/21/1824
In Georgetown, on the 13th May, instant, in the 26th year of her age, Mrs. Agnes Peter, the wife of Maj. George Peter.	05/22/1824
On the 15th inst., in the 31st year of his age, at his residence, Mount Airy, Richmond county, Virginia, John Tayloe, Jr., Esq., late a lieutenant in the Navy of the United States. He was one of those gallant young heroes who participated in the glorious exploit of Capt. Hull and the double capture of so handsomely achieved by Capt. Stewart.	05/22/18241
At Montgomery, Alabama, on the 16th of April last, Mr. Charles Crawford, brother of the Secrettary of the Treasury, aged about 47	05/22/1824

Marriage and Death Notices	Date
years.	
Last evening, William Warner, Esq., long a respectable citizen and bookseller, in this city.	05/24/1824
At St. Jago de Chili, in August last, Joseph Garcier Cadiz, merchant, formerly of this city.	05/24/1824
At St. Jago de Cuba, April 10, Mr. Charles Coleman, 40, son of Mr. David Coleman, of Nantucket.	05/25/1824
On Thursday evening last, by the Rev. Dr. Roberts, Mr. John Gothrop, to Miss Jane Logan, both of this city.	05/26/1824
Last evening, by the Rev. Mr. Healey, Mr. John Lynch, to Mrs. Elizabeth Read, both of Baltimore county.	05/28/1824
22nd May, instant, aged one year and ten months, Rosalie O'Donnel Finley, second daughter of E. L. Finley, Esq.	05/28/1824
At Cahauba, Alabama, Miss Rebecca Travers, formerly of Baltimore.	05/28/1824
At Port au Prince, aboard the schooner Medal, of Baltimore, on the 11th inst., after an illness of four days, of the yellow fever, Aaron Parker, a native of Accomac county, Virginia.	05/28/1824
On Thursday evening last, by the Rev. Mr. Payton, Mr. James Leak, to Miss Elizabeth, eldest daughter of Mr. James Peregoy, all of this city.	05/29/1824
On Thursday evening, by the Rev. Mr. Guest, Mr. Charles Horsman, to Miss Catherine Smith, all of this city.	05/29/1824
On Thursday evening, 27th inst., by the Rev. John Valiant, of Baltimore, Mr. John Mumma, of Christiana, to Miss Maria Ann Lucas, both of Baltimore county.	05/29/1824
Departed this transitory life, at the Laurel Mills, near Baltimore, on the 17th inst., after 5 months acute indisposition, which he bore with pious fortitude and resignation, Robert Hezlitt, aged 44 years. He has left a loving and affectionate wife to lament his irreparable loss.	05/29/1824
Departed this life, Friday morning, 21st May, in the 20th year of her age, after a long and painful illness, which she bore with Christian fortitude and resignation, Caroline Margaret Cook, daughter of Mr. William Cook, of this city.	05/29/1824

Marriage and Death Notices	Date
On Tuesday last, 25th inst., by the Rev. Dr. Roberts, Capt. John Beard, to Miss Elizabeth N. Reese, both of this city.	05/31/1824
On Tuesday evening last, 25th inst., by the Rev. Mr. Mitchell, Mr. Joshua Hutchins, merchant, of this city, to Caroline R., second daughter of Luke W. Barber, of St. Mary's county, Md.	05/31/1824
On Thursday, 27th instant, at Recess, Elk Ridge, by the Rev. A. H. Dashiell, Dr. Michael S. Baer, of this city, to Miss Matilda Chase, youngest daughter of the late Judge Ridgely.	05/31/1824
On the evening of the 29th inst., after an illness of three days, James Steward, of this city, leaving an affectionate wife and three small children to mourn their irreparable loss.	05/31/1824
On Friday, the 28th inst., at his residence, in Baltimore county, Mr. Underwood Guyton, in the 90th year of his age.	05/31/1824
On the 26th ultimo, at Friends Meeting, at Waterford, Loudon county, Virginia, Dr. George Harris, late of Baltimore, to Sarah Ann Littler, of the former place.	06/01/1824
On Sunday last, by the Rev. Mr. Wilson, Mr. Stephen Grimes, to Miss Susan Grimes, all of Baltimore county.	06/01/1824
Suddenly, on Saturday morning, 29th inst., in the 65th year of his age, Mr. John B. Gauline, a native of Marseilles, and long a respectable citizen of Baltimore.	06/01/1824
On Thursday evening last, by the Rev. Mr. Walton, Mr. Benjamin W. Foster, formerly of Boston, to Mrs. Mary Connor, of this city.	06/02/1824
On Monday evening, in the seventy-fifth year of his age, Mr. Lewis Pascault, a native of France, and one among the oldest and most respectable citizens of Baltimore – whose great usefulness is too well remembered to need any eulogy. In him dwelt a noble soul. His spirit too pure for earth, has sought its natural Heaven, leaving all its terrestrial turmoils to rest in the peaceful asylum prepared for the just, there to enjoy eternal bliss, and with the sanctified spirits of God, to praise forever the Holy Trinity.	06/02/1824
On Thursday, the 27th ult., Miss Jeannette Lee Glaggett. The character of this young lady was such, that a long and studied eulogium is not needed to preserve a grateful and affectionate remembrance of it among those to whom she was known. In addition to one of the most sweet and	06/02/1824

Marriage and Death Notices	Date
amiable dispositions, she was enriched and adorned with all the graces and virtue of our holy religion. The doctrines and promises of the gospel, constituted her support and consolation during the protracted illness which preceded her decease; and the holiness of her life, the devotion of her spirit, together with her meek and uniform submission to the will of Heaven, afforded to her mourning friends, comforting and satisfactory evidence of her personal interest in that Savior, who ascended to prepare mansions for all his followers, in "a building of God; a house not made with hands, eternal in the Heavens."	
On Sunday evening last, by the Rev. Mr. Smith, Mr. Thomas F. Clony, to Miss Mary Ann C. Byrne, both of this city.	06/03/1824
On Tuesday evening last, by the Rev. Dr. Roberts, Mr. John Austin, of Nashville, Tennessee, to Miss Mary Ann Rode, of this city.	06/03/1824
At Philadelphia, of pulmonary consumption, Joseph Delaplaine, Esq., a gentleman generally known and much esteemed.	06/03/1824
At New Orleans, on the 10th ult., William Kenner, Esq., of the firm of William Kenner & Co., of that city.	06/03/1824
Last evening, by the Rev. Mr. Guest, Mr. Elisha W. R. Sink, to Miss Mary Hughes, both of this city.	06/04/1824
Early yesterday morning, after a lingering illness, Mrs. Ann Niles, wife of Hezekiah Niles, editor of the Register, aged nearly 44 years. If a prompt and strict performance of the duties of daughter, wife, mother, sister, and relative; if a charitable heart glowing with benevolence bounded only by the means of exerting it; and a willing attention to the relative connections of society without ostentation; and a mild and meek observance of the principles of Chrisianity, confer value on woman, it may be said that the subject of this notice possessed them in an eminent degree, and will most certainly insure the reward of *"the god and faithful servant."*	06/04/1824
On Thursday evening last, by the Rev. Dr. Roberts, Mr. Philip Bonn, to Miss Sarah Grant, all of this city.	06/05/1824
On Thursday evening last, by the Rev. Dr. Wyatt, Dr. John Stafford, to Miss Mary Elizabeth, eldest daughter of Capt. Saml. Sylvester, of this city.	06/08/1824
Yesterday afternoon, Mr. Alexander Stevenson, in the 35th year of his	06/08/1824

Marriage and Death Notices	Date
age, after a very short illness.	
Last evening, by the Rev. Bishop Soule, Mr. Frederick Niebling, to Miss Elizabeth, eldest daughter of Mr. George Myers, all of this city.	06/09/1824
The recent death of Ferdinand Bullitt, Esq., at Bogota, far from his family and friends, is another melancholy example of the "vanity of human wishes." 'Tis but a short time since he left his friends in Maryland, with his uncle Anderson, for the capital of Columbia, in the dawn of manhood, his heart beating high with the anticipation of scenes, about to be unfolded to him, his imagination pourtraying visions, alas! never to be realized. Educated as this young man had been, in the bosom of an affectionate family, where none but virtuous impressions had ever reached him, he might have bid defiance to the snares, which the world was preparing to throw around him, but it has pleased Providence to remove him from its temptations, and though our first impulse cannot but arraign the decree which has consigned Ferdinand to the tomb, reason and religion much teach us submission and adoration.	06/10/1824
Died, near Manfield Farm, Baltimore county, on the 17th ult., Mrs. Anna De St. Ceran, wife of Tullins De St. Ceran, aged 17 years, leaving an affectionate and bereaved husband, and a lovely infant, just entered into life. This amiable woman will long be remembered with kindness and affection, by all who enjoyed her acquaintance.	06/10/1824
On Thursday evening last, by the Rev. Dr. Roberts, Mr. William Gibbs, to Miss Susan Armstrong, all of this city.	06/11/1824
On Tuesday night last, by the Rev. Mr. Charles W. Gardner, Mr. William Watkins, to Miss Henrietta Russell, both of this city.	06/11/1824
Departed this life, on the 31st May last, Mr. Peter Clark, of this city, in the 33rd year of his age.	06/11/1824
On Thursday evening last, by the Rev. Mr. Payton, Mr. William Blake, to Miss Elizabeth Jane Beard, all of this city.	06/12/1824
On Thursday evening last, by the Rev. Mr. Guest, Mr. Jeremiah Elder, to Miss Elizabeth Jones, all of this city.	06/12/1824
At Philadelphia, by the Rev. G. T. Bedell, Mr. Stevenson Smith, senior Editor of the Philadelphia Gazette, to Miss Mary, daughter of the late John C. Elselen, of Baltimore.	06/14/1824
Last evening, after a severe illness of about 48 hours, Jesse Pouder, son	06/14/1824

Marriage and Death Notices	Date
of Leonard Pouder, in the 14th year of his age. His friends and acquaintances are requested to attend his funeral, from Mrs. Germans, north Howard st., on Tuesday, the 15th inst., at 3 o'clock P. M.	
On the 13th inst., by the Rev. Mr. Payton, Mr. Stephen Jay, of Harford county, to Miss Sarah Ives, of this city.	06/15/1824
At New York, Mr. G. F. Hyatt, recently of Baltimore Theatre, to Mrs. E. M. Perry.	06/16/1824
On the 14th inst., by the Rev. Mr. Payton, Mr. George Williams, to Miss Mary Tarr, both of this city.	06/17/1824
On Deer Creek, Harford county, on the 10th inst., by the Rev. Mr. Finney, Mr. John Wilson, to Miss Elizabeth Wilson, all of this place.	06/17/1824
On Thursday last, by the Rev. Mr. Guest, Mr. George Wilson, to Mrs. Elizabeth Cooper, all of this city.	06/18/1824
Yesterday evening, Charles W. Reis, son of the Rev. Edmund J. Reis, in the 18th year of his age – the funeral will take place from his father's dwelling, tomorrow afternoon, at 3 o'clock. The friends and acquaintance are respectfully invited to attend.	06/18/1824
At his farm, near Hagerstown, on Saturday afternoon last, David Cooke, Esq., formerly of Marietta, Pennsylvania, of which place he was the founder, aged about 74 years. Through a long life, he sustained the noblest of all characters, that of an "honest man."	06/18/1824
On Thursday evening, the 17th inst., by the Rev. Dr. Roberts, Mr. Charles D. Gorsuch, to Elizabeth, daughter of Andrew Brunner, Esq., all of this city.	06/19/1824
At Newtown, L. I., on the 14th inst., by the Rev. E. M. Johnson, Mr. George Carr Grundy, of Baltimore, to Miss Mary L. Billop, of the former place.	06/19/1824
At Jackson, Mississippi, on the 23rd May, after a tedious illness, Mr. Gassaway E. Lusby, formerly of Maryland.	06/19/1824
On Tuesday evening, 13th inst., by the Rev. Mr. Guest, Mr. Joshua Tibbitt, to Miss Ann Rutter Dallas, both of this city.	06/22/1824
On the 19th inst., at Easton, Talbot county, by the Rev. Joseph Scull, Mr. Jacob Cronmiller, to Miss Rebecca Kirby.	06/22/1824

Marriage and Death Notices	Date
On Sunday evening last, by the Rev. D. E. Reis, Mr. John W. Prince, to Miss Catherine Braneman, all of this city.	06/22/1824
At the house of Wm. Free, near Baltimore, on Saturday evening, the 19th June, of a long illness, Mr. William Ripple, hatter, formerly of Wilksburg, Penn.	06/22/1824
At Washington, on the evening of Saturday last, the 19th instant, Mr. William Brown, bricklayer, a native of Hull, England, and for the last 8 or 9 years of his life, a respectable inhabitant of this city. The circumstances of his death are calculated to leave a lasting impression on the minds of the living. Whilst engaged at his business, on or about the 15th ultimo, he accidentally trod on the point of a nail, which penetrated through his shoe, and pierced the sole of his foot. The wound was considered unimportant, and was suffered to heal up, without having extracted the poisonous effects of the nail. He continued assiduously in the pursuit of his business, until about the 8th or 9th of the present month, when his foot became sore, and the muscular parts of his body greatly affected; the lock jaw ensued, and finally terminated the existence of a worthy, active, and useful member of society, leaving a wife and three small children to deplore the loss of an affectionate husband and a tender father.	06/23/1824
Last evening, by the Rev. Mr. Guest, Mr. William H. Morling, to Miss Mary Orem, all of this city.	06/24/1824
On Tuesday evening last, by the Rev. Mr. Nevins, Mr. James J. Atkinson, to Miss Mary Virginia, only daughter of the late Capt. Thomas Cole.	06/24/1824
On Friday last, after a short, but severe illness, which he bore with Christian fortitude and resignation, Mr. William G. Rutter, in the 28th year of his age, leaving one child and a numerous circle of friends and relations to lament his death. Honesty, faith, and benevolence, were the presiding tokens that illuminated through the shadows of this world his passage to the tomb, but notwithstanding his amiable qualities they could not preserve life; such was the purity of his soul, that death to him could bring no terrors, but kindly gave him a friendly passport to another and a better world; to that blessed abode "where the weary are at rest, and the wicked doth cease from troubling."	06/24/1824
At Litchfield, Conn., May 21st, Mr. John Cotton, *aged one hundred and eight years*, a revolutionary pensioner. Mr. C. served seven years in the old French war, and seven years in the revolutionary war.	06/24/1824

Marriage and Death Notices	Date
On Tuesday evening, by the Rev. Mr. Soule, Mr. Alanson Webb, to Louisa, second daughter of Mr. Jacob Myers.	06/25/1824
On Wednesday, the 16th, at the residence of his mother, in Taney Town, Frederick county, John H. Bentley, Esq., of this city. It will be consoling to his numerous friends to learn that in his last moments he participated in the blessed sacrements of the Holy Church of which he was a member, administered by the hands of the Rev. Mr. Zockey, Roman Catholic pastor of the place. His remains were interred in the burying ground attached to the Catholic Church.	06/25/1824
On Friday last, by the Rev. Dr. Roberts, Mr. Archibald Roe, to Miss Harriet Beebee, all of this city.	06/26/1824
At New York, by the Rev. John Hargrove, of Baltimore, the Rev. Manning B. Rorke, of Philadelphia, to Miss Sarah E., eldest daughter of Mr. Henry Howard, of New York and recently of Baltimore.	06/26/1824
On Thursday evening last, by the Rev. Mr. Guest, Mr. James Freeman, of Virginia, to Miss Charlotte Ann Berry, of this city.	06/26/1824
On the 31st May last, Rachael Slatter, consort of Daniel Slatter, aged 55 years, long a respectable inhabitant of Calvert County, Md.	06/26/1824
On Thursday evening last, by the Rev. Mr. Wells, Mr. Edwin H. Alford, to Miss Mary Brown, both of this city.	06/28/1824
On Wednesday, the 23rd inst., Mr. Andrew Clopper, in the 53rd year of his age.	06/28/1824
On Tuesday evening, the 15th instant, by the Rev. F. N. Smith, James E. Barroll, Esq., of Chestertown, to Miss Henrietta J. B. Hackett, of Queen Anne's county.	06/29/1824
At Louisville, Ken., on the 10th inst., A. S. Roger, formerly of this place.	06/29/1824
Yesterday morning, by the Rev. Mr. Merwin, J. P. Krafft, Esq., his Prusian Majesty's Consul, to Eliza, third daughter of John Brice, Esq., all of this city.	06/30/1824
On Wednesday evening last, by the Rev. Mr. Bartow, Mr. James Maloy, to Mrs. Mary Brice, all of this city.	06/30/1824
In this city, on Monday, Miss Ann Eliza Weeks, aged 16.	06/30/1824

Marriage and Death Notices	Date
At Philadelphia, in the 26th year of his age, Richard R. Thomson, Esq., Consul for the United States at Canton. The deceased had arrived in this port the day previous to his death, having struggled with his disease only to resign his breath in his native country.	06/30/1824
Yesterday, at Christ Church, by the Rev. Dr. Wyatt, John Crawford, Esq., His Britannic Majesty's Consul for this state, to Miss Harriet M'Intosh, daughter of John M'Intosh, late of the Bahama Islands.	07/01/1824
On Monday evening last, by the Rev. Mr. Bartow, Mr. Abner Hayden, to Miss Brunetha Hayden.	07/01/1824
On Monday evening last, by the Rev. Mr. Bartow, Mr. John H. Williams, to Miss Ann Danson, all of Lancaster county, Virginia.	07/01/1824
At Poplar Mount, near Baltimore, on the 27th inst., Mrs. Ann Peirce, consort of Humphrey Peirce, Esq., formerly merchant of this city.	07/01/1824
At Philadelphia, aged 50 years, Joseph Scattergood, a member of the Religious Society of Friends. The deceased was a man of unblemished integrity, and a sound and practical believer in the redemption which comes of Jesus Christ.	07/01/1824
On the 24th ult., at half past two o'clock, at his residence near Portsmouth, after an illness of ten days, Richard C. Archer, Esq., Purser in the United States Navy, leaving a wife and many friends and acquaintance to lament his death.	07/01/1824
In New York ciy, Guysbert B. Vroom, Esq., Cashier of the Merchant's Bank.	07/01/1824
Last evening, by the Rev. Mr. Guest, Mr. David Clark, of Lynchburg, Va., to Miss Adaline Massy, of this city.	07/02/1824
On the 1st inst., Mr. John P. Entwisle, aged 28, a man whose liberality and affability secured him the respect and esteem of all who knew him. It is not fulsome flattery, but and act of justice, to the memory of the deceased, to say that in the death of J. P. Entwisle, we deplore a serious loss to society. In all the social relations of life, he was known as an exemplary and a most estimable character in the walks of private life. Prompt and ready, his hand and purse was ever open to protect and defend the afflicted.	07/02/1824
At City Point, on Sunday night last, after a short illness, Capt. Perkins, of the brig Floyd, of Boston.	07/02/1824

Marriage and Death Notices	Date
At Annapolis, Thursday evening, July 1st, by the Rev. Dr. Davis, Mr. Albert Benton, Otsego county, N. Y., to Mary Albright, daughter of Capt. Geo. Barber, of Annapolis.	07/03/1824
On the evening of Friday, the 18th ult., by the Rev. Dr. Glendy, Mr. Bernard McCain, Merchant, to Miss Cecilia Malone, of this city.	07/03/1824
This morning, after a lingering illness, Jonathan Harvey, for many years a respectable resident of this city. His friends and acquaintance are invited to attend his burial, to meet so as to leave the house of Ann Scott, No. 33½ German, near Eutaw street, tomorrow evening, at 6 o'clock.	07/03/1824
On the 1st inst., Mr. Joseph Young, of Baltimore, aged 58 years; a more amiable, affectionate, charitable, and honest man, never left this world.	07/03/1824
In this city, on Monday, lamented by all who knew her, Miss Ann Eliza Weeks, sixteen years of age, after an illness of sixteen days. In her, all the virues that adorn the human character shone in a preeminent degree; most amiable in her disposition, she was the friend of the oppressed, and whenever she beheld an object of compassion the tear of sympathy stole profusely down her lovely cheeks. In her relations as daughter and sister, she was peculiarly distinguished – a most dutiful and affectionate child, her filial affection was unsurpassed – as a sister she was most sincerely attached – in a word, all the virtues of the human character appeared to be concentrated in her. May she rest in peace as the prayer of one who knew how to appreciate her worth.	07/03/1824
On Thursday morning, the 15th July, by the Rev. Mr. Tidings, Mr. Bennett M. Billingslea, Merchant, of Abingdon, Harford county, to Miss Elizabeth F. Garrittson, of this city.	07/06/1824
On Thursday morning, the 24th ult., at the Warren Factory, in Baltimore county, Mr. Joseph Cooper. He has left a wife and seven children to lament their loss.	07/06/1824
On Tuesday evening, 6th inst., by the Rt. Rev. Archbishop Mareschal, Dr. John Frederick Huttner, to Miss Maria Francisa Driscoll, all of this city.	07/07/1824
On Tuesday evening, 6th inst., by the Rev. Dr. Roberts, Mr. John Purdy, late of Washington, to Miss Ann Christopher, all of this city.	07/07/1824
At Philadelphia, on Saturday morning, the 3rd July, of a pulmonary consumption, in the 27th year of her age, Catherine, wife of Joseph M.	07/07/1824

Marriage and Death Notices	Date
Sanderson, the keeper of the Merchant's Coffee House.	
Suddenly, on Tuesday evening last, Mr. Samuel Curry, Printer, in the 22nd year of his age. {A long sorrowful poem follows the short notice.}	07/09/1824
On Thursday evening, by the Rev. Mr. Kerney, Mr. George Twinhan, to Miss Ann Wheatley, all of this city.	07/10/1824
On the evening of the 9th inst., Mrs. Mary Flint, consort of Thomas Flint, aged 26 years.	07/10/1824
On the 9th inst., William Henry, youngest son of Mr. R. H. Osgood.	07/10/1824
On Friday morning, after a lingering and painful illness, William, oldest son of Wm. M'Conkey, Esq., in the 28th year of his age.	07/12/1824
On Friday morning, after a very painful and protracted illness, which he bore with Christian fortitude and resignation, Mr. Robert Toneley Rigby, in the 58th year of his age, an old and respectable inhabitant of this city. In all the relative duties of life, he could not be surpassed – an affectionate father, a kind husband, and a sincere friend, to whom the tale of sorrow could not be told without exciting visible emotions of sympathy; and it may be well said, that in him the indigent widow and orphan always found a protector and liberal benefactor. In short, he possessed all the amiable and virtuous qualities that adorn the human mind; and fit the soul for Heaven.	07/12/1824
At Elkton, Francis Gillespie, Sheriff of Cecil county, Maryland.	07/12/1824
On Friday morning, after a short and painful illness of 46 hours, Thomas, eldest son of George Coulter, in the 5th year of his age. His death was occasioned by drinking the oil of vitriol which he got in a bottle, and soon put an end to his existence. It is hoped this will be a warning to persons using the like liquid in the business, or occupation, to keep it secure from their children, lest they should participate the same trouble.	07/13/1824
On Sunday evening last, by the Rev. Mr. Helfenstein, Mr. Edwin Thomas, to Miss Hannah Jarvis, all of this city.	07/14/1824
On Sunday, the 4th inst., by the Rev. John Valiant, Mr. Elijah D. Kline, to Miss Mary Alter, all of this city.	07/14/1824
By the Rev. John Valiant, on Friday evening last, Mr. James Carpenter Ferrell, to Miss Ann Bergen, of Baltimore county.	07/14/1824

Marriage and Death Notices	Date
By the Rev. John Valiant, on Sunday evening last, Mr. Edward Wyman, to Miss Elizabeth Sindall.	07/14/1824
On Tuesday evening last, by the Rev. Mr. Elbers, Mr. Louis Muller, of this city, to Miss Elenora Kinneman, of the Eastern Shore of Maryland.	07/15/1824
On Tuesday evening, 13th inst., by the Rev. John P. Peckworth, Mr. Washington Hanway, of Harford County, to Miss Elenor Lindsey, of this city.	07/15/1824
Last evening by the Rev. Mr. Gibson, Mr. Abraham Hutz, of Lancaster, Pennsylvania, to Miss Elizabeth Burk, of this city.	07/15/1824
On the 17th May last, at Amiens, in France, the Rev. John Francis Moranville, late Rector of St. Patrick's Church, Fell's Point, in the 53rd year of his age.	07/15/1824
On Sunday, the 11th instant, at Reading, Pennsylvania, the Rev. George Shenfelter, Pastor of the Roman Catholic Church in that place, in the 30th year of his age.	07/17/1824
At New Orleans, June 8: Hudson Curtis, of New York, aged 11; John Fleming, Philadelphia, 33; Mary Baldwin, Ireland, 27; John Forrest, Connecticut, 35; Hiram H. Root, New York, 25; Charles Lock, Connecticut, suicide, opium, 40. June 24: Benjamin Adams, New York, 23; Peter Staily, N. York, 28. June 16: Charles Petevey, N. York, 40; Abm. Boyer, Philad.; John Mullen, Ireland; Richard Gilmore, Baltimore; Joseph Peppernell, do.; Moses O'Neal, Ireland; Nancy Curtis, N. York, 35; David Lyel, England. At Point Coupee, 23rd June, the Hon. Julian Poydras.	07/17/1824
On Tuesday evening last, by the Rev. Mr. Payton, Mr. Joseph Peregoy, to Miss Jarusha Randall, all of this city.	07/19/1824
At Philadelphia, on Saturday morning last, Tench Cox, Esq., in the 69th year of his age.	07/19/1824
In Salem, Capt. Joseph Moreridge, of the Navy of the Columbia Republic, to Miss Margaret Baker, of Salem. Mr. Daniel Brimmer to Miss Sally Chandler.	07/20/1824
On board the U. S. ship Hornet, lying off Old Point Comfort, Thomas N. Mann, Esq., diplomatic agent from this government to Guatimala.	07/20/1824
On Thursday evening last, by the Rev. Mr. Kurtz, Mr. John Steigers to	07/21/1824

Marriage and Death Notices	Date
Miss Ann Penn.	
At New Mills, N. J., on the 18th ult., Lt. Charles Lacey, of the U. S. Navy, aged 38 years.	07/21/1824
On the 21st inst., Mrs. A. M. Wyant, widow of the late Peter Wyant, of a lingering and painful illness, aged 66 years. She possessed in an eminent degree every virtue which adorns the female character and secured to herself the affectionate esteem of all who knew her.	07/22/1824
On Saturday last, William H. Webster, comedian, formerly of the Baltimore and Philadelphia Theatres. As a vocalist, few, if any, were more admired by gentile audience, for fine powers, than was the subject of this notice.	07/22/1824
On Saturday night last, on board the U. S. Ship Hornet, lying off Old Port Comfort, Thomas N. Mann, Esq., Diplomatic Agent from this Government to Guatimala. His complaint was of a pulmonary character, which, as is usual in that disease, flattered him to the last moment with a promise of returning health. His remains were landed at Old Point, yesterday afternoon, at 4 o'clock, minute guns being fired from the ship from the time the corpse left her side until it reached the shore. A procession was then formed of the officers of the ship; the officers of the U. States corps of Artillery at Fortress Monroe; the seaman from the Hornet; all the privates of the Artillery Corps not on duty; strangers on the Point; and many citizens of Norfolk, on a visit there. The whole preceded by the artillery band, playing a solemn dirge. The body was deposited in the cemetery attached to the Fortress. Mr. Mann was a native of North Carolina, a gentleman of fine talents, and possessing great urbanity of manners. He was greatly respected by the officers of the ship, who deeply regret his loss.	07/22/1824
Last evening, by the Rev. Dr. Wyatt, Mr. John C. Draper, to Miss Sarah, daughter of Mr. Alexander B. Hanna, of this city.	07/23/1824
On the 20th inst., at the residence of Mr. Fred'k Lauderman, Mr. Samuel George Cooper, a native of Bermuda, in the 23rd year of his age. The deceased was deservedly esteemed by all who knew him, and fully resigned to quit this for another and a better world.	07/23/1824
OBITUARY. It has been remarked that, when a good man dies, his loss is that of the whole community in which he lived. And in the death of the Rev. John Francis Moranville, this remark appears but too well verified. The sentiments of grief pervading the beloved and effectionate flock which so long experienced the watchful solicitude, and paternal	07/24/1824

Marriage and Death Notices	Date
love of the zealous minister of the Church of Christ, present a melancholy and yet grateful proof of the extent of the bereavement which has been occasioned by his decease. On Wednesday last, the solemn rite of the Church, for the repose of the soul of its departed minister, was performed in the temple which had so often heard his pious exhortations and fervent prayers – and the heart-touching spectactle of a congregation in tears but too plainly told their poignant grief for the loss of him whom the ravages of disease and the terrors of surrounding death could not deter from administering the kind attentions of the friend, and the consolations of the sacred gospel. When in a distant land, his thoughts were still with the Congregation which had for so many years been the object of his pastoral charge and his prayers on his death bed for their welfare prove that he did not forget them. His earthly career is now closed! Many are the hearts which will respond to the prayer, *"May he rest in peace."*	
Died, on 8th inst., in Augusta, Georgia, of the prevailing fever, Mr. William Hennaman, in the 26th year of his age, a native of this city.	07/24/1824
Mrs. Ann Stocket, wife of Joseph Noble Stocket, Esq., of Anne Arundel county. Mrs. Martha Coulter, wife of Mr. Henry Coulter, of Annapolis.	07/26/1824
On the 14th ultimo, at Pensacola, Florida, by the Rev. Mr. Maenhout, Capt. Richard M. Sands, of the United States' Army, of Baltimore, to Miss Adele Senac, daughter of Mr. Pierre Senac, of that city.	07/26/1824
In Queen Ann, Prince George county, Md., on Thursday, the 17th inst., after a painful illness of about ten days, Bennas Harrison, Esq., Postmaster of that village.	07/26/1824
On Sunday evening last, by the Rev. Mr. Stansbury, Mr. Thomas Slade, to Miss Rachel Allsworth, both of this city.	07/26/1824 07/27/1824
On Friday night, in her 32nd year, Susan, wife of Charles Guildener, of this city leaving a husband and three small children to mourn their irreparable loss.	07/27/1824
In St. Peter's Church, Sharp street, on Sunday evening last, by the Rev. Mr. Henshaw, Mr. Henry Hewlit, merchant, to Miss Mary Harpur, all of this city.	07/28/1824
On Monday evening last, by the Rev. Mr. Shane, Mr. William Glover, to Mrs. Susan Sewell, both of this city.	07/28/1824

Marriage and Death Notices	Date
On the 25th inst., aged 10 months, Mary Randolph, youngest daughter of E. L. Finley, Esq.	07/29/1824
Yesterday, Mr. John P. Spies, after a lingering and painful sickness – a respectable inhabitant of this city for 20 years.	07/29/1824
Near Cincinnati, Ohio, Capt. William Parsons, formerly of Baltimore, a useful citizen, and whose loss will be severely felt by the public. A man best known as the most experienced steam boat builder in the Western country.	07/29/1824
In the death of Mrs. A. M. Wyant, society has lost one of its brightest ornaments, the Christian Church one of its most zealous devotees, & her friends a model worthy of imitation. She was the daughter of Mr. George Steig, of York, Pa., a wealthy and respectable inhabitant of that place, whose paternal care and virtuous life, was evinced by the peculiar pleasure he took in instilling into the minds of his children, at an early age, a proper sense of their moral and religious duties, and of their accountability to God. His care and exertions were by no means lost on the subject of this notice. As her age matured, so also did her knowledge in the depravity of our nature and utter unworthiness in the sight of God – which gave rise to a lively faith in the merits of Christ, and a sincere conformity to his gospel requisitions, as the only means of salvation. Through the whole course of her long life, her professions and actions have been consistent. She early united herself to the German Reformed Church, by receiving the sacrament of the Lord's Supper, and earnestly through life endeavoured to comply with all the vows then made, and the whole tenor of her life warrants the inference that her success was as great as the infirmities of our nature would admit of. In all the relations of life, she acted from consciencious motives, and it is believed, in a manner acceptable both to God and man. As a child, she was respectful and duiful – as a wife, affectionate and kind; as a mother, she devoted all the energies of a strong mind to the inculcation of Gospel precepts in the youthful minds of her children, and to the excitement of a desire in them, to acquire a knowledge of such refinements and such branches of educations, as would contribute to their usefulness and comfort in this world, and secure for them a happy immortality in that which is to come; as a nerighbor, she was obliging, respectful, and respected; and as a Christian, she was humble, benevolent, and and faithful. Her disease was one which left no hope of recovery – it was lingering and poignant, and yet she bore it with exemplary patience, fortitude, and resignation. She died at the advanced age of 66 years, with ample faith in the atoning blood of Christ, and an humble hope for the endless enjoyment of felicity beyond the grave.	07/30/1824

Marriage and Death Notices	Date
On Thursday evening, 29th inst., by the Rev. Mr. Guest, James Everitt, to Ann Eliza Moore, all of this city.	07/31/1824
In Statesville, N. C., on the 20th ult., James M'Lelland, Esq., attorney at law, to Miss Mary Ann M'Jimsey, formerly of Baltimore.	07/31/1824
On Thursday, 29th inst., Mrs. Mary D. Crabbin, in the 75th year of her age, after having borne with truly Christian fortitude and resignation, all the painful feelings incident to a spasmatic complaint. The deceased was a resident of this city for the last thirty years, during which time she discharged all the duties of a mother, friend, and protector of the poor, in such an exemplary manner, as to endear her to the memory of her surving friends, which death alone can obliterate. The author of this was well acquainted with her virtues, and as a feeble tribute to departed worth, tenders this obituary to lament excellence.	07/31/1824
On Wednesday evening last, in Harford County, Md., after a severe illness, Mrs. Elizabeth Quarles, consort of John Quarles, Esq., of this city.	07/31/1824
On Friday morning, the 30th instant, Mr. James Callender, of a consumption, in the 42nd year of his age.	07/31/1824
Died, in this city, on the 24th inst., in the 33rd year of her age, of a painful and lingering disease, which she bore throughout with pious fortitude and exemplary resignation, Miss Francis Catherine Cole, a native of Fulvanna county, state of Virginia.	07/31/1824
On Friday, 30th July, in the fifth year of her age, Frances Elizabeth, only daughter of Capt. N. Baden, of the U. S. army.	08/02/1824
At Mount Prospect, Calvert county, on Tuesday last, 27th ult., by the Rev. Mr. Willis, Basil Burke, to Mary T. Mackenzie.	08/02/1824 08/03/1824
On Sunday evening, by the Rev. Mr. Kurtz, Mr. Peter Corbin, of Virginia, to Miss Susan Swan, of this city.	08/03/1824
On the 27th July, by the Rev. Dr. Roberts, Enoch Burnett, to Margaret Remmey, both of this city.	08/04/1824
Last evening, by the Rev. Dr. Glendy, Capt. William P. Young, to Miss Susan W., youngest daughter of Mr. James Taylor, all of this city.	08/04/1824
On Tuesday morning, 3rd inst., Isabella, aged 15 months and 17 days, youngest daughter of Mr. John H. Poor.	08/04/1824

Marriage and Death Notices	Date
On Sunday morning last, by the Rev. Mr. Walton, Mr. William Armstrong, to Miss Eliza Jane Mason, both of this city.	08/05/1824
At Charlotte Hall, St. Mary's county, Md., James Miltimore, Esq., to Nancy R. Eilgour, both of that place.	08/05/1824
OBITUARY. With no ordinary emotions of regret, we record the departure of our late worthy citizen, John Brevitt, who died on the 24th inst., after a severe illness of several weeks, in the 64th year of his age. We mention his death as a subject of information, or custom, for his virtuous character stands in no need of news-paper eulogy. He was well known as one of the oldest and most respectable inhabitants of Baltimore, and during a long and useful life, exhibited so unblemished a character and such a course of honorable and upright conduct, as casts a dignity on human nature itself. In private life, his social virtues were of the first order and his friendships of the most valued kind. He was an officer during the American Revolution, and joined the army at the age of 19. For the last 25 years of his life, he was an active member of the Methodist Episcopal Church, and in his religious career, evinced so much piety, and such an evenness and consistency of deportment that the tongue of slander itself never lisped a reproach against him. He died without an enemy and in the full assurance of eternal bliss. "The chamber where the good man meets his fate, Is privileged beyond the common walk Of virtuous life, quite in the verge of Heaven."	08/05/1824
"Heaven gives us friends to bless the present scene; resumes them to prepare us for the next." Died, on Wednesday, the 28th ult., at the residence of her mother, in Harford county, Maryland, after a lingering illness, which she bore with Christian resignation, Mrs. Elizabeth Quarles, consort of John Quarles, Esq., of this city. This truly amiable woman left this city in the early part of June, to pay a visit to her mother and other relations at Deer Creek, the place of her birth. She set off in her usual good spirits, without taking a formal leave of all her friends, as she expected to return in a very short time. But alas she was not gone more than two or three days, before she was seized with the prevailing epidemic of the neighborhood, which terminated in her lamented death. In the demise of Mrs. Quarles, we regret no common subject of regret. She has left a blank in the circle of her friends, which will not soon be filled. She possessed all those qualities, both social and intellectual which adorn the character of her sex. Few persons had more friends than the deceased, for whoever knew her was her friend. Her constancy to her attachments affords to her friends a convincing proof that there is more friendship in the world than cold philosophers allow. Such was the	08/05/1824

Marriage and Death Notices	Date
excitement which the death of the deceased produced, that the whole neighborhood of Deer Creek was in tears on the occasion. On the day in which the last sad tribute was paid to her remains, all business was suspended; and her funeral, which was very numerously attended, was peculiarly solemn and affecting. X.	
Lately, in Fairfield District, S. C., Charles D. Bradford, aged 90 years. It is thought that the deceased was the oldest surviving soldier and officer belonging to the Provincial troops of South Carolina.	08/05/1824
At Pittsburg, 27th ult., Mrs. Nancy Findlay, consort of Wm. Findlay, Esq., late Governor of the Commonwealth of Pennsylvania.	08/05/1824
On Thursday evening last, by the Rev. Dr. Glendy, Mr. William F. Smith, to Miss Ann Peale, both of this city.	08/06/1824
On Sunday evening last, by the Rev. Mr. Hargrove, Mr. James Burgess, to Miss Mary Crockett, all of this city.	08/06/1824
On Tuesday evening last, by the Rev. Mr. Greenfield, Mr. Charles Canaan, to Miss Keziah, second eldest daughter of William Bishop, Esq., all of Baltimore county.	08/07/1824
On Thursday evening, July 22, by the Rev. Dr. Roberts, Mr. George West, to Miss Sarah Blair, all of this city.	08/07/1824
On Friday morning, 6th inst., after a short illness of ten days, Emily Jane Alfred, only daughter of Thomas Alfred, of this city.	08/07/1824
At Philadelphia, Elisha Spencer Sergeant, Esq., aged 38.	08/07/1824
On the 17th July, at his residence near Canton, Ohio, John Shorr, Sr., Esq., for many years a respectable merchant of this city. His death was occasioned by the falling off a beam, whilst superintending the erection of a Church, in his neighborhood.	08/07/1824
This morning, at one o'clock, after a short illness, Capt. John Campbell, of the Union Line Steam Boat Philadelphia. His friends and acquaintance are requested to attend his funeral, this evening, at half past 5 o'clock, from Capt. Benjn. Ferguson's dwelling, Forrest st.	08/09/1824
On Saturday morning, the 7th inst., James Kean, aged 35 years, brother of Stephen B. Kean, merchant tailor, of this city.	08/09/1824
Suddenly, at Providence, R. I., on the 30th ult., the Hon. David Howell, L. L. D., Judge of the U. States, for the District of the R. Island, aged 77	08/09/1824

Marriage and Death Notices	Date
years.	
On Saturday evening last, Zebulon Hollingsworth, Esq., formerly Associate Judge of the sixth Judicial District of the State of Maryland, in the 63rd year of his age.	08/10/1824
At Norfolk, Dr. Wilmot F. Rogers, aged 33, of the U. S. Navy. At Richmond, Mrs. Sarah, wife of the Rt. Rev. Bishop Moore.	08/10/1824
On the passage from Marseilles, on board brig Spartan, James Crawford, Esq., of Georgetown, D. C.	08/10/1824
In Marblehead, Capt. Benjamin Trevett, aged 39 years. Capt. T. served several years in the U. S. Navy, and was considered an active and useful officer, and for several years past commanded the U. S. Revenue Cutter, at Eastport.	08/10/1824
At St. Louis, Mo., June 23, Mr. William Wheatcroft, from Cincinnati. He belonged to a company of men who were exhibiting, at St. Louis, a number of Wild Beasts, and came to his death in consequence of a wound on one of his hands, occasioned by a bite from a lion.	08/10/1824
On the 7th inst., after a long and painful illness, Mrs. Rebecca Armstrong, consort of Mr. George Armstrong, merchant, of this city.	08/11/1824
At his residence, in Baltimore county, on the 3rd of August, in the 72nd year of his age, after a long and painful illness, Col. William Hutchins.	08/12/1824
On Sunday morning, in the 68th year of his age, Mr. Benjamin Francis, for many years a respectable inhabitant of this city.	08/12/1824
Suddenly, at his residence, at Still Pond, Kent county, Md., Lt. Col. Amos Reed.	08/12/1824
Life is, of all things, the most uncertain. When the infirmities of age, and the decay of mental and corporal faculties, strongly indicate the approaching dissolution of the "earthly tabernacle," when the ravages of lingering disease, speak in silent admonition, the slow, but certain advance of the awful moment of death, even under such circumstances, frail humanity shudders at the consummation, and almost sinks under the weight of its affliction. How much more heart-rending, the sorrow of those, who, without these prepatory warnings, are called to witness the sudden departure of a near and beloved relative, torn from them at a period of life, when those interesting traits of character begin to display themselves to be hereafter	08/13/1824

Marriage and Death Notices	Date
perfected, in the vigour and strength of maturity. Such are the reflections occasioned by the recent, untimely, death of Charles Carter Armistead McMechen, youngest son of the Hon. Judge McMechen, in the 16th year of his age. The victim of a violent bilious attack, in the short space of three days, he sunk beneath the shock, too powerful for a constitution naturally weak and delicate. Amiable and affectionate in his disposition, he had endeared himself to all who knew the goodness of his heart, whence emanated the warm feelings of friendship, benevolence, and love. Exemplary in the duties of son, and brother, he had so won the attachment of his whole family, that no lapse of time can obliterate the recollection of the many excellent qualities of this lamented youth. His success in the attainment of literary acquirements, gave promise of future respectability, for his intellectual capacity, needed but diligent application to have insured an abundant harvest. Though thus cut short, in the opening blossom, the flower has not withered, but has been transplanted into a celestial vineyard, there to flourish in rich perfection, moistened by the dews of Heaven. Parents! you have suffered a grievous dispensation, but weep not for your loss in his gain! His spirit, too pure for a terrestrial abode, has sought an asylum more congenial to its nature, and is now reposing in that region of bliss, where the souls of the just, are made perfect in holiness. 13h Aug. 1824 *A Friend*	
On Thursday evening, 12th inst., by the Rev. Mr. Helfenstein, Mr. Alonzo Lilly, merchant, formerly of Ashfield, Mass., to Miss Mary Ann, second eldest daughter of Philip Entler, Esq., both of this city.	08/14/1824
On Thursday evening last, by the Rev. Mr. Guest, Capt. John Repeto, to Miss Frances Johnson, all of this city.	08/14/1824
On Sunday evening last, by the Rev. Mr. Guest, Capt. William Mason, to Miss Eliza Manning, all of this city.	08/14/1824
On Monday morning, by the Rev. Mr. Henshaw, Mr. Simeon Leonard, of Bridgetown, W. New Jersey, to Miss Margaret Davis, of Patapsco Mills, Baltimore county.	08/14/1824
Last evening, by the Rev. Mr. Bartow, Mr. John Coster, to Miss Maria Downs, all of this city.	08/15/1824
On Tuesday evening, by the Rev. Mr. Kurtz, Mr. Thomas Saddler, to Miss Mary Ann Finley, of this city.	08/16/1824

Marriage and Death Notices	Date
At Cambridge, E. S. Maryland, Mr. Hector Scott, son-in-law of Luther Martin, Esq., in the 52nd year of his age. The deceased was father to one of the proprietors of the Cambridge Chronicle, and removed there, but a few months since. During a visit to Baltimore, he was attacked with a bilious complaint, with which he lingered until Monday morning last, when he exchanged this for a better and happier clime. His obituary is recorded in the hearts of all who knew him.	08/17/1824
By the Rev. Dr. Glendy, on the 4th of July last, Mr. Samuel Duer, to Miss Matilda Owings, both of Baltimore county.	08/18/1824
By the Rev. Mr. Glendy, on the 14th inst., Mr. Thomas White to Miss Mary Ann Haslup.	08/18/1824
In Salem, Capt. Charles Millet to Miss Sarah, daughter of Capt. Nathaniel Archer. Mr. John Kelman to Mrs. Henzibah Parris.	08/18/1824
Last evening, by the Rev. Dr. Roberts, Mr. Samuel Stellings, to Miss Lydia Poland, both of this city.	08/18/1824
At New York, Mr. Greenbury Dorsey of New Orleans, to Miss Elizabeth Packwood, of that city. By the Rev. Mr. Schroeder, John O'Donnell, of Baltimore, to Miss Mary Palmer, of that city.	08/18/1824
On Saturday evening last, in Dorchester, by the Rev. Mr. Baine, Mr. George Fisher, merchant, of Baltimore, to Miss Mary Ann, youngest daughter of Col. John Jones, of the former place.	08/20/1824
On Thursday evening last, by the Rev. Dr. Wyatt, Mr. John Logan to Miss Margaret Humphries, both of this city.	08/20/1824
On Sunday morning last, after a short illness of 16 hours, Mr. Benjamin Armitage, aged 52 years, a native of New York, but for many years a worthy and respectable inhabitant of this city. In him were combined an affectionate husband, a fond father, and a sincere friend – his death being lamented by a disconsolate widow and six children, and by those to whom he was universally known.	08/20/1824
This morning, in St. Paul's Church, by the Rt. Rev. Bishop Kemp, Charles Thorndike, Esq., of Boston, to Mary M., youngest daughter of the late Isaac Burnell, of Caroline County, Maryland.	08/21/1824
On Sunday evening last, by the Rev. Dr. Jennings, Mr. John U. Bond, to Miss Sarah Ann Randel, all of this city.	08/21/1824

Marriage and Death Notices	Date
On Thursday evening last, by the Rev. Dr. Roberts, Mr. Alies M'Leane, to Miss Mary Ready, all of this city.	08/21/1824
At New York, Mr. John C. Valesent, of Baltimore, to Miss Eleanor Schenck.	08/23/1824
On Tuesday morning last, at 5 o'clock, at his residence, in Newark, Delaware, in the 43rd year of his age, James Andrews, Esq., senior editor of the Elkton Press.	08/23/1824
At New Orleans, on the 26th day of July last, of yellow fever, Mr. Samuel Dana Ingraham, son of Nathaniel G. Ingraham, of New York, in the 32nd year of his age.	08/23/1824
At Mobile, William A. Fales, Esq., aged 35, attorney at law, recently of Boston.	08/24/1824
On Thursday evening last, by the Rev. Mr. Murvent, Mr. Samuel Dryden, to Miss Sabina Crownover, all of this city.	08/25/1824
At Marietta, Pennsylvania, on Wednesday morning last, Dr. James A. Boggs, after a protracted illness, in the 22nd year of his age.	08/25/1824
Lately, at Jackson, Louisiana, William F. Scott, Esq., respected and beloved by all his friends.	08/25/1824
Lately, at Nashville, the Hon. James Trimble, a firm friend and enlightened citizen.	08/25/1824
On Saturday, 14th August, 1824, Mrs. Margaret C. Triplett, consort of Dr. Thomas Triplett, of Fauquier county, Va.	08/25/1824
On Friday, the 13th inst., at his residence, in Montgomery county, Md., Robert D. Dawson, Esq., in the 66th year of his age.	08/25/1824
On the 18th of July, at the residence of C. Frazee, in Baldwin county, Alabama, Capt. Joseph H. Ashbridge, formerly of Philadelphia, aged 33.	08/25/1824
At his residence, in Lexington, Oglethorpe county, Geo., on the 3rd inst., Stephen Upson, in the 40th year of his age. He was a native of the sate of Connecticut.	08/25/1824
Another Revolutionary Soldier Gone. While we are enjoying the blessings our fathers achieved for us, we are often forgetful that under Providence it was such men as Benjamin Francis, who were the instruments that obtained our freedom and consequent happiness by	08/25/1824

Marriage and Death Notices	Date
their bravery. The subject of these remarks was born in Massachusetts, near Boston; and at the age of 18, at the battle of Bunker's Hill, he flew to arms, and continued to serve his country until the capture of Fort Washington, when he was, with his unfortunate fellow prisoners, conducted to New York, and was there condemned to undergo all the sufferings that could be inflicted by a merciless British soldiery; and had it not been for his robust constitution, his bones long ere this would have whited the shores of that city. His suffering, at that time, made such an inroad to his constitution that the writer of this small tribute to his memory has often heard him say, that the ill treatment received while a prisoner with the British, was the cause of his affliction, which at last terminated his existence, on Sunday morning, the 8th inst., after a few days illness, aged 68 years. He had lived many years in Baltimore, and was so well known for his honesty and integrity, that his word was sufficient with all that knew him. The widow, the orphaned, and the distressed, always found him ready to assist them to the utmost of his ability.	
On Saturday morning, the 21st inst., at the house of Mr. Dorsey, of this city, Miss Amanda Matilda, daughter of the late Nathaniel Lightner, Esq., of Lancaster county, Pa., in the twentieth year of her age, after a short, but severe illness, which she bore with unabated fortitude – and departed his life with the full assurance of enjoying eternal happiness in the arms of her maker. This amiable female was on a visit to this city, when she was thus suddenly torn away. Her mild and unassuming manners had drawn around her a circle of acquaintances, who will never cease to deplore the irreparable loss they have sustained. Breathe not a sigh for me when I am gone, But let my grave-place be Dreary and lone; Let the rude tempst rave a requiem oe'r my grave; But sing thou none. Yet place a wild rose near my narrow bed; Emblem of *one* too dear, still dear, though dead! Cherish its tender root, Let no rude straner's foot Bow down its head. Yes! 'Twas a lovely flower my bosom wore: Vast wast its beauty's pow'r – Alas! Tis o'er. Death, in a gloomy hour, tore it from Love's own bower, To bloom no more. Winter will blight the rose thou plants for me! Spring will new-life disclose t'will flourish free; And my heart's flower shall bloom Bnrightly beyond the tomb, eternally! The editor of the Lancaster Journal will please give the above an insertion.	08/26/1824

Marriage and Death Notices	Date
On Wednesday evening, 25th inst., by the Rev. Mr. Bester, Mr. Joseph Hisky, to Miss Helena, eldest daughter of Mr. John Geissenderffer, all of this city.	08/27/1824
On Saturday morning last, by the Rev. Mr. Healey, Mr. Henry Selby, to Miss Elizabeth Cordery, both of this city.	08/27/1824
Last evening, by the Rev. Mr. Healey, Mr. Hicks Rook, to Miss Esther Wilson, of Anne Arundel county.	08/27/1824
On Sunday evening last, 22nd inst., in Prince George's county, Md., by the Rev. Aloysius Mudd, Mr. Luke Howard, merchant, of Tuscumbia, Alabama, to Miss Harriot, youngest daughter of the late Henry Brooke, Esq., of said county.	08/27/1824
On the 11th inst., at Mt. Holly, N. J., by John Blackwood, Esq., Mr. Levi Bates, of Philadelphia, to Miss Maria Stiff, of Baltimore.	08/27/1824
On Thursday evening, by the Rev. Mr. Helfenstein, Mr. William Mumma, to Miss Ann Aupold, both of Baltimore county.	08/28/1824
On Thursday evening last, by the Rt. Rev. Bishop Kemp, Mr. Frederick Horze, to Miss Eliza Ann Ellis, all of this city.	08/28/1824
On the 24th instant, at the late residence of Mr. Samuel Phillips, of Prince George's county, Mrs. Sarah Phillips, aged 30 years, eldest daughter of Wm. Ashman, of this city, after a short illness, which she bore with Christian fortitude, and in full assurance of everlasting rest; the realities of which she fully enjoyed in the affliction; and resigned her peaceful soul in the bosom of her dear Redeemer – lamented and much esteemed by all who knew her worth.	08/28/1824
In Newton, Mass., on Sunday last, while on a visit to her father, Gen. William Hull, Mrs. Caroline, wife of Rufus K. Page, Esq., of Hallowell, Me., aged 32.	08/28/1824
On the 25th inst., Mrs. Mary Pleasants, wife of Mr. John P. Pleasants, in the 31st year of her age. We forbear the attempt to do justice to the character of the deceased for rational piety, benevolence, and sweetness of manners, because to those who knew her well, the praise would appear inadequate; to those who knew her not, it might seem the ordinary, unmeaning, and unmerited adulation which injudicious friendship heaps on the memory of the departed.	08/30/1824
At Church-hill, Queen Ann's county, Md., on the 17th of August,	08/31/1824

Marriage and Death Notices	Date
William H. Jacobs, Esq., in the 38th year of his age. He was for a number of years past a useful member of the Methodist Episcopal Church. He was remarkable for his hospitality and kindness to ministers traveling through the village in which he lived; and did as much as he could for the promotion of their comfort and happiness. As a man and a citizen, he was amiable and greatly respected; as a friend, sincere; as a father, affectionate; and, as a husband, devoted, attentive, and kind. The day before his death, he took an affectionate leave of his wife and children, assuring the former, that he had a firm and unshakable confidence in the mercy of his God, and the certainty of a blessed immortality; while, therefore, we mingle our tears with those of his disconsolate and agonizing widow, and deeply sympathize with his infant children in their irreparable loss; we have the unspeakable consolation that their loss is his eternal gain. The unexpected death of a fellow citizen cut down in the meridian of life should teach us to remember the uncertain tenure under which we hold all the pleasure and enjoments of this life, and to stimulate us to *be also ready to give an account of our stewardship.*	
On the 18th ultimo, at his residence, in Concordia, near Natchez, Mis., Walter S. Parker, Esq., in the 31st year of his age, formerly a respectable merchant of this city.	09/01/1824
On the 26th ult., at Church Hill, Md., Mrs. Ellenor Lamb, in the 65th year of her age. She lived respected and died regretted by all by all who knew her.	09/02/1824
Yesterday evening, at 5 o'clock, of a short, but severe illness, which he bore with the utmost patience and resignation, Michael Kimmel, in the forty second year of his age, and for many years a respectable merchant of this city. His friends and acquaintance are respectfully invited to attend his funeral, this day, at 3 o'clock P. M., from his late dwelling, Great York street, opposite the Friends' burying ground.	09/03/1824
On Thursday evening last, by the Rev. Mr. Reese, Mr. Charles Seth, to Miss Mary Duling, both of this city.	09/04/1824
On Thursday evening last, by the Rev. Mr. Reese, Mr. James Crocker, to Miss Sarah Parker.	09/04/1824
Suddenly, yesterday morning, in the tanyard of Mr. Hitzelberger, in Fish street, where he was employed, Frederick M'Comas. One of the coroners, Lambert Thomas, Esq., was called to view the body, when after an examination by the jury, a verdict was returned, "that he had	09/04/1824

Marriage and Death Notices	Date
come to his death by a fit of some kind unknown to the jury."	
At Richmond, Mrs. Mary, wife of Mr. John Williams, late of Baltimore, but formerly a merchant of Petersburg, Va.	09/04/1824
At New York, of consumption, at No. 48 Courtland street, Mr. Charles Coffin, aged about 20, born in Baltimore, and a seaman, on board the brig Catherine.	09/06/1824
Departed this life, on Tuesday afternoon, the 7th inst., Christopher Hughes, Esq., in the 80th year of his age. Mr. Hughes has been, for the last fifty four years, a citizen of Baltimore and by his enterprise and industry has largely contributed to its growth and prosperity.	09/08/1824
Died, on the 1st inst., William, only son of Thomas Dance, of this city, aged 5 years and 7 months.	09/08/1824
Departed this life, on Tuesday morning last, after a long and painful illness, in the 25th year of her age, Mrs. Elizabeth Robins, consort of Mr. James Robins, of this city. By this dispensation of Divine Providence, society has been deprived of a valuable and useful ornament, a husband of a fond and dear companion, a parent of a dutiful and attentive child. Her memory will long be cherished, and her death deplored by her friends whose grief speaks her eulogy. Her hopes of immortality were built on Christ, placing her trust by faith in Him, she was enabled in the "hour and article of death," to meet the "king of terrors" with the triumphant song of the Christian, O Death where is thy sting, O grave where is thy victory!"	09/09/1824
Departed this transitory life, on Friday evening last, Mr. Thomas Armstrong, in the 60th year of his age, long a respectable inhabitant of this city, leaving a disconsolate Widow and 6 children to lament his loss. As a husband and a father, he was kind and affectionate, as a friend sincere. It is a matter of great consolation to those who witnessed the closing scene of his life to believe that he attained mercy through the merits of his Lord and Savior.	09/09/1824
In Beverly, Mrs. Mary Goodridge, widow of Mr. Joseph Goodridge. She had lain down, preparatory to watch with a sick neighbor, but feeling unwell, got up about 9 o'clock, and took some drops of *Prussic acid*. The effects were such as might have been expected to a person unused to that *deadly poison*; she was soon thrown into convulsions, and died at midnight.	09/09/1824

Marriage and Death Notices	Date
Departed this life, on the 14th ult., at the residence of the late Walter S. Parker, in Concordia, near Natchez, Mississippi, Miss Mary Parker, after a short, but severe illness, which she bore with Christian resignation. It is a source of much consolation to her friends under the present dispensation, to know that during her life she attended to those things which make for eternal happiness, and has now only gone to receive the reward of her many labors of love and deeds of charity. "Blessed are the dead which die in the Lord; yea saith the spirit, for they rest from their labors, and their works do follow them."	09/09/1824
Departed this life, on Friday, 3rd inst., after a long and painful illness, Mrs. Letitia Small, in the 50th year of her age.	09/10/1824
On Thursday evening last, by the Rev. Mr. Guest, Mr. Peter B. Lucas, to Miss Elizabeth Hopkins, both of this city.	09/11/1824
On Thursday evening last, by the Rev. J. M. Duncan, Mr. Lloyd M. Miller, to Miss Ann M. Conway, all of this city.	09/11/1824
On the 11th inst., at Woodbine, her late residence in Baltimore county, Mrs. Sophia Price, relict of Mr. Wm. Price, aged 74 years.	09/15/1824
Departed this life, this morning, 17th inst., Thomas Kilbreth, of a protracted disease, which he bore to the last with Christian fortitude. The deceased has been long a respectable resident of this city. His friends and acquaintance are requested to attend the funeral, from his late dwelling, Eutaw street, tomorrow morning, at 9 o'clock.	09/17/1824
On Monday, the 13th inst., at Havre de Grace, Harford county, Md., at the residence of Wm. Cole, Esq., after a distressing and protracted pulmonary disease, Mrs. Eliza Ann St. Victor, in the 31st year of her age. The deceased was dearly beloved by all who knew and could esteem her worth, she bore her illness without a murmur and left this world in the confident belief, that she was destined to another, where, through the blessed Redeemer Jesus Christ, she would meet with eternal happiness.	09/17/1824
On Sunday last, at his late residence in Anne Arundel county, in the 84th year of his age, Maj. William Brogden, a truly venerable and respectable member of the community. Mr. B. served in the cause of his country during the Revolutionary War, and subsequently as a member of the Legislature of Maryland.	09/17/1824
This morning, Mr. James Hayden, in the 51st year of his age. Mr. Hayden spent the last 30 years of his life in this city, where he was very	09/18/1824

Marriage and Death Notices	Date
generally known and respected as an industrious, honorable, and skillful mechanic, and a pious and sincere Christian. He has left a splendid monument of his mechanical skill in the Cathedral, the construction of which he superintended, with distinguished zeal and industry, under the direction of that eminent architect, B. H. Latrobe, whereby he has secured to his memory the gratitude and respect of the numerous congregation of that Church, who are hereby invited, with his other friends, to attend his funeral, tomorrow, Sunday afternoon, at 3 o'clock, from his residence, Pennsylvania avenue.	
This morning, at half after six o'clock, Mr. Benjamin Sterrett, in the 57th year of his age, for many years a respectable merchant of this city. His friends and acquaintances generally are respectfully invited to attend his funeral, from his dwelling, North Charles st., tomorrow morning, at half past 8 o'clk.	09/18/1824
On Tuesday last, in Frederick, Md., after a lingering illness, Mr. Frederick Getz, in the 42nd year of his age. On the following day, his remains were interred with masonic and military honors.	09/20/1824
Died, at Mount Pleasant farm, near Snow Hill, Md., on the evening of the 7th inst., after an illness of a very few days, Mrs. Mary Smith, consort of Samuel R. Smith, Esq., in the 25th year of her age. In closing her short lived career, this amiable and interesting female has left a melancholy void in the circle of her friends and acquaintance; a fond parent has lost a darling and an only daughter; a disconsolate husband his greatest source of earthly felicity, and a numerous train of friends and relations an example of virtue beyond her years; but they have no cause to sorrow as those without hope, having a comfortable and heart-cheering assurance, that her departed spirit is now enjoying the smiles of that Saviour of whom she was a follower, and in the redemption of whose blood she had long since made a public profession.	09/20/1824
From the Charleston Courier. Died at Sullivan's Island, Mr. Wm. Eveleth, aged 35 years, son of Joseph Eveleth, Esq., of Salem, Mass., a young man respected and beloved by all who knew him. He has left father, mother, brothers and sister, to mourn the loss of a son and brother endeared to them by the many virtues he possessed. Although he died far from his native home, without a parent's tender eye to watch, or hand to close his dying eyes, he was surrounded by those who administered to his wants with the hands of true friendship. He suffered a painful and distressing illness of four days, when on the morning of Sunday last, the 5th inst. "His God, the God of peace and love, Poured kindly solace from above,	09/20/1824

403

Marriage and Death Notices	Date
And soothed his soul to rest."	
On Thursday, the 16th inst., in the 59th year of his age, Thomas Dinsmoore, after a short illness, for many years a respectable merchant of this city, generally beloved by all his acquaintances.	09/21/1824
At Philadelphia, Mr. Thomas Jefferson, of the Philadelphia Theatre, in the 27th year of his age.	09/21/1824
On Tuesday evening, by the Rev. Mr. Henshaw, Mr. Frisby Roberts, to Miss Maria Brown, both of this city.	09/22/1824
At Capt. Moffitt's, last evening, by the Rev. Dr. Roberts, Mr. Merritt Martin, to Mrs. Mary Ann Beard, both of this city.	09/22/1824
On Tuesday evening last, the 21st inst., by the Rev. Dr. Wyatt, John Milner, Esq., of Philadelphia, to Miss Eliza Donaldson, of Baltimore.	09/23/1824
On Saturday morning last, after a long and severe illness, John Wood, in the 48th year of his age leaving a wife and six children to mourn the loss of a tender husband and kind and affectionate father.	09/23/1824
At the mansion of his father, Judge Sherburne, in Portsmouth, N. H., on Tuesday last, the 14th inst., after a short and painful sickness, Mr. William Whipple Sherburne, aged 32.	09/23/1824
On Sunday evening last, by the Rev. Dr. Roberts, Mr. Samuel Gladding, to Miss Sarah Baker.	09/24/1824
On Thursday, the 16th inst., by the Rev. Mr. Guest, Capt. T. W. Brotherton, of the Columbian Navy, to Miss Phoebe T. Cox, of Harford county, Md.	09/24/1824
At Hagerstown, on the 20th inst., the Rev. John Lind, Pastor of the Presbyterian congregation of that place, in the 41st year of his age.	09/24/1824
At the residence of the Rev. Charles G. M'Lean, in Cumberland township, on the 20th inst., after 16 days illness, the Rev. James Gray, D. D., in the 54th year of his age.	09/24/1824
OBITUARY. Departed his life, at Alexandria, D. C., on the 25th August, in the 32nd year of her age, Mrs. Sarah Cannell, wife of Mr. Isaac Cannell, merchant of that place. {The long obituary continues, extolling her virtues and lamenting her death.}	09/24/1824

Marriage and Death Notices	Date
On the 18th inst., at Port Tobacco, Md., Mr. Peter F. Campbell, in the 25th year of his age, formerly of Marietta, Lancaster county, Penn., much beloved and regretted by all who knew him.	09/25/1824
On Thursday evening last, by the Rev. Mr. Duncan, Mr. William Tiffany, to Miss Mary S. Marean, both of this city.	09/27/1824
In this city, on Saturday last, after a short, but illness of only nine days, Miss Lydia Stone, in the 25th year of her age, formerly of Talbot county, Md.	09/28/1824
At St. George the Martyr, Queen square, London, Samuel M'Culloh, Esq., of Baltimore, in the United States, to Eleanor M'Culloh, of Great Ormond st., and formerly of Charlton, in Kent.	09/29/1824
At New Orleans, of yellow fever, Dr. J. B. Wilkinson, formerly of Kentucky; Alexander M. Cumming, printer, of Philadelphia; William Dillon, 30, New York; Nathaniel Peckham, 24, Vt.; Elisha Smith, N. J.; William Michel; Thomas Brown; John Casey, 29, Ireland; Laurent Seur, native; Bernard Largury, Ireland; Louisa Nagel, native; Patrick Comins, 36, Ireland; Julia Le Roy, 19, France. At New Orleans, of casualty, William Bradford, of New York, aged 30.	09/30/1824
On the 2nd September, by the Rev. Dr. Wyatt, Mr. Jonathan Shockley, to Miss Caroline P. Cole, all of this city.	10/01/1824
OBITUARY. Died, in the Gulph of Mexico, on the first instant, on board the schooner Col. Tenant, of and for Baltimore, from Alvarado, George Bier, late master and supercargo of the above vessel, in the 34th year of his age. The writer of the above notice, although aware that there is nothing wanting to perpetuate the memory of the deceased, in the breasts of his fellow citizens, cannot do justice to those sentiments of high regard and esteem, which he has long cherished for him, without making a few brief remarks on his life and character. Having for a considerable length of time previous to his late departure from Baltimore, had the honour of an acquaintance with Capt. George Bier, I have had an opportunity of observing in various instances, with a high degree of admiration those exalted traits that nobleness of soul and amiableness of character and manners, which alone are counterparts of the great mind and which made him the delight of his acquaintances and the endearing hope of an adorned and loving wife, and affectionate family. Noble, generous, and candid himself, he, as is frequently the case, entertained exalted opinions of the virtues of others, and was always found to stand forth the champion of his fellow men, with a philanthropy and disinterestedness which did honor to the human	10/01/1824

Marriage and Death Notices	Date
character. He was indeed the pride and delight of his family and friend, and an ornament to the circle in which he moved; but alas! how fallacious are the hopes and expectations of human life – how like the delusive vision of the night, which fills the mind with a momentary rapture, whilst we are enveloped in sleep and which vanishes forever with the first break of morning. Alas! how little did the regretted subject of this memoir think, as he pressed the quivering lips of the beloved partner of his life, and wiped away the trembling tear which told her grief at the thought of a temporary absence, that he was taking his last and final leave – and she, to whom I have alluded, as she watched his lessening sail, until the misty eye could no longer discern it in the dim horizon that ere again it met her longing sight, he who steered its course over the vast blank of the trackless ocean, should find his grave beneath its profound abyss, enshrouded forever from her ravished gaze! Oh! the thought is too painful; 'tis enough to make every chord of the heart which vibrates to the call of sympathy, bleed for his untimely fate. I deem it unnecessary further to multiply words in order to pourtray the merits of our departed fellow citizen, as his worth and integrity, are too well illustrated to need further commemoration, and shall conclude this brief narrative, by wishing that his name may long be remembered, and his virtues emulated by a large portion of his countrymen.	
On Tuesday last, at New York, Mr. George I. Mankin, merchant, of Baltimore, to Miss Ann F. Strong, daughter of Roger Strong, Esq.	10/02/1824
On Wednesday evening last, by the Rev. John Valiant, Mr. Joseph Howe, to Miss Hannah Fletcher.	10/04/1824
On Thursday evening, by the Rev. John Valiant, Mr. John Hawk, to Mary Ann Poole, of Anne Arundel county.	10/04/1824
On Thursday evening last, by the Rev. Mr. Bartow, Mr. James Tyler, to Miss Mary Lake, all of this city.	10/04/1824
On Thursday evening last, by the Rev. Mr. Payton, Mr. John T. N. Douglass, to Miss Eliza C. Chandley.	10/04/1824
On Sunday evening, September 26th, by the Rev. Mr. Nevins, Mr. Stanislas Audibert, to Miss Amelia Fulton, all of this city.	10/04/1824
On Wednesday evening last, by the Rev. Mr. Peckworth, Mr. John Burnham, to Miss Keziah Todd.	10/04/1824

Marriage and Death Notices	Date
In Frederick county, on Tuesday evening, 28th Sept., by the Rev. Alfred Griffith, Mr. Israel Griffith, merchant, of Baltimore, to Miss Sarah Ann, daughter of Col. Philemon Griffith, of the former place.	10/04/1824
On the 23rd inst., at the residence of Capt. Dooley, by the Rev. Mr. Stier, Mr. Thomas O'Denny, of West River, to Miss Elizabeth T. M'Donnell, of Baltimore.	10/04/1824
On Tuesday last, in Washington county, Md., William Schley, Esq., Attorney at Law, of Frederick, to Miss Ann, daughter of Gen. Samuel Ringgold, of the former place.	10/04/1824
Departed this life, on Friday morning last, after a tedious and painful illness, which she bore with truly Christian fortitude and patience, Mrs. Ann Hoskyns, universally beloved, for meekness of temper, and mildness of disposition.	10/04/1824
Departed this transitory life, on Saturday, the 11th ulto., Mrs. Elizabeth, consort of Capt. Joseph Gardner, in the 35th year of her age – after a short, but painful illness – which she bore with Christian fortitude and resignation, looking forward for the reward of a well spent life. She has left behind her an affectionate husband and a large family of children to deplore her irreparable loss.	10/04/1824
On Sunday evening, 3rd inst., by the Rev. Dr. Jennings, Mr. Samuel Taylor, to Miss Margaret Carey, all of this city.	10/05/1824
Departed this life, on Thursday night, after a short and painful sickness, Mrs. Anna Myers, in the 46th year of her age, consort of Jacob Myers, of Fell's Point. She has left a disconsolate husband and a large family of children to deplore her loss.	10/05/1824
Departed this life, on Friday morning, 1st int., at the country seat of B. J. Von Kapff, Esq., Miss Mary McGaghy, a native of Bedford, Penn., in the 38th year of her age. She died universally regretted by her acquaintances; and the family which sustains her loss, will long have to bewail her afflicting bereavement.	10/05/1824
On Tuesday evening, 5th inst., by the Rev. Dr. Roberts, Mr. William Pierce, to Miss Ellen Bell, all of this city.	10/09/1824
On Tuesday evening last, after a short illness, Mrs. Charlotte, the wife of Capt. Pearle Durkee.	10/09/1824
Departed this life, on 4th inst., of a bilious remittent fever, in the 26th	10/09/1824

Marriage and Death Notices	Date
year of his age, Mr. Thomas Russell, lately of New York, formerly of Drimeny, Donegall county, Ireland.	
On the 29th Sept., in St. Mary's county, Col. Athanasius Fenwick, late a Senator of Maryland.	10/11/1824
On the 6th inst., at Middletown, Md., Thomas Dunn, Sergeant at arms of the House of Representatives of the United States.	10/11/1824
At Charleston, on the 10th September, Mr. Asa B. Norris, in the 24th year of his age.	10/11/1824
On Tuesday evening, by the Rev. Mr. Smith, Mr. Hugh Simpson, to Miss Sarah Cashin, both of this city.	10/14/1824
On Tuesday evening, by the Rev. Mr. Richards, Edward C. Pinkney, Esq., to Georgiana, daughter of Marcus McCausland, Esq.	10/14/1824
On Tuesday evening last, by the Rev. Mr. Hemphill, Mr. Charles Howard, to Miss Ann Veter Shipley, daughter of Mr. Richard A. Shipley, all of this city.	10/14/1824
On Tuesday evening, 5th inst., by the Rev. Mr. Guest, Mr. Samuel Guest, to Miss Susan Sheerwood, all of this city.	10/14/1824
On Tuesday evening last, by the Rev. Dr. Roberts, Mr. Joshua Royston, to Ellen, daughter of Mr. Walter Crook.	10/14/1824
In St. Mary's County, Md., at his residence, Clover Hills, on the 1st instant, Mr. Edward Millard, in the 30th year of his age. This young gentleman was an ornament to society, and no man was more respected and esteemed. His loss is truly deplored.	10/14/1824
On Thursday evening last, by the Rev. John P. Peckworth, Mr. Ebenezer Lewis, to Mrs. Mary Ross, all of this city.	10/15/1824
On Thursday evening last, by the Rev. W. E. Wyatt, Mr. Benjamin Greble, of the City of Philadelphia, to Miss Ellen Hatton, of this city.	10/16/1824
On Thursday evening last, by the Rev. Mr. Kurtz, Mr. Thomas Gambell, to Miss Catherine Warner, all of this city.	10/18/1824
Yesterday, Dr. John Owen. His friends are invited to attend his funeral, from his late residence, in Chatham street, this afternoon, at 4 o'clock precisely.	10/19/1824

Marriage and Death Notices	Date
At Doylestown, Penn., on the 11th inst., after a short illness, Wm. C. Rogers, Esq.	10/19/1824
In this city, on the 16th inst., Col. Shubael Butterfield, late of Sacket's Harbor, New York, aged 41. He was a meritorious officer through the whole of the late war; a kind and affectionate husband and father respected and endearing in all the relations of life. He has left an afflicted family, and a numerous circle of friends and acquaintance to mourn and lament his loss.	10/21/1824
Died, suddenly, on Saturday evening last, at the residence of her father, Col. Tenant, in the 22nd year of her age, Mary, the wife of John P. Kennedy, Esq. We know not in what language to speak of a clamamity which has ravished from the bosom of affection, in the bloom of her youth and the plenitude of her hopes, this lovely, intelligent, and accomplished female. Her obituary is written in the heart. Her loss is indescribable. Gifted with no ordinary powers of intellect, she blended with the endowments of education, the purest charities of life – society at large acknowledged the influence of those feminine virtues which particularly shed happiness over the domestic circle. We have deply felt the daily beauty of an existence, that crowded in its brief span, all those qualities which endear their possessor to the world, and render irreparable to her family, the bereavement, which it is our lot to record.	10/21/1824
Died, at St. Thomas, on the 27th of September, Capt. Eugene Fenton, in the 32nd year of his age, a native of Ireland, but for many years a resident of Baltimore. Few persons perhaps have died more universally regretted than the deceased. We forbear the attempt to do justice to the character of the subject of this obituary for he possessed all that nobleness of soul, and cheerfulness of disposition added to goodness of heart which drew him friends, and besides the art of making them, he possessed the more uncommon talent of retaining them. May his afflicted and disconsolate wife, and all who lament his irreparable loss, seek comfort, and consolation in that religion that administered to all his wants and sweetened all his sorrows. It is hoped he died without an enemy, and in the full assurance of eternal happiness. "The chamber where the good man meets his fate is priviledged beyond the common walk of virtuous life, quite in the virge of heaven."	10/21/1824
At Fredericktown, Md., on Saturday week, the Rev. Patrick Davidson. He was a native of Pennsylvania; graduated at Dickinson College; was twenty seven years in the ministry; and died in the 49th year of his age. For nearly 15 years, he was the pastor of the Presbyterian Church in Fredericktown.	10/21/1824

Marriage and Death Notices	Date
At New Orleans, on the 19th ult., Mr. Samuel Tweedy, of Delaware, and late of Baltimore, of the prevailing fever. He has left a wife and child to deplore his irreparable loss.	10/21/1824
On Tuesday evening last, by the Rev. Mr. Bartow, Capt. William C. Tilden, to Miss Ruth McKenzie, all of this city.	10/22/1824
On Wednesday afternoon, after a protracted illness, Mrs. Ann, consort of Col. Jacob Small, in the 52nd year of her age, a victim of parental affection. This is the fourth case of mortality that has occurred in the family, within the short space of one year. The fatigue consequent to the arduous attention which she bestowed on the declining health of those of her family, who have trodden the path of death before her, produced the fatal effect on her constitution, nor could the evident inroads of disease on her system, prevent her from discharging the duties of an affectionate parent with the greatest assiduity. In the death of Mrs. Small, her family and friends have sustained a great and irreparable loss. She was friendly and affectionate, and in her the poor have lost one of their best friends. Her obituary will not soon be erased from the hearts of those who knew her.	10/22/1824
Departed this life, on Thursday morning, 21st inst., in the 42nd year of her age, Mrs. Lydia Allen, wife of Capt. John Allen, of Nantucket, of a lingering consumption, which she endured with meek resignation, as the will of her Creator. "Why should we mourn departed friends, Or shake at death's alarms? 'Tis but the voice, that Jesus sends, To call them to his arms."	10/22/1824
The recent death of Dr. John Owen is a severe loss to the city of Baltimore. In the 50th year of his age, in the vigor of life and usefulness, he has been suddenly arrested by the hand of fate. The heart, whose philanthropy embraced the universe with the circle of its affections, has ceased its pulsations; the hand "which open as day to melting charity" was ever extended to relieve the distressed, lies cold within its tenaments of clay. The scenes which mark the individual, and serve to attache his friends so strongly to him, are to line only "in the memory of days that are past." His elogium as a Physician might rest with those who have come within the scope of his widely diffused practice. An almost intuitive knowledge of the source of diseases – ardent and indefatigable exertions to remove them – coolness and deliberation in seizing the favorable moment for applying the proper remidies – These were the qualities that gained so much the confidence of his patients, that no family that which had once employed him ever after dispensed	10/23/1824

410

Marriage and Death Notices	Date
with his services. These were the qualities which rendered his success as a practitioner almost without parallel. In critical cases, he was consulted by his brethren in the last resort; and in a profession, whose members are supposed to to be peculiarly tenacious, there was such an understanding of his skill and probity, that the bitterness of jealousy rarely brought him in collision with any of them. That benevolence, which pervaded his life, was a shield in his professional career. As a public servant and director of the Penitentary, his loss will be felt by the state for under his management, more than of any other, have grown up the regulations which governed that institution – and his fostering hand mainly contributed to provide the subordinate inducements to ameliorate the morals of the criminals and fit them for society. These things may be bitter in perusal, but must be sweet in reflection to those relatives who depended on him for support and looked up to him for protection.	
On Tuesday, 19th, by the Rev. Mr. Merwin, Mr. Isaac Reynolds, to Miss Harriet A. Kell, all of this city.	10/25/1824
At Labrador, on the 3rd of February last, in the 33rd year of her age, Mrs. Cordelia Taylor, late consort of William Taylor, of Baltimore, step daughter of Richard Jennings, Esq., of New York, and daughter of Dr. Daniel Ledyard, deceased.	10/25/1824
On the 22nd inst., by the Rev. Dr. Roberts, Mr. Edward Needles, of this city, to Miss Rachel Green, formerly of Philadelphia.	10/26/1824
On Sunday evening last, by the Most Rev. Archbishop Mareschal, Capt. Samuel D. Legrand, to Miss Sarah Lynch, both of this city.	10/26/1824
By the Rev. Dr. Jennings, on the 6th inst., Mr. Daniel Chase, to Miss Elizabeth Walter.	10/26/1824
By the Rev. Dr. Jennings, on Sunday evening last, Mr. Albert G. M'Comas, to Miss Sarah Mortimer.	10/26/1824
On Wednesday last, the 20th inst., at his residence, near Reisterstown, in Baltimore county, after a severe indisposition of a few days, Mr. Charles C. Cockey, in the 28th year of his age. In the bloom of youth, and vigor of life, we are but in death.	10/26/1824
Departed this transitory life, on Friday, the 22nd inst., after a severe indisposition of four weeks, John Cockey, Esq., in the 67th year of his age.	10/26/1824

Marriage and Death Notices	Date
On Friday last, after a short, but painful illness, in the 29th year of her life, Miss Mary Merrick. To make comment upon her virtues would be unnecessary, as they were so well known by those with whom she was acquainted. She acted for a long time as a mother to the Orphan children of this city, and with as much attention as if they were her own. Her death has caused a loss that is irreparable.	10/26/1824
On Tuesday, 19th inst., by the Rev. Mr. Hoskins, Mr. Benjamin M. Duckett, to Miss Mary Anne, daughter of Mr. Fielder Cross, all of Prince George's county.	10/27/1824
On the 5th inst., at the residence of his father, near Princess Anne, Somerset county, George T. Slocombe, late of Baltimore, in the 34th year of his age.	10/27/1824
At New Orleans, on the 19th ult., of yellow fever, Mr. Robert Briggs, printer, aged 28. Oft has the weary Printer lock'd Death's Daily Record* in his Chase, Now Death has lock'd the Printer up, Within his cold and sad embrace. *The deaths by yellow fever are published daily in New Orleans.	10/27/1824
By Dr. Roberts, on the 26th, Benjamin Hiss, to Miss Susan M. H. Brown, all of this city.	10/28/1824
On Thursday evening, the 21st inst., by the Rev. Mr. Larken, William B. Pittenger, of Frederick county, to Miss Louisa, daughter of Capt. Dunkin, of this city.	10/29/1824
At Petersburg, Va., after an illness of three days, of the bilious fever, Georgiana P. Williams, daughter of Mr. John Williams, late of Baltimore.	10/29/1824
On Thursday evening, by the Rev. Dr. Wyatt, Capt. Solomon Rutter, to Frances, daughter of the late Thomas Rutter, Esq.	10/30/1824
On Sunday evening last, by the Rev. Mr. Helfenstein, Mr. John Shreck, to Miss Mary Ann Kelly, both of this city.	11/01/1824
On the 18th ult., at Chestertown, Md., by the Rev. Mr. Jackson, Richard Ringgold, Esq., to Mrs. Catherine Hand, all of that place.	11/01/1824
On the plantation of Henry M'Call, Esq., 25 miles below New Orleans, on Sunday, 26th Sept., William Hardusty, a native of the state of	11/01/1824

Marriage and Death Notices	Date
Maryland, aged about 30 years.	
On Tuesday evening, the 2nd instant, by the Rev. Andrew Hemphill, the Rev. William W. Chapman, to Miss Rebecca, daughter of Caleb Merryman, Esq., all of Baltimore county.	11/05/1824
On Tuesday evening last, by the Rev. Dr. Hall, John Vergis, Esq., to Miss Flora Galloway, both of this city.	11/05/1824
On Wednesday evening, by the Rev. Mr. Bartow, Henry Bennet, Esq., to Miss Rosanna Thompson, all of this city.	11/05/1824
In Hartford county, on the 28th of Oct. last, by the Rev. Mr. Webster, Mr. Wm. J. Mead, to Miss Elizabeth Ann Lawder, all of this city.	11/05/1824
On Wednesday, 3rd inst., by the Rev. Dr. Roberts, Mr. George Bartlett, merchant, to Miss Vashti Robinson, all of this city.	11/05/1824
This morning, after a long and painful illness, Mrs. Abigail M'Ginnis, in her 49th year, widow of the late John M'Ginnis. Her friends and acquaintances are requested to attend her funeral, tomorrow, Saturday, evening, at 2 o'clock, from her late dwelling.	11/05/1824
On Saturday, 9th October, at Middleton, Charles county, Mrs. Ann Ferguson, consort of Mr. Robert Ferguson, in the 45th year of her age, after a painful illness, which she bore with Christian fortitude and resignation, leaving a disconsolate husband and two children to lament her irreparable loss.	11/05/1824
On Saturday, the 30th Oct. last, at Clifton, his residence, near Baltimore, Samuel Howard Moale, in the 22nd year of his age. In noticing the death of this young gentleman, we are deeply sensible of incompetency of an obituary notice to afford consolation to his family and friends. Mr. Moale was the only son of one of the most respectable members of the Baltimore bar, of a father who regarded him with all a father's fondness. He was a young husband, who was every day more and more realizing the interesting and responsible relations in which he stood to his family and society; he was just throwing off the ardour and impetiousity incident to youth; and the change to calmness and thoughtfulness so likely to be produced by the example afforded him by his respectable father, was rapidly taking place, and in a few years his friends would have realized their fond anticipation of his being as much endeared to society at large as he was to his family.	11/05/1824

Marriage and Death Notices	Date
On the night of the 2nd inst., at the residence of Mr. Charles White, Millenton Mill Seat, Miss Henrietta L. Moore, in the 27th year of her age, after a short illness, which she bore with Christian fortitude and resignation.	11/05/1824
On Thursday last, by the Rev. Mr. Guest, Mr. George James, to Miss Lydia Sharewood, both of this city.	11/06/1824
On Thursday evening last, by the Rev. Mr. Parish, Samuel S. Briggs, to Miss Ann Bullin, all of this city.	11/06/1824
Yesterday morning, in the 40th year of his age, Samuel Claggett, Esq., of Prince George's county.	11/06/1824
On Tuesday evening last, by the Rev. Mr. Austin, Mr. Edward A. Cockey, to Miss Eurith C. Owings, youngest daughter of Samuel Owings, Esq., all of Baltimore county.	11/09/1824
On Thursday evening, the 4th inst., by the Rev. Dr. Roberts, Mr. Joseph Sturges, to Miss Mary Ann Miller, daughter of Mr. Jacob Miller, all of this place.	11/09/1824
On Thursday evening last, at Trenton, New Jersey, by the Rev. Mr. Smith, Mr. Don Carlos Hall, of Baltimore, to Miss Ann Elizabeth Roberts, of Trenton.	11/09/1824
On Sunday evening last, by the Rev. Mr. Vanhouse, Capt. Richard M. Fernald, to Miss Mary E. Golibart, both of this city.	11/10/1824
On Thursday, the 21st ult., by the Rev. Mr. Richardson, Capt. David Parrot, of Baltimore, to Miss Rebecca Gildea, of Abingdon, Harford county.	11/10/1824
On the 23rd, by the Rev. Mr. Webster, Mr. William Mead, of the city of Baltimore, to Miss Ann Elizabeth Lander, of Bush river Neck.	11/10/1824
Departed this life, on Monday, the 8th inst., at half past 6 P. M., Mrs. Ann Hollingsworth, in the 68th year of her age.	11/10/1824
On Tuesday evening last, by the Rt. Rev. Archbishop Mareschal, at the residence of Thomas Hillen, Esq., in Baltimore county, John Hunter, Esq., of Prospect Hill, to Miss Jennet, daughter of Thomas Hillen.	11/11/1824
On Tuesday evening last, by the Rev. Mr. Van Horsigh, Mr. William Johnson, to Miss Teresa Clautice, all of this city.	11/11/1824

414

Marriage and Death Notices	Date
On Tuesday, 2nd inst., by the Rev. Dr. Jennings, Mr. William Hopper, of Baltimore county, to Miss Matilda Ann Sudoi, of this city.	11/11/1824
Last Sunday morning, in her 15th year, Miss Susan Malehorn, daughter of Casper Malehorn, of Baltimore county.	11/11/1824
At New Orleans, Oct. 9th, Sarah F., daughter of Peter Coffin, Esq., of Boston, aged 18. At the same place, Oct. 11th, Col. Wm. Boyd, merchant, formerly of Portsmouth, N. H., and latterly from this city.	11/11/1824
Last evening, by the Rev. Mr. Nevins, Christopher Rankin, Esq., Representative in Congress from Mississippi, to Julianna, daughter of Gen. Stricker, of this city.	11/12/1824
Yesterday morning, after a lingering illness, which she bore with Christian fortitude, Mrs. Elizabeth Solomon, in the 68th year of her age.	11/12/1824
At Mount Healthy, on Tuesday evening last, by the Most Rev. Dr. Mareschal, John Hunter, Esq., to Miss Janett H., eldest daughter of Thomas Hillen, Esq., both of Baltimore county.	11/13/1824
On Thursday evening last, by the Rev. Mr. Snyder, Mr. William Schwatka, to Miss Rachel Amich, all of this city.	11/13/1824
On Sunday evening, the 14th inst., by the Rev. Mr. Bartow, Capt. Henry M. Waddell, of Pennsylvania, to Miss Ann Maria Monkur, of this city.	11/15/1824
At New York, Henry White, of Baltimore, to Mary, daughter of the late Jacob Le Roy, Esq.	11/15/1824
In Washington, Mississippi, Oct. 10th, Mr. Andrew Cole, tailor, formerly of Baltimore.	11/15/1824
Last evening, Mrs. Catherine Cronmiller, wife of Mr. Thomas Cronmiller, in the 67th year of her age. The friends and acquaintance of the deceased are requested to attend the funeral, from her late dwelling, Camden street, tomorrow afternoon, at 3 o'clock.	11/16/1824
Last evening, by the Rev. Mr. Helfenstein, Mr. John Lewis, to Miss Jane Cunningham, all of this city.	11/17/1824
On Monday evening last, by the Rev. Dr. Wyatt, Mr. James Crook, to Miss Mary Ann, eldest daughter of Capt. Joseph Holbrook, all of this city.	11/17/1824

Marriage and Death Notices	Date
Last evening, by the Rev. Dr. Wyatt, Mr. George Witman, to Elizabeth, second daughter of Mr. John Readel, all of this city.	11/17/1824
On Monday evening last, by the Rev. Mr. Stansbury, Mr. James Sweetman, to Miss Eliza Thompson, all of this city.	11/17/1824
On Tuesday evening, the 16th inst., by the Rev. Mr. Smith, Mr. Charles Godard, to Miss Mary Ann, eldest daughter of James Gordon, Esq., all of this city.	11/18/1824
On Sunday evening last, by the Rev. Dr. Roberts, Mr. Cornelius Deems, to Miss Eliza Brown, all of this city.	11/19/1824
On Thursday, the 18th instant, Mr. Adam Gantz, in the 74th year of his age, and one amongst the oldest and most respectable merchants of this city.	11/19/1824
Yesterday, James Hough, in the 26th year of his age. His friends and acquaintance are respectfully invited to attend his burial, to leave the house of Rachel Hough, No. 60 Pratt street, at 3 o'clock, this afternoon.	11/19/1824
On Tuesday evening last, by the Rev. Mr. Helfenstein, Mr. Samuel Hart, to Miss Arianna Trueman, all of this city.	11/20/1824
On Thursday, the 18th inst., Miss Sarah Darrinton, in the 43rd year of her age.	11/20/1824
At New York, on the 18th inst., Capt. Joseph Bainbridge, son of Commodore Bainbridge.	11/22/1824
On the morning of Saturday last, at an advanced age, Caleb Merryman, Esq., of Baltimore county. He was much esteemed for his honesty and integrity of character – and his memory will long be cherished by his many friends who have experienced his hospitality and goodness of heart.	11/23/1824
On the 31st ult., at Wellfield, the seat of her father, aged 6 years and 1 month. Catherine Embury, second daughter of Mr. Isaiah Mankin; a lovely and interesting child. From her uncommon mind and sweetness of disposition, she bid fair to become a bright ornament to Society, but alas! the happy temporal anticipations of her fond parents are cut off, and the only consolation they have, is in knowing that her happy spirit rests in the bosom of her Savior. "Farewell sweet babe! thou wert an angel here, But now a seraph in a higher sphere."	11/23/1824

Marriage and Death Notices	Date
On Sunday evening last, by the Rev. Dr. Jennings, Mr. Uriah Hannan, to Miss Martha Groom, all of this city.	11/24/1824
Last evening, by the Rev. N. Wilson, Mr. Reuben Benson, to Miss Margaret Adrion, both of Baltimore county.	11/24/1824
On Saturday evening, of consumption, on board the brig Osprey, from Leghorn and Gibraltar, Capt. J. Lufkin, a passenger, late master of the ship Draco, of Boston.	11/24/1824
In Snowhill, Md., Matthew Hopkins, Esq., Register of Wills, for Worcester County. He filled that office for many years with distinguished ability and success.	11/24/1824
On Sunday evening last, by the Rev. Mr. Peyton, Mr. Wiley Lankford, to Miss Martha Hodges, all of this city.	11/25/1824
On Tuesday evening last, by the Rev. Dr. Wyatt, Thomas B. Grundy, Esq., to Miss Caroline, third daughter of the late Mark Pringle, Esq.	11/25/1824
On Monday morning last, Julius C. Mann, eldest son of Dr. Anthony Mann, in the 35th year of his age, lamented by those who knew him.	11/25/1824
Longevity. Departed this transitory life, on Tuesday evening last, 23rd inst., Mr. John Fishpaw, in the 108th year of his age. It would be unnecessary to attempt to eulogize the character of this worthy man; suffice it to say that he lived as he died, a pattern of Christian piety. He was enabled to say that he had fought the good fight, he had finished his course, he had kept the faith; hence he was about to receive the reward.	11/25/1824
On Sunday evening last, by the Rev. Mr. Guest, Mr. William Roberts, of this city, to Miss Emily Corry, of Philadelphia.	11/26/1824
On Thursday evening last, by the Rev. Dr. Roberts, Mr. Ward Sears, to Miss Hannah W. Larabee, all of this city.	11/27/1824
On Saturday evening, 20th inst., by the Rev. John Peckworth, Mr. Francis Wagner, to Miss Charlotte Dawson, all of this city.	11/27/1824
By the Rev. John Peckworth, on Tuesday evening, the 23rd inst., William Adams, to Miss Abigail Baxley, both of Baltimore county.	11/27/1824
In this city, on Thursday evening last, by the Rev. Mr. Vanasey, Mr. Wm. P. Hanson, to Miss Theresa Manson, both of this city.	11/27/1824

Marriage and Death Notices	Date
On Thursday, in the fifty eighth year of his age, Mr. William Ryland, formerly a respectable merchant of this city. Mr. Ryland was a native of England, and has two brothers, respectable and rich manufacturers, residing at Birmingham. The deceased had suffered much from poverty and indisposition, during several of his latter years, and has left a very distressed family.	11/27/1824
At her residence, in Cecil county, Mrs. Hannah Stump, consort of John Stump, Esq., on Saturday, the 20th instant, in the 63rd year of her age, leaving a disconsolate husband, and a numerous family of children and grand children, to deplore her death.	11/27/1824
Last evening, by the Rev. Mr. Merwin, Mr. David Ramsay, to Miss Ann Phillips, all of this city.	11/29/1824
On Thursday, 25th inst., by the Rev. Mr. Guest, Mr. Theodore Webb, of Anne Arundel county, to Miss Mary Haslett, of this city.	11/29/1824
Suddenly, on Thursday morning last, S. Carpenter, Esq., Mayor of the city of Lancaster, Pennsylvania, in the 60th year of his age.	11/29/1824
Last Sunday evening, by the Rev. Mr. Bartow, Capt. George C. Baker, to Mrs. Sophia Veasey, all of this city.	11/30/1824
At Friends' Meeting house, Deer Creek, on the 25th inst., Joshua Matthews, merchant, of this city, to Mary Hopkins, of Harford county.	11/30/1824
This morning, at 1 o'clock, Owen Dorsey, Esq., in the fiftieth year of his age. His friends and acquaintance are respectfully invited to attend his funeral, from his late dwelling, in Green street, tomorrow morning, at 11 o'clock. The male part of the procession will proceed on foot to the place of interment. AC	11/30/1824
Last evening, of a short illness, which he bore with Christian fortitude, Mr. William Browning, aged 48 years; he was an affectionate husband, the orphan's father, and the poor man's friend. His friends and acquaintance are requested to attend his funeral, this afternoon, at 3 o'clock, from his late dwelling, at the corner of Fish Market and Market Space.	11/30/1824
On the 24th inst., at his residence, in Harford county, Mr. James M'Comas, in the 29th year of his age leaving a wife and a number of small children to lament his death.	11/30/1824
On Monday evening last, by the Rev. Mr. Henshaw, Col. Thomas	12/02/1824

Marriage and Death Notices	Date
Barber, to Miss Ellen Maccubben, both of this city.	
By the Rev. Dr. Glendy, on the evening of Tuesday last, Edward Lloyd, Jr., Esq., of Talbot county, Md., to Alecia, eldest daughter of Michael McBlair, Esq., of this city.	12/02/1824
By the Rev. Mr. Tyng, at Bel Air, Prince George's county, Md., on Tuesday, 23rd instant, Julius Forrest, of Marlboro', to Sophia, daughter of Benjamin Ogle, Esq.	12/02/1824
On Saturday morning last, in the eighty-first year of his age, Mr. James Norris, Sr., a native of this city. The deceased was an officer in the Maryland militia, during the revolutionary war. By his Christian virtues and correct deportment, he acquired the esteem and confidence of all who knew him. He has left a numerous offspring, consisting of twelve children, sixty-three grand children, and fifteen great grand children to mourn their loss.	12/02/1824
On Wednesday morning, in the 42nd year of his age, Mr. William Courtenay, of this city.	12/02/1824
On the 17th ult., Mr. Peter Megar, in the 40th year of his age, after a short illness, which he bore with exemplary fortitude.	12/02/1824
On the 24th ult., Mr. John Young, a native of Easton, Md., in the thirty-fifth year of his age.	12/02/1824
On Friday, the 26th ult., at Church-hill, Md., after a short, but painful illness, which he bore with Christian fortitude and patience, characteristic to him, Mr. Robert Sands, in the 35th year of his age, late of this city.	12/02/1824
Last evening, by the Rev. Dr. Roberts, Mr. Thomas E. Hambleton, to Sarah Ann, eldest daughter of Jesse Slingluff, Esq., all of Frederick county.	12/03/1824
At Springfield, Baltimore county, on Tuesday evening last, by the Rev. Mr. Guest, Mr. Daniel Chambers, Jr., to Miss Susan T. Howard, both of Baltimore county.	12/03/1824
On Thursday evening last, by the Rev. Dr. Roberts, Mr. Jacob Stahl, of Wilmington, Del., to Miss Harriet White, of this city.	12/04/1824
On Thursday evening last, by the Rev. Mr. Kurtz, Mr. Charles Guildener, to Miss Hannah Herwig, all of this city.	12/04/1824

Marriage and Death Notices	Date
On Thursday morning, the 2nd inst., after a lingering disease, which he bore with the fortitude and resignation of a Christian, Mr. Nathaniel Walton, aged 41 years – the deceased has left a wife and large family with numerous friends to lament their irreparable loss.	12/04/1824
On Tuesday evening last, by the Rev. Dr. Wyatt, Mr. Thomas Snowden, Jr., of Prince George's County, to Ann Rebecca, only daughter of the late Mr. Richard Nicols, of this city.	12/06/1824
In Fredericktown, on last Thursday morning, by the Rev. Mr. Martin, Mr. Wm. Clemmons, of Baltimore, to Miss Charlotte Gibson, of Frederick county.	12/06/1824
On Tuesday, the 1st inst., by the Rev. John Summerfield, Mr. William Hance, of Calvert county, Md., to Miss Mary Ann, daughter of Alexander Russel, Esq., of this city.	12/07/1824
On Friday morning last, after a severe illness, Emeline Rebecca Marriott, the only daughter of Mr. Joshua Marriott, of this city, in the 6th year of her age.	12/07/1824
On Sunday evening last, in the 56th year of his age, Jeremiah Cosden, Esq., formerly of Elkton, Cecil county, but recently of this city.	12/07/1824
Departed this transitory life, on Friday last, after a long and painful illness, which he bore with manly fortitude and Christian resignation, Mr. Nicholas Shannon, long a respectable inhabitant of this city, in the 29th year of his age. He has left a disconsolate widow and three children to mourn their irreparable loss.	12/07/1824
On Thursday evening last, by the Rev. Dr. Wyatt, Dr. Robert Goldsborough, Jr., of Queen Anne's county, to Miss Eleanor D. Lux, of this city.	12/08/1824
On Thursday evening last, by the Rev. Mr. Montgomery, at the seat of Chanddler Price, Esq., Mr. Benjamin Tevis, merchant, to Miss Mary M., daughter of the late Wm. Hunter, all of Philadelphia.	12/08/1824
On the 6th December, at Washington City, Mrs. Elizabeth Stewart, aged 53 years, consort of the late David C. Stewart, Esq., of Baltimore.	12/08/1824
By the Rev. Dr. Glendy, on the evening of Thursday last, Mr. James P. Ford, to Miss Margaret Brannon.	12/09/1824
By the Rev. Dr. Glendy, on the evening of Thursday last, Mr. Robert	12/09/1824

Marriage and Death Notices	Date
Queen, to Miss Priscilla Trusly, all of this city.	
On Tuesday evening, by the Rev. Dr. Roberts, Joseph J. Ogden, Esq., to Miss Maria, daughter of Mr. Paul Ruckle, of this city.	12/09/1824
On Tuesday evening last, by the Rev. Dr. Jennings, Mr. Daniel Stiltz, to Miss Eleanor M'Ginn.	12/09/1824
On Tuesday morning, the 10th inst., at Newark, Delaware, by the Rev. Mr. Russel, Wm. S. Hays, Esq., Attorney at Law, of Harford county, to Miss Sarah McBeth, of the former place.	12/09/1824
In this city, on Thursday evening, the 9th inst., by the Rev. Mr. Henshaw, John Wroth, Esq., of Sassafras Neck, to Miss Eliza Cox, of the same place.	12/10/1824
Departed this life, last evening, Mr. Wm. Fisk, in the 43rd year of his age.	12/10/1824
On Thursday evening last, by the Rev. Mr. Henshaw, Mr. Thomas Welsh, to Miss Maria Pogue, all of this city.	12/11/1824
Suddenly, on the 10th instant, Ann Kirby, daughter of George Stannard, of Georgetown, D. C., aged 7 years. Death had never a lovelier victim – nor friends a more bitter bereavement.	12/11/1824
On the 7th instant, Robert Fisher, of this city, in the 59th year of his age.	12/11/1824
On the 4th instant, at Mount Pleasant, near Chester-Town, in Kent county, James Cruikshanks, Esq. leaving a widow and six children, to lament the loss of a tender husband and an affectionate father.	12/11/1824
In Winchester, Mrs. Keziah, wife of Mr. Alvin Jewell. She had been confined about two weeks previous by the birth of two lovely sons, both of whom, together with the mother, languished until they fell asleep in death; and all three were buried in one grave.	12/11/1824
On Thursday evening last, by the Rev. Mr. Snyder, Mr. John S. Eichelberger, of this city, to Miss Maria Eichelberger, of Anne Arundel county.	12/13/1824
On Thursday, the 9th inst., at Wilmington, Del., Mr. Samuel Hays, of Elkton, to Miss Ann B., daughter of Mr. Thomas Warrington, of the former place.	12/14/1824

Marriage and Death Notices	Date
On Thursday evening, 25th November, by the Rev. Mr. Snyder, Mr. William Numsen, to Miss Mary, third daughter of the Rev. Mr. Snyder, all of this city.	12/14/1824
On Monday, the 22nd November, at his residence, in Harford county, Mr. Thomas Poteet, Sr., at the advanced age of 86 years, of an illness of three days, which he bore with Christian fortitude and resignation. In the death of this amiable man, his friends and relations have sustained an irreparable loss; but our loss is his infinite gain – he was a man of virtue, sobriety, integrity, and punctuality, he was a tender and affectionate husband and a loving father – but, alas, he is no more, he has gone the way that all flesh must that is human.	12/14/1824
At the Union Factory, on Sunday last, by the Rev. Mr. Hemphill, Mr. David Atkinson, to Miss Airey T. Waters.	12/15/1824
At Newark, Del., Mr. William S. Hays, Esq., of Belle-Air, Md., to Miss Sarah Macbeth.	12/15/1824
In Talbot county, Mr. Wm. Rice to Miss Frances Blake. Mr. A. C. Leaman, of Baltimore, to Miss Susannah Hardcastle.	12/15/1824
On board the ship Huntress, at Canton, Robert Snow Brower, in the 21st year of his age, youngest son of John Brower, of New York.	12/15/1824
On Tuesday morning, by the Rev. Mr. Bartow, Mr. Jonathan Sleeper, to Georgiana, only daughter of Mr. Stephen Clark, of this city.	12/16/1824
On Tuesday evening last, by the Rev. Dr. Wyatt, Capt. Washington Carlile, of Harford county, to Miss L. M. Delmass, of this city.	12/16/1824
At Chestertown, Md., on Sunday last, by the Rev. James Ridgaway, Mr. Owen C. Jones, to Miss Julia Ann Coleman.	12/16/1824
At Chestertown, Md., on Sunday last, by the Rev. Thomas Smith, Mr. Joseph F. Merriken, to Miss Alphonso Hall, all of Kent county.	12/16/1824
On Saturday, the fourth inst., Elizabeth, wife of Mr. Bernard Coskery, endeared to all who knew her by the suavity of her manners; she during a lingering illness beheld the gradual approaches of that moment which was to sever her from all that she held dear on earth, with a resignation which noting but pure religion and the recollection of a life well spent, could inspire. An humble confidence that she has gone to enjoy the blissful reward of her many virtues, is the sole consolation of afflicted relatives.	12/16/1824

Marriage and Death Notices	Date
At Montpelier, Washington county, Md., John Thompson Mason, Esq.	12/16/1824
Last evening, by the Rev. Mr. Finley, Mr. John Harris, to Miss Lydia, daughter of Alexander Marr, Esq., all of this city.	12/17/1824
At Airy Hill, near Chestertown, on the 7th inst., by the Rev. Mr. Jackson, William C. Tilghman, to Sarah N., daughter of Judge T. Worrel.	12/17/1824
On Thursday evening last, by the Rev. Dr. Roberts, Mr. Caleb Hissey, to Mrs. Jane Brewer, all of Baltimore.	12/20/1824
On Thursday evening last, by the Rev. Mr. Merwin, Nathan Bradford, Esq., to Miss Sarah Stansbury, daughter of the late Rev. Nicholas Swamstead, deceased, all of Anne Arundel county.	12/20/1824
Departed this life, last evening, William Buchanan, Esq., Register of Wills, in the 78th year of his age. His friends and acquaintances are requested to attend his funeral, from his late residence, in Barnet street, on Tuesday morning, at ten o'clock.	12/20/1824
At Swan Creek, in Kent county, on Wednesday, 8th inst., after a long and most afflicting illness, which was sustained with the most exemplary patience, Mrs. Hester Crane, consort of Wm. Crane, Esq., in the 51st year of her age, leaving to lament her loss a most indulgent & affectionate husband, with a large circle of friends and acquaintance. Sensible to her approaching dissolution, she calmly communicated it to her afflicted husband, to her attending friends, and to her domestics, and with and assurance that death has no terrors for a true Christian, she resigned with the most perfect composure her soul into the hands of a blessed Redeemer. Long, very long, will the acts of beneficence and the charities of the deceased be remembered in the circle of those who stood in want of her kindness. It may be truly said that she "visited the sick, clothed the naked, and fed the hungry." Her hospitable house was a sure asylum for the orphan. Blessed are the dead who died in the Lord, for they rest from their labours, and their works do follow them."	12/22/1824
On Tuesday evening, Dec. 21st, by the Rev. E. J. Reis, Mr. Robert A. M'Comas, of Harford county, to Miss Sarah Ann Taylor, of this city.	12/23/1824
By the Rev. Dr. Glendy, on Tuesday last, Dr. Adolphus Dunan, to Miss Emily, third daughter of Maj. Haslett, all of this city.	12/23/1824
At Washington, Pa., Mr. Lucius W. Stockton, of Baltimore, to Miss Rebecca, daughter of Mr. Daniel Moore, of that place.	12/23/1824

Marriage and Death Notices	Date
On Tuesday evening last, by the Rev. J. Larkin, Mr. William Grover, to Miss Ann Walf, all of Baltimore county, Md.	12/24/1824
On Tuesday evening last, by the Rev. Dr. Wyatt, Capt. Richard Edwards, to Miss Abarilli, eldest daughter of Mr. Jacob Graf, all of this city.	12/24/1824
On Thursday evening last, by the Rev. Mr. Habb, Mr. Peter Blatchly, of Baltimore county, to Mrs. Elizabeth Barkman, of this city.	12/24/1824
On Saturday last, in Prince George's county, Mrs. Mary Mullikin, in the 69th year of her age.	12/24/1824
On Thursday evening last, by the Rev. Dr. Wyatt, Mr. John Reynolds, of Frederick county, to Miss Susannah B. Winn, of this city.	12/28/1824
At Philadelphia, on Thursday, 23rd inst., by the Rev. Mr. Hurley, Dr. A. B. Tucker, to Elizabeth Henrietta, eldest daughter of Charles Carroll, Esq., of Baltimore.	12/28/1824
By the Rev. Mr. Gibson, Mr. Michael M'Blair, to Miss Mary Margaret Hoyle, niece of Capt. George Ellis.	12/28/1824
Last evening, in the 78th year of his age, sailing master, John Nants, of the U. States Navy. The friends and acquaintance of the deceased, and particularly his masonic brethren, are invited to attend the funeral, from his late residence, in Exeter street, tomorrow morning, at 11 o'clock.	12/28/1824
Yesterday afternoon, of a short illness, Mrs. Ann Elizabeth, widow of the late Henry Augustine, in the 72nd year of her age. Her friends and acquaintances are invited to attend her funeral, from her late dwelling, Lombard street, this afternoon, at 3 o'clock.	12/28/1824
Yesterday morning, after a short illness, Mr. Henry Bride, in the 47th year of his age.	12/28/1824
On the 25th inst., Mrs. Mary Allbright, in the 95th year of her age.	12/28/1824
On Monday night, the 20th inst., Charles Winchester, in the 34th year of his age. Such was the high estimation in which this most amiable man was held by his family and his friends that panegyric is wholly superfluous. He died in Baltimore, the place of his nativity, after an illness of but two days —his family and his friends, have for their consolation, a full conviction that he now enjoys a happier society, for Christ has said "He that believeth in me, though he were dead, yet shall	12/28/1824

Marriage and Death Notices	Date
he live."	
At Matanzas, on the 4th of October, Mrs. Catherine Conn, daughter of the late John Wilhelm, and wife to Mr. Henry Conn, who had recently arrived at that place, with his family from Baltimore. Mrs. Conn was the first American female victum to the yellow fever ever known in that city. Her remains were attended from the Catholic church to the burying ground by one of the most respectable assemblages of people ever witnessed in Matanzas.	12/28/1824
On Tuesday evening, 28th inst., by the Rev. Mr. Dansforth, Mr. William F. Moore, to Mrs. Reganer Repperd, all of this city.	12/29/1824
On the 24th inst., in Philadelphia, Mrs. Harriet Lucas Huger, wife of Col. Francis K. Huger, and daughter of Gen. Thomas Pinckney, of South Carolina.	12/29/1824
On Tuesday evening last, by the Rev. Mr. Greenwood, Alexander C. Bullitt, Esq., to Mary D., daughter of Edward Denison, Esq., all of this city.	12/30/1824
Last evening, by the Rev. Mr. Allen, William B. Donaldson, Esq., of this city, to Miss Julianna Hartley, of Cecil county, Maryland.	12/30/1824
Departed this life, on Wednesday, the 22nd inst., after a lingering illness, which she bore with Christian fortitude, Mrs. Anne Sclatter, aged 64 years. Of this worthy woman, it may be truly said, that she was a friend to the needy. Her disease was protracted and severe, but through all her sufferings, she was never heard to murmur or repine, and in her death her children and friends should not sorrow, knowing that though absent from them, she is now present with the Lord, enjoying those consolations, which are the sure and certain reward of the righteous, for "Blessed are they who died in the Lord."	12/30/1824

Coroner's Reports	Date
There were nine persons in all, lost by the wreck of the Helen, viz. Capt. Huguet, the steward and the cabin boy, drowned in the cabin. Passengers, Maj. Sterry, of Baltimore, son in law of Mr. James Arden, of this city, late consul at Rochelle; Messrs. Michel Porringer, Casspell, Kronemanche, Colieve, and Odesta. Forunately, Mr. Sterry's family, who were expected, did not embark with him. The bodies have all been found; that of Capt. Huguet was brought to town on Sunday morning for interment. *Mer. Adv.* {Articles in previous issues provide significant detail about the ship, cargo, voyage, and wreck.}	01/29/1820
Suicide. On Thursday night, a man, who a short time since, had enlisted in the United States service, hung himself, by means of his handkerchief, in a lumber yard on M'Elderry's wharf. *American.*	02/05/1820
A Coroner's inquest was yesterday held, at the head of Frederick street dock, on the body of a white woman commonly called Mary – the verdict was that she had come to her death by intemperance.	05/10/1820
CASUALTY. Yesterday afternoon, James Phillips, aged 14, a fine promising youth, the son of Richard Phillips, of this city, with some boys of his acquaintance, went to the Spring Gardens for the purpose of bathing; while in the water, he was seized, as it is supposed, with the cramp, and was drowned before assistance could be afforded. His body was recovered, and brought to the house of his agonized father. *Telegraph.*	06/17/1820
Suicide. A young man who reported himself to be a native of Ireland, by the name of Christopher Whelan, put a period to his existence yesterday morning – it was supposed by administering laudanum to himself the day previous.* A paper was found in his pocket book stating that he had committed the deed of suicide, adding nearly in these words, 'let the law remain silent – let the suspicion sleep, &c.' He was a Printer by a profession, and was last from Kingston, in the state of New York, where he worked on the "Ulster Plebian." From the editor of which paper, he had strong recommendations, as a young man of correct deportment, very well educated, and possessing respectable talents. *Ib.* *Verdict of the Coroner's inquest.	06/23/1820
A Coroner's Inquest was held, yesterday morning, at the lower end of Strawberry Alley, Fell's Point, on the body of Adam Consort, seaman,	06/26/1820

Coroner's Reports	Date
about 46 years of age, said to be a native of Philadelphia, and that his relatives reside in that place. Verdict of the Jury that he came to his death by accidentally drowning, being in a fit of intoxication at the time.	
Georgetown, D. C., July 13. ACCIDENT. A man by the name of Arnold was drowned on Tuesday evening last, having fallen from the wharf in a state of intoxication.	07/15/1820
This morning, about 3 o'clock, in Liberty street, Old Town, a man by the name of Charles Pindell, formerly a Constable, committed suicide, by cutting his throat with a razor. We do not learn the causes which drove him to this act of desperation.	07/20/1820
A Corner's Inquest was held yesterday morning, in Strawberry Alley, Fell's Point, on the body of a new-born female infant child, which was thrown into a privy, by its mother, Sarah Dickson. It was understood, that the woman had resided for some time in Market Space, in Town. The verdict of the Jury was that the said female child came to its death, in consequence of its being thrown into a privy and suffocated by its mother, Sarah Dickson.	07/22/1820
A Coroner's Inquest was held this morning in the 1st Ward, by James B. Stansbury, Esq., over the body of John Peale, about 8 years of age, who fell from the wharf into the dock while fishing, and was drowned. Verdict of the Jury that he came to his death by being accidently drowned.	08/12/1820
A Coroner's Inquest was held yesterday afternoon, by James B. Stansbury, Esq., at the Coffee-House wharf, Second Ward, over the body of John Batiste, colored boy, about 9 years of age. Verdict of the Jury that he came to his death by being accidently drowned.	08/17/1820
A Coroner's Inquest was held yesterday evening, by James B. Stansbury, Esq., over the body of William Kerr, aged 6 years, son of Capt. Archibald Kerr, who was drowned in the dock adjoining the Coffee House wharf, Second Ward. Verdict of the Jury that he came to his death by accidently falling into the dock, and was drowned. *Baltimore, August 23, 1820.*	08/23/1820
Last evening, a sailor by the name of Schwartz, fell from the Baartscheer's wharf, Fell's Point, attempting to get on board of the	09/19/1820

Coroner's Reports	Date
Dutch brig William, and was drowned. He belonged to the brig.	
A Coroner's Inquest. Was held this morning, by James B. Stansbury, Esq., on the body of John Schwartz, seaman, belonging to the Dutch brig William de Eersten, lying at Baartscheer's wharf. In attempting to go on board, last night about 10 o'clock, being much intoxicated, he accidently fell over-board, and was drowned. Verdict of the Jury that he came to his death by accidentally falling over-board, being in a state of intoxication, and was drowned. *September 19th, 1820.*	09/20/1820
A Coroner's Inquest was held this morning, by James B. Stansbury, Esq., over the body of John Wood, bay trader. In going on board his vessel last night, about 10 o'clock, at the County wharf, Second Ward, he accidently fell over the wharf and was drowned.	09/23/1820
A Coroner's Inquest was held on Thursday evening, by Lambert Thomas, Esq., on the body of Solomon Williams, a free colored man, at Stansville, about two miles from the city on the Belle Air road. The verdict of the jury states that he came to his death by a fall from a chestnut tree.	10/07/1820
A Coroner's Inquest was held by Lambert Thomas, Esq., on Saturday evening last, on the body of Henry Leonard, a free colored man, in Gordon street, near the Alms House – verdict of the jury that he came to his death by intemperance.	10/10/1820
A Coroner's Inquest was held, by Morgan Browne, Esq., on Tuesday last, on the body of Liny Pleasant, a colored woman, in Tyson street, near the Alms House. Verdict of the jury that she came to her death by intemperance.	10/18/1820
A Coroner's Inquest was held by Lambert Thomas, Esq., on Saturday last, in the prison of Baltimore county, on the body of John, alias Charles Miffleton. He was committed on the first of October as the supposed murderer of Thomas Hungerford, of the state of Virginia. On the 19th of this month, he showed a considerable perturbation of mind; and calling to him a fellow prisoner, confessed to him the perpetration of the crime for which he stood committed! The verdict of the jury was that, "he had come to his death by the hand of God." The attendant physician is of the opinion that his mental, more than his bodily	10/23/1820

Coroner's Reports	Date
infirmities, were the cause of his death.	
A Coroner's Inquest was held yesterday afternoon, by J. B. Stansbury, Esq., in Spring street, on the body of Jeremiah Blue, a man of small stature, and apparently about 30 years of age, had lost his left arm. Verdict of the jury that he came to his death from the effects of intemperance.	10/27/1820
A Coroner's Inquest was held on Monday last, by Morgan Browne, Esq., on the body of William Barnet, found in the Basin, near Hughes' Quay. Verdict of the jury that he came to his death by accidental drowning.	11/08/1820
A Coroner's Inquest was held this morning, by James B. Stansbury, Esq., at the Draw-Bridge, over the body of a white man, name unknown, who was drowned last night between the hours of 9 and 10 o'clock. He is apparently about 40 years of age, black hair and fair complexion, had on a blue cloth coat, and pantaloons, brown cloth vest, and a great-coat of brown cloth with a large cape – had the letters K. M. marked on his linen. Verdict of the Jury that he came to his death by drowning. *November 17, 1820.*	11/18/1820
A Coroner's Inquest was held on Sunday last, by Lambert Thomas, Esq., on the body of Rosina Kelnor, in East st., Old Town. The verdict of the jury was that she had come to her death by intemperance.	11/28/1820
A Coroner's Inquest was held on Wednesday evening last, by James B. Stansbury, Esq., at Mr. James Ramsay's wharf, over the body of Caldwell Scott, aged 16 years. Verdict of the jury that he came to his death by being accidentally drowned.	12/01/1820
Mrs. Webb, living in Primrose alley, on Sunday afternoon, committed suicide by hanging herself with a bed cord. No cause has been assigned for this rash procedure. We understand she was a very respectable woman, and has left a husband and two children. *Telegraph.*	12/19/1820
A Coroner's Inquest was held by Morgan Brown, Esq., on Friday last, over the body of John Mullingar, a coloured man, in Sugar alley. Verdict of the Jury that he came to his death by intemperance and the inclemency of the weather, for the want of sufficient clothing.	01/27/1821

Coroner's Reports	Date
A Coroner's Inquest was held by Morgan Browne, Esq., on Friday last, over the body of a female infant, about twenty-four hours old, in Hill street, found in the cellar of a house occupied by John Fountain. Verdict of the Jury, that she came to her death by violence used by Mary Jones, the mother, and John B. Bya, according to the testimony that was produced before them.	02/26/1821
A Coroner's Inquest was held by Morgan Browne, Esq., on Wednesday last, over the body of Kitty Johnson, a colored woman, found in the water at Hughes' Quay. Verdict of the Jury that she came to her death by accidental drowning.	04/19/1821
A Coroner's Inquest was held by James B. Stansbury, Esq., this morning, corner of Bank and Spring streets, second ward, over the body of Caleb Green, a coloured infant child, about four months old. Its death could not be accounted for, as there was no marks of violence on the body. Verdict of the Jury that it came to its death from some unknown cause.	04/21/1821
A Coroner's Inquest was held last evening, by Lambert Thomas, Esq., over the body of William Raymond, taken out of M'Elderry's dock. Verdict of the Jury that he was accidently drowned. This is the same person who was advertised as missing a few days ago.	04/25/1821
A Coroner's Inquest was held on Saturday morning, by Lambert Thomas, Esq., over the body of Patrick M'Laughlin, found in Frederick street dock. Verdict of the Jury that he came to his death by drowning. The deceased had been missing for a week past.	04/30/1821
A Coroner's Inquest was held on Friday evening, by Lambert Thomas, Esq., over the body of Edward Nicholson, a child about four years of age, the son of Michael Nicholson, corner of Wolf and Fleet streets, F. P., who was drowned in Frederick street dock. The father had taken the child on board a vessel in the dock, in which he was employed, and whilst he was sitting in the cabin in conversation with a gentleman, the child went upon the deck unobserved and fell overboard – when found, the body was still warm, but all efforts to restore it to life proved unavailing. The verdict of the Jury was that he came to his death by drowning.	05/07/1821

Coroner's Reports	Date
A Coroner's Inquest was held yesterday morning, by Lambert Thomas, Esq., over the body of Adam Stewart, Jr., aged about 17 years, found drowned near Burke's wharf, F. P. Verdict of the Jury, "accidental death by drowning."	05/31/1821
A Coroner's Inquest was held yesterday morning, by James B. Stansbury, Esq., in Apple alley, over the body of Anna Maria Shale. Verdict of the Jury that she came to her death from some unknown cause.	06/04/1821
A Coroner's Inquest was held on Thursday afternoon, by Lambert Thomas, Esq., near the Sugar House Harris' creek, over the body of a white woman supposed to be about 25 years of age – her dress was a dark calico gown, white cotton stockings, black morocco shoes, and a calico sunbonnet – her linen was marked M. M. Verdict of the jury, "Death by drowning."	06/09/1821
Coroner's Report. A jury of inquest was impannelled at Charleston, S. C., on 10th inst., to enquire into the cause or causes which led to the death of Charles Johnson, a native of Baltimore, aged 35 years. Verdict – death by intemperance.	06/18/1821
A Coroner's Inquest was held yesterday morning, by James B. Stansbury, Esq., at the County wharf, F. P., over the body of John W. Brown, aged about 30 years, who has left a wife and two children to lament his untimely fate. Verdict of the Jury that he came to his death by being accidentally drowned.	06/27/1821
A Coroner's Inquest was held by John Aisquith, Esq., on Saturday last, on the body of Hetty Janeway, a white woman found dead. The verdict was that her death was occasioned by receiving a deep wound in the fore-part of her head, above the left eye, from a brick bat, thrown designedly by a certain George Reintzell, without any cause or provocation.	07/02/1821
A Coroner's Inquest was held by Morgan Brown, Esq., on Sunday Evening last, over the body of John Delvacchio, aged 6 years, found in the dock at Hughes' Quay. Verdict of the Jury that he came to his death by accidentally drowning.	07/17/1821

Coroner's Reports	Date
A Coroner's Inquest was held by Lambert Thomas, Esq., on Wednesday evening last, over the body of James M'Caberly, at Webb's Soap Factory, in Old Town. Verdict of the jury was that "he came to his death by the act of God."	08/04/1821
A Coroner's Inquest was also held on Thursday morning, in a house near the Hay Scales, by the same, over the body of George Stinson, a native of Wilmington, Delaware – verdict of the jury was that "he came to his death by intemperance.	08/04/1821
An inquest was also held on Thursday evening, by James B. Stansbury, Esq., at Mr. Charles Wirgman's wharf, Fell's Point, over the body of Isaac Handy, a free coloured man, about 35 years of age – verdict of the jury, "that he came to his death by being accidentally drowned."	08/04/1821
A Coroner's Inquest was held by James B. Stansbury, Esq., yesterday morning, at Thames street wharf, over the body of Chester Brown, a free coloured man, about 35 years of age. Verdict of the Jury that he came to his death by being accidentally drowned.	08/19/1821
A Coroner's Inquest was held on Thursday, by Lambert Thomas, Esq., over the body of Lucy Anderson, a colored woman, about 60 years of age, in Apple Alley, between Alisanna and Lancaster streets. Verdict of the Jury was "that the deceased came to her death by the ill-treatment of a certain John Manuel, a Portuguese negro, by throwing her on the floor, on the 29th inst., she being in a diseased state, and exposed to the rain of the previous evening." Manuel has since been apprehended and placed in confinement.	09/01/1821
Coroner's Report, September 4. An inquest was held at the house of Samuel H. Rogers, No. 73, Gold street, on the body of Peter Neilson, who was found dead in the house directly opposite. Verdict of the Jury, suicide by taking laudanum. He was a very industrious man, a native of Scotland, aged twenty-five years, and has left a wife to lament his untimely end. *Com. Adv.*	09/07/1821
At an Inquisition held by John Aisquith, Esq., this morning, on the body of Henry Cook, a free colored man, the Jury found that the deceased came to his death by accidentally falling overboard from a schooner, into Dugan's dock.	09/11/1821

Coroner's Reports	Date
A Coroner's Inquest was held on Tuesday morning, at Pratt street bridge, by Lambert Thomas, Esq., over the body of James McGouran, about 15 years of age – verdict of the jury was that he had come to his death by accidental drowning.	10/03/1821
A Coroner's Inquest was held by Morgan Brown, Esq., on Tuesday morning last, over the body of Hannah Howard, found in the water at Light st. wharf. Verdict of the Jury that she came to her death by being accidentally drowned.	10/04/1821
An Inquest was held yesterday morning, by Lambert Thomas, Esq., at the Bellona Powder works, over the bodies of John Young, Francis Kelly, Charles Bagen, and Abraham Caution, a colored man. The verdict of the Jury was that they came to their death by the accidental blowing up of the stamping-mill of the Powder works. The explosion took place about 4 o'clock in the afternoon. From the testimony given to the Jury of Inquest, it appears that Mr. Young, the superintendant, had stopped the mill for a few minutes, in order to make some repair, and while in the act of driving a wrought nail with a copper hammer, the explosion took place, created, it is believed, by a spark from the nail. There were six persons in the mill, four of whom (the above named) died a few hours after the explosion; the remaining two, William Alexander, the foreman, and Patrick Clark, are so severely burnt, that their lives are despaired of. The deceased have left families of helpless widows and young children, who are fit objects of charitable notice. Great praise is due to Dr. Josiah Marsh, for his kindness and unremitted attention to the unfortunate victims of this distressing calamity. *American.*	10/17/1821
A Coroner's Inquest was held yesterday morning, in Salisbury street, by Lambert Thomas, Esq., over the body of Sarah Hughes, about 28 years of age. Verdict of the Jury, "that she had come to her death by drinking a quantity of laudanum, being in a state of intoxication." *Am.*	10/30/1821
Coroner's Report. On the 10th inst., an inquest was held at the house of James Wilkie, corner of Cherry and Governeur streets, on the body of Michael G. Kains, who was found at No. 301, Cherry street. Verdict of the Jury that he came to his death by intemperance. He was a native of Ireland and aged 66 years.	11/14/1821

433

Coroner's Reports	Date
A Coroner's Inquest was held on Sunday, by Lambert Thomas, Esq., about 5 miles on the York road, over the body of a negro man named William, supposed about 45 years of age. Verdict of the jury that "he had perished from exposure to the storm on Saturday night last."	11/27/1821
A Coroner's Inquest was held yesterday morning, by James B. Stansbury, Esq., on board the United States schooner Asp, over the body of John J. Seimson, about 30 years of age. Verdict of the Jury that he came to his death from the effects of intemperance.	12/05/1821
Coroner's Office, Dec. 14, 1821. *A Child Burnt.* The coroner was called yesterday to view the body of Margaret Hopper, a black child, aged seven years, who was burnt to death on Wednesday last. The jury returned a verdict "that the child came to its death by its clothes taking fire accidentally, and not otherwise." It was stated before the jury that the child was left alone in a room where a fire was burning, and before proper means was used to extinguish the clothes, the child was past recovery.	12/21/1821
A Coroner's Inquest was held by James B. Stansbury, Esq., on Tuesday evening, at the lower end of Market street, Fell's Point, over the body of Theophilus James Norton – verdict of the Jury that he came to his death from the effects of intemperance.	12/27/1821
A Coroner's Inquest was held yesterday morning, by James B. Stansbury, Esq., on the east side of Harris' Creek, over the body of Mr. John Young. Verdict of the Jury that he came to his death by being accidently drowned.	03/04/1822
A Coroner's Inquest was held by James B. Stansbury, Esq., yesterday morning, in Liffe street, over the body of Thomas Ehern, about 38 years of age. Verdict of the Jury that he came to his death by being drowned.	05/10/1822
A Coroner's Inquest was held by James B. Stansbury, Esq., on Wednesday afternoon, in Baltimore street (east) over the body of John Trazen, alias D. Juan Dugac de Palma, about 28 years of age, and said to be an Italian by birth. He came to Baltimore in the schooner Stirling from Jeremie, about a week since. Verdict of the Jury that he came to his death by having his neck dislocated, occasioned by a fall from his horse.	05/17/1822

Coroner's Reports	Date
A Coroner's Inquest was held by James B. Stansbury, Esq., on Saturday morning last, on the north side of Queen street, over the body of William Smith, about 8 years of age, who was drowned in the city dock. Verdict of the Jury that he came to his death by being accidentally drowned.	06/03/1822
A Coroner's Inquest was held before William Hines, Esq., Coroner in Kent county, Md., on the 2nd instant, on the body of a transient person, found drowned in a pond, in the Southern District of that county. He had about one dollar in cash in his pocket, and by papers in his pocket book his name appeared to be Nicholas Vedder, of the state of New York. He had several letters of recommendation as to his sobriety and moral character, from several gentlemen of New York, and also one from Selleck Osborn, Esq., Editor of the *Delaware Watchman*. He was a native of Montgomery county, N. Y. He had one letter from William Ross, dated Newbourgh, February 15, 1821, to Walter Case, Esq., in Congress and others of less consequence. The verdict of the jury was accidental death by drowning. It is desirable that printers, between Baltimore and Albany, should notice this event that his friends may hear of the circumstances of his death.	06/07/1822
A Coroner's Inquest was held on Sunday morning last, by James B. Stansbury, Esq., at the County wharf, Fell's Point, over the body of Richard Taylor, aged about 22 years, a native of Liverpool and sailmaker of the ship Mary, of Liverpool, who was drowned the previous evening by the upsetting of a boat. By the same, yesterday morning, over the body of Andrew Simpson, aged about 24 years, a native of Scotland, and a carpenter of the above-mentioned ship, and drowned out of the same boat, as above stated. Verdict of the Juries that they came to their deaths by the upsetting of the boat, and were accidentally drowned.	07/23/1822
A Coroner's Inquest was held yesterday, by John Aisquith, Esq., at Richard Ratcliff's, Montgomery street, on the body of a white young man, of the name of James Ratcliff. Verdict of the Jury was accidental death. It is supposed he was thrown from a cart, which was drawn over his body.	08/01/1822
A Coroner's Inquest was held by Lambert Thomas, Esq., on Saturday morning last, near the Steam Mills, lower end of McElderry's dock,	09/09/1822

Coroner's Reports	Date
over the body of a white man, supposed to be Levi Thomas, of Choptank – he was missing on Wednesday night. The verdict of the Jury was accidental death by drowning.	
A Coroner's Inquest was held this morning, by Lambert Thomas, Esq., at the corner of Eden and Pitt streets, over the body of Joseph Lowery, aged about 34 years. Verdict of the Jury, that he came to his death by discharging a pistol, loaded with shot, into his head, entering just above his right ear. It appears by a paper found upon him, written by himself, that extreme poverty was the cause of this desperate act.	09/17/1822
A Coroner's Inquest was held by Lambert Thomas, Esq., at the house of John Hughes, in Liberty street, Old Town, over the body of a coloured woman by the name of Charlotte Anderson, about twenty years of age. The verdict of the jury was that she had come to her death by intemperance and taking laudanum.	10/18/1822
A Coroner's Inquest was held on Wednesday night, on the Frederick Turnpike road, at the house of Daniel Whitney, near the 7th mile stone, by Lambert Thomas, Esq., over the body of Adam Alter. The verdict of the Jury was that he had come to his death from intemperance, and ill treatment from the hands of some person or persons unknown to them. The deceased was about the premises of Mr. Whiney a day or two, and it is but justice to state, that he received from Mr. W. and family every kindness and attention, which his situation appeared to require. *American.*	11/08/1822
A Coroner's Inquest was held by James B. Stansbury, Esq., yesterday morning, in Apple alley, over the body of Richard Johnson, a free colored man, found dead in a garret. Verdict of the Jury that he came to his death from the effects of intemperance and exposure to cold.	12/06/1822
A Coroner's Inquest was held yesterday morning, on M'Elderry's dock, by Lambert Thomas, Esq., over the body of John M. Crisman, a white man. The verdict of the Jury was, "that he came to his death by drowning in M'Elderry's dock." A few articles found in his pockets are in the hands of the Coroner, and will be delivered to his friends when called for.	04/16/1823
A Coroner's Inquest was held by Lambert Thomas, Esq., yesterday morning, near Pratt street Bridge, over the body of Michael M'Gauran.	04/17/1823

Coroner's Reports	Date
Verdict of the Jury that he came to his death by accidentally drowning in Jones' Falls. It will be recollected that an inquest was held over the body of his son, near the same spot, in the year 1821.	
A Coroner's Inquest was held by Lambert Thomas, Esq., yesterday afternoon, in Union street, over the body of a colored woman named Milley Dorsey. Verdict of the jury, "that she came to her death by the visitation of God."	04/23/1823
A Coroner's Inquest was held on the 20th May, by Morgan Browne, Esq., over the body of John Davis, on the Fort road, near the Powder House. Verdict of the Jury that he came to his death by intemperance.	05/21/1823
A Coroner's Inquest was held by James B. Stansbury, Esq., on Sunday, 1st June, at Harris' Creek, over the body of Thomas Waterman, a lad about 13 years of age. Verdict of the Jury, accidental death by drowning.	06/03/1823
A Coroner's Inquest was held on Wednesday last, by Lambert Thomas, Esq., at Grace's Quarter, Middle River Neck, Baltimore County, over the bodies of negro Rachel, aged 26, and her female infant, aged one month. The verdict of the jury was that they had come to their deaths by accidental drowning in attempting to cross Dundee, a branch of Gunpowder Falls, in a small boat.	06/20/1823
A Coroner's Inquest was held by Lambert Thomas, Esq., yesterday morning, in Belvidere street watch house, over the body of Robert Williams, late of New York. The verdict of the jury was that he came to his death by taking a dose of arsenic.	06/25/1823
A Coroner's Inquest was held yesterday afternoon, by James B. Stansbury, Esq., at Wilson's wharf, Fell's Point, over the body of John Berry, about six years of age. Verdict of the jury that he came to his death by being accidentally drowned.	06/28/1823
A Coroner's Inquest was held yesterday evening, by James B. Stansbury, Esq., on the shore, between Mr. Trotter's Pottery and the Sugar House, over the body of Patrick Quigly, a native of Ireland, about 28 years of age, who went into the river for the purpose of bathing, and almost instantly sunk. Verdict of the Jury that he came to his death by	07/11/1823

Coroner's Reports	Date
being accidentally drowned.	
This morning a Coroner's Inquest was held by the same, at the draw bridge, over the body of John Gidelman, about 5 years of age, son of John Gidelman, in Still-house street, Old Town – the child had been missing from yesterday afternoon about 7 o'clock. Verdict of the jury, accidental drowning.	07/11/1823
A Coroner's Inquest was held by Morgan Browne, Esq., this morning, at Hughes' Quay, over the body of Gabriel Wickes. Verdict of the Jury, accidental drowning.	07/19/1823
A Coroner's Inquest was held on Sunday afternoon, by Lambert Thomas, Esq., over the body of Mr. John Hargus, aged 18 years, who was drowned in Herring run, near the Harford Turnpike, whilst in the act of bathing.	07/22/1823
A Coroner's Inquest was held by Morgan Browne, Esq., on Sunday morning last, over the body of Samuel Smith, aged six years, found in the Basin, Light street wharf, near House and Woolen's lumber yard. Verdict of the Jury, accidental drowning.	07/22/1823
A Coroner's Inquest was held on Monday evening, in Back River Neck, by Lambert Thomas, Esq., over the body of Mingo Jones, a free coloured man, aged about seventy years. Verdict of the jury – death, by the visitation of God. The deceased was in the field, attending a harrow – the attention of his fellow workman was attracted by his calling out, and when he came to the deceased, he saw blood gushing from his mouth. Five minutes before, he appeared to be in perfect health.	08/06/1823
A Coroner's inquest was held last evening, near Camp Fairfield, by Lambert Thomas, Esq., over the body of Benjamin Fremon, of this city, aged about 15 years. Verdict of the jury, "that he came to his death by receiving a wound under the right eye and below the right knee, by the accidental explosion of a small cannon" – with which the deceased and several of his companions from the city had been amusing themselves, and which (being about six inches in length) had been nearly filled with old nails, &c. at the time of he explosion.	08/18/1823
A Coroner's Inquest was held by Lambert Thomas, Esq., on Wednesday night, at Mr. John Mycroft's place, near the York road, over the body of	08/22/1823

Coroner's Reports	Date
David Floyd, a white man, aged about 28 years. Verdict of the Jury that he came to his death by intemperance.	
A Coroner's Inquest was held by Lambert Thomas, Esq., on Tuesday evening, over the body of a new born female infant, found in the vault of a privy in an unoccupied house in Second street. Strong circumstantial evidence was produced to prove that the child belonged to a mulatto woman residing in the neighbourhood. The verdict of the jury was "that they believe the said new born female infant was the child of Calista Ward, coloured woman, and that it came to its death by the neglect of the above named Calista Ward or some person unknown.	08/29/1823
A Coroner's Inquest was held by Morgan Browne, Esq., over the body of Margaret Hill, on Thursday last, at Whetstone Point. Verdict of the Jury that she came to her death by an assault and battery, committed on her by John Everitt, in the presence of William Crayle.	08/29/1823
A Coroner's Inquest was held by Morgan Browne, Esq., on Tuesday last, over the body of Jacob Wing, found in the Light street dock. Verdict of the Jury, accidental drowning.	08/29/1823
A Coroner's Inquest was held yesterday morning, by Lambert Thomas, Esq., over the body of Edward M'Cosker, a workman in the laboratory of Messrs. Tyson & Simms. The verdict of the jury was "that he had come to his death by accidental drowning in Jones' Falls, near the drawbridge.	09/03/1823
A Coroner's Inquest was held by James B. Stansbury, Esq., yesterday morning, in Baltimore County Jail, over the body of Eliza McDowle, about 20 years of age. Verdict of the Jury, "that she came to her death by hanging herself with her under jacket, tied round her neck and over the hinge of the cell door."	09/04/1823
A Coroner's Inquest was held on Friday morning, at McElderry's wharf, by Lambert Thomas, Esq., over the body of a white man, named Blake, late residence in Mulberry, near Calvert street. Verdict of the Jury, accidental drowning.	09/13/1823
A Coroner's Inquest was held on Saturday evening, by Lambert Thomas, Esq., on Dugan's wharf, over the body of negro Marshall, a slave to Francis Turbin, of Dorchester county. Verdict of the Jury,	09/15/1823

Coroner's Reports	Date
accidental drowning.	
A Coroner's Inquest was held by James B. Stansbury, Esq., on Sunday Morning last, over the body of Wm. Stevens, a free colored man, about 37 years of age – who was found dead near the corner of Gough and County streets. Verdict of the Jury that he came to his death from some unknown cause.	11/04/1823
A Coroner's Inquest was held on the 3rd instant, by Daniel Pendleton, Esq., over the body of a colored woman, in Frederick street, named Rebecca Bond. The verdict of the jury was that she came to her death by being burnt, from her clothes accidentally catching fire the night previous.	11/05/1823
A Coroner's Inquest was held by James B. Stansbury, Esq., yesterday evening, at Chase's wharf, over the body of Amos Stow, about 40 years of age, a seaman, attached to the brig Chase, of Salem. He was born in Beverly, near Salem, Massachusetts, where he has left a large family to bemoan his untimely fate. Verdict of the Jury that he came to his death by accidentally falling off the wharf, and was drowned.	12/24/1823
An Inquest was held this morning, by Coroner Stansbury, in Bond street, over the body of John Peter, free colored man, about 35 years of age. Verdict of the Jury that he came to his death from the effects of intemperance.	12/24/1823
A Coroner's Inquest was held yesterday, by Lambert Thomas, Esq., on the new cut Harford Road, over the body of Jane Jones, a coloured child, about nine years of age. The verdict of the Jury was "that she came to her death by receiving a gore from a cow in the left side" – she instantly died.	02/10/1824
A Coroner's Inquest was held by James B. Stansbury, Esq., yesterday afternoon, at the County wharf, lower end of Ann street, Fell's Point, over the body of William Baker, a native of London, aged about 26 years. Verdict of the Jury that he came to his death by drowning.	02/20/1824
A Coroner's Inquest was held by Lambert Thomas, Esq., on Saturday night, at Frederick street dock, over the body of Hugh Foy. It appeared by the evidence that he had been heard to fall into the dock, the night being very dark. Efforts, as speedily as circumstances would admit,	02/23/1824

440

Coroner's Reports	Date
were made to extricate him, but he was drowned before he was taken from the water. The verdict of the jury was "death by accidental drowning."	
A Coroner's Inquest was held on the 21st inst., by Daniel Pendleton, Esq., over the body of Patrick McDonnell. The verdict was that he came to his death by being accidently drowned, having fallen into Jones' Falls.	05/22/1824
A Coroner's Inquest was held by Lambert Thomas, Esq., on Friday morning, at the lower end of Dugan's wharf, over the body of Benjamin Willis, slave of Capt. Partridge, of St. Mary's county, at the mouth of the Patuxent river. Verdict of the jury – death by accidental drowning, having fallen overboard from the schooner Messenger.	05/29/1824
A Coroner's Inquest was held on Friday night, 4th instant, by Lambert Thomas, Esq., at Belvidere street bridge, over the body of Hugh Kernan, a white boy, about 9 years of age. Verdict of the Jury that he came to his death by accidental drowning in Jones' Falls. Edward Holland, about 15 years of age, the son of Mr. John Holland, of East street, Old Town, who was fishing a short distance from the spot, plunged into the relief of the deceased and brought him to the shore, but too late to save his life.	06/07/1824
A Coroner's Inquest was held this morning, by Morgan Browne, Esq., over the body of Jesse Bunch, near the Glass House. Verdict of the Jury that he came to his death by being struck by lightning.	06/29/1824
A Coroner's Inquest was held on the 2nd inst., by John Aisquith, Esq., over the body of Chas. Howard, a free colored man, lying dead in South Liberty st. An inquest was held by the same, on the 3rd, over the body of Eliza Jacobs, a white woman, lying dead in South Frederick street. Verdict of the Jury that they came to their deaths by intemperance.	07/06/1824
A Coroner's Inquest was held yesterday, near Howard's Park, by Lambert Thomas, Esq., over the body of Thomas Henley, aged about 84 years. Verdict of the Jury – death by the visitation of God. The deceased left his home yesterday morning, with the intention of consulting a physician respecting an ailment of his breast. On his return home, it is supposed he passed through the Park, as he was found there,	07/10/1824

Coroner's Reports	Date
lying dead under a tree.	
A Coroner's Inquest was held yesterday morning, in the Centre Market, by Lambert Thomas, Esq., over the body of a white man, by the name of Patrick Carroll. The verdict of the Jury was, "that he came to his death by intemperance."	08/28/1824
A Coroner's Inquest was held yesterday morning, in Union street, Old Town, by Lambert Thomas, Esq., over the body of Susanna George. The verdict of the Jury was that "she came to her death by hanging herself with a silk handkerchief to the tester of a high post bedstead."	09/25/1824

Surname Index

___ker, 105
Abbott, 68
Abercrombie, 22, 351
Abey, 319
Acy, 114
Adams, 36, 97, 105, 164, 165, 176, 207, 209, 235, 242, 280, 303, 376, 387, 417
Addison, 89
Adgate, 243
Adrean, 262
Adreon, 70, 93
Adrion, 417
Afflick, 336
Ahasverus, 258
Aiken, 322
Aitkin, 68, 91
Alberger, 342
Albers, 15
Albert, 168
Albridge, 222
Albright, 57, 385
Alcock, 125, 204
Alden, 21
Alder, 270
Alderdice, 32
Aldridge, 195
Alexander, 14, 51, 73, 92, 96, 105, 188, 194, 433
Alford, 162, 383
Alfred, 393
Algeyer, 25
Allan, 234
Allbright, 424
Allein, 39
Allen, 42, 52, 56, 71, 76, 147, 154, 158, 185, 189, 314, 344, 352, 356, 371, 374, 410
Allender, 67, 161, 164, 364
Aller, 154
Allison, 186, 188
Allmand, 191
Allston, 61
Allsworth, 389
Almacost, 163
Alricks, 104

Alsop, 109
Alsten, 327
Alter, 386, 436
Alteroff, 295
Altfather, 336
Alwood, 299
Amelung, 94
Ames, 214
Amey, 117, 196
Amich, 415
Amos, 97, 114, 253, 373
Amoss, 107, 175, 220, 337
Anderson, 32, 71, 73, 74, 97, 142, 182, 331, 364, 366, 376, 432, 436
Andrew, 91, 357
Andrews, 59, 83, 105, 238, 292, 397
Angell, 237
Ankeney, 148
Appleby, 11, 105, 137
Applegarth, 26, 264
Appold, 288
Arcambal, 40
Archer, 206, 384, 396
Arden, 426
Arey, 306
Argust, 99
Armager, 16
Armat, 257
Armengast, 15
Armitage, 396
Armstrong, 26, 39, 64, 103, 130, 176, 265, 306, 380, 392, 394, 401
Arnest, 24, 72
Arng, 205
Arnold, 105, 202, 203, 427
Arthur, 281
Ash, 64
Ashbaugh, 53
Ashbridge, 397
Ashbury, 17
Asher, 351
Ashly, 21
Ashman, 190, 399
Ashmead, 9

Bazlin, 168
Beachem, 235
Beale, 200
Beall, 37, 97, 138, 276, 315, 343
Bealmear, 294
Beam, 175, 343
Bean, 280, 289
Beanes, 212
Beard, 84, 123, 163, 185, 378, 380, 404
Beasman, 327, 354, 357
Beasten, 44
Beatty, 118, 151, 234, 235, 260, 337
Beaumont, 87
Beck, 24, 160, 260, 277
Beckett, 329
Beckley, 84, 364
Beckwith, 195
Bedford, 31
Beebee, 383
Beecher, 142
Beeman, 203
Behn, 273
Belford, 41, 365
Bell, 92, 110, 156, 407
Belt, 138, 202, 261, 268
Belts, 197
Bend, 129
Benett, 98
Benezet, 38
Bennet, 320, 413
Bennett, 23, 24, 41, 109, 200, 223, 245, 373
Benney, 142, 169
Benson, 26, 32, 223, 307, 312, 417
Bentalou, 206
Benteen, 45
Bentley, 383
Benton, 107, 385
Bentz, 366
Benzinger, 244
Bergen, 386
Bermudez, 154
Bernard, 216
Berry, 30, 137, 383, 437
Berryman, 62
Bessell, 155
Betterton, 104

Betts, 59, 135, 301
Bevans, 342
Bevard, 154, 195, 294
Bever, 310
Beveridge, 146
Biays, 44, 51, 344
Bibb, 280
Bicknell, 97
Biddison, 46
Biddle, 15, 181
Bier, 184, 405
Bigeo, 178, 179
Biggert, 71
Biggs, 194
Billingslea, 344, 385
Billop, 381
Birckhead, 273, 329
Bird, 159
Birely, 126, 151
Birgan, 342
Biscoe, 119, 168
Bishop, 328, 329, 393
Bison, 105
Bivens, 39
Bixby, 244
Bixler, 15
Bizouard, 367
Black, 78
Blackburn, 318
Blackestone, 112
Blackiston, 261
Blackstone, 152
Blackway, 54
Blade, 341
Blades, 174
Blagge, 80
Blair, 393
Blake, 151, 173, 331, 380, 422, 439
Blakely, 136
Blanchard, 204
Bland, 361
Blandy, 98
Blasden, 260
Blatchly, 424
Bliss, 299
Blizzard, 262

Block, 105
Bloomer, 277
Blue, 429
Blyden, 349
Boarman, 152
Bodartha, 46
Boddily, 89
Bodensick, 176
Boding, 205
Boehm, 205
Boeugher, 257
Bogen, 56
Boggs, 303, 397
Bohn, 208
Boisseau, 275
Bolster, 129
Bolton, 261
Bonaparte, 269, 298
Bond, 18, 66, 74, 125, 156, 160, 178, 195,
    302, 312, 313, 343, 375, 396, 440
Bonn, 379
Bonsall, 10
Boon, 55, 120, 169, 358
Booth, 45, 182, 200, 237, 261
Bosley, 41, 186, 192, 348, 371
Boss, 337
Boston, 309, 313
Boswell, 153
Bosworth, 268
Boteler, 17, 148, 188
Boughan, 59, 352
Bouldin, 265
Bourne, 341, 372
Boury, 43, 296
Bouzee, 193
Bovey, 259
Bowden, 83
Bowdle, 278, 313, 367
Bowen, 31, 312
Bowers, 78, 248, 254, 363
Bowersox, 341
Bowie, 24, 78, 268
Bowman, 164
Bowyer, 248
Boyce, 103

Boyd, 75, 82, 83, 84, 112, 124, 159, 191,
    244, 254, 258, 274, 301, 317, 415
Boyer, 77, 321, 346, 387
Boyle, 290, 329, 341
Bozman, 295
Bra__nan, 185
Bradenbaugh, 167, 203, 339
Braderhous, 102
Bradford, 214, 309, 393, 405, 423
Bradley, 105
Bradshaw, 24, 272
Brady, 31
Brag, 245
Bragonier, 103, 138
Braneman, 382
Brannoch, 59
Brannock, 24
Brannon, 420
Branson, 54, 78
Brant, 50
Brawner, 84, 90, 109
Bray, 251
Brazer, 274, 275
Brazier, 98
Breckenridge, 325
Breerwood, 161
Bremerman, 345
Brent, 207, 214
Brevitt, 392
Brewer, 9, 21, 63, 72, 93, 103, 294, 423
Brewster, 274
Brian, 237
Brice, 278, 347, 383
Brickhead, 175
Bride, 424
Bridges, 296
Briggs, 341, 412, 414
Brimmer, 387
Brindley, 56
Brinkman, 317
Briscoe, 152, 210, 305
Brister, 40
Britton, 146
Briz, 255
Broadfoot, 257
Brockemiller, 120

448

Cummins, 84, 232
Cunningham, 166, 415
Cunninham, 294
Currie, 105, 325, 356
Currier, 217
Curry, 99, 386
Curson, 256, 375
Curtage, 62
Curtain, 16, 54
Curtin, 272
Curtis, 195, 250, 291, 387
Cushman, 254
Cutcher, 98, 288
Cutsail, 20
D'Anmour, 284
Dabbs, 208
Dabney, 41
Dade, 174
Daffin, 352
Dagen, 91
Dailey, 105
Daily, 214, 277
Dalck, 237
Daley, 266, 293
Dall, 140
Dallam, 67, 98
Dallas, 332, 381
Dalrymple, 132, 340
Daly, 304
Dance, 81, 401
Dangerfield, 154
Daniel, 157
Danley, 313
Dannenberg, 29
Danskin, 369
Danson, 384
Danyer, 105
Darby, 23
Darrinton, 416
Dashiell, 26, 165, 224, 375
Daste, 113
Daugherty, 77, 211
Davenport, 91
Davidge, 362
Davidson, 39, 97, 138, 155, 159, 234, 293, 409

Davies, 39, 135, 303
Davis, 47, 55, 59, 68, 83, 95, 100, 105, 107, 109, 110, 126, 129, 137, 143, 155, 168, 178, 185, 203, 210, 231, 234, 239, 253, 254, 262, 263, 265, 270, 278, 287, 293, 294, 309, 395, 437
Davy, 234, 282
Dawes, 43, 60
Dawson, 83, 137, 192, 210, 241, 277, 315, 397, 417
Day, 84, 105, 169, 184, 189, 243
Dayhuff, 30
de Armas, 335
de Bernabeu, 349
De Garis, 125
de Kalb, 369
De La Ree, 278
de Palma, 434
De Rosenkrantz, 369
De Spada, 363
De St. Ceran, 263, 380
De Valengin, 204
De Witt, 30
Deal, 202
Dean, 96
Deaver, 291, 294, 301
Decamp, 50
Dechamp, 367
Dechert, 275
Decker, 66, 338
Deems, 416
Deer, 96
Deford, 257
Delahay, 266
Delahy, 164
Delaplaine, 379
Delaplane, 32
Delcher, 311
Delehay, 151
Delmass, 422
Deloughery, 135
Delprat, 139
Delpry, 347
Delsher, 345
Delvacchio, 431
Demoiny, 93

Floyd, 267, 438
Focke, 117, 205
Foder, 205
Fogle, 20
Follin, 26
Foltz, 15, 29, 79
Forbes, 23
Ford, 28, 93, 156, 261, 263, 302, 313, 420
Foreman, 18
Forman, 105, 166
Forney, 134, 145, 146
Forrest, 387, 419
Forrester, 9, 34
Forster, 315
Forsyth, 262
Fort, 135
Forwood, 189
Foss, 84
Fossett, 366
Foster, 57, 145, 264, 378
Fouble, 313
Foulds, 291
Foulk, 10, 188
Fountain, 306, 430
Fowble, 129, 295, 314, 316
Fowler, 79, 101, 328
Fox, 97, 213, 304
Foxcraft, 105
Foxcroft, 244
Foy, 356, 440
Foye, 181
Frailey, 239
Frampton, 48
Francis, 394, 397
Francois, 325
Frank, 277
Franklin, 191, 237, 263, 338
Frazee, 397
Frazier, 106, 186
Free, 382
Freeland, 25
Freeman, 43, 270, 383
Freize, 154
Fremon, 438
French, 43, 255
Frey, 271

Frink, 295
Frisbie, 210
Frizzell, 66
Frost, 126
Frow, 281
Fry, 251
Fuhrman, 15
Fullard, 119
Fuller, 121
Fulton, 42, 324, 353, 406
Furlong, 329
Furneaux, 283
Fusselbaugh, 37, 122
Gable, 233
Gaddess, 151
Gade, 343
Gaffney, 268
Gaither, 30, 32, 73, 243
Gallagher, 68, 74
Gallatin, 371
Gallaway, 242, 371
Gallion, 288
Gallop, 275
Galloway, 31, 294, 413
Gallup, 83
Galt, 276
Gambell, 408
Gamble, 55, 206
Gambrill, 30, 79, 312
Ganettson, 269
Gant, 301
Gantt, 30, 81, 287
Gantz, 295, 416
Gardiner, 21, 114, 375
Gardner, 136, 144, 365, 407
Garey, 250
Garish, 293
Garner, 278
Garnett, 348
Garret, 175
Garretson, 335
Garrett, 107, 306
Garrison, 30, 57, 105, 229, 296, 323
Garritee, 314
Garrittson, 385
Garts, 17

Gartside, 347
Garver, 68
Garvin, 26
Gassaway, 36
Gatch, 104
Gatchell, 107, 227
Gates, 155, 192
Gauline, 378
Gavitt, 34
Gawthrop, 13
Geddes, 51
Geddis, 144
Geiger, 150
Geissenderffer, 399
George, 9, 148, 442
Gerhart, 185
German, 65
Gerrard, 308
Gerrell, 71
Gerrish, 231
Getz, 403
Getzendanner, 96
Ghequiere, 313, 375
Ghequire, 246
Gheselin, 246
Gibbins, 371
Gibbs, 380
Gibsen, 372
Gibson, 12, 68, 83, 122, 137, 324, 329, 332, 420
Gidelman, 438
Gilbert, 73, 97
Gildea, 414
Giles, 165, 340
Gill, 84, 101, 165
Gilles, 247, 262
Gillespie, 386
Gillespy, 25
Gillingham, 256, 320
Gillmore, 137
Gilmier, 29
Gilmor, 108, 166
Gilmore, 98, 387
Gilpin, 33
Gird, 270
Gist, 142, 174

Gitt, 314
Gittings, 20, 93, 166, 189, 207, 254, 312, 315, 341, 354, 367
Gladding, 404
Glaggett, 378
Glasgow, 319
Glenn, 64, 76, 253, 347
Glover, 84, 389
Godard, 416
Goddard, 75
Godman, 140
Goff, 68
Goging, 52
Goldsborough, 30, 32, 71, 89, 167, 208, 420
Goldsmith, 108, 150, 184
Goldthwait, 131
Golibart, 414
Gomber, 29
Gomer, 208
Good, 107, 186
Goodd, 297
Goodding, 81
Gooden, 55
Gooding, 134, 170, 344
Goodman, 192
Goodrich, 188
Goodrick, 363
Goodridge, 401
Goodwin, 13, 94, 124, 160, 262, 376
Gordon, 172, 264, 416
Gore, 132
Gorman, 225
Gorsuch, 15, 31, 104, 181, 189, 292, 343, 381
Gorton, 63
Gosnell, 14, 53, 303, 348
Gosse, 93
Gothrop, 377
Gott, 221, 266, 308, 325, 375
Gough, 66, 206
Gould, 55, 188, 229, 277, 292
Gover, 30, 154, 213
Gower, 154
Grace, 211
Gracie, 36
Graf, 424

Hans, 13
Hanson, 70, 170, 337, 345, 417
Hanway, 387
Hardcastle, 254, 422
Harden, 27, 59, 83, 151
Hardester, 101, 173
Hardesty, 30
Harding, 18, 23
Hardister, 253
Hardusty, 412
Hardy, 241, 357, 373
Hared, 287
Harford, 33
Hargus, 438
Harington, 306
Harland, 118
Harper, 97, 258, 304
Harpur, 389
Harr, 316
Harramon, 54
Harrington, 287
Harris, 13, 18, 91, 108, 112, 195, 208, 244,
    252, 256, 314, 327, 328, 332, 348, 378,
    423
Harrison, 16, 19, 22, 55, 164, 165, 192, 195,
    201, 208, 226, 346, 389
Harrop, 14, 15
Harry, 187
Harryman, 294, 312
Hart, 37, 215, 416
Hartley, 267, 425
Hartman, 22
Harvey, 89, 99, 188, 206, 298, 329, 385
Harwood, 255, 277, 303, 353
Haskins, 142, 265, 329
Haslett, 30, 122, 256, 418, 423
Haslin, 143
Haslup, 396
Hassan, 150
Hassell, 20
Hassen, 288
Hastings, 196
Hatch, 78, 107
Hatcheson, 261, 342
Hathaway, 340
Hatten, 160

Hatton, 176, 351, 408
Haubert, 195, 242
Haughey, 268
Hawk, 406
Hawken, 186, 188
Hawkes, 105
Hawkins, 33, 71, 76, 160, 183, 262, 374
Haword, 74
Hawskins, 189
Hay, 211
Hayden, 384, 402
Hayes, 107, 169, 240, 310
Hayne, 324
Hays, 83, 157, 313, 421, 422
Hayward, 185, 268
Hayworth, 145
Hazel, 302
Hazlehurst, 32
Headinger, 260
Headley, 301
Heafer, 324
Heaps, 199
Heart, 351
Heath, 157
Heaton, 178
Hebb, 56, 99
Hebert, 141
Heddinger, 292
Heddrick, 25
Heden, 260
Hederick, 298
Hedge, 96
Hedrick, 201
Heever, 261
Heide, 191
Heidelbach, 331
Heidelback, 117
Helm, 160
Helmton, 229
Hemphill, 37, 260
Hemsley, 175
Henderson, 10, 78, 117, 188, 330, 366
Henley, 441
Hennaman, 389
Hennick, 163
Henning, 36

Henry, 106, 274
Herbert, 43
Hermange, 348
Hermitage, 54
Herring, 37
Hertzog, 282
Hervey, 62
Herwig, 140, 419
Heslip, 50
Hesselius, 35, 374
Heugh, 196
Hewes, 33
Hewit, 153
Hewitt, 181, 242, 316
Hewlett, 239
Hewlit, 389
Heyward, 346
Hezlitt, 377
Hickey, 174
Hickly, 192
Hickman, 109
Hicks, 272, 330
Hide, 9
Higgins, 55, 164, 296
High, 348, 376
Highland, 115
Higinbotham, 21, 225
Hignat, 184
Hildebrand, 374
Hildebrandt, 259
Hill, 72, 178, 195, 198, 200, 210, 262, 439
Hillen, 42, 330, 362, 414, 415
Hills, 270
Hilton, 63, 197, 263
Hindman, 168
Hines, 288
Hinkley, 69, 267
Hintze, 172
Hisky, 399
Hiss, 103, 412
Hissey, 423
Hitchcock, 135
Hite, 147
Hitzelberger, 400
Hixley, 121
Hoban, 226

Hobbs, 160, 173
Hobby, 101, 340
Hobson, 38
Hodges, 145, 186, 417
Hodgewerff, 274
Hodgkinson, 40
Hodskiss, 39
Hodson, 184
Hody, 31
Hoffman, 10, 89, 114, 140, 165, 176, 186, 195, 314, 375
Hofleich, 123
Hogan, 53
Hogarthe, 258
Hogmire, 82
Hohne, 55, 78
Hoke, 83, 344
Holbrook, 286, 415
Holdam, 50
Holding, 230
Holdruff, 173
Holland, 27, 28, 132, 178, 328, 441
Holliday, 109
Hollingsworth, 143, 226, 394, 414
Hollins, 157
Hollman, 365
Holloson, 341
Holmes, 78, 175, 244, 300, 363
Holt, 141, 262
Holton, 56
Holtz, 61
Holtzman, 291
Honsaker, 338
Hook, 19, 66, 70, 94, 161, 289
Hooper, 184
Hoover, 351, 364
Hope, 161, 190
Hopkin, 264
Hopkins, 78, 142, 203, 219, 229, 238, 264, 273, 306, 331, 362, 402, 417
Hopkinson, 329
Hopper, 82, 85, 199, 236, 277, 415, 434
Hornamer, 374
Hornsby, 61
Horre, 200
Horsey, 210, 277, 356

Horsman, 377
Horton, 56, 64, 182, 293
Horves, 107
Horze, 399
Hose, 157
Hoskinson, 265
Hoskyns, 407
Hough, 313, 316, 416
House, 14
Houser, 185, 251
Houston, 176
Howard, 51, 66, 70, 71, 78, 103, 150, 167,
    195, 227, 235, 245, 283, 288, 310, 312,
    315, 383, 399, 408, 419, 433, 441
Howe, 159, 406
Howell, 23, 137, 265, 372, 393
Hoxter, 151
Hoxton, 30, 347
Hoyle, 424
Hubbal, 357
Hubbard, 78, 206, 208, 314
Hubly, 200
Hucorn, 296
Huff, 32
Huger, 425
Hughes, 37, 46, 92, 97, 122, 188, 195, 227,
    261, 313, 341, 379, 401, 433, 436
Hughy, 206
Huguet, 426
Huinrickhouse, 39
Hull, 65, 93, 376, 399
Hulse, 63, 71
Hultz, 35
Humbert, 269
Humes, 22, 51
Humphreys, 51, 98, 112
Humphries, 396
Humrickhouse, 253
Hungerford, 428
Hunt, 22, 71, 153, 195, 330, 349
Hunter, 14, 27, 74, 104, 312, 330, 414, 415,
    420
Hupfeld, 316
Hupfild, 355
Hurst, 19, 101
Husband, 324

Hussey, 151, 203
Huston, 269
Hutchins, 89, 378, 394
Hutson, 134
Huttner, 385
Hutton, 265
Hutz, 387
Hyatt, 184, 289, 381
Hyde, 74
Hynson, 118, 203, 245, 246, 291
Hyson, 348
Hyter, 164
I'Anson, 215
Ingalls, 274
Inglis, 353
Ingraham, 301, 397
Inloes, 113, 202
Ireland, 131, 347
Irvine, 91, 150, 340
Irwin, 20, 117
Iseminger, 138
Islehart, 255
Ives, 335, 381
Jack, 45
Jackson, 22, 47, 51, 59, 60, 105, 185, 224,
    269, 288, 319
Jacobs, 175, 225, 399, 441
Jacobsen, 176
James, 10, 18, 42, 87, 140, 161, 173, 184,
    188, 210, 245, 340, 342, 352, 376, 414
Jameson, 101
Jamieson, 210
Jamison, 137, 150, 154
Jandine, 90
Janeway, 431
Janney, 219
Janvier, 44
Jarett, 253
Jarrett, 79, 243
Jarvis, 386
Jay, 381
Jefferson, 110, 404
Jeffrey, 294
Jeffries, 303
Jenifer, 199

Jenkins, 52, 75, 84, 153, 159, 172, 236, 278, 292, 327, 347
Jenkinson, 157, 208
Jenne, 26
Jenney, 348
Jennings, 46, 57, 68, 78, 98, 142, 178, 227, 266, 309, 336, 411
Jenoweth, 25
Jessop, 263, 371
Jesup, 273
Jewell, 421
John, 132
Johns, 19, 64, 93, 95, 127, 206, 225, 374
Johnson, 28, 31, 33, 35, 56, 62, 63, 64, 69, 72, 75, 77, 79, 82, 84, 88, 101, 105, 124, 137, 146, 155, 184, 199, 201, 208, 225, 228, 230, 247, 251, 253, 256, 261, 293, 295, 325, 334, 338, 342, 345, 351, 375, 395, 414, 430, 431, 436
Johnston, 30, 42, 309, 321
Joice, 293
Jollie, 157
Jolliffe, 226
Jonea, 396
Jones, 26, 39, 47, 68, 82, 90, 105, 109, 123, 130, 131, 135, 147, 150, 164, 166, 181, 185, 186, 192, 196, 211, 226, 239, 253, 263, 314, 324, 335, 370, 380, 422, 430, 438, 440
Jordan, 58, 271, 311
Joyce, 349
Joynes, 252
Judah, 45
Juden, 176
Jugall, 260
Jump, 99
Jury, 141
Kadle, 186, 188
Kains, 433
Kalbfus, 140, 365
Kampf, 115
Kane, 196
Karrick, 211
Kauffman, 10, 22, 188
Kay, 209
Kaylor, 366

Kean, 393
Keatinge, 14
Keatting, 299
Keck, 327
Keech, 155, 191
Keen, 340, 343
Keence, 310
Keene, 20, 136, 173, 356
Keener, 69
Keepers, 261
Kehlenbeck, 87
Keiffel, 27
Keirn, 271
Keisacker, 63
Keithley, 264
Kell, 411
Kellar, 150
Keller, 118, 144, 148
Kelley, 345
Kelly, 143, 154, 179, 186, 234, 242, 345, 412, 433
Kelman, 396
Kelnor, 429
Kelso, 137, 308
Kemp, 176, 303, 326, 357
Kempe, 283
Kempfer, 36, 37
Kendal, 200
Kendle, 67
Kenley, 255
Kennard, 18, 192, 202, 376
Kennedy, 27, 31, 76, 107, 166, 193, 200, 216, 259, 279, 349, 409
Kenner, 50, 379
Kenney, 19
Kent, 60
Keplinger, 376
Keppler, 95
Kerfoot, 161, 164
Kerlinger, 345
Kerman, 342
Kernan, 129, 220, 441
Kerr, 24, 121, 172, 174, 363, 427
Kerrl, 28
Kersey, 65
Kessler, 261

Ketsall, 172
Key, 11, 144, 170, 242, 253, 302, 305, 335
Keyes, 304
Keyser, 33, 102
Kiersted, 221
Kilbourne, 273
Kilbreth, 402
Kilmon, 370
Kilty, 54, 141
Kimball, 268
Kimble, 87
Kimmel, 227, 245, 272, 400
Kinch, 252
King, 9, 58, 95, 98, 131, 169, 234, 252, 265, 266, 274, 277, 356, 364, 371
Kingsmore, 130
Kinkade, 188
Kinnamont, 83
Kinneman, 387
Kinsey, 104
Kirby, 277, 292, 319, 370, 376, 381
Kirk, 92
Kirkland, 98
Kirkpatrick, 46
Kirkwood, 53, 255
Kittlewell, 160
Kizer, 132
Kliendenstin, 35
Kline, 386
Klinefelter, 178, 321, 374
Klunk, 167
Knafe, 185
Kneeland, 299
Knight, 50, 79, 96, 205, 296
Knipe, 312
Knotts, 67
Knox, 44, 84, 171, 191
Konig, 94, 249
Koonts, 18
Koontz, 53, 94
Koster, 76
Kotman, 254
Krafft, 383
Kraft, 365
Kramer, 357
Krebs, 196, 256

Kreider, 375
Krepps, 182
Kreps, 181
Krise, 246
Kronemanche, 426
Krouse, 338
Kursey, 103
Kurstendorf, 181
Kurtz, 91, 197, 278
La Fontaine, 351
Labes, 37
Labome, 211
Labourde, 226
Lacey, 388
Lafferty, 176
Lafon, 57
Laidler, 251
Lainhart, 21
Laird, 243
Lake, 87, 269, 406
Lakin, 365
Lamb, 308, 400
Lambdin, 307
Lambert, 279, 313
Lamden, 181
Lamson, 296
Lancaster, 53, 65, 191
Lander, 414
Landsdale, 332
Lane, 45, 166, 214, 237, 332
Langdon, 15, 241
Langley, 162
Lankford, 417
Lannay, 53
Lansfield, 324
Larabee, 417
Largury, 405
Larouraudais, 145
Larsh, 244
Lash, 16
Lassell, 350
Latimer, 78, 144
Latorunau, 281
Latrobe, 402
Latschaw, 63
Laty, 255

Laudeman, 201
Laudenslager, 169, 333
Lauderman, 311, 388
Laudsberry, 150
Lavary, 227
Lavely, 220
Lavitt, 31
Law, 87, 220
Lawder, 413
Lawes, 28
Lawrence, 40, 102, 179, 221, 365
Lawrenson, 215
Lawson, 299, 326, 336
Layton, 174
Le Compt, 161
Le Compte, 198
Le Roy, 405, 415
Lea, 267
Leach, 277
League, 203, 258
Leahy, 223
Leak, 377
Leake, 352
Leaken, 83
Leakin, 306
Leaman, 168, 240, 422
Lear, 370
Learned, 192
Leary, 206
Leatherberry, 117
Leatherwood, 49, 122
Lebon, 367
Lecompte, 155
Leddon, 191
Ledley, 310
Ledyard, 411
Lee, 28, 36, 93, 103, 158, 167, 188, 257, 298, 328
Lefaver, 51
Lefeber, 185
Lefevre, 253
Leggett, 127, 138
Leggitt, 95
Legrand, 411
Leig, 230
Leigh, 114

Leisure, 148
Leloup, 9, 96
Lemmon, 272, 353
Lemoine, 292
Lenox, 61, 141, 262
Leonard, 16, 372, 395, 428
Leothold, 48
Leroy, 187
Leslie, 305
Lesourd, 340
Letournau, 276
Levant, 119
Levely, 146
Levering, 57, 128, 223, 289
Lewis, 78, 89, 105, 210, 262, 331, 408, 415
Leypold, 227
Liddle, 190
Lidy, 247
Lightner, 398
Lilly, 395
Lind, 198, 404
Lindenberger, 55
Lindsey, 387
Lingenfelter, 27
Linthicum, 34, 277
Linvill, 310
Lippincott, 151
Litle, 241
Littig, 16
Little, 11, 188, 202
Littlejohn, 324
Littler, 378
Littleton, 110
Livers, 230
Livingston, 282, 302
Lloyd, 33, 419
Loane, 129
Lock, 219, 351, 387
Locker, 164
Lockwood, 254
Logan, 56, 188, 377, 396
Lohary, 144
Loney, 50, 82, 112
Long, 176, 193, 202, 325, 358
Longman, 39
Lorman, 81, 146

Lorre, 129
Lose, 63
Loudenslager, 19
Loudon, 140
Loughridge, 219
Love, 21, 183, 237, 331
Loveday, 34, 119, 157
Lovelace, 298
Lovell, 128, 298
Low, 296
Lowe, 248
Lowens, 324
Lowery, 141, 436
Lowndes, 248, 282
Lowrey, 60
Lowry, 17, 129
Lucas, 32, 46, 69, 126, 377, 402
Luckett, 34
Ludden, 79
Lufkin, 417
Lughman, 267
Luke, 51, 277
Lusby, 40, 51, 267, 381
Lusbz, 243
Luscomb, 203
Lutz, 201
Lux, 237, 308, 420
Lyel, 387
Lyles, 60
Lynch, 14, 258, 377, 411
Lynn, 58, 73
Lyon, 98, 144, 319
Lyons, 36, 104
Lytle, 84
M'Ardle, 64
M'Aulister, 105
M'Blair, 424
M'Cabe, 121
M'Caberly, 432
M'Call, 354, 412
M'Cannon, 85, 179
M'Causland, 21, 281
M'Causlin, 306
M'Ceney, 331
M'Clanahan, 79
M'Clean, 141

M'Cleery, 191
M'Clellan, 325
M'Clenachen, 93
M'Cleod, 338
M'Clestal, 81
M'Clure, 87
M'Comas, 53, 56, 400, 411, 418, 423
M'Conkey, 386
M'Connell, 88, 181, 273
M'Cormick, 252, 283
M'Cosker, 439
M'Coskry, 159
M'Coull, 228
M'Coy, 93, 150
M'Crearey, 343
M'Cristall, 211
M'Cubbin, 341
M'Culley, 102
M'Culloh, 405
M'Daniel, 156
M'Donald, 32
M'Donnel, 140
M'Donnell, 407
M'Dowell, 219
M'Eldery, 129
M'Eleget, 286
M'Faddon, 195
M'Fadon, 323, 343
M'Fall, 109
M'Farland, 271
M'Farquhar, 227
M'Gary, 330
M'Gauran, 436
M'Gibbon, 122
M'Ginn, 421
M'Ginney, 155
M'Ginnis, 21, 152, 413
M'Gloshe, 122
M'Guire, 288, 373
M'Henry, 103
M'Intire, 373
M'Intosh, 158, 384
M'Jimsey, 391
M'Kay, 376
M'Kean, 82
M'Keane, 147

Martinberry, 29
Martindale, 26, 36, 48, 99
Marvin, 250
Mason, 155, 309, 328, 343, 392, 395, 423
Mass, 75
Massaneau, 277
Massay, 248
Massey, 64, 84, 202, 249
Massy, 384
Matchett, 27
Mather, 19, 98, 249
Mathews, 341
Mathewson, 193
Mathias, 29
Mathiot, 314
Matthews, 110, 181, 189, 234, 300, 323, 349, 418
Matthewson, 350
Matthieu, 187
Mattingly, 132
Maul, 181
Maund, 155, 305
Maxwell, 151, 273, 282, 329, 332
May, 100, 200
Maydwell, 62, 249
Mayer, 29, 227, 257
Mayger, 43
Mayhew, 251, 340
Maynard, 26, 228
Mayo, 55
McBeth, 421
McBlair, 419
McCain, 385
McCaler, 352
McCall, 335
McCandless, 226
McCannon, 32
McCausland, 163, 408
McCeney, 259
McClasky, 371
McCleary, 363
McCleine, 363
McClellan, 21
McCleskey, 178
McClure, 342
McComes, 214

McConkey, 201
McCormic, 281
McCormick, 174
McCoy, 34, 288, 328
McCrone, 304
McCubbey, 271
McCulloch, 363
McCullough, 137
McCully, 269
McCurdy, 219, 311
McDermot, 61
McDermott, 192
McDonald, 137, 343
McDonnell, 441
McDowell, 214, 262
McDowle, 439
McElfresh, 23
McElroy, 363
McElwee, 370
McFadden, 209
McFaul, 9
McGaghy, 407
McGaw, 280
McGibbon, 338
McGirr, 372
McGouran, 433
McGowan, 267
McGuire, 63
McHenry, 241, 245, 300
McKaa, 42
McKage, 262
McKee, 202
McKeel, 304
McKenney, 103, 162
McKenzie, 410
McKey, 51
McKoen, 71
McLaughlin, 11, 185
McManus, 28
McMaster, 249
McMechen, 256, 376, 394
McMullan, 232
McMullin, 342
McNulty, 43, 192
McPherson, 145
McQuiller, 371

Morrison, 158, 178, 267, 343
Morrow, 89
Mortimer, 411
Morton, 213, 361
Moss, 41
Mother, 268
Mott, 36
Motter, 122
Mowberry, 164
Mowbray, 138
Muckelwee, 178
Mugers, 214
Muir, 42
Mullen, 313, 373, 387
Mullenix, 85
Muller, 387
Mullican, 363
Mullikin, 141, 146, 165, 277, 424
Mullingar, 429
Mulvey, 287
Mumford, 275
Mumma, 150, 377, 399
Mummy, 347
Mundell, 28
Mungan, 63
Munn, 99, 132
Munroe, 23, 27, 29, 311
Murcan, 185
Murdoch, 19, 347
Murdock, 129, 230
Murphy, 42, 56, 159, 169, 188, 226, 254, 349
Murray, 70, 79, 118, 127, 140, 146, 179, 301, 304, 362, 370
Murry, 35
Muse, 101
Musgrave, 346
Musgrove, 268
Mycroft, 438
Myer, 15, 221, 338
Myers, 23, 122, 134, 151, 153, 185, 218, 228, 231, 234, 236, 313, 341, 348, 368, 380, 383, 407
Nabb, 46, 125, 141, 215, 219, 298
Nagel, 405
Nagle, 34, 78, 227, 306

Nants, 424
Napp, 274
Nash, 283
Neal, 44, 105, 208
Neale, 10, 157, 208, 296, 312, 365
Needham, 14
Needles, 411
Neill, 54
Neilson, 113, 186, 256, 432
Nelson, 56, 66, 186, 270, 350
Nennemacher, 103
Neril, 100
Nesbitt, 104
Nevil, 71
Nevins, 253
Newbury, 262
Newcarric, 280
Newcomb, 266
Newcomer, 185, 261
Newman, 31, 50, 301
Newton, 34, 226, 286
Niccle, 306
Nicholls, 30, 282
Nichols, 57
Nicholson, 24, 62, 70, 236, 239, 272, 295, 331, 430
Nicodemus, 292
Nicol, 40
Nicoll, 173
Nicols, 189, 420
Niebling, 380
Niles, 26, 379
Nind, 233
Ninde, 228
Noel, 192
Nokes, 304
Noland, 313
Norbury, 278, 297
Norris, 36, 52, 53, 72, 157, 169, 173, 253, 264, 304, 327, 354, 408, 419
North, 180
Norton, 363, 434
Norwood, 30, 133, 264, 368
Nowland, 92
Numsen, 422
Nussear, 372

Pendleton, 263
Penn, 105, 276, 387
Penniman, 145
Pennington, 348
Pentz, 214
Peppernell, 387
Peregoy, 194, 377, 387
Perine, 289, 296
Perkins, 18, 167, 222, 278, 384
Perley, 52
Perry, 92, 305, 381
Peter, 376, 440
Peterman, 61
Peters, 85, 97, 162, 249, 318, 348
Peterson, 10, 150
Petevey, 387
Pettigreu, 351
Peyton, 186, 329
Pfeiffer, 29, 268
Phenix, 282, 315
Phifer, 232
Philips, 105, 129, 291
Phillips, 73, 190, 227, 287, 349, 399, 418, 426
Philpot, 202
Phipps, 264
Phoenix, 187
Phrow, 128, 305
Pickens, 105
Pickering, 26
Pidgeon, 267
Pierce, 244, 290, 364, 407
Pierre, 328
Piet, 250
Pike, 73, 339
Pinckney, 425
Pindell, 134, 261, 427
Pine, 204
Pinkney, 147, 274, 408
Pinor, 362
Pinter, 193
Piper, 256
Pise, 63, 225, 230
Pistol, 304
Pitcock, 300
Pitt, 16, 314

Pittenger, 412
Pitts, 74, 80
Placide, 293
Plains, 277
Plater, 66, 199
Platt, 137
Pleasant, 428
Pleasants, 399
Plummer, 62, 119, 126, 141, 160
Pocock, 101
Poe, 317, 340
Pogue, 154, 421
Poland, 396
Polk, 79, 296
Pollard, 115
Pool, 21, 195, 227, 302
Poole, 26, 406
Poor, 353, 391
Pope, 150, 260
Porringer, 426
Porsher, 289
Porter, 137, 151, 155, 281, 309, 367
Posey, 191
Poteet, 422
Poteete, 290
Pottenger, 123, 157
Potter, 305, 323
Potts, 188, 199, 227, 303
Pouder, 274, 380
Pouge, 176
Poulletiere, 248
Poultney, 35, 328
Pour, 152
Powel, 326, 375
Powell, 23, 122, 126, 313
Powers, 51, 54, 72, 123
Powles, 88
Poydras, 387
Prather, 273
Pratt, 94, 136, 257, 272, 320
Prehol, 146
Prendergast, 141
Prentiss, 59
Presbury, 131, 166
Presstman, 179
Prestman, 251

473

www.ingramcontent.com/pod-product-compliance
Lightning Source LLC
Chambersburg PA
CBHW060127280326
41932CB00012B/1443